Why Do You Need This New Edition?

The requirements, strategies, and tools for college writing assignments have changed in many ways since the last edition of *Ancient Rhetorics for Contemporary Students* published, so make sure you're up to date! If you're still wondering why you should buy this new edition, here are a few more great reasons:

❶ The *progymnasmata* have now been interspersed throughout the book so that you can practice scaffolded rhetorical exercises in context and strengthen your rhetorical practice as you move through the text and the term.

❷ Revised and updated activities in every chapter ask you to work through concepts and build on in-text examples by analyzing or revising contemporary texts in both popular media and academic journals—offering you the opportunity to strengthen your use of rhetoric in college and beyond.

❸ New examples illustrating the current state of rhetoric in the U.S. that include John Stewart on CNN's *Crossfire* and Sheryl Crow in *The Times* provide you with contemporary s spoken and written rhetoric in broadcas in order to help you recognize rhetorical at work in different communication mec

❹ The updated *progymnasmata* on Con presents new examples both from ancie that compare Achilles and Hector and cu sources that compare Barack Obama and Rodham Clinton in order to help you see

rhetors throughout history have made effective use of this strategy.

❺ New student texts illustrate *kairos* by examining campus shootings and the use of Native American figures as sports mascots so that you can see how your peers have used rhetorical history and timing in their own writing.

❻ Revised coverage of the enthymematic argument analyzes new, contemporary examples such as Apple marketing campaigns and speeches made by President Bush after 9/11 in order to help you recognize examples of this ancient method of argument in everyday culture.

❼ A refreshed *progymnasmata* on Introduction of Law uses the new example of an assault rifle ban to help you link your academic work to broader issues of citizenship and democracy outside of college.

ed
ess
c-
f
r
.

PEARSON
Longman

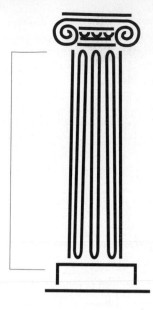

FOURTH EDITION

ANCIENT RHETORICS FOR CONTEMPORARY STUDENTS

SHARON CROWLEY
Arizona State University

DEBRA HAWHEE
University of Illinois at Urbana-Champaign

PEARSON
Longman

New York   San Francisco   Boston
London   Toronto   Sydney   Tokyo   Singapore   Madrid
Mexico City   Munich   Paris   Cape Town   Hong Kong   Montreal

Acquisitions Editor: Lauren A. Finn
Senior Supplements Editor: Donna Campion
Senior Marketing Manager: Sandra McGuire
Production Manager: Bob Ginsberg
Project Coordination, Text Design, and
     Electronic Page Makeup: Pre-Press PMG
Cover Design Manager: Wendy Ann Fredericks
Cover Designer: Kay Petronio
Cover Art: istockphoto.com
Photo Researcher: Ilene Bellovin
Manufacturing Buyer: Roy Pickering
Printer and Binder: Courier/Westford
Cover Printer: Coral Graphic Services, Inc.

For permission to use copyrighted material, grateful acknowledgment is made to the
copyright holders on pp. 448–449, which are hereby made part of this copyright page.

Library of Congress Cataloging-in-Publication Data

Crowley, Sharon, 1943–
     Ancient rhetorics for contemporary students/Sharon Crowley,
Debra Hawhee.—4th ed.
          p. cm.
     ISBN 0-205-58954-5
     1.   English language—Rhetoric. 2.   Rhetoric, Ancient. I. Hawhee,
Debra. II. Title.

PE1408.C725 2008
808'.042—dc22   2007046167

Visit us at www.ablongman.com.

ISBN-13: 978-0-205-57443-8
ISBN-10:   0-205-57443-2

45678910—CRW—11 10

Contents

CHAPTER 3

Stasis Theory: Asking the Right Questions   71

CHAPTER 4

The Common Topics and the Commonplaces: Finding the Available Means   117

PART THREE: STYLE, MEMORY, AND DELIVERY

CHAPTER 10

Style: Composition and Ornament   *327*

PREFACE

Welcome to the fourth edition of *Ancient Rhetorics for Contemporary Students* (called "*ARCS*" for short by its authors and editors). Thanks to all the teachers and students who have said nice things about *ARCS*, and thanks as well to those who have offered constructive criticisms. We have tried to incorporate those in this edition wherever possible.

Here is a list of the changes we made to this edition. The book has been rewritten for clarity throughout. Several of the chapters include newly rewritten sections; these include the introduction as well as the chapters on *kairos*, stasis, *ethos*, *pathos*, and arrangement. The *progymnasmata* (preliminary exercises) and imitation exercises have been redistributed throughout the book as featured sections in order to better achieve a balance between principles and practice. New examples were embedded throughout with attention to currency. The figure-by-figure history that appeared in the first chapter of earlier editions has been cut to reduce bulk. Instead, we refer readers to the Appendix, which features "signposts" of ancient rhetoric, and also to the newly revised list of suggested readings in the back of the book.

Since this book is about a very old way of thinking, some confusion has arisen about our use of terms relating to time. We do not typically use the term *modern* in a generic sense meaning "the present." For that use we employ the term *contemporary*. Throughout, we use *modern* to indicate a specific set of beliefs about composition and composing. Since we use *modern* somewhat disparagingly, we want to be clear that we are not talking about contemporary students or teachers when we use that term. Rather, we are referring to the habits of mind that still inform ways of thinking about composing. The distinction between modern and contemporary is difficult to maintain, though, since modern ideas still persist in contemporary teaching practices. As a result, the terms we use become slippery because different oppositions are at work: ancient versus modern, modern and contemporary, modern versus postmodern. We write in a postmodern era, an era that embraces change and accepts intellectual discord; hence it demands flexible communication strategies. Most of today's students and many teachers, raised in a complex and stimulating technological and ideological age, hold postmodern attitudes toward composing and composition. We believe ancient rhetorics, which are of course premodern, offer an interesting starting point from which postmodern rhetors might think about discourse anew.

While writing *Ancient Rhetorics for Contemporary Students,* we adopted three ancient premises about composing: first, that nobody thinks or writes without reference to the culture in which he or she lives; second, that human beings disagree with one another often and for good reasons; and third, that people compose because they want to affect the course of events. We appealed to ancient rhetoric as the source of our thinking for this book because ancient rhetoricians invented and taught an art that was immersed in the daily traffic of human events and in communal discourse about them. In this the art differed markedly from the modes of composition ordinarily taught in school today, which present writers and speakers with an abstracted set of pseudoscientific rules that dictate how a finished discourse ought to look.

Ancient rhetoricians began their instruction about composing by considering the occasions that generated a desire to write or speak. Modern teachers, in contrast, too frequently begin (and end) their instruction with consideration of forms or genres, asking students to begin by composing outlines, thesis statements, or essays. We think that the rich fund of theories and strategies that can be found in ancient rhetorics, particularly instruction about how to address rhetorical situations and how to find arguments (called **invention** in ancient thought) is far more helpful to students in the stage of the composing process that is most difficult for novices: beginning.

We hope that this book will show writers and speakers that their rhetorical practice and their ethical obligations are always communal. The need to compose arises from composers' desire to insert their voices into the differences of opinion that occur within the discourse of a community. When they are read or heard, compositions enter into that discourse, either to maintain and reinforce it or to disrupt it. Compositions produced in college are as communal as any other writing. Teachers and peers read student writing or listen to student speeches, and these compositions become part of classroom discourse.

Ancient rhetoricians knew that audiences are never neutral: that is, they never receive a rhetor's discourse neutrally or objectively. The reception accorded any discourse depends as much upon the rhetor's relation to the community and her relation to the issue discussed as it depends upon the content of her discourse. Modern rhetorics, particularly the version taught in college, pretend that this is not the case, that compositions on any topic can be made available to any educated reader, who can consume them without prejudice. Ancient rhetoricians, in contrast, taught their students how to analyze the contexts for which they composed and how to adapt their composing processes to fit these contexts as closely as possible. They never assumed that a given discursive situation could be adequately met by employment of generic formulas.

Because we have adopted the ancient assumption that rhetoric cannot be fruitfully studied and practiced apart from the issues that engage the communities it serves, this book introduces its readers to some contested topics in contemporary political and ethical discourse. Its examples are drawn from popular and academic writing about controversial issues. We realize that to engage students in talk about values is a departure from traditional approaches to composition instruction. However, we feel that rhetoric cannot be taught without addressing the issues that vitally concern the people who use it. We are aware as well that some of our examples will soon become dated. However, it should not be difficult for teachers and students to supply their own contemporary examples in places where the immediate relevance of our examples is no longer apparent.

The book also includes some features of ancient rhetoric that have not received much attention in modern accounts of its teachings. For example, the book contains a thorough treatment of ancient discussions about figures of thought. There are chapters that show how to compose proofs from character and appeals to the emotions, which, so far as we know, are not treated at length in any other contemporary textbook, even though both are commonly practiced in contemporary political and commercial rhetorics.

Nearly half of this book (seven chapters) is devoted to invention. This proportion reflects the lavish attention given to invention by ancient rhetoricians. Of the three books in Aristotle's *Rhetoric*, two are devoted to invention; the third treats delivery, style, and arrangement. Of the twelve books of Quintilian's *Institutes of Oratory*, five are devoted to invention, two are devoted to style, delivery and memory get a chapter each, and the rest of the work concerns the proper education of an orator. Cicero's *On Invention*, obviously, treats nothing else. These proportions testify to the importance of the first canon in ancient rhetorics. We represent that importance here because all the means of invention defined by ancient rhetoricians are still in use in public discourse.

In ancient rhetorics, a person who was inventing arguments might or might not make use of writing, depending upon the quality of his memory. It is likely that ancient rhetors composed arguments aloud and stored them in memory. The only ancient revision practices that are similar to literate revision occurred when students were working with the elementary exercises called *progymnasmata*. They copied passages onto wax tablets, working either from memory or from a text. They then tried out variations in writing. No doubt they memorized the variations that won the most approval.

However, literate revision practices can be built into the ancient system. Students can compose trial arguments as they work their way through this book, and they can revise their work as they master new rhetorical strategies. In other words, the ancient inventional schemes can all be worked out in writing, and so anyone can produce a great deal of writing while using this book. It is organized just as the ancients organized their rhetorical instruction, following the order of the canons of rhetoric: invention, arrangement, style, memory, and delivery. Even though its organization dimly reflects modern descriptions of the composing process—which is sometimes characterized as moving through prewriting, writing, revision, and editing—people who use this book will soon discover that the linear economy of the modern composing process is far too simple to accommodate ancient notions of composing. Ancient teachers emphasized copiousness, or the art of having more to say or write than a **rhetor** needs for a single occasion. Ancient composing processes did not aim toward the production of a finished product; rather, they equipped rhetors with arguments and materials that would be readily available whenever they needed to compose for a given occasion.

Given our emphasis on invention rather than convention or form, it follows that students and teachers in both writing and speech classes can use this book profitably. We mean the terms *composing* and *composition* generically, to refer to work done by people who are preparing to deliver either oral or written discourse. All of the exercises included here are appropriate for classes in public speaking; indeed, our emphasis on ancient rhetorics harmonizes with the rhetorical approach often used by teachers of speech and communication.

Finally, as we mentioned earlier, we have organized this edition with the idea of mixing art with practice. To this end, each chapter ends with two sets of exercises: rhetorical activities and exercises in composing. Appearing first are rhetorical activities. These are designed to encourage further reflection on the principles of art in that chapter. They ask students to employ what they have learned in their own reading and writing, or to find and consider a particular rhetorical principle at work in their everyday lives. There are no drills or canned exercises; that is, students are never asked to analyze or comment on prose written by other people. The book's most important pedagogical feature, we think, is that it provides students with motives for composing.

Equal partner to those motives are lots of opportunities for practice composing. At the very end of each chapter, we have included composition exercises. These exercises focus on two important ancient modes of practice: *progymnasmata*, the ancient term for "preliminary exercises, " and exercises in imitation. We explicate each exercise, supply classical and modern examples, and make composing suggestions for each. In this book, these exercises follow a progression, and they are also keyed to the concepts and principles in the main chapters. We include them because we follow the ancient belief that lots of patterned practice at composing can further enliven rhetorical habits of mind. If students follow ancient instructions for preparing and composing arguments, they will generate a lot of writing.

Too often modern classrooms treat such activities and exercises as "busy work, " something to fill time between "real" assignments. We believe this is because of a heavy emphasis in twentieth-century classrooms on writing as product. By contrast, the ancients placed less emphasis on the product—the speech or the piece of writing—and more emphasis on constant activity and practice. The best comparison for the ancient model of rhetorical education is the immersion technique of foreign language learning, wherein students speak only the language being learned. Likewise, these activities and exercises encourage you to see rhetoric all around you, to engage rhetoric analytically, and to practice improving your use of rhetoric when you speak and write. Because this book aims at comprehensiveness, it contains more activities, exercises, and approaches than can be crammed into a semester or quarter.

This book also differs in some respects from the few contemporary textbooks about ancient rhetorics that are currently available. It does not treat all the rhetorics produced during antiquity as a monolithic theory of discourse. Nor does it assume that the principles and techniques isolated by ancient rhetoricians can be usefully transferred to contemporary situations without qualification. Throughout the book we attempt to alert readers to the fact that cultures that are widely separated in time and space differ from one another, even though the cultures under study here are regarded as the sources of what is now called "Western civilization." In the first chapter, we address some important differences between modern and ancient thought about knowledge and its production. We updated or abandoned altogether the features of ancient rhetorics that are simply too foreign to be of use. For example, we altered translations to mitigate the sexism manifested by ancient teachers as well as their modern translators. Where that was not possible, we pointed out the sexism.

Throughout, we followed ancient practice in assuming that everyone who wishes to speak or write possesses something to write or speak about insofar as he or she participates in the common discourse of the communities to which he or she belongs. As a result, this book never asks students to write personal essays or to generate expressive discourse. We do not accept the assumption that writing should begin with personal expression and move outward into expository and persuasive modes. To the contrary, we agree with the ancients that there are no purely personal opinions, just as there can be no private language.

We hope that this book will interest its readers in further study of ancient rhetorics themselves. The major works of several ancient rhetoricians—Aristotle, Isocrates, Cicero, and Quintilian—are now available in relatively inexpensive paperback editions. A few anthologies are also available that include portions of their work, along with related ancient treatises on literary composition and elementary exercises. Accompanied by readings in ancient texts, this book might profitably be used in humanities or critical thinking classes as an introduction to ancient ways of knowing and thinking. Of course, it should also prove useful in undergraduate and graduate courses designed to introduce students to ancient rhetorics. In our experience, contemporary students find ancient texts difficult to read unless they are contextualized with history and commentary about ancient times. This book attempts to fill that need, although its history of ancient rhetorics is quite brief. Those who are interested in the histories of ancient Greece and Rome and their rhetorical traditions should consult the work of historians listed in the bibliography.

The bibliography also lists the citation sources of classical texts. For the most part we opted to put these titles in a concluding list rather than cluttering up the text with long citations. Prose and poetry by early modern English writers are generally cited from the standard works, where these exist, or collected works.

We included a glossary that defines ancient or technical terms and supplies pronunciation guides for a few terms that have no ready equivalent in English. Such terms are printed in **bold type** when they first appear in the text, as a few do in this preface. The appendix offers a more detailed outline of major developments in ancient rhetorics themselves. The bibliography lists modern sources of our quotations of ancient texts and supplies some suggestions for further reading in ancient rhetorics.

Perhaps a word about our use of the term *we* is in order. It is a departure to use a familiar pronoun in a textbook. However, we wanted to insure that our readers were regularly reminded that statements put forward in this book issue from actual, fallible people rather than from some unavailable site of teacherly authority. Usually, the term *we* refers to Sharon Crowley and Debra Hawhee, particularly when we are giving advice and instruction or rendering opinions about current affairs. However, the use of *we* can slip into a "royal *we*," taking on precisely the voice we wish to avoid—that of an indisputable authority. We tried to be aware of this use and to eliminate it wherever possible, but we probably did not succeed. In any case, we hope that readers of this book will want to argue with us throughout, and that's one reason why we wrote it in the first person.

The Instructor's Manual offers supplementary suggestions for teaching *ARCS*. To this end, it tries to help teachers help students meet the challenges posed by a study of ancient rhetoric, offers a repertoire of strategies for linking ancient rhetorical concepts to contemporary issues, and provides additional insight into what the authors were thinking when they wrote the textbook. In addition to suggestions for daily use, the manual features sample syllabi and assignment ideas.

ACKNOWLEDGMENTS

Once again, Sharon thanks Debbie for intellectual inspiration, hard work, and moral support (which are the qualities necessary to maintenance of a good *ethos*, after all). My father used to say that one of the great pleasures of teaching was watching one's students surpass their teachers, and Debbie has borne out the wisdom of his observation. I also express my appreciation to my colleagues in rhetorical studies for intellectual stimulation and the delightfully good talk that always attends rhetoricians' meetings. Katherine Heenan is owed special thanks for helping me to understand how to teach ancient rhetorics better, and for helping me to survive in the entrepreneurial university. For a sort of help that can't be readily articulated, I thank my faithful writing companion Margaret Fuller, who has now slept through the composition of four editions of this book. White Guy helped, too, by reminding me when it was time to eat.

Debbie continues to be grateful to Sharon for so many things: her sage advice on "associate professorland," her lively phone conversations, her remarkable penchant for infusing old stuff with new life. Thanks to colleagues in Communication and at the Center for Writing Studies at Illinois for their ongoing collegial support and interest. I owe a debt of gratitude to the International Society for the History of Rhetoric and the Rhetoric Society of America for offering a three-day seminar on the *progymnasmata* tradition, as well as to Manfred Kraus, who led it, to Lawrence Green who organized it, and to the lively group of colleagues who participated in it. The discussions in that seminar inspired this edition's redistribution of the ancient exercises, whose promise has endured. Closer to home, thanks to Tillie and Jada for making me go outside. Thanks, too, to John Marsh. I am repeatedly astonished by his ability to remember the most subtle rhetorical strategies, who used them, where, and when. Even Simonides would be impressed.

We both extend warm thanks to Lauren Finn for seeing us through this edition, and to Kathleen Lamp, whose research abilities and cheerful endurance made this book a whole lot better. We would also like to thank all the people who wrote reviews:

Hugh Burns, Texas Woman's University; Joe Zeppetello, Marist College; Jessica Enoch, University of Pittsburgh; Kimberly Harrison, Florida International University; Walter Jost, University of Virginia; John Harwood, Penn State University; Susan Miller, University of Utah

SHARON CROWLEY
DEBRA HAWHEE

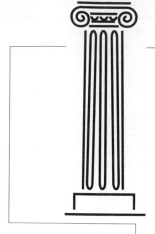

ANCIENT RHETORICS: THEIR DIFFERENCES AND THE DIFFERENCES THEY MAKE

For us moderns, rhetoric means artificiality, insincerity, decadence.

—H. I. Marrou

WHEN AMERICANS HEAR the word **rhetoric,** they tend to think of politicians' attempts to deceive them. Rhetoric is characterized as "empty words" or as fancy language used to distort the truth or tell lies. Television newspeople often say something like "There was more rhetoric from the White House today," and editorialists write that politicians need to "stop using rhetoric and do something," as though words had no connection to action. Many people blame rhetoric for our apparent inability to communicate and to get things done.

But that isn't the way **rhetoricians** defined their art in ancient Athens and Rome. In ancient times, people used rhetoric to make decisions, resolve disputes, and to mediate public discussion of important issues. An ancient teacher of rhetoric named Aristotle defined rhetoric as the power of finding the available arguments suited to a given situation. For teachers like Aristotle or practitioners like the Roman orator Cicero, rhetoric helped people to choose the best course of action when they disagreed about important political, religious, or social issues. In fact, the study of rhetoric was equivalent to the study of citizenship. Under the best ancient teachers, Greek and

1

Roman students composed discourse about moral and political questions that daily confronted their communities.

Ancient teachers of rhetoric thought that disagreement among human beings was inevitable, since individuals perceive the world differently from one another. They also assumed that since people communicate their perceptions through language—which is an entirely different medium than thoughts or perceptions—there was no guarantee that any person's perceptions would be accurately conveyed to others. Even more important, the ancient teachers knew that people differ in their opinions about how the world works, so that it was often hard to tell whose opinion was the best. They invented rhetoric so that they would have means of judging whose opinion was most accurate, useful, or valuable.

If people didn't disagree, rhetoric wouldn't be necessary. But they do, and it is. A rhetorician named Kenneth Burke remarked that "we need never deny the presence of strife, enmity, faction as a characteristic motive of rhetorical expression" (1962, 20). But the fact that rhetoric originates in disagreement is ultimately a good thing, since its use allows people to make important choices without resorting to less palatable means of persuasion—coercion or violence. People who have talked their way out of any potentially violent confrontation know how useful rhetoric can be. On a larger scale, the usefulness of rhetoric is even more apparent. If, for some reason, the people who negotiate international relations were to stop using rhetoric to resolve their disagreements about limits on the use of nuclear weapons, there might not be a future to deliberate about. That's why we should be glad when we read or hear that diplomats are disagreeing about the allowable number of warheads per country or the number of inspections of nuclear stockpiles per year. At least they're talking to each other. As Burke observed, wars are the result of an agreement to disagree. But before people of goodwill agree to disagree, they try out hundreds of ways of reaching agreement. The possibility that one set of participants will resort to coercion or violence is always a threat, of course; but in the context of impending war, the threat of war can itself operate as a rhetorical strategy that keeps people of goodwill talking to each other.

Given that argument can deter violence and coercion, we are disturbed by the contemporary tendency to see disagreement as somehow impolite or even undesirable. We certainly understand how disagreement has earned its bad name, given the caricature of argument that daily appears on talk television.

Thanks to these talk shows, argument has become a form of entertaining drama rather than a means of laying out and working through differences or discovering new resolutions. We are apparently not the only ones who feel this way. In October of 2004—three weeks before the presidential election—Jon Stewart, the host of Comedy Central's *The Daily Show with Jon Stewart*, appeared live on CNN's political "argument" show named *Crossfire* to register his disappointment with the state of argument in America. In what has now become a famous plea (thanks to viral video on the Internet), Stewart asked then-*Crossfire* hosts Paul Begala and Tucker Carlson to "Stop, stop, stop, stop hurting America." How, exactly, does Stewart think that *Crossfire* is hurting America? Here is a segment from the show's transcript:

STEWART: No, no, no, but what I'm saying is this. I'm not. I'm here to confront you, because we need help from the media and they're hurting us. And it's—the idea is . . .

[APPLAUSE]

[CROSSTALK]

BEGALA: Let me get this straight. If the indictment is—if the indictment is—and I have seen you say this—that . . .

STEWART: Yes.

BEGALA: And that CROSSFIRE reduces everything, as I said in the intro, to left, right, black, white.

STEWART: Yes.

BEGALA: Well, it's because, see, we're a debate show.

STEWART: No, no, no, no, that would be great.

BEGALA: It's like saying The Weather Channel reduces everything to a storm front.

STEWART: I would love to see a debate show.

BEGALA: We're 30 minutes in a 24-hour day, where we have each side on, as best we can get them, and have them fight it out.

STEWART: No, no, no, no, that would be great. To do a debate would be great. But that's like saying pro wrestling is a show about athletic competition.

Stewart's **analogy**, in which professional wrestling is to athletic competition as *Crossfire* is to debate, is worth dwelling on in part because the move from engaged performance of sports or debate to the sheer entertainment and antics of World Wrestling Entertainment (WWE, formerly the World Wrestling Federation) is a move from "real" to "mere." In other words, what could become earnest rhetorical engagement becomes instead a staged spat, "mere" theater. *Theater*, in fact, is the word that Stewart settles on to describe *Crossfire* later in his appearance. That a current WWE show called *Smackdown* has a title that could well be mistaken for a cable "debate" show helps underscore Stewart's point: like WWE, shows like *Crossfire* seem to exist to dramatize conflict solely for entertainment purposes. In doing so, the so-called debate shows effectively distance argument further from the American public, placing it on the brightly lit set of a television show, making it seem as if "argument" has distinct winners and losers, and playing up the embarrassment of "losing."

It is interesting to note that after Stewart's appearance on *Crossfire*, CNN canceled the show altogether, but they did not replace it with what Stewart—or we—would consider a debate show. We wholeheartedly agree with Stewart's criticism. Shows like *Crossfire* perpetuate rhetoric's bad name, because the hosts and guests don't actually argue; rather, they shout

commonplaces at one another. Neither host listens to the other or to the guest, who is rarely allowed to speak, and then only intermittently. Even the transcript quoted here shows how because of the hosts' frequent interruptions, Stewart must work very hard to maintain a point. Shouting over one another is an extremely unproductive model of argument because doing so rarely involves listening or responding, and seldom stimulates anyone to change his or her mind.

Engaging in productive argument is much different from shouting tired slogans. For one thing it is hard intellectual work, and for another, it requires that all parties to an argument listen to positions stated by others. Despite its difficulty, people who live in democracies must undertake productive argument with one another, because failure to do so can have serious consequences, ranging from inaction on important issues, such as global warming, to taking serious actions such as going to war. Consider this *New York Times* account of a rather uproductive encounter between two well-known celebrities and President George W. Bush's deputy chief of staff, Karl Rove:

BUSH AIDE'S CELEBRITY MEETING BECOMES A GLOBAL WARMING RUN-IN

Put celebrity environmental activists in a room with top Bush administration officials and a meeting of the minds could result. At least that is a theoretical possibility.

The more likely outcome is that an argument will break out, as it did at the White House Correspondents' Association dinner on Saturday night between Karl Rove, the president's deputy chief of staff, and the singer Sheryl Crow and Laurie David, a major Democratic donor and a producer of the global warming documentary featuring Al Gore, "An Inconvenient Truth."

Ms. Crow and Ms. David, who have been visiting campuses in an event billed as the Stop Global Warming College Tour, approached Mr. Rove to urge him to take "a fresh look" at global warming, they said later.

Recriminations between the celebrities and the White House carried over into Sunday, with Ms. Crow and Ms. David calling Mr. Rove "a spoiled child throwing a tantrum" and the White House criticizing their "Hollywood histrionics."

"I honestly thought that I was going to change his mind, like, right there and then," Ms. David said Sunday, The Associated Press reported.

Ms. Crow was at the dinner as a guest of Bloomberg News. Ms. David and her husband, Larry David, a creator of "Seinfeld," were guests of CNN. Mr. Rove was a guest of The New York Times.

The one thing all three parties agree on is that the conversation quickly became heated.

As Ms. Crow and Ms. David described it on the Huffington Post Web site on Sunday, when Mr. Rove turned toward his table, Ms. Crow touched his arm and "Karl swung around and spat, 'Don't touch me.'"

Both sides agreed that Ms. Crow told him, "You can't speak to us like that, you work for us," to which Mr. Rove responded, "I don't work for you, I work for the American people." Ms. Crow and Ms. David wrote that Ms. Crow shot back, "We are the American people."

In their Web posting, Ms. Crow and Ms. David described Mr. Rove as responding with "anger flaring," and as having "exploded with even more venom" as the argument continued.

"She came over to insult me," Mr. Rove said Saturday night, "and she succeeded."

Mr. Rove did not respond to a request for comment on the women's Internet posting on Sunday.

Tony Fratto, a White House spokesman, said, "We have respect for the opinions and passion that many people have for climate change." But, Mr. Fratto said, "I wish the same respect was afforded to the president."

He accused Ms. Crow and Ms. David of ignoring the president's environmental initiatives, like pushing for alternative fuels, and for "going after officials with misinformed assertions at a social dinner."

"It would be better," Mr. Fratto said, "to set aside Hollywood histrionics and try to help with the problem instead of this baseless, and tasteless, finger pointing." (*New York Times*, April 23, 2007, A16)

We offer this account of the heated exchange as an example of a simultaneous faith in rhetoric—Laurie David claims she "honestly thought" she "was going to change his mind, like, right there and then"—and a refusal of rhetorical engagement (Rove's alleged "don't touch me"). Indeed, Americans often refuse to talk with each other about important matters like religion or politics, retreating into silence if someone brings either subject up in public discourse. And if someone disagrees publicly with someone else about politics or religion, Americans sometimes take that as a breach of good manners. Note the White House spokesman's moral offense that such a matter would come up at "a social dinner," suggesting that Crow and David committed an etiquette violation by mixing arguments with hors d'oeuvres.

Americans tend to link a person's opinions to her identity. We assume that someone's opinions result from her personal experience, and hence that those opinions are somehow "hers"—that she alone "owns" them. For example, when Whitehouse spokesman Tony Fratto refers to Crow's and David's approach as "Hollywood histrionics," he effectively reduces their stance on global warming to a small demographic, invoking a **commonplace** about out-of-touch Hollywood, and referring to their confrontation as a type of acting. Rhetoric gives way to personal insult, engagement to hand-waving dismissal.

Too often opinion-as-identity stands in the way of rhetorical exchange. If someone we know is a devout Catholic, for example, we are often reluctant to share with her any negative views we have about Catholicism, fearing that she might take our views as a personal attack rather than as an invitation to discuss differences. This habit of tying beliefs to an identity also has the unfortunate effect of allowing people who hold a distinctive set of beliefs to belittle or mistreat people who do not share those beliefs.[1]

The intellectual habit that assumes religious and political choices are tied up with a person's identity, with her "self," also makes it seem as though people never change their minds about things like religion and politics. But as we all know, people do change their minds about these matters; people convert from one religious faith to another, and they sometimes change their political affiliation from year to year, perhaps voting across party lines in one election and voting a party line in the next.

The authors of this book are concerned that if Americans continue to ignore the reality that people disagree with one another all the time, or if we pretend to ignore it in the interests of preserving good manners, we risk undermining the principles on which our democratic community is based. People who are afraid of airing their differences tend to keep silent when those with whom they disagree are speaking; people who are not inclined to air differences tend to associate only with those who agree with them. In such a balkanized public sphere, both our commonalities and our differences go unexamined. In a democracy, people must call into question the opinions of others, must bring them into the light for examination and negotiation. In communities where citizens are not coerced, important decisions must be made by means of public discourse. When the quality of public discourse diminishes, so does the quality of democracy.

Ancient teachers called the process of examining positions held by others "**invention**," which Aristotle defined as finding and displaying the available **arguments** on any **issue**. Invention is central to the rhetorical process. What often passes for rhetoric in our own time—repeatedly stating (or shouting) one's beliefs at an "opponent" in order to browbeat him into submission—is not rhetoric. Participation in rhetoric entails that every party to the discussion be aware that beliefs may change during the exchange and discussion of points of view. All parties to a rhetorical transaction must be willing to be persuaded by good arguments. Otherwise, decisions will be made for bad reasons, or **interested** reasons, or no reason at all.

Sometimes, of course, there are good reasons for remaining silent. Power is distributed unequally in our culture, and power inequities may force wise people to remain silent on some occasions. We believe that in contemporary American culture people who enjoy high socioeconomic status have more power than those who have fewer resources and less access to others in power. We also hold that men have more power than women and that white people have more power than people of color (and yes, we are aware that there are exceptions to all of these generalizations). We do not believe, though, that these inequities are a natural or necessary state of things. We do believe that rhetoric is among the best ways available to us for rectifying power inequities among citizens.

The people who taught and practiced rhetoric in Athens and Rome during ancient times would have found contemporary unwillingness to engage in public disagreement very strange indeed. Their way of using disagreement to reach solutions was taught to students in Western schools for over two thousand years and is still available to us in translations of their textbooks, speeches, lecture notes, and treatises on rhetoric. Within limits, their way of looking at disagreement can still be useful to us. The students who worked with ancient teachers of rhetoric were members of privileged classes for the most part, since Athens and Rome both maintained socioeconomic systems that were manifestly unjust to many of the people who lived and worked within them. The same charge can be leveled at our own system, of course. Today the United States is home not only to its native peoples but to people from all over the world. Its non-native citizens arrived here under vastly different circumstances, ranging from colonization to immigration to enslavement, and their lives have been shaped by these circumstances, as well as by their genders and class affiliations. Not all—perhaps not even a majority—have enjoyed the equal opportunities that are promised by the Constitution. But unfair social and economic realities only underscore the need for principled public discussion among concerned citizens.

The aim of ancient rhetorics was to distribute the power that resides in language among all of its students. This power is available to anyone who is willing to study the principles of rhetoric. People who know about rhetoric know how to persuade others to consider their point of view without having to resort to coercion or violence. For the purposes of this book, we have assumed that people prefer to seek verbal resolution of differences to the use of force. Rhetoric is of no use when people determine to use coercion or violence to gain the ends they seek.

A knowledge of rhetoric also allows people to discern when **rhetors** are making bad arguments or are asking them to make inappropriate choices. Since rhetoric confers the gift of greater mastery over language, it can also teach those who study it to evaluate anyone's rhetoric; thus the critical capacity conferred by rhetoric can free its students from the manipulative rhetoric of others. When knowledge about rhetoric is available only to a few people, the power inherent in persuasive discourse is disproportionately shared. Unfortunately, throughout history rhetorical knowledge has usually been shared only among those who can exert economic, social, or political power as well. But ordinary citizens can learn to deploy rhetorical power, and if they have a chance and the courage to deploy it skillfully and often, it's possible that they may change other features of our society, as well. In this book, then, we aim to help our readers become more skilled speakers and writers. But we also aim to help them become better citizens. We begin by offering a very brief account of the beginnings of ancient rhetorical thought and then move to considering some important differences between ancient and modern thinking about rhetoric.[2]

ANCIENT RHETORIC: THE BEGINNINGS

Something quite remarkable happened in the small Greek city of Athens during the sixth, fifth, and fourth centuries BCE. During this period, the citizens of that community evolved a form of government they called *demokratia* (*demos* ["people"] and *kratos* ["political power"]). Any Athenian who was defined as a citizen played a direct role in making important decisions that affected the entire community: whether to go to war, to send ambassadors to neighboring countries, to raise or lower taxes, to build bridges or walls, to convict or acquit people accused of crimes against the state or other citizens.

In the Athenian political system, citizenship was determined by birthright and thus was awarded to any adult male who could establish his Athenian heritage, whether he was wealthy or not, aristocratic or not. These were very inclusive requirements for the time, even though they excluded the bulk of the population who were women, foreign-born men, or slaves. Because of these requirements, classical Athens can hardly be said to have been a democracy in our more inclusive sense, although we remind readers that for almost half of its history, the United States limited suffrage to white males. Nor was Athens a representative democracy, as ours is said to be, since the few hundred people who were defined as Athenian citizens participated directly in making political and judicial decisions rather than acting through elected representatives.

The citizens met in the Assembly to make political decisions and acted as jurors at trials. Athenian men apparently took their civic responsibilities seriously. Despite the difficulties entailed in meeting this responsibility—leaving work undone for several days, traveling to the city from outlying farms—as many as five hundred or more citizens could be expected to attend and vote in the Assembly when it was in session.

Sometime during the fifth century BCE, all citizens earned the right to speak in the Assembly. This right was called *isegoria* ("equality in the agora" or assembly place). Most likely, very few citizens exercised their right to speak. When five hundred Athenians met to deliberate on important issues, not everyone could speak at once, nor was everyone sufficiently informed about the issue at hand to speak effectively. The task of filling in the details and of arguing for a course of action fell to people who were trained in speaking, who had sufficient education to understand the issues, and who had the leisure to study the issues at hand. These were the professional *rhetores*. In the fifth-century, the term *rhetor* referred to someone who introduced a resolution into the Assembly, but by the fourth century BCE the term meant something like "an expert on politics." Later it came to mean "one skilled in public speaking" as well. In this book, we refer to people who practice rhetoric as rhetors. We refer to people who teach it or theorize about it as rhetoricians.

SOME DIFFERENCES BETWEEN ANCIENT AND MODERN THOUGHT

The great age of ancient rhetorics dictates that there will be differences between them and modern thinking about rhetoric. One such difference is that ancient rhetoricians did not value factual proof very highly, while **facts** and **testimony** are virtually the only proofs discussed in modern rhetorical theory (see the chapter on **extrinsic proofs**). Ancient teachers preferred to use arguments that they generated from language itself and from community beliefs during an intellectual process they called "invention." They invented and named many such arguments, among them commonplaces, examples, **conjectures**, maxims, and enthymemes (see the chapters on **stasis,** commonplaces, and on rhetorical reasoning). Another difference is that ancient rhetoricians valued opinions as a source of knowledge, whereas in modern thought opinions are often dismissed as unimportant. But ancient rhetoricians thought of opinions as something that were held not by individuals but by entire communities. This difference has to do with another assumption that they made, which was that a person's character (and hence her opinions) were constructions made by the community in which she lived. And since the ancients believed that communities were the source and reason for rhetoric, opinions were for them the very stuff of argument.

A third difference between ancient and modern rhetorics is that ancient rhetoricians situated their teaching in place and time. Their insistence that local and temporal conditions influenced the act of composition marks a fairly distinct contrast with the habit in modern rhetoric of treating rhetorical occasions as if they were all alike. For example, modern rhetoric textbooks insist that every composition display a thesis. Ancient teachers, in contrast, were not so sure that every discourse has a thesis to display. For example, people sometimes write or speak in order to determine what alternatives are available in a given situation. In this case they are not ready to advance a thesis. And if a rhetor has a hostile audience, after all, it might be better (and safer) not to mention a thesis at all, or at least to place it near the end of the discourse (see the chapter on **arrangement** for advice about the selection and placement of arguments generated by invention).

A last difference between ancient and modern rhetorics has to do with ancient teachers' attitude toward language. Modern rhetoricians tend to think that language's role is limited to the communication of facts. Ancient rhetoricians, however, taught their students that language does many things. Cicero, who was an extremely skilled and influential speaker in the days of the Roman Republic, asserted that the ends of language use are to teach, to give pleasure, and to move. But the point of instructing or delighting audiences is, finally, to move them to accept or reject some thought or action.

Just the Facts, Please

From an ancient perspective, one of the most troublesome of modern assumptions about the nature of argument goes like this: if the facts are on your side, you can't be wrong, and you can't be refuted. Facts are statements that somebody has substantiated through experience or proved through research. Or they are events that really happened, events that somebody will attest to as factual. Facts have a "you were there" quality; if the arguer doesn't have personal knowledge of the facts, he is pretty sure that some expert on the subject does know them, and all she has to do in that case is to look them up in a book. Here are some examples of factual statements:

1. Water freezes at 32 degrees Fahrenheit.
2. The moon orbits the earth.
3. On April 16, 2007, Virginia Tech student Cho Sueng-Hui killed 32 people and himself on his campus in Blacksburg, Virginia.

These are facts because they can be verified through experience or by means of testimony. Individuals can test the accuracy of the first statement for themselves, and all three statements can be confirmed by checking relevant and reliable sources.

No doubt the importance given to facts derives from the modern faith in science or, more technically, from faith in empirical proofs, those that are available to the senses: vision, smell, taste, touch, and hearing. During the nineteenth century, rhetoricians came to prefer so-called scientific or empirical proofs to all the other kinds outlined in ancient rhetoric. After 1850, American rhetoric textbooks began to reduce the many kinds of evidence discriminated by ancient rhetoricians to just two: empirical evidence and testimony. Both of these kinds of evidence have the you-are-there quality: empirical evidence derives from someone's actual sensory contact with the relevant evidence; testimony involves somebody's reporting their acquaintance with the facts of the case. During the twentieth century, rhetoric textbooks enlarged testimony to include accounts by persons recognized as experts or authorities in specialized fields of study. The modern reverence for facts and testimonies explains why students are often asked to write research papers in school—their teachers want to be sure they know how to assemble empirical evidence and expert testimony into a coherent piece of writing.

There are some problems with the approving modern attitude toward empirical evidence. For one thing, it ignores the possibility that the evidence provided by the senses is neither reliable nor conclusive. People are selective about what they perceive, and they continually reconstruct their memories of what they perceive, as well. Moreover, people don't always agree about their sensory perceptions. The Older Sophist Protagoras pointed out that a blowing wind could feel cold to one person and hot to another and that honey tasted bitter to some people although it tastes sweet to most.

Perceptions, and thus testimony about them, can also be influenced by an observer's perspective. Over the years during which we have been writing and revising this book, the National Football League has changed its policy on the use of instant replay several times. In instant replay, the referees watch video tapes of a controversial play taken from several different angles in order to decide what penalties to assess, if any. Even though professional referees are trained observers of the game, sometimes they simply cannot see whether a defensive player used his arms illegally or whether a receiver managed to keep his feet within bounds while he caught the ball. The problem with instant replay, though, is that sometimes television cameras are not well positioned to see a contested play, either. In terms used in this book, the supposedly factual or empirical account yielded by instant replay is often no better at resolving disagreements about violations than is the testimony given by referees. Currently the NFL uses a rather complicated combination of taped replays and referee judgements to make decisions about contested plays. In other words, the NFL has opted to combine facts and testimony as evidence for opinions rendered about close calls. This example interests us because fans seem to trust referees' judgements less than they do that of the television camera operators. Indeed, fans often accuse referees of having an interest in one outcome or another, assuming that this interest influences their perception of events. This suggests in turn that football fans may trust machines rather more than they trust human experts, even though the machines are, after all, constructed and operated by human beings. One seldom hears complaints that CBS or Fox placed its cameras in positions that might serve its own interests, at least in the context of football games.

This example highlights the even more interesting observation that the facts of the physical world don't mean much to anybody unless they are involved in some larger **network of interpretation.** In football the relevant network of interpretation is the rules of the game. Without these rules, the exact placement of a player's arm or the exact point at which his feet touched the ground pretty much loses its relevance. (Sometimes football players suddenly switch to a network of interpretation that allows them to read an arm in the face as an act of aggression. When this happens, referees have to assess more penalties until the game's more usual network of interpretation can be restored.)

Here's another example that demonstrates that facts are not very interesting or persuasive unless they are read within a network of interpretation: geologists use the fossil record as evidence to support the theory of evolution. They point to boxes and crates of mute, stony facts—fossilized plants and animals—as evidence that species have evolved over time. But the fossil record itself, as well as the historical relationships that geologists have established among fossils from all over the world, is a network of interpretation. That is, geologists have read a series of natural objects in such a way as to construe them as evidence for a huge natural process that nobody could actually have witnessed. If you want to object that a fossil is a fact, please do. You are quite right. Our point is that it is not a very useful (or interesting) fact apart from its interpretation as a fossil, rather than a rock, and its location within the network of interpretation called evolutionary theory. Using other networks of interpretation, a fossil can just as easily be read as a doorstop or a weapon.

In contrast to moderns, ancient philosophers understood the usefulness of empirical facts quite differently from moderns. Early Greek thinkers were skeptical about the status of phenomena, the name they gave to the facts of the physical world—stuff like trees, fossils, rocks, honey, cold winds, and the like. They argued about whether such things existed at all, or whether they existed only when perceived by the human senses. Most agreed that human perception of the facts of the physical world necessarily involved some distortion, since human thoughts and perceptions and language are obviously not the same things as physical objects like rocks.

Perhaps because of their skepticism about the nature of facts, ancient teachers of rhetoric were equally skeptical about the persuasive potential of facts. Aristotle wrote that facts and testimony were not truly within the art of rhetoric; they were *atechnoi*—"without art or skill"—and hence extrinsic to rhetoric. Extrinsic proofs were not developed through a rhetor's use of the principles of rhetoric but were found in existing circumstances. Aristotle defined an extrinsic proof as "all such as are not supplied by our own efforts, but existed beforehand" (*Rhetoric* I ii 1356a). Such proofs are extrinsic to rhetoric, then, because no art is required to invent them. A rhetor only has to choose the relevant facts or testimony and present them to an audience.

Because facts are relatively mute in the absence of a relevant network of interpretation, rhetors seldom argue from a simple list of facts.[3] Today, practicing rhetoricians invent and use a wide variety of nonfactual arguments with great effectiveness. Take a trivial illustration: many MP3 player advertisements are arguments from **example.** Advertisers show a silhouette of a woman dancing energetically, hair flying, while wearing headphones and holding a distinctive-looking MP3 player in her hand. They assume that the attractive example will make people reason as follows: "Well that woman listens to a particular brand of MP3 player, and look at how she moves, how cool she is, and how much fun she's having. If I listen to that kind of player, I'll be a sleek, dancing, fun-having person too." The ad writers hope that viewers will generalize from the fictional example to their own lives, and draw the conclusion that they should buy the MP3 player. There are no facts in this argument—indeed it is a fiction, a digitally-mastered silhouette, constructed by scriptwriters, graphic designers, directors and others—and yet it is apparently persuasive, since this type of advertisement endures.

Rhetors who rely only upon facts and testimony, then, place very serious limits on their persuasive potential, since many other kinds of rhetorical argument are employed daily in the media and in ordinary conversation. These arguments are invented or discovered by rhetors, using the art of rhetoric. Aristotle described invented arguments as *entechnoi*—"embodied in the art" of rhetoric. This class of proofs is **intrinsic** to rhetoric, since these proofs are generated from rhetoric's principles.

In rhetoric, intrinsic proofs are found or discovered by rhetors. **Invention** is the division of rhetoric that investigates the possible means by which proofs can be discovered; it supplies speakers and writers with sets of instructions that help them to find and compose arguments that are appropriate for a given rhetorical situation. The word *invenire* meant "to find" or "to come upon" in Latin. The Greek equivalent, *heuriskein,* also meant "to find out" or "discover." Variants of both words persist in

English. For instance, the exclamation "Eureka!" (derived from *heuriskein*) means "I have found it!" This word was so popular during the nineteenth-century gold rush that a town in California was named "Eureka." The Greek word has also given us *heuristic,* which means "an aid to discovery," and we refer to anyone who has new ideas as an "inventor," from the Latin *invenire.*

A **proposition** (Latin *proponere,* "to put forth") is any arguable statement put forward for discussion by a rhetor. A proof is any statement or statements used to persuade an audience to accept a proposition. Proofs are bits of language that are supposed to be persuasive. Ancient rhetoricians developed and catalogued a wide range of intrinsic rhetorical proofs, most of which relied on rhetors' knowledge of a community's history and beliefs. The Older Sophists contributed the notions of commonplaces and **probabilities.** Aristotle contributed **enthymemes, examples, signs,** and **maxims,** and Hermagoras of Temnos is credited with the invention of **stasis theory.**

Aristotle discriminated three kinds of intrinsic rhetorical proofs: *ethos, pathos,* and *logos.* These kinds of proofs translate into English as ethical, pathetic, and logical proofs. Ethical proofs depend on the rhetor's **character;** pathetic proofs appeal to the emotions of the audience; and logical proofs derive from arguments found in the issue itself. Our words *logic* and *logical* are derived from the Greek *logos,* which meant "voice" or "speech" to early Greek rhetoricians. Later, *logos* also became associated with reason.

Here is an example. Like water and air pollution, light pollution has lately been receiving attention, perhaps because the issue of climate change has caused the American people to pay more attention to environmental issues. In 2003, in fact, *The Simpsons* aired an episode called "Scuse Me While I Miss the Sky," in which Lisa Simpson, having decided to become an astronomer, is an outspoken opponent of light pollution. In making her case to the people of Springfield, Lisa Simpson could have made any of several interesting arguments in support of a "dark-sky" ordinance, which would reduce the amount of light emitted into the night sky by streetlights and billboards. She could point out that current light levels from these sources interfere with astronomers' ability to observe the night sky through their telescopes. The association of astronomy with science gives her a strong appeal from ethos, because scientists are generally respected in our culture (and, of course, as a member of the Simpson family, Lisa enjoys her own unique **situated ethos** in the town of Springfield). She can also make an emotional appeal by reminding her audience that human-made lighting interferes with the ordinary person's ability to see the moon and stars clearly, thus decreasing his enjoyment of the night sky. In addition, there are a good many logical proofs available to her in the issue itself. She can reason from **cause to effect:** city lighting causes so much interference with telescopes and other instruments that the quality of observational work being carried out at the observatory is diminished. Or she can reason from a **parallel case:** "a dark-sky ordinance was enacted in the town down the road, and the quality of astronomical observations has improved enormously there. The same thing will happen in Springfield if we install a dark-sky ordinance here." If Lisa made these arguments, she would rely on only one fact: that current light levels from the city interfered with her ability to make astronomical observations. Interested citizens could contest even this statement (which the ancients would have called a **conjecture**), since it obviously serves the interests of someone who needs a dark sky to complete her observations.

Recently, the dark-sky campaign has moved into the U.S. national parks, as the following excerpts from an article by Alison Fromme demonstrate:

CRUSADERS OF DARKNESS

Chad Moore isn't afraid of the dark. On moonless nights, while many backpackers are sitting around campfires, the 36-year-old park ranger is humping 65 pounds of specialized gear along inky mountain trails. He heads for high, open spaces—treeless ridgetops are perfect—and unloads a wide-field digital camera, motorized tripod, laptop, and enough wires and batteries to jump-start a bus. Moore assembles the gear quickly, his routine honed by forays into dozens of backcountry locales from Nebraska's Agate Fossil Beds to California's Lassen Volcanic National Park. He isn't a hobbyist pursuing astronomy, however. As head of the National Park Service's Night Sky Team, Moore is giving up his sleep so backpackers can enjoy darker nights and more stars. . . .

Preserving dark skies and quantifying light pollution has been Moore's focus for most of his 12 years as a ranger. When he founded the Night Sky Team in 1999, his goals were too ambitious for the available camera technology. So Dan Duriscoe, the project's technical leader, built a motorized tripod and camera mount that could be used to take sky surveys. This system has generated thousands of night-sky images to yield light-pollution baselines for many park units. Moore has presented these results at astronomy conferences, and published his data in a 2007 scientific paper and on the web (nature.nps. gov/air/lightscapes). For many park rangers and scientists, the team's description of widespread light pollution isn't new. But Moore's energetic campaign has won new converts, including bigwigs at NPS headquarters who responded by increasing the team's funding. After running his operation on a minuscule budget for several years, Moore received a $4 million, 4-year NPS grant in 2006. "I think the Park Service takes pride in being a leader in this fight," he says.

Reducing light pollution isn't as easy as switching off a few floodlamps. Light can travel hundreds of miles, spoiling views far from its source. And since no one's pulling the plug on Vegas, saving starry nights for backpackers in Death Valley calls for more creative solutions. Moore understands this challenge. "We're not here to tell people to turn off all the lights," he says. Instead, his team wants to help the public adopt smarter, more efficient, and in the long run, more economical lighting options. . . . Like his colleagues racing to preserve endangered animals and plants, Moore knows he's defying the headlong rush of civilization. But there's one important difference, he notes. Darkness isn't subject to extinction, only a temporary loss of intensity. The night sky will always be recoverable; we just need to dim the lights. (43–44)

Chad Moore has been successful in making light pollution matter—to backpackers as well as to the National Park Service. His efforts involve a good deal of data collection, as is evident from the opening paragraph of the article, but the data collection is usually not enough; numbers also need arguments. For example, it is very important for Moore to present himself as a reasonable person and to be clear in advance about what he is proposing, and what he is not, as he does with this assertion: "We're not here to tell people to turn off all the lights." This sentence is a small but persuasive argument found within the rhetorical situation, what Aristotle called an intrinsic proof.

Ancient students of rhetoric practiced inventing a wide variety of intrinsic proofs while they were in school. By the time they finished their education, invention strategies were second nature to them, so that whenever they were called on to construct a speech or to compose a piece of written discourse, they could conduct a mental review of invention processes. This review helped them to determine which proofs would be useful in arguing about whatever issue confronted them. The means of inventing rhetorical proofs can still provide rhetors with an intellectual arsenal to which they can resort whenever they need to compose. Anyone who becomes familiar with all of them should never be at a loss for words.

To become adept at invention is not easy, though. Invention requires systematic thought, practice, and above all, thoroughness. But careful attention to the ancient strategies for discovering arguments will amply repay anyone who undertakes their study and use. Hermogenes of Tarsus wrote that "nothing good can be produced easily, and I should be surprised if there were anything better for humankind, since we are logical animals, than fine and noble *logoi* and every kind of them" (*On Style* I 214). In other words, to invent arguments is essentially human. But invention also has a less lofty, more practical aim: rhetors who practice the ancient means of invention will soon find themselves supplied with more arguments than they can possibly use.

That's Just Your Opinion

There is another category in popular notions about argument that deserves our attention. This is the category called "opinion." People can put a stop to conversation simply by saying, "Well, that's just your opinion." When someone does this, he implies that opinions aren't very important. They aren't facts, after all, and furthermore, opinions belong to individuals, while facts belong to everybody. Another implication is this: because opinions are intimately tied up with individual identities, there's not much hope of changing them unless the person changes her identity. To put this another way, the implication of "Well, that's just your opinion" is that Jane Doe's opinion about, say, energy use and global warming is all tied up with who she is. If she thinks that driving a Humvee is morally wrong, well, that's her opinion and there's not much we can do about changing her belief or her practice.

The belief that opinions belong to individuals may explain why Americans seem reluctant to challenge one another's opinions. To challenge a person's opinion is to denigrate his character, to imply that if he holds an unexamined or stupid or silly opinion, he is an unthinking or stupid or silly person. Ancient teachers of rhetoric would find fault with this on three grounds. First, they would object that there is no such thing as "just your opinion." Second, they would object to the assumption that opinions aren't important. Third, they would argue that opinions can be changed. The point of rhetoric, after all, is to change opinions.

Ancient rhetoricians taught their students that opinions are shared by many members of a community. The Greek word for common or popular opinion was *doxa*, which is the root of English words like *orthodoxy* ("straight opinion") and *paradox* ("opinions alongside one another"). Opinions develop because people live in communities. A person living alone on an island needs a great many skills and physical resources, but she has no need for political, moral, or social opinions until she meets up with another person or an animal, since politics, morality, and sociality depend upon our relations with beings that think and feel.

Let's return to the example of energy conservation in relation to climate change. Here is an article written by *Addison County Independent* reporter Megan James, entitled "Step It Up for Global Warming."

MIDDLEBURY—When Lincoln resident Stacey Lee-Dobek saw "An Inconvenient Truth," the film about Al Gore's fight against climate change, for the first time last December, she knew it was time to take action against global warming.

"I stood up and said out loud to myself, 'I have to do something more than changing my light bulbs,'" she said. "It became a New Year's Resolution."

So Lee-Dobek sat down at her computer to begin researching the issue, and before she knew it, she'd found Step It Up, Ripton environmentalist Bill McKibben's nation-wide virtual demonstration to send the U.S. government a singular message on Saturday, April 14: "Step it up, Congress! Cut carbon emissions 80 percent by 2050."

Over the last five months, McKibben and his crew of six recent Middlebury College graduates have helped facilitate the organization of more than 1,200 actions to take place simultaneously in all 50 states that day. From the tops of melting glaciers and the steps of town halls, demonstrators will upload digital images of their actions to the Step It Up Web site at www.stepitup2007.org, and those images will be compiled and delivered straight to Congress.

Lee-Dobek fell in love with the idea immediately, and in her excitement, signed herself up for two different demonstrations. Realizing she couldn't be in two places at once, she dropped the idea she'd planned for Burlington, and focused instead on organizing a primary rally for Middlebury.

"My focus is letting Vermonters know what they can do to help," she said. "I'm concerned about mankind and coastal cities, especially where the economy is really poor. I've got kids, and they're going to have kids and I want their quality of life to be just as good as ours."

For Lee-Dobek, the first key to fighting global warming locally is "aggressive conservatism" of energy.

"Carpooling is one of the most effective things we can do as Vermonters," she said. "It's amazing how much we drive in this state."

Middlebury's rally will begin this Saturday at 2 p.m. on the town green, where demonstrators will convene with banners, posters and possibly even drums. They will then walk to the Marble Works footbridge, where they will pose for the group photo, and continue to the municipal gym, where from 3 to 5 p.m., area renewable energy activists and musicians will hold an environmental fair.

The activities will begin with a performance by Ripton-based folk trio Bread and Bones, featuring Richard Ruane, Beth Duquette and Mitch Barron. Middlebury College english and environmental studies professor John Elder will give a short presentation about what Vermonters can do to lessen their impact on the environment and how to affect change in Congress. Representatives from area environmental organizations will set up informational booths.

"What I've been impressed by is how much is going on in Addison County," Lee-Dobek said. "Until the bug bit me I had no clue."

She is excited to see all of these local efforts to combat climate change showcased in one room on Saturday, including Central Vermont Public Service (CVPS) Cow Power, Bristol-based IdleFree Vermont, Addison County Relocalization Network (ACoRN) and SolarFest, a Middletown Springs nonprofit that uses art to build renewable energy education in its community.

With Step It Up, area residents have a unique opportunity to send their message directly to Congress. Lee-Dobek urges everyone to join a demonstration on Saturday, whether it is in Middlebury or at one of the 64 actions planned for Vermont. The ones in area towns will take place in:

- Brandon, where a bike ride against global warming will begin in front of the Brandon Free Public Library and a pinwheel parade will take place at the gazebo in the park by the falls at 10 a.m.

- East Middlebury, where residents will gather at the Gorge at the Middlebury River at 11 a.m.

- Orwell, where Singing Cedars Farmstead will host a seed-planting event starting at 10 a.m.

- Ripton, where students from the North Branch School will serve a potluck lunch at the Ripton Community House at 11 a.m. and people will gather at Spirit In Nature off Ripton-Goshen Road at noon.

- Salisbury, where residents will gather at Camp Keewaydin at noon and then offer a couple of interpretive hikes in the area.

- Vergennes, where people at Vergennes Union Middle School will spend the day, starting at 8 a.m., writing to legislators and creating an art project focused on global warming.

And if all of these are still too far to drive, Lee-Dobek suggested that interested Vermonters create their own demonstration. To do so, go to the Step It Up Web site for information on how to register a new action.

"It's not too late for people to host their own actions," she said. "People can climb to the top of Mount Abe or Camel's Hump. The important thing is to get a banner with the slogan and to upload a photo from wherever you are." *(Addision County Independent)*

If we return to our earlier discussion of Jane Doe equipped with the notion of shared opinion, we can see that Jane's opinion about global warming is not "just hers." Rather, she shares it with other people like Laurie David and Al Gore, whose film inspired Stacey Lee-Dobek, the focus of this particular article, to become more resolute and outspoken for the cause. She shares it with singer Sheryl Crow, author and activist Bill McKibben, and a host of students at Middlebury College, as well. She also shares her opinion with thousands of people whom she has never met—with everyone who believes, as she does, that it is wrong to continue such excessive use of fuel without regard for global warming. And Vermont, where Stacey goes to school, is particularly hospitable to environmental concerns and has taken a leadership position among states. It might be easier for someone like Jane to care about global warming in a Vermont community as opposed to, say, a community in a state such as Texas, where the oil industry has a stronghold. And if her opinion is not just hers, it follows that, should she wish to, Jane can change her opinion without changing her identity.

This is not to deny that changing one's opinion, particularly about deeply held religious or political beliefs, is very hard work. But it can be done, and it can be done by means of a systematic examination of the available positions on an issue. Environmental activism is an interesting example in this regard because it was until recently a minority belief and practice. Arguments supporting minority beliefs and practices must actively be sought out; often they are not available in venues that convey more dominant opinions, such as mainstream media. As few as five years ago, it took work to find arguments against the wastefulness of American lifestyles, and environmental activists could only become so after rejecting a more dominant view. Opinions and practices that are dominant, on the other hand, can be accepted without much thought or investigation. Most Americans born after the Second World War grew up believing in the infinite availability of gasoline and electricity, often driving long distances on vacations and idling at drive-thrus waiting for food that was shipped to the restaurant. That individuals and major corporations have very recently felt the need to examine their "carbon footprints"—and that the phrase "carbon neutral" has now entered into the mainstream—indicates that previous practices have met with a rhetorical challenge significant enough to threaten their status as commonplaces, that is, as dominant, mainstream beliefs that used to "go without saying" (see the chapter on commonplaces).

If we locate opinions outside individuals and within communities, they assume more importance. If a significant number of individuals within a community share an opinion, it becomes difficult to dismiss that opinion as unimportant, no matter how much we like or detest it. Nor can we continue to see opinions as unchangeable. If Jane got her opinion about climate change from somebody she knows, something she read, or a film she saw, she can modify her opinion when she hears or reads or sees a different opinion from somebody else. For example, perhaps her economics professor may caution that the American economy will take a nosedive if legions of Americans suddenly begin to pay attention to carbon footprints and the like. Communication researchers have discovered that people generally adopt the opinions of people they know and respect. Opinions are likely to change when we lose respect for the people who hold them or when we meet new people whom we like and respect and who have different opinions.

The modern association of facts with science, and opinion with everything else, draws on a set of beliefs that was invented during the seventeenth century. Science was associated with empirical proofs and rational problem solving, while nonscientific methods of reasoning began to be considered irrational or emotional. It was also during this period that the modern notion of the individual emerged, wherein each person was thought to be an intellectual island whose unique experiences rendered his or her opinions unique. While the modern notion of the individual is attractive in many ways, it does cause us to forget that opinions are widely shared. Too, the modern distinction between reason and other means of investigation keeps us from realizing how many of our beliefs are based in our emotional responses to our environments. Indeed, our acceptance of our most important beliefs—religious, moral, and political—probably have as much to do with our desires and interests as they do with rational argument. The reason/emotion distinction also keeps us from realizing how often we are swayed by appeals to our emotions or, more accurately, how difficult it is to distinguish between a purely rational appeal and a purely emotional one. And the notion of the unique individual makes it difficult for us to see how many of our opinions are borrowed from the beliefs that we share with other members of our communities.

Ancient teachers of rhetoric believed that rhetorical reasoning, which is used in politics, journalism, religious argument, literature, philosophy, history, and law—to name just a few of its arenas—is fully as legitimate as that used in any other field. And even though it utilizes appeals to community opinion and to emotions, if it is done responsibly, rhetorical reasoning is no more or less valid than the reasoning used in science. In fact, scientific reasoning is itself rhetorical when its propositions are drawn from beliefs held by the community of trained scientists.

On Ideology and the Commonplaces

We suggested earlier that networks of interpretation—the way people interpret and use the facts—have persuasive potential, while facts by themselves do not. Postmodern rhetoricians use the term *ideology* to name networks of interpretation, and that is the term we use in the rest of this book.

An ideology is a coherent set of beliefs that people use to understand events and the behavior of other people; these beliefs are also used to predict events and behaviors. Ideologies exist in language, but they are worked out in practices. They are sets of statements that tell us how to understand ourselves and others and how to understand nature and our relation to it, as well. Furthermore, ideologies help us to decide how to value what we know—they tell us what is thought to be true, right, good, or beautiful in a community.

Each of us is immersed in the ideologies that circulate in our communities once we begin to understand and use language. Hence ideologies actually produce "selves"; the picture you have of yourself has been formed by your experiences, to be sure, but it has also been constructed by the beliefs that circulate among your family, friends, the media, and other communities that you inhabit. You may think of yourself as a Christian, Jew, New Ager, or atheist. In each case, you adopted a set of beliefs about the way the world works from some relevant community (in the last case, you may have reacted against dominant ideologies). Even though identities are shaped by ideologies, they are never stable, because we can question or reject ideological belief. As we have suggested, people do this all the time: they undergo religious conversion; they adopt a politics; they decide that UFOs do not exist; they stop eating meat; they take up exercise because they have become convinced it is good for them. Often, it is rhetoric that has brought about this ideological change. Ideology is the stuff with which rhetors work.

We mean no disrespect when we say that religious beliefs and political leanings are ideological. Quite the contrary: human beings need ideologies in order to make sense of their experiences in the world. Powerful ideologies such as religions and political beliefs help people to understand who they are and what their relation is to the world and to other beings.

Sometimes people make small changes because the ideological bias of a customary practice has been called into question by the community with which they identify. For example, the first edition of this book used a BC/AD dating system. This nomenclature is ideological because it is particularly Christian (*BC* stands for "before Christ" while *AD* abbreviates the Latin *anno Domini*, "in the year of the Lord," and is used to designate the years after the birth of Christ). In the second edition, we adopted a new and increasingly customary dating system, BCE/CE, which stand for "before the Common Era" and "Common Era" respectively. We realize, as one of our critics has pointed out to us, that changing the naming system still does not alter the calendar itself. The year "zero" is still associated with the birth of Christ. But in changing from BC/AD to BCE/CE, we made an ideological choice to use a secular dating system. In doing so, we follow our own beliefs as well as scholarly convention—the common practice in a broad community of scholars. (If this were a book about the history of Christianity, we might have made a different choice.)

Ideologies are made up of the statements that ancient rhetoricians called commonplaces. The distinguishing characteristic of a commonplace is that it is commonly believed by members of a community. These beliefs are "common" not because they are cheap or trivial but because they are shared "in common" by many people. Commonplaces need not be true or accurate (although they may be true and they are certainly thought to be so within the communities that hold them). Some commonplaces are so thoroughly embedded in a community's assumptions about how the world works that they are seldom examined rhetorically. Here are some examples of commonplaces that circulate in American discourse:

> Anyone can become president of the United States.
>
> All men are created equal.
>
> Everyone has a right to express his or her beliefs because free speech is protected by the Constitution.

Please note that even though these statements are widely accepted in American discourse, they are not necessarily true for all Americans. In other words, outside the communities that subscribe to them, commonplaces may be controversial. If you disagreed with us earlier when we asserted that "men have more power than women," your disagreement should alert you to the presence of a commonplace that is accepted in some community to which we belong but not in the communities with which you identify. In a case like this, the commonplace is contested. Contested commonplaces are called **issues** in rhetoric, and it is the point of rhetoric to help people examine and perhaps to achieve agreement about issues.

Most people probably subscribe to commonplaces drawn from many and diverse ideologies at any given time. Because of this and because our subscription to many of our beliefs is only partially conscious, our ideological beliefs may contradict one another. For instance, if John believes on religious grounds that abortion is murder, he may find that belief to be in conflict with his liberal politics, which teach that women have the right to determine whether or not they wish to carry a pregnancy to term. Thus John's ideology contains a potential contradiction. This is not unusual, because ideology is seldom consistent with itself. In fact, it may be full of contradictions, and it may (and often does) contradict empirical states of affairs as well. For example, the commonplace that affirms that "anyone can become president of the United States" overlooks the reality that all presidents to date have been white men.

Rhetorical Situations

Ancient rhetoricians defined knowledge as the collected wisdom of those who know. In ancient thought, knowledge was not supposed to exist outside of knowers. Teaching and learning began with what people already knew. People talked or questioned each other, and worked toward new discoveries by testing them against what was already known (Aristotle, *Posterior Analytics* I i). Ancient rhetoricians assumed that anyone who wanted to compose a discourse had a reason for doing so that grew out of his life in a community. Young people studied rhetoric precisely because they wanted to be involved in decisions that affected the lives of their family, friends, and neighbors. Students of ancient rhetoric did engage in a good deal of practice with artificial **rhetorical situations** taken from history or literature or law (the rhetorical exercises were called *progymnasmata* and *declamation*). However, this practice was aimed at teaching them something about the community they would later serve, as well as about rhetoric. In other words, they did not study rhetoric only to learn its rules. Instead, their study was preparation for a life of active citizenship.

A rhetorical situation is made up of several elements: the issue for discussion; the audience for the discussion and their relationship to the issue; as well as the rhetor, her reputation, and her relation to the issue. Rhetors must also consider the time and the place in which the issue merits attention (see Chapter 2, on *kairos*).

Because of its emphasis on situatedness, on location in space and time, and on the contexts that determine composition, ancient rhetorical theory differs greatly from many modern rhetorical theories which assume that all rhetors and all audiences can read and write from a neutral point of view. The notion of objectivity would have greatly puzzled ancient rhetors and teachers of rhetoric, because it implies that truth and accuracy somehow exist outside of people who label things with those words. What interested ancient rhetoricians were issues: matters about which there was some disagreement or dispute. In other words, nothing can become an issue unless someone disagrees with someone else about its truth or falsity, or applicability, or worth. Issues do not exist in isolation from the people who speak or write about them.

LANGUAGE AS POWER

Many modern rhetoric textbooks assert that language is a reliable reflection of thought. Their authors assume that the main point of using language is to represent thought, because they live in an age that is still influenced by notions about language developed during the seventeenth century. In 1690 John Locke argued influentially that words represent thoughts and that the function of words was to convey the thinking of one person to another as clearly as possible. The assumption that language is transparent, that it lets meaning shine through it, is part of what is called a **representative theory of language.** The theory has this name because it assumes that language represents meaning, that it hands meaning over to listeners or readers, clear and intact.

Ancient rhetoricians were not so sure that words only or simply represented thoughts. As a consequence, they had great respect for the power of language. Archaic Greeks thought that the distinguishing characteristic of human beings, what made them different from animals, was their possession of *logos*, or speech. In archaic Greek thought, logos was tightly linked to identity, a person's *logos* was her name, her history, everything that could be said about her. Another word for *logos* was *kleos*, "fame" or "call." Thus, to be *"en logoi"* was to be taken into account, to have accounts told about one, to be on the community's roster of persons who could be spoken, sung, or written about. Any person's identity consisted in what was said about her. Someone's name, or tales told about her, defined the space in which she lived.

In keeping with the archaic Greek emphasis on language as the source of knowledge, the Older Sophist Protagoras taught that "humans are the measure of all things." By this he apparently meant that anything that exists does so by virtue of its being known or discussed by human beings. Because knowledge originates with human knowers, and not from somewhere outside them, there is no absolute truth that exists separately from human knowledge. Moreover, contradictory truths will appear, since everyone's knowledge differs slightly from everyone else's, depending on one's perspective and one's language. Thus Protagoras taught that at least two opposing and contradictory *logoi* (statements or accounts) exist in every experience. He called these oppositions *dissoi logoi*.

The Older Sophist Gorgias apparently adopted Protagoras's skepticism about the relationship of language to truth or to some absolute reality. In his treatise on the nonexistent, Gorgias wrote: "For that by which we reveal is *logos*, but *logos* is not substances and existing things. Therefore we do not reveal existing things to our neighbors, but *logos*, which is something other than substances" (Sprague 1972, 84). In other words, language is not things, and language does not communicate things or thoughts or anything else. Language is not the same thing as honey or fossils or cold winds, nor is it the same as thoughts or feelings or perceptions. It is a different medium altogether. What language communicates is itself—words, syntax, metaphors, puns, and all that other wonderful stuff. Philosophers are mistaken when they argue that justice or reality exist; they have been misled into thinking that justice or reality are the same for everyone by the seeming unity and generality of the words *justice* and *reality*.

Ancient rhetoricians were aware that language is a powerful force for moving people to action. Gorgias went so far as to say that language could work on a person's spirit as powerfully as drugs worked on the body. He taught his students that language could bewitch people, could jolt them out of their everyday awareness into a new awareness from which they could see things differently. Hence its persuasive force. As he said, language can "stop fear and banish grief and create joy and nurture pity" ("Encomium to Helen" 8). If you doubt this, think about the last time you went to a movie that made you cry, or saw a commercial that induced you to buy something, or heard a sermon that scared you into changing your behavior.

Isocrates argued that language was the ground of community, since it enabled people to live together and to found cultures ("Nicocles" 5–9). Communication was the mutual exchange of convictions, and communities could be defined as groups of human beings who operate with a system of roughly similar convictions. For Isocrates, language was the *hegemoon* (prince, guide) of all thought and action. He pointed out that language makes it possible for people to conceive of differences and to make distinctions like man/woman or good/bad. It also allows them to conceive of abstractions like justice or reality.

The Greek notion of *logos* was later translated into Latin as *ratio* (reason), and in Western thought the powers that were once attributed to language became associated with thinking rather than with talking or writing. Cicero blamed the philosophers for this shift:

> [Socrates] separated the science of wise thinking from that of elegant speaking, though in reality they are closely linked together. . . . This is the source from which has sprung the undoubtedly absurd and unprofitable and reprehensible severance between the tongue and the brain, leading to our having one set of professors to teach us to think and another to teach us to speak. (*De Oratore* III xvi 60)

The notion that thought can be separated from language began with the philosopher Socrates, who was the teacher of Plato, who was the teacher of Aristotle.

In one of his treatises on logic, Aristotle wrote that "spoken words are the symbols of mental experience and written words are the symbols of spoken words" (*On Interpretation* 16a). This passage made two important assumptions: that mental experiences are independent of language and that the role of language is to symbolize or represent mental experiences. The passage also suggested that written words are representations of spoken words, as though speech is somehow closer to thinking than writing. In the *rhetoric*, Aristotle wrote that style and delivery—the rhetorical canons having to do with expression—were secondary to the substance of an argument (1404a). Even though it was necessary to study style and delivery, because these forms of expression were persuasive, according to Aristotle the first prerequisite of style was clarity, which implied that whatever thoughts were being expressed should be immediately apparent to readers (1404b).

Here Aristotle expressed his subscription to a representative theory of language. The notion that a style can be clear, that language allows meaning to shine through it without distortion, makes sense only if language is thought to represent something else. Naturally enough, philosophers are less interested in the rhetorical effects produced by language than they are in using language to say what they mean, as clearly and exactly as possible. That's why they prefer to argue that language somehow represents thought or reality. However, this argument presents a problem to rhetoricians, since the representative theory of language implies that some piece of language can be found that will clearly express any thought. So if a piece of language is not clear to an audience, anyone who subscribes to this model of language must blame its author, who either had unclear thoughts or was unable to express them clearly. The only other possible explanation for misunderstanding is that the audience has not read the language carefully enough or is for some reason too inept to understand it.

Aristotle's attitude toward clarity also assumed that rhetors can control the effects of language—that they can make language do what they want it to do, can make listeners or readers hear or read in the way they intended. Furthermore, Aristotle's attitude about clarity seriously underestimated the power of language. People who assume that it is "the thought that counts" must also assume that language is the servant of thought and, hence, that language is of secondary or even negligible importance in the composing process. This attitude sometimes causes teachers to blame unintelligible compositions on a student's faulty thinking, when the difficulty might be that the student's language had more and different effects than she intended.

Ancient teachers never assumed that there is only one way to read or interpret a discourse. Audiences inevitably bring their ideologies, their linguistic abilities, and their understandings of local rhetorical contexts to any reading or listening they do. Contexts such as readers' or listeners' experiences and education or even time of day inevitably influence their interpretation of any discourse. This is particularly true of written discourse, which, to ancient ways of thinking, was set adrift by authors into the community, where people could and would read it in as many ways as there were readers (Plato, *Phaedrus* 275). Today, however, people sometimes think that texts can have a single meaning (the right one) and that people who don't read in this way are somehow bad readers. This attitude is reinforced by the modern assumption that the sole purpose of reading is to glean information from a text, and it is repeated in school when students are expected to take tests or answer a set of questions about their reading in order to prove that they comprehended the assignment.

But people do many things when they read a text for the first time, and determining what it says is only one of these things. When you read any text, especially a difficult one, you simply can't find out what it says once and for all on your first trip through it. You can't consume written words the way you consume a cheeseburger and fries. When written words are banged up against one another, they tend to set off sparks and combinations of meanings that their writers never anticipated. Unfortunately, writers are ordinarily not present to tell readers what they intended to communicate.

Sometimes unintended meanings happen because written letters and punctuation marks are ambiguous. There are only twenty-six letters in the English alphabet, after all, and just a few marks of punctuation in the writing system. So most of these letters and marks must be able to carry several meanings. For example, quotation marks can signify quoted material:

"Get lost," he said.

But they can also be used for emphasis:

We don't "cash" checks.

Or they can be used to set off a term whose use a writer wants to question:

This is not a "liberal" interpretation.

In speaking, the work done by punctuation is conveyed by voice and gesture, but writers do not have the luxury of conveying meaning through their bodies; instead they must rely on stylistic and other indicators to negotiate meaning in their writing (see Chapter 13, on **delivery**).

The meanings of words differ, too, from person to person and from context to context. Indeed, the meanings of words are affected by the contexts in which they appear. In current political discourse, for example, words such as *patriotism*, *freedom*, and *justice* can mean very different things to the people who use them, depending upon whether they subscribe to conservative or liberal ideologies. The slogan "Support our troops" has been used by those in favor of the war in Iraq as well as by those who oppose it. Because people are different from one another, they have different responses to the same discourse.

When we listen to someone speaking, we have several contextual advantages that readers do not have. If we misunderstand a speaker, we can ask her to repeat or to slow down. This is why press conferences or lectures usually feature a question-and-answer session. Our chances of misunderstanding spoken language are also decreased by the fact that we can see and hear the person who is speaking and we can interact with her, as well. Thus we can support our interpretation of the meanings of her words with our interpretations of her facial and bodily gestures and the loudness and pitch of her voice. Too, we are often acquainted with people who speak to us, while often we do not know writers personally. And even if we don't know a speaker well, we do understand our relationship to her. If a speaker is your mother rather than your teacher or boss or fitness instructor, you can rapidly narrow down the range of possible meanings she might convey when she commands you to "shape up!" All of these kinds of contexts—physical and social—help us to interpret a speaker's meaning.

But these contexts are not available in any writing that is composed for an audience of people who are not known to the writer. So writers have to guess about the contexts that readers will bring to their reading. Usually those contexts will be very different from the writer's, especially in the case of a book like this one that introduces readers to a new field of discourse. Our experience as teachers has taught us that our familiarity with rhetoric and its terminology often causes us to take some of its fundamental points for granted. When we do this in a classroom, students can ask questions until they are satisfied that they understand. But readers cannot do this. So even though we have tried very hard to make the contexts of ancient rhetorics clear in this book, people are bound to understand our text differently from each other and perhaps differently from what we tried to convey. Ancient rhetorics were invented by cultures that have long since disappeared, and that is one potential source of differential understanding in this particular text. But writers always fail to match their contexts with those of readers, and this kind of differential understanding is universal. It arises simply because writers can only imagine readers—who they are, what they know.

To put all of this another way: writers and speakers always fail to put themselves precisely in their readers' and listeners' shoes. This potential for differential understanding is not a curse, as modern rhetorical theory would have it. Rather, it is what allows knowledge to grow and change. The ancients understood this, and that's why they celebrated copiousness—many arguments, many understandings.

Because ancient rhetoricians believed that language was a powerful force for persuasion, they urged their students to develop *copia* in all parts of their art. *Copia* can be loosely translated from Latin to mean an abundant and ready supply of language—something appropriate to say or write whenever the occasion arises. Ancient teaching about rhetoric is everywhere infused with the notions of expansiveness, amplification, abundance. Ancient teachers gave their students more advice about the divisions, or **canons,** of rhetoric—invention, arrangement, style, memory, and delivery—than they could ever use. They did so because they knew that practice in these rhetorical arts alerted rhetors to the multitude of communicative and persuasive possibilities that exist in language.

Modern intellectual style, in contrast, tends toward economy (from Greek *oikonomia,* "a manager of a household or state," from *oikos,* "house"). Economy in any endeavor is characterized by restrained or efficient use of available materials and techniques. Of course the modern preference for economy in composition is connected to modern insistence that clarity is the only important characteristic of style. People who bring modern attitudes about clarity and economy to the study of ancient rhetorics may be bewildered (and sometimes frustrated) by the profuseness of ancient advice about everything from invention to delivery.

They also miss an important aspect of ancient instruction: that messing around with language is fun. Composition need not be undertaken with the deadly seriousness that moderns bring to it. Moderns want to get it right the first time and forget about it. Ancient peoples fooled around with language all the time. The Greeks sponsored poetry contests and gave prizes for the most daring or entertaining elaborations on a well-known theme. Romans who lived during the first centuries CE held rhetorical contests called declamations, the object of which was to compose a complicated and innovative discourse about some hackneyed situation involving pirates or angry fathers. The winner was the person who could compose the most unusual arguments or who could devise the most elaborate amplifications and ornamentations of an old theme.

Practice, Practice, Practice

To return to the positive side of Jon Stewart's analogy equating competitive athletics with real debate—or, in this book's terms, with rhetorical engagement—it is interesting to note that many teachers of rhetoric in ancient Athens and Rome found it useful to think of rhetorical training and performance as roughly analogous to athletic competition. As one of us argues in another book, the ancients deemed the struggle of competition (*agonism*) to be productive and beneficial, and in the context of rhetoric, they believed

hard work paid off. Many ancients devoted themselves to devising conceptual tools and training methods that would help their fellow citizens
become strong rhetors, active citizens equipped to think about issues of the
day. All the rhetors and rhetoricians mentioned in this book believe that
rhetoric is a complex and flexible art that can nevertheless be learned and
taught. And while there was much disagreement among the ancients about
the best way to learn rhetoric, most of them agreed on three points: practice, practice, and practice. Contemporary rhetorical theorist David Fleming
points out that in ancient rhetorical education, practice had three main components: exercise, imitation, and composition (2003, 107).

Too often modern classrooms treat such activities and exercises as
"busy work," something to fill time between "real" assignments. We believe
this is because of a heavy emphasis in twentieth-century classrooms on
writing-as-product. In case it isn't clear by now, the ancients placed less
emphasis on the product—the speech or the piece of writing—and more
emphasis on constant activity and practice. The best comparison for the
ancient model of rhetorical education is the immersion technique of foreign
language learning, wherein students speak only the language being
learned. Likewise, these activities and exercises encourage students to see
rhetoric all around them, to engage rhetoric analytically, and to practice
improving their use of rhetoric when they speak and write.

Aelius Theon, one of the early developers of *progymnasmata*, had strong
faith in their effectiveness:

> It is quite evident that these exercises are altogether beneficial to those who
> take up the art of rhetoric. For those who have recited a narration and a fable
> well and with versatility will also compose a history well . . . Training through
> the chreia not only produces a certain power of discourse but also a good and
> useful character since we are being trained in the aphorisms of wise persons.
> Both the so called commonplace and description have benefit that is conspic-
> uous since the ancients have used them everywhere. . . . (*Progymnasmata*
> Preface 1)

Ancient rhetoric teachers believed their students would become the best
rhetors if they combined study of rhetorical principles with lots of practice
composing. This book is designed to strike that balance as well. It makes
sense that ancient rhetorical training spanned years—sometimes a decade
or more.

The *progymnasmata* brought to the students' attention patterns in
language. The regular and varied practice at composing often has the surprising effect of making people enjoy writing and speaking just by making
them more familiar as activities. *Progymnasmata*, as the classicist Ruth Webb
argues, did not key to the "end result" but rather sought to cultivate rhetorical sensibility through constant—and constantly changing—rhetorical
activity (2001, 300).

Even more than *progymnasmata*, though, the imitation exercises might feel
strange to contemporary students. When asked to imitate a passage written by

an author you admire, you might feel as if you are violating some sort of rule about copying. Beliefs about rhetorical style have, in many ways, gone the direction of opinions and argument: style has become an "individual," ineffable thing. We disagree. And so would the ancients. We would never encourage students to violate copyright laws or university plagiarism policies, but we also believe that imitation has nothing to do with stealing. Imitation exercises, if practiced in the way that the ancients practiced them, can lead you to a more finely tuned rhetorical method of reading and listening. That is, when reading and listening rhetorically, we read and listen as much for *how* a writer or speaker builds an argument with words, sentences, paragraphs, and sections, as for *what* the writer or speaker is arguing. And what is more, while plagiarizing (copying work from someone else) is easy (that's why people do it), imitation exercises can be extremely difficult. This is because imitation exercises ask you to try new approaches and to innovate within those approaches. Imitation exercises can be as challenging as they are fun.

Professional rhetors know that much more work is produced during invention than is actually presented to audiences. That is, not everything that is composed actually ends up in a finished piece. Some ancient exercises are for practice, while others draw attention to style. Still others increase understanding of rhetorical principles. Practice is not wasted effort because everything a rhetor composes increases copiousness—a handy supply of arguments, available for use on any occasion.

RHETORICAL ACTIVITIES

1. Look around you and listen. Where do you find people practicing rhetoric? Watch television and read popular newspapers or magazines with this question in mind. Jot down one or two of the rhetorical arguments you hear or see people making. Presidents and members of Congress are good sources, but so are journalists and parents and attorneys and clergy and teachers. Do such people try to support these arguments with facts? Or do they use other means of convincing people to accept their arguments?

2. Consider Jon Stewart's point about the state of argument in America today. Have you encountered any examples recently of argument-that's-not-really-argument? How can you tell the theatrical sort of argument from the rhetorically engaged?

3. Think about a time when you tried to convince someone to change his or her mind. How did you go about it? Were you successful? Now think about a time when someone tried to get you to change your mind. What arguments did the person use? Was he or she successful?

4. Try to answer this question: what counts as persuasion in your community? Here are some questions to start from: Think of a time when you changed your mind about something. How did it happen? Did

somebody talk you into it, or did events cause you to change the way you think? How do the people you know go about changing their minds? How does religious conversion happen, for example? What convinces people to stop smoking or to go on a diet? How do people get to be racists or become convinced they ought to stop being racist? How does a president convince a people that they ought to support a war? Make a list of arguments that seem convincing in these cases.

5. The Roman teacher Quintilian underscored the importance of rhetorical situations to composing when he suggested that students should consider

> what there is to say; before whom, in whose defence, against whom, at what time and place, under what circumstances; what is the popular opinion on the subject; and what the prepossessions of the judge are likely to be; and finally of what we should express our deprecation or desire. (IV 1 52–53)

If you are at a loss for something to say or write, you can use Quintilian's list as a heuristic, or means of discovery. Begin by thinking about the communities of which you are a part: your families, relatives, and friends; your street, barrio, town, city, or reservation; your school, college, or university; groups you belong to; your state, country, or nation and the world itself. What positions do you take on issues that are currently contested in your communities? This exercise should help you to articulate what you think about such issues.

a. Start with this question: what are the hotly contested issues in the communities you live in (the street, the barrio, your hometown, the university you work in, the reservation, the state, the nation)? Make a list of these issues. (If you don't know what these issues are, ask someone—a parent, teacher, friend—or read the editorial and front pages of a daily newspaper or watch the local and national news on television or access news sources on the Internet.)

b. Pick one or two issues and write out your positions on them. Write as fast as you can without stopping or worrying about grammar and spelling. Use a computer if you have access to one and are a fast typist, or write by hand if that is more comfortable for you. At this point you are composing for your use only. So don't worry about neatness or completeness or correctness; write to discover what you think about these issues. Write for as long as you want to, but write about each issue for at least 15 minutes without stopping. Remember that thinking is exercise, just like running or bicycling, so don't be surprised if you tire after a few minutes of doing this work.

c. These writings should give you a clearer view of what you think about one or two urgent issues. Let them sit for awhile—an hour is good but a couple of days is better. Then read them again. Now use Quintilian's questions to find out your positions on community issues. What is the popular opinion on each issue? What is the position taken by people in authority? What is your position on the issue? Are there policies or practices you advocate or reject? With which members of your communities do you agree? Disagree? On what issues? What positions are taken by people who disagree with you? How will the community respond to your propositions?

d. Now you should have an idea about which issue interests you most. Be sure to select an issue that you can comfortably discuss with other people. Write about it again for awhile—say 15 minutes.

e. Give what you've written to someone you trust; ask him or her to tell you what else he or she wants to know about what you think. Listen carefully and take notes on the reader's suggestions. Don't talk or ask questions until the reader finishes talking. Then discuss your views on the issue further, if your reader is willing to do so. If your reader said anything that modifies your views, revise your writing to take these changes into account.

f. Keep these compositions as well as your original list of issues. You can repeat this exercise whenever you wish to write about an issue or when you are asked to write for a class.

6. Begin recording in a journal or notebook the arguments that you commonly hear or read.

PROGYMNASMATA I: OVERVIEW, FABLE, AND TALE

As we mentioned in this chapter, rhetoric teachers used the series of exercises called *progymnasmata* (preliminary exercises) over a very long stretch of time.

The term first appears in the sophistic *Rhetoric to Alexander,* written during the fourth century BCE (unless this is a later insertion in the manuscripts). The author furnished a relatively long list of rhetorical tactics, and suggested that "if we habituate and train ourselves to repeat them on the lines of our preparatory exercises, they will supply us with plenty of matter both in writing and in speaking" (1436a 25). His casual reference suggests that exercises were routinely used in the rhetorical schools of the time. In fact, Cicero testifies that Aristotle used an exercise called "thesis" to train his rhetoric students "so that they might be able to uphold either side of the question in copious and elegant language" (*Orator* xiv 46). If Cicero's information is correct, thesis was used even in schools of philosophy during the fourth century BCE. It was still being practiced in Rome some five centuries later, as Quintilian testifies in the second book of the *Institutes,* and it was still in use in some European schools at least as late as the sixteenth century CE.

Aside from brief descriptions that appear in global accounts of ancient rhetorics, such as Quintilian's *Institutes,* four ancient manuscripts devoted solely to the *progymnasmata* have survived. The oldest of these is attributed to Aelius Theon, a sophist who lived in Egyptian Alexandria during the first century CE. Hermogenes of Tarsus wrote another, probably during the second century CE; this treatise, as translated into Latin by the grammarian Priscian, was very popular during the European Middle Ages. A Byzantine sophist named Nicolaus produced another Greek *progymnasmata* during the fifth century CE. However, the most complete list of elementary exercises we possess is the one put together by Aphthonius, who taught rhetoric in Antioch around the fifth century CE. Translated into Latin, this treatise was enormously popular in Europe during the Renaissance. Scholars have established that the educations of famous writers such as St. Augustine, William Shakespeare, and John Milton included extensive practice with preliminary exercises (Woods 2002; Desmet 2005).

In ancient Greece and Rome, when boys became old enough to go to school, their parents placed them with a teacher who was a grammarian. (This ancient association of elementary study with grammar explains why American elementary schools are still sometimes called "grammar schools.") While they studied with a grammarian, young students practiced imitating and elaborating on fables, tales, *chreia*, and **proverbs**. When they graduated to higher education in rhetoric, they composed sample parts of orations such as confirmations or refutations, sometimes imitating famous speeches and sometimes following a standard arrangement of parts. They also composed **commonplaces, descriptions** *(ekphrasis)*, characters *(ethopoeia)*, **comparisons** *(synkresis)*, and speeches of praise *(**encomia**)* and blame (*psogos*, **invective**). When students matured, they were set to composing more difficult exercises in deliberative and forensic rhetoric, called thesis and **introduction of law**.

The *progymnasmata* remained popular for so long because they are carefully sequenced: they begin with simple paraphrases (like the ones considered in the last chapter) and end with sophisticated exercises in deliberative and forensic rhetoric. Each successive exercise uses a skill practiced in the preceding one, but each adds some new and more difficult composing task. Ancient teachers were fond of comparing the graded difficulty of the *progymnasmata* to the exercise used by Milo of Croton to gradually increase his strength: "Milo lifted a calf each day. Each day the calf grew heavier, and each day his strength grew. He continued to lift the calf until it became a bull (*Institutes* I xi 5)."

Relentless practice in these exercises seems to have produced rhetorical superheroes, whose skill with words was on a par with Milo's strength; classical scholar Ruth Webb writes that those trained in this tradition were "relentlessly eloquent, able to compose a declamation on any theme, often at a moment's notice, thoroughly imbued with the classical past" (2001, 289). In other words, the exercises encouraged facility in an astonishing breadth of flexible rhetorical patterns.

The *progymnasmata* may look and feel artificial or formulaic to contemporary writers. However, the directions for amplification that accompany some of them are meant to be freely interpreted; for example, not every encomium must have the same number of parts, and the parts need not always appear in the same order. This freedom of interpretation and arrangement is what distinguishes classical exercises from the prescriptive formulas laid down in modern school rhetoric. Practice in these exercises should be neither formulaic nor dull.

In this first section, we offer two *progymnasmata*, fable and the tale. In doing so, we adhere to the order presented by Hermogenes, Aphthonius, and Nicolaus the sophist. According to Nicolaus, "those who arranged these things [i.e., the *progymnasmata*] . . . put the fable first among them as being naturally plain and simpler than the others and having some relationship to poems" (Kennedy 2003 133). In antiquity, poetry and myth served the purpose that fairy tales and storybooks do today for young children in the United States. College students are, of course, much older than the students to whom Nicolaus and company wrote, but the earlier exercises can still be fun if taken in the spirit of play.

As you work through the *progymnasmata* here and in the next eight chapters, we suggest that you adapt them to contemporary themes or issues that interest you. We give a few suggestions for doing this along the way. In his description of the exercises, Theon encourages students to inhabit these forms by experimenting, to "expand" and then "compress" the stories and tales—their own and others'. In doing so, he emphasizes the elasticity of language and rhetorical formats. The object of these exercises, then, is manifold: they present opportunities for focused practice and allow developing rhetors to explore rhetorical possibilities while achieving *copia* or abundance.

FABLE

All cultures produce fables, little stories used to teach moral behavior to children. Aesop's tale of the country mouse and the city mouse, written thousands of years ago, is still part of childhood lore. Native American cultures have produced especially rich traditions of fables that display a fascinating range of human and animal characters such as the trickster coyote and the sturdy turtle.

Fables are fictitious stories meant to teach moral lessons. This exercise was very popular among teachers of younger students, and exercises in the composition of fables endured in European schools throughout the Middle Ages and the Renaissance. A sixteenth-century teacher named Erasmus praised fables in this way: "their attraction is due to their witty imitation of the way people behave, and the hearers give their assent because the truth is set out vividly before their very eyes" (631). Here, Erasmus elaborates on the phrase Nicolaus the sophist uses to describe what fable does. According to Nicolaus, "it images the truth" (Kennedy

2003, 133). Its appeal is similar, then, to that achieved by means of vivid description, or *enargeia* (see the chapter on pathos).

In the eighteenth century, a scholar and critic named Samuel Johnson defined a fable as "a narrative in which beings irrational, and sometimes inanimate, are, for the purpose of moral instruction, feigned to act and speak with human interests and passions" (283). The great French fabulist Jean de la Fontaine composed a more poetic definition:

> Fables in sooth are not what they appear;
> Our moralists are mice, and such small deer.
> We yawn at sermons, but we gladly turn
> To moral tales, and so amused we learn. (*Selected Fables* iii)

The attraction of the fable, then, is that it renders a moral lesson easy to swallow by wrapping it in an amusing tale.

The rhetoric teacher Aphthonius divided fables into two kinds: those that use human characters and those that use animal characters. The comic strips *Doonesbury, Pogo,* and *Life in Hell* are or were continuing

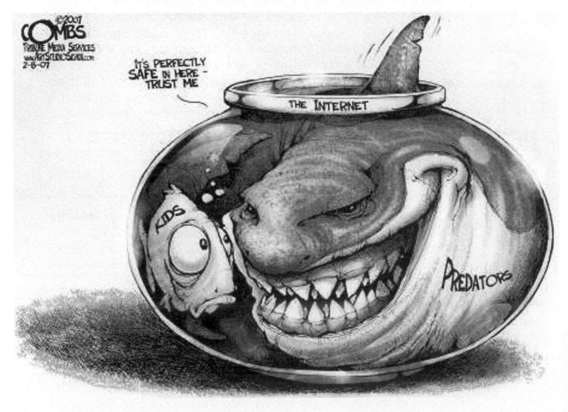

FIGURE 1.1
Source: Paul Combs, Tribune Media Services, February 8, 2007.

fables that commented on current affairs; *Doonesbury* uses human characters, while *Pogo* was an animal fable and *Life in Hell* used both humans and animals.

Fabulous uses of animals sometimes appear in political cartoons, as well. In the cartoon in Figure 1.1, a shark, used to represent predators, is stuffed inside a fishbowl with a wide-eyed little yellow fish, used to represent children on the Internet. Young Internet users can be vulnerable to reassurances made by an adult. The cartoonist suggests this possibility by means of an animal fable.

In Figure Figure 1.2 the frog—an animal commonly used in fabulous fairy tales—is singing a new version of a *Sesame Street* song. Whereas the previous version, "It's Not Easy Bein' Green," begins by lamenting the ordinariness of the color green, this version plays on the newer, environment-friendly meaning of "green." In the context of the extraordinarily high gasoline prices in early summer 2007, the cute little frog has a point.

FIGURE 1.2

Source: Dick Locher Copyright Tribune Media Services, Inc. All rights reserved. Reprinted with permission.

Fables are popular with children, of course, and that's why the list of *progymnasmata* begins with them. Ancient teachers asked their very young students to imitate the fables of Aesop. However, older students may enjoy paraphrasing extant fables or even creating their own stories that make some moral or political point.

Here is an ancient fable in the Aesopian tradition put into verse by the Roman writer Babrius:

THE FIRE-BEARING FOX

Someone caught a fox, the enemy of his vines and garden. Wishing to punish him with a new kind of torment, he set fire to his tail, after tying some flax upon it, and let him loose to run. But the spirit of Retribution that keeps watch over such acts guided the fox with his burden of fire straight into the grain fields of the man who had done him harm. It was the season of standing crops, and the grain was fruitful, fair, and full of promise. The owner ran after the fox, bemoaning the loss of his hard work, and the grain never saw his threshing floor.

One must be calm and not unbounded in one's anger. There is a certain retribution for anger—and may I guard against it—bringing loss upon such men as lose their tempers. (*Fables* 11.1–11.12)

This fable, or any fable, can be used in several rhetorical exercises. You can imitate or paraphrase it, perhaps using human characters. You can compose a moral for it, or write a different interpretation than that implied by Babrius. Could setting fire to the fox's tale also represent unduly harsh and rash punishment, or even torture?

Here is a fable used by Aphthonius:

AN ETHICAL FABLE OF THE CICADAS AND ANTS, EXHORTING THE YOUNG TO TOIL

It was the height of summer and the cicadas were offering up their shrill song, but it occurred to the ants to toil and collect the harvest from which they would be fed in the winter. When winter came on, the ants fed on what they had laboriously collected, but the pleasure of the cicadas ended in want. Similarly, youth that does not wish to toil fares badly in old age. (Kennedy 2003, 96)

In this short fable, the passing of time is represented by a change in seasons. The ancients commonly used seasons of spring and summer to represent youth, whereas winter represented old age.

If you want to stretch your creative abilities, compose a fable that is analogous to some current event or state of affairs about which you are concerned. For example, you can compose a version of Aphthonius's fable that makes a different point about work and age. In that case, you might want to use different animals than cicadas and ants. Hermogenes recommended that beast fables employ animals whose actions can be plausibly compared to human activities: "if the contention be about beauty, let this be posed as a peacock; if some one is to be represented as wise, there let us pose a fox; if imitators of the actions of men, monkeys" (*Progymnasmata* 24). [trans. Baldwin]

We composed a fable about energy resources. In keeping with Hermogenes' advice, we chose a monkey as an imitator of human actions:

> There was once a monkey who lived in a lush jungle where lots of vegetation grew, especially beautiful and rare flowers. He loved flowers so much that he wanted to have them all for himself. He would spend entire afternoons gathering the elegant flowers and taking them back to his little patch of jungle. Occasionally, he would invite other monkeys to come and marvel at his collection of flowers. Soon, though, he amassed all the flowers in the area, and the bees that worked among the flowers had no other reason to live there and so moved on to another place. After the bees left, there was no more honey, which made the bears very angry. The bears searched high and low for the flowers and, finding the monkey amidst the piles of lovely bouquets, stamped into the ground and chased the monkey away.

The moral here is about how unnecessary and thoughtless wastefulness can be harmful for others and ultimately to oneself.

Fables are usually quite brief; the composer simply presents a bare narrative. If you wish to expand a fable, add descriptions of the setting or compose dialogue for the characters, as we suggest below. Of course, any fable you compose can be used for purposes of illustration or analogy in a larger composition.

COMPOSING FABLES

1. Visit one of the websites listed here and read some of the fables collected there. Then choose one and alter it in some way—change the descriptions of the setting, add or alter the dialogue, change the animals or the moral.

   http://www.literature.org/authors/aesop/fables/
   http://www.bartleby.com/17/1/
   http://classics.mit.edu/Aesop/fab.html

2. Compose a fable with a lesson that might be useful for college students at the beginning of a term.

3. Look through a current magazine or newspaper and choose an issue that is of concern to your local community or to the broader public. Compose a fable with a moral or lesson that speaks to that issue.

TALE

The second preliminary exercise involved students in retelling stories from history and poetry.

Nicolaus the sophist claims that narrative is "more argumentative than fable" but still not as complex as the other exercises. Aphthonius saw a narrative as part of a larger narration, and offers this analogy: "Narrative differs from narration as a piece of poetry differs from a poem. The *Iliad* as a whole is a poem, the making of the arms of Achilles [an incident within the *Iliad*] is a piece of poetry. In other words, narrative describes one action or event that may fit into a larger sequence" (Nicolaus in Kennedy 2003, 136). Narratives can be mythical, historical, or fictive. Since narrative plays an important role in persuasive discourse, it is important that rhetors know how to compose skillful stories, whether these are historical or fictional (see the chapter on arrangement). Aelius Theon pinpointed six elements of narration: "the person, whether that be one or many; and the action done by the person; and the place where the action was done; and the time at which it was done; and the manner of the action; and sixth, the cause of these things" (Kennedy 2003, 28). He believed that a narrative missing any one of these components was deficient.

The composition of narrative is not simple or artless, and we should not be misled by the fact that in ancient times very young students were set this task. Of course, very young students were asked to imitate or paraphrase only the very short narratives that they found in their reading. As we shall see later on in the exercises on imitation, highly skilled adult poets such as Virgil and John Dryden were able to imitate much longer narratives, such as Homer's *Iliad*. Surely they were introduced to this skill in their childhoods, when they were asked to compose tales. Here is Aphthonius's example of a short mythical tale:

A DRAMATIC NARRATIVE CONCERNING THE ROSE

Let anyone who admires the rose for its beauty consider Aphrodite's wound. The goddess was in love with Adonis and Ares in turn was in love with her, and the goddess was to Adonis what Ares was to her: a god was in love with a goddess and a goddess was pursuing a mortal. The emotion was the same even if the species was different. Struck with jealousy, Ares wanted to do away with Adonis, thinking the death of Adonis would be the end of the love. Ares attacks Adonis. Learning what had been done, the goddess hurried to his rescue, and in her haste, falling on a rose, she stumbled among the thorns and pierces the bottom of her foot. The blood from the wound dripped on the rose and changed its color to the now familiar appearance; the rose, originally having been white, changed to the appearance it now has. (Kennedy 2003, 97)

Writers can imitate or paraphrase this short tale. But Quintilian also suggested that students change the order of events in such stories, telling them backwards or starting in the middle, in order to improve their memories (*Institutes* II iv 15).

Quintilian's exercise is useful for improving writers' skills at arrangement, as well. What happens when events are given in a different order than that chosen by Aphthonius? What if the teller were to narrate the story about the rose before she provided the information about the love triangle?

> One day, as the goddess Aphrodite was hurrying through the woods, she stumbled into a rosebush because of her haste. She fell among the thorns and the flat of her foot was pierced. Flowing from the wound, the blood changed the color of the rose to its familiar appearance, and the rose, though white in its origin, came to be as it now appears. Aphrodite was hurrying because the god Ares, who loved her, was attacking the mortal man she loved, Adonis. Ares thought that if he could kill Adonis, Aphrodite would forget her mortal lover.

We reordered the events of the story and removed the embellishments given it by Aphthonius. This arrangement presents an entirely different impression of Aphrodite, we think. Which version do you prefer?

Aphthonius's version of the tale omitted the fate of Adonis. According to ancient myth, Aphrodite warned her mortal lover to be careful while hunting, but he ignored her warning and was gored to death by a boar. That part of the story can easily be told in one sentence, as we have just done. Compare our spare version to Ovid's lovely narrative:

> Since she believed her warning had been heard,
> The goddess yoked her swans and flew toward heaven—
> Yet the boy's pride and manliness ignored it.
> His hunting dogs took a clear path before them
> And in the forest waked a sleeping boar;
> As he broke through his lair within a covert,
> Adonis pricked him with a swift-turned spear.
> The fiery boar tore out the slender splinter
> And rushed the boy, who saw his death heave toward him.
> With one great thrust he pierced the boy's white loins
> And left him dying where one saw his blood
> Flow into rivulets on golden sands. (*Metamophoses X*)

Ovid added touches of description and characterization. Do these additions change the effect of the tale? Can you tell it differently? Can you tell it better? You can find the whole story of Aphrodite and Adonis in any collection of ancient Greek or Roman myths (the goddess is called "Venus" in Roman mythology) or in Shakespeare's poetic retelling entitled "Venus and Adonis."

You needn't go to ancient literature to find short tales to imitate or paraphrase; they abound in our culture. While we prefer telling jokes to writing them down, composing different versions of jokes can be a useful exercise. We can also write and revise or reorder tales about events from our own lives. Often we tell these to friends for their amusement; why not try writing them? There are also fairy tales. Walt Disney Studios has a long history of amplifying these little stories into two-hour animated films, complete with well-developed characters and more complex plot lines than are featured in the originals. Compare the versions of well-known fairy tales found in Grimm or Hans Christian Andersen to those told by Disney, whose versions are ordinarily less gruesome than the originals. Why is this so, do you think? For practice in narrative composition, write a version of a fairy tale that uses bits of Disney along with bits of earlier versions. Or compose your own version of a well-known fairy tale. Update the story of Little Red Riding Hood or the Little Mermaid. Find a copy of the ancient story of Hercules, and compare it to Disney's recent movie.

A curious sort of tale that exists today is the "urban legend." Urban legends are eerie, often difficult-to-believe stories, usually circulated by word of mouth (though a good number can be found on the Internet and via e-mail), that often feature a friend of a friend who has experienced a change of fortune. Another regular component is a twist of corporate conspiracy. One recent legend in circulation, for instance, claimed that a known corporate entity—at various times Microsoft, Nike, Disney—had developed a sophisticated e-mail tracing program, and offered $1,000 each to the first thousand recipients of the "chain" email.

A tale circulated in the mid-1990s alleging that Neiman Marcus charged an inordinate amount for its cookie recipe. And this turned out to be a version of an urban legend from the mid-1980s about Mrs. Fields' cookie recipe, which was in turn a version of a rumor about the Waldorf-Astoria's red-velvet cake recipe; that rumor dated back (some say) to the 1950s. Some urban legends, however, are local and involve a familiar place (the campus library, an old dormitory), and some resemble horror stories. These are often hoaxes and are often told for the sake of telling. It might be fun to write down an urban legend currently in circulation and share it with the class. Or write down two and look for the narratives' shared features.

Writers of contemporary nonfiction conventionally employ small narratives in the beginnings of books or chapters. Here, for example, is the opening of a chapter of *How Doctors Think*, a discussion of the way physicians diagnose their patients through a kind of "pattern recognition," written by Jerome Groopman, M.D.:

> On a spring afternoon several years ago, Evan McKinley was hiking in the woods near Halifax, Nova Scotia, when a pain in his chest stopped him in his tracks. McKinley was a forest ranger in his early forties, trim and extremely fit, with straw-blond hair and chiseled features. He had had a growing discomfort in his chest for the past few days, but nothing as severe as this. He wasn't sweating or lightheaded, and didn't feel feverish. But each time he took a breath, the pain got worse. McKinley slowly made his way back through the woods to the shed that housed his office. He sat and waited for the pain to pass, but it didn't. As a forest ranger, he was used to muscle aches from scaling a steep rocky trail or jogging with a loaded pack on his back. But this was different, and he decided he should see a doctor immediately. (2007, 41)

The narrative continues into the emergency room, where the physician on duty misdiagnosed McKinley. This narrative stimulates readers' interest in the fairly specialized subject of the chapter—the challenges of making a correct medical diagnosis. Compare the impact of the opening narrative to the section just following: "Chest pain is the second most common reason for a patient to visit an emergency room (abdominal pain is number one). . . . But despite its frequency, chest pain is one of the most challenging symptoms for the clinician to unravel" (2007, 43). Had the chapter begun with this material, fewer readers would finish it. Obviously Groopman, like many writers of nonfiction, is aware of the power of narrative to entice and hold readers.

Aspiring rhetors can learn much from reading the skillful historical narratives composed by writers such as Taylor Branch, Jon Krakauer, or Doris Kearns Goodwin. Historical novels are currently very popular, as well: Phillipa Gregory, Charles Johnson, Margaret George, and Sharon Kay Penman are only four of the many skilled historical novelists whose work frequently makes the best-seller lists.

PROGYMNASMATA, TALE

1. Research the outbreak of a disease like tuberculosis, influenza, or malaria. Try to develop an imaginative narrative that can draw readers into a discussion of the research.

2. As a useful exercise in summary paraphrase, condense the narrative of a history or novel you are reading for another class into a short tale.

3. Compare the narrative thread of a film to the book it is based on. What did the filmmakers include, and what did they leave out? Did they add anything?

4. Try your hand at telling the story of some contemporary event: a concert, a snowstorm or tornado, a politician's visit to another country, an athletic event, an accident.

NOTES

1. This reasoning is an example of what we call "ideologic." As we explain more fully in the chapter on ideology and the commonplaces, we coin the term *ideologic* to describe reasoning that works from ideological premises (that is, from commonplaces).

2. We encourage readers who are interested in the history of ancient rhetorics to consult Appendix A, where we include a discussion of ancient rhetoric's signposts. If you are interested in a slightly more extensive (and chronological) history of rhetoric, we recommend that you consult some of the histories cited in the bibliography at the end of the book. If you are interested in reading the works of the ancient rhetors and rhetoricians themselves, inexpensive editions of many of these can be found in the classics or literature sections of many bookstores, and they are available in libraries, too. The bibliography also lists modern editions of the major works of the most influential ancient rhetors and rhetoricians.

3. Recital of the facts connected with an argument does reinforce a rhetor's *ethos*, or persuasive character. If a writer or speaker demonstrates that she knows the facts of a case, her listeners or readers will increase their respect for her and her argument (see Chapter 6 for more on *ethos*).

WORKS CITED

Babrius. *Fables: Babrius and Phaedius*. Trans. Ben E. Perry. Cambridge: Harvard University Press, 1990.

Burke, Kenneth. *The Rhetoric of Motives*. Berkeley: University of California Press, 1969.

Desmet, Christy. "Progymnasmata." In *Classical Rhetorics and Rhetoricians: Critical Studies and Sources*, 296–304. Edited by Michelle Ballif and Michael G. Moran. Westport, Conn.: Praeger, 2005.

Fleming, David. "The Very Idea of a Progymnasmata." *Rhetoric Review* 22:2 (2003): 105–120.

Fontaine, Jean de La. *Selected Fables*. Mineola: Dover Publications, 2000.

Fromme, Alison. "Crusaders of Darkness." *Backpacker* (June 2007): 43–44.

Groopman, Jerome. *How Doctors Think*. New York: Houghton Mifflin, 2007.

Johnson, Samuel. "Life of Gay" in *Lives of the English Poets*. (1779–81); ed. George Birkbeck Hill, vol. 2. p. 267–85.

"Jon Stewart's America." *Crossfire*. CNN, Atlanta. Original airdate: October 15, 2004. Transcript: http://transcripts.cnn.com/TRANSCRIPTS/0410/15/cf.01.html.

Kennedy, George. *Progymnasmata: Greek Textbooks of Prose Composition and Rhetoric*. Leiden: Brill, 2003.

"'Scuse Me While I Miss The Sky." *The Simpsons*. Fox, New York. Original airdate: March 30, 2003.

Sprague, Rosamond Kent. *The Older Sophists*. Columbia: University of South Carolina Press, 1972.

Webb, Ruth. "The Progymnasmata as Practice." In *Education in Greek and Roman Antiquity*, 289–316. Edited by Y. L. Too. Leiden: Brill, 2001.

Woods, Marjorie Curry. "Weeping for Dido: Epilogue on a Premodern Rhetorical Exercise in the Postmodern Classroom." In *Latin Grammar and Rhetoric: From Classical Theory to Medieval Practice*, 284–294. Edited by Carol Dana Lanham. London: Continuum Books, 2002.

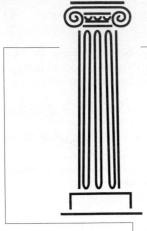

CHAPTER 2

KAIROS AND THE RHETORICAL SITUATION: SEIZING THE MOMENT

ANCIENT RHETORICIANS RECOGNIZED the complexity of rhetoric, and they realized that teaching such a multivalent art was a difficult task. Rhetoric cannot be reduced to a handy list of rules on writing or speaking, because each **rhetorical situation** presents its own unique set of challenges. Because each rhetorical situation is unique, each occurs in a time and place that can't be wholly anticipated or replicated. The proverb that tells us to "strike while the iron is hot" is certainly applicable to rhetoric: issues sometimes seem to appear overnight; others, such as capital punishment and abortion, seem remarkably enduring in American discourse. Sometimes issues are available for discussion, but audiences who are ready to hear about them cannot be found; at other times an audience for a given issue seems to coalesce overnight. A few years ago, for example, almost no one in the corridors of power was interested in hearing about global warming, and although scientists had been publishing their concerns about climate change for many years, their work reached only a small audience of committed environmentalists. As we write, however, Americans in general are becoming more aware of the issue. Magazines and newspapers have begun to feature articles on climate change, and television news makes frequent reference to it. And now it seems that public officials are beginning to pay attention, too. In rhetorical terms, the issue of climate change has finally found a national audience.

Rhetors must always be prepared, then, to meet the moment and find the place where the sometimes-sudden conjunction of issues with their appropriate audiences appears. The ancients knew this, and they had a name for the right rhetorical moment: they called it *"kairos."* A multidimensional and flexible term, *kairos* suggests a special notion of space and/or time. Since American English does not have a term quite like *kairos*, a bit of explanation is in order.

ANCIENT DEPICTIONS OF KAIROS

The Greeks had two concepts of time. They used the term *chronos* to refer to linear, measurable time, the kind with which we are more familiar, that we track with watches and calendars. But the ancients used *kairos* to suggest a more situational kind of time, something close to what we call "opportunity." In this sense, *kairos* suggests an advantageous time, or as lexicographers put it, "exact or critical time, season, opportunity" (Liddell and Scott 1996, 859). The temporal dimension of *kairos* can indicate anything from a lengthy time to a brief, fleeting moment. In short, *kairos* is not about duration but rather about a certain *kind* of time. In Roman rhetoric, the Latin word *opportunitas* was used in a similar manner; its root, *port–*, means an opening, and from it we get English verbs such as *import* and *export* as well as an old-fashioned word for a door or window, *portal. Kairos* is thus a "window" of time during which action is most advantageous. On Wall Street, there are *kairotic* moments to buy, sell, and trade stock to maximize gains. Victorious sprinters often accelerate at just the right time to pass their opponents. The success of a joke or funny quip depends upon its timing, or the *kairos* of its delivery.

Kairos was so important for ancient thinkers that it became a mythical figure. Lysippos, the famous ancient sculptor of athletes, chose to "enroll Kairos among the gods" (Himerius 759). It is little wonder that someone knowledgeable about competitive athletics—where timing and an awareness of the situation are critical—would render *kairos* into human form. The picture of Kairos in Figure 2.1 provides a good way to think about the rhetorical situation. Indeed, the rhetor is much like Kairos, bearing many different tools. Not just anybody can balance precariously on a stick while displaying a set of scales on a razor blade in one hand and depressing the pan with the other; such balance takes practice. As you can see in Figure 2.1, a depiction of a relief at Turin, Kairos is concerned about balancing the particulars of the situation, just as he perches tenuously on edge. His winged back and feet suggest the fleeting nature of time and situations. Perhaps the most remarkable and well-known characteristic of Kairos, however, is his hairstyle. Kairos was said to have hair only in the front, suggesting that one must keep an eye

FIGURE 2.1

Kairos, from a bas-relief in Turin. Reprinted from Zeus: A Study in Ancient Religion *by Arthur Bernard Cook.*

out for the opportune moment and seize it by grasping the forelock before it passes.

Figure 2.2 shows another depiction of Kairos, still with wings, this time holding a wheel, suggesting movement again. In this depiction, found on a Theban limestone relief, Kairos is flying on the back of another mythical figure: Pronoia, the figure of foresight. Sitting dejected in the background is her counterpart, Metanoia, who is the figure of afterthought or hindsight. This scene, like the forelock in Figure 2.1, suggests the importance of anticipating opportunities and seizing them before they pass. These figures underscore the many dimensions of *kairos*.

The ancients were certainly aware of its relevance to the art of rhetoric. Indeed, the Older Sophist Gorgias was famed for having based his theory of rhetoric on it. The Greek writer Philostratus tells us that Gorgias may have invented extemporaneous speaking:

> For coming into the theater of the Athenians, he had the boldness to say "suggest a subject," and he was the first to proclaim himself willing to take this chance, showing apparently that he knew everything and would trust to the moment [*toi kairoi*] to speak on any subject. (Sprague 1972, 30)

By acknowledging the importance of *kairos*, Gorgias's rhetorical theory accounted for the contingencies of rhetorical situations, for the timely conjunction of issues and audiences. Gorgias studied the particularities of each situation as means of invention; that is, his awareness of the right time and place helped him to discover compelling things to say.

FIGURE 2.2

Kairos, from a bas-relief in Thebes. Reprinted from Zeus: A Study
in Ancient Religion *by Arthur Bernard Cook.*

Isocrates, too, emphasized the importance of *kairos*, claiming that people need to discuss prevailing issues before their currency dissipates:

> The moment for action has not yet gone by, and so made it now futile to bring
> up this question; for then, and only then, should we cease to speak, when the
> conditions have come to an end and there is no longer any need to deliberate
> about them. ("Panegyricus" 5:2)

For Isocrates, the urgency and currency of a situation demand action in
the form of lively rhetorical exchanges about an issue. But if an issue has
lost its immediacy, then the rhetor must not only deliberate about the issue
but make a case for the issue's relevance.

KAIROS, CHANGE, AND RHETORICAL SITUATIONS

Alongside the Older Sophists, we believe that the world is always changing and that knowledge itself is full of contraries—that is, never certain.

Kairos draws attention to the mutability of rhetoric, to the ever-changing
arguments that can be found in connection with a particular issue. The
available arguments on a given issue change over time because the people
who are interested in the issue change—their minds, their beliefs, their ages,

their locations, their communities, and myriad other things. Individuals can become deeply interested in issues and then they grow disinterested—people change their tastes in music and food and clothing over time, and they change their beliefs and interests as well. An individual may be religiously observant as a child, and grow utterly indifferent to religion as an adult (or vice versa). A second individual may have no interest whatever in politics until she joins a community—friends, neighbors, roommates—that is passionately engaged in political activity. Shared or communal belief changes as well, although this apparently happens more slowly. Americans have been arguing about gun control off and on for more than 200 years, but national interest in the issue waxes and wanes. Interest usually grows when some event, such as a school shooting, turns the nation's attention to the issue. That is to say, a school shooting can open a *kairotic* moment in which discussion of gun control seems more urgent than it does at other times.

Kairos also points to the situatedness of arguments in time and place and the way an argument's suitability depends on the particulars of a given rhetorical situation. The particulars of a rhetorical situation include the rhetor of course: her opinions and beliefs, her past experiences, as well as her position on an issue at the time she composes a discourse about it. But the rhetorical situation also includes the opinions and beliefs of her audience at that time and in that place, as well as the history of the issue within the communities that identify with it. Aristotle claimed that rhetoric seeks the available proofs, and these proofs are made available by the interactions of human beings who find themselves in particular sets of circumstances. That is, rhetorical situations create the available arguments. No one would care about gun control if people were not killed and injured by guns; no one would argue about climate change if it did not impact human lives or the lives of species on which we depend (such as fish) or about whose future we care (such as penguins and polar bears).

A *kairos*-based rhetoric cannot seek or offer certainty prior to composing, then. Rather, *kairos* requires that rhetors view writing and speaking as opportunities for exploring issues and making knowledge. A rhetoric that privileges *kairos* as a principle of invention cannot present a list of rules for finding arguments, but it can rather encourage a kind of ready stance, in which rhetors are not only attuned to the history of an issue (*chronos*) but are also aware of the more precise turns taken by arguments about it and when the arguments took these turns. One way to consider the *kairos* of an issue, then, is to explore the history of the issue; another is to pay careful attention to the arguments made by other parties about the issue, in order to cultivate a better understanding of why people are disagreeing at a particular time and in a particular place. In short, the rhetor must be aware of the issue's relevance to the time, the place, and the community in which it arises. Rhetors who understand all of the contexts in which issues arise will be well equipped to find convincing arguments in any given situation. In order to demonstrate how attention to *kairos* can guide analysis of an issue, we look at a set of events that occurred recently at the University of Illinois.

For many years, sports teams at Illinois have been represented by a mascot named Chief Illiniwek. This mascot has become a controversial figure, as the following editorial from *The Daily Illini*, the school's student newspaper, makes clear:

> Much like the Chief is a symbol for the University, the controversy surrounding his image has come to represent the administration's inability to act unless their hand is forced by a third party. Now that it has been forced, the time has come for closure.
>
> No matter where any of us fall on the debate, Chief Illiniwek as we know him is all but dead. As such, we see no compelling reason to put the issue off any longer. With each passing day, the distraction grows larger and the problem more serious.
>
> The Oglala Sioux tribe's recent request that the University return the regalia undermines the validity of the pro-Chief argument. If the University were to refuse the request, pro-Chief advocates could no longer claim that the Chief honors the American Indian tradition. If the University were to acquiesce, then the Chief would truly become a white man made up like an Indian.
>
> Chief Illiniwek symbolized the honor and integrity of the school for more than 80 years. He has represented the academic and athletic achievement of the University, performing at football, basketball and volleyball games in buckskin regalia adorned with a headdress.
>
> The current portrayal of the Chief began with Gary Smith, former director of the Marching Illini, who purchased the regalia in 1982 for $3,500 from Frank Fools Crow, an Oglala Sioux tribe member. The regalia included moccasins, a tunic, breastplate, leggings, peace pipe pouch and a war bonnet adorned with eagle feathers. Last Wednesday, the tribe's five member executive committee adopted a resolution by a 3–0 vote demanding the University return the feathers and regalia. Despite the confusion about the exact whereabouts of the various pieces of the Chief's dress, the important fact remains that the Oglala Sioux tribe, with whom the Chief has been closely linked, has demanded that the University cease their use of Chief Illiniwek.
>
> The University has become a popular target over the issue of American Indian representation ever since the NCAA handed down a ruling last year prohibiting the University from hosting postseason events as long as it continues using the Chief, calling it a "hostile and abusive" mascot. The regalia incident also comes on the heels of embarrassing student statements encouraging violence and intolerance on a pro-Chief Facebook group.
>
> These embarrassing incidents are a direct result of the University administration's refusal to make a decision on the Chief, even as tensions escalated. These tensions are not limited to the campus community. Alumni and other concerned parties have waged this debate far outside the area between Lincoln and Neal [sic]. Those outside this community are largely responsible for framing the argument as simply pro- or anti-Chief. The absence of leadership at the highest levels of this school's governing body has allowed the factions at the extreme ends of the issue to dominate the public discourse.
>
> The University didn't take advantage of its students, who represented the entire spectrum of the debate. Numbering more than 40,000, the students were the best chance the University had to find an acceptable compromise. The University failed the students and community by allowing this largely symbolic argument to overshadow actual pressing issues.

The situation should have been handled once and for all after the NCAA penalized the University in August 2005.

The University Board of Trustees has promised a decision will be made this year. But for the silent majority, those who are not committed to either side of the debate but desperately seek resolution, the wait has already been too long. Instead of retiring the Chief long ago in a respectful manner when it had the chance, the Board has allowed the issue to fester, the rift to widen and its credibility to rot.

The next meeting of the University Board of Trustees will be held on March 13 at 9 a.m. in Urbana. The time for a respectable solution has long since passed, and the only way the University can move forward is to put Chief Illiniwek out of his misery. (2007)

As we inserted this example into our chapter on *kairos*, it was painfully apparent to us that the issues surrounding Chief Illiniwek are in one sense strictly local—the only people who know what "between Lincoln and Neail" means are associated with the University of Illinois. (The phrase refers to streets that mark the boundaries of the campus.) For Illinois sports fans, who call themselves the "Fighting Illini," the chief's performances are part of school spirit. In another sense, however, the issue has national implications because other college and professional sports teams have mascots whose costumes and performances refer to Native American cultures. In fact, in 2005 the National Collegiate Athletics Association (NCAA) took a position on this issue, defining Chief Illiniwek and similar mascots at 17 other schools as "hostile and abusive" representations of American Indians. Other national groups, such as the National Association for the Advancement of Colored People (NAACP), the Modern Language Association (MLA), and the National Education Association (NEA) have asked that the chief be retired. Members of the university's faculty have also petitioned the University of Illinois Board of Trustees to get rid of the chief, and they were joined in this desire by some, but by no means all, students at Illinois. The chief gave his last performance at a basketball game in February 2007.

Paradoxically, rhetors can step into a *kairotic* moment when it appears only if they are well prepared to do so. Rhetorical preparedness includes an awareness of the communities who are interested in an issue, as well as awareness of their positions on it. Until the chief was retired, many communities had a stake in this issue: the students, faculty, staff, administration, and the University of Illinois Board of Trustees; the Illiniwek, the Sioux, and members of other local Native American tribes as well as members of tribes located elsewhere who are concerned about the impact of such representations on their lives and cultures; fans and supporters of the University and its sports programs; the townspeople and the municipal government of Champaign-Urbana, where the University is located; the Illinois state legislature and the governor of the state; the NCAA; other schools on the NCAA's list, and, conceivably, sports fans everywhere; and last, people and groups like the NAACP, the American Civil Liberties Union (ACLU), the MLA, and NEA who are concerned about racist discourse and its associated practices. This is a very long list of relevant communities, but it indicates the sort of initial homework that must be done by a rhetor who wants to understand the *kairos* of an issue.

A list of interested communities can serve as a **heuristic**, because it can be used to ascertain the available arguments that are in circulation among interested parties. For example, residents of Champaign-Urbana might be interested in the chief for many reasons—his performances might encourage tourism, or they might encourage more people to turn out for sports events, allowing local people to make money by parking cars in their yards. On the other hand, town residents might share the concerns felt by some participants in this discussion—that the chief's performance has racist dimensions. Where this is the case, the money generated by tourists and sports fans is probably a secondary consideration. Financial incentives might also have been at work in the situation faced by the board of trustees. The chief is apparently very popular among some students, boosters, and alumni, and, of course, satisfied boosters and alumni donate money to universities. On the other hand, the imposition of NCAA sanctions on postseason sports events, including the lucrative Bowl Championship Series (BCS), represented a potentially heavy financial loss for the university. This dilemma may have led to the delay criticized by the editors of the *Daily Illini*.

Preparedness also includes some knowledge of the history of the issue. Chief Illiniwek had a long history at Illinois; his first performance took place in 1926. Over an 80-year period, more than 30 students successfully auditioned for the role, all of them men except for one woman who performed the chief's role in 1943, when most college-aged men were in the military. Over the years, not all sports fans enjoyed the chief's performances: protests against them began in the 1970s, and in 1989, Charlene Teters, a graduate student and a member of the Spokane tribe, demonstrated at sports events where the chief was scheduled to perform.

But the earlier history of the state of Illinois is also crucial to gaining an understanding of this issue. In the early nineteenth century, some Illiniwek were forcibly relocated from their native lands in what is now the state of Illinois, and today fewer Native Americans live in Illinois than in many other states, such as Arizona. Oddly enough, the regalia most recently worn by the chief is not Illiniwek but Oglala Sioux, which suggests that those who support the chief's performances may not be interested in differences among Native cultures.

Kairos as a Means of Invention

We generated the material contained in the previous paragraphs by thinking about the times, places, and communities that are concerned with Chief Illiniwek's relation to the University of Illinois. Clearly, then, *kairos* can serve as a means of **invention**. Invention, remember, is the art of discovering all of the arguments made available by a given rhetorical situation. *Kairos* is but one of several means of invention we explore in this book—others are **stasis theory,** the **commonplaces,** and the **topics.** All of these means of invention can generate heuristics, which are usually lists of questions that help rhetors to investigate issues systematically.

Because *kairos* is not only temporal but spatial, its exploration can generate questions such as these:

1. Have recent events made the issue urgent right now, or do I need to show its urgency or make it relevant to the present? Will a history of the issue help in this regard?

2. What arguments seem to be favored by what groups at this time? That is, which communities are making which arguments? How are their interests served by these arguments?

3. What venues give voices to which sides of the issues? Does one group or another seem to be in a better position—a better place—from which to argue? In other words, what are the power dynamics at work in an issue? Who has power? Who doesn't? Why?

4. What lines of argument would be appropriate or inappropriate considering the prevailing needs and values of the audience?

5. What other issues are bound up with discourse about this issue right now, in this place and in this community? Why?

How Urgent or Immediate Is the Issue?

Usually, urgency depends on the audience as well as the existing situation—on recent activity around the issue. In recent years, arguments for and against retention of Chief Illiniwek became more and more urgent. The first widely heard arguments against the chief apparently emerged during the 1970s, when, not coincidently, Native Americans gained sufficient mainstream visibility to participate in the national discourse. The urgency of the issue accelerated as dissenting arguments circulated among other groups, and when the NCAA imposed a postseason events ban on the university in 2005, the discussion became a very hot topic at UI and at other schools as well. But interest eventually fades, even from the hottest topics. In an interesting take on this argument, Justin Breen muses about its future impact:

> Years from now, a dusty videotape of the University of Illinois' Chief Illiniwek will surface, someone will pop it in an outdated VCR, watch it and probably utter: "What were they thinking?"
>
> Illiniwek provided his final halftime performance at Wednesday's Illinois–Michigan men's basketball game. After two decades of complaints, protests and voting, the chief said so long.
>
> It's about time.
>
> The chief, an offensive portrayal of Native Americans, should have been dismissed years ago. Instead, for more than 80 years, a dancing, painted-and-feathered student provided entertainment for fans—and a nice cash flow for the university—at the expense of real honor.
>
> I don't remember much from my college days down in Champaign-Urbana, but one distinct recollection was watching the documentary "In Whose Honor?" during a sociology class. The film showed how Spokane Indian and Illinois graduate Charlene Teters and her two children were offended by the chief, and how it mocked Native Americans.

And she was absolutely right.

Teters responded by crusading against Illiniwek, trying to get rid of him once and for all. And now, finally, she and others in a vast minority can have some peace.

For the most part, the decision to remove Illiniwek is an unpopular one.

All I say is this: Imagine if your religion—your highest beliefs—were mocked right in front of your face, while others cheered and celebrated. You'd be pretty ticked, too. And, hopefully, you'd want something done about it.

One day, hopefully, all offensive mascots and these ridiculous traditions will be removed.

And the only memories of them will be on tapes collecting dust on an antique shelf. (2007)

Like VCRs and videotapes, some issues have a relatively short shelf life. *Kairos* is fickle, and as is suggested by his winged shoes, he is also fleeting. The first edition of this book was written in 1990, and we have now revised it several times. Each time we revise, we update the issues we use to illustrate our points so that they will be familiar to our current readers. Most of the issues we dealt with in earlier editions no longer seem urgent. On the other hand, one or two—such as abortion—appear to have real staying power within American discourse.

If you become interested in an issue that does not seem urgent at the moment, it might help to remember that *kairos* is akin to the Latin term *opportunitas*, an opening. Is there an opening for you to begin making new arguments on a particular issue? If not, can you create such an opening? Charlene Teters took advantage of a *kairotic* moment when no one else seemed to be concerned. Nearly 20 years later, her effort paid off.

Arguments and Interests

The specific arguments that are currently circulating about a particular issue play an important role in creating *kairos*. Who makes what arguments and why? For example, what **interest** might motivate someone to object to Chief Illiniwek's association with the University of Illinois? In the editorial we quoted previously, Justin Breen suggests that rejecting the chief is a matter of honor. That is, Breen appeals directly to a traditional value. Of course, supporters of the chief can also appeal to this value, although they read it a bit differently, as the sporting honor of the Fighting Illini.

We have already suggested that financial considerations often motivate arguments. What motives or values might have fueled the interests of those, like the editors of the *Daily Illini*, who want the chief to be retired? What groups would accept or reject their position? Why?

Considering the interests at stake in an issue can help a rhetor decide the most advantageous way to frame an argument for a particular audience at a particular time. Most issues that capture our attention are highly complex, and they resonate differently among groups with differing political and social agendas. Before launching an argument about a hot social issue, then, a rhetor who wishes to argue persuasively would do well to tune in to arguments already in circulation. Furthermore, he should interrogate the values and assumptions that drive those arguments. A rhetor who does this can maintain a *kairotic* stance that readies him to speak to various sides of the issue, supporting those that he finds convincing and refuting those with which he disagrees.

In order to demonstrate how consideration of the values and interests in circulation around an issue can help rhetors to generate arguments, we now turn to a frightening event: a shooting at Virginia Tech University. Early on the morning of April 16, 2007, police were called to a dorm room on that campus, where they found two people dead from gunshot wounds. Two hours later, a gunman opened fire in a classroom building, killing 30 more people before killing himself. It did not take long for this event to trigger speculation about gun control. Adam Gopnik suggested that the shootings offered us a *kairotic* moment:

> The cell phones in the pockets of the dead students were still ringing when we were told that it was wrong to ask why. As the police cleared the bodies from the Virginia Tech engineering building, the cell phones rang, in the eccentric varieties of ring tones, as parents kept trying to see if their children were O.K. To imagine the feelings of the police as they carried the bodies and heard the ringing is heartrending; to imagine the feelings of the parents who were calling—dread, desperate hope for a sudden answer and the bliss of reassurance, dawning grief—is unbearable. But the parents, and the rest of us, were told that it was not the right moment to ask how the shooting had happened—specifically, why an obviously disturbed student, with a history of mental illness, was able to buy guns whose essential purpose is to kill people—and why it happens over and over again in America. At a press conference, Virginia's governor, Tim Kaine, said, "People who want to . . . make it their political hobby horse to ride, I've got nothing but loathing for them . . . At this point, what it's about is comforting family members . . . and helping this community heal. And so to those who want to try to make this into some little crusade, I say take that elsewhere."
>
> If the facts weren't so horrible, there might be something touching in the Governor's deeply American belief that "healing" can take place magically, without the intervening practice called "treating." The logic is unusual but striking: the aftermath of a terrorist attack is the wrong time to talk about security, the aftermath of a death from lung cancer is the wrong time to talk about smoking and the tobacco industry, and the aftermath of a car crash is the wrong time to talk about seat belts. People talked about the shooting, of course, but much of the conversation was devoted to musings on the treatment of mental illness in universities, the problem of "narcissism," violence in the media and in popular culture, copycat killings, the alienation of immigrant students, and the question of Evil.
>
> Some people, however—especially people outside America—were eager to talk about it in another way, and even to embark on a little crusade. The whole world saw that the United States has more gun violence than other countries because we have more guns and are willing to sell them to madmen who want to kill people. Every nation has violent loners, and they tend to have remarkably similar profiles from one country and culture to the next. And every country has known the horror of having a lunatic get his hands on a gun and kill innocent people. But on a recent list of the fourteen worst mass shootings in

Western democracies since the nineteen-sixties the United States claimed seven, and, just as important, no other country on the list has had a repeat performance as severe as the first.

In Dunblane, Scotland, in 1996, a gunman killed sixteen children and a teacher at their school. Afterward, the British gun laws, already restrictive, were tightened—it's now against the law for any private citizen in the United Kingdom to own the kinds of guns that Cho Seung-Hui used at Virginia Tech—and nothing like Dunblane has occurred there since. In Quebec, after a school shooting took the lives of fourteen women in 1989, the survivors helped begin a gun-control movement that resulted in legislation bringing stronger, though far from sufficient, gun laws to Canada. (There have been a couple of subsequent shooting sprees, but on a smaller scale, and with far fewer dead.) In the Paris suburb of Nanterre, in 2002, a man killed eight people at a municipal meeting. Gun control became a key issue in the Presidential election that year, and there has been no repeat incident.

So there is no American particularity about loners, disenfranchised immigrants, narcissism, alienated youth, complex moral agency, or Evil. There is an American particularity about guns. The arc is apparent. Forty years ago, a man killed fourteen people on a college campus in Austin, Texas; this year, a man killed thirty-two in Blacksburg, Virginia. Not enough was done between those two massacres to make weapons of mass killing harder to obtain. In fact, while campus killings continued—Columbine being the most notorious, the shooting in the one-room Amish schoolhouse among the most recent—weapons have got more lethal, and, in states like Virginia, where the N.R.A. is powerful, no harder to buy.

Reducing the number of guns available to crazy people will neither relieve them of their insanity nor stop them from killing. Making it more difficult to buy guns that kill people is, however, a rational way to reduce the number of people killed by guns. Nations with tight gun laws have, on the whole, less gun violence; countries with somewhat restrictive gun laws have some gun violence; countries with essentially no gun laws have a lot of gun violence. (If you work hard, you can find a statistical exception hiding in a corner, but exceptions are just that. Some people who smoke their whole lives don't get lung cancer, while some people who never smoke do; still, the best way not to get lung cancer is not to smoke.)

It's true that in renewing the expired ban on assault weapons we can't guarantee that someone won't shoot people with a semi-automatic pistol, and that by controlling semi-automatic pistols we can't reduce the chances of someone killing people with a rifle. But the point of lawmaking is not to act as precisely as possible, in order to punish the latest crime; it is to act as comprehensively as possible, in order to prevent the next one. Semi-automatic Glocks and Walthers, Cho's weapons, are for killing people. They are not made for hunting, and it's not easy to protect yourself with them. (If having a loaded semi-automatic on hand kept you safe, cops would not be shot as often as they are.)

Rural America is hunting country, and hunters need rifles and shotguns—with proper licensing, we'll live with the risk. There is no reason that any private citizen in a democracy should own a handgun. At some point, that simple truth will register. Until it does, phones will ring for dead children, and parents will be told not to ask why. (2007)

Gopnik's essay answers our first question, about urgency: when it was published two weeks after the shootings, recent events had indeed made the issue of gun control urgent once again. Gopnik begins, in fact, by offering his readers a list of *kairotic* issues, issues that are often raised whenever a disastrous event occurs—breaches of national security, the dangers of smoking, failure to use seat belts—reminding us that while these issues are all urgently important to the nation, they seldom remain in the news for long after some event has brought them to our attention. He also addresses one of the power dynamics in this situation: his citation of remarks made by the governor of Virginia implies that public figures often ignore *kairotic* moments because they would rather not have thorny issues brought front and center when they are not ready to discuss them. Gopnik then surveys incidents of mass murder that have occurred recently in European countries, thus supplying us with a brief international history of the issue. He notes that in each case gun laws were tightened in response to mass shootings. This is not the case in America, even though there have been several recent instances of mass murders in the United States—instances that Gopnik reviews. The gunman at Virginia Tech used two automatic handguns during his killing spree, which enabled him to fire off nearly 200 shots in less than ten minutes' time. He apparently purchased the handguns at a nearby gunshop with no difficulty.

Gopnik ends his essay by noting that automatic handguns do not necessarily protect those who wield them, and he notes as well that hunters do not use such weapons. These are, of course, arguments that are often used by opponents of gun control legislation, and so Gopnik is here refuting arguments that he knows will be made by those who oppose his position. In the process he gives a partial answer to our second question: which arguments seem to be favored by which groups at this time?

Ted Nugent is adamantly opposed to gun control, and so his essay on the Virginia Tech shootings stands in stark contrast to Gopnik's work:

> Zero tolerance, huh? Gun-free zones, huh? Try this on for size: Columbine gun-free zone, New York City pizza shop gun-free zone, Luby's Cafeteria gun-free zone, Amish school in Pennsylvania gun-free zone and now Virginia Tech gun-free zone.
>
> Anybody see what the evil Brady Campaign and other anti-gun cults have created? I personally have zero tolerance for evil and denial. And America had best wake up real fast that the brain-dead celebration of unarmed helplessness will get you killed every time, and I've about had enough of it.
>
> Nearly a decade ago, a Springfield, Oregon, high schooler, a hunter familiar with firearms, was able to bring an unfolding rampage to an abrupt end when he identified a gunman attempting to reload his. 22-caliber rifle, made the tactical decision to make a move and tackled the shooter.
>
> A few years back, an assistant principal at Pearl High School in Mississippi, which was a gun-free zone, retrieved his legally owned Colt. 45 from his car and stopped a Columbine wannabe from continuing his massacre at another school after he had killed two and wounded more at Pearl.

At an eighth-grade school dance in Pennsylvania, a boy fatally shot a teacher and wounded two students before the owner of the dance hall brought the killing to a halt with his own gun.

More recently, just a few miles up the road from Virginia Tech, two law school students ran to fetch their legally owned firearm to stop a madman from slaughtering anybody and everybody he pleased. These brave, average, armed citizens neutralized him pronto.

My hero, Dr. Suzanne Gratia Hupp, was not allowed by Texas law to carry her handgun into Luby's Cafeteria that fateful day in 1991, when due to bureaucrat-forced unarmed helplessness she could do nothing to stop satanic George Hennard from killing 23 people and wounding more than 20 others before he shot himself. Hupp was unarmed for no other reason than denial-ridden "feel good" politics.

She has since led the charge for concealed weapon upgrade in Texas, where we can now stop evil. Yet, there are still the mindless puppets of the Brady Campaign and other anti-gun organizations insisting on continuing the gun-free zone insanity by which innocents are forced into unarmed helplessness. Shame on them. Shame on America. Shame on the anti-gunners all.

No one was foolish enough to debate Ryder truck regulations or ammonia nitrate restrictions or a "cult of agriculture fertilizer" following the unabashed evil of Timothy McVeigh's heinous crime against America on that fateful day in Oklahoma City. No one faulted kitchen utensils or other hardware of choice after Jeffrey Dahmer was caught drugging, mutilating, raping, murdering and cannibalizing his victims. Nobody wanted "steak knife control" as they autopsied the dead nurses in Chicago, Illinois, as Richard Speck went on trial for mass murder.

Evil is as evil does, and laws disarming guaranteed victims make evil people very, very happy. Shame on us.

Already spineless gun control advocates are squawking like chickens with their tiny-brained heads chopped off, making political hay over this most recent, devastating Virginia Tech massacre, when in fact it is their own forced gun-free zone policy that enabled the unchallenged methodical murder of 32 people.

Thirty-two people dead on a U.S. college campus pursuing their American Dream, mowed-down over an extended period of time by a lone, non-American gunman in possession of a firearm on campus in defiance of a zero-tolerance gun ban. Feel better yet? Didn't think so.

Who doesn't get this? Who has the audacity to demand unarmed helplessness? Who likes dead good guys?

I'll tell you who. People who tramp on the Second Amendment, that's who. People who refuse to accept the self-evident truth that free people have the God-given right to keep and bear arms, to defend themselves and their loved ones. People who are so desperate in their drive to control others, so mindless in their denial that they pretend access to gas causes arson, Ryder trucks and fertilizer cause terrorism, water causes drowning, forks and spoons cause obesity, dialing 911 will somehow save your life, and that their greedy clamoring to "feel good" is more important than admitting that armed citizens are much better equipped to stop evil than unarmed, helpless ones.

Pray for the families of victims everywhere, America. Study the methodology of evil. It has a profile, a system, a preferred environment where victims cannot fight back. Embrace the facts, demand upgrade and be certain that your children's school has a better plan than Virginia Tech or Columbine. Eliminate the insanity of gun-free zones, which will never, ever be gun-free zones. They will only be good guy gun-free zones, and that is a recipe for disaster written in blood on the altar of denial. I, for one, refuse to genuflect there (2007).

Nugent begins his essay with a history of the issue told by means of two lists of examples. The first list alludes to several well-known events wherein unarmed participants in "gun-free zones" were slaughtered by well-armed attackers; the second lists instances wherein armed participants slew would-be assassins with guns of their own. Like Gopnik, Nugent cites the Virginia Tech shootings as the urgent impetus for his essay, but he connects that episode to many others where "bad guys" prey upon innocent "good guys." Like the history given by Gopnik, Nugent's history also goes back a long way—Richard Speck murdered eight women in 1966. This tells us that both writers expect their audiences to be old enough, or well-connected enough, to remember events that occurred more than 40 years ago.

Nugent has an interesting way of making arguments by implication. The arguments about McVeigh and Dahmer and Speck—all convicted mass murderers—are arguments from analogy: the implication is that if we don't ban Ryder trucks and fertilizer (used by McVeigh to blow up the Federal Building in Oklahoma City in 1995), we should not outlaw guns simply because evil or deranged people use them to kill. This argument rephrases a commonplace favored among those who want no legal controls over gun sales and distribution: "guns don't kill people, people do." Nugent also gives us some arguments that he thinks drive his opponents: they disrespect the Second Amendment, they are control addicts, they are in denial, and gun control legislation makes them "feel good." Nugent does not seem to care if he offends people who disagree with him; that is, he does not seem to mind if his arguments are received by his opponents as inappropriate.

Neither of these essays offers direct clues as to why their authors believe as they do on the issue of gun control. That is, it is difficult to determine from an examination of these texts alone to what communities either author belongs. We can make educated guesses, though; members of the National Rifle Association often take positions and make arguments similar to Nugent's, while members of the Brady Campaign to Control Gun Violence will sympathize with Gopnik's remarks. These assumptions can lead us to search engines and other research tools that will direct us toward more arguments used by those who are interested in the issue of gun control and that will allow us to define more carefully the groups that are invested in the issue.

Nationally known public figures are also expected to voice opinions about shattering events. Often, they seem to feel that it is not in their best interests to take sides on an issue as controversial as gun control. Shortly after the shootings at Virginia Tech, Edward Epstein and Carla Marinucci published an account of the reactions of prominent Democrats and Republicans to the Virginia Tech shootings:

The Virginia Tech campus massacre may reignite a national debate over gun control, but with an election year looming and a powerful gun lobby geared for battle, Democrats probably will be reluctant to push such a divisive issue that could threaten their control of Congress and effort to win back the White House.

"Democrats tend to be worried about their electoral prospects with the gun-owning public," said Bob Levy, a senior fellow and constitutional scholar with the conservative CATO Institute, a Washington think tank. "They haven't been particularly vocal, because they understand that people in this country want their guns."

But Ladd Everitt of the Coalition to End Gun Violence said American voters, battered by the painful replays of Virginia Tech and other shooting deaths, want action.

"I don't know what the tipping point is," he said. "At some point, the public will just have to stand up and say 'enough.' "

The White House reaction this week to a question about gun control relating to the campus tragedy underscored President Bush's support for and from gun owners—a vital constituency for the Republican Party.

"The president believes that there is a right for people to bear arms, but that all laws must be followed," spokeswoman Dana Perino said Monday afternoon.

On the Democratic side, California Sen. Dianne Feinstein expressed her sorrow and issued a statement saying she hoped that the killings would "reignite the dormant effort to pass commonsense gun control regulations in this country."

Feinstein, who sponsored the 1994 federal assault weapons ban that expired in 2004, was joined in the effort by Rep. Carolyn McCarthy, D-N.Y., whose husband was killed and son wounded by a shooter in 1996 on a Long Island commuter train.

McCarthy, who was elected to the House on a strong gun control platform, admitted the matter is "a tough sell," even in the wake of the national trauma over the worst massacre by a single gunman in American history.

Politicians in Congress aren't the only ones struggling with the issue: on the presidential candidate stage, Republican former New York City Mayor Rudolph Giuliani has spoken in favor of gun control in the past; former Massachusetts Gov. Mitt Romney recently declared himself a "lifelong" hunter and National Rifle Association member.

GOP consultant Dan Schnur said that "for years, half of the political world has rushed to gun control as the answer, and the other half has rushed to tougher penalties for criminals using guns—and never the twain shall meet."

Because the 2008 presidential election campaign is already underway, Schnur said, "The candidate who does the best job of bridging that debate is the one who benefits."

The Democratic mood on Capitol Hill Tuesday, just 24 hours after the Virginia Tech killings, was pragmatic about gun control. Lawmakers said the shootings will revive interest in legislation, but they said they will move cautiously before pushing ahead into a politically volatile area.

Gun control divides Democrats in Congress, and it is an issue that anti-gun-control Republicans have used effectively in House and Senate races. In the Democratic-controlled House, where the party's majority is due in part to victories in November in conservative to moderate districts formerly represented by Republicans, the party's winning candidates often campaigned as advocates of gun owners' rights.

Leadership aides concede privately that leaders are unlikely to push major gun control legislation because keeping the majority depends on reelecting members from districts where gun control is a losing issue.

"The country and the Congress will have additional discussions, as is always the case, after these incidents," House Majority Leader Steny Hoyer of Maryland told reporters. "But right now we're focused on the incident itself.

"I don't want to get into a debate about what we need to do less than 24 hours after the incident. We need to focus on the victims of this tragedy, on the students, the teachers and their families."

Senate Majority leader Harry Reid of Nevada agreed, saying, "I hope there's not a rush to do anything. We need to take a deep breath."

He said he wanted local, state and federal investigations to continue into the guns, the ammunition and the shooter in the Virginia Tech killings before pushing any legislation. But Reid spoke favorably about a bill sponsored by California Sen. Barbara Boxer to improve school safety.

Boxer said the latest university killings have motivated her to push that bill, which she has introduced in past Congresses.

"Virginia Tech reminds all of us that our kids are at risk in schools," she said.

She said Congress should look at two issues, "guns that are in the wrong hands, and security at these campuses."

Democrats this week, however, recalled that Feinstein's assault weapons ban was allowed to lapse before the 2004 election, even though Bush said he would sign an extension if the Republican Congress sent him such legislation. The widespread view was that the GOP Congress blocked an extension of the ban so the president wouldn't have to upset the gun lobby by signing it or gun control advocates by going back on his pledge.

Even Feinstein didn't spell out exactly what she would like to see done.

"Down the road, we should learn more about this crime, how it was perpetrated, and what lessons can be learned from it," she said Tuesday.

Everitt, of the Coalition to Stop Gun Violence, said there are reasons for gun reform groups to be optimistic. He noted 188 mayors in 44 states organized to push for gun control, and cited efforts by New York's McCarthy to improve background checks on guns sales. He also said there was hope for more support on behalf of legislation—already enacted in California—to "close the gun-show loophole," which allows buyers in 33 states, including Virginia, to buy guns at such expositions "without background checks or paperwork, cash and carry and (in many cases) you don't have to fill out a form."(2007)

In general, these powerful people did not want to commit to an opinion on the issue of control, at least during the moment of highest urgency. Some mentioned moderate alternatives to the most radical positions available, but, as Gopnik noticed, nearly all counseled patience. The questions of *kairos* should lead us to ask: why do political figures avoid taking positions on controversial issues? How are their interests served by doing so?

Power Dynamics in a Rhetorical Situation

In some ways, Ted Nugent's essay about gun control is all about power: gun users have it; people who work in "gun-free zones" don't. And so he laments the power that has supposedly accrued to the antigun lobby that would, in his opinion, disarm people of weapons they need to protect themselves and their families. Nugent associates this lobby with the Brady Campaign, a group named after James Brady, who was seriously wounded when an assassin shot President Ronald Reagan in 1981. In an apparent effort to limit their power with the national discourse, Nugent excoriates gun-control activists in scathing terms: they are mindless, greedy, insane.

To examine and invent arguments using *kairos* is to consider the power dynamics at work in a particular issue in addition to the recent events and arguments that press on it. The questions to ask here are:

Which arguments receive more attention?

Who is making these arguments?

What arguments receive less attention?

Who is making these arguments?

When gun control arises as an issue, reporters often request statements from groups already organized, such as the National Rifle Association or the Brady Campaign. Organized groups often have more power to be heard in given rhetorical situations than do people who are unaffiliated with a relevant group. Government leaders, too, are asked to make known their stances on such issues. Here, for example, is Senator Dianne Feinstein's reaction to the Virginia Tech incident:

> "My heart nearly stopped when I heard that more than 30 people had been killed at Virginia Tech today.
>
> In an instant, the hopes and dreams of students were destroyed by a cowardly and terrible act of insane violence. My deepest condolences go to all those touched by this violence.
>
> This mass shooting will be seared into our memories, alongside Columbine, 101 California, the University of Texas Clock Tower, and the shooting at a McDonald's in San Ysidro, California.
>
> It is my deep belief that shootings like these are enabled by the unparalleled ease with which people procure weapons in this country. And I believe this will reignite the dormant effort to pass common-sense gun regulations in this nation." (2007)

Feinstein represents the state of California, and so she is careful to mention incidents of gun violence that occurred in that state. Unlike other public officials, she connects the violence at Virginia Tech directly to the gun control issue, giving *kairos* its due as a spatial concept.

The arguments made by the governor of Virginia probably had more impact than those made by Feinstein, given his responsibility for the welfare of the citizens of Virginia and his relative proximity to Virginia Tech. On the other hand, we rarely hear or read the opinions of young people about gun control. Students on the campus were repeatedly asked about their emotional responses to the shootings, and they were asked as well to give factual accounts if they were in a position to do so. But reporters for the national media who wrote about the incident often did not bother to ask about the opinions of those who will some day make decisions about gun control. How do we account for the absence of the voices of the young from public discourse about gun control? Could it be that this group is apathetic? Or does their nonvoting status have something to do with the undervaluing of their position? All of these questions and more are raised by consideration of the power dynamics at work in any rhetorical situation (see the chapter on *ethos* for more discussion of powerrelations in rhetoric).

A Web of Related Issues

Rhetorical situations are complex. A rhetor who is attuned to *kairos*, then, must demonstrate awareness of the many values and the differential power dynamics that are involved in any struggle over an issue. The stakes in an argument can shift according to who is speaking, as is illustrated by the contrasting arguments on gun control that we cited. A rhetor attuned to *kairos* should consider a particular issue as a set of different political pressures, personal investments, and values, all of which produce different arguments about an issue. These diverging values and different levels of investment connect to other issues as well, producing a weblike relationship with links to other, different, new—but definitely related—rhetorical situations. The issue of gun control is linked to the issue of violence, of course, and those who are charged to prevent violence, such as the police and the courts, have a large stake in seeing to it that really dangerous weapons, such as automatic handguns, are kept out of the wrong hands.

The incident at Virginia Tech opened up other issues as well, including but not limited to the appropriate procedures for recognizing disturbed people who are potentially dangerous to themselves and others. But some mental health professionals worried as well about the impact on viewers of repetitive television coverage of the event. Here, for instance, is an entry from Natalie Reiss' blog, posted a few days after the event:

> Just like everyone else, I am struggling to make sense of the VA Tech shootings. If you haven't already, I encourage you to read the pieces on Mental Help Net written by Dr. Dombeck and Dr. Schwartz. In my humble opinion, each of these pieces are much more informative and thought-provoking than the incredibly short sound bytes and quotes being presented by the news media as "analysis" of the tragedy. No matter how well-spoken or authoritative someone appears or sounds, a few minutes or a few sentences is simply not enough time to coherently and appropriately analyze something as complex as what would drive a young man to engage in this horrifying display of rage and destruction.
>
> In my blog, I'd like to bring up a different twist on the issue. I'd like you, the reader, to take a step back and really think about your own emotional and mental reaction to this tragedy. What emotions are you experiencing today? Shock, sorrow, numbness, fear, anger, disillusionment, grief? A combination? Do your emotional reactions change over the course of the day? Are you having trouble sleeping, concentrating, eating, or remembering even simple tasks? Do you feel panicked or frantic? Are you having nightmares? Are you having repetitive thoughts about the world as an unsafe and uncontrollable place?

These are all common reactions to a stressful event, and you should not feel guilty about these reactions, even if you didn't personally know the professors and students that were killed. To cope with your feelings and reactions, it is important to share your thoughts and feelings with others; eat healthy, rest and exercise; periodically TURN OFF THE TV or STOP READING OR LISTENING TO COVERAGE OF THE EVENT (particularly graphic photos or writings); and find a way to focus on and help others. These feelings and thoughts should dissipate over the course of the next days or weeks. . . .

We probably will never have a satisfactory answer to why this tragedy occurred. We don't live in a just world, and life is simply not fair. Human behavior is multi-factorial and complex, and a few people who desperately need help will always slip through the cracks of our mental health system. Please don't compound the tragedy by failing to seek help for yourself if you need it (2007).

Reiss's concern about mental health connects to other issues, such as the relative usefulness and potential harm of relentless media coverage of tragic events. These and other related issues form a web that provides seemingly endless possibilities, or "openings," for arguments.

We are not suggesting that a rhetor should address all the values and actions pressing on a particular issue at a particular time. Rather, we recommend that rhetors be aware of the issue's ever shifting nuances, which might lead to new opportunities for rhetorical arguments. Considering the wealth of possibilities produced by attention to an issue's *kairos*, it is no wonder that Gorgias was bold enough to say to the Athenians, "Suggest a subject," and remain confident that he could make a rhetorical argument about it on the spot.

RHETORICAL ACTIVITIES

1. Survey a variety of magazines and newspapers and select a handful of articles on a given issue. How does each article draw on or create *kairos*? Is the issue so pertinent or urgent that little needs to be done to establish the article's relevance? Do some writers or speakers use an opportune moment to "change the subject" and argue about a separate but related set of issues?

2. Using a library periodical database such as LexisNexis or the Internet, look for a few recent articles on gun control or offensive sports mascots. How has the *kairos* surrounding these issues changed since we wrote this book? Has the Illinois situation spawned similar studies and actions in other states, or has its *kairos* "fizzled"? Has talk about gun control faded from the national news?

3. Choose an issue and read broadly about it, keeping track of the various perspectives. Then, make a visual "map" of the arguments, tracking how the main issue gives rise to others. The map may look like two sets of lists, or it may be more sprawling with lots of offshoots, like a broad web. Be sure to include in the map the arguments people are making, who the people are, and what values they seem to be asserting.

4. Choose an issue and compose an opening paragraph that shows how the issue matters for people you may be addressing.

PROGYMNASMATA II: CHREIA AND PROVERB

The Spanish novelist Miguel de Cervantes once observed that "A proverb is a short sentence based on long experience." Experience—and observations based on experience—informs the next two *progymnasmata* practiced by the ancients: *chreia* and tale. The ancients' fondness for pithy sayings, quotable quotes, and memorable actions still endures today. Nowadays it is common practice to append a proverb like quotation to an e-mail signature or to personalize Web pages, Facebook pages, and MySpace pages with favorite proverbs or maxims. Such quotations can serve as the starting point for these exercises, which ask that short statements be elaborated.

Chreia

A *chreia*, as described by Aelius Theon, is a brief saying or action that makes a point. It is always attributed to a specific person and as such often reads like a maxim or proverb attributed to a person (Aelius Theon, Kennedy 2003, 15). Its name comes from the Greek word for *useful* (*khreiōdēs*). Hermogenes defined *chreia* as "a concise exposition of some memorable saying or deed, generally for good counsel" (Kennedy 2003, 26). Nicolaus the Sophist writes that *chreia* should be "well aimed." Hence it is not surprising that the examples of *chreia* offered in the extant educational treatises have to do with education, so that students could take pointed lessons from the sayings or deeds they were asked to interpret and to amplify (*Institutes* I ix 4–6).

Aphthonius offers this example of a *chreia* that is a saying: "Plato said the twigs of virtue grow by sweat and toil" (Kennedy 2003, 97). Ancient teachers regularly cited the following example of a famous deed, attributed variously to Diogenes or Crates: a man, on seeing a young boy misbehave, struck the boy's teacher. The moral, of course, is that teachers are ultimately responsible for the behavior of their students. Nicolaus the Sophist observes that some *chreia* are just as clever as they are useful. He offers this one as an example: "Damon the trainer, they say, had twisted feet and when he lost his shoes at the baths he expressed the hope that they would fit the feet of the thief" (141). We also rather like this *chreia* of his: "Aesop the fabulist, having been asked what is the strongest thing in human society, said 'Speech'" (Kennedy 2003, 141).

In *chreia*, ancient students moved from composing narratives to amplifying them, sometimes by fleshing out the bare narrative, but more often by adding commentary on famous deeds or utterances. The ability to amplify on a theme was much prized in antiquity and throughout the premodern period, because it demonstrated the fruits of a rhetor's long study and well trained memory. In his sixteenth-century textbook on *copia*, Erasmus wrote that amplification was "just like displaying some object for sale first of all through a grill or inside a wrapping, and then unwrapping it and opening it out and displaying it fully to the gaze" (572).

Ancient rhetors could amplify any theme in order to meet situational constraints, such as resistant audiences who needed a good deal of convincing. They could also shorten their compositions if time limits were imposed on them. Amplification evolved into something of an art form in Roman rhetoric. Seneca the Elder told a story about a rhetor named Albucius, who could amplify a single theme so fully that he could speak through three soundings of the trumpet (the trumpet blew at the end of each three-hour watch during the night). Seneca reported that Albucius wished "to say not what ought to be said but what is capable of being said. He argued laboriously rather than subtly; he used argument to prove arguments, and as though there were no firm ground anywhere confirmed all his proofs with further proofs" (*Controversiae* 7 pref. 1).

Because of the importance of amplification, Hermogenes and Aphthonius both supplied a list of instructions for amplifying on a simple account of a historical event or speech. The fully amplified *chreia* was to begin with praise of a famous speaker or doer of deeds; then there was to be an explanation or paraphrase of the famous saying or action; the composer next supplied a reason for the saying or doing; then she compared and contrasted the famous saying or doing to some other speech or event; next, she added an example and supported the saying or doing with testimony; last, she concluded with a brief epilogue.

Aphthonius supplied the following example of a fully developed *chreia*. The famous saying, taken from the work of Isocrates, is "The root of education is bitter, but sweet are its fruits."

(PRAISE FOR THE AUTHOR, OR *ENCOMIUM*): It is fitting that Isocrates should be admired for his art, which gained for him an illustrious reputation. Just what it was, he demonstrated by practice and he made the art famous; he was not made famous by it. It would take too long a time to go into all the ways in which he benefitted humanity, whether he was phrasing laws for rulers on the one hand or advising individuals on the other, but we may examine his wise remark on education.

(PARAPHRASE OF SAYING): The lover of learning, he says, is beset with difficulties at the beginning, but these eventually end as advantages. That is what he so wisely said, and we shall wonder at it as follows.

(CAUSES OR REASONS FOR SAYING): The lovers of learning search out the leaders in education, to approach whom is fearful and to desert whom is folly. Fear waits upon the boys, both in the present and in the future. After the teachers come the attendants, fearful to look at and dreadful when angered. Further, the fear is as swift as the misdeed and, after fear, comes the punishment. Indeed, they punish the faults of the boys, but they consider the good qualities only fit and proper. The fathers are even more harsh than the attendants in choosing the streets, enjoining the boys to go straight along them, and being suspicious of the marketplace. If there has been need of punishment, however, they do not understand the true nature of it, but the youth approaching manhood is invested with good character through these trials.

(A CONTRAST): If anyone, on the other hand, should flee from the teachers out of fear of these things, or if he should run away from his parents, or if he should turn away from the attendants, he has completely deprived himself of their teaching and he has lost an education along with the fear. All these considerations influence the saying of Isocrates that the root of learning is bitter.

(A COMPARISON): For just as the tillers of the soil throw down the seeds to the earth with hardship and then gather in a greater harvest, in like manner those seeking after an education finally win by toil the subsequent reknown.

(AN EXAMPLE): Let me call to mind the life of Demosthenes; in one respect, it was more beset with hardships than that of any other rhetor but, from another point of view, his life came to be more glorious than any other. For he was so preeminent in his zeal that the adornment was often taken from his head, since the best adornment stems from virtue. Moreover, he devoted to his labors those energies that others squander on pleasures.

(TESTIMONY): Consequently, there is reason to marvel at Hesiod's saying that the road to virtue is hard, but easy it is to traverse the heights. For that which Hesiod terms a road, Isocrates calls a root; in different terms, both are conveying the same idea.

(EPILOGUE): In regard to these things, there is reason for those looking back on Isocrates to marvel at him for having expressed himself so beautifully on the subject of education. (Nadeau 266–267)

We encourage our readers to imitate or paraphrase this *chreia*; surely it is possible to write a better or more up-to-date amplification of Isocrates' observation about education.

PROGYMNASMATA: CHREIA

1. Copy the famous saying by Isocrates—"The root of education is bitter, but sweet are its fruits"—and then, following Aphthonius's instructions, amplify the *chreia*.

2. Try amplifying a famous historical deed—perhaps George Washington's act of cutting down the cherry tree or Benjamin Franklin's flying his famous kite.

3. Choose a song lyric by your favorite musical artist and cast it as a *chreia* (remember that the distinguishing mark of *chreia* is that the saying is attributed to a particular person or group of people—this could well apply to a band). Then amplify the lyric according to Aphthonius's instructions.

4. Elaborate some favorite saying, or some habit, of a relative or a friend; or you can use sayings from editorials in newspapers or magazines; or you can develop a *chreia* of action from a news story.

5. Quintilian suggested yet another kind of exercise with *chreia*: try to determine the causes of some well known symbolic relationships. His examples were these: Why in Sparta is Venus represented as wearing

armor? or Why is Cupid believed to be a winged boy armed with arrows and a torch? (II iv 26) Here are a couple of modern examples of this sort of question, around which a *chreia* could be developed: Why is justice represented as blind? Why does the Statue of Liberty bear a lighted torch? Find out the answers to these questions, and compose a *chreia* that amplifies on the justness of these decisions. Remember the *chreia* differs from tale because the story taken from history is supposed to point out a lesson or moral and can be based on actions or statements or—in these instances—physical characteristics.

Proverb

Proverbs are common sayings that nearly every member of a culture knows: "A stitch in time saves nine," "Haste makes waste," and the like. (Aristotle regarded proverbs as maxims, and he discusses them as a means of proof—see the chapter on rhetorical reasoning). Hermogenes defined a proverb as "a summary saying, in a statement of general application, dissuading from something or persuading toward something, or showing what is the nature of each" (27). That is, proverbs are either persuasive or expository. Examples of contemporary proverbs that persuade people to action are: "The squeaky wheel gets the grease", "Wake up and smell the roses," and "The early bird catches the worm." Proverbs that dissuade people from doing things are "Friends don't let friends drive drunk" and "Don't count your chickens before they hatch." Explanatory proverbs include "Rolling stones gather no moss" and "The spirit is willing, but the flesh is weak."

Any of these proverbs can be amplified according to the ancient directions for doing so: begin by praising either the wisdom of the proverb or its author (if the author is known), paraphrase or explain the proverb's meaning, give proof of the proverb's truth or accuracy, give comparative and contrasting examples, supply testimony from another author, compose an epilogue. Donald Lemen Clark's study of ancient rhetoric during the English Renaissance includes an example of this exercise composed by the seventeenth-century poet John Milton, who elaborated on the proverb "In the morning rise up early."

> (*ENCOMIUM*): Tis a proverb worn with age, "it is most healthy to rise at break of day." Nor indeed is the saying less true than old, for if I shall try to recount in order the several advantages of this, I shall seem to undertake a task of heavy labor.
>
> (PARAPHRASE): Rise, then, rise, thou lazy fellow, let not the soft couch hold thee forever.
>
> (CAUSE): You know not how many pleasures the dawn brings. Would you delight your eyes? Look at the sun rising in ruddy vigor, the pure and healthful sky, the flourishing green of the fields, the variety of all the flowers. Would you delight your ears? Listen to the clear concert of the birds and the light humming of the bees. Would you please your nostrils? You cannot have enough of the sweetness of the scents that breathe from the flowers.

(ANOTHER CAUSE): But if this please you not, I beg you to consider a little the argument of your health; for to rise from bed at early morn is in no light
degree conducive to a strong constitution; it is in fact best for study, for then
you have wit in readiness.

(COMPARISON): Besides, it is the part of a good king not to pamper his
body with too much sleep, and live a life all holidays and free from toil, but to
plan for the commonwealth night and day.

(ANCIENT TESTIMONY): As Theocritus wisely urges "It is not well to
sleep deep." And in Homer the Dream thus speaks to Agamemnon "Sleepest
thou, son of a wise-minded, horse-taming Atreus? 'Tis not well for a man of
counsel to sleep all night through."

(EXAMPLE): Why do the poets fable Tithonus and Cephalus to have loved
Dawn? Surely because they were sparing of sleep; and, leaving their beds, were
wont to roam the fields, decked and clad with many colored flowers.

(CONTRARY): But to extirpate somnolence utterly, to leave no trace of it, I
shall attempt to lay bare the numberless inconveniences that flow to all from it.
It blunts and dulls keen talent, and greatly injures memory. Can anything be
baser than to snore far into the day, and to consecrate, as it were, the chief part
of your life to death?

(CONCLUSION): But you who bear rule, you especially should be wide
awake, and utterly rout gripping sleep as it creeps upon you. For many, coming upon enemies, whelmed by heavy sleep, and as it were, buried therein,
have smitten them with slaughter, and wrought such havoc as it is pitiful to see
or hear of. A thousand examples of this kind occur to me which I could tell with
an inexhaustible pen. But if I imitate such Asiatic exuberance, I fear lest I shall
murder my wretched listeners with boredom. (1948, 235–246)

We think the Milton example is careful and funny. But for something a little more contemporary, we decided to compose our own amplification of a
proverb.

For this exercise we chose a proverb that might be relevant for the lives
of our readers:

"Never put off till tomorrow what you can do today."

(PRAISE OF THE PROVERB/AUTHOR): Thomas Jefferson penned this
wise maxim in his "Decalogue of Canons for Observation in Practical Life."
Jefferson, is of course, well known for his labors on liberty, and it's certainly the
case that his views on liberty and basic freedom likely informed his views on
diligence that motivate this proverb. The virtue of this quotation is what
remains unsaid, namely the direct ties to personal freedom. One must work to
remain free, or else one risks becoming oppressed by worry resulting from
work undone. As an example, once we hit upon this proverb as one to amplify,
we nearly let the mere discovery stand as our work for the day. That's right, we
almost put off the amplification until tomorrow. And then deciding not to
waste too much time musing over the irony of what we'd nearly done, we set
to work expanding the proverb.

(PARAPHRASE AND EXPLANATION): Jefferson, then, in listing this piece
of advice at the very top of his observations on practical living, urges us to tend
to business that needs to be tended to and not to defer it just because it's easy
to do so. Of course this maxim is not just appropriate to business matters, or

matters of schooling, but personal matters as well, like that phone call to your grandmother or an overdue lunch with a friend. The main question here is, why delay? Get things done in a timely manner. These days, people write entire books on how to get things done, and they are all expansions of Jefferson's pithy but simpler rule of thumb.

(PROOF): Pressing tasks really ought to be handled sooner rather than later, in part because you never know what other matters will arise tomorrow to prevent you from doing that which you deferred in the first place.

(EXAMPLE): Consider this scenario: In June of 1776, a committee appointed by Continental Congress delegated to Jefferson the task of drafting the Declaration of Independence. What if Jefferson, feeling a little overwhelmed by the task, had convinced his friends Madison and Adams to join him at a pub instead? "Oh, I can get started tomorrow," he might have assured them, "the vote for independence hasn't even happened yet, anyway." And then what if the next day Jefferson slept late and woke up with a terrible headache and finding himself unable to focus properly, decided to put off beginning the draft yet another day? Instead, Jefferson set right to work, completing a draft in plenty of time for his colleagues John Adams and Benjamin Franklin and the rest of the committee members to revise it and to present it to the Continental Congress in late June. Had Jefferson not followed his own advice, we might be celebrating Independence Day in mid-August, closer to Thanksgiving, or not at all.

(TESTIMONY): We say not at all because as Martin Luther, another producer of a timely document, once said, "How soon 'not now' becomes 'never.'" There's also the famous saying "Procrastination is the grave in which opportunity is buried." And Jefferson's colleague, Benjamin Franklin, to whom the previous proverb is sometimes attributed (most likely because someone put off checking his sources), also said, "You may delay, but time will not." Perhaps most compellingly, Martin Luther King Jr. makes good use of antideferral logic where civil rights are concerned. In "Letter from Birmingham Jail," he writes,

> For years now I have heard the word "Wait!" It rings in the ear of every Negro with piercing familiarity. This "Wait" has almost always meant "Never." We must come to see, with one of our distinguished jurists, that "justice too long delayed is justice denied.

"Too true. Kings's testimony confirms our belief that liberty undergirds Jefferson's proverb.

(EPILOGUE): Now that we have completed this amplification, we will have the afternoon free. Perhaps we will discover something else that can be done today.

Proverb, *chreia*, tale, and fable were the exercises used by grammarians to help younger students master the basic composing skills, and you might have noticed along the way that these early exercises have a strong moral component, illustrating the ancients' concern about producing upstanding people who will use rhetoric ethically. After all, as we saw with the *chreia* attributed to Diogenes, teachers were often held accountable for their students' actions. When students matured, they moved on to study with a teacher of rhetoric, who saw to it that they practiced exercises in the achievement of *copia* that were directly related to composing skills they would need as rhetors.

PROGYMNASMATA: PROVERB

Visit one of the following Web sites (or another one you locate through a search). Select a quotation and amplify it following our example.

http://www.quotationspage.com/

http://www.bartleby.com/

http://www.brainyquote.com/

http://en.thinkexist.com/

WORKS CITED

Breen, Justin. "Chief Illiniwek Needed to Disappear." *NWI Times* [IN], February 22, 2007. http://nwitimes.com/articles/2007/02/22/columnists/justin_breen/docc89f8e2c31a6f1a38625728900824a29.txt (accessed June 5, 2007).

Clark, Donald Lemen. *John Milton at St. Paul's School: A Study of Ancient Rhetoric in English Renaissance Education.* New York: Columbia University Press, 1948.

Daily Illini Editorial Board. "The Chief Should Finally Rest in Peace." *Daily Illini*, January 24, 2007. http://media.www.dailyillini.com/media/storage/paper736/news/2007/01/24/Editorials/The-Chief.Should.Finally.Rest.In.Peace-2670760.shtml (accessed May 24, 2007).

Epstein, Edward, and Carla Marinucci. "Virginia Tech Massacre; Gun Control: Democrats, Eyes on Majority, Apt to Go Slow on Restrictions." *San Franciso Chronicle*, April 18, 2007. http://www.sfgate.com/cgibin/article.cgi?file=/chronicle/archive/2007/04/18/MNGOUPAJ141.DTL&type=politics (accessed May 22, 2007).

Feinstein, Dianne. "Statement of Senator Dianne Feinstein on the Mass Shooting at Virginia Tech." Feinstein's official Web site, January 16, 2007. http://feinstein.senate.gov/public/index.cfm?FuseAction=NewsRoom.PressReleases&ContentRecord_id=fc6adefc-9b7a-525a-b67d-24447a8403fc&Region_id=&Issue_id= (accessed May 22, 2007).

Gopnik, Adam. Shootings. *The New Yorker*, April 30, 2007. http://www.newyorker.com/talk/comment/2007/04/30/070430taco_talk_gopnik (accessed May 22, 2007).

Kennedy, George. *Progymnasmata: Greek Textbooks of Prose Composition and Rhetoric.* Leiden: Brill, 2003.

Liddell, Henry George and Robert Scott. *A Greek-English Lexicon.* New York: Oxford University Press, 1996.

Nugent, Ted. "Nugent: Gun-Free Zones Are Recipe for Disaster." CNN official Web site, April 20, 2007. http://www.cnn.com/2007/US/04/19/commentary.nugent/index.html (accessed May 22, 2007).

Reiss, Natalie. "A Mental Health Reader: Mental Health News and Commentary." The MentalHealth.Net Directory, May 20, 2007. http://www.mentalhelp.net/poc/view_doc.php?type=weblog&wlid=6&id=211&cn=109. (accessed May 22, 2007).

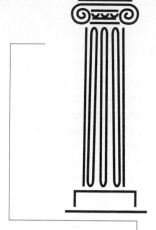

CHAPTER 3

STASIS THEORY: ASKING THE RIGHT QUESTIONS

How is Cato to deliberate "whether he personally is to marry," unless the general question "whether marriage is desirable" is first settled? And how is he to deliberate "whether he should marry Marcia," unless it is proved that it is the duty of Cato to marry?

— Quintilian,
Institutes III 13

STUDENTS WHO WANT a systematic way of asking questions about rhetorical situations can use stasis theory. This means of invention provides rhetors with a set of questions that, when asked systematically, can help them to determine just where it is that the disagreement between themselves and their audience begins. Determining the point of disagreement is an obvious starting point for rhetorical invention, which is always stimulated by some difference of opinion.

Staseis (questions or issues in Greek) were probably part of rhetorical lore as early as the fourth century BCE (Aristotle, *Rhetoric* III 17). But the popularity of this system of invention in Hellenistic and Roman rhetoric was probably due to Hermagoras's codification of the process during the second century BCE. His textbook is lost, so scholars have reconstructed his theory of invention from discussions of it that appear in Cicero, Quintilian, and other ancient and medieval authorities.

The term *stasis* (Latin *status* or *constitutio*) is derived from a Greek word meaning "a stand." Thus a stasis can refer to the place where one rhetor takes a stand. Seen from the point of view of two disputants, however, the stasis marks the place where two opposing

71

forces come together, where they rest or stand in agreement on what is at issue (hence the appropriateness of the Latin term for stasis, *constitutio*, which can be translated as a "costanding" or a "standing together"). An agreement to disagree must occur in every rhetorical situation; as Quintilian put it, "Every question is based on assertion by one party and denial by another" (III vi 7). But this resting place is only temporary, suspended as it is between conflicting movements, until a skilled writer or speaker comes along to move the argument away from stasis. The most satisfactory modern equivalent for stasis seems to be the term *issue*, which we define as the point about which all parties to an argument can agree to disagree: this is what is at issue.

Determining the point of stasis is crucial to any rhetorical argument. However, figuring out the stasis is more difficult than it may seem at first glance. Most people who are engaged in arguments want to advance their own position as quickly and forcefully as possible. And so they do not want to take the time to find all the available arguments, as stasis theory and other ancient means of invention require. However, this hasty approach can lead to stalemate (or shouting or even violence), as has happened in public arguments over abortion—which we examine in detail in this chapter. Rhetors who do take the time to find all the available arguments can be assured both that their position is defensible and that they have found the best evidence to support it.

The very old systematic investigative procedures described in this book were used for thousands of years to help rhetors figure out what arguments are available to them, and we hope that they will help you to determine the issues you want to argue, as well. We recommend that you begin by trying to answer the questions outlined below. Consider all the statements you generate as you work through the questions to be potential propositions. If you work systematically and thoroughly, you should produce a full and useful analysis of the issue you have chosen to examine. Doing all of this intellectual work has several advantages. Rhetors who work through the questions raised by this heuristic in systematic fashion will find that the process:

1. Clarifies their thinking about the point in dispute
2. Forces them to think about the assumptions and values shared by members of their targeted audience
3. Establishes areas in which more research needs to be done
4. Suggests which proofs are crucial to the case
5. Perhaps even points the way toward the most effective arrangement of the proofs

What this or any heuristic will not provide, however, is a draft of a paper or speech. Ancient rhetors spent a good deal of time in preparation for writing or speaking, trying out one inventional scheme or another. They did not mind if these trials produced false starts, because they knew that the false starts turned up in one case could most likely be used in a different rhetorical situation. Contemporary debaters work in a similar fashion, preparing all relevant arguments in advance in case they ever need to use them, and to limit as well the chance that a skilled opponent will use an argument they are not prepared to answer. It is important to remember, then, that practice with this (or any heuristic) also supplies the rhetor with *copia*. Proofs generated in practice with any heuristic system may prove useful at some other time.

THE *STASEIS* AND CONTRARY ARGUMENTS

The Older Sophists believed that every argument had at least one contrary argument. According to the ancient historian Diogenes Laertius, "Protagoras was the first to say that on every issue there are two arguments opposed to each other" (Sprague 1972, 21). Some collections of sophistic arguments have come down to us. Characteristically, the arguments in these collections are arranged in contradictory pairs, since the sophists taught their students how to argue both sides of any question. (This pedagogical tactic distressed philosophers, who characterized it as "making the weaker case seem the stronger.") Students using these arguments learned from them how to create a proof favorable to one party in a litigation or to argue for adoption of a proposal before the assembly. Then they would use a set of opposing arguments to prepare a case for the other side or to argue for rejection of the proposal they had just supported.

The sophistic treatise called *"Dissoi Logoi,"* or *"Countervailing Arguments"* illustrated the sophists' conviction that contradictions pervade rhetorical situations. Here are some sample arguments from that treatise:

> Some say that the good is one thing and the bad another, but others say that they are the same, and a thing might be good for some persons but bad for others, or at one time good and at another time bad for the same person. I myself side with those who hold the latter opinion, and I shall examine it using as an example human life and its concern for food, drink, and sexual pleasures: these things are bad for a man if he is sick, but good if he is healthy and needs them. And, further, incontinence in these matters is bad for the incontinent but good for those who sell these things and make a profit. And again, illness is bad for the sick but good for the doctors. And death is bad for those who die but good for the undertakers and gravediggers. (Sprague 1968, 155)

The rhetor continued in this way, listing examples showing that good and bad are the same, depending on circumstances and point of view. The topic in this case is "things that are good for some persons but bad for others." The rhetor simply applied this generalization to all the examples he could think of within the set he chose, in order to flesh out the argument that good and bad are the same. Then he did a turnabout, demonstrating that good and bad are different:

> I think it [would] not be clear what was good and what was bad if they were just the same and one did not differ from the other; in fact such a situation would be extraordinary. And I think a person who says these things would be unable to answer if anyone should question him as follows: "Just tell me, did your parents ever do you any good?" He would answer, "Yes, a great deal." "Then you owe them for a great deal of evil if the good is really the same as the bad." . . . Come and answer me this: isn't it the case that you are both pitying beggars because they have many evils, [and] again counting them lucky because they have many goods, if good and bad are really the same thing? . . . I shall go though the individual cases, beginning with eating, drinking and sexual pleasures. For the sick these things are [bad to do, and again] they are good for them to do, if good and bad are really the same. And for the sick it is bad to be ill and also good, if good is really the same as bad. And this holds for all the other cases which were mentioned in the previous argument. (156–57)

The topic in this case is "Things that are good for some people cannot be bad for them, too." The rhetor simply applied this generalization to all the specific cases he could think of in order to amplify support for the other side of the original argument, that good and bad are different.

The abstract, nonspecific nature of this argument—whether or not good and bad are relative to each other—suggests that the *"Dissoi Logoi"* were part of a school exercise. They were sample amplifications, used to show aspiring rhetors how to exploit systematically the argumentative possibilities inherent in an issue. When rhetors argued cases or debated before the assembly, of course, they dealt with much more specific issues, and they supported only one position on any issue.

For Gorgias and other Older Sophists, contradictory arguments provided fruitful starting points for the exploration of a particular issue. Moreover, the doctrine of *dissoi logoi* points to the situational nature of discourse recognized by *kairos*. In rhetorical situations, positions on important issues are always championed by people who disagree with one another. In other words, there are always at least two sides to every argument. The people who take those sides can and do change their minds, depending upon the time and place in which they engage in argument. A systematic exploration of any issue by means of stasis theory can reveal not only the available and often contradictory positions that may be taken up with regard to it; examination of the *staseis* can also reveal that there are often more than just two sides to any issue.

THEORETICAL VERSUS PRACTICAL QUESTIONS

Ancient rhetoricians divided questions into two kinds: theoretical and practical. Some questions concern what people should do (action), but these are always related to questions about why people should do something (theory). Cicero gave this example of a theoretical question in his treatise the *Topics* (xxi 82):

> Does law originate in nature or in some agreement and contract between people?

This is the sort of abstract theoretical question that is discussed today by law school professors and their students when they talk about what grounds or centers the law. It is an important question because certain practical actions follow from any answer that may be given. If law is grounded in nature, it cannot easily be changed. If, on one hand, law is natural, it is also difficult to argue that a given law is incorrect or unfair; a rhetor's only option in this case is to argue that the law in question is unnatural. To get an idea of how difficult this is, imagine yourself arguing in court that laws against speeding are unnatural. The argument from nature is used on occasion: motorcycle riders who opposed legislation requiring them to wear helmets have argued—without much success—that such laws violate the natural human desire for freedom from restraint. If law results from human contract, on the other hand, it is much easier to justify alterations to laws, because a rhetor can appeal to the expressed opinions or desires of the majority as support for her argument that a law should be changed.

Unlike theoretical questions, which address the origins and natures of things, practical questions always concern what people should do. Cicero gave this example of a practical question:

> Should a philosopher take part in politics?

Notice that this question concerns what people who study philosophy ought to do; it does not raise questions about the nature or aim of philosophy or politics, as a theoretical question would.

The English word *theory* derives from a Greek word *(theorein)* which literally means "to sit in the highest row of the arena." More freely translated, the term meant something like "to observe from afar." A theoretical question, then, allows rhetors to view questions "from afar," as though they had no immediate relevance for daily affairs and putting aside for the moment their practical effects. Many times theoretical investigations provide positions on more practical issues. But they also take rhetors far afield from everyday events. Take this very practical (and very specific) question, for instance:

> Should Jane study this weekend?

To answer this question, a rhetor needs to consider Jane's options (partying, visiting home, and so on) and the consequences attached to each choice. But this practical question has theoretical underpinnings:

> Is studying more important than having fun or visiting family?

To answer this theoretical question is more difficult because a rhetor must take into account not only Jane's immediate desires but her longer-term goals, her values, her personal history, and so on.

Another way to think about the difference between theoretical and practical questions is to consider the level of generality at which an issue may be addressed. Greek rhetoricians used the term *hypothesis* to name a specific question that involved actual persons, places, or events. They used the term *thesis*, in contrast, to name general questions having wide application—matters suited to political, ethical, or philosophical discussion—which don't refer to actual persons or events. The classic example of a **general issue** was:

Should anyone marry?

The classic specific question was:

Should Cato marry?

Here are some contemporary examples of general and specific questions:

1. *General:* Is the sale of assault weapons just?

   Specific: Should college student Cho Sueng-Hui have been able to so easily attain the assault weapons used to commit this country's worst single-person killing spree to date?

2. *General:* Should people convicted of murder be put to death?

   Specific: Should Timothy McVeigh have been put to death for blowing up the Murrah building in Oklahoma City on April 19, 1995, an act which resulted in the deaths of 168 people?

3. *General:* Is a thriving national economy more important than the protection of natural resources and the climate?

   Specific: Should the United States ratify the Kyoto Protocol to the United Nations Framework Convention on Climate Change, a series of scientist-recommended efficiency measures for restoring the earth's greenhouse gas emissions to levels below what they were in the 1990s?

The ancient distinction between a theoretical question and a question of action is a binary distinction—that is, it allows for only two possibilities. However, general and more specific questions are more helpfully thought of as lying along a spectrum or range from very general to very specific. There are many levels of generality and specificity at which any issue can be stated. Hence the generality or specificity of a given claim is never absolute; it follows that statements of a question are general or specific only in relation to each other. For example:

General: Is conservation of the environment more important than economic development? *(Note that this is a theoretical as well as a very general question—stated this way, the question raises issues for contemplation and discussion rather than action.)*

More Specific: Should the United States sacrifice industries that negatively impact its environment—logging, manufacture of certain chemicals and plastics, nuclear power plants—in order to conserve the environment? *(This question, while still general, is no longer simply theoretical; answers to it imply actions to be taken by the United States.)*

Even More Specific: Should the city council of Ourtown reject an application to build a large discount department store if this requires clear-cutting five acres of forest?

Very Specific: Should I take time to recycle plastics, paper, and aluminum even though to do so costs money and time? *(The last three versions of the claim raise practical questions, insofar as they imply human actions; but each successive claim involves fewer people, so each is more specific than the one that precedes it.)*

The level of generality at which a question or issue is stated determines the amount of research needed and the kinds of proofs that must be composed in order to argue it persuasively. On one hand, more general questions require broader knowledge and usually require a longer and more complex treatment. To answer the general question about conservation given here, for example, would require at least a book-length discussion. On the other hand, the very specific question, involving a personal decision, at minimum requires some private reflection and a bit of hands-on research. To answer this very specific and very practical question would require the rhetor only to recycle plastics, paper, and aluminum for awhile to see how much time and/or money is required to recycle these substances and to compare these results to the time and money required in having unsorted garbage hauled away by the city. A paper or speech answering this question could simply state a proposition ("Recycling is expensive and time-consuming for me") and report the results of this research. As you can see, though, answers given to this very specific question depend upon answers given to more generally stated questions, including the first, very general question stated previously. Whether you recycle or not depends, ultimately, upon your values: is preservation of the environment more important to you than your time or your budget? (Here we've restated the very specific question just a bit more generally.)

The relation of general to specific issues was a matter of debate among ancient rhetoricians. As Quintilian pointed out, every special issue presupposes a general one: for example, the question of whether Cato ought to marry really couldn't be answered satisfactorily unless the general question, "Should a person marry?" had also been considered (III v 13). Too, there are questions that hover somewhere between the very general and the very specific: for example, "Should an older person marry?" For ancient rhetoricians, questions like these were ethical ones, having to do with a person's character and the right course of conduct for certain characters. Ethical questions still concern us, of course. We regularly read or hear arguments about whether young people ought to marry, for example, and there is a good deal of contemporary argument about when or if people should have children. Often these arguments are cast as personal or financial choices, but they have ethical aspects too, since decisions about marriage and reproduction affect many people, not just those who make them.

Of course any decision you make about the level of generality at which you will pursue an issue is always affected by the rhetorical situation for which you are composing. Who is the audience for the paper or speech? What is the setting? How does the audience feel about the issue? What do they know already, and what will the rhetor have to tell them? And so on.

PUTTING THESE DISTINCTIONS TO WORK

Rhetors can use the set of questions developed by ancient rhetoricians as a means of clarifying for themselves exactly what is at issue between them and their projected audience. And if they choose and frame the question carefully, rhetors can begin the argument from their own ground, rather than an opponent's. Let us return, for example, to the case of the astronomer who argues that the city council should adopt a dark-sky ordinance. When she prepares her case, she asks: are we disagreeing about a general or a specific issue? She can define the issue specifically, as follows:

> Ourtown should adopt a dark-sky ordinance.

As stated, this is a specific issue because it names a particular city and urges the adoption of a particular action. It also provides an advantage to the astronomer because it permits her to take a stand on her own ground; that is, she defines the point at issue in such a way that the ensuing argument must revolve around adoption of a dark-sky ordinance, rather than issues of safety or of the advertising revenue brought to the city from lighted billboards.

The astronomer might prefer, however, to state the issue in more general or theoretical terms. In that case, she could raise a question about community values:

> Which is more important to us: the accumulation of scientific knowledge made available by a darkened night sky or the revenue which is brought to advertisers by lighted billboards?

This statement of the general issue is theoretical. She could also state the more general issue in practical terms, though:

> Should we give priority to advertisers when we pass city ordinances?

To state the issue in general terms gives the astronomer a persuasive advantage, since her audience might view as self-serving the particular statement of the issue ("Ourtown should adopt a dark-sky ordinance so that astronomers can make night-time observations"). Stated generally, the issues raise questions that concern the entire community, not just astronomers.

Stating the Issue
The Practical Question Framed Specifically
Should Ourtown adopt a dark-sky ordinance?

The Practical Question Framed More Generally

> Should cities value scientific knowledge over advertising revenues?

The Specific Question Framed as Theory

> Should the city council of Ourtown give priority to astronomers or to advertisers when it passes city ordinances?

The Specific Question Framed in Practical Terms

> Will Ourtown profit more from a dark-sky ordinance than from revenue brought in by billboard advertising?

Very Specific, Very Practical Questions

> Will the astronomers who work at Ourtown's observatory close down the facility if they cannot get a sufficiently dark night-time sky? Can Ourtown afford to lose the prestige and money brought into town by the observatory? Does the revenue brought in by billboard advertising offset this loss of revenue?

Opponents of the astronomer's proposal can follow exactly the same procedure. For example, the city police could anticipate the astronomer's statement of the particular issue and simply state it negatively:

> Ourtown should not adopt a dark-sky ordinance.

But this tactic gives an advantage to the astronomer, since it takes up the stand on her turf, so to speak. Thus the police might prefer to begin by defining the issue so that the stand occurs on their ground:

> Lowering the level of light in Ourtown will endanger citizens who must travel the streets at night.

Once again, this is a specific statement of the issue, since it refers to a specific place and implies a single potential action. It is also practical, since it involves human activity. The police might also prepare to argue the case from the vantage point of a general theoretical stance, addressing values:

> The safety of citizens is more important than the accumulation of scientific knowledge.

Or they might choose a general, practical stance that counsels a principle for action:

> When the council of Ourtown passes ordinances, its members should always give top priority to the safety of citizens.

Stating the question this way adds to the *ethos* of the police, since it shows their concern not for the added work they must do if lower levels of light are permitted but for the safety of the community at large.

There are, of course, other specific and general, theoretical and practical, questions that can be generated from this issue. A thorough examination of the arguments available to the astronomer can be generated through use of the *staseis* discussed further on in this chapter. And other arguments are available to other interested parties—advertisers, billboard companies, environmentalists, and other concerned citizens.

A good way to decide which kind and level of question you wish to argue is to imagine the kind and level of question your opponent may advance. Will he argue a theoretical question? In that case, you must be prepared to consider the question on that level, in order to meet him in stasis. The level of generality you choose will also be dictated by the rhetorical situation in which you find yourself. Do the police of Ourtown have an amicable working relationship with the city council? Are their spokespeople trusted by council members? Does their ethos outweigh that of the astronomers at the observatory? Will their concerns about citizen safety carry greater weight with the council than the scientific concerns of the astronomers? And so on. (For more discussion about audiences, see Chapter 7, on *pathos*.) As you have probably guessed by now, heuristics do not work as reliably as mathematical formulas. There is no guarantee that your consideration and development of theoretical and practical or general and specific questions will provide you with exactly the proposition that you wish to argue. In many cases, you will continue to refine the issue and to develop nuances of your proposition as you work through each of the rhetorical canons. In fact, invention can begin all over again during late stages of the composing process—arrangement, revision, or even editing. However, attention to the heuristics described in this book will certainly enrich your stock of arguments—your intellectual *copia*. And systematic, thoughtful consideration of the issue at hand just may provide you with precisely the proposition you are looking for, as well as arguments you can use to support it.

WHAT HAPPENS WHEN STASIS IS NOT ACHIEVED?

Contemporary public discourse about abortion provides a stunning example of an argument that has been sustained for many years but that shows no sign of being resolved.

Public debate about abortion began in earnest more than thirty years ago, when the Supreme Court legalized the practice in 1973. Ever since that time, those who oppose the availability of abortion, usually on moral grounds, have employed a number of legal (and illegal) tactics in order to get the procedure banned, while at the same time, those who support the availability of abortion have fought to keep the practice, as they say, "safe, legal, and rare." Those who oppose abortion are called "pro-life" because of their belief that abortion is murder; those who support it are called "pro-choice" because they believe that women should be able to choose their methods of controlling reproduction.

For more than thirty years, those who oppose and those who support abortion rights have battled one another in both the judicial and legislative arenas. In 2005, for example, the state legislature of South Dakota passed a bill making it a felony for a doctor to perform an abortion anywhere in the state. The legislation allowed no exceptions whatever: abortions were not permitted when a mother's health was at stake (unless her life was in danger), and citizens of South Dakota who had suffered rape or incest were denied this option as well. Abortion rights activists succeeded in placing a resolution on the ballot during the election of 2006 that would strike down this law, and the people of South Dakota supported the resolution. The law had been expressly designed by its advocates to produce a test case that would challenge *Roe v. Wade*, the 1973 decision that legalized abortion.

One reason that this argument has not been resolved is that it cannot be, as long as the central propositions put forward by those involved in it are not in stasis. People who line up against the legalization of abortion offer the following statement as their major proposition: abortion is murder. People who argue that abortion should maintain its current status as a legal operation put the following statement forward as their major proposition: women have the right to choose what happens to their bodies, including terminating a pregnancy.

Keeping in mind that reaching stasis means finding the place where opponents agree to disagree, even a cursory examination of these statements shows that they are not in stasis. On one hand, a rhetor who wishes to find stasis with someone who believes that abortion is murder should argue (a) that abortion is not murder; or (b) that abortion is legal so therefore it cannot be murder, because murder is illegal in America; or (c) that abortion is not murder, because a fetus is not a human being; or some other proposition that defines abortion in such a way that it can be excluded from the category "murder."

Stasis Achieved: Rhetors Can Now Agree to Disagree

A. Abortion is murder.

B. Abortion is not murder.

A rhetor who wishes to find stasis with someone who believes that women have a right to decide what happens to their bodies, on the other hand, must argue that (a) women do not have that right, at least when they are pregnant; or (b) that the right to life of a fetus outweighs a woman's right to choose what happens to her body; or (c) that the right to life extends to fetuses and takes primacy over any other human right; or some other similar proposition about the priority ordering of human rights.

Stasis Achieved: Rhetors Can Now Agree to Disagree

A. Women have the right to decide what happens to their bodies, including terminating a pregnancy.

B. Women do not have the right to decide what happens to their bodies when they are pregnant because a potential life is at stake.

While the propositions we turned up in our stasis analysis do appear in contemporary discourse about abortion, they are seldom offered in the systematic, head-to-head way we have listed them here; that is, they are seldom put in stasis. It is not for nothing that opponents of abortion are called "pro-lifers," while those who want to keep abortion legal are called "pro-choicers." Surely those who support legal abortion do not want to be known as "anti-life," and those who oppose abortion do not want to be known as "anti-choice." As this juxtaposition of terms suggests, stasis analysis establishes that the participants in this argument are arguing right past each other. That is to say, the major propositions they put forward do not address the same issue.

Interestingly the statements that would achieve stasis in this argument are a bit shocking: pro-choice advocates do not often directly address the pro-life position by saying "Abortion is not murder." Nor do pro-life advocates often say in public forums that "women do not have the right to determine what happens to their bodies." This reluctance to admit the implications of its propositions may be another reason why the argument is not in stasis. Those who frame the abortion issue as a question of murder are compelled to argue that abortion, defined as murder, outweighs a woman's right to choose an abortion. They frequently support their position by making reference to religious, moral, or natural laws. Those who support legal abortion, in contrast, have recourse to the political discourse of rights, arguing that individuals have a right to conduct private business without interference from the state. They assume further that deciding to have an abortion is a private, not a public, matter. Another way to articulate this failure to achieve stasis is to say that people who oppose abortion are arguing from philosophical or theological assumptions about the point at which life begins; people who defend women's rights are arguing from political grounds about the rights of individuals and the relation of those rights to community goods. The point to be made here, however, is that as long as the major propositions in this discourse remain out of stasis, the argument will continue.

For more than thirty years, both sides have adapted their tactics in order to bring the argument into stasis, or at least into the appearance of stasis. The following article, written by Robin Toner for the *New York Times*, illustrates how a 2007 Supreme Court ruling upholding a ban on late-term abortion made it possible for antiabortion activists to position their stance as pro-woman, subtly shifting the terms of the abortion debate.

ABORTION FOES SEE VALIDATION FOR NEW TACTIC

For many years, the political struggle over abortion was often framed as a starkly binary choice: the interest of the woman, advocated by supporters of abortion rights, versus the interest of the fetus, advocated by opponents of abortion.

But last month's Supreme Court decision upholding the Partial-Birth Abortion Ban Act marked a milestone for a different argument advanced by anti-abortion leaders, one they are increasingly making in state legislatures around the country. They say that abortion, as a rule, is not in the best interest of the woman; that women are often misled or ill-informed about its risks to their own physical or emotional health; and that the interests of the pregnant woman and the fetus are, in fact, the same.

The majority opinion in the court's 5-to-4 decision explicitly acknowledged this argument, galvanizing anti-abortion forces and setting the stage for an intensifying battle over new abortion restrictions in the states.

This ferment adds to the widespread recognition that abortion politics are changing, in ways that are, as yet, unclear, if not contradictory. Even as the anti-abortion forces relish their biggest victory in the Supreme Court in nearly 20 years, they face the possibility of a Republican presidential nominee, former mayor Rudolph W. Giuliani of New York, who is a supporter of abortion rights.

The anti-abortion movement's focus on women has been building for a decade or more, advanced by groups like the conservative Justice Foundation, the National Right to Life Committee and Feminists for Life.

"We think of ourselves as very pro-woman," said Wanda Franz, president of the National Right to Life Committee. "We believe that when you help the woman, you help the baby."

It is embodied in much of the imagery and advertising of the anti-abortion movement in recent years, especially the "Women Deserve Better Than Abortion" campaign by Feminists for Life, the group that counts Jane Sullivan Roberts, the wife of the chief justice, among its most prominent supporters.

It is also at the heart of an effort—expected to escalate in next year's state legislative sessions—to enact new "informed consent" and mandatory counseling laws that critics assert often amount to a not-so-subtle pitch against abortion. Abortion-rights advocates, still reeling from last month's decision, argue that this effort is motivated by ideology, not women's health.

"Informed consent is really a misleading way to characterize it," said Roger Evans, senior director of public policy litigation and law for Planned Parenthood. "To me, what we'll see is an increasing attempt to push a state's ideology into a doctor-patient relationship, to force doctors to communicate more and more of the state's viewpoint."

Nancy Keenan, president of NARAL Pro-Choice America, said, "It's motivated by politics, not by science, not by medical care, and not for the purposes of compassion."

The Guttmacher Institute, a research group and an affiliate of Planned Parenthood, said recently that "a considerable body of credible evidence" over 30 years contradicted the notion that legal abortion posed long-term dangers to women's health, physically or mentally.

But Allan E. Parker Jr., president of the Justice Foundation, a conservative group based in Texas, compares the campaign intended for women to the long struggle to inform Americans about the risks of smoking. "We're kind of in the early stages of tobacco litigation," Mr. Parker said.

All sides agree that the debate reached a new level of significance when Justice Anthony M. Kennedy, writing the majority opinion in the Supreme Court case last month, approvingly cited a friend-of-the-court brief filed by the Justice Foundation.

The foundation, a nonprofit public interest litigation firm that has handled an array of conservative causes, has increasingly focused on abortion through its project called Operation Outcry. Mr. Parker said the group began hearing from women in the late 1990s who considered themselves victims of legalized abortion—physically and emotionally—and wanted to tell their stories. Operation Outcry, which grew to include a Web site, a national hot line and chapters around the country, eventually collected statements from more than 2,000 women, officials said.

In its friend-of-the-court brief, the group submitted statements from 180 of those women who said that abortion had left them depressed, distraught, in emotional turmoil. "Thirty-three years of real life experiences," the foundation said, "attests that abortion hurts women and endangers their physical, emotional and psychological health."

The case before the Supreme Court involved a specific type of abortion, occasionally used after the first trimester, that involves removing a fetus intact after collapsing its skull. Justice Kennedy upheld that ban on narrower, legal grounds, but he used the Justice Foundation brief to write more broadly about the emotional impact of abortion on women.

"While we find no reliable data to measure the phenomenon, it seems unexceptionable to conclude some women come to regret their choice to abort the infant life they once created and sustained," Justice Kennedy wrote, alluding to the brief. "Severe depression and loss of esteem can follow."

Given those stakes, the justice argued, "The state has an interest in ensuring so grave a choice is well informed."

Many, on both sides, viewed that as an invitation from a newly conservative court to pass tough new counseling and informed-consent laws intended for women seeking abortions—"a green light for enhanced informed consent," in the words of Clarke D. Forsythe, president of Americans United for Life, a leader in that legislative effort.

The abortion-rights side was caught off guard, in part because its strategists believe the scientific debate has been so decisively settled against the Justice Foundation's argument over the years. "We thought that brief was so extraneous that we didn't even bother coming up with a response to it," said Mr. Evans of Planned Parenthood.

In her dissenting opinion, Justice Ruth Bader Ginsburg agreed. "The court invokes an anti-abortion shibboleth for which it concededly has no reliable evidence," she wrote.

But Mr. Parker at the Justice Foundation said the point of view being promoted by his group had already had an impact in states debating informed consent and other abortion regulations, including South Dakota.

That state's law, currently being challenged in federal court, requires women seeking an abortion to be told that the procedure will terminate a "whole, separate, unique, living human being," and that it carries a variety of psychological and physical risks to the woman.

Other new "informed consent" proposals in the states would require women to receive an ultrasound before their abortion; according to NARAL, 10 states have considered such legislation this year. South Carolina has been debating proposals that encourage, if not require, a woman to go a step further and review the sonogram.

This focus on women by the anti-abortion movement has real power, many experts said. Reva B. Siegel, a Yale law professor and a supporter of abortion rights who recently conducted a study of this effort, said it combined "the modern language of trauma and women's rights" with "some very traditional ways of understanding women."

But Geoffrey Garin, who conducts polls for abortion-rights groups, said, "Once you get past the verbiage, women get that the motivation here is political as opposed to medical."

History suggests that the way the abortion struggle is framed has a significant effect, over the years, on legislative and political outcomes. In the late 1980s, the NARAL slogan "Who Decides?" was widely credited with helping the abortion-rights movement capture the voters of the center. A decade later, the campaign to outlaw what critics call partial-birth abortion—symbolizing a broader argument that the right to an abortion had gone too far—helped the anti-abortion movement widen its support and win significant victories in Congress, state legislatures and the court.

The anti-abortion movement clearly hopes this emphasis on women as victims of abortion has similar influence, although some of its strategists acknowledge it is a huge task; there are an estimated 1.3 million abortions a year in the United States, according to the Guttmacher Institute.

Mr. Parker said his organization planned to make its legal argument, and the accompanying testimonials from women, available to more state legislatures. Every time he speaks on the issue, he said, he receives more phone calls from women who have had abortions. (2007)

As of the time we are writing, it is too soon to determine the rhetorical effects of the Supreme Court's ruling, but responses from Justice Ginsberg and other pro-choice activists suggest that it may be challenging for antiabortion activists to fully reconcile a pro-woman stance with a pro-life stance. As Justice Ginsberg's dissenting opinion intimates, the court offers at best partial evidence. It may well be that this shift in argumentative ground will reopen the question of what is in fact in women's "best interests."

THE FOUR QUESTIONS

The process of asking questions does not conclude once the point of stasis has been identified. Ordinarily, the determination of the question for debate will give rise to other questions. Ancient rhetoricians devised a list of four questions, or *staseis*, that would help them refine their grasp on the point at issue:

1. CONJECTURE *(stasis stochasmos)*—Is there an act to be considered?
2. DEFINITION *(stasis horos)*—How can the act be defined?
3. QUALITY *(stasis poiotes)*—How serious is the act?
4. POLICY *(stasis metalepsis)*—Should this act be submitted to some formal procedure?[1]

If someone is accused of theft, for example, the first question that must be raised is **conjecture:** "Did she do it or not?" If all parties agree that she took the property in question, the stasis moves to a question of **definition:** "Was it theft?" (She might have borrowed the supposedly stolen item.) And if everyone agrees that the act can be defined as theft, the stasis becomes: "Was it right or wrong?" (The theft might be justified on any number of grounds—she took liquor from the house of a friend who is an alcoholic, for instance.) The ancients called this stasis **quality,** and we will use this term as well. Last, if the question of quality is agreed upon, the stasis then becomes: "Should she be tried for the offense?" This is the question of procedure or **policy**.

THE FOUR QUESTIONS

Conjecture: Does it exist? Did it happen?

Definition: What kind of thing or event is it?

Quality: Was it right or wrong?

Policy: What should we do?

When a rhetor begins to examine an issue, according to Cicero, he should ask the following:

> Does the thing about which we are disputing exist? (Latin *an sit*)
> If it exists, what is it? (*quid sit*)
> What kind of thing is it? (*quale sit*)

Cicero said that the first is a question of reality, the second of definition, and the third of quality (*On the Parts* xviii 62). If, for example, a rhetor were concerned with the theoretical issue of justice, she might employ the three questions as follows:

A. Does justice exist in nature, or is it merely a human convention?

B. Can justice be defined as that which benefits the majority?

C. Is it advantageous to live justly or not?

The first question forces the rhetor to conjecture about whether justice exists and, if so, where; the second, how it can be defined; and the third, what its value is, and to whom. Cicero and Quintilian insisted that only the first three questions were really necessary to the preparation of arguments to be used outside the courtroom. Nevertheless, the fourth stasis, policy, is sometimes useful in nonlegal settings. People who deliberate in assemblies often have to decide how to regulate practices.

Stasis theory is as useful to writers as it is to speakers, since rhetors must assess the probable response of an audience to their work. Cicero recommended that speakers and writers work through the questions in order. The process of working through questions of conjecture, definition, and quality, in order, will help rhetors to find the points about which they and their audience agree; it will also establish the point from which they must begin the argument—the point where they disagree. In the first stasis, the rhetor determines whether or not he and his audience agree about the existence of some being or the commission of some act. If they do, this stasis is no longer relevant or useful, having been agreed to—waived—by both parties. In the second stasis, the rhetor determines whether or not he and his audience agree about the classification of the being or the act; if so, the stasis of definition may be passed by. Third, the rhetor determines whether he and his audience agree about the value of the being or the seriousness of the act. That is, what is its relevance to the community as a whole? According to Cicero, in the third stasis, there is a controversy about the nature or character of an act when there is both agreement as to what has been done and certainty as to how the act should be defined, but there is a question nevertheless about how important it is or in general about its quality: for example, was it just or unjust, profitable or unprofitable? (*De Inventione* I viii 12).

ELABORATING THE QUESTIONS

Each of the four questions can be elaborated into other sets of questions. According to Cicero, there are four ways of dealing with a question of conjecture (*Topics* xxi 82). One can ask the following:

Does the thing exist or is it true?

What is its origin?

What cause produced it?

What changes can be made in it?

Some modern rhetoricians call the issue of conjecture "the question of fact." However, the Greek term *stochasmos* is more literally translated as "a guess" or "an inference." Since the term *fact* connotes the sort of hard physical evidence we discussed in the first chapter of this book, it is misleading here. The stasis of conjecture does not establish anything at all about the truth or fact of the matter under discussion; rather, it represents an educated guess about what might be or about what might have occurred. And since reality may be perceived very differently by people who occupy different social and political positions, people may paint very different pictures of that reality. For example, a man who tells a dirty joke to his colleagues at work may think that he is only being friendly, while a woman colleague who hears the joke may feel that it belittles women. Or, in another example of conjecture, a recipient of Aid to Families with Dependent Children (AFDC) might describe a welfare check as the only means she has for feeding her children. A politician who is opposed to welfare, however, might characterize that very same check as a handout to freeloaders. These people have all offered conjectures about the way the world is or how people behave. In the examples given here, each party has some stake or **interest** in picturing the joke or the welfare check in the way that they do. Their disagreement about these facts is what renders conjecture rhetorical.

Questions of Conjecture

Does it exist? Is it true?

Where did it come from? How did it begin?

What is its cause?

Can it be changed?

For an example, let's return to the case being prepared by the astronomer who wants a dark-sky ordinance to be passed in her city. Under the question of conjecture, the astronomer can ask the following:

Does light pollution exist in the city?

What is the origin of the pollution?

What causes it?

What will change it?

When she tries to answer these questions, the astronomer learns that she will probably need to provide evidence that light pollution does indeed exist. She will need to provide further evidence that the pollution is not natural (that is, that it doesn't originate from moonlight or starlight). She will have to establish that the pollution is caused by billboards and streetlights, and she will need to establish further that elimination of these two sources will produce a level of light that will make astronomic observation possible.

Use of the stasis of conjecture is often productive in just this way—that is, it demonstrates to rhetors what evidence they need in order to mount their arguments. Sometimes, use of the stasis of conjecture also establishes that there is no issue, or that a rhetor has framed the issue incompletely, or that he wants to change his mind about the issue. Because heuristics often produce surprises—that is what they are for, after all—rhetors must be prepared for shifts in their thinking. When using the *staseis* or any means of invention, then, rhetors should always allow time for intellectual development to occur.

If all parties to the discussion agree about the conjecture—the description of the state of things—the search for stasis moves on to matters of definition.

Questions of Definition

What kind of thing or event is it?

To what larger class of things does it belong?

What are its parts? How are they related?

Definitions are rhetorical because they can determine on whose ground the question will be taken up (see Chapter 9, on the sophistic topics, for more about definition). In this case, the astronomer can take advantage of the rhetorical aspect of definition to compose one that suits her interest. She is probably the only party, other than thieves and lovers, who has an interest in defining light pollution.

Definition requires that the astronomer name the particular or proper quality of light pollution and divide it into its parts. Let's say that she defines light pollution as "that level of light which is sufficient to interfere with astronomical observations." She might then divide such light levels into light caused by

> billboards,
>
> streetlights,
>
> home lighting, and
>
> natural sources.

This **division** demonstrates to her that she needs evidence that establishes the level of pollution caused by each of these sources (see the chapter on the sophistic topics for more about division). It tells her further that if the evidence demonstrates that natural light is not an important factor in creating light pollution, she can concentrate her major arguments on the other sources of light, all of which can be mitigated by a dark-sky ordinance. As it does here, the stasis of definition will sometimes produce a way of dividing up the discourse—producing what ancient rhetoricians called the **partition** (see Chapter 10, on arrangement, for more about partitions).

Other parties concerned about this issue might, on one hand, return to the question of conjecture to assert that there is no such thing as light pollution, in an attempt to render the astronomer's definition irrelevant. If they succeed in this, she too will be forced to return to the stasis of conjecture if all parties wish to continue the discussion. If they accede to her definition, on the other hand, the argument is in stasis and all parties can turn to the next stasis, quality. If they do accept that light pollution exists and that it can be defined as the astronomer asserts, she has been able to set up the discussion in terms that favor her interest.

Questions of quality may be asked in two ways: simply or by comparison. Simple questions of quality attempt to determine the worth of the issue—its justice or rightness or honor—or how much the community desires it. Comparative questions of quality put the issue in the context of other qualities, comparing it with related issues in order to determine its priority among the community's values. If asked simply, then, the question of quality is "Is light pollution a good or a bad thing?" If asked comparatively in this case, the question could become "Is the safety of citizens more important than the needs of astronomers?"

According to Cicero, there are three kinds of simple questions of quality:

what to seek and what to avoid,

what is right and what wrong,

what is honorable and what base. (*Topics* xxi 84)

Questions of Quality

Simple Questions of Quality

Is it a good or a bad thing?

Should it be sought or avoided?

Is it right or wrong?

Is it honorable or dishonorable?

Comparative Questions of Quality

Is it better or worse than something else?

Is it more desirable than any alternatives?

Is it less desirable than any alternatives?

Is it more or less right than something else?

Is it more or less wrong than something else?

Is it more honorable than something else?

Is it less honorable than something else?

Is it more base than something else?

Is it less base than something else?

Thus our astronomer might ask the following simple questions of quality:

Should lower levels of light pollution be sought, or should they be avoided?

If the lower levels of light affect other situations, like citizens' safety, should they then be avoided?

That is, is it right or wrong to ask for lower levels of light?

Is it honorable to put the needs of astronomers above those of ordinary citizens?

Is it dishonorable to deprive citizens of a source of safety?

Thinking comparatively, the rhetor compares the importance of her issue to other related issues. In the astronomer's case, for example, a general comparative question of quality is:

Should the present state of affairs, which includes light pollution, be preferred to a state of affairs in which light pollution has been lessened?

A comparative specific question is:

Should the present state of affairs in Ourtown, which includes lighted bill-boards, be maintained in preference to an imagined state of affairs (or the actual state of affairs in Othertown) where lighted billboards have been elimi-nated so that astronomers can see better?

Since questions of comparison are of two kinds—similarity and differ-ence—the astronomer will ask herself what differences will be brought about in her observations of the night sky if light pollution is reduced; under the head of similarity, she also will consider what problems might remain even if light pollution is reduced. If she is systematic in her use of the *staseis*, she must produce all the available arguments, even those that oppose her position. She can be sure that those who disagree with her will produce these arguments, and so she must be prepared to answer them. For example, her use of the stasis of comparative differ-ence will produce this question: will the reduction of light pollution, thus giving us a better view, alter our previous descriptions of the night sky? In other words, will astronomers be forced to revise our earlier work if we can see better?

As this example makes clear, the *staseis* of quality are ordinarily very productive. Using them, the astronomer has generated some questions that should stimulate her to compose good arguments. The *staseis* often allow rhetors to articulate assumptions that they take for granted but that may be controversial to others. For example, the astronomer might simply assume, without thinking about it, that other citizens value a dark sky as much as she does. Other citizens, however, will not take this proposition for granted. The police will be concerned about safety, and billboard companies will be concerned about possible loss of revenue if they cannot light their advertising signs at night. Use of the stasis, then, demonstrates to the astronomer that she must prepare arguments that defend the importance she places on a dark sky, should it become neces-sary to do so.

The fourth stasis, policy, is relevant in the astronomer's case, as well. In questions of policy, the rhetor proposes that some action be taken or that some action be regulated (or not) by means of a policy or law. Questions of policy are usually twofold: they are both deliberative and forensic. That is, a rhetor who wishes to put forward a question or issue of policy must first deliberate about the need for it and then argue for its implementation.

Questions of Policy

Deliberative Questions

Should some action be taken?

Given the rhetorical situation, what actions are possible? Desirable?

How will proposed actions change the current state of affairs? Or should the current state of affairs remain unchanged?

How will the proposed changes make things better? Worse? How? In what ways? For whom?

Forensic Questions

Should some state of affairs be regulated (or not) by some formalized policy?

Which policies can be implemented? Which cannot?

What are the merits of competing proposals? What are their defects?

How is my proposal better than others? Worse?

Using the deliberative questions of policy, our astronomer is forced to ask herself some hard questions. She has already decided that some action should be taken. She needs now to ask herself whether her proposal to enact a dark-sky ordinance can be implemented and whether it is a good thing for the community it will affect. She needs to consider changes that its implementation might bring about—loss of revenue to Ourtown, possibly dangerous situations for citizens—and determine whether the seriousness of these changes outweighs the merits of her proposal. Turning to the forensic questions of policy, the astronomer realizes that she can enhance both her ethical and logical appeals by presenting the council with a draft of a proposed dark-sky ordinance. The draft demonstrates the depth of her concern about the situation, since she took the time to compose it. It also strengthens the possibility that her audience will use part or all of her draft when they write the ordinance, since busy people are likely to make use of work that has already been done. She can find arguments for implementing her proposal by showing how it will improve the current state of things, by showing how alternative proposals are not as satisfactory as her own, and by showing that implementation of her proposal is entirely possible. For example, she should try to counter the opposing argument that lowered levels of light can endanger citizens' safety. If possible, she should point out in her proposal that current levels of light from streetlights do not pose a problem to astronomical observation.

So if you wish, on one hand, to recommend that a policy or procedure be implemented, you must compose it. Find out how similar policies are enacted in similar situations, and compose a plan for implementing the one that you suggest. You should also determine how the policy that you recommend can be enforced. If you are recommending, on the other hand, that some public practice be implemented or changed, you must first compose your recommendation. Then find out who can make the changes you suggest, and find out what procedures must be followed in order to make the recommended change. You should also try to find out how your recommended change can be implemented and enforced and offer suggestions for achieving this.

USING THE *STASEIS*

The *staseis* still prove surprisingly useful for beating a path through the thicket of issues that often surround a controversy. We suggest that rhetors begin by asking themselves what sort of question they are facing: general or specific? theoretical or practical? Try to formulate the question in each of these terms in succession. Then compare them in order to determine which seems the most effective approach given the rhetorical situation for which you are preparing. Once you have decided upon the level of generality at which you wish to argue and have examined possible points of stasis, you should then formulate your question in terms of each of the four questions: conjecture, definition, quality, and policy. Again, compare these formulations: Do any seem to capture the point at issue? Do any hold out the possibility of helping you with further investigation? Do any tell you something about issues that might be raised by a member of the audience or by someone who disagrees with you? Do any help you to begin to develop an argument? Remember that this procedure is intended only to help you decide where to start. Its use does not guarantee that you will generate any useful proofs, much less that you can begin to draft a speech or paper at this stage of your preparation.

In the sample analyses that follow, we used stasis theory to find out what issues reside in two contemporary controversies: abortion and hateful speech. The examples are intended to demonstrate how this heuristic can help someone who is just beginning to think about a rhetorical problem. We did no formal research on these issues before we began this analysis, although of course we had heard them discussed in conversation and had read news articles about them. There are many more propositions and arguments available within these issues than those we found by using stasis theory. However, even a preliminary use of this heuristic discloses its rich argumentative possibilities and points out as well the research and composition that are necessary to argue it persuasively. Our examples should not be followed slavishly, as though they model all possible uses of the system. As you will see when you study the examples, we have used the *staseis* very differently in each one. This happened because the rhetorical situations that gave rise to each of the controversies were very different. Because of the situatedness of rhetoric, then, stasis theory cannot be applied mechanically. The issues or problems it turns up will differ from situation to situation, so any rhetor who uses it must be alert to all the possibilities it raises in any case. Rhetors should always be ready to follow any tangent thrown up by their consideration of the *staseis*.

The First Example: Abortion

Because most Americans are familiar with the terms of arguments about abortion, we return to this issue as our first illustration of how stasis theory can work. In what follows, we back up a bit and assume that a rhetor who is examining this issue has not yet developed a position on it. In other words, we use stasis theory here as a heuristic—a means of discovery. We state the issue both theoretically and practically and consider what happens when we state its available propositions at various levels of generality. Then we subject its available propositions to Hermagoras's questions to see if we can discover persuasive arguments that may be useful on occasions when we wish to enter into discussions about abortion.

Step 1. *Decide whether to formulate the question in theoretical or practical terms.*

Possible Theoretical Questions

Seen "from afar," what is the nature of abortion?

What are its origins? Its ends?

Possible Practical Questions

Where and when do abortions occur? Who is involved?

Why do people practice abortion?

What and whose interests are served by the practice of abortion?

What and whose interests are denied by the practice of abortion?

Your answers to these questions may yield propositions that you wish to support or reject. If you try to answer the theoretical questions, you will probably discover that you do not know all that you need to know about this issue in order to argue responsibly about it. To answer the first theoretical question, for example, you need a medical dictionary that will tell you just what this procedure entails. Answers to the second require you to know something about the history and contemporary use of the practice.

Answers to the practical questions lead to **lines of argument**—the related issues that we discussed in Chapter 2, on *kairos*. For example, the second practical question might be answered as follows: people practice abortion as a means of birth control. This answer suggests a line of argument: since there are other means of contraception available, why do people resort to abortion for this purpose? Is there some feature of the state of affairs that keeps people from using these other means?

Step 2. *Decide whether to formulate the question generally or specifically.*

Possible General Formulations of the Question

Do abortions occur? (conjecture)

What is abortion exactly? (definition)

Is it a good or a bad thing? (quality)

Should abortion be regulated? (policy)

Possible Specific Formulations of the Question

Do abortions occur in Ourtown? (conjecture)

Can the abortions done in Ourtown be classified as medical procedures? Murders? Methods of contraception? (definition)

Is the availability of abortion a good thing or a bad thing in Ourtown? (quality)

Should the practice be regulated in Ourtown? (policy)

This analysis reveals something about the scope or size of the available arguments on this issue. That is, a rhetor who undertakes this exercise learns how much research will be necessary to tackle the question on either a theoretical or practical level. To answer the theoretical question of conjecture requires empirical research. Additional research would be necessary to determine, for instance, the number of abortions practiced prior to *Roe v. Wade*. Answers to the second theoretical question require the composition of a definition suitable to the rhetor's position on the issue, although a careful rhetor will look for definitions advanced by others as well so that he is prepared to argue for the superiority of his own definition. (See Chapter 9, on the sophistic topics, for advice about composing definitions.) The third and fourth theoretical questions require at least book-length examination, and indeed, many books have been written about both of them. The practical and specific questions cover less-daunting amounts of space and time and hence require a rhetor to do less research. The specific questions may also be more interesting to the immediate community of Ourtown.

Step 3. *Decide which of the four staseis best describes the point at issue in the rhetorical situation at hand.*

In arguments over abortion both the conjectural and the definitional questions are very much at issue. People who are pro-choice conjecture abortion to be among the rights granted to citizens. Those who are pro-life find this position unacceptable (some feminists suspect that pro-lifers do not conjecture women as citizens). The second stasis, definition, is crucial for the prolife position because the pro-life definition of abortion as murder is precisely the point at issue in this argument. Other definitions thrown up by the stasis of definition (abortion is a method of contraception; abortion is a medical procedure) are not acceptable to the pro-life position, and any rhetor who argues that position should find arguments against both during invention because opponents will surely use them. Pro-lifers and pro-choicers also struggle over the definitional issue when they contest how exactly to define a fetus. Is it a human life even though it cannot survive without the woman who carries it? The question of quality often forms the point of stasis in this argument as well, as when the question arises whether the ready availability of abortion is a good or a bad thing for a given community. The question of policy has already been decided in American courts of law (abortion is currently legal), although pro-life advocates are seeking to change the policy. It is hard to generalize about which question will prove most useful in a given case, because the rhetorical situation dictates which of the propositions yielded by the *staseis* will prove most useful to a rhetor (see Chapter 2, on *kairos*, for more about rhetorical situations).

In order to illustrate the process of determining which of the four *staseis* best describes the point at issue in a given argument, we turn to yet another example of an argument about abortion. In the following report for *Time* magazine by Nancy Gibbs, the ostensible question under discussion is fetal pain.

CAN A FETUS FEEL PAIN?

In the rhetorical trenches of the culture wars, sometimes the best way to ambush your enemies is to echo them. Read some of the arguments in support of the Federal Unborn Child Pain Awareness Act, which the lame duck Congress debated on Wednesday, and you'll be forgiven if you think they were drafted by a liberal crusader for women's rights. The law is presented as protecting a woman's right to know, and to make an informed consent. "Women should not be kept in the dark," argues Kansas Senator Sam Brownback, a sponsor of the bill whose stated purpose is "to ensure that women seeking an abortion are fully informed regarding the pain experienced by their unborn child."

Lawmakers and activists opposed to abortion naturally want to make sure that women know as much as possible about the procedure, the risks, and the alternatives. Each layer of restriction, from waiting periods to parental notification, reinforces the message that this is not a decision to be made lightly. The movement to make ultrasounds more available reflects the belief that women who see an image, watch a heart beat, are much less likely to go through with an abortion. More than 20 years ago, the video *The Silent Scream* helped to shift the public focus from the horror stories of women who had suffered back-alley abortions to the horror movie of a fetus undergoing one.

Now it all comes together: Brownback and Congressman Chris Smith argue for a woman's right to understand the experience of the fetus. Their bill would require abortion providers to tell patients that by 20 weeks after fertilization a fetus can feel pain, and to ask if she would like anesthesia for the baby. If she refuses, she would have to sign a waiver. Doctors who fail to follow the rules could face fines up to $250,000. "There is substantial evidence that by this point, unborn children draw away from surgical instruments in a manner which in an infant or an adult would be interpreted as a response to pain," the text of the bill states. "Congress finds that there is substantial evidence that the process of being killed in an abortion will cause the unborn child pain, even though you receive a pain-reducing drug or drugs."

It's hard to argue with a bill that aims to reduce suffering; but in this case it's also easy to sense an ulterior motive. The bill's supporters, which include most anti-abortion lawmakers and organizations, can argue that so long as abortion remains legal, the least we can do is make it merciful. But the bill's language makes it clear that in this case mercy is for monsters: it invites women to request pain relief for her baby, so that it will hurt less when, as the law states, "the unborn child's body parts are grasped at random with a long-toothed clamp. The fetal body parts are then torn off of the body and pulled out of the vaginal canal." The text notes that this concern for the unborn child's possible pain is in keeping with laws having to do with the humane slaughter of livestock and lab animals.

Most people have no problem with pain being part of the abortion discussion: a Zogby poll found that 77% of the public supported the idea of giving pregnant women information about fetal pain. Even NARAL Pro-Choice America issued a statement saying it would not oppose the measure: "Pro-choice Americans have always believed that women deserve access to all the information relevant to their reproductive health decisions. For some women, that includes information related to fetal anesthesia options."

The question, however, is what information. Already the two sides of the abortion wars argue over state laws requiring doctors to warn of a heightened risk of breast cancer linked to abortion, despite something like a medical consensus that this link has not been proven. In this case there is dispute among researchers about when a fetus's nervous system and brain are mature enough to allow for pain, with some saying this occurs around 26 weeks, not the 20 weeks the bill stipulates. (An article in the *Journal of the American Medical Association* suggested pain was unlikely before 29 weeks; but the bill's defenders pointed out that some of the paper's authors were abortion rights activists with a clear conflict of interest.)

Another point of contention is that the law dates a pregnancy as beginning at the moment an egg is fertilized, as opposed to the standard definition, the point at which it implants in the womb. Were that to become a legally accepted definition, then those forms of contraception that may prevent a fertilized egg from implanting could be categorized as a form of abortion. That belief is what propels opposition to emergency contraception like Plan B.

Finally, the value of protecting a fetus from possible pain will in practice be balanced against the cost to the woman. A great many abortion providers would probably not be trained, equipped or insured to provide the kind of anesthesia the law gives women the right to demand. While it may reduce a fetus' pain, it also increases the woman's risk. Some women who might not be able to afford the added cost would be left only with the added guilt.

While the National Organization for Women denounced "this deceptive bill [that] will put women's health at risk and add one more barrier to abortion access," even some abortion foes questioned this particular strategy. Douglas R. Scott, president of Life Decisions International, worried that the offer of anesthesia might make women *more* likely to go through with an abortion. "The mother can believe she is making a benevolent choice, even as she simultaneously participates in a heinous act," he wrote on Christian Newswire. "I can hear it now. 'At least the fetus didn't feel pain . . . '"

There's nothing wrong with people opposed to abortion trying to discourage women from having them. But when the discouragement carries the force of law, it must be based on fact. Pain in adults is something of a mystery and a quandary; aware and articulate, we can describe what we feel—a sharp stab, a dull ache, a twinge, a pang, an agony—and yet still physicians argue over what to do and how to treat. Unlocking the secrets of the womb is surely harder, and the stakes for the mother high as well.

All those who have grown weary of these wars will be grateful that this may be the last for a while. With the G.O.P. still in control of Congress these last few weeks, they were eager to bring this to a vote; the activists believe in the value of the issue, the strategists in the value of forcing Democrats to vote against proposals that large majorities of Americans support. In the new Congress, the

Democrats' agenda does not include placing new restrictions on abortion or making women think harder before having one. But that just means the argument will be moving to new battlegrounds. (2006)

The rhetorical struggle occurring here concerns pain, its meaning, and its connections to the idea of life. If pro-life advocates can establish that early-term fetuses are able to feel pain, then they are one step closer to defining the fetus as a human being. This proposed change in abortion practice cleverly detours the line of argument so that related issues—pain and its treatment—can be used as covers for the underlying stasis desired by those who hold the pro-life position. Pro-choice advocates are aware of this sleight of hand, asking why advocates don't care about the pain caused to the fetus during medical birthing procedures, such as caesarian sections and the administering of epidurals. Even though the proposed legislation was voted down, states such as Arizona and Minnesota enacted laws requiring that women seeking abortion be informed of the risks of fetal pain. Arguments ensued about the viability of the claim, resulting in several medical studies on when exactly pain can be felt. The problem is that elected officials are moving to the stasis level of policy prematurely, which is to say they are failing to resolve the subargument about pain and fetal development, which rests at the stasis points of definition and conjecture: what is pain (definition), and does fetal pain exist? (conjecture).

We are now in a position to determine which of the four *staseis* best represents the point at issue.

Conjecture

Is there an act to be considered? The examples we consider in this chapter concern legislation that was passed at some level (federal or state). Still, the fact remains that every proposal we consider has opponents, which suggests that the arguments underlying this issue have to do with other questions. So an interested rhetor should investigate the questions of conjecture to see whether they yield useful propositions.

Conjectural Questions to Ask

1. Does abortion exist? Pro-life people often say that more than 4 million "babies" have been "killed" since *Roe v. Wade* became law. Is this figure correct? Is it current? Under what conditions are abortions performed? Because of pressure from antiabortion activists, fewer doctors and hospitals will perform abortions. Are private clinics still performing abortions? If so, how many are there? Pro-life advocates have produced a popular license plate that recommends adoption rather than abortion, and so a rhetor interested in the conjecture "whether adoption exists" instead of, or in place of, abortion may need some statistics or examples about the relation of these practices in order to argue any side of the question of relation. How many pregnant women opt for adoption instead of abortion?

2. How did it begin? Abortion has been used as a method of birth control for thousands of years. Recently, however, safer, more effective means of birth control have been found, and the use of abortion as a means of contraception has become increasingly controversial. The example of fetal pain legislation is an example of a tactic recently resorted to by opponents of abortion rights—to adopt legislation in related matters that may effect changes in *Roe v. Wade* stated earlier. When did opponents of abortion rights adopt this practice? Why did they do so? Will they find it useful in the future?

3. What is its cause? In some cases, of course, abortions are performed because they are required in order to save women's lives. Although contested, this cause does not seem to be so controversial as cases in which abortion is used as a means of birth control. Here the question of cause asks us to consider what causes people to choose abortion rather than other available means of contraception. Those who support the legality and availability of abortion suggest a number of causes for its use: lack of education about birth control, lack of access to birth control, women's fear of rejection or abuse if they use other means of birth control, and women's lack of control over their reproductive choices—the most glaring example of which is rape. Those who oppose abortion conjecture its causes quite differently: as irresponsibility, lack of the correct values, and disrespect for a familial tradition.

4. Can it be changed? It is an interesting question whether the practice of abortion will ever cease or whether the number of abortions, legal or illegal, can be changed by regulation. Abortion has been legal in America for about thirty years, which suggests that it can be made illegal again. States have limited access to abortion by mandating a twenty-four-hour waiting period, for example. And on the national level, opponents of abortion rights have attempted to outlaw certain kinds of abortions. These are legal means of seeking change, as are demonstrations and parades and petitions. Some antiabortion actions have on occasion been found to be illegal, such as protests held too close to clinics. Conjecture about the possibility of change in this case raises further interesting questions: Can illegal procedures—such as the bombing of abortion clinics or murder of doctors who perform abortions—effect a change in law? If not, why do the perpetrators of such acts engage in them?

Definition

How can the act be defined? As we have seen, this is a crucial stasis in the debate over abortion. In this issue the question of definition requires rhetors to examine their moral positions—something that is ordinarily very difficult. Perhaps the question of definition is seldom raised in public discussion about abortion because of the very difficulty and seriousness of the questions it raises. If a rhetor accepts the definition of abortion as murder, she can argue propositions that treat abortion like other instances of murder. It would follow that similar punishments should be meted out to those found guilty of performing the act. A rhetor who supports abortion rights cannot allow the argument to be taken up at the stasis of definition if his opponents argue that abortion is murder. If he does, he will inevitably find himself in the unenviable and untenable position of defending acts of murder. If he accepts some other definition of abortion, certain other consequences follow. If he defines it as a woman's right, for example, he can compare it to other rights enjoyed by citizens, such as the right to vote and the right to free speech. If he defines abortion as a woman's health issue or as a reproductive issue, other arguments appear. If abortion is defined as a feature of health care for women, for example, a rhetor can argue that its practice ought to be supported legally and perhaps even financially.

Definition Questions to Ask

1. What kind of a thing is it? Is abortion an act of murder? Is it a medical practice? A means of birth control? An affront to family values? A feminist issue?

2. To what larger class of things does it belong? Is a fetus a human being with all the rights to which humans are entitled? Or is a fetus not human if it is not viable outside the womb? What is a human being, anyway? What is the essence of being human? Is abortion a crime against humanity? Is resistance to legal abortion part of a disabling set of patriarchal prescriptions against women?

3. What are its divisions? Currently, federal law proscribes medical intervention in a pregnancy beyond the first trimester (three months) unless it is warranted by some overriding concern (such as the mother's life or health). Is this the best temporal division that can be devised? There are other ways to apply division to the issue of abortion—who practices it, places where it is illegal and for whom, and so on.

Quality

How serious is the act? Answers to questions of quality always depend upon the values maintained in the community. There are few issues currently under public debate that so deeply involve community values as abortion does. For many religious people who oppose abortion, its practice is a sin. But people who support legalized abortion take the issue seriously, too, arguing that its practice is part of the larger issue of women's control of their reproductive lives.

Simple Quality Questions to Ask

1. Is abortion good or bad? No one who is party to this argument thinks that abortion is a good thing. Those who oppose it want it banned completely. Those who support it want it to be safe and legal, but they would prefer that women not have to resort to it as a means of birth control.

2. Should abortion be sought or avoided? Are there any cases in which abortion ought to be sought? Or should abortion always be the choice of last resort?

3. Is abortion right or wrong? Those who oppose abortion say that the practice is always wrong. Can you imagine a hypothetical situation in which this is not the case? In other words, are there any situations in which abortion is the right choice?

4. Is abortion honorable or dishonorable? Those who are opposed to abortion have tried to shame doctors who perform the procedure by convincing them that it is a dishonorable act. Some doctors refuse to perform the procedure, while others consider it a mark of courage and pride that they are willing to continue performing abortions under frightening and sometimes dangerous conditions. Are they behaving honorably or dishonorably?

Comparative Questions of Quality

1. Is it better or worse than some alternative? A pregnant woman has only a few alternatives to abortion: parenthood, adoption, or abandonment. Keeping in mind that situations differ, try to rank these alternatives in terms of their relative goodness and badness.

2. Is it less or more desirable than any alternative? Most parties to this discussion think that abortion is the least desirable alternative of those listed above. Can you think of situations in which abortion may be the most desirable alternative?

3. Is it more or less right or wrong than any alternative? Those who support abortion rights often argue that abortion is preferable to bringing an unwanted child into the world. In other words, they say that abortion is less wrong than giving birth to an unwanted child. Is this argument valid? With whom might it be effective?

4. Is it more or less honorable or base than some alternative?

Policy

Abortion is currently a legal medical procedure. However, there is much contemporary debate about policies related to abortion (for example: Should so-called "partial-birth" abortions remain legal? Should women under the age of eighteen be forced to tell their parents about a planned abortion?) As is the case with any issue, rhetors who wish to advocate or oppose adoption of a policy must first deliberate the need for the policy or procedure and, second, must study how it would be implemented (or removed).

Deliberative Questions of Policy

1. Should some action be taken? Should abortion remain legal? Should it be made illegal? Should it be made illegal in some cases only? People have proposed to issue license plates that say "Choose Life" and to

extend the definition of childhood to the moment of conception. Should either of these actions be taken? In the case of the license plates, only two alternatives are available: accept or reject the proposal (although presumably the measure could be tabled for a time). In the case of the redefinition of childhood, there is a range of available alternatives between conception and birth that could be designated as the moment when a fetus becomes a child.

2. Given the rhetorical situation, what actions are possible or desirable? Is it possible to outlaw abortion?

3. How will the proposed actions change the current state of affairs? Or should the current state of affairs remain unchanged? Or is the status quo satisfactory? Desirable? If not, how will the new license plates affect community opinion about abortion? Will the administration's proposal, if adopted, affect other legislation? Will these changes be desirable? Satisfactory? To whom?

4. How will the proposed changes make things better? Worse? How? In what ways? For whom? The proposed redefinition of "when life begins" will force reconsideration of *Roe v. Wade* and other legislation related to the practice of abortion that depends upon the division of pregnancy into trimesters. It could also affect the practice of contraception, because the argument could be made that if life begins at conception, any means of contraception is murder. If any of this happens, will the world be a better place? How so?

Forensic Questions of Policy

1. Should some state of affairs be regulated (or not) by some formalized procedure? The practice of abortion is currently legal, although it is regulated by a variety of state and local laws. Those who oppose abortion, obviously, would like to see it made illegal so that all the regulatory procedures that attend illegal operations (the police, courts, prisons) can be brought to bear on those who participate in abortion.

2. Which policies can be implemented? Which cannot? Given the current ideological climate in America, the legality of abortion must be defended against those who would outlaw it. So it does not seem likely that a proposal that recommends free abortions for everyone will be readily accepted. Rather, proposals such as those exemplified here, intended to limit or deter access to abortion, have been successful in recent years.

3. What are the merits of competing proposals? What are their defects? Those who support abortion rights have often argued that better and more widely available sex education and wide distribution of free contraceptives would markedly reduce the number of abortions that are performed in this country. Are they right? If their proposals were adopted, could abortion then be made illegal?

A Second Example: Hateful Speech

We attempt to demonstrate the use of stasis theory by turning to yet another example of a controversial argument in American civic discourse. The First Amendment to the U.S. Constitution reads as follows: "Congress shall make no law respecting an establishment of religion, or prohibiting the free exercise thereof; or abridging the freedom of speech or of the press; or the right of the people peaceably to assemble, and to petition the Government for a redress of grievances." This amendment guarantees that American citizens have the right to practice whatever religion they wish, to say whatever they wish, and to associate with whomever they please. It also guarantees that no limits can be placed on journalists' freedom of speech or on citizens' ability to seek compensation from government for wrongs suffered.

The First Amendment clause insuring freedom of speech concerns us here. During the 1990s a number of American universities adopted policies regulating the use of so-called "hateful speech," that is, language or acts that offend members of certain groups. Rodney Smolla, an attorney who is an authority on the First Amendment, defines hateful speech as "a generic term that has come to embrace the use of speech attacks based on race, ethnicity, religion, and sexual orientation or preference" (1993, 152).

We now prefer to call this sort of discourse "hateful speech" because this term captures the effects of such speech on those who are subjected to it. While hateful speech traditionally takes the form of a face-to-face interaction, it has now found its way online, into hateful sites that single out people of a specific race, nationality, religion, or sexual orientation. Hateful speech has also showed up on video sites like YouTube and popular networking sites like Facebook. Controversy over the University of Illinois team mascot, Chief Illiniwek (discussed in the chapter on *kairos*), gave rise to a Facebook page that brought this emotionally intense issue into the realm of hateful speech. The following article, written by Matt Spartz and published in the online version of the student newspaper at the University of Illinois, points out some of the controversial issues raised by the use of hateful speech on such sites.

FACEBOOK POSTINGS ALARM UI OFFICIALS: GROUP BRINGS RACIAL TENSIONS TO FOREFRONT

The University's struggle for racial tolerance took another hit, this time from comments made on a pro-Chief Facebook group's wall.

Two students posted derogatory comments towards American Indians on the wall of the "If They Get Rid of the Chief I'm Becoming a Racist" group and threatened a University graduate student. These students could face disciplinary action from the University or legal actions for hate crimes.

The pro-Chief group has since been removed from Facebook but was formed as far back as early November. The first controversial post was written on Nov. 20.

"What they don't realize is that there was never a racist problem before," wrote one of the students. "But now I hate redskins and hope all those drunk, casino owning bums die."

But action was prompted from a second post on Dec. 2.

"Apparently the leader of this movement is of Sioux descent. Which means what, you ask? The Sioux indians are the ones that killed off the Illini indians, so she's just trying to finish what her ancestors started. I say we throw a tomahawk into her face."

A press release by the University's American Indian Studies program and Native American House brought these threats to light on Jan. 8, calling for the University to take legal and disciplinary action against these students.

Chancellor Richard Herman sent a mass e-mail to the members of the C-U [Champaign-Urbana] community explaining that the University has spent 140 years creating a "welcoming environment" and that he "will not tolerate such violent threats."

The incident has been referred to the Office of Student Conflict Resolution, which will determine if the student code can apply disciplinary action to these students. Herman said in his e-mail the University "will take all legal and disciplinary action available."

But not every student in the group knew it harbored such extreme views. Lizzy Cunningham, freshman in LAS, was one of the 110 members but had never seen the postings before the issue blew up.

"I don't know what the people were thinking when they wrote them," she said. "But they were really inappropriate."

Other pro-Chief organizations have addressed this issue, too. Students For Chief Illiniwek, a registered student organization at the University, came to the forefront of the conflict, attempting to separate themselves from the negative stigma these students put onto the pro-Chief group.

"Our organization and its members are not involved in or responsible for the comments in question," wrote Paul Schmitt, vice president of the student group, in a press release. "We feel that these comments highlight the need for further education on the history of the Chief Illiniwek tradition . . ."

But others feel these threats towards a American Indian student illustrate a larger problem at the University. Wanda Pillow, director of the Native American House and American Indian Studies program, said this incident shows the need for campus administration and the Board of Trustees to address the issues of race on campus, along with resolving the debate over the Chief.

"The anti-Indian attitudes that were expressed on the webpage demonstrate the hostile and abusive environment which persists for people of color at the University," said Pillow in an e-mail interview.

There are Facebook groups for students who are anti-Chief, or more broadly, against racism. Lindsey Bever, senior in LAS, created the group "Students Against Racist Mascots." She said the Facebook group shows how the Chief can make people unattached to what the Chief should represent.

"They may have thought it (the post) was funny at the time," she said. "But now they may realize that it was dumb to write."

But there are other groups that try to further the fight to abolish the use of the Chief. Ronu Ghoshal, a University alum, created an anti-Chief group with the hope to bring more attention to the fight against the Chief.

"I do not believe that most Chief supporters are racist or hateful individu-als," he said in an e-mail interview. "Rather, I felt that through this group, I could express just how strongly many of us feel about the need to remove the Chief."

The issues of race-relations on the C-U campus has been noted specifically by James Kaplan, chairman of the Illinois Board of Higher Education. He said the University is the only one in the state that he knows of with specific race-related incidents, referring also to the exchange earlier in the year between the Zeta Beta Tau fraternity and Delta Delta Delta sorority.

Kaplan said the board works to promote diversity as a "valuable element at universities." About the Facebook incident, he said, "When you belittle any of us, you belittle all of us."

Chancellor Herman in his e-mail invited the community to a forum address-ing the ways to create a more welcoming campus environment. The forum will be held on Feb. 1 at 4 p.m. in Foellinger Auditorium.

"The plans for the forum are already in place due to some theme parties we had earlier," said Herman, adding that he hopes this will be "a way forward, a way to declare our shared values and make sure we act on them every-day." (2007)

A typical response to sites that single out people with hateful comments, or even—in this case—threats of harmful action, is to remove the sites. Videos are removed from YouTube regularly, some for similar reasons. Sites like Facebook, MySpace, and YouTube have developed policies governing such posts, but when site managers can control sites and remove content posted by others, this inevitably raises the issue of censorship.

The question raised by hateful speech, then, is whether it should be included under the definition of free speech cited in the First Amendment In general, U.S. courts have held that an American citizen may say any-thing she wishes unless her words create real and immediate danger for others (Walker 1994, 64–65). With this exception American courts have, historically, offered First Amendment protection to the content of speech or expressive acts. Until recently, for example, the courts treated flag burning and cross burning alike as expressions that are protected by the First Amendment. The act of burning a flag usually expresses anger at, or dis-agreement with, the policies of a government. The act of burning a cross has long been associated with the Ku Klux Klan and is widely regarded as a threat to groups singled out by the Klan for persecution: blacks, gays, Jews, and Catholics. You can readily see, then, how an act such as wearing Klan-like robes to a campus party could be taken by some as an act of hate speech—a symbolic attack on a group. However, distasteful as they may be to some people, flag burning and cross burning are both expressions of political or ideological speech, and hence they are ordinarily protected by the First Amendment, as they were in the Viktora case examined elsewhere in this book.

Examination of the issue of hateful speech by means of stasis theory dis-closes its available propositions and suggests as well the level and extent of preparation necessary to argue any of these. Often, rhetors have opinions about controversial issues before they are ever called to write or speak about them. If this is the case, a rhetor may use stasis theory to discover whether his opinion, expressed in a proposition, can be supported with strong and persuasive arguments. Use of the *staseis* will also disclose arguments that can be used against his position, so that he can anticipate and refute these.

Step 1. *Decide whether to formulate the question generally or specifically.*

Possible General Formulations of the Question

Does hateful speech occur? (conjecture)

What is hateful speech exactly? (definition)

Is hateful speech a good or a bad thing? (quality)

Should hateful speech be regulated? (policy)

Possible Specific Formulations of the Question

Does hateful speech occur on my campus or in my community? (conjecture)

What forms does it take on my campus or in my community? (definition)

Is hateful speech a bad thing on my campus or in my community? (quality)

Should hateful speech be regulated here? (policy)

This analysis demonstrates that very different kinds of research are necessary to argue the question as a thesis and as a hypothesis. The general questions require the rhetor to examine the state of affairs on campuses across the country, to examine American values regarding good manners and the limits of expression, and to consider whether regulation of hateful speech violates other American practices and policies (such as freedom of speech). A thorough discussion of the question at this level of generality would require at least a book-length treatment and a good deal of specialized knowledge as well—knowledge about constitutional law, for instance.

The specific questions would require much less preparation and composition, although their scope is still quite large. To answer the first or second hypothetical questions would require some informal research: questioning friends or acquaintances, reading through back issues of the local newspapers. More formal research might include compiling a list of questions to ask of people who claim to have heard hateful speech or assembling an attitude survey about its effects on the discursive climate of campus or the community. The article quotes an e-mail by the chancellor of the University of Illinois, in which he refers to parties into which students were invited to wear costumes portraying racial stereotypes. For a rhetor investigating the local climate, such parties could become part of the context of behavior on campus. Once a rhetor has documented a list of occurrences of hateful speech, she can define it as it occurs on her campus and classify its forms. Either of these questions could be answered in a discourse of three or four pages. Answers to the third hypothetical question, however, are more difficult to compose since they require an understanding of the educational values of the university in question and of its students. Answers to the fourth require study of the university's existing policies in this area, as well as an understanding of how such policies are generated, implemented, and enforced.

Circumstances sometimes force rhetors to use particular questions even when a general question might produce a more powerful argument. If the rhetor is president of the student body at Illinois, for instance, she might be suspected of evading her responsibility to represent students at that campus if she chooses to argue the general question. But circumstances may also prevent use of the particular questions. If no instances of hateful speech can be documented on his campus, a rhetor who wishes to address the issues raised by its regulation must retreat to a more general formulation. The general formulations of the question do present him with some rhetorical advantages. If he chooses to argue any of them, he takes up the stand on his ground, which always works in a rhetor's favor. For example, a proposition based on the first general question might be constructed as follows:

> Hateful speech occurs with increasing frequency on American campuses.

Anyone who disagrees with this is forced to argue negatively, which is always more difficult:

> Hateful speech never occurs on American campuses.

This is demonstrably untrue, since the controversy surrounding hateful speech would not arise at all unless someone, somewhere, had used it. This rhetor can modify his negative stance a bit:

> Hateful speech occurs so seldom that its use is unimportant or negligible.

This is still a weak proposition, since its probability is diminished by the very fact that hateful speech is being discussed.

Step 2. *If you choose to treat the question generally, decide whether to state it theoretically or practically.*

Theoretical questions ask why people behave as they do; practical questions investigate actual human behavior.

A General Question, Stated Theoretically

Is the use of hateful speech natural (or unnatural) to human beings?

Or

Do people use hateful speech because of their upbringing or education or habits, or because their friends and acquaintances use it?

A General Question, Stated Practically

What happens when people use hateful speech?

This analysis reveals that, as usual, the practical question would be much easier to prepare and argue (although none of these questions are simple ones). The practical question requires only a study of the practice and its effects, while the theoretical questions inquire into human psychology and sociology. A successful answer to the practical question requires only some empirical evidence about what happens when people use hateful speech.

Steps 1 and 2 demonstrate the scope of various arguments on a given question. That is, they show the size of various questions and, hence, supply a quick estimate of the work and time required to compose an argument in support of each one. Rhetors can also use stasis theory to get a sense of how much research will be necessary in order to argue a given issue. Practicing rhetors need to know whether they have the resources to do justice to a given formulation of an issue. Use of the *staseis* will help them to decide very quickly.

Step 3. *Decide which of the four staseis best describes the point at issue in the rhetorical situation at hand.*

Conjecture

Is there an act to be considered? That is, has someone used hateful speech in some relevant situation? If hateful speech has occurred, try to describe the incidents as accurately and as persuasively as possible (see Quintilian's advice for doing this in Chapter 10, on arrangement). If no incidents of hateful speech have occurred, this stasis is not relevant in this case. Move to the next stasis. If such incidents have occurred, however, an examination of conjecture may produce useful arguments.

Questions to Ask About Conjecture

1. Does hateful speech exist? Someone who is opposed to regulation of hateful speech could argue that it doesn't exist. To do so, this rhetor can resort to the question of definition in order to define hateful speech in such a way that whatever incident stimulated the discussion is not included. For example, rhetors at Auburn or Michigan State could define "hateful speech" so that the term excludes wearing clothing that is offensive to some groups. How widespread is its use? Is it confined to a few small groups of people, or is the general climate permeated with it? A rhetor who supports the regulation of hateful speech should catalogue as many incidents of its use as she can find.

2. How did it begin? Answers to this question require some empirical research. When did hateful speech first occur in the relevant situation?

3. What causes it? Proponents of regulation can argue that hateful speech originates in some unsavory source such as racism, sexism, or religious bigotry. Opponents of regulation can argue that it stems from less offensive sources such as carelessness or high spirits.

4. Can it be changed? Proponents of regulation can argue that implementation of a policy prohibiting the use of hateful speech can change
   students' behavior, thus stopping its use. Opponents can argue that
   such regulations will not change behavior or will only force students to
   utter hateful remarks in private.

Definition

How can the act be defined? If white students dress up as members of the
Ku Klux Klan for a party, for example, is that hateful speech? How would
a rhetor have to define hateful speech in order to include this behavior? If
you think that something that happened on your campus is an instance of
hateful speech, compose a definition of hateful speech that can include it
(see the discussion of definition in Chapter 9). Your definition should also
allow you to take up your stand on defensible ground. For example, if you
define hateful speech as "all utterances that are offensive," you risk including justifiable criticism of someone's behavior under the heading of hateful
speech. In case there are no relevant instances of hateful speech to be
defined, move to the next stasis.

Questions to Ask About Definition

1. What kind of thing is it? Is hateful speech an example of racist, sexist,
   or bigoted behavior or attitudes? Or is it an example of high spirits,
   careless good fun, blowing off steam? Must an utterance be backed by
   an intent to offend in order to be classed as hateful speech? Someone
   who supports regulation of hateful speech might define those who
   oppose him as insensitive clods who underestimate the power of language to wound and offend others. An opponent of its regulation
   might define those who support regulation as extraordinarily sensitive
   persons who mistake idle chatter for offensive language.

2. To what larger class of things does it belong? Perhaps hateful speech
   belongs among the kinds of speech protected by the First Amendment
   to the Constitution. In this case, it can't be regulated in America.
   Indeed, many hateful speech codes enacted in American universities
   during the 1990s were found unconstitutional by the courts. Some
   European countries, in contrast, have recently taken steps to curb the
   proliferation of hateful speech on the Internet. They can do so either
   because their constitutions have no free-speech clause or because their
   court systems have interpreted *free speech* more narrowly than do
   American courts.

3. What are its parts? Are racist, sexist, heterosexist, and religiously bigoted remarks the only kinds of hateful speech? Does hateful speech
   include remarks that slur a person's abilities? His or her appearance?
   Do "offensive utterances" include pornography? Slang? Four-letter
   words? Do they include acts, such as wearing Klan robes or burning
   crosses? Does the use of racist remarks bear any relation to the use of
   sexist or heterosexist remarks? To religiously bigoted remarks?

Quality

How serious is the act? This is a challenging question with regard to the issue of hateful speech. Answers to questions of quality nearly always depend on what is valued in a given community. Depending on their ideology, some rhetors may hold that the use of hateful speech is very serious indeed, since it violates the American belief that everyone has the right to be treated equally and with respect (see Chapter 4, on ideology and the commonplaces). Others may feel that even though hateful speech is serious, it is primarily a violation of good manners. Others may think it's not very serious at all. Some people may feel that some instances of hateful speech are worse than others; women, for example, may feel quite offended by gender-biased representations. A few years back at Harvard some women were offended by a nine-foot snow sculpture of an erect penis, arguing that the sculpture symbolized masculinist power to control or harm women. Depending on their circumstances and ideology, some persons will think this is not hateful speech at all, or at least that it is not as serious as the use of words like *fag, bitch,* or *cripple.* Others, like the women at Harvard, take it very seriously indeed.

Simple Questions of Quality

1. Is hateful speech good or bad? Hateful speech is widely regarded as a bad practice, since it breeds divisiveness and unhappiness. Conceivably, a rhetor who opposes the regulation of hateful speech could argue that its use is sometimes a good thing, since verbal wounds are not as serious as physical ones. That is, he could argue that people must be allowed to express their hatred verbally so that they need not resort to physical violence.

2. Should hateful speech be sought or avoided? Rhetors who support regulation of hateful speech can argue that rules prohibiting it will force people to avoid its use. Rhetors who oppose regulation of hateful speech can argue that rules forbidding it will cause people to seek out instances of its use in the hope of bringing users to justice.

3. Is hateful speech right or wrong? Answers to this question of quality depend upon a rhetor's religious or moral beliefs. For example, a rhetor might, on one hand, cite Jesus Christ's teaching that humans should love their neighbors as themselves; the use of hateful speech is wrong in terms of this religious injunction. On the other hand, a rhetor might cite the First Amendment, which protects the right of Americans to utter their opinions without fear of reprisal, and argue that the use of hateful speech is protected by this legal injunction.

4. Is hateful speech honorable or dishonorable? If, on one hand, a rhetor has defined hateful speech as an attempt to belittle others, its use is certainly not honorable. If she has defined it as a satisfactory alternative to violence, on the other hand, its use is honorable.

Comparative Questions of Quality

1. Is the unregulated use of hateful speech better or worse than a related state of affairs? An opponent of regulation might argue that if the use

of hateful speech is regulated, students will not feel free to express their opinions on anything. This repressive state of affairs is certainly not preferable to that wherein all speech, even hateful speech, is tolerated.

2. Is the use of hateful speech more or less desirable than alternatives? A proponent of regulation can argue that the current state of affairs, wherein hateful speech runs rampant, is less preferable than one in which students think carefully before they utter remarks that offend others.

3. Is the state of affairs where hateful speech is unregulated better or worse than alternatives? This question calls upon rhetors to establish priorities among their values. Is absolute freedom of speech more important than the less offensive climate brought about by regulation of speech?

4. Is the state of affairs in which hateful speech is unregulated more or less honorable than alternatives? People who oppose regulation can argue that the existence of policies controlling speech demonstrates that the policy makers do not trust individuals to behave honorably. People who support regulation can argue that people have demonstrated by their use of hateful speech that they cannot behave honorably without regulation by external authority.

Policy

Should this act be submitted to some formal procedure? Or how can this policy be implemented? This stasis is relevant in this case only if a rhetor supports or rejects the implementation of a policy regarding hateful speech. If you simply wish to take a position on the use, definition, or value of hateful speech, careful and thorough use of the first three stases is sufficient to raise the relevant questions. If you wish to implement a policy that will regulate hateful speech, however, you must compose it, and be sure to demonstrate how it will serve its intended function. To do this, you can look at the policies used at other universities. Here, for instance, is a policy on intolerance that was adopted at Penn State:

Purpose

The University is committed to creating an educational environment which is free from intolerance directed toward individuals or groups and strives to create and maintain an environment that fosters respect for others. As an educational institution, the University has a mandate to address problems of a society deeply ingrained with bias and prejudice. Toward that end, the University provides educational programs and activities to create an environment in which diversity and understanding of other cultures are valued.

Acts of intolerance violate the principles upon which American society is built and serve to destroy the fabric of the society we share. Such actions not only do untold and unjust harm to the dignity, safety and well-being of those who experience this pernicious kind of discrimination but also threaten the reputation of the University and impede the realization of the University's educational mission.

Definition

An act of intolerance refers to conduct that is in violation of a University policy, rule or regulation and is motivated by discriminatory bias against or hatred toward other individuals or groups based on characteristics such as age, ancestry, color, disability or handicap, national origin, political belief, race, religious creed, sex, sexual orientation, gender identity or veteran status.

Policy

The Pennsylvania State University is committed to preventing and eliminating acts of intolerance by faculty, staff and students, and encourages anyone in the University community to report concerns and complaints about acts of intolerance to the Affirmative Action Office or the Office of the Vice Provost for Educational Equity, and in cases involving students, reports also may be made to the Office of Judicial Affairs.

If any violation of University policy, rule or regulation is motivated by discriminatory bias against or hatred toward an individual or group based on characteristics such as age, ancestry, color, disability or handicap, national origin, political belief, race, religious creed, sex, sexual orientation, gender identity or veteran status, the sanction will be increased in severity and may include termination or expulsion from the University.

Retaliation constitutes a separate violation and may result in a sanction independent of the outcome of a complaint.

Expression of Opinion

The expression of diverse views and opinions is encouraged in the University community. Further, the First Amendment of the United States' Constitution assures the right of free expression. In a community which recognizes the rights of its members to hold divergent views and to express those views, sometimes ideas are expressed which are contrary to University values and objectives. Nevertheless, the University cannot impose disciplinary sanctions upon such expression when it is otherwise in compliance with University regulations. (2007)

As you can see, Penn State's administration defines intolerance in fairly sweeping terms. However, in the final paragraph the authors of the policy qualify their intolerance for intolerance when it comes to speech, saying that the university cannot discipline "expression of opinion" that is contrary to university values if it does not break other campus codes. This is a clever way to regulate offensive behavior while allowing for freedom of speech. Clearly the authors of this statement have given a good deal of thought to the formulation of rules and procedures that will contribute to a congenial campus climate.

If you want to implement, change, or rescind a policy or a procedure, you should find out how policies are generated and implemented at your university or in your community: that is, what committees make policy, where and how policies are published, and who enforces them once they are in place.

RHETORICAL ACTIVITIES

1. Select one of the issues you worked with in the last exercise of Chapter 1. Try to frame the theoretical and practical questions it raises. To determine the theoretical questions, ask yourself, What is the nature or origin of this issue? To determine the practical questions, ask yourself what effects the issue has on people, what is expected of people, what people should do.

   Now try to frame the issue in general, specific, and very specific terms. When you finish this exercise, you should have a list of questions that help you see how much work will be required to argue the issue you have chosen at any level of generality and in theoretical or practical terms. You may discover ways to argue about this issue that you had not thought about before. You should also have a sense of how much research you will need to do to argue the question you eventually choose to pursue.

2. Select one of the issues you worked with in the last exercise in Chapter 1 and examine it using the questions suggested by stasis theory. The first time you try this, you may wish to use our examples as models. But since every issue is different (because every rhetorical situation is different), you will soon discover that our models don't raise all the relevant questions for your issue and that they do raise some questions that are not relevant to your issue.

3. Find a compelling letter or op-ed piece on the editorial page of your college or community newspaper. Write a brief analysis of the argument that appears in this letter. Here are some questions to ask: What is the issue under debate? Given the writer's account of the issue, can you determine at what stasis the argument seems to lie? That is, does the argument rest at conjecture (X exists; X is a problem)? Definition (X is this kind of thing or event)? Quality (X is a good or a bad thing)? Policy (what should we do)? Can you determine the position that is being argued against? That is, what position or positions is the writer attacking? Can the writer achieve stasis with his opponents, given the way he has stated the issue and the ground upon which he has taken his stand?

PROGYMNASMATA III: CONFIRMATION AND REFUTATION

The first of the strictly rhetorical exercises engaged students in composing the main parts of arguments: confirmation and refutation. Confirmation is the section of a composition that lays out the composer's arguments and her support for them.

The section called refutation answers the anticipated arguments of those who oppose the rhetor's point of view. Matters of fact are not suitable for this exercise since they need not be confirmed, nor can they be refuted. Discourses that are obviously fictional are not suitable for confirmation or refutation, either.

Quintilian suggested that students compose confirmations and refutations using the same historical materials they worked with in the elementary exercises before they graduated to the composition of confirmations and refutations for use in actual rhetorical situations (II iv 18–19). For example, he suggested that students write compositions confirming or refuting the legend that "a raven settled on the head of Valerius in the midst of a combat and with its wings and beak struck the eyes of the Gaul who was his adversary."

According to Aphthonius, both exercises—confirmation and refutation—include "all the power of the art (of rhetoric)" (Kennedy 2003 101, 104). Aphthonius taught that a rhetor's first duty in refutation was to state the "false assertion of the opposition," and then to write a brief exposition of the situation. The opposites of these topics (that is, certainty, credibility, possibility, consistency, propriety, and convenience) can be used in confirmation. A confirmation begins with an account of the good reputation enjoyed by the doer of the deed, presents an exposition of the situation, and employs the opposite topics used in refutation: certainty, believability, possibility, consistency, propriety, convenience.

Following Aphthonius's instructions, we composed a sample confirmation and refutation about a contemporary event also considered in the chapter on *kairos*. On January 11, 2003, George Ryan, the governor of Illinois, citing problems with the Illinois justice system, commuted the sentences of those on the state's death row. Here is our confirmation of his action:

> *Assertion to Be Confirmed:* Governor Ryan was right to commute the sentences of death row inmates in Illinois.
>
> *Encomium:* Governor George Ryan is an honorable person who makes decisions based on ethics rather than politics.
>
> *Exposition of the Situation:* On January 11, 2003, Governor George Ryan (R) of Illinois commuted the sentences of his state's entire death row. The decision came after a three-year study revealed major problems with the state's judicial system, including revelations that at least seventeen inmates were innocent, and that some inmates' confessions had been elicited by use of torture. Faced with what he called "startling information," Governor Ryan proclaimed, "I have acted today in what I believe is in the interest of justice. It is not only the right thing to do, I believe it is the only thing to do."
>
> *Certainty:* It has been repeatedly established that Illinois's judicial system is unreliable and corrupt. No one should be sentenced to death in such a system.
>
> *Credibility:* Governor Ryan has been evaluating the justice system and weighing the prospects for death row inmates for over three years. Because Ryan was previously a proponent of the death penalty, this decision was made based strictly on the facts at hand rather than on political grounds.

Possibility: It is quite possible that the people whose sentences were commuted were innocent. Evidence could still emerge (as it has with others who had already been executed) proving their innocence.

Consistency: Governor Ryan's action was consistent with a tradition in which presidents and governors may commute sentences at any time.

Propriety: Governor Ryan's commutation was appropriately timed, because he was about to be replaced by a governor who had indicated he would not commute the sentences.

Convenience: The commutations were convenient, since it saved the government from considering the sentences on a case-by-case basis, a process that may have taken years.

Here is a refutation of Governor Ryan's action:

False Assertion to Be Refuted: Governor Ryan was right to commute the sentences of death row inmates in Illinois.

Exposition of the Situation: On January 11, 2003, Governor George Ryan (R) of Illinois commuted the sentences of his state's entire death row. The decision came after a three-year study revealed major problems with the state's judicial system, including revelations that at least seventeen inmates were innocent, and that some inmates' confessions had been elicited by use of torture. Faced with what he called "startling information," Governor Ryan proclaimed, "I have acted today in what I believe is in the interest of justice. It is not only the right thing to do, I believe it is the only thing to do."

Uncertainty: It is not certain that the inmates are innocent; therefore each case should be examined carefully.

Incredibility: It is hard to believe that the Illinois justice system is so flawed as to convict innocent people.

Impossibility: It is now impossible for the families of the crime victims to have a sense of closure.

Lack of Consistency: The commutations are inconsistent with Ryan's previous stance on the death penalty.

Impropriety: Governor Ryan has had a vexed political career; this action is inappropriate because he is merely trying to improve his reputation before he leaves office.

Inconvenience: The commutations were inconvenient for other governors facing similar situations in their own states.

Remarkably, our systematic use of the ancients' suggested topics produced most of the arguments that were made in the press and elsewhere in regard to this event.

PROGYMNASMATA: CONFIRMATION AND REFUTATION

1. Go to the periodical or newpaper section of your school's library (or a public library if it's more convenient) and browse through magazines and newspapers for a local or national issue that is getting a lot of

attention. Develop a statement related to the issue, and, following the instructions and our example, write a confirmation and a refutation of the statement.

2. Select a debatable question from history and write a confirmation and refutation on the question. Some examples might include: Should the United States have entered the Vietnam War? Should President Truman have used atomic weapons to end World War II? Was Christopher Columbus's arrival on American shores a good thing?

NOTE

1. The system of questions given here does not appear in any ancient thinker's work. We have generalized the four questions we feature out of primary and secondary classical sources (for an illuminating if complex account of competing ancient traditions of stasis, see Quintilian's painstaking discussion in the third book of the *Institutes*). Our system is a hybrid, although it is the same one that George Kennedy reconstructs for Hermagoras's lost treatise (307–08). In particular, our consideration of policy along with the other three *staseis* is a departure from ancient stasis theory, since the ancients usually classed policy with questions of law (forensic rhetoric), while the first three staseis we discuss were ordinarily associated with deliberative rhetoric.

WORKS CITED

Gibbs, Nancy. "Can a Fetus Feel Pain?" *Time*, December 6, 2006. http://www. time. com/time/nation/article/0,8599,1566772,00.html (last accessed June 9, 2007).

Kennedy, George. *The Art of Persuasion in Greece.* Princeton: Princeton University Press, 1963.

Pennsylvania State University. "Statement on Intolerance." Updated January 1, 2007. http://guru. psu. edu/policies/AD29. html (accessed June 14, 2007).

Smolla, Rodney. *Free Speech in an Open Society.* New York: Vintage, 1993.

Spartz, Matt. "Facebook Postings Alarm UI Officials: Group Brings Racial Tensions to Forefront." *Daily Illini* January 17, 2007. http://media. www. dailyillini. com/media/storage/paper736/news/2007/01/16/ News/Facebook. Postings. Alarm. Ui. Officials-2633563. shtml (last accessed June 9, 2007).

Sprague, Rosamond Kent. "*Dissoi Logoi,* or *Dialexis.*" *Mind: A Quarterly Review of Psychology and Philosophy* 77, (no. 306 April 1968): 155–167.

Sprague, Rosamond Kent, trans. *The Older Sophists.* Columbia: South Carolina University Press, 1972.

Toner, Robin. "Abortion Foes See Validation for New Tactic." *New York Times.* May 22, 2007, national edition, sec. A.

Walker, Samuel. *Hate Speech: The History of an American Controversy.* Lincoln: Nebraska University Press, 1994.

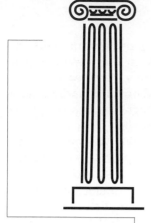

THE COMMON TOPICS AND THE COMMONPLACES: FINDING THE AVAILABLE MEANS

For just as all kinds of produce are not provided by every country, and as you will not succeed in finding a particular bird or beast, if you are ignorant of the localities where it has its usual haunts or birthplace, as even the various kinds of fish flourish in different surroundings, some preferring a smooth and others a rocky bottom, and are found on different shores and in diverse regions . . . so not every kind of argument can be derived from every circumstance, and consequently our search requires discrimination.

—Quintilian,
Institutes V x 21

PERHAPS THE SYSTEM of invention most often associated with ancient rhetoric is that referred to by both ancient and modern rhetoricians as the topics (Greek *topos*, "place") or the commonplaces (Latin *locis communis*). The word *place* was originally meant quite literally. Lists of topics were first written on papyrus rolls, and students who were looking for a specific topic unrolled the papyrus until they came to the place on the roll where that topic was listed. Later, this graphic meaning of *place* was applied conceptually, to mean an intellectual source or region harboring a proof that could be inserted into any discourse where appropriate. Even later, the terms *topic* and *place* referred to formal or structural inventive strategies, like definition, division, or **classification** (see Chapter 9, on sophistic topics, for more information about the formal topics).

Ancient rhetoricians often described the places as though they were hidden away somewhere. Quintilian, for example, defined the topics as "the secret places where arguments reside, and from which they must be drawn forth" (V x 20). Just as hunters and fishermen need to know where to look for specific kinds of prey, rhetoricians need to be skilled at tracking down suitable proofs. Quintilian's

117

students must have used the topics much as hikers use trail markers—to point them in the right direction to take through the wilderness of all possible proofs. As Cicero wrote to his friend Trebatius, "It is easy to find things that are hidden if the hiding place is pointed out and marked; similarly if we wish to track down some argument we ought to know the places or topics" (*Topics*, 17).

Some modern scholars treat the topics as representations of structures in the human mind, arguing that they describe the processes everybody uses to think with. But this interpretation gives the topics a modern coloring, because it focuses invention on minds or brains rather than on language. The only ancient treatises that lend themselves to such a reading are Aristotle's *Rhetoric* and *Topics*. However, Aristotle also discussed topics drawn from the operations of the Greek language (as in *Topics* I vii, for example), and he drew as well from the ethical and political issues that confronted fourth-century Athenians (as in *Rhetoric* I iv).

There are two ancient terms for these features of ancient rhetorical theory because ancient rhetors spoke both Greek and Latin. We will take advantage of this duality by using the terms *topic* and *commonplace* to mean different things, even though the terms were used interchangeably in ancient thought. We adopt the term *topic* to refer to any specific procedure that generates arguments, such as definition and division or comparison and contrast. We use the term *commonplace* to refer to statements that circulate within ideologies. This should not be taken to imply that topics are not implicated with ideology, however, because the very processes we think with— difference and similarity and the like—may be ideologically constructed.

Nor should the ancient topics be confused with the modern use of the term *topic*. In modern thought, topics exist either in a body of knowledge that must be learned or in a thinker's review of her experiences. When modern teachers ask students to assemble a list of topics to write about, they mean that students are to select some piece of knowledge found in books, or in other research, or in some personal experience, as subjects that can be discussed in writing. For ancient rhetoricians, in contrast, topics existed in the structures of language or in the issues that concerned the community. That is why they were called *common*—they were available to anyone who spoke or wrote the language in which they were couched and who was reasonably familiar with the ethical and political discussions taking place in the community. Since the topics yield propositions and proofs drawn from daily discussion and debate—the common sense of a community—they cannot easily be separated from consideration of political, ethical, social, economic, and philosophical issues.

ANCIENT TOPICAL TRADITIONS

Humans have used topics for a very long time. Some historians of rhetoric think they may be related to a memory device used during very ancient times by poets called "rhapsodes," who traveled about the countryside reciting epic and lyric poetry and telling stories of the gods. Before the time when writing was readily available to most people, rhapsodes recited long poems from memory, and they accomplished this partly by relying on bits of lines or images that they could insert into any recitation wherever they needed a transition or a description or a way to fill out the meter of a line. The poets who are now known collectively as "Homer" probably repeated phrases like "rosy-fingered dawn" and "the wine-dark sea" to help them remember what came next while they recited lengthy poems (see Chapter 12, on memory).

By the sixth or fifth centuries BCE, rhetoricians might have used topics in the same way, memorizing a stock of arguments that were general enough to be inserted into any speech. Because they had this stock, rhetors were ready to speak on the spot whenever necessary simply by combining and expanding upon the appropriate topics. By examining several topics and amplifying each one, rhetors could lengthen any speech to fit the time allotted them by a rhetorical situation. In the dialogue called *Menexenus*, Plato gives us a glimpse of how this might have been done:

> Yesterday I heard Aspasia composing a funeral oration about these very dead. For she had been told, as you were saying, that the Athenians were going to choose a speaker, and she repeated to me the sort of speech which he should deliver—partly improvising and partly from previous thought, putting together fragments of the funeral oration which Pericles spoke, but which, as I believe, she composed. (236b)

In other words, Aspasia used parts of an earlier, similar speech she had composed in making up a new one. These fragments may have been what were later called "topics" or "commonplaces." They would certainly include arguments that praised the dead, and there might be topics of blame used against people thought to have caused the death, as well. Praise and blame are **epideictic** topics, suitable for use on ceremonial occasions such as funerals. Ancient rhetors and rhetoricians also developed topics appropriate for use in the courtroom and in the assembly, where **forensic** and **deliberative** discourse are practiced.

After writing became readily available, lists of topics that had previously served as memory devices could more easily be preserved. Ancient rhetoricians produced at least three topical traditions. One of these is ordinarily identified with sophistic teachers like Tisias and Corax, Theodorus, or Thrasymachus, who may have written the first rhetorical handbooks. No one knows for sure whether any of the Older Sophists wrote handbooks, but if they did, the sections on invention probably contained lists of stock arguments or topics that could be inserted into any discourse. Aristotle developed this sophistic tradition into a complete theory of topical invention, as we shall see later in this chapter.

Two topical traditions were in use during the Hellenistic period and in Roman rhetoric, and both were based on Aristotelian texts. The first was drawn from the *Rhetoric*, the second from the *Topics*. The second tradition appeared prominently in Cicero, Quintilian, and minor rhetoricians and is the system most often referred to by modern rhetoricians when they discuss classical invention. Some of the topics delineated in this tradition—division, classification, and **similarity/difference**—survive in modern composition textbooks, where they are usually treated as means of arrangement rather than invention. We discuss these sophistic topics in a later chapter of this book because they can be used as means of arrangement as well as invention.

ARISTOTLE'S TOPICAL SYSTEM

The topical system delineated in Aristotle's *Rhetoric* is tightly bound to the system of logical proofs that he erected in his treatises on logic, dialectic, and poetry as well as those on rhetoric and the topics. These treatises taken together reveal in great detail his assumptions about how language can be put to work as a heuristic, a method of finding proofs to use when debating any issue. Like the sophistic topics, Aristotle's topics comply with intellectual assumptions that are far distant in time and space from our own. Thus they display the foreignness of ancient rhetorical thought more graphically than many of its other features. Nevertheless, Aristotle's topical system is still useful when updated to account for the commonplaces used in contemporary ideologies.

Aristotle probably did not invent the topics that appear in the *Rhetoric*. They had most likely been in circulation for many years among traveling sophists and teachers. His contribution was to devise a classification scheme for the topics. He divided rhetorical topics into two kinds: those that were suited to any argument at all (the *koina* or **common topics**) and those that belonged to some specific field of argument (the *eide*, or **special topics**) (*Rhetoric* I ii 21). The three common topics follow:

1. Whether a thing has (or has not) occurred or will (or will not) occur;
2. Whether a thing is greater or smaller than another thing, and
3. What is (and is not) possible.

Scholars call these common topics **past/future fact; greater/lesser,** or magnitude; and **possible/impossible.** For simplicity's sake we refer to them here as conjecture, **degree,** and **possibility.** You will note some conceptual overlap with the questions delineated in stasis theory. That is not surprising, because ancient teachers of rhetoric were eclectic; they adopted any useful teaching tactic that came to hand without being careful to distinguish sophistic traditions from each other or from Aristotelian thought. We thought it important to retain the term *conjecture* even at the risk of some confusion between systems of invention, because it best conveys the special meaning that ancient teachers conveyed when speaking about things or events perceived in the world.

According to Aristotle, the common topics belonged exclusively to rhetoric because they do not discuss any particular class of things; rather, they are useful for discussing anything whatever. Aristotle apparently developed the category of common topics in order to support his argument that rhetoric was a universal art of investigation. Some authorities on the *Rhetoric* argue that the common topics represent all the kinds of rhetorical questions that can be debated. In other words, an issue has to fall into one of these three categories in order to be available for discussion at all. Other scholars argue that the common topics help people to invent proofs for propositions drawn from the specific arts, chiefly politics and ethics, to which the universal art of rhetoric is most closely related (I ii 1356a). Whatever Aristotle intended the common topics to do, they can still prove useful to people who are looking for good arguments.

The special topics, in contrast, dealt with specific arts and sciences. Aristotle delineated a great many special topics belonging to fields of discourse such as politics, ethics, and law. The special topics of politics, for example, are "finances, war and peace, national defense, imports and exports, and the framing of laws" (*Rhetoric* I iv 7; Kennedy 1991, 53). He pointed out that rhetors need a good deal of specific knowledge to argue from special topics. One who would discuss war and peace, for example, must be able to assess the strength of his country's defenses and that of supposed enemies; must know the history of relations between the two countries; and must study the war-making capabilities of anyone "with whom there is the possibility of war" (I iv 9; Kennedy 1991, 54). We have departed from Aristotle, and from rhetorical tradition altogether, by treating Aristotle's special topics under the heading of "commonplaces."

The Topic of Past and Future Fact (Conjecture)

The English word *fact* is ordinarily used to translate the Greek term for "conjecture." However, the facts that can be uncovered by this commonplace are not irrefutable physical facts in the modern sense; rather, they are educated guesses about something that probably took place in the past or present or about something that will take place in the future. The topic of past conjecture is useful in courtrooms, where it is often necessary to speculate about whether something happened or did not happen, while the topic of future conjecture is often used in deliberative assemblies, such as state legislatures, which have the responsibility to make policy that will be binding on future generations.

Contemporary rhetors resort to the topic of conjecture in order to describe the way things are: what people are like, what the world is like, what society is like.[1] Such conjectures may include portraits of a community's history (past conjecture), as well as pictures of its future (future conjecture). Proponents of a given political position can use this topic to argue that certain features of a given society exist, while others don't. For instance, proponents of the current state of economic affairs can conjecture that even though the national economy is not as strong as it previously was, it is still functioning: the stock market has not closed and inflation has been held at bay. Critics of the current state of affairs, in contrast, can conjecture that the stock market is not the best predictor of economic health and that the level of unemployment, which is a more accurate indicator, is rising. Here are some statements to consider:

The Common Topic of Conjecture

What exists

What does not exist

The size or extent of what exists

How things used to be (past conjecture)

How things will be in the future (future conjecture)

Strange as it may seem, rhetors often disagree vigorously about what exists and how extensive it is. As we write, the fifth anniversary of the invasion of Iraq by the United States and other countries has come and gone, and the occupation of Iraq continues. This was a war that began on the basis of a conjecture. In 2002, leaders of the United States and other countries conjectured that Iraq had stockpiled weapons of mass destruction to an extent that is not acceptable under international law. Iraq's leader at the time said it had not done so, and he produced a large study to substantiate this claim. Leaders of the United States and other countries, on the other hand, conjectured that Iraq has stockpiled illegal amounts of these weapons, but they never offered proof of that claim.

Here is another example of an argument about conjecture: One of us taught a class concerning the rhetoric of political correctness. A few students in the class argued that there is no such thing as political correctness, while others argued that political correctness did indeed exist on our campus and that it exerted pressure on students to be careful not to say anything that offended identifiable groups of people. When asked to define "political correctness," members of the class settled on this definition: "Political correctness means not giving offense." We read some books about political correctness whose authors agreed that it exists but disagreed both about what it is and about its extent or seriousness. In *Illiberal Education*, Dinesh D'Souza argued that political correctness is "an unofficial ideology" that generates pressure to conform among students and faculty at American universities (1992, xv). According to John K. Wilson, however, conservatives like D'Souza use the term "to convey the image of a vast conspiracy controlling American colleges and universities" (1995, 4). When used by contemporary conservatives, according to Wilson,

> political correctness described a broad movement that had corrupted the entire system of higher education. By this transformation the conservatives accuse universities of falling under the influence of extremist elements. For conservatives, "I'm not politically correct" became a badge of honor, a defense against a feared attack—even though no one had been seriously accused of being politically incorrect. (4)

In other words, D'Souza conjectured political correctness as a powerful ideology that stifles freedom of speech on American campuses. Wilson conjectured political correctness as itself a rhetoric mounted by conservatives in order to brand universities as hotbeds of coercive liberal or leftist thought. Both of these conjectures take the issue of political correctness far more seriously than did the students who conjectured it to be a matter of etiquette—a way of speaking that doesn't give offense.

From a rhetorician's point of view, nothing is to be gained by trying to determine which of these conjectures about political correctness is true. Persons who accept either of them believe they are true because each stems from and affirms a worldview—an ideology. What is important for rhetors is (a) to understand the commonplaces deployed in each of these conjectures and how they are implicated in ideological positions, and (b) to determine the actual or potential effects of each conjecture in order to decide which causes the least public harm.

Here is another example of the way conjecture works in contemporary American discourse. Stephanie Coontz, who teaches courses about the history of the family, asks her students to write down images of "the traditional family." In her book *The Way We Never Were*, Coontz lists some of those images:

> One is of extended families in which all members worked together; grandparents were an integral part of family life, children learned responsibility and the work ethic from their elders, and there were clear lines of authority based on respect for age. Another is of nuclear families in which nurturing mothers sheltered children from premature exposure to sex, financial worries, or other adult concerns, while fathers taught adolescents not to sacrifice their education by going to work too early. Still another image gives pride of place to the couple relationship. In traditional families, my students write—half derisively, half wistfully—men and women remained chaste until marriage, at which time they extricated themselves from competing obligations to kin and neighbors and committed themselves wholly to the marital relationship, experiencing an all-encompassing intimacy that our more crowded modern life seems to preclude. (1992, 8)

Needless to say, all of these images are conjectures that are associated with the commonplace of "traditional family values." Coontz argues in her book that the rhetorical conjecture of the traditional family had practical, real-life downsides for both men and women, downsides that never appeared on *Leave It to Beaver* and *The Donna Reed Show:*

> All women, even seemingly docile ones, were deeply mistrusted. They were frequently denied the right to serve on juries, convey property, make contracts, take out credit cards in their own name, or establish residence. A 1954 article in *Esquire* called working wives a "menace"; a *Life* author termed married women's employment a "disease." Women were excluded from several professions, and some states even gave husbands total control over family finances. There were not any permissible alternatives to baking brownies, experimenting with new canned soups, and getting rid of stains around the collar.

Men were also pressured into acceptable family roles, since lack of a suitable wife could mean the loss of a job or promotion for a middle-class man. Bachelors were categorized as "immature," "infantile," "narcissistic," "deviant," or even "pathological." Family advice expert Paul Landis argued: "Except for the sick, the badly crippled, the deformed, the emotionally warped and the mentally defective, almost everyone has an opportunity (and, by clear implication, a duty) to marry."(32–33)

Coontz's argument is itself a mixture of conjectures and the extrinsic proofs called "testimony." For rhetoricians, it is worth asking what rhetorical, and actual, practical effects would have occurred if Coontz's conjecture about family life in the 1950s had been portrayed in media of the period more frequently than it was. In movies such as *Mona Lisa Smile* (2003), *Far From Heaven* (2002), and *Revolutionary Road* (2008), directors and producers have portrayed the American family of the 1950s as Coontz conjectures it to have been. This suggests, perhaps, that sufficient time has passed so that the commonplace conjectures about traditional American family life associated with Beaver Cleaver have become available for argument.

The Common Topic of Greater/Lesser (Degree)

Aristotle anchored his discussion of the topic of greater and lesser in his notion of the golden mean. We know that which is great, he wrote, when it is compared to the normal; likewise for that which is small (*Rhetoric* I vii 1363b). "Greater" and "smaller" are always relative to each other: greatness can be measured by the fact that it exceeds something else, while smallness is always exceeded by something else. The relation of these terms is easy enough to illustrate with examples from the physical world: if the average person is about five feet eight inches tall, then the average basketball player will be taller since this class of people is marked to some extent by the requisite of tallness. But more difficult, and more interesting, applications of the topic occur when we move to the realm of values. To call someone "a great leader" implies a norm against which greatness is measured—the average leader. The implied existence of such a norm also opens the possibility that lesser leaders exist.

Ancient Athenian citizens apparently agreed on a list of common public values. At any rate, ancient rhetoric texts regularly list goodness, justice, honor, and expediency as important values. While these terms obviously do not mean the same thing to us as they meant to ancient rhetors and teachers, we can still use them to name values that are commonly cited in our own public discourse. Certainly, contemporary rhetors often try to establish that their position is good, just, honorable, or expedient. These values can be phrased in terms of their opposites as well—what is bad, unjust, dishonorable, or inexpedient. The common topic of degree, which Aristotle called "greater and less" can be used, then, to establish the relations between degrees of goodness, justice, and so on. Rhetors can argue that some state of affairs is better, more just, more honorable, or more expedient than another, or less so. Using the topic of degree, they can also argue that changes in these values have occurred over time: some state of affairs is less good than it used to be, or will deteriorate in the future.

To return to an economic example we used in discussing conjecture: using the topic of degree, all parties in a discussion may agree that the present economic situation is not good compared to that of the recent past; however, they may disagree about whether or not this is relatively a good, just, honorable or expedient state of affairs. For example, a proponent of the current state of affairs, on one hand, can argue that economic decline is better than recession, since most people are still employed and can feed and clothe their families, thus stimulating the economy by spending. A critic of the current state of affairs, on the other hand, can use the same topic to argue that the relative good of gradual economic decline is offset by the fact that the very rich profit far more in periods of decline than do the poor and middle classes.

As this example demonstrates, the topic of greater/less can be applied generally or selectively: a rhetor can argue that what is good for one segment of the community is good for all, or she can argue that what is good for one group isn't necessarily good for everyone or isn't good for other groups in the community.

The Common Topic of Degree

What is greater than the mean or norm

What is lesser than the mean or norm

What is relatively greater than something else

What is relatively lesser than something else

What is good, just, beautiful, honorable, enjoyable, etc.

What is better, more just, etc.

What is less good, less just, etc.

What is good, etc., for all persons

What is good, etc., for a few persons or groups

What has been better, etc., in the past

What will be better, etc., in the future

The topic of degree obviously lends itself to questions of value. Let us return, then, to the issue of abortion in order to illustrate its argumentative possibilities. The analysis that follows touches on only a few of the many arguments opened by this rich topic.

Using degree, rhetors who oppose the legal status of abortion can argue that more abortions are performed when the practice is legal (that is, the number of abortions is greater under the current circumstances); a rhetor who supports the status quo can argue, though, that there are fewer unsafe abortions performed when the operation is legal. But greater and lesser are not only relative to each other; there are relative degrees of magnitude and minuteness. So, the first rhetor could rejoin that if abortions were illegal, fewer abortions would be performed overall; this decrease in turn would reduce the relative number of unsafe abortions.

Tying the topic of degree to values, an opponent of abortion can argue that legal abortion is not a good thing; nor is it just, or enjoyable, or beautiful. Furthermore, relative to other means of birth control, abortion is less good. His opponent can argue, on the other hand, that abortion is better than bringing unwanted children into the world; that justice means extending the same rights to women that are extended to men (on the ground that men's reproductive practices are not legislated by the state); that while abortion is of course neither enjoyable nor beautiful, it is sometimes the only available practical alternative.

An opponent of abortion can argue that while abortion may be good for individual women, it is obviously not good for the fetus; less obviously, it is not good for members of an immediate family or for society at large; a rhetor who supports abortion rights can argue that the availability of the practice is nonetheless better for women, who currently constitute a majority of the population. A rhetor who is opposed to abortion can argue that things were better (and more just and more honorable) in the past when abortion was not legal and women were forced either to bear every pregnancy to term or to undergo an illegal abortion. A rhetor who supports abortion rights, in contrast, can argue that things were worse in the past when alternative means of birth control were not available and women were forced either to bear every pregnancy to term or to seek out some back-alley practitioner. Finally, a rhetor who opposes abortion can argue that legal abortion is not good for future generations, who will lack the proper respect for human life if abortion becomes a routine option. A rhetor who supports abortion rights can argue that the future will be better if unwanted and uncared-for children are never brought into that world.

Our balanced list of value arguments about abortion may give the impression that we are indecisive or heartless (see Chapter 6, on ethos). We are not indecisive about this issue, and we are not insensitive to the emotional costs of abortion for all concerned parties. If we were actually arguing the issue of abortion for an audience, we would never present all of the arguments produced by the topic of degree. We would not even present all of the arguments in favor of our own positions (see Chapter 10, on arrangement). Here, however, for purposes of demonstration we have used the topic of degree as a heuristic in order to discover the wide range of arguments that are available on this or almost any issue. Our analysis also demonstrates that if rhetors examine all available arguments raised by the topics, they will come across arguments that follow from their position which may be distasteful to them. In other words, rhetors who use the topics vigorously and thoroughly must be prepared to turn up arguments that they do not like. Warning: thorough examination of an issue has been known to cause rhetors to change their minds.

The Common Topic of Possible/Impossible (Possibility)

Rhetors resort to the topic of possible/impossible in order to establish that change either is or isn't possible, now or in the future. For example, proponents of the current economic state of affairs might use this topic to argue that it is impossible for inflation to occur during a period of gradual economic decline. Critics can argue the opposite position, that it is possible for inflation to occur at such times. Rhetors using this topic can argue that it is impossible for the economy to become unstable today, but it might become so in six months or a year. A critic, though, can argue that it is entirely possible that current economic strategies will bring about instability in the marketplace. Strange as it may seem, rhetors can also argue about past possibilities; anthropologists do this when they argue about whether it was possible for some hypothetical set of events to have occurred in the past: Was it possible for *homo sapiens* to have developed a larger brain without an opposable thumb? Without an upright posture? Writers of popular nonfiction are especially fond of the commonplace of the past possible: Is it possible that an extraterrestrial vehicle crashed in the desert around Roswell, New Mexico, in 1947? Is it possible that President John F. Kennedy was killed not by a lone assassin but by a band of conspirators? Use of this topic also admits degrees of possibility or impossibility. While it may not be possible to stabilize economic prosperity for all groups, it may be more (or less) likely that this can be done in the future.

The Common Topic of Possibility

> What is possible
>
> What is impossible
>
> What is more or less possible
>
> What is possible in the future
>
> What is impossible in the future
>
> What was possible or impossible in the past

There are, no doubt, other ways to pose questions under the topic of possibility, but these should suffice to get you started.

We return to the issue of hateful speech to illustrate the uses of this rich topic. Is it possible that hateful speech occurs on our campus? A rhetor who opposes the implementation of a speech code could argue that it is impossible that students at Our State University would be tactless or insensitive enough to use language that offends people. An opponent could argue that, given the strain of student life, it is possible that ordinarily tactful and sensitive people could, on occasion, utter an offensive remark unless they were aware that the possibility exists that they could be punished for saying offensive things. Or, noting the existence of some group that is known for its opposition to another group, she could argue that it is quite possible that members of the first group could utter offensive remarks. Or, noting the currency of racism or sexism in our culture, she could argue that it is quite possible that hateful speech would be used on some occasion. Rhetors who oppose implementation of a speech code could argue that it is possible that such a code will stifle free speech. Arguing from relative possibilities, those who support a code could argue, alternatively, that its implementation increases the possibility that those who might otherwise utter offensive remarks will keep these to themselves.

The topic of possibility is also used regularly in discussions of abortion. Proponents of choice argue that it is not possible to stop women from having abortions by means of legislation against it. Opponents argue that it is possible to stop women from having abortions, and they seek to do so either by passing laws against it or by bringing the moral authority of the community to bear.

COMMONPLACES AND IDEOLOGY

Contemporary rhetoricians have a way of speaking about the *sensus communis,* or the common sense that is shared among members of a community: they call it **ideology.** As we suggested in the first chapter of this book, ideologies are bodies of beliefs, doctrines, familiar ways of thinking that are characteristic of a group or a culture. They can be economic, ethical, political, philosophical, or religious. When we call someone a capitalist or a socialist, we assume that she subscribes to a set of coherent beliefs about the best way to structure an economy. If we say that someone is a Christian, Muslim, or Jew, we imply that she holds a recognizable set of religious values. If we describe someone as a conservative or as a liberal, we imply that her political practices are guided by a distinct set of beliefs about human nature. If we refer to someone as a feminist or an environmentalist, we imply that his ethical, economic, social, and political practices are governed by a coherent philosophical position. Capitalism and socialism; Christianity, Islam and Judaism; conservatism and liberalism; feminism; and environmentalism are examples of ideologies.

As the preceding examples illustrate, some ideologies are more sweeping than others, some are highly respected in given cultures, and some are older or more powerful than others. In rhetoric, the power of an ideology is measured by the degree to which it influences the beliefs and actions of relatively large groups of relatively powerful people. Ideologies that are subscribed to by large groups of people are called "dominant" or "hegemonic" (from Greek *hegemoon,* "prince" or "guide"). Ideologies subscribed to by small or marginalized groups are called "subordinate" or "minority." The relations between dominant and subordinate ideologies are complex and they change over time. Forty years ago, for example, environmentalism influenced the discourse and practice of only a few people; it was a distinctly subordinate or minority discourse in America. In the process of gaining wider support, environmentalism has challenged the hegemony of other, far more powerful discourses—chiefly those of individualism and capitalism. It has not yet succeeded in becoming a dominant ideology, precisely because it calls into question hegemonic discourses that are central to American thought. Environmentalism has not had much impact on the discourse of individualism, for example, as is attested by the resistance Americans have shown to buying smaller, less-polluting vehicles and to cutting back on the amount of driving they do.

Even more confusing, several ideologies can be referred to by a single term: there are varieties of Judaism, Christianity, and Islam, just as there are different kinds of feminism and environmentalism. All are subscribed to with varying degrees of faithfulness by people who are influenced by them. Some ideologies are so pervasive or have been in place for so long that the people who subscribe to them seldom actually articulate the beliefs that constitute them. *To articulate* can mean both "to speak" and "to connect to nearby things or concepts," and we hope that our readers will keep both meanings in mind when we use this word. As a general rule, the need to articulate deeply held ideological beliefs comes about only when some new ideological construct challenges an older one. Such is the case currently with vegetarianism, which has recently challenged the centrality of meat eating within American dietary beliefs and practices.

Ideologies can be held by a small group or an entire culture. No doubt the ideology held by each person results from life experiences and education. But even though ideologies grow out of experience, none is unique, because experiences, and our memories of them, are influenced by prevailing cultural attitudes about ethnicity, gender, class, appearance, and occupation, among a host of other things.

Commonplaces that make up an ideology sometimes contradict one another. Some thinkers about ideology argue that its function is precisely to smooth over contradictions in our lives. How can Americans be persuaded to go to war, for example, where the probability is high that the lives of loved ones will be put in danger? A skilled rhetor who urges our going to war can deploy commonplaces drawn from American patriotism to downplay fears of injury or death and to cause people to forget about the horrors of war.

Groups often coalesce around ideologies, such as environmentalism (Greenpeace, the Sierra Club) or fascism (American Nazi Party, skinheads). Groups also coalesce around specific issues: members of Operation Rescue are united by their opposition to abortion; members of NOW (the National Organization for Women) are united by their desire to enact legislation that will secure equality for women. Members of each of these groups may or may not share the same ideologies, however. Some members of Operation Rescue, for example, appear to oppose abortion on religious grounds, while others oppose it for moral or political or social reasons. Members of NOW may subscribe to a variety of feminisms—liberal, radical, cultural, materialist, third-wave, postmodern—and it is conceivable that a member of NOW may not be a feminist at all.

Some rhetoricians think that entire cultures may subscribe to a common ideology. E. D. Hirsch, for example, claims that there is a perceptible

American ideology that centers on values embedded in the Declaration of Independence and the Constitution of the United States. Hirsch describes America's "civil religion," as he calls it, as follows:

> Our civil ethos treasures patriotism and loyalty as high, though perhaps not ultimate, ideals and fosters the belief that the conduct of the nation is guided by a vaguely defined God. Our tradition places importance on carrying out the rites and ceremonies of our civil ethos and religion through the national flag, the national holidays, and the national anthem (which means "national hymn"), and supports the morality of tolerance and benevolence, of the Golden Rule, and communal cooperation. We believe in altruism and self-help, in equality, freedom, truth telling, and respect for the national law. Besides these vague principles, American culture fosters such myths about itself as its practicality, ingenuity, inventiveness, and independent-mindedness, its connection with the frontier, and its beneficence in the world (even when its leaders do not always follow beneficent policies). It acknowledges that Americans have the right to disagree with the traditional values but nonetheless acquiesce in the dominant civil ethos to the point of accepting imprisonment as the ultimate means of expressing dissent. (1987, 98–99)

Has Hirsch captured Americans' commonplace sense of what it means to be an American? Remember that commonplaces are not necessarily true—the distinguishing mark of a commonplace, rather, is that it is widely believed. Remember too that the commonplaces that make up an ideology sometimes contradict one another.

Take the value called "patriotism," for example. During the Vietnam war, those who opposed the United States' participation in that war were widely castigated as unpatriotic. A popular slogan, "America: love it or leave it," suggested that anyone who did not support the war did not support America and hence was not wanted in the country. Those who opposed the war, however, thought of themselves precisely as patriots—as people who loved their country and showed as much by dissenting from its foreign policy (an act that is quintessentially American, according to Hirsch). Some opponents of the war actually went to prison in order to express their dissent. The boxer Muhammad Ali, who was then called Cassius Clay, is probably the most famous person who was imprisoned for refusing to serve in the war. But thousands of other men were also incarcerated for burning their draft cards or otherwise refusing to be inducted into military service.

For rhetoricians, the point of this example is that while Americans may disagree about what counts as a patriotic act, the value of patriotism—love of country—circulates in American discourse with such power that it affects lives and actions. Disagreements about what patriotism is or about the specific acts that can be classified as patriotic (voting? serving in the military? speaking well of friends and ill of perceived enemies?) are arguments; that is, they can be subjected to invention (conjecture and definition in these examples), and rhetors can work toward achieving agreement about them. Patriotism itself, in contrast, has a second important status in rhetoric if it is a fundamental tenet of American ideology—that is, if it is a commonplace in that ideology.

During the 1960s, conjectures about patriotism became available for argument; that is, there was sufficient disagreement about what constitutes patriotism that fierce discussion and even violence erupted over its meaning. That people were willing to do verbal and physical battle over this value suggests that its status as a commonplace was then in jeopardy. People do not generally make arguments about values that are so fundamental to their belief systems that they literally "go without saying" or can be "taken for granted." Both phrases in quotes are shorthand ways of describing an interesting feature of commonplaces, which are so basic to a mode of thought and behavior that people who subscribe to them may remain unaware of their allegiance to them. Commonplaces are, literally, "taken for granted"—they are statements that everyone assumes already to be satisfactorily proven. So no one bothers to discuss them. Immediately after the events of September 11, 2001, patriotism briefly returned to its status as a commonplace that virtually "goes without saying," and although the intensity of the feeling has since diminished, its manifestation was so powerful for a time that some 90 percent of the American people supported a war of retaliation on the suspected perpetrators. Counterarguments were difficult to find, and audiences for them were scarcer yet.

Here is another list of American commonplaces, written this time by Howard Zinn, whose politics are to the left of Hirsch's:

> We grow up in a society where our choice of ideas is limited and where certain ideas dominate: We hear them from our parents, in the schools, in the churches, in the newspapers, and on radio and television. They have been in the air ever since we learned to walk and talk. They constitute an American *ideology*—that is, a dominant pattern of ideas. Most people accept them, and if we do, too, we are less likely to get into trouble.
>
> The dominance of these ideas is not the product of a conspiratorial group that has devilishly plotted to implant on society a particular point of view. Nor is it an accident, an innocent result of people thinking freely. There is a process of natural (or, rather *unnatural*) selection, in which certain orthodox ideas are encouraged, financed, and pushed forward by the most powerful mechanisms of our culture. These ideas are preferred because they are safe; they don't threaten established wealth or power.
>
> For instance:
>
> "Be realistic; this is the way things *are*; there's no point thinking about how things *should be*."
>
> "People who teach or write or report the news should be *objective*; they should not try to advance their own opinions."
>
> "There are unjust wars, but also just wars."
>
> "If you disobey the law, even for a good cause, you should accept your punishment."
>
> "If you work hard enough, you'll make a good living. If you are poor, you have only yourself to blame."
>
> "Freedom of speech is desirable, but not when it threatens national security."

"Racial equality is desirable, but we've gone far enough in that direction."

"Our constitution is our greatest guarantee of liberty and justice."

"The United States must intervene from time to time in various parts of the world with military power to stop communism and promote democracy."

"If you want to get things changed, the only way is to go through the proper channels."

"We need nuclear weapons to prevent war."

"There is much injustice in the world but there is nothing that ordinary people, without wealth or power, can do about it."

These ideas are not accepted by all Americans. But they are believed widely enough and strongly enough to dominate our thinking. (1990, 3–4)

Zinn's list shows that commonplaces do change. For instance, commonplaces about the threat of communism now are not so powerful nor so widespread as they were prior to the collapse of Soviet Communism, and the threat of nuclear war does not now seem so menacing as it once did. However, versions of these commonplaces still circulate, although the threat named in them is different: today we fear terrorism rather than communism, and global warming rather than nuclear winter. In other words, the commonplaces Zinn lists have enjoyed currency within American discourse in the past, and versions of most of them are still in circulation.

Even though Hirsch and Zinn do not agree precisely about what beliefs constitute an American ideology, they do agree that it exists. Whether we can list its contents precisely or not, everyone who lives in America is affected by its ideology, since its values are embedded in our public discourse. Our coinage says "From many, one" and "In God we trust"; our elementary schoolbooks tell us that "all men are created equal"; our national anthem tells us that America is "the land of the free and the home of the brave." Action movies tell us that life's problems can be solved by violence—the more spectacular the better. Whether we believe these commonplaces or not, they provide the terms within which American discourse works. Rhetors cannot escape the commonplaces of American public discourse, and they overlook them at their peril.

An understanding of ideology, of the common sense of a group or a whole culture, is important to rhetors because people do not respond to a rhetorical proposition out of context. Their responses are determined by the ideologies to which they subscribe. People use commonplaces to express ideological positions. Contemporary commonplaces range from well-worn slogans ("tax and spend," "family values," "When guns are outlawed only criminals will have guns") to sophisticated texts that encapsulate key beliefs of a given ideology (the platform of a political party, a bible, a constitution). The persuasive power of rhetorical commonplaces depends upon the fact that they express assumptions held in common by people who subscribe to a given ideology. For example: a first principle of environmental philosophy is preservation of the earth's ecosystem. Within the environmentalist community, people have developed commonplaces that express this principle: "Earth first"; "Good planets are hard to find." These slogans represent the received wisdom of the environmental community in a shorthand that reminds its members of their shared beliefs. They can be deployed whenever the group needs to be energized or reminded of its ideological commitments or when its members wish to persuade others to adopt their ideology.

Rhetorical commonplaces have heuristic potential as well, since they give rise to an inexhaustible supply of proofs. They can be used as major premises for arguments (see our discussion of enthymemes in Chapter 5, on reasoning), and like all rhetorical proofs, they can also be used to persuade others to join the community and to accept its commitments. For instance, the appeal to family values is a well-worn commonplace. Even though it was initially put into circulation by conservatives, it has since been adopted by people who subscribe to other political ideologies. A first principle of contemporary American conservativism is that morality is best transmitted across generations when people live in a nuclear family headed by two parents in which moral authority rests with the father. Hence a conservative rhetor is likely to argue that Americans could solve problems as diverse as high rates of teenage pregnancy, drug abuse, or inadequate public schools if only we would return to traditional family values. The commonplace of family values is a shorthand way for conservatives to express their dismay that most Americans no longer live in nuclear families; its use also strengthens their sense of community. Like all commonplaces, however, the appeal to family values is very general—which explains why it has so easily been appropriated by liberals. Nor is it necessarily a good causal explanation for issues such as dilapidated schools and drug abuse, issues which may or may not be caused by a perceived decline in so-called family values. Nevertheless, this commonplace was so pervasive for awhile it even appeared on a bumper sticker: "Hatred is not a family value."

Like most commonplaces, the commonplace of family values also has heuristic potential. Using it, a rhetor can think through his position on almost any political issue, from AIDS research (Does AIDS threaten families?) to abortion (Is this practice antifamily?) to defense systems (How much and what kind of defense is required to keep American families safe?).

The power of ideology and commonplaces stems from the fact that they reside in the very language we speak and the symbols we rely on. For that reason many of our ideological values are hidden from our conscious awareness, just as Quintilian said they were. Take, for example, the response of the American people to the first President Bush's declaration of war against Iraq in 1991. People who remembered the country's negative reaction to the Vietnam war predicted that Americans would not support another interventionist war. But President Bush's rhetoricians succeeded in associating the war with American values by arguing that it would restore democracy and freedom to the Kuwaiti people. They invoked powerful symbols of American patriotism—the flag and yellow ribbons—and suggested that anyone who did not support the war did not support American soldiers. This strategy, focusing on traditional American values and symbols, diverted attention away from the hard facts of war itself—death and destruction, hunger and privation. For a time, the president's popularity soared, thanks to his rhetoricians' skillful use of commonplace symbols drawn from the rhetoric of American patriotism. The second President Bush's war with Iraq did not succeed in winning widespread support because, according to dissenters, the reasons for it were never clearly articulated. There had been no aggressive action by Iraq such as the invasion of Kuwait in the 1990s. In his struggle to gain support for the war, Bush made repeated appeals to patriotism and its connected values of freedom and democracy.

COMMONPLACES IN AMERICAN POLITICAL RHETORIC

As we have pointed out, Aristotle gave the name *special topics* to places drawn from specific fields of discourse, such as politics, ethics, and law. However, we are using the term *commonplace* to refer to such field-dependent topics. As a way of illustrating the importance of commonplaces to rhetorical invention, we have worked out an analysis of the commonplaces typically used in contemporary American political rhetoric. We chose politics rather than ethics or law because political commonplaces are in somewhat wider circulation today than are commonplaces used in other fields.

Conventionally, political ideologies may be distinguished from one another if they are placed along an imaginary line or spectrum.

An American Political Spectrum

Left	Center	Right

Political theorists decide whether to place a given position on the left or right side of this spectrum depending on its adherents' views about a number of issues. Political positions such as socialism, democratic socialism, some versions of communism (Castroism, for example), and liberalism are conventionally placed on the left wing of the ideological spectrum. We list these positions in order of their decreasing leftward leaning: socialism is farthest left, while liberalism is only slightly left of center (from our point of view, anyhow—we are conjecturing, remember). On the right wing of the spectrum are fascism, American neoconservatism (the "new right"), and old or traditional conservatism. We list these ideologies in order of their decreasing rightward leaning: traditional conservatism is just right of center on the political spectrum, while fascism is farthest right.

An American Political Spectrum

Left	Center	Right

[*socialism—democratic socialism—liberalism   conservatism—neoconservatism—fascism*]

Of course the range of political possibilities is much more complex than we have suggested here. American neoconservatism at present has at least two manifestations, called the "new right" and the "religious right." Many more positions on the spectrum are represented in the world than appear in America; Italy, for example, has over one hundred political parties, each representing a slightly different position on the spectrum.

In current American rhetoric there is debate about the following issues, stated very generally.[2]

1. What is the appropriate foreign policy (nationalism, internationalism, interventionism, pacifism)?

2. What is the role of the federal government in legislation, as opposed to the roles of state and local governments?

3. What level of fiscal responsibility do citizens bear toward federal, state, and local government?

4. What social and economic relations are appropriate among citizens (more or less personal freedom: more or less economic equality among classes, races, and genders)?

5. What levels of political and legal equality should exist among genders, races, classes, sexualities (none, some, full equality)?

6. What is the appropriate relation to authority (acceptance, questioning, skepticism, rejection)?

7. What is the appropriate role for government to play in legislating moral issues (none, some, a lot)?

8. What is or should be the relation of human beings and governments to the environment?

The answers given to these questions by individuals or groups give clues about the ideologies to which they subscribe, although these clues are not infallible.

Two ideologies have in the recent past dominated contemporary American political discourse: liberalism and conservatism. There are fascists, anarchists, libertarians, social democrats, and socialists in America, but their views are generally not sufficiently widespread within mainstream American discourse to generate national commonplaces. In what follows, we attempt to describe commonplaces that are generally accepted by persons who subscribe to liberalism or conservatism. This task has become increasingly difficult, however. In the early years of the twenty-first century, the U.S. House of Representatives and the Senate were nearly evenly balanced between Republicans and Democrats. But the commonplace assumption that Republicans are conservative and Democrats are liberal has become much more difficult to maintain. In the last years of the twentieth century, mainstream Democrats moved to the center of the political ideological spectrum, adopting some conservative positions—particularly with regard to economic issues—while many Republicans moved further toward the right. In fact, it seems to us that nowadays fewer and fewer Americans identify themselves as liberals. To the extent that this assessment is correct, it testifies to the success of conservative attacks on "the L-word," as well as the ability of conservative rhetoricians to persuade Americans to accept their arguments about the rightness of conservative thought. Hence a more accurate depiction of the contemporary political spectrum might name two poles in commonplace American political thought as "conservative" and "not conservative." This assessment must immediately be complicated by the observation that conservatives profess many beliefs that are products of liberal thought. This is so because the founding documents of the United States were written by people who wove liberal beliefs into them. Historically, the belief that all men are created equal is a liberal notion, although many Americans who think of themselves as conservative can, and do, hold this belief as a commonplace.

One more qualification: the lists that follow are not meant to imply that all persons calling themselves "liberal" or "conservative" subscribe to every commonplace named in those categories. Nor are they meant to imply that someone who subscribes to one or more liberal or conservative commonplace is perforce a liberal or a conservative. In short, *conservative* and *liberal* do not refer to identities; rather they depict positions on an ideological spectrum. That is to say, what follows is a series of conjectures about contemporary American political discourse.

Contemporary American liberalism tends to support capitalism, but people who subscribe to liberal politics usually feel more secure if business can be regulated by government. Sometimes people who accept liberalism will support policies that lean toward socialism—for instance, some argue that there should be tax-supported health care for all citizens who cannot afford it. Liberalism tends to be internationalist insofar as its supporters want to maintain good relations with other countries. Those who subscribe to liberalism may, in fact, oppose war of any kind—that is, they may be pacifists. The core of American liberalism, however, is support for a high degree of individual freedom and advocacy of social and economic equality for all. Liberalism promotes a positive view of human nature; its proponents believe that human beings are naturally good or at least tend toward good action. If people do not behave well, the liberal assumption is that there is or has been some impediment or lack in their lives and surroundings that have kept them from fulfilling their potential. Liberalism tends to be skeptical of authority (this is in keeping with the high value that it places on individuality). Those who accept liberalism usually advocate government intervention in social and economic issues to correct what they perceive as unfair distribution of wealth, but they generally resist intervention by any authority into moral choices. They tend to characterize moral choices as "private" matters, in keeping with their emphasis on individual freedom and their skepticism about authority.

People who accept the tenets of contemporary American conservatism part company with liberalism on most of these issues. Support of capitalism and business are important conservative values. Conservatism tends to be nationalist insofar as its adherents want the United States to be the most important nation in the world, and people who accept conservatism will support military intervention in the affairs of other nations in order to further the goal of U.S. supremacy. People who subscribe to conservative commonplaces support personal freedom, but they care less about individual rights than liberals do, since they think that the greater good of the group is more important than individual desire. This is in keeping with conservative respect for tradition and authority, especially that of the family and of religion. Conservatism is skeptical about the perfectibility of human nature—its adherents generally do not assume that everyone is naturally good or capable of moral improvement. Nonetheless, a central tenet of conservatism is that people must take responsibility for their actions. Conservatism also assumes that people who do not take such responsibility must accept the community's decisions regarding their actions. People who subscribe to traditional conservatism do not care for government intervention in social or economic matters, arguing instead that free enterprise will take care of poverty and social inequality. At present, however, people who subscribe to the ideology called "neoconservatism" do advocate government intervention in moral matters on occasion.

The positions we ascribe to conservatives and liberals are commonplaces within those discourses. Thus, in conservative rhetoric, appeal to traditional family values is a commonplace, while appeal to personal freedom for individuals—now usually cast in the discourse of "individual rights"—is a commonplace in liberal rhetoric. For heuristic purposes, we now explore how people who accept liberal and conservative commonplaces, respectively, would answer the questions named earlier as major issues in American rhetoric. Remember that we are operating on the level of the commonplace. The positions we delineate are positions that follow ideologically from liberal and conservative rhetoric. That is to say, we are working out their ideologic (for more on ideologic, see the later section of this chapter). Since commonplaces do change, sometimes relatively rapidly, our conclusions may not apply at all times and in all places to people who identify themselves as liberals or conservatives.

1. *What is the appropriate foreign policy?* Generally, liberalism favors peaceful interaction with other countries. Liberals ordinarily support the United Nations and other global political organizations. Conservatism is not so inclined to favor global diplomacy and intervention, especially if these efforts are perceived to interfere with America's political preeminence in the world. Liberalism is not inclined to support military intervention into the affairs of other countries, while conservatism will support military intervention into foreign affairs if such intervention can be characterized as necessary to the preservation of America's position as a world leader. There are exceptions, of course, as there are to any commonplace. Liberals in the Kennedy and Johnson administrations maintained and escalated the Vietnam war, for instance.

2. *What is the role of the federal government in legislation as opposed to the roles of state and local governments?* Currently, people who describe themselves as conservative say they are opposed to "big government," and during the last years of the twentieth century conservatives in the United States Congress supported legislation that passed fiscal responsibility for social programs such as welfare onto state and local governments. Conservative rhetoric typically depicts liberals as favoring federal intervention into many aspects of cultural and social life. Conservative rhetors have argued, for instance, that liberals saddled Americans with restrictions on their right to personal freedom when they imposed affirmative action and environmental regulation. Conservative rhetors would prefer that individuals and corporations undertake such initiatives as are necessary to protect the environment and to advance those who cannot advance by themselves; conservatism assumes that market pressures will urge individuals and corporations to see to it that these things happen. Liberalism, in contrast, typically supports legislation that is intended to correct what its adherents perceive as social wrongs. Social Security, civil rights legislation, affirmative action, Medicare, and Medicaid were all sponsored by liberals.

3. *What level of fiscal responsibility do citizens bear toward federal, state, and local government?* Currently, rhetors who subscribe to conservatism argue that the tax burden borne by citizens should be lessened, while rhetors who accept liberal beliefs argue that certain initiatives are so important to social and economic progress that taxpayers must continue to shoulder the burden of financing them (hence the conservative commonplace used to describe liberal administrations: "tax and spend"). Rhetors who accept liberalism generally argue that these social initiatives should include at least Social Security and Medicare.

4. *What social and economic relations are appropriate among citizens?* The rhetoric of liberalism champions social and economic equality. In fact, the American doctrine that "all men are created equal" is borrowed from eighteenth-century liberal thought. Given its distrust in the perfectability of human nature, conservatism is not sure that all people are created equal to one another in intelligence and ability. However, contemporary conservatism does defend the fundamental American principle that all citizens are equal before the law.

5. *What levels of political and legal equality should exist among genders, races, classes, sexualities?* In keeping with their faith in equality, those who accept liberalism profess that all citizens—no matter their gender, race, class, sexuality, ability, or age—should be treated equally, at least in law. For those who accept conservatism—and especially for those who respect tradition and authority—equality among genders, races, and sexualities is a more complicated and troublesome issue. Strict adherence to traditional beliefs requires an American conservative to assume that men best fulfill their social and moral duties, if not their nature, when they take care of and protect women. Traditional conservatism assumes further that heterosexuality is a norm. Hence people who

accept this position are not sure that full legal equality should apply to women or to homosexuals.

6. *What is the citizen's appropriate relation to authority?* In keeping with their respect for instituted authority and their emphasis on personal responsibility, conservative rhetors tend to take tough stands on crime and punishment and on enforcement of the law. In keeping with their respect for individual rights and the potential perfectibility of human nature, liberal rhetors, in contrast, tend to advocate prevention and rehabilitation rather than punishment for offenders. It makes ideological sense that people who subscribe to liberalism would be more skeptical of received religious wisdom or traditional notions about family structure than are those who subscribe to conservative positions.

7. *What is the appropriate role for government to play in legislating moral issues?* People who subscribe to liberalism tend to resist government intervention into realms that they define as "private." This is why liberal rhetors generally support abortion rights and why many persons of liberal persuasion think that the use of marijuana and perhaps other proscribed drugs should be legalized. These days conservative rhetors, if they share conservatism's elevation of the good of the community over individual rights, tend to support legislative intervention into realms that liberals define as "private." Hence, they are generally opposed to the legalization of drugs and abortion on the ground that drug use and abortion negatively affect the community at large even though they may benefit specific individuals. Liberal rhetors tend to argue against censorship on the ground that censorship is a restriction of the right to free speech. Conservative rhetors tend to support censorship on the ground that the circulation of some materials—pornography, for example—is deleterious to the public good. It is not always easy to predict liberal and conservative positions on moral issues, however. For instance, some liberal feminists support restriction of the distribution of pornography on the ground that pornography is injurious to women. This position conflicts with the liberal belief that everyone—even a pornographer—has a right to free speech. Another contradiction can be found in conservative and liberal responses to no-smoking or gun-control legislation. Despite their support for the right of freedom of assembly and the personal freedom to indulge habits of choice, liberal rhetors tend to support restrictions on smoking in public areas and on the sale of some types of weapons because they perceive these as serving the public good. Conservative rhetors, on the other hand, tend to oppose such measures on the ground that people who object to smoke in public areas should take responsibility for dealing with this situation without asking government to interfere. Conservatives' objection to gun control is usually based on a loose interpretation of the Second Amendment, which concerns citizens' right to bear arms.

8. *What is or should be the relation of human beings and governments to the environment?* It is hard to delineate conservative and liberal positions on environmental issues. The term *conservation* is etymologically related to the term *conservative*, which suggests that the desire to conserve or preserve

natural phenomena is or should be a conservative position. Protection of the common good is also a conservative goal, and preservation of the environment would seem to serve that goal as well. However, in today's political economy, environmentalists tend to be liberal or left-of-liberal. Conservative disinterest in this issue may have to do with conservatism's general support of business, which often finds itself at odds with environmental protection. Liberal rhetors, however, have traditionally favored legislative intervention to correct what they perceive to be wrongs, and so it is they who have typically proposed environmental regulations. However, support for environmentalism can place liberals in difficult rhetorical positions, since environmentalists would like to limit the use of automobiles (thus restricting the individual right to freedom of movement) and place limits on human reproduction (thus restricting the freedom of individuals to have as many children as they wish).

USING COMMON TOPICS AND COMMONPLACES TO INVENT ARGUMENTS

As we suggested earlier, ideologies vary and change over time because people are differently located in terms of gender, age, ethnicity, class, economic situation, religious beliefs, education, and the political or cultural power they possess. A rhetor who uses the common topics should take careful account of whether or not her arguments will be well received by an audience whose ideological affiliations may prescribe very different versions of what exists, what is good, and what is possible than those espoused by the rhetor. This holds doubly for rhetors who want to use commonplaces to build arguments. We are treating the commonplaces as equivalents of the topics that Aristotle called "special," by which he meant topics that circulate within specific sorts of rhetorical discourse, such as that used in legislatures, courtrooms, and at community events. Aristotle insisted that use of special topics required rhetors to be very knowledgeable about the history, practices, and values important to that community. We agree.

In order to use commonplaces as means of invention, it is helpful to think of them as statements that form bits or pieces of ideologies. In Chapter 5, on reasoning, we employ a term from logic, the **premise,** to talk about general statements that govern the generation of other related but more specific statements. A **major premise** is any statement that is assumed or supposed prior to the beginning of a discussion, negotiation, or argument. In this chapter we defined commonplaces as assumptions that "go without saying," by which we mean that they are often so deeply held by communities that they are not subjected to discussion or argument. As we demonstrate in the chapter on reasoning, rhetors can create arguments by combining or chaining statements together. We think that reasoning of this sort occurs within ideology as well. We give the name *ideologic* to the kind of reasoning in which commonplaces are yoked together, strung, or chained into a line of argument. In ideologic, commonplaces may be combined with other sorts of statements—such as conjectures or definition, testimony or evidence—but the persuasive force of the argument is generally carried by the commonplaces. Aristotle thought that people more readily accepted lines of argument relying on commonplaces because audiences feel that they are actually participating in the construction of the argument when they adhere to beliefs used by a rhetor to advance his position.

Because ideologic relies so heavily on commonplaces, it is seldom fully articulated. However, to work out the ideologic functioning within a statement or argument is ordinarily quite easy. Take, for example, the slogan from the Vietnam war era that we alluded to earlier: "America: love it or leave it." Ideologically, this statement forms a conclusion to a chain of reasoning that goes something like this:

1. American citizens love their country.
2. People who love their country do not disagree with its policies.
3. The war in Vietnam is American policy.
4. People who protest the policy and hence the war do not love their country.
5. People who do not love their country do not deserve to enjoy its benefits.
6. People who do not love their country should not continue to live in it (that is, "love it or leave it").

The third statement had the status of a statement of fact during the Vietnam war, although its status as fact was hotly contested because people opposed to the war argued that the Tonkin Gulf Resolution may not have constituted the necessary congressional authorization for continuing the war. In other words, the third statement is perhaps better categorized as a conjecture. For our purposes here, though, the important point about this bit of ideologic is that most of its premises are commonplaces. Certainly all but the third meet the tests of commonplaces: they are widely believed and they are not often submitted to argument. People do not often work through the ideologic of a statement or assertion, but it is a worthwhile exercise for rhetors because it reveals much about the ideology of people who use it.

Using the commonplaces that appear in contemporary versions of conservativism and liberalism and armed with the notion of ideologic, we can now illustrate how Aristotle's two means of invention can still work to help rhetors find "the available means of persuasion" (*Rhetoric* I ii 1). First, we work out how conservatives or liberals might use Aristotle's topics of conjecture, degree, and possibility to find proofs for pressing issues. We present very brief lists of arguments that may be found on a variety of issues by using the common topics. Then we apply them more extensively and systematically to an exemplary issue. We conclude with some exercises in ideologic, that is, in detecting chains of commonplaces that operate in common lines of argument.

We recommend that, after studying our examples, readers choose some issue that interests them and work slowly through Aristotle's common topics, using them to probe for proofs on the issue. As Quintilian warned, not all of the topics will be appropriate for use on every issue. Practice and experience are the best guides to their proper use.

The Common Topic of Conjecture

Disagreement often stems from the fact that rhetors interpret reality differently in the service of their interests. Conservative rhetors interpreted the Vietnam war as a fight against the spread of international communism (in keeping with the more general conservative stance in support of a strong national defense), while liberal rhetors viewed America's role in the conflict as an intrusion into a local civil war (in keeping with liberalism's general laissez-faire tolerance for letting other nations do as they wish). Today, conservative rhetors depict countries such as Iraq, North Korea, and Iran as a threat to the security of the United States, while opponents of the war with Iraq believe that the war stems from greed for its oil or as an unnecessary act of aggression against a sovereign nation.

Liberal rhetors believe social welfare programs offer necessary support for those who cannot support themselves; conservative rhetors interpret such programs as an oppressive system that keeps people from achieving self-reliance. Such assumptions can also influence the depictions of major national events. After Hurricane Katrina made landfall in late August 2005, breaking the levees protecting the city of New Orleans and causing unprecedented flooding and a mass evacuation, conservative rhetors blamed the people of New Orleans for not heeding evacuation orders. Senator Rick Santorum, for example, wondered if there needed to be "tougher penalties on those who decide to ride it out and understand that there are consequences to not leaving" (2005). Liberal rhetors, on the other hand, argued that people in the poorer areas like the Lower Ninth Ward could not afford to leave. Many did not own or have access to cars, and public transportation was not an option. Liberal rhetoricians argued that scientists and government officials knew that the historically black and poor neighborhoods were the most vulnerable to damage should the levees breach, and still they failed to develop a plan to assist with evacuation of those areas. While conservative rhetors blamed the natural disaster and the people who "refused" to leave, liberal rhetors blamed racist policies and conservative head-turning for the storm's tragic aftermath.

The Common Topic of Degree

Using this topic, a rhetor can argue that even though poverty exists in the United States, it isn't as severe as that experienced in other countries. He can argue as well that it is relatively easy (or relatively difficult) to solve the problem of poverty, compared to other problems the world faces. If she is a liberal, she may argue that it is better to address poverty than to fund defense spending. If she has conservative leanings, she may argue that it is better for poverty to be addressed by local or state agencies or by free enterprise, while defense spending is necessarily a federal priority because it protects the community as a whole. If a rhetor is forced by circumstances to admit that a given situation is less good, or right, or just, or preferable than some other state of affairs, she can use the topic of degree to argue that these negative features are actually a relative good. Conservative rhetors who are forced to acknowledge the existence of poverty and unemployment sometimes argue that the poor deserve their lot, since they refuse to take responsibility for themselves. Liberal rhetors counter this conjecture by arguing that since a capitalist economy dictates that a certain percentage of the citizenry will inevitably suffer from poverty, government is obligated to support its poorer citizens. Finally, using the topic of degree, a liberal rhetor can argue that the achievement of financial equity for all people is more important than accumulation of wealth by the few. Conservative rhetors can argue that free enterprise is preferable to the socialist desire to redistribute wealth, since a free market enhances initiative and bolsters economic growth.

The Common Topic of Possibility

This topic is regularly put to use in contemporary discussions about environmental protection. Corporations and factory owners, on one hand, often argue that it is not possible for them to conform to clean-air regulations and maintain their present levels of production. Sometimes they argue that while conformity may be possible in the future, it is not possible at the present time. Environmentalists argue, on the other hand, that it is entirely possible that human activity is causing global warming. They argue further that it is impossible for the environment to survive present levels of pollution and degradation.

AN EXTENDED EXAMPLE

In order to give an extended illustration of how the common topics and the commonplaces work, we return to the issue we analyzed in the previous chapter: the regulation of hateful speech. This is chiefly an ethical issue, although it can become a legal issue when hateful speech is defined as speech protected by the First Amendment. In any case, rhetors who address it can use liberal and conservative commonplaces having to do with personal freedoms, relationship to authority, and social equality. As was demonstrated by our use of stasis theory on this issue in the previous chapter, a rhetor can treat hateful speech as an issue of conjecture, definition, or quality, depending upon the rhetorical situation in which he finds himself. Here we treat it as a procedural question, that is, as a question of policy. Two broad procedural positions are available on this issue: a rhetor may favor regulating the use of hateful speech or, conversely, he may oppose its regulation. Our example does not illustrate uses of all the available commonplaces, although all are theoretically available for use on any issue.

Using the Common Topic of Conjecture

What exists?

What does not exist?

What is the size or extent of what exists?

Did it exist in the past?

Will it exist in the future?

Using the topic of "what exists," a rhetor who wishes to regulate hateful speech can paint a picture of the university as beset by an epidemic of slurs against certain groups. She can mention epithets painted on walls, shouted from windows, and posted on social networking sites. Using the topic of size or extent, she can try to show that the problem is widespread and that it represents a general Climate of hatred on campus. Using the topic of past conjecture, she may argue that the climate is worse than it used to be, and she may use the topic of future conjecture to show that the situation contains little promise of improvement unless something is done. A rhetor who opposes regulation, in contrast, can describe the campus scene as peaceful and harmonious, or can argue that incidents of hateful speech are isolated and do not occur very often or that they are the work of just a few people who can be disciplined and removed from the scene, if necessary. He may argue that the situation is better than it was in the past, since a few guilty persons have been removed from the scene. He can point out that this local action mitigates the need for a blanket policy regarding hateful speech, which, after all, anticipates that a need for regulation will arise in the future. If the rhetor who opposes regulation is conservative, she may conjecture that students are responsible people who do not need policies to keep them from behaving badly. A conservative who favors regulation, in contrast, can point out that groups often need to adopt rules and enforce them in order to regulate the behavior of individuals who, inevitably, cannot restrain themselves. A liberal rhetor who favors regulation has much precedent for his argument, since liberal procedure historically has been to adopt regulations that are intended to protect defenseless people from harm. This rhetor, then, can conjecture the campus as a scene where frequent belittling remarks injure students' self-esteem. A liberal who opposes regulation, of course, can always appeal to the individual right to free speech.

Using the Common Topic of Degree

What is greater than the mean or norm?

What is lesser than the mean or norm?

What is relatively greater than something else?

What is relatively lesser than something else?

What is good, just, beautiful, honorable, enjoyable, etc.?

What is better, more just, etc.?

What is less good, less just, etc.?

What is good, etc., for all persons?

What is good, etc., for a few persons or groups?

What has been better, etc., in the past?

What will be better, etc., in the future?

A rhetor who favors regulation of hateful speech can use the topic of degree to show why hateful speech should be regulated. Generally, she can take the positions that hateful speech is bad, unjust, dishonorable, or inexpedient and that regulation of it is therefore good, just, honorable and expedient. Not all of these topics will be useful or necessary in any given case, of course, but in general each should produce arguments for any case. For example, a rhetor can argue that the use of hateful speech is unjust on the ground that it discriminates among persons according to unacceptable criteria such as gender or appearance. Or she can argue that the use of hateful speech is inexpedient since it can foment uneasiness and even violence on campus.

Relative arguments from degree are also many: a rhetor can argue that regulation of hateful speech, even though it impedes personal freedom, is better than unbridled expression of racist or sexist opinions, for example. Or he might argue that regulation is not a good, since it affects everyone on campus, while the expression of hateful speech affects only a few. If the rhetor who favors regulation is a liberal, he faces a quandary, given that liberals think of individual freedoms (including freedom of speech) as good, just, and expedient. However, liberals also think of social equality as a good, and hateful speech can be construed as an attack on the right of equal access for certain groups. He can resolve this dilemma by using the topic of degree: in other words, he can decide which of his liberal values—freedom of speech or social equality—is more important to him. Or he can argue that hateful speech is so disruptive and so immoral that an exception must be made to his general support for freedom of speech. Whether or not he can support regulation of hateful speech depends on whether he defines it as a political or ethical issue, since liberals generally support intervention that regulates matters of social equity but do not approve of legislation of moral matters.

If the rhetor who favors regulation is a conservative, she also faces a dilemma. She is not likely to be impressed by the argument that hateful speech impedes progress toward social equality, since this is not high on her list of goods. However, she may favor regulations that curtail abusive verbal behavior by individuals in the interests of maintaining harmony among the wider community.

Using the topic of degree, a rhetor who opposes regulation of hateful speech may argue that such regulation is neither good, just, honorable, nor expedient. It would be difficult for him to argue that hateful speech is good, just, and honorable, but use of this topic shows that such positions are available to him if he wishes to defend any of them. A more defensible topic is available to this rhetor, however. He may argue that a policy of regulation imposes the values of some onto the entire group and, for that reason, regulation is unjust. If this rhetor is a liberal, he can characterize those who use hateful speech as exercising their right to free speech, although he faces the same dilemma as the liberal rhetor who favors regulation, insofar as he has to decide whether individual freedom is more important than social equity in this case. If the rhetor who opposes regulation is a conservative, she can use the topic of degree to argue that university policies are not appropriate means for regulating hateful speech, which should be policed instead by family and religious authority; this rhetor can also argue that students have a personal responsibility to behave respectfully toward others.

Using the Common Topic of Possibility

What is possible?

What is impossible?

What is more or less possible?

What is possible in the future?

What is impossible in the future?

What was possible or impossible in the past?

Using the topic of possibilities, the rhetor who favors regulation of hateful speech must address the question of whether it is possible to curtail hateful speech by such means. He must also examine whether such a policy will have the desired effect in the future as well. The rhetor who opposes regulation, of course, can argue that it is not possible to regulate verbal behavior; she can suggest as well that it was impossible for hateful speech to have occurred in the past since the term itself is of recent invention.

THE EXAMPLE EMBEDDED IN A RHETORICAL SITUATION

In the chapter on stasis, we mentioned flag burning and cross burning as examples of speech that have in the past been protected by the First Amendment. Recently, however, the Supreme Court heard a case about cross burning in which something quite remarkable happened. Here is an account of the event written by Linda Greenhouse for the *New York Times*:

AN INTENSE ATTACK BY JUSTICE THOMAS ON CROSS-BURNING

Washington, Dec. 11—The question for the Supreme Court in an argument today was whether a state may make it a crime to burn a cross without at the same time trampling on the protection that the First Amendment gives to symbolic expression. The case, concerning a 50-year-old Virginia law, raised tricky questions of First Amendment doctrine, and it was not clear how the court was inclined to decide it—until Justice Clarence Thomas spoke.

A burning cross is indeed highly symbolic, Justice Thomas said, but only of something that deserves no constitutional protection: the "reign of terror" visited on black communities by the Ku Klux Klan for nearly 100 years before

Virginia passed the law, which the Virginia Supreme Court declared unconstitutional a year ago.

A burning cross is "unlike any symbol in our society," Justice Thomas said.

"There's no other purpose to the cross, no communication, no particular message," he continued. "It was intended to cause fear and to terrorize a population."

During the brief minute or two that Justice Thomas spoke, about halfway through the hourlong argument session, the other justices gave him rapt attention. Afterward, the court's mood appeared to have changed. While the justices had earlier appeared somewhat doubtful of the Virginia statute's constitutionality, they now seemed quite convinced that they could uphold it as consistent with the First Amendment.

Justice Thomas addressed his comments to Michael R. Dreeben, a deputy federal solicitor general who was arguing in support of Virginia's defense of its statute. But he did not have questions for Mr. Dreeben, who in any event agreed with him in nearly all respects. The threat of violence inherent in a burning cross "is not protected by the First Amendment" but instead is "prohibited conduct," Mr. Dreeben had just finished arguing.

Rather, Justice Thomas appeared driven to make the basis for his own position unmistakably clear.

"My fear is you are actually understating the symbolism of and effect of the burning cross," he said, adding, "I think what you're attempting to do is fit this into our jurisprudence rather than stating more clearly what the cross was intended to accomplish."

It was a gripping made-for-television moment—except, of course, for the fact that television cameras are not permitted inside the courtroom. Justice Thomas speaks in a rich baritone that is all the more striking for being heard only rarely during the court's argument sessions. His intervention, consequently, was as unexpected as the passion with which he expressed his view.

He referred to an opinion he wrote in 1995, concurring with the majority that the City of Columbus, Ohio, had no basis for refusing permission to the Klan to place a cross among other Christmastime displays in a downtown park that served as an open forum for religious expression. In that opinion, Justice Thomas said he was joining the decision despite his belief that the Klan's cross was not a form of religious expression but rather "a symbol of white supremacy and a tool for the intimidation and harassment" of racial and religious minorities.

There was a suggestion in his remarks today that perhaps he now regretted his effort in that case to meld his own views into the court's jurisprudence and, after 11 years on the court, no longer felt obliged to try.

Afterward, Justice David H. Souter addressed Rodney A. Smolla, the lawyer for three men who were convicted under the cross-burning statute in two incidents. Mr. Smolla, a well-known First Amendment scholar at the University of Richmond, had just argued that the government could make it a crime to brandish a gun but not to burn a cross because a gun has physical properties that make it dangerous while the danger inherent in a burning cross comes from the ideas it symbolizes and not its physical properties.

That might have been a winning argument two centuries ago, Justice Souter said, "but how does your argument account for the fact that the cross has acquired potency at least akin to a gun?"

Justice Souter called a burning cross "a kind of Pavlovian symbol, so that the person who sees it responds not to its message but out of fear." He added that "other symbols don't make you scared," suggesting that a burning cross might be "a separate category."

Mr. Smolla recalled the court's decision upholding a First Amendment right to burn an American flag.

"You must concede," he said, that the cross itself "is one of the most powerful religious symbols in human history." As with burning the flag, the act of burning a cross involves "calling on that repository of meaning" to make a symbolic point, he said.

Justice Ruth Bader Ginsburg objected that there was "a big difference" between the two acts.

"The flag is a symbol of the government," Justice Ginsburg said, and it is inherent in the constitutional system that "anyone can attack the government." But burning a cross means "attacking people, threatening life and limb," she said.

The Virginia law prohibits burning a cross "with the intent of intimidating any person or group of persons." Mr. Smolla said it would be effective as well as constitutional to make threats and intimidation a crime without singling out a particularly threatening symbol.

"A burning torch and a burning cross—what's the difference?" he asked, evidently intending to emphasize the expressive nature of cross-burning. But Justice Anthony M. Kennedy found a different answer. "One hundred years of history," he said.

Mr. Smolla made the best of the moment, saying, "Thank you, Justice Kennedy, and that 100 years of history is on the side of freedom of speech."

William H. Hurd, Virginia's state solicitor, argued on behalf of the statute in *Virginia v. Black*, No. 01-1107.

"We have not tried to suppress freedom of speech," Mr. Hurd said. "All we've tried to do is protect freedom from fear." (2002)

Here Justice Thomas apparently argued that a burning cross exists in a class by itself, quite different from a burning flag, because of its history as a threat "to life and limb," as Justice Ginsberg put it. Other justices seemed receptive to this argument, although the lawyer for the defendants in the case—who is an authority on the First Amendment—seemed to be made very uneasy by this situation. Why was this?

Let's imagine that two rhetors are trying to develop arguments in this case. One—let's call her Catherine—wishes to argue alongside Justice Thomas that there is something special about cross burning that exempts it from First Amendment protection. The other—call him Rodney—wishes to define cross burning as an expressive act that should be classified as free speech and therefore entitled to protection under the amendment. We attempt to find available arguments in this case by using the common topics and a few of the commonplaces in circulation about free speech in American discourse. As always, our use of this heuristic is only suggestive; that is to say we do not develop all of the arguments that would appear in a full and systematic investigation of the common topics.

Using the common topic of conjecture, Catherine and Rodney can ask:

Does cross burning exist or not?

What is the size or extent of what exists?

Did it exist in the past?

Will it exist in the future?

Clearly cross-burning exists. In one August 2006 case, Neal Chapman Coombs was charged with knowingly and willfully intimidating an African-American family that was negotiating for the purchase of a house in Hastings, Florida, by threat of force and the use of fire. Specifically, it was alleged that Coombs's actions were motivated by the family's race and that he burned a cross on property adjacent to the house ("Florida Man Sentenced in Cross Burning"). In Tennessee in June of 2006, someone burned a cross in the yard belonging to a gay man ("Prosecutor"). Gays and lesbians, it should be noted, are not protected under the federal law discussed earlier.

Cross burning existed in the past, as justices Thomas and Ginsberg pointed out, when it was used as a means of threatening violence to groups of people singled out by the Klan. Twenty-five hundred documented cases of lynchings of African American men and women occurred between 1880 and 1930, and, Michael Bronski argues, this was always done "by a white mob driven by hate and often with the influence, support, backing, or direct help of the Ku Klux Klan. During this time, the Klan, and groups like it, used burning crosses as a potent symbol that they could—and would—get away with it" (2002). This unsavory history is what renders the contemporary act of burning a cross so frightening. However, even if cross burning is made illegal on First Amendment or any other ground, the practice may continue in the future. If the court rules that the practice is not protected by the First Amendment, people who burn crosses will be liable to prosecution for the first time in American history. Such a ruling would compromise the court's historical stance that the content of speech cannot be regulated, and this possibility makes proponents of current interpretations of the First Amendment, like Rodney, uneasy.

Using the topic of past and future fact as relative measures, Rodney can argue that no matter how vicious the symbol of a burning cross was in the past, things have changed for the better. In the cases before the Virginia court, for example, no one was hurt; the victims were only frightened by the burning crosses. That is to say, times have changed, and African Americans, gays, Jews, and Catholics are no longer subjected to regular and continuing threat of bodily harm by the KKK. Here Rodney can also conjecture that the scope (the extent of what exists) of the problem has changed: Klan membership is much smaller and far less powerful than it used to be. Catherine, however, can use this topic (the extent of what exists) to point out that Klan-inspired lynchings have occurred as recently as 1981, and because of its violent history the mere presence of a burning cross is still a threat to those it is intended to intimidate even though the practice is now less widespread and perhaps less dangerous than it was in the past.

Alternately, Rodney can switch focus and, on the one hand, use the common topic of conjecture to investigate past, current, and future interpretations of the First Amendment. He can argue, for example, that heretofore cross burning was defined as political speech and hence was afforded First Amendment protection. He can argue that its status as political speech must be protected now and in the future on the ground that to exclude cross burning from First Amendment protection will have the effect of excluding other expressions or acts that have heretofore been protected as political speech, such as burning a flag. Catherine can use this topic, on the other hand, to argue that burning a cross has no content; that is, it expresses no message in the way that burning a flag expresses a message. Therefore, American courts should define cross burning now and in the future as something other than political speech—as the threat of intimidation or violence, perhaps.

Next our rhetors can investigate the common topic of degree. Under this topic they can ask questions such as the following:

What is greater than the mean or norm?

What is lesser than the mean or norm?

What is relatively greater than something else?

What is relatively lesser than something else?

What is good, just, beautiful, honorable, enjoyable, etc.?

What is better, more just, etc.?

What is less good, less just, etc.?

What is good, etc., for all persons?

What is good, etc., for a few persons or groups?

What has been better, etc., in the past?

What will be better, etc., in the future?

In general, the topic of degree raises this question: how is cross burning valued in the community? More specifically, is the practice good or bad, just or unjust, beautiful or ugly, honorable or dishonorable? And who assigns each of these values to the practice? While arguments can be developed from all of these values (apparently a nighttime cross burning can be conjectured by some people as a beautiful sight, for instance), these days a majority of Americans agree that cross burning is bad, unjust, ugly, and dishonorable. If they did not feel this way, there would be no laws such as the one being contested in Virginia. Even advocates of First Amendment protection for cross burning agree that it is a despicable act. When Rodney and Catherine consider the way in which this practice is valued within and across communities, they can ask, Is cross burning good or bad, just or unjust, and so on for some group of persons? Their answers to these more situated questions yield some interesting arguments. For instance, Christians might construe the practice to be blasphemous because of the importance of the cross to their beliefs. Obviously cross burning holds some good for those who practice it, while those against whom it is used suffer from it.

Viewed this way, it becomes clear that the courts are being asked to choose between the conflicting values of two or more groups as they rule on this practice.

The topic of degree is productive of other arguments when values are thought of relative to one another: for example, is cross burning better or worse than something else? Using this topic, Rodney can argue that a cross burning ceremony is a ritual occasion during which those in attendance can shout and generally let off steam, thus curbing the potential for more violent behavior. Of course Catherine can use the same topic to argue that this ritual actually inspires violence, as history shows; in other words, as a ceremonial practice cross burning is worse than almost anything else that can be imagined. Last, under the common topic of degree, our rhetors can ask: Do values change? Will we value cross burning differently in the future than we do now or did in the past? Will this change be for the better or worse? History demonstrates that fewer people now value the practice than did in the past. And the *New York Times* editorial cited previously argues that if the Supreme Court upholds the Virginia law, it is conceivable that cross burning will come to be widely defined as "an imminent threat of violence to real people, for whom the threat is not abstract." That is, it will no longer be defined as the sort of speech that is protected by the First Amendment but rather as the sort of "fighting words" that have long been held to be illegal. If legality or illegality is viewed as a consolidation or affirmation of the values held by a majority of the people, then this change will indicate that the way in which the community values cross burning has changed.

Which brings us to the common topic of possibility. Using this topic, Catherine and Rodney can ask:

What is possible?

What is impossible?

What is more or less possible?

What is possible in the future?

What is impossible in the future?

What was possible or impossible in the past?

The topic of possibility raises some interesting questions in this case. Is it possible to regulate the practice of cross burning? Can this be done by making it illegal? Is it possible or impossible that rendering cross burning illegal will eliminate the hatred that motivates it? Is it more or less possible to legislate the practice out of existence than to eliminate the values that motivate it? Is it possible or impossible that community values will change so much in the future that hatred of groups designated by the Klan will disappear along with the Klan itself? Is it possible that if cross burning had been more responsibly regulated in the past that the motives underlying the practice would have disappeared sooner?

We turn from our examination of the common topics to a look at the commonplaces circulating within this rhetorical situation. At this moment, the Virginia case in some ways reinforces commonplace arguments surrounding cross burning and other forms of hateful speech. Typically, liberals have argued for an inclusive definition of First Amendment protection. The Bill of Rights, after all, was inspired by liberals who valued rights such as the freedom of speech and assembly because of their insistence on the general freedom of individuals to speak and do as they please. And so liberals are generally willing to extend First Amendment protection to expressive acts such as cross burning and pornography even though they may find these practices odious. This causes a dilemma for contemporary liberals, on one hand, who generally oppose racism and sexism because it can be argued that cross burning and pornography give particular offense to African Americans and some religious groups or to women. On the other hand, conservatives have been anxious to narrow the definition of free speech so that it does not protect expressive acts such as flag burning, which is thought to criticize authority or tradition. That is to say, conservatives have been inclined to regulate some political speech. Conservative justices have in the past, however, consistently awarded First Amendment protection to cross burning, as they did in *RAV v. Minnesota*, on the ground that it is political speech. Justice Thomas, who is conservative, is thus behaving consistently with conservative values in arguing that a particular act should not be protected, thus narrowing the range of expressions and acts that are covered by the First Amendment. However, his insistence that a burning cross "was intended to cause fear and to terrorize a population" implies that the content of speech should be regulated, not because it attacks authority or tradition but because it gives offense to certain members of the community. That is, he adopts the politically correct argument often condemned by conservatives who have consistently exempted so-called offensive speech from regulation. Presumably, if adopted, this argument not only would include racist speech or expressive acts but could possibly lead to further narrowing of First Amendment protection for acts of speech that are determined offensive to other groups. That is, conceivably, feminists could use this precedent to argue that pornography should be regulated because it is offensive and possibly dangerous to women; and conservatives could argue that flag burning and war protests should be regulated because they are offensive to conservatives and threaten the ideological integrity of the community.

RHETORICAL ACTIVITIES

1. Reread the descriptions of American ideology given by E. D. Hirsch and Howard Zinn in this chapter. Whose description seems more accurate to you? Can you tell from these descriptions whether Hirsch and Zinn lean toward the right or left of the political spectrum? How can you justify your placement of either writer on the political spectrum?

2. Find a large parking lot. Copy down the bumper stickers that you see on the vehicles parked there, such as "My SUV ♥s Iraqi Oil," "Nobody Died When Clinton Lied," "A Family Needs a Father," "Parenting by Choice, Not Chance," "I'm for the Separation of Church and Hate," "If

you can read this, thank a teacher," and "Guns Don't Kill People, Abortion Clinics Kill People." Each of these commonplaces makes an argument and implies an ideologic. Try to figure out the arguments and ideologics that underlie bumper stickers you have seen. If a vehicle sports several bumper stickers, does the collection suggest contrary or conflicting ideologies? This exercise also works with vanity license plates—"FLYNHI," "BIGDOG," "CHSLIFE." What do these phrases suggest about the ideologies of their owners? What happens when a commonplace is not commonplace enough?

3. Think about a specific rhetorical situation in which you recently participated. Writing as fast as you can, describe this situation: the people who participated, their relationships to each other (friends, family members, and so on), the place, the time, the issue. Now examine the position taken by one participant in the rhetorical situation (not yourself). Write down as many of his or her arguments as you can remember. What beliefs or values undergird the position he or she took in the argument? See if you can list these. Do any of them look like conservative or liberal commonplaces? Is the person open to persuasion on any of them? If so, how might a rhetor persuade that person to change his or her mind about any of his or her arguments?

4. Use Aristotle's common topics to analyze some issue that you want to understand better. Ask each of the questions listed in this chapter under conjecture, degree, and possibility. Take your time, and write down all of the answers that come to you. Remember, the point of a heuristic is to help you find all of the available arguments. If you are thorough, systematic use of the topics should turn up more arguments than you need.

5. Read the front page of a daily newspaper that covers both local and national news. Read this week's news magazines, watch the news on TV, listen to radio news programs, or surf the Internet. This ought to familiarize you with the issues that are currently being debated in the American public sphere. Then read some magazines that are avowedly partisan in order to see how they treat currently controversial issues. In our opinion *The New Republic, The American Spectator,* and the *Wall Street Journal* are conservative; *The Nation, Dissent,* and *The Village Voice* are liberal or left-of-liberal. Compare the treatments of the same issue that appear in conservative and liberal magazines. Now try to answer these questions: What is the ideological bias (if any can be detected) of your hometown newspaper? Of the news desk of your local TV station? The *New York Times? USA Today? Time* magazine? *Newsweek?* CNN? Network television news? Oprah? Bill O'Reilly? Dr. Laura? Rush Limbaugh? Conan O'Brien? Howard Stern? Keith Olbermann? Stephen Colbert?

   This exercise will help you to compile an inventory of the commonplaces that appear in American rhetoric. You may draw on this list in two ways: it should help you to understand the ideologic that undergirds the arguments that are presented to you, and you can use it to build your own arguments.

PROGYMNASMATA IV: COMMON-PLACE

This exercise should not be confused with the commonplaces of invention, though there is some conceptual overlap. In the context of the *progymnasmata*, common-place elaborates on a commonly held belief, particularly with regard to a generic action. Some ancient authors held that the action amplified can be good or evil, as Aelius Theon wrote: commonplace "is of two kinds: one is an attack on those who have done evil deeds, for example, a tyrant, traitor, murderer, profligate; the other in favor of those who have done something good: for example, a tyrannicide, a hero, a lawgiver" (Kennedy 2003, 42–43). Nicolaus the Sophist seems to favor elaborating only evil actions, but still acknowledges others' views that common-place can go both ways. "Commonplace," writes Nicolaus, "is an amplification and attack on an acknowledged evil; or as others define it, an amplification of an acknowledged evil or human goodness" (Kennedy 2003, 148). Aphthonius appears to favor a focus on evil, while Hermogenes believes the exercise can just as easily apply to good and bad actions. Hermogenes helpfully explains: "it is called 'common'-place because (what we say) applies to every temple robber or every war hero" (Kennedy 2003, 79). Nicolaus elaborates:

> it is 'common' because it is not directed against a specified person, for example, against Timarchus for prostitution or Lycophron for adultery, but simply against any prostitute or adulterer. It is called *topos* because rhetorical arguments are called topos . . . or because, as though setting out from some common spot, we easily compose attacks on specified kinds of practices. (Kennedy 2003, 148)

Nicolaus's explanation helpfully reminds us of the place-based meaning of *topos*.

When practicing common-place, students can use the argumentative skills they acquired in the confirmation and refutation, but here they do not argue the facts of an actual case. Rather, they argue against some vice or moral fault such as treachery or theft or greed, or they argue for virtues such as honor or justice. The facts of any case used in this exercise are assumed, and so there is no need to spend time establishing that, say, murder has occurred. The object is rather to elaborate on the moral qualities of a virtue or vice. Ancient teachers used this exercise to give their students practice in writing perorations, the last and most emotional part of persuasive discourses.

Aphthonius suggested that the composition of a common-place begin with a prologue. Then the composer should provide a contrary, then an exposition that interests the listener, and a comparison that attaches blame to the accused. This was to be followed by an attack on the doer's motives and a digression that castigated his past life. Finally the composer rejected any feeling of pity for the doer, and reminded his audience of the standard topics that were relevant to the common-place being amplified: legality, justice, expediency, practicability, honor, or result. John of Sardis, who lived during the ninth century CE and who wrote elaborate commentary on the various *progymnasmata*, sees an interesting relationship between common-place and fable. Both aim at lessons about morality and have strong preference for showcasing bad actions. Common-places differ from fables, however, in two ways. First, common-places offer generalized accounts of evil actions rather than fictionalized accounts. Second, common-places frequently include an exhortation to punishment, while a fable merely advises avoidance of such actions." (Kennedy 2003, 205).

Next we give an example of a common-place composed against a ruler or group of people who commits genocide, the intentional and systematic destruction of an ethnic, national, racial, or religious group; we imagine an audience of an international tribunal.

(PROLOGUE): Since certain international laws have been established to keep nations in check, to prevent evil from developing regardless of national borders, and since those laws apply when leaders of nations commit crimes of humanity against groups within their own countries, these laws surely must be considered when a nation's leaders systematically destroy or condone the destruction of certain peoples.

(CONTRARY): It seems to us that you will have a better picture of the conditions that lead to such a dreadful act if you consider the intentions of the United Nations when it developed international laws to prevent persecution. Since at different times different nations come under systems of rule that alter an otherwise fair and humane course of governance, and since deep hatred has been known to form across religious, racial, or ethnic differences, resulting in mass persecution of peoples on the basis of their race, religion, ethnicity, or nationality, the United Nations sought to balance the inequities of history with uniform laws. They devised standards of rule to work against evil and persecution; these are laws to which all nations under its jurisdiction would be held accountable.

(EXPOSITION): However, a leader or group of leaders who either commit or comply with genocide shows no regard for law, humanity, or the rest of the world. Such people have in effect let their hatred of a group of people rise above international law. They have effectively said to themselves "a group of humans deserves to be extinguished on the basis of their different appearance, beliefs, or political commitments, which we believe to be wrong." The only wrong here is the senseless destruction of a people. Such thinking is not only evil but is unfathomable.

(COMPARISON): A tyrant is dreadful, but one who condones or commits genocide is worse. The former is hungry for power; the latter for mass destruction.

(INTENTION): Most people who commit dreadful acts at least distinguish their intention from their action, but the same cannot be said about groups involved with genocide, because those who act in compliance do so knowingly and deliberately. If such a group had unknowingly been part of mass and systematic killing, perhaps it could be excused from trial, but since the act has been planned and executed over a period of time, it cannot be dismissed.

(DIGRESSION): If a person committed such an atrocious act as an aberration from his previous actions, then perhaps that person could be excused. But any group that participates in planning and carrying out murder on such a massive scale could never have lived a good life.

(REJECTION OF PITY): Perhaps you will soften in the face of a group of well-dressed, well-groomed humans, humans like yourselves. And it might be tempting to give in when the children of those responsible weep and beg for a lighter punishment. But it would be worse to condone such behavior in front of the next generation, for genocide itself must be extinguished.

(LEGALITY): If it is custom to praise those who protect people, then it follows that it is right to punish those who destroy them.

(JUSTICE): It is therefore just for those to submit in your court to the appropriate punishment.

(ADVANTAGE): The prosecution of those who have committed genocide will have long-term benefits; for international law will be upheld, and further destruction may be prevented.

(POSSIBILITY): It will be easy to punish those who commit genocide, for while the act committed took ample planning and manpower, the power to punish that act lies in the court's hands and can be accomplished with a decision.

Sadly, despite the passing of a UN resolution against genocide in 1948 in response to the Holocaust, genocide persists even today, and the deeds of those responsible can still inspire compositions against injustice. But common-places can concern other vices or virtues than genocide; honorable and dishonorable actions, actions that cause evil results, or actions that endanger others can all provide subjects for common-places.

PROGYMNASMATA: COMMON-PLACE

1. Following Aphthonius's instructions as carefully as you can, compose a common-place against the regrettable features of one of the following: someone who commits acts of terrorism; someone who cheats on tests or papers; someone who bullies classmates.

2. Compose a common-place extolling the virtues of the following: a philanthropist, someone who volunteers for charitable organizations, someone who helps strangers in distress.

NOTES

1. We relied on ancient thought as well as Goran Therborn's *The Ideology of Power and the Power of Ideology* (London: National Library Board, 1980) for the analysis that follows.
2. We do not pretend that this list is exhaustive. And it will change with the passage of time (see the chapter on *kairos*). In the first edition of this book, for example, our list began with this question: "What is the appropriate kind of economy?" We removed that question from subsequent editions because virtually all American political ideologies that have a public voice currently accept capitalism as the preferred economy for America.

WORKS CITED

Bronksi, Michael. "'Dworkin Avenged: 'Long Dong' Silver Fan Clarence Thomas Echoes the Arguments of Anti-Porn Feminists to Ban Cross-Burning." *Boston Phoenix*, December 19–26, 2002. http://72.166.46.24/boston/news_features/other_stories/multipage/documents/02598657.htm (accessed June 14, 2007).

Coontz, Stephanie. *The Way We Never Were: American Families and the Nostalgia Trap.* New York: Basic Books, 1992.

D'Souza, Dinesh. *Illiberal Education: The Politics of Race and Sex on Campus.*New York: Vintage, 1992.

"Florida Man Sentenced in Cross Burning." U.S. Department of Justice, January 31, 2007. http://www.usdoj.gov (accessed June 4, 2007).

Greenhouse, Linda. "An Intense Attack by Justice Thomas on Cross Burning." The *New York Times*, National Desk (December 12, 2002). nytimes.com.

Hirsch, E. D. *Cultural Literacy: What Every American Needs to Know.* Chicago: Chicago University Press, 1987.

Kennedy, George. *Aristotle on Rhetoric: A Theory of Civic Discourse.* New York: Oxford University Press, 1991.

—. *Progymnasmata: Greek Textbooks of Prose Composition and Rhetoric.* Leiden: Brill, 2003.

"Prosecutor calls TBI on cross burning at homosexual's home." Associated Press, July 20, 2006. http://www.wreg.com/Global/story.asp?s=5177508&nav=3ltve

Wilson, John K. *The Myth of Political Correctness: The Conservative Attack on Higher Education.* Durham: Duke University Press, 1995.

Zinn, Howard. *Declarations of Independence.* New York: Harper Collins, 1990.

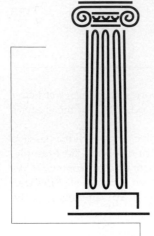

LOGICAL PROOF: REASONING IN RHETORIC

> In some oratorical styles examples prevail, in others enthymemes; and in like manner, some orators are better at the former and some at the latter. Speeches that rely on examples are as persuasive as the other kind, but those which rely on enthymemes excite the louder applause.
>
> —Aristotle, *Rhetoric* I ii 20

ARISTOTLE TAUGHT THAT three kinds of arguments or proofs are convincing in rhetoric: arguments found in the issue itself, arguments based on the rhetor's character and reputation, and arguments that appeal to the emotions (*Rhetoric* I i 2). He called these three sorts of arguments *logos*, *ethos*, and *pathos*. We discuss *ethos* and *pathos* in the next two chapters. Here we are concerned with arguments from *logos*, the logical or rational proofs that can be found by examining issues. The Greek word *logos* gives us the English words *logic* and *logical*. *Logos* meant "voice" or "speech" in archaic Greek. Later it came to refer to "reason" as well, and it carries this sense in English in words such as *logic*. When someone says "Be logical," she means "Think things through—be rational." However, the Greek word's early reference to speaking or language also appears in English words such as *ideology* and *psychology*, where the suffix *-logy* means "words about" or, more loosely, "study of." Hence *ideology* literally means "words about ideas" or "study of ideas"; psychology is "words about the mind" (Greek *psyche*) or "study of the mind."

In his methodology (literally, "ways of reasoning") Aristotle developed four logical methods to help people argue their way through complex issues. The four methods were scientific demonstration, dialectic, rhetoric, and false or contentious reasoning. Aristotle taught that in each of these kinds of reasoning the arguer began with a statement called a premise. This word is derived from Latin words which mean "to send before." Thus a **premise** is any statement laid down, supposed, or assumed before the argument begins. Premises are then combined with other premises in order to reach conclusions. Arguers can ensure that their arguments are valid (that is, correctly reasoned), if they observe certain formal rules of arrangement for the premises. Conclusions reached by this means of reasoning are true only if their premises are true.

In scientific demonstration, according to Aristotle, argument began from premises that are true or that experts accept as true. The premises of scientific argument or demonstration must be able to command belief without further argument to support them. For example: "Water freezes at 32 degrees Fahrenheit" and "The moon orbits the earth" are simple scientific premises. In dialectical reasoning, the arguers are less certain about the truth of the premises; here the premises are accepted by people who are supposed to be especially wise. For example, Socrates' dictum that "the unexamined life is not worth living" is a dialectical premise, as is Jesus's teaching that human beings ought to love each other. In rhetorical reasoning, premises are drawn from beliefs accepted by all or most members of a community. According to Aristotle, false or contentious reasoning differs from scientific, dialectical, and rhetorical reasoning because it relies on premises that only appear to be widely accepted. False reasoning also uses premises that are mistakes or lies.

The premises in rhetorical reasoning always involve human action or belief. Cicero's arguments in Roman courts and in the Senate, for example, usually involved premises about human action—whether Milo actually murdered someone or whether Caesar should be allowed to become a dictator. "Our town should adopt a dark-sky ordinance," "Hateful speech is a harmful practice within a university community," and "Abortion is murder" are rhetorical arguments, rather than scientific or dialectical ones, because they deal with human action and/or beliefs.

Some rhetorical premises are commonplaces; that is, they are widely accepted by the relevant community. When the premises of rhetorical arguments draw on commonplaces, rhetorical reasoning can be called ideological, the name we gave to such reasoning in the previous chapter, on the commonplaces. "Convicted criminals should be punished" and "Anyone can become president of the United States" are commonplace premises. Many Americans take commonplace premises for granted, accepting arguments and conclusions that follow from them as forceful and persuasive. Their taken-for-grantedness qualifies them as commonplaces in American ideology, and that in turn qualifies them as premises in ideologic, a kind of rhetorical reasoning.

PROBABILITIES

For our purposes the salient difference among scientific, dialectical, and rhetorical premises has nothing to do with some external criterion for truth. Rather, the difference among them depends upon the degree of belief awarded them by the people who are arguing about them. Ancient teachers of rhetoric began the reasoning process with premises that were widely accepted as certain, and moved to those that were less certain. In fact, Quintilian defined arguments in rhetoric and logic as methods "of proving what is not certain by means of what is certain" (V x 8). Thus, such arguments enable "one thing to be inferred from another"; they also confirm "facts which are uncertain by reference to facts which are certain" (11). Without some way of moving from the certain to the uncertain, Quintilian argued, we'd have no way of proving anything.

Greek rhetoricians called any kind of statement that predicts something about human behavior a statement of probability (*eikos*). Probabilities are not as reliable as certainties, but they are more reliable than chance. Furthermore, rhetorical probabilities differ from mathematical probabilities in that they are both more predictable and less easy to calculate. Compare, for example, the relative probability that you will draw a winning poker hand to the relative probability that your parents, spouse, or partner will be upset if you get home late from the game. The chances of drawing to an inside straight are relatively remote, although they can be mathematically calculated. The chance that parents or a spouse or partner will be upset if you arrive home later than you promised are relatively greater than your chance at drawing to an inside straight, but this chance cannot be calculated by mathematical means. If you want to estimate the probability of their reaction, you need to know something about their attitudes toward promise keeping, the quality of their relationship to you, and the record of promise keeping you have built up over the years.

The reason for the relative certainty of statements about probable human action is that human behavior in general is predictable to some extent. Aristotle wrote that people can reason about things that happen "as a rule." As a rule, family members become upset when promises made to them are broken. Moreover, people cannot reason about things that happen by chance, like drawing to an inside straight. Since rhetorical statements of probability represent the common opinion of humankind, we ought to place a certain degree of trust in them. Thus statements of probability are pieces of knowledge, and as such they provide suitable premises for rhetorical proofs.

Plato credited the legendary Tisias with the invention of the argument from probability (*Phaedrus* 273b). Whether this attribution is correct or not, probability must have been a sophistic tactic, given its emphasis on human behavior rather than human nature (which is what Plato would have preferred). Since the premises used in rhetoric deal with human action, they are only usually or contingently true. In antiquity the most famous argument from probability was this one:

A small weak person will not physically attack a large strong person.

This is a rhetorical premise, since it articulates some common sense about the way people generally behave. In this case, it is not certain that a weaker person will leave a stronger one alone; it is only probable. The smaller person could hire others to act for him, or he could be so driven by desperation or anger that he attacks a man who is sure to injure him, anyway. A sophist would likely argue from probability in the other direction as well: a small weak person might attack a larger more powerful one, even though she was bound to be injured, since no one would suspect that she had done such a dangerous thing. Her doing so, in other words, was not probable. Our pronoun gender switch may alert you to a probability that is a commonplace in American discourse: we assume that an assailant is probably male.

Quintilian named four kinds of premises that could be regarded as certain:
   those which involved things perceived by the senses;
   those which involved things about which there is general agreement, such as children's duty to love their parents;
   those which involved things that exist in law or in custom, such as the custom of punishing convicted criminals;
   those which are admitted by either party to the argument. (V x 12–14)

A sophist might have disagreed with Quintilian about this, however. As we noted earlier, things perceived by the senses are not always certain, since our senses may not be functioning properly: when someone has a cold, it is difficult for him to smell the roses. Moreover, an observer may not be in a position to use her senses properly, or she might not be paying attention. Nor is it true that things existing in law always have certain outcomes; these days, even if someone is convicted of a heinous crime, it is not certain that he will serve the designated sentence. Executions are even more uncertain. The outgoing governor of Illinois in 2003 pardoned or commuted the sentences of several people on death row, a few of whom had been there for many years, because of his uneasiness over the methods used to convict them. Customs are not always certainly adhered to, either, because they change quite rapidly. Men no longer open doors for women, as a rule; women may now ask men for a date, as a rule. Neither of these was a probability thirty years ago. Last, parties to an argument may have extrinsic reasons for accepting a premise as a given: they may have been bribed, or they may think that a premise is irrelevant to their case. In insanity defenses, for example, the defense attorneys sometimes admit that their clients are guilty of the crime they have been charged with. This admission has no bearing on the certainty or likelihood that a client did indeed commit a crime.

In short, very little is certain in the realm of human action. Quintilian regarded three sorts of statements as probable:

those which involved what usually happens (children are usually loved by their parents);

those which were highly likely (a person who is healthy today will be alive tomorrow);

those in which nothing worked against their probability (a household theft was committed by some resident of the household). (16–17)

These sorts of premises are suitable for use in rhetoric, because they are statements about the probable conduct of human beings.

ARISTOTLE ON REASONING IN RHETORIC

For Aristotle, argument took place in language. Arguers placed premises in sequence in order to determine what could be learned from the procedure. He wrote that "a statement is persuasive and credible either because it is directly self-evident or because it appears to be proved from other statements that are so" (I ii 11). Aristotle taught his students how to reason from knowledge that was already given to that which needed to be discovered. People who wished to discover knowledge in any field did so by placing premises in useful relations to one another.

Deduction

In rhetoric, as well as in dialectic and science, the discovery process moves in two directions. Aristotle called these directions **reasoning** (*syllogismos*) and **induction** (*epagoge*). He defined reasoning (also called **deduction**, from a Latin word meaning "to lead down") as "a discussion in which, certain things having been laid down, something other than these things necessarily results through them" (*Topics* I i). The most famous example of this sort of reasoning goes as follows:

1. All people are mortal.
2. Socrates is a person.
3. Therefore, Socrates is mortal.

The first statement is a general premise accepted by everyone. This premise is general because it makes an observation about an entire class: all people. In **syllogisms** set up like the example about Socrates, the first general premise is called the major premise. The second statement is a particular premise accepted by everyone. This premise is particular because it refers to only one person out of the class of people. This premise is called the **minor premise**. The last statement is a **conclusion**, arrived at by comparing the premises: if Socrates fits in the class "people," he also fits in the class "mortal," and thus his death is inevitable. The reasoner has moved down from a generalization ("All people are mortal") to statements concerning a particular person, Socrates.

Aristotle assumed that premises did two kinds of work: they named classes of things (**generalizations** or classifications) and they named **particulars** (one instance of a thing). A **class** is any number of people or things grouped together because of certain likenesses or common traits.

The Class "Cats"

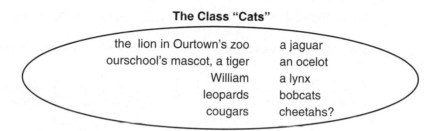

the lion in Ourtown's zoo	a jaguar
ourschool's mascot, a tiger	an ocelot
William	a lynx
leopards	bobcats
cougars	cheetahs?

All members of this class share certain traits: they are predatory flesh-eating mammals, usually having soft fur whiskers, four legs each with five toes, and so on. The cheetah has many feline (catlike) characteristics but many doglike characteristics as well. So it is a marginal member of the class "cats."

When logicians make classes or categories, they like to know how completely its members have been enumerated. So any premise beginning with the word *all* must designate a class for which all the members are known or can be found. When a complete class is put into a premise in logic, whatever is predicated of it should be true of every member of the class, as well, as in "All people are mortal." Classes can be divided into subclasses, which indicate groups within a class; members of a subclass should all have the characteristic or characteristics that define the class, but they may differ in some characteristics from members of other subclasses. Individual members of classes or subclasses are called "particulars." For example, the class of "all mortal entities" includes people, animals, and plants.

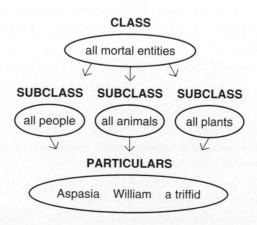

CLASS

all mortal entities

SUBCLASS   SUBCLASS   SUBCLASS

all people   all animals   all plants

PARTICULARS

Aspasia   William   a triffid

Syllogisms worked in ancient logic because logicians thought that the relations between classes and the particulars were a fundamental element of human thinking. So they often began by naming classes, groups that belonged to those classes, and individuals that belonged to those groups:

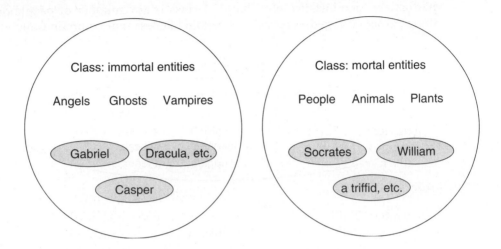

Rhetors are not so concerned as logicians are that the members of classes be completely enumerated, since rhetorical classes are intended to be persuasive rather than mathematically or dialectically accurate. Complete enumeration of every item in a class would soon put audiences to sleep (*Rhetoric* I i 1357a). For persuasive purposes, almost any items can be grouped together to be made into a class, depending on the rhetorical situation. The class "politicians" logically includes anyone who runs for public office; but a rhetor might want to include campaign managers or spin doctors in this class, as well, in order to make a more sweeping judgment about the whole group. Here are some examples of complete deductions:

Major Premise: Ghosts and vampires are immortal creatures.

Minor Premise: Casper and Dracula are a ghost and a vampire, respectively.

Conclusion: Casper and Dracula are immortal creatures.

Major Premise: No politician can be trusted.

Minor Premise: John is a politician.

Conclusion: John can't be trusted.

Major Premise: The death penalty cannot be justified if innocent people are sentenced to death.

Minor Premise: Governor Ryan of Illinois discovered that innocent people are in fact sentenced to death.

Conclusion: The death penalty cannot be justified.

Induction

Aristotle recognized another movement between premises, and he defined it as "the progress from particulars to universals." Later logicians called this movement induction (Latin *inducere*, "to lead into." Induction leads away from particulars and into a general conclusion). A particular is any individual that can be put into a class. Particulars are also called "**instances**" or "examples." Aristotle supplied this example of inductive reasoning:

> If the skilled pilot is the best pilot [particular premise]
> and if the skilled charioteer the best charioteer [particular premise]
> then the skilled person is the best person in any particular sphere [conclusion].
> (*Topics* I 12)

The inductive reasoner can continue to pile up particulars that reinforce the conclusion by naming skilled athletes, weavers, flute players, engineers, and so on. Induction provides certainty only when all the particulars that belong to a class have been enumerated—something that would be difficult to do in this example, which would require a rhetor to name every sphere of human work. However, rhetoricians do not require complete enumeration of particulars, since a piece of inductive reasoning may be persuasive if enough particulars have been named to convince most people to accept the conclusion drawn from them.

Here is an example of inductive argument from Samuel Walker, who is an authority on hateful speech:

> The 1920s are remembered as a decade of intolerance. Bigotry was as much a symbol of the period as Prohibition, flappers, the stock market boom, and Calvin Coolidge. It was the only time when the Ku Klux Klan paraded en masse through the nation's capital. In 1921 Congress restricted immigration for the first time in American history, drastically reducing the influx of Catholics and Jews from southern and eastern Europe, and the nation's leading universities adopted admission quotas to restrict the number of Jewish students. The Sacco and Vanzetti case, in which two Italian American anarchists were executed for robbery and murder in a highly questionable prosecution, has always been one of the symbols of the anti-immigrant tenor of the period. (1994, 17)

Walker begins this paragraph with a conclusion about the high level of bigotry and intolerance in America during the 1920s and then, working inductively, cites a series of examples—the Klan and restrictions on immigration—to support it.

Aristotle had a good deal more to say about reasoning in rhetoric, all centered on the relation of general premises to particular ones. Using this scheme, he invented four types of reasoning that are special to rhetoric: enthymemes, examples, signs, and maxims.

Enthymemes

The premises used in constructing rhetorical proofs differ from those used in dialectic and science only in the degree of certainty we can attach to them. In dialectic and science, deductive arguments are called syllogisms. In rhetoric, they are called enthymemes. The word *enthymeme* comes from the Greek *thymos*, "spirit," the capacity whereby people think and feel. Ancient Greeks located the *thymos* in the midsection of the body. Quite literally, then, an enthymematic proof was a visceral appeal.

Rhetors ordinarily use some widely held community belief as the major premise of their argument. Then they apply that premise to the particular case in which they are interested. Here, for example, is an enthymeme that could be used to develop the argument about hateful speech:

Major Premise: Racist slurs directed against innocent people are offensive and ought to be punished.

Minor Premise: Members of Gamma Delta Iota wore Klan outfits, stood on the commons, and shouted racist epithets at people passing by.

Conclusion: Members of Gamma Delta Iota engaged in offensive behavior and ought to be punished.

Here the major premise is a rhetorical probability, since it is not certain that everyone is offended by the use of racist slurs. The rhetor counts on the fact that most people accept this premise. Those who do not accept it may be reluctant to admit as much; if so, the rhetor's major premise has a greater chance of winning acceptance by an audience. In this case the conclusion also turns on a probability, given the rhetor's assumption that her audience probably agrees that wearing Klan garb and shouting racist epithets is offensive.

There are many sorts of relations that may obtain among premises. Sometimes, a minor premise is an example of the major premise, as it is in the enthymeme about offensive behavior. Sometimes, though, the minor premise states a reason for acceptance of the conclusion:

Major Premise: Secondhand smoke can cause lung cancer.

Minor Premise: Because people are allowed to smoke in our workplace, secondhand smoke is present there.

Conclusion: Smoking should be banned from our workplace.

The relations between major and minor premises, then, often take one of these two forms:

a.   Y (minor premise) is an example of X (major premise).
b.   Y (minor premise) is a reason for X (major premise).

And, as is the case in our examples about hateful speech and smoking, the conclusion of an enthymeme often has the relation of "thus it follows that," a relation that can by indicated by "therefore."

Standard Enthymematic Patterns

Y is an example of X.

Therefore, it follows that Z.

Or

> Y is a reason for X.
>
> Therefore, it follows that Z.

Here is an argument built on the first pattern, arguing from a single example:

> My brother-in-law spends his unemployment check on booze.
> All welfare recipients cheat.

This inductive argument is neither logical nor convincing, because there is a large gap between the minor and major premises. The rhetor has assumed that what is true of one particular, "my brother-in-law," is true of the class of "all welfare recipients." The only audiences who will accept this argument are those who are already convinced of its worthiness. Despite its flaws, people make arguments similar to this one every day.

Here is an instance of an argument built on the second pattern, arguing from a reason:

> Men have the power in Hollywood.
> That's why there are so few good roles for actresses.

The first and major premise generalizes about the gender of all powerful people in Hollywood, while the rhetor draws the conclusion that there are few good roles for actresses from a suppressed middle premise. Can you figure out what it is? It goes something like this:

> Men aren't interested in finding good roles for women.

In order to determine whether this argument from a reason is accurate or convincing, the middle premise must be articulated; once it is articulated, a rhetor who wants to be convincing can determine whether or not it can or needs to be supported by evidence. Such an examination in this case shows that at least a few examples should be assembled in order to shore up both the major and the minor premise.

The enthymematic patterns of example and reason are not and need not be followed slavishly. Sometimes an enthymematic argument begins with its conclusion:

> Because alternative music usually finds its way into pop culture, suburban dwellers like hip-hop and Johnny Cash songs can be heard on the streets of New York City.

The pattern here, then, is

> Because Z, X and Y.

The conclusion (Z), that alternative music becomes part of popular culture, is supported by two examples (X and Y) about the crossover popularity of hip-hop and country music. Whether this argument is convincing depends upon whether audiences think the examples are actually particulars that fit into the class asserted in the conclusion.

The advertisement for Apple products—"Think different"—is a highly truncated enthymeme in which only the conclusion is stated. The other premises are presented in various ways, including images of animated computer hardware, as well as images of historical figures made famous by their innovative approaches and unique messages: Albert Einstein, Martin Luther King Jr., John Lennon, Mohammad Ali, Ghandi, and Sarah Bernhardt, among others. Nonetheless, the entire enthymeme can be articulated in language:

> All geniuses are different from regular people.
>
> Apple products are different from other computer products.
>
> Apple is the genius of computers.

But that's not all: in urging the broader public to "think different," Apple is suggesting that its products may well be the first step toward innovative thinking. "Think different" therefore becomes a first premise, with the conclusion taking the form of an image of a shiny new Apple computer. The longer version goes something like this:

> Think different.
>
> Apple is different.
>
> Think Apple.

This enthymeme depends for its impact on a number of American commonplaces and attitudes: our reverence for novelty, for athletes and inspirational leaders, for creativity, assertiveness, and self-reliance. All of these commonplaces could be adduced as a chain of major premises that underlie the Apple ads. If we replace the word *think* with the word *buy*, then we have the kernel of the message: buy our product. This is the implicit or explicit conclusion offered by most advertising.

Presidential rhetoric is often a good place to look for enthymemes. Rhetorician Craig Allen Smith offers a helpful analysis of the speeches delivered by President George W. Bush in the wake of 9/11 and also in the 2004 presidential campaign. These speeches show President Bush creating an "enthymeme of evil" that allows a country like Iraq to be included in the sweeping post-9/11 condemnations. Smith shows how quickly Bush's enthymeme developed by offering this timeline:

> Transcendence of the attacks evolved quickly. At 9:30 a.m., Bush announced that "our country" had been attacked; at 2:30 p.m., that "freedom itself" had been attacked; and by 9:30 p.m., it was "our way of life, our very freedom" that had been attacked. In a similar manner, the attacks attributed at 2:30 p.m. to "a faceless coward" had by 9:30 p.m. been perpetrated by "evil." On the night of September 11, our response would be to "go forward to defend freedom and all that is good and just in our world"; but at the National Day of Prayer and Remembrance Service held on September 13, we would "rid the world of evil."

The rhetorical transformation from a coward's attack on our country to a mission to rid the world of evil had taken barely 48 hours. . . .

Rhetorically, the most effective path toward justification of a two-stage offensive against unspecified enemies who may or may not have had anything to do with the attacks of 9/11 was a rapid transformation of our response from *an attack on our country* to *ridding the world of evil*. From the outset, President Bush had characterized the acts as *evil*. By early October, he was talking about *evildoers* rather than the attackers. At his October 11 press conference, Bush said, "After all, on our TV screens the other day, we saw the evil one threatening—calling for more destruction and death in America." By *the evil one*, did the president mean bin Laden or was he invoking memories of the 9/11 photographs that purported to show Satan's face in the smoke and fire above the Twin Towers? Or perhaps he meant Saddam Hussein, of whom Bush had said earlier in the same press conference, "There's no question that the leader of Iraq is an evil man. After all, he gassed his own people. We know he's been developing weapons of mass destruction. And I think it's in his advantage to allow inspectors back in his country. . . . We're watching him carefully."

On November 2, Bush reiterated that "our war that we now fight is against terror and evil. It's not against Muslims. . . . Our struggle is going to be long and difficult, but we will prevail. We will win. Good will overcome evil." Bush went on to say that "we are fighting evil, and we will continue to fight evil, and we will not stop until we defeat evil." (2005, 38–39)

What Smith means by "enthymeme of evil" can be made clear by drawing out Bush's premises even further, like this:

Major premise: Evil ought to be defeated.

Minor premise: The perpetrators of the 9/11 attacks are evil.

Conclusion: The perpetrators of the 9/11 attacks ought to be defeated.

The first statement is a general premise, drawn from common-sense beliefs held by the community. The minor premises are particular premises, since they refer to individuals—the perpetrators of 9/11. The third statement is a conclusion derived from comparing the premises.

The frequent suppression of a minor premise allows for other minor premises, such as one that names other countries that Bush placed along the "axis of evil" in a speech delivered on January 29, 2002. The above enthymeme can be informed by a number of other enthymemes, which, when charted would look like this:

Major Premise: Anyone who would stockpile weapons of mass destruction and gas his own people must be evil.

Minor Premise: Saddam Hussein has stockpiled weapons of mass destruction and has gassed his own people.

Conclusion: Saddam Hussein is evil.

When the second enthymeme joins with the first one, an invasion of Iraq would be the conclusion Bush expected his audience to draw. Still other conclusions could be drawn from the premises of this enthymeme: that defeating evil requires support from the American people, and that they should do what they can to support the nation's response. Obviously, Bush and his speechwriters hoped that voters would draw these further conclusions.

As is apparent from this example, the placement of premises in rhetoric does not require the rigorous formal analysis that is necessary in logic. Nor are rhetors obligated to offer only two premises and a conclusion, as logicians are. Rather, an enthymeme may contain as many premises as are needed to secure the audience's belief in the conclusion. Furthermore, some premises might not hold up under scrutiny. For example, the *9/11 Commission Report*, as well as other sources, have since argued that the claim about weapons of mass destruction was unfounded.

Ordinarily, rhetors do not state all of the premises and conclusions of an enthymematic argument. Bush's "enthymeme of evil" was carefully constructed so it was ambiguous, allowing room for a host of premises. From the administration's point of view, the argument about Saddam Hussein was a very successful argument, because Congress backed a plan to invade Iraq and remove its leadership. From a rhetorician's point of view, however, it is an example of what Aristotle called "false reasoning," because its premises were not true. Rhetoricians are ethically obligated to avoid using premises that are not true.

Enthymemes are powerful because they are based in community beliefs. Because of this, whether the reasoning in an enthymeme is sound or whether the statements it contains are true or not, sadly enough, often makes little difference to the community's acceptance of the argument. Enthymemes work best when listeners or readers participate in constructing the argument—that is, if their prior knowledge is part of the argument, they are inclined to accept the entire argument if they are willing to accept the rhetorician's use of their common, prior knowledge. Bush's use of "we" in the statement "We know he's been developing weapons of mass destruction" marks the knowledge as specialized, obtained perhaps by national intelligence. And yet enough common sentiment in favor of going to war persisted at the time so that this remark was allowed to pass without much comment. Immediately after 9/11, certain common-sense responses and beliefs were heightened: fear of future attacks, mourning from loss, the need for national protection, a sense of moral outrage on behalf of the victims and their families—all of which funneled into the major premise about the need to defeat "evil."

Enthymematic arguments do not have to be spelled out completely, either. The rhetorician may even omit premises or conclusions. The audience will enjoy supplying the missing premises for themselves, and may be more readily persuaded by the argument because they have participated in its construction.

Take this enthymeme, for example: "Good people do not commit murder; Ethica is a good person; therefore Ethica did not commit murder."

While delivering this argument, the rhetor might omit the minor premise, saying only this: "Since good people do not commit murder, obviously Ethica is not guilty." Or he might omit the conclusion: "Good people do not commit murder, and Ethica is a good person." It is easy for the audience to supply the implied conclusion. As is true of all rhetorical premises, the major premise of this enthymeme is a probability rather than a certainty, and thus exceptions to it do exist.

The placement of premises in rhetoric does not require the rigorous formal analysis that is necessary in logic. And ordinarily, rhetors do not state all of the premises and conclusions of an enthymematic argument. Nor are rhetors obligated to offer only two premises and a conclusion, as logicians are. Rather, an enthymeme may contain as many premises as are needed to secure the audience's belief in the conclusion.

Cicero pointed out that while experienced rhetoricians know how to trace out all the arguments that appear in enthymemes, they do not present them according to the strict arrangement of their premises developed during invention. Rather, when it came to arrangement and delivery, a rhetor should chain premises together in the most effective way. The important thing, for Cicero, was to take a variety of approaches to laying out arguments for audiences. He counseled that a rhetor should

> use induction at one time and deduction at another; and again, in the deductive argument not always employ all . . . possible parts nor embellish the parts in the same fashion, but sometimes to begin with the minor premise, sometimes use one of the . . . proofs, sometimes both, and finally, use now this and now that form of conclusion (*De Inventione* I xli 76).

In other words, enthymemes may begin sometimes with premises or conclusions, depending on which is most effective in a given rhetorical situation. Furthermore, rhetors may omit premises that are self-evident to an audience. Cicero maintained that a few practice sessions would demonstrate just how easy it is to compose effective enthymemes.

Rhetorical Examples

Aristotle's word for example was *paradeigma* ("model"). A rhetorical example is any particular that can be fitted under the heading of a class and that represents the distinguishing features of that class. One of us lives with a cat named Margaret, who is an example of the class "cat" because she bears the distinguishing characteristics of this class. Lions and tigers (but not bears) are also examples of this class.

As Quintilian defined it, an example adduces "some past action real or assumed which may serve to persuade the audience of the truth of the point which we are trying to make" (V xi 6). If, for instance, a rhetor wants to convince her neighbor that he should keep his dog inside the fence that surrounds his property, she can remind him of a past instance when another neighbor's dog, running free, spread another neighbor's garbage all over both front yards. Rhetorical examples should not be confused with the particulars used in inductive reasoning. This rhetor has no interest in generalizing about all dogs in the neighborhood but is only concerned to compare the actual behavior of one dog running free to the probable behavior of another in similar circumstances. A rhetor who uses examples is reasoning only from part to part, or like to like, or like to unlike, and not from a particular to a generalization as he does in induction.

Rhetorical examples are persuasive because they are specific. Since they are specific, they call up vivid memories of something the audience has experienced. This effect works well if the rhetor gives details that evoke sensory impressions, that mention familiar sights, sounds, smells, tastes, or tactile sensations. In the following passage, Victor Villanueva, a teacher himself, gives us a portrait of a teacher who influenced him:

> An appreciation for literacy comes from Mr. Del Maestro. He teaches drama, though he ventures into poetry on occasion. A Robert Culp-like fellow, square jawed, thin but not skinny, reading glasses halfway down his nose, thin brown hair combed straight back, large hands. He had been a makeup man in Hollywood, he says. Brings movie-making to life. And for me, he brings Julius Caesar to life, removes the mist from "Chack-es-piri," as *abuela* would say it. And for those in the room not as fascinated by Julius Caesar or Prince Hamlet or poor Willy Loman as I am, those who are—in teacher talk—disruptive, Mr. D forgoes the pink slip to the principal, meets the disrupter downstairs, in the gym, twelve-ounce gloves, the matter settled. He has a broad definition of art. He knows the world—and he understands the block, *el bloque*, what kids today call "the hood." Mr. D was as close to color as any teacher I had known in school. (1993, 1–2)

Notice how the details in this example evoke readers' memory of their own teachers.

Examples also work well when they evoke memories of specific historical events that are fresh in the memories of members of the audience. Here is an exerpt from Nancy Gibbs's report on the events of the Virginia Tech shootings in April of 2007, written for *Time*:

> The winds were April cruel in Blacksburg on Monday: too strong for helicopters to evacuate the most badly wounded that morning, too strong for candles that night. The vigils would have to wait; the students grieved in the privacy of their dorms. The stately, sprawling campus of Virginia Tech was littered with broken branches; yellow police tape ribboned through a tree as if the gusts had tied it there, mourning those who would not be coming back. The locals said the winds rose to carry the angels down so they could take the children home.
>
> Hindsight blows just as strong through events like this. It's the nature of tragedy that it comes packaged in irony, sharp little stabs of coincidence that make it hurt even more: there was the Holocaust survivor who died trying to save his students from a mass murder committed on Holocaust Remembrance Day. There was the international-studies student who had seen the carnage at the Pentagon on 9/11 and wanted to be a peacemaker; he died in French class.

> There was the killer who signed into English class with a question mark, known by the few who knew him at all as one who hardly ever said a word to anyone—until the day he chose to start screaming and ended by shooting himself in the face, a final act of deletion. (2007)

Notice how Gibbs specifies and gives life to the generalization in the middle of this passage—"It's the nature of tragedy that it comes packaged in irony"—by listing example after example of sad coincidences.

When a rhetor reasons by means of example, she ordinarily uses a well-known instance to illuminate or explain one that is less well known. Aristotle, Cicero, and Quintilian all use this illustration of reasoning from example:

> To prove that Dionysius is aiming at a tyranny, because he asks for a bodyguard, one might say that Pisistratus before him and Theagenes of Megara did the same, and when they obtained what they asked for, made themselves tyrants. All the other tyrants known may serve as an example of Dionysius, whose reason, however, for asking for a bodyguard we do not yet know. (*Rhetoric* I ii 1357b)

If a rhetor wishes to turn this argument from example into an inductive argument, he can mention as many examples as he needs to be convincing, and then assemble them under a universal proposition: "One who is aiming at a tyranny asks for a bodyguard." He could immediately apply this generalization to new particulars if he wished: "We should beware, then, when Pericles asks for a bodyguard."

Historical Examples—Brief and Extended

Aristotle pointed out that successful examples may be drawn from history. For instance, people who opposed the Persian Gulf War in 1991 used the historical example of Vietnam to argue that America should not become involved again in a localized quarrel in which America had no direct involvement. Later, presidents Bush and Clinton both used the example of Vietnam as a reason for their hesitation to intervene in a local war between ethnic groups in Bosnia. People who opposed George W. Bush's plan to invade Iraq have also called on the example of Vietnam to caution against unilateral involvement in the affairs of other nations. Or, if a rhetorician were interested in arguing that politicians ought not to be trusted, she could briefly mention a number of examples taken from history—Nathan Hale, Benedict Arnold, or Richard Nixon, who, whether fairly or not, was called "Tricky Dick." The brief argument from example works because people respond to the specificity of examples. It works best when the examples selected (Hale, Arnold, Nixon) seem to squarely represent the class (politicians who were traitors).

Using a procedure called "extended example," a rhetor mentions only one of these figures and establishes his untrustworthiness by naming and describing several instances of it. For instance, Nixon lied to the American people on at least two occasions, he broke several laws, and he destroyed evidence that would implicate him in illegal acts. A rhetor can give as many vivid details as possible in order to evoke the audience's memory of the incident and thus to induce their sympathy with his argument. In the following passage, taken from the first chapter of *The Footnote*, Anthony Grafton has fun with the point he wants to make by citing extensively from the example set by the great eighteenth-century historian Edward Gibbon:

In the eighteenth century, the historical footnote was a high form of literary art. No Enlightenment historian achieved a work of more epic scale or more classic style than Edward Gibbon's *History of the Decline and Fall of the Roman Empire*. And nothing in that work did more than its footnotes to amuse his friends or enrage his enemies.[1] Their religious and sexual irreverence became justly famous. In his *Meditations*, says Gibbon the historian of the emperor Marcus Aurelius, husband of the notoriously gallant Faustina, he thanks the gods, who had bestowed on him a wife, so faithful, so gentle, and of such a wonderful simplicity of manners.[2] The world, urbanely reflects Gibbon the annotator, has laughed at the credulity of Marcus; but Madam Dacier assures us (and we may credit a lady) that the husband will always be deceived, if the wife condescends to dissemble.[3] The duty of an historian, remarks Gibbon in his ostensibly earnest inquiry into the miracles of the primitive church, does not call upon him to interpose his private judgment in this nice and important controversy.[4] It may seem somewhat remarkable, comments Gibbon in a footnote which drops all pretense of decorum, that Bernard of Clairvaux, who records so many miracles of his friend St. Malachi, never takes any notice of his own, which, in their turn, however, are carefully related by his companions and disciples.[5] The learned Origen and a few others, so Gibbon explains in his analysis of the ability of the early Christians to remain chaste, judged it the most prudent to disarm the tempter.[6] Only the footnote makes clear that the theologian had avoided temptation by the drastic means of castrating himself—and reveals how Gibbon viewed this operation: As it was his general practice to allegorize scripture; it seems unfortunate that, in this instance only, he should have adopted the literal sense.[7] Such cheerfully sarcastic comments stuck like burrs in orthodox memories and reappeared to haunt their author in the innumerable pamphlets written by his critics.[8]

Gibbon's artistry served scholarly as well as polemical ends—just as his footnotes not only subverted, but supported, the magnificent arch of his history.[9] He could invest a bibliographical citation with the grave symmetry of a Ciceronian peroration: In the account of the Gnostics of the second and third centuries, Mosheim is ingenious and candid; Le Clerc dull, but exact; Beausobre almost always an apologist; and it is much to be feared that the primitive fathers are very frequently calumniators.[10] He could supply a comic parallel with a gravity usually reserved for the commendation or condemnation of a major historical figure: "For the enumeration of the Syrian and Arabian deities, it may be observed, that Milton has comprised, in one hundred and thirty very beautiful lines, the two large and learned syntagmas, which Selden had composed on that abstruse subject."[11] And he could salute the earlier scholars, good Christians all, whose works he drew upon for a thousand curious details, with a unique combination of amused dismissal of their beliefs and genuine respect for their learning.[12] Gibbon was certainly right to think that comprehensive account of his sources, written in the same style, would have been susceptible of entertainment as well as information.[13] Though his footnotes were not yet Romantic, they had all the romance high style can provide. Their instructive abundance attracted the praise of the brilliant nineteenth-century classical scholar Jacob Bernays as well as that of his brother, the Germanist Michael Bernays, whose pioneering essay on the history of the footnote still affords more information and insight than most of its competitors.[14]

1. See in general G. W. Bowersock, "The Art of the Footnote," *American Scholar*, 53 (1983–84), 54–62. For the wider context, see the remarkable older study by M. Bernays, "Zur Lehre von den Citaten and Noten," *Schriften zur Kritik und Litteraturgeschtchte*, IV (Berlin, 1899), 255–347 at 302–322.

2. E. Gibbon, *The History of the Decline and Fall of the Roman Empire*, chap. 4; ed. D. B. Womersley (London, 1994), I, 108–109.

3. Chap. 4, n. 4; ibid., 109.

4. Ibid., chap. 15; I, 473.

5. Chap. 15, n. 81, ibid., 474.

6. Ibid., 480.

7. Chap. 15, n. 96, ibid. For a recent critical discussion of the story of Origen's self-castration, see p. Brown, *The Body and Society* (New York, 1988), 168 and n. 44.

8. This point is well made by Bernays. For more recent studies along the same lines, see F. Palmeri, "The Satiric Footnotes of Swift and Gibbon," *The Eighteenth Century*, 31 (1990), 245–262, and P. W. Cosgrove, "Undermining the Footnote: Edward Gibbon, Alexander Pope, and the Anti-Authenticating Footnote," *Annotation and Its Texts*, ed. S. Barney (Oxford, 1991), 130–151.

9. For two helpful case studies see J. D. Garrison, "Gibbon and the 'Treacherous Language of Panegyrics,'" *Eighteenth-Century Studies*, i 1 (1977–78), 4062; Garrison, Lively and Laborious: Characterization in Gibbon's Metahistory, *Modern Philology*, 76 (1978–79), 163–178.

10. Chap. 15, n. 32; I, 458.

11. Chap. 15, n. 9, ibid., 449.

12. See e.g. n. 98 to chap. 70, in which Gibbon expertly reviews and assesses the work of the indefatigable historian and editor of texts Ludovico Antonio Muratori, "my guide and master in the history of Italy." "In all his works," Gibbon comments, "Muratori approves himself a diligent and laborious writer, who aspires above the prejudices of a Catholic priest" (Muratori himself would have claimed that writing accurate history lay within a good priest's duties); ed. Womersley, III, 1061. On Muratori himself see S. Bertelli, *Erudizione a storia in Ludovico Antonio Muratori* (Naples, 1960).

13. "Advertisement," I, 5 (this text first appears, under the same title, on the verso of the half title to the endnotes in the first edition of the first volume of the *Decline and Fall* ([London, 1776]).

14. The phrase "lehreiche Fulle" is Jacob Bernays', as quoted with approval by Michael Bernays (305, n. 34). The relationship between the two deserves a study. Jacob mourned his brother as dead when he converted to Christianity: but Michael nonetheless emulated Jacob's analysis of the

manuscript tradition of Lecretius in his own geneological treatment of the editions of Goethe. For Jacob, see A. Momigliano, "Jacob Bernays," *Quinto contributo alla storia degli studi classici e del mondo antico* (Rome, 1975), 127–158; for his work on Lucretius, see S. Timpanaro, *la genesi del metodo del Lachmann*, 2nd ed. (Padua, 1985). For Michael Bernays, see W. Rehm, *Spate Studien* (Bern and Munich, 1964), 359–458, and H. Weigel, *Nur was du nie gesehn wird ewig dauern* (Freiburg, 1989). So far as I know, the third brother, Freud's father-in-law Berman, did not venture an opinion on Gibbon's footnotes. (1997, 1–4)

Notice how Grafton peppered his text with learned footnotes of his own, in order to reinforce the message conveyed by his extended example: "historians' arguments must still stride forward or totter backward on their footnotes" (4).

Fictional Example

Aristotle pointed out that successful examples can also be found in fiction. He drew his fictional examples from Aesop:

> A horse was in sole occupation of a meadow. A stag having come and done much damage to the pasture, the horse, wishing to avenge himself on the stag, asked a man whether he could help him to punish the stag. That man consented, on condition that the horse submitted to the bit and allowed him to mount him javelins in hand. The horse agreed to the terms and the man mounted him, but instead of obtaining vengeance on the stag, the horse from that time became the man's slave. (*Rhetoric* II xx 1393b)

According to Aristotle, Aesop used this fictional example to warn people that they should not give power to a dictator simply because they wished to take revenge on an enemy.

Fictional examples include fables and analogies (*paraboge*, "comparisons"). Fables may be drawn from literature or film, or a rhetor may compose her own stories for illustrative purposes (see the *progymnasmata* at the end of Chapter 1 for help in composing fables). Aristotle wrote that fables are easier to use than historical examples, because fables may be invented when no historical parallels are available which fit the rhetor's case. Advertisers often use animals or fabulous human beings to sell their products. One has only to recall Mr. Peanut or the Keebler Elves to realize how effective these fabulous images can become. Joe Camel and the Marlboro Man were used to sell cigarettes in the days when cigarette smoking was more fashionable than it is today. There is a good deal of argument over whether these fictional examples actually caused people to buy cigarettes, but certainly they did contribute to name recognition of the products they represent.

Fabulous examples work best if the narratives from which they are drawn are well known and liked by the audience. A rhetorician, on one hand, who is interested in establishing the possibility that UFOs are piloted by friendly extraterrestrials, for example, might revive his audience's memory of the vivid scenes of such visitations portrayed in popular films such as *E.T.* or *Close Encounters of the Third Kind*; rhetors who want to portray aliens as hostile, on the other hand, can turn to the vivid depictions of this scenario in *Signs, Alien,* or *The X-Files.* Fables are most effective when morals, or generalizations, can be drawn from them. So the rhetor who utilizes the movie fables mentioned here should point out exactly how these fictions reinforce the notions that the intentions of extraterrestrial visitors are friendly or hostile. He should also directly connect the lessons taught by the films with the point of his argument.

Analogy

In an **analogy** a rhetor places one hypothetical example beside another for the purposes of comparison. Aristotle borrowed his illustration of analogy from Socrates:

> It is as silly to argue that leaders should be chosen by balloting as it would be to argue that Olympic athletes or the pilots of ships should be chosen by lot.

By means of this comparison with examples, wherein choosing by ballot could produce disastrous results, the rhetor implies the conclusion that when leaders are chosen by ballot, there is no assurance that they will possess the skills requisite to leadership. He also manages to imply that leaders must have skill levels comparable to those of athletes and pilots of ships.

In a simple analogy like this one, a rhetor simply compares two or more things or events. President Lyndon Baines Johnson, in a commencement address delivered at Howard University in 1965, used the following simple analogy to underscore the need for affirmative action:

> You do not take a person who for years has been hobbled by chains and liberate him, bring him up to the starting line of a race and then say, "you're free to compete with all the others," and still justly believe that you have been completely fair. Thus it is not enough just to open the gates of opportunity. All our citizens must have the ability to walk through those gates. . . . We seek not . . . just equality as a right and a theory but equality as a fact and equality as a result.

Here President Johnson compared those who could benefit from affirmative action to a runner unable to exercise. This analogy became so popular among advocates of affirmative action programs and policies that it assumed the status of a commonplace in that discourse.

In complex analogies, in contrast, two examples exhibit a similar relation among their elements. The physician William Hervey, who is credited with discovering the circulation of the blood in human beings, used a complex analogy to do so. He reasoned that if sap circulates in vegetables and keeps them alive, it was reasonable to assume that blood circulates in animals and performs a similar function for them. Here the similarity lies in the relationship of circulation, rather than between the items mentioned—sap and blood, vegetables and animals.

Cicero included an example of complex analogical reasoning in the *De Inventione*. He told a story about an ancient rhetor named Aspasia who used a series of complex analogies to convince a couple to be satisfied with their marriage. First Aspasia prompted the wife to admit that, while she would prefer to have the gold ornaments and fine dresses possessed by a neighboring woman if they were better than her own, she would not covet that woman's husband, even though he be a better husband. In other words, since ornaments and fine dresses do not bear the same relation to happiness as does marriage to a fine husband, they do not bear the same relation to a woman's well-being or happiness. Aspasia then used a complex analogy to demonstrate to the husband that, while he might prefer to own the better horses and the better farm possessed by a neighboring man, he would not prefer the man's wife, even though she be a better wife than his own. Aspasia concluded:

> You, madam, wish to have the best husband, and you, Xenophon, desire above all things to have the finest wife. Therefore unless you can contrive that there be no better man or finer woman on earth, you will certainly always be in dire want of what you consider best, namely, that you be the husband of the very best of wives, and that she be wedded to the very best of men. (II xxxi 52)

The reasoning in this complex analogy goes like this:

> Any spouse who wants the best spouse must also become the best spouse because part of being wedded to "the best spouse" is being the "best spouse there is."

Because of the mutual relation of spouses to one another, each can be only as good a spouse as the other. The complex analogy resides, then, in the relationship of spouseness itself, rather than in the qualities of either husband or wife. Cicero thought that the force of this conclusion is undeniable, since it is very like the undisputed conclusions about jewelry and livestock that preceded it. He noted further that Socrates used this method "because he wished to present no arguments himself, but preferred to get a result from the material which the interlocutor had given him—a result which the interlocutor was bound to approve as following necessarily from what he had already granted" (53).

Here is an example of a complex analogy, put forward by columnist Maureen Dowd.

HOW WE'RE ANIMALISTIC—IN GOOD WAYS AND BAD

The odd thing is that conservatives wear pinstriped suits. They love the ancients so much that they really should be walking around in togas. The main contribution of the Greeks to modern American politics may have been Michael Dukakis, who once climbed the Acropolis in wingtips.

But that doesn't stop conservatives—especially the Straussians who pushed for going into Iraq—from being obsessed with ancient Greece, and from believing that they are the successors to Plato and Homer in terms of the lofty ideals and nobility and character in American politics—while Democrats merely muck about with policies for the needy.

Harvey Mansfield, a leading Straussian who taught political science at Harvard and who wrote a book called "Manliness" (he's for it), gave the Jefferson lecture recently at the National Endowment for the Humanities in Washington.

It was an ode, as his book is, to "thumos," the Greek word that means spirit-edness, with flavors of ambition, pride and brute willfulness. Thumos, as Philip Kennicott wrote in *The Washington Post*, "is a word reinvented by conservative academics who need to put a fancy name on a political philosophy that boils down to 'boys will be boys.' "

In his prepared remarks, Mr. Mansfield did not mention the war, which is a downer at conclaves of neocons and thumos worshippers. But he explained that thumos is "the bristling reaction of an animal in face of a threat or a possible threat." In thumos, he added, "we see the animality of man, for men (and especially males) often behave like dogs barking, snakes hissing, birds flapping. But precisely here we also see the humanity of the human animal" because it is reacting for "a reason, even for a principle, a cause. Only human beings get angry."

The professor used an example, naturally, from ancient Greece to explain why politics should be about revolution rather than equilibrium: "What did Achilles do when his ruler Agamemnon stole his slave girl? He raised the stakes. He asserted that the trouble was not in this loss alone but in the fact that the wrong sort of man was ruling the Greeks. Heroes, or at least he-men like Achilles, should be in charge rather than lesser beings like Agamemnon who have mainly their lineage to recommend them and who therefore do not give he-men the honors they deserve. Achilles elevated a civil complaint concerning a private wrong to a demand for a change of regime, a revolution in politics." Mr. Mansfield concluded: "To complain of an injustice is an implicit claim to rule."

The most recent example of the Hellenization of the Bush administration is the president's choice for war czar, Army Lt. Gen. Douglas Lute, who says he loves the Greek military historian Thucydides.

Other Thucydides aficionados include Victor Davis Hanson, who was a war-guru to Dick Cheney when the vice president went into the bunker after 9/11 and got into his gloomy Hobbesian phase. (Hobbes's biggest influence was also Thucydides.)

Donald Kagan, a respected Yale historian who has written authoritatively on the Peloponnesian War, is the father of Robert Kagan, a neocon who pushed for the Iraq invasion, and Frederick Kagan, a military historian who urged the surge.

I called Professor Kagan to ask him if Thucydides, the master at chronicling hubris and imperial overreaching, might provide the new war czar with any wisdom that can help America sort through the morass of Iraq.

Very much his sons' father, the classicist said he was disgusted that the White House, after a fiasco of an occupation designed by Rummy, "is still doing one dumb thing after another" by appointing General Lute, a chief skeptic of the surge.

Professor Kagan said that one reason the Athenians ended up losing the war was because in the Battle of Mantinea in 418 B.C. against the Spartans, they sent "a very inferior force" and had a general in command who was associated with the faction that was against the aggressive policy against the Spartans.

"Kind of like President Bush appointing this guy to run the war whose strategy is opposed to the surge," he said dryly.

With cold realism, Thucydides captured the Athenian philosophy in the 27-year war that led to its downfall as a golden democracy: "The strong do what they can and the weak suffer what they must."

What message can we take away from Thucydides for modern times?

"To me," Professor Kagan said, "the deepest message, the most tragic, is his picture of civilization as a very thin veneer. When you punch a hole in it, what you find underneath is hollow, the precivilized characteristics of the human race—animalistic in the worst possible way." (2007)

Compared to Iraq, the Peloponnesian War was a cakewalk. Dowd cleverly begins the analogy between conservative leaders and the ancients by pretending to be perplexed at the different fashion choices—pinstripe suits and wingtips aren't quite togas. But her analogy becomes more complex as she explores the main analogy: that between the Iraq War and the Peloponnesian War. She begins by examining the ancient anecdote made by the conservative political theorist Harvey Mansfield, which, according to Dowd points to a hypermasculine model of power. While Dowd doesn't mention it, her analysis hearkens back to California Governor's Arnold Schwarzenegger's favorite epithet for Democrats: "girlie men." Digging more deeply into ancient history, she contacts a Yale historian known for his four-volume work on the Peloponnesian War who also happens to be the father of two highly ranking military officials. Throughout, Dowd hints at the conservative desire for empire, and with the last line suggests that the "Road to Empire" might well be more complicated now compared to what it was in ancient times.

Similar and Contrary Examples

Quintilian distinguished between examples that work by comparing two like instances, which he called "**simile**," and those that work by comparing unlike cases or "**contraries**." His example of simile was "Saturninus was justly killed, as were the Gracchi" (V xi 7). The Gracchi were famous brothers, Tiberius and Gaius, who led revolts against constituted Roman authority. Quintilian's comparison implied that the lesser-known and less respected Saturninus belonged in the class of persons who are important enough to pose a threat; it also implied that even though he was a lesser person, he nevertheless deserved a punishment similar to that meted out to the members of the famous Gracchus family.

A contemporary rhetorician might argue from simile as follows: *Survivor* and *American Idol* were rigged. So don't expect me to watch *America's Next Top Model*. The argument implied by the comparison among these examples of so-called "reality TV" is that if two were rigged, others will be, as well, and are hence not worth watching. A contemporary rhetorician who is skeptical about official explanations of the assassinations of public figures might make a more complex argument from comparative possibility as follows: "If it was possible to capture and imprison the assassin of Robert Kennedy, it ought to be possible to capture and imprison the assassins of Martin Luther King Jr. and John F. Kennedy as well." The comparison suggests that even though suspects were captured and imprisoned in the latter two cases, neither was the actual assassin.

To argue from example by contrary is trickier but nevertheless effective. Quintilian's illustration of contrary example was this: "Marcellus restored the works of art which had been taken from the Syracusans who were our enemies, while Verres took the same works of art from our allies" (V xi 6). This example reflects very negatively on the character of Verres, who, in contrast to Marcellus's generosity to former enemies, stole from friends. One of us recently saw a bumper sticker that argues through contrary example in the form of an intricate enthymeme: "Nobody died when Clinton lied." The implied subject here is the Bush administration's mistruths about weapons of mass destruction, which led to deaths of U.S. soldiers, allied troops, as well as Iraqi citizens. The lie Clinton told about his sexual activity, by comparison, seems less objectionable—at least to the driver who bought the bumper sticker.

USING EXAMPLES

Aristotle preferred enthymemes to examples as a kind of proof, no doubt because enthymemes were similar to the fundamental unit of proof in his logical system—the syllogism. However, he wrote that if no enthymemes are available to a rhetor, she must use examples since they do produce conviction (II xx 9). If enthymemes are available, he recommended that a rhetor support them with examples and that she put the examples last since they are likely to induce belief. If a rhetor must begin with examples, she should include several; however, if she uses them last, in support of an enthymeme, one example will do.

Aristotle's preference for logical reasoning seems to have overtaken his usual good sense at this point. Modern audiences are ordinarily impressed by examples. The argument from example is certainly a favorite of advertisers—think, for instance, of the ads for beer that show people drinking beer and having a good time. Many contemporary journalists and writers of nonfiction also begin their arguments with extended examples. Here are the opening paragraphs from an article about global warming written by Chad Harbach for the magazine *n+1*:

> Over the course of the past century, mean global temperatures increased by 0.6°C. This change seems slight but it isn't: in the winter of 1905 my great-grandfather, a coppersmith, installed the roof on a new reef-point lighthouse two miles from Lake Michigan's shore. Each morning he drove out across the open ice in a horse and buggy laden with his copperworking tools; today the water that far from the shore never freezes, much less to a depth that could support a horse's weight.
>
> Well into the 1990s, such changes had happened gradually enough to seem salubrious, at least in the Upper Midwest—a karmic or godly reward, perhaps, for hard work and good behavior. No snow in October! Another fifty-degree day in February! It was as if the weather, too, partook of the national feeling of post-WWII progress: the economy would expand, technology would advance, the fusty mores of a black-and-white era would relax, and the climate, like some index or celebration of all this, would slowly become more mild. This was America. Our children would not only have bigger cars, smaller stereos, a few extra years to themselves—they'd have better weather, too.
>
> Now we know what we've done. (2006, 1)

Notice how Harbach uses an extended example here to dramatize events in his narrative, events that he could not have witnessed personally but that he nevertheless knows about through stories passed down through generations in his family. This use of extended example creates a stark picture of climate change, providing a suitable frame for his argument that global warming is "worse than you think," which entices the reader to read further into the narrative.

If well chosen, examples cause audiences to recall similar circumstances in which they have participated or in which they would like to participate. The rhetorician can hope that the vividness of the comparison will also cause his audience to draw the conclusions at which he has only hinted. The rhetors who design beer ads obviously hope that viewers will connect use of the product with the fun shown in the ad.

Maxims

Maxims are wise sayings or proverbs that are generally accepted by the rhetorician's community. Ancient maxims were often drawn from poetry or history, as with Aristotle's "There is no man who is happy in everything," by the playwright—Euripides, or "The best of omens is to defend one's country" from the poet Homer (II 21 2 and 11). But maxims also arise from the common wisdom of the people: the proverb "Birds of a feather flock together" was old even when Quintilian cited it two thousand years ago (V xi 41). Modern examples of maxims include such hoary sayings as "A stitch in time saves nine," "Better late than never," "Rolling stones gather no moss."

In ancient times, when literacy was not widespread, much popular wisdom was contained in oral sayings. Many of these were drawn from lines composed by respected poets, especially Homer. A rhetorician could utter a line from Homer and his audience would immediately recognize the context and the point of the quotation. This is still possible to a certain extent, although modern audiences are not as well acquainted with lines from poetry as people once were. However, many of us do know maxims taken from the Christian Bible such as "an eye for an eye," and most of us have heard the line "To be or not to be" at least once in our lives, although fewer people know that it is the first line of a speech uttered by a character created by Shakespeare named Hamlet. This phrase could well serve as the opening line of a defense attorney's opening speech; in fact a rhetor could use it to organize a list of options in any discourse urging that some action be taken. We do remember lines from speeches, such as Martin Luther King's "I have a dream" or John F. Kennedy's "Ask not what your country can do for you" or George W. Bush's "axis of evil." Such lines serve subsequent rhetors as a rhetorical shorthand that can evoke whole political philosophies.

According to Aristotle, maxims are general statements which deal with human actions that should be chosen or avoided (II xxi 2). The first two modern maxims listed earlier recommend actions: "A stitch in time saves nine" counsels us to be as well prepared as possible in order to save ourselves extra trouble. "Better late than never" implies that doing something too late is better than never doing it at all. The "rolling stones" maxim implies that people who submit to wanderlust don't pile up responsibilities; since wanderlust as a way of life might be either appealing or repulsive to a given audience, the action recommended here is culturally ambiguous. A rhetor who relies on the persuasive power of this maxim would do well to clarify whether she approves of wanderlust and why.

Maxims can be found in dictionaries of proverbs or collections of quotations. Their rhetorical force derives from their commonness. Since they are commonly held, they seem to be true. As Quintilian pointed out, "sayings such as these would not have acquired immortality had they not carried conviction of their truth to all mankind" (V xi 41). And as Aristotle noted, somewhat cynically, maxims are especially convincing to audiences who like to hear their beliefs confirmed. Aristotle's example is this: a person who happened to have bad neighbors or children would welcome anyone's statement that nothing is worse than having neighbors or more stupid than to beget children (II xxi 15). This feature of maxims provides a clue as to how to hunt for appropriate ones: a rhetor should try to determine whether his audience has any preconceived opinions that are relevant to his point. If so, he should find an appropriate maxim that generalizes these preconceived opinions. For example, the maxim "Rolling stones gather no moss" would be appropriate for an older audience who disapproves of the way younger Americans tend to move frequently from community to community and from job to job. Their very general nature makes maxims applicable to a wide variety of situations. In fact, part of their persuasive force lies in their generality—when applied to a specific case, a maxim can impart its own persuasive force to that case. For example, Marine officers use the motto of the corps, *Semper fidelis* ("Always faithful"), to breed camaraderie among their troops and to convince them to go into battle. The motto is an abbreviated reference to the entire history of the Marine Corps—it reminds Marines of the corps's martial history and of its tradition of brotherhood under fire. Thus, though general, the motto can be effectively used in any specific situation when the troops need to be urged forward. Its use is such a commonplace among Marines and ex-Marines that saying "*Semper fi*" establishes an immediate relation of trust between even recent acquaintances.

Aristotle noted that maxims are often the premises or conclusions of an enthymeme. Here is an argument from a news editorial using an enthymeme that employs the maxim "Better late than never" as its conclusion:

> Last year Mr. Bush finally conceded that global warming existed. This year he conceded that human beings were to blame, and the damage was going to be severe. At this rate, next year he'll start to champion policies that will begin to put a dent in climate change—such basic steps as higher gas-mileage standards for American cars and trucks, more research into renewable energy, and tougher enforcement of the Clean Air Act instead of Mr. Bush's attempts to weaken it.
>
> Better late than never. But for an administration that views energy conservation as nothing more than a personal virtue, you probably shouldn't count on it. ('Get Used to It')

Maxims can serve effectively as the major premises of enthymemes, as well, since they represent the common wisdom of a community. Here is an example:

Major Premise: A stitch in time saves nine.

Minor Premise: There is a small crack in the windshield of Felix's car.

Conclusion: Felix should have the crack buffed out, or else it will spread and he will have to replace the entire windshield.

Note how, in this case, the maxim predicts the particular conclusion so readily that the rhetorician could safely omit the conclusion when she presents the argument.

One cautionary note about maxims is in order: Aristotle warned that maxims should not be used by young people, who run the risk of appearing to espouse something in a maxim that they have not learned through experience.

Signs

Signs are physical facts or real events that inevitably or usually accompany some other state of affairs. For example, if someone has a fever, this is a sign that he is ill; if someone bears a physical scar, this is a sign that he was once injured. If, as in these examples, the connection between the sign and the inferred state of affairs always exists, we have what Aristotle called an infallible sign (*tekmerion*) (I ii 16). But not all signs are infallibly connected to some state of affairs. We can argue, for instance, that a defendant's bloody clothing is a sign that she committed the murder for which she is being tried. However, the defense attorney could plausibly argue that the defendant suffers from frequent nosebleeds and thus that the bloodied clothing is a sign of that problem, rather than her participation in a murder.

The argument from sign can be very effective in an argument for the same reason that examples are effective. Arguments from sign appeal to the daily experiences that we share with members of our audience. The trick for a rhetor who uses the argument from sign is to convince an audience that the sign in question is (or is not) inevitably connected to the state of affairs he is trying to establish. Because of this difficulty, Quintilian recommended that the argument from sign be accompanied by other support (V ix 9). If the prosecuting attorney can prove that the defendant was an enemy of the murdered man, had threatened his life, and was in his house at the time of the murder, then all of these strengthen the connection of the bloody clothing to murder, rather than to a bloody nose.

We rely on arguments from sign more than we perhaps realize. We take a cloudy sky as a sign of an impending storm; if a friend is listless and uninterested in his surroundings, we take that as a sign of depression; when the pilot of an airplane in flight turns off the light that says "Fasten seat belt," we take that as a sign that it is safe to get out of our seats. But as these examples suggest, it is not always safe to rely on signs as though they were infallible. A darkened sky may result from pollution; our listless friend may be coming down with the flu; sudden unexpected turbulence may make us wish we hadn't taken the pilot's message so casually. If someone who is accused of making hateful remarks has made them on previous occasions, this may or may not be a sign that she harbors racist or sexist attitudes.

The argument from sign has a *kairotic* element, insofar as signs change over time. In the 1960s, a man's long hair was taken as a sign that he was a hippie who believed in free love and using drugs. These days, however, the length of a man's hair does not reliably signify much of anything. Indeed, an important part of contemporary rhetorical argument involves the disassociation of signs from their commonplace referents. Today, rhetors are at pains to point out that tattoos or body piercings are not necessarily a sign of rebelliousness, or that being on welfare is not necessarily a sign of laziness or unwillingness to work. Some extremely conservative groups are trying to establish that refusing to pay one's taxes is a sign of patriotism. Signs differ from place to place as well. In the midwestern and southern states, people ask strangers about their parents and family as a sign of friendliness. In western states, however, such curiosity may be taken as a sign of nosiness or even of very bad manners. And there are cases in which we turn things or events into signs even though we have no idea what they signify. For example, cattle mutilations and the large designs that have appeared in crop fields all over the world have been taken as signs of something, but no one is exactly sure what.

RHETORICAL ACTIVITIES

1. Find an article from a popular magazine or newspaper and examine its use of enthymemes, examples, maxims, or signs. How effectively are these proofs used?

2. Create an enthymeme to use in some composition you are currently working on. Find a maxim that supports your proposition and work out the argument that connects the maxim to your position. Find a historical example that supports your position and include it. Find or invent a fictional example that supports your position and include it (see Chapter 15, on the *progymnasmata*, for advice about writing fictions). Find an argument from sign that supports some conclusion in your argument.

3. Some popular slogans are conclusions or premises of enthymemes. The statement that "Elvis has left the building" is part of a long enthymematic argument whose other premises are never stated. Can you articulate them?

PROGYMNASMATA V: ENCOMIUM AND INVECTIVE

While commonplace engaged students in composing discourses that examined general vices or virtues, the next two exercises of the *progymnasmata* asked students to compose discourses in which they either praised or abused some specific person or thing. Greek rhetors called a discourse of praise "panegyric," but it is still known in English by its Latin name, *encomium*. A discourse that blames or abuses something or someone, on the other hand, is called "invective." Both kinds allow students to practice composing epideictic rhetoric. Rhetors have many opportunities both to praise good actions or persons and to heap blame on less honorable persons and activities, and so these exercises provide excellent practice for real rhetorical situations. Quintilian observed that such compositions are often imposed on us, as when we are asked to give eulogies at funerals (a discourse of praise) or when we are asked to serve as character witnesses in court, in which case we may be asked either to praise or to blame an accused person (III vii 2).

Encomium and invective were commonly practiced by the ancient Greeks and Romans. Encomiums were featured in many religious and cultural celebrations in both cultures, and famous rhetors often gave speeches of praise or denunciation to large audiences in order to display their oratorical abilities. Isocrates' *Panegyricus* and *Panathenaicus* are encomiums of the city of Athens. Gorgias and Isocrates, among others, composed encomiums about Helen, whose abduction by Paris initiated the Trojan War. Popular interpretations of Homer's account of that war suggested that Helen was responsible for starting it. But these famous sophists argued the opposite case in their speeches of praise for her.

Encomiums and invective are still being composed today, although we don't call them that. Most Fourth of July speeches are encomiums to the United States, while speeches and editorials composed for Memorial Day praise those killed in war. Mothers' Day inspires endless essays about the virtues of motherhood, which are examples of encomiums to an abstract ideal. Obituaries are encomiums to deceased persons, and letters of reference may praise the character of the person being recommended. Toasts at weddings and retirement parties usually offer praise for the guests of honor. Invective, which exposes evils or heaps blame on someone who has done wrong, is used in political campaigns when candidates heap blame on one another even more frequently than they praise their own efforts.

Invective is also a regular feature of letters written to the editors of newspapers and magazines. Political leaders sometimes use invective when trying to incite people in their area to unite against another person or group of people. President George W. Bush, with the help of his speechwriters, issued an invective when he used the phrase "axis of evil" to refer to different areas in the Middle East and Asia. Sometimes biographies, histories, and journalistic books are extended encomia or invectives. For example, Al Franken's *Lies and the Lying Liars Who Tell Them: A Fair and Balanced Look at the Right* (2003) is an invective about the American Right, especially the Bush administration's 2000 campaign and the so-called War on Terror. Unauthorized biographies of famous people are popular precisely because they contain large doses of invective.

Aphthonius, on one hand, defined an encomium as "a composition expository of inherent excellences." He listed its proper subjects as "persons, things, times, places, animals, and also plants: persons like Thucydides or Demosthenes, things like justice or moderation, times like spring or summer, places like harbors or gardens, animals like a horse or an ox, and plants like an olive or a vine." Hermogenes, on the other hand, suggested that students compose encomiums about a race (such as the Greeks), a city, or a family.

Ancient teachers defined an elaborate set of directions for composing encomiums and invectives: Theon, for example, listed thirty-six possible encomiastic headings for amplification. The standard list of headings for an encomium of a person was as follows: a prologue; announcement of the class of person or thing to be praised or blamed; consideration of the person's origins (nationality, native city, ancestors, parents); education and interests; achievements (virtue, judgement, beauty, speed or strength, power, wealth, friends); comparison; and epilogue. Both Apthonius and Nicolaus the Sophist note that encomia should be both extensive and exhaustive; an encomium, according to Nicolaus, "is developed through an account of all the virtues and all the excellences of what is being praised" (155). The same topics can be used to compose invectives. Here is Aphthonius's encomium on the ancient historian Thucydides:

> To honor the inventors of useful things for their very fine contributions is just, and just it is that the light coming forth from those men be turned with good reason upon those who displayed it. Accordingly, I shall laud Thucydides by choosing to honor him with the history of the man himself. Moreover, it is a good thing that honor be given to all benefactors, but especially to Thucydides about others, because he invented the finest of all things. For it is neither possible to find anything superior to history in these circumstances, nor is it possible to find one more skillful in history than Thucydides.
>
> Accordingly, Thucydides came from a land that gave him both life and a profession. For he was not born from an indifferent quarter but from whence history came, and by gaining Athens as his mother of life, he had kings for ancestors, and the stronger part of his good fortune proceeded from his earlier ancestry. By gaining both force of ancestry and democratic government, the advantage from one supplied a check upon the other, preventing his being rich unjustly through political equality and concealing public poverty through the affluence of his descent.
>
> Having come upon the scene with such advantages, he was reared under a civil polity and laws that are by nature better than others. Knowing how to live both under arms and under law, he determined to be in one and the same person both a philosopher and a general, neither depriving history of military experience nor placing battles in the class of intellectual virtue. Further, by combining things that were naturally separate, he made a single career in things for which he had no single set of rules.
>
> As he arrived at manhood, he kept seeking an opportunity for the display of those qualities in which he had been well disciplined. And fortune soon produced the war, and he made the actions of all the Greeks his personal concern. He became the custodian of the things that the war brought to pass, for he did not allow time to erase the deeds separately accomplished. Among these, the capture of Plataea is famous, the ravages of Attica were made known, the Athenian circumnavigation of the Poloponnesus was described, and Naupactus was a witness to sea battles. By collecting these things in writing, Thucydides did not allow them to escape notice. Lesbos was won, and the fact is proclaimed to this day; a battle was fought against the Ambraciotes, and time has not obscured the event; the unjust decree of the Lacedaemonians is not unknown. Sphacteria and Pylos, the great achievement of the Athenians, has not escaped unseen.
>
> Where the Corcyraeans speak in the assembly at Athens, the Corinthians present answers to them. The Aeginetans go to Lacedaemon with accusations. Archidamus is discreet before the assembly, but Sthenelaides is urging them on to war. And to these examples, add Pericles, holding a Spartan embassy in no esteem and not allowing the Athenians to make trouble when they were suffering. Once and for all, these things are preserved for all time by Thucydides' book.
>
> Does anyone really compare Herodotus with him? But Herodotus narrates for pleasure, whereas this man utters all things for the sake of truth. To the extent that entertainment is less worthy than a regard for the truth, to that degree does Herodotus fall short of the virtues of Thucydides.

There would be many other points to mention about Thucydides, if the great number of his praises did not prevent the enumeration of all of them. (Matsen, Rollinson, and Sousa 1990 276–77)

A careful reading of this encomium will show that Aphthonius included a prologue, stated the kind of encomium he has composed (praise of a single person), and commented on his subject's birth and upbringing as well as his studies and achievements. The encomium concludes with a comparison and a summarizing epilogue.

Thomas L. Friedman composed an encomium on the class of 2007 that reflects on a kind of quiet courage he sees in recent college graduates. We include an excerpt of it here.

THE QUIET AMERICANS

Since my daughter is graduating from college today, I am thinking a lot about the class of 2007 and the world they are about to enter. I'm not sure what they call this generation. Is it generation "X" or "Y" or "Zero" or "Me"? Having taken part in two other commencements this season, though, and knowing enough about what my own daughter's friends are doing, I can say that there is something quietly impressive about this cohort. In fact, if I were giving them a label I'd call them the "Quiet Americans"—not in the cynical way Graham Greene meant it, but in a very positive sense.

They are young people who are quietly determined not to let this age of terrorism curtail their lives, take away their hopes or steal the America they are about to inherit. They don't take to the streets much—in part, I suspect, because they do a lot of their political venting online. But it seems to me that they go off and volunteer for public service or for military service with as much conviction as any generation, if not more.

Four years ago, when my wife and I dropped our daughter off at college, I wrote that I was troubled that I was dropping her off into a world that was so much more dangerous than the one she had been born into—and I worried that she would not be able to travel in the carefree way that I had when I was her age. Her two summers teaching and researching in India have cured me of that misapprehension. Now I know how my mother felt.

"I don't know where these kids find lepers, but they find them and they read to them," said Stephen J. Trachtenberg, the departing president of George Washington University.

"I've been a college president for 30 years, and these kids are more optimistic about the future than any I have seen—maybe more than they have reason to be," he said. "They still believe that the world is their oyster and go abroad with abandon. Notwithstanding everything, they remain optimistic." (2007 p. 11)

Friedman provides a brief history of this year's graduating class, praises their strengths, and marvels at the futures they have planned. In addition, he supports his generalizations with testimony from a university president.

Quintilian suggested that praise of persons include praise of place of birth, parents, and ancestry (III viii 10). This may be handled in two ways: the rhetor may show that someone lived up to the high standards of her place of birth or that her deeds have made her place of birth even more praiseworthy. Someone's character, physical endowments such as beauty and strength, or deeds and achievements can furnish topics for praise (or abuse). Accidental advantages, such as wealth or power, should not be praised for themselves but only if the person put such advantages to honorable use. The only deeds deserving of praise are those that were done for the sake of others, not on the person's own behalf. Sometimes reputations increase (or decrease) after persons have died; in this case, Quintilian says, it is appropriate to point out that "children reflect glory on their parents, cities on their founders, laws on those who made them, arts on their inventors and institutions on those that first introduced them" (18).

The same topics can be used in denunciations of persons. People who came from privileged backgrounds can be blamed if they squandered those resources or if they used them to engage in vice. While we no longer approve of denouncing persons because of their physical appearance, we can blame someone who demonstrates an immoral character or who engages in reprehensible acts. Quintilian pointed out that the reputations of bad or immoral persons redounds upon their children and their homelands as well (21). We may not like to admit this, but we (the authors) think it is still true that we condemn innocent people who are associated by birth or circumstance with individuals who commit immoral acts.

Cities are praised or blamed in the same way. A city's founder can be made responsible for the habits of its citizens in the same way that parents are responsible for their children. Quintilian remarked that great age usually brings fame to a city, as do their settings, public works, and buildings or fortifications. Buildings should be praised for their "magnificence, utility, beauty and the architect or artist must be given due consideration" (27). As an example of an encomium on a place, Quintilian cited Cicero's praises of Sicily in his Verrine orations:

> When Sicily was at the height of its prosperity, and abounded in wealth and resources, there were many fine workshops on the island. For, before Verres' tenure as governor, there was not a home somewhat well off in which there could not be found such things as silver dishes with decorative medallions and figures of the gods, silver bowls used by the women in performing rituals, and a censer, even though there may not have been much else in the way of silver plate. These things were, moreover, executed in a classic style of exquisite craftsmanship; one would be led to believe that the Sicilians had, at one time, owned many other things of equal value, but, that incurring their loss through changed fortunes, they still retained the objects associated with religious worship. (IV, 21)

Notice how skillfully Cicero managed to praise the Sicilians at the same time as he blamed Verres for their impoverished condition.

In his remarks on the composition of encomiums, Aristotle made a subtle point that does not appear in ancient textbooks: discourses of praise or blame must be carefully suited to their audiences (*Rhetoric* I 9). He quoted Socrates, who is supposed to have said that "it is not difficult to praise Athenians in Athens" (1367b). What is considered honorable in Athens can be an object of blame among Scythians or Laconians. Of course, the same point holds true today. To praise Americans in America is easy enough to do; such a composition would be received quite differently elsewhere in the world. The same holds true for invective; it is easy to blame Americans when writing for other audiences. During the Persian Gulf War, Judith Williamson wrote the following passage for a British publication called *The Guardian*:

> It is the unreality of anywhere outside the US, in the eyes of its citizens, which must frighten any foreigner. Like an infant who has yet to learn there are other centres of self, this culture sees others merely as fodder for its dreams and nightmares. . . . The hyped-up concern over US children's fears ("Will Saddam kill me Mommy?") is obscene when you consider that American bombs are right now killing Iraqi children. It isn't that Americans don't care (God knows they care) but that for most of them, other lands and people cannot be imagined as real. (1991, 21)

Americans who accept the accuracy of Williamson's invective may nevertheless be put off by her criticism.

Distinct groups of persons also hold differing sets of values. Quintilian observed that "much depends on the character of the audience and the generally received opinion, if they are to believe that the virtues of which they approve are preeminently characteristic of the person praised and the vices which they hate of the person denounced" (III vii 23). The boundaries between virtue and vice are also notoriously hard to define; acceptable behavior in one setting may be utterly unacceptable in another (25). The wise rhetor will keep these differences in mind as he composes encomiums or invective.

The composition of encomiums and invective was a popular exercise among educated persons during late antiquity and throughout the Renaissance. Erasmus's *Praise of Folly* (in Latin, *Encomium Moriae*, 1509) is a satiric encomium about foolishness. John Milton composed paired poems called "Joy" and "Thoughtfulness" when he was quite young. The poem about joy contains an invective about melancholy, or sadness, that connects its origins with death:

> Hence loathed Melancholy
> Of Cerberus, and blackest midnight born,
> In Stygian Cave forlorn.
> 'Mongst horrid shapes, and shrieks, and sights unholy,
> Find out some uncouth cell,
> Where brooding darkness spreads his jealous wings,
> And the night-Raven sings;
> There under Ebon shades, and low-brow'd Rocks,
> As ragged as thy Locks,
> In darks Cimmerian desert ever dwell.
>
> —John Milton, "L'Allegro"

The poem about thoughtfulness, in contrast, contains a lengthy encomium to melancholy. We quote only its opening lines:

> But hail thou Goddess, sage and holy,
> Hail divinest Melancholy,
>   Whose Saintly visage is too bright
> To hit the Sense of human sight;
>   And therefore to our weaker view,
> Ore laid with black staid Wisdoms' hue.
>
> —John Milton, "Il Penseroso"

Once again, Milton's performance suggests that arguments can be found to attack or defend anything or anybody, depending on the situation.

Rhetors can adapt Aphthonius's suggestions to any contemporary topic: you can practice writing discourses that praise or blame nations, cities, families, persons, animals, or things. For a relatively simple exercise, choose a favorite relative, a favorite pet, or even a plant and use Aphthonius's topics to develop a discourse raising it. This exercise does not have to be serious; funny essays can be written in praise or blame of inanimate objects. Isocrates complained about rhetors who composed encomiums to salt and bumblebees ("Helen" 12).

Lighthearted encomia and invective are still popular. Erma Bombeck, the columnist, often composed very funny encomiums or invectives about household objects such as vacuum cleaners and garage door openers. Here's a contemporary encomium, this time on a cookbook, written by Lloyd Fonvielle. It appeared in the online magazine salon.com.

ODE TO "JOY"

On the Internet recently I tracked down a mint copy of "The Joy Of Cooking" from the early '50s—the edition I remember as a fixture in my family's kitchen in those times.

Its resonance as an object is oddly powerful to someone of my generation— deeper even than reruns of "The Mickey Mouse Club"—one of those artifacts of civilization that becomes invisible through familiarity and hard to collect because of use. You have to pay a premium for a vintage copy of the book that isn't splattered and stained with food or split open at the entry for meatloaf.

I was moved to own a copy because the title was recently included on one of those lists of the 100 most important books of the 20th century.

This struck me as a brilliant insight, and a deeply logical one. This is a book that moved with women as they left their old communities, and served in loco parentis in the kitchen, as Dr. Spock served them in the nursery.

It also introduced an ambition for sophistication and a kind of defensive professionalism into domestic cooking at a time when all things domestic were being devalued in the culture at large.

In my mind now, it serves as an emblem of my mother's time in the kitchen, the unrecorded epic of her domestic labor, which in childhood was the clearest expression I knew of absolute love and absolute security.

We dismiss the almost mystical reverence for such labor by the Victorians as insincere sentimentality, a sop to the oppressed, but any child knows differently.

The book remains useful. I recently consulted it for instruction on how long to boil hardboiled eggs. The awesome ignorance this revealed was touching to me, as it also revealed the awesome knowledge of those who don't need it for such things and the bewilderment of those who found that knowledge suddenly underappreciated.

The book is really about the sacredness of cooking. Not cuisine, but cooking—the invisible work done in the kitchen on any ordinary Wednesday. (2000)

In his encomium on the best-selling *Joy of Cooking*, Fonvielle offers an account that situates the book personally as well as culturally—diagnosing its long-standing appeal. Who knew a cookbook could mean so much to someone?

No subject is off limits in this exercise. In fact, its versatility is one of its strengths. Quintilian remarked that compositions of praise or blame were "profitable in more than one respect. The mind is exercised by the variety and multiplicity of the subject matter, while the character is molded by the contemplation of virtue and vice" (IV iv 20).

PROGYMNASMATA: ENCOMIUM AND INVECTIVE

1. Develop an encomium or an invective about the city council or other leaders of your town or state.

2. A United States senator has been accused of sexual harassment: write an invective that denounces him for this behavior, or compose an encomium that excuses him from these charges on the basis of his origin, character, or achievements.

3. Compose an encomium or an invective about abstract ideas or issues: how about an encomium to rhetoric?

WORKS CITED

Dowd, Maureen. "How We're Animalistic—In Good Ways and Bad." *New York Times*, May 30, 2007. Sec. A col. 1 p. 21.

Friedman, Thomas L. "The Quiet Americans." *New York Times*, May 27, 2007, Sec. 4, p. 11.

Fonvielle, Lloyd. "Ode to Joy." *Salon* 7 (March 2000). http://archive.salon.com/mwt/sust/2000/03/07/joy/.

"'Get Used to It': President's New Philosophy on Global Warming." *Record* (June 4, 2002): L12. North Jersey Media Group, specifically Passaiz + Bergen Counties, NJ.

Gibbs, Nancy. "Darkness Falls." *Time*, April 17, 2007. http://www.time.com/time/magazine/article/0,9171,1612715,00.html.

Grafton, Anthony. *The Footnote: A Curious History*. Cambridge: Harvard University Press, 1997.

Harbach, Chad. "The Intellectual Situation: An Interruption." *n+1*. 1, no. 4 (Spring 2006): 1–7.

Johnson, Lyndon B. Commencement Address at Howard University: "To Fulfill These Rights?" http://www.lbjlib.utexas.edu/johnson/archives.hom/speeches.hom/650604.asp.

Matsen, Patricia P., Philip B. Rollinson, and Marion Sousa. *Readings from Classical Rhetoric*. Carbondale: Southern Illinois University Press, 1990.

National Commission on Terrorist Attacks. *The 9/11 Commission Report: Final Report of the National Commission on Terrorist Attacks Upon the United States*. New York: W.W. Norton, 2004.

Smith, Craig Allen. "President Bush's Enthymeme of Evil: The Amalgamation of 9/11, Iraq, and Moral Values." *American Behavioral Scientist* 49, no. 1 (2005): 32–47.

Villanueva, Victor Jr. *Bootstraps: From an American Academic of Color*. Urbana: National Council of Teachers of English, 1993.

Walker, Samuel. *Hate Speech: The History of an American Controversy*. Lincoln: Nebraska University Press, 1994.

Williamson, Judith. "It's the Mad Bad Saddam vs. the Scudbusters." *Guardian*, January 31, 1991, 21.

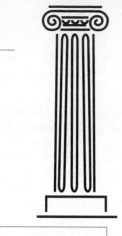

ETHICAL PROOF: ARGUMENTS FROM CHARACTER

As regards the orator, the qualities which will most commend him are courtesy, kindliness, moderation and benevolence. But, on the other hand, the opposite of these qualities will sometimes be becoming to a good man. He may hate the bad, be moved to passion in the public interest, seek to avenge crime and wrong, and, in fine, as I said at the beginning, may follow the promptings of every honorable emotion.

—Quintilian,
Institutes XI i 42

ANCIENT RHETORICIANS KNEW that good arguments were available to them from other sources than *logos*. As early as the fourth century BCE, Greek teachers of rhetoric gave suggestions about how a person's character (Greek *ethos*) could be put to persuasive uses, and rhetorical theorists continued to discuss the uses of ethical proofs throughout the history of ancient rhetoric.

We use the terms *character* and *ethical proof* in this chapter to refer to proofs that rely on community assessments of a rhetor's character or reputation. According to Webster's dictionary, the English word *character* retains three of the important senses it carried for ancient rhetoricians: (1) "the pattern of behavior or personality found in an individual or group"; (2) "moral strength; self-discipline, fortitude, etc"; (3) "a good reputation." The modern term *personality* does not quite capture all the senses of the ancient Greek term *ethos*, since it carried moral overtones and since, for the Greeks, a character was created by a person's habits and reputation rather than by her experiences.

195

To give our readers a sense of how effective this proof can be and of how important it was to ancient orators, we quote at length from the opening of Isocrates' *Panegyricus*:

> Many times have I wondered at those who first convoked the national assemblies and established the athletic games, amazed that they should have thought the prowess of human bodies to be deserving of so great bounties, while to those who had toiled in private for the public good and trained their own minds so as to be able to help also their fellow humans when they apportioned no reward whatsoever, when, in all reason, they ought rather to have made provision for the latter; for if all the athletes should acquire twice the strength which they now possess, the rest of the world would be no better off; but let a single man attain to wisdom, and all men will reap the benefit who are willing to share his insight. Yet I have not on this account lost heart nor chosen to abate my labors; on the contrary, believing that I shall have a sufficient reward in the approbation which my discourse will itself command, I have come before you to give my counsels on the war against the barbarians and on concord among ourselves. I am, in truth, not unaware that many of those who have claimed to be sophists have rushed upon this theme, but I hope to rise so far superior to them that it will seem as if no word had ever been spoken by my rivals upon this subject. (1–3)

Contemporary rhetors may shy away from such unabashed praise of themselves. Nevertheless, it must be admitted that in this passage Isocrates established his character as a very serious man whose important work is underestimated. At the same time he separated himself from persons who had spoken less well than he does.

Contemporary rhetors also create an ethos for themselves, although they are generally not as openly self-congratulatory as Isocrates. Here, for example, is John Cloud, writing about cultural changes in the city of Dallas, Texas:

> When I was a kid in Arkansas in the 1980s, we viewed Dallas with something approaching reverence. Mine was a fairly conservative family, aspirational. We passionately golfed and occasionally visited Neiman Marcus, the Dallas clothier that taught the South how to wear Versace and an air of profligacy. I wanted to drive a Mercedes and order bourbon and branch the way J. R. Ewing did. I wanted to go out with a Cowboys cheerleader with marcelled blond hair. The summer I was 13, Ronald Reagan was renominated in Dallas, and I signed up to be a young volunteer (2007, 55).

Cloud paints this picture of his younger self in order to establish the important cultural role played by the glamorous ideal of Dallas, Texas, in the South during his youth. All the details he gives are intended to show readers how very conventionally upper-middle class he was then, and how he learned to participate in this culture by emulating what he knew of Dallas. If readers are intrigued or charmed by Cloud's ethos in this opening paragraph, they will surely continue reading.

ETHOS IN ANCIENT RHETORICS

The term *ethos* was used in several ways over the long history of ancient rhetoric. The author of the *Rhetoric to Alexander* cautioned rhetors to be careful about their personal conduct, "because one's manner of life contributes to one's powers of persuasion as well as to the attainment of a good reputation" (XXXVIII 1445b 30). This passage implies that a rhetor's ability to persuade is connected to his or her moral habits—a connection that was more fully developed by Roman rhetoricians. Aristotle, in contrast, was not so concerned about the way rhetors lived as he was about the appearance of character that they presented within their discourse (*Rhetoric* I ii 1356a). Perhaps in keeping with Plato's injunction that rhetors must know what types of souls men have (*Phaedrus* 271d), Aristotle also provided a long list of the "characters" of audiences, depending on their age, station in life, and so on.

Aristotle's student, Theophrastus, wrote descriptions of possible character traits, a practice that critics later called *ethopoeia* ("fabricating character"). These descriptions typically began with a definition and listed examples of behavior that typified the character being described. Here, for instance, is Theophrastus's account of the character of a tactless person:

> Now tactlessness is a pain-giving failure to hit upon the right moment; and your tactless person . . . will accost a busy friend and ask advice, or serenade a sweetheart when she is sick of a fever. He will approach someone who has gone bail and lost it, and ask that person to be his security for a loan; and will come to bear witness after the verdict is given. Should you bid him to a wedding, he will inveigh against womankind. Should you be but now returned from a long journey, he will invite you to a walk. He is given to bringing you a merchant who, when your bargain is struck, says he would have paid more had you asked; and to rising from his seat to tell a tale all afresh to such as have heard it before and know it well. He is forward to undertake for you what you would not have done but cannot well decline. If you are sacrificing and put to great expense, that is the day he chooses to come and demand what you owe him. At the flogging of your servant he will stand by and tell how a servant of his hanged himself after just such a flogging as this; at an arbitration he will set the parties against each other when both wish to be reconciled; and when he would dance, lay hold of another who is not yet drunk enough to behave foolishly. (XII)

Theophrastus provides us with many amusing details that show us how tactless persons are out of touch with *kairos*. Theophrastus's characters were probably used to teach students how to analyze character, and they provided moral instruction as well. Later on, Hellenistic teachers of rhetoric encouraged their students to compose "characters" for historical or fictional persons as part of the rhetorical exercises they called the *progymnasmata* (included at the end of this chapter).

Aristotle recognized two kinds of ethical proof: invented and situated. The distinction probably depends on Aristotle's prior distinction between intrinsic and extrinsic proofs, or invented and found proofs (1355b). According to Aristotle, rhetors can invent a character suitable to an occasion—this is invented *ethos*. However, if rhetors are fortunate enough to enjoy a good reputation in the community, they can use it as an ethical proof—this is situated *ethos*. But situated *ethos* is extrinsic to the issue; that is, a rhetor brings it to the rhetorical situation. Interestingly enough, this distinction parallels two primary senses of the term *character* in ancient Greek thought. The Greeks assumed that a good character could be constructed by the habitual practice of virtuous acts, and hence parents were urged to find tutors for their children who would both model and demand good behavior. But *character* also referred to the community's assessment of a person's habits, that is, to her reputation. Because an individual's character had as much to do with the community's perception of her actions as it did with her actual behavior, it was conceivable, at least among the Greeks, that a bad actor could deceive the community into awarding him a good character. But the Romans would have none of this. Quintilian argued that a bad person could never become a respected orator, and so the wisest course for an aspiring rhetor was to maintain a good character, both in fact and by repute.

Today we may feel uncomfortable with the notion that rhetorical character can be constructed, since we tend to think of character, or personality, as fairly stable. We generally assume as well that character is shaped by an individual's experiences. The ancient Greeks, in contrast, thought that character was constructed not by what happened to people but by the moral practices in which they habitually engaged. An *ethos* was not finally given by nature, but was developed by habit *(hexis)*. Thus it was important for parents and teachers not only to provide children with examples of good behavior but to insist that young persons practice habits that imprinted their characters with virtues rather than vices. The notion that character was formed through habitual practices endured throughout antiquity. Quintilian devoted many pages of the *Institutes* to the importance of carefully selecting a teacher for very young children, a teacher whose character would set a suitable example for them and whose practices would develop positive moral habits in them (I i v).

Because the ancients thought that character was shaped by one's practices, they considered it to be much more malleable than we do. Within certain limits imposed by class and gender restrictions, one could become any sort of person one wished to be, simply by engaging in the practices that produced that sort of character. It followed, then, that playing the roles of respectable characters enhanced one's chances of developing a respectable character. Playing a virtuous character, in turn, increased the chance that the rhetor would enjoy a positive, and hence persuasive, situated ethos.

According to Quintilian, Roman rhetoricians who relied on Greek rhetorical theory sometimes confused *ethos* with *pathos*—appeals to the emotions—because there was no satisfactory term for *ethos* in Latin (VI ii 8).

Cicero occasionally used the Latin term *persona* ("mask"), and Quintilian simply borrowed the Greek term. This lack of a technical term is not surprising, because the requirement of having a respectable character was built into the very fabric of Roman oratory. Early Roman society was governed by a number of important families, and a direct line of descent from one of these families lent authority to their offspring. And so a person's lineage had everything to do with what sort of ethos he could command when he took part in public affairs. Under the Republic and the Empire the family requirement softened a bit, but it was still necessary for someone to maintain a reputation for good character in order to be heard. In fact, Quintilian equated the skillful practice of rhetoric with a good character: "No person can speak well who is not good" (II xv 35). Cicero, the practitioner, was more sympathetic to the Greek position that a suitable *ethos* could be constructed for a rhetorical occasion, although in *De Oratore* one of the participants remarks that "merit, achievements or reputable life" are "qualifications easier to embellish, if only they are real, than to fabricate where non-existent" (II xlii 182).

In later antiquity, *ethos* became associated almost wholly with style. Hermogenes of Tarsus, for example, furnished a long list of the virtues or characters of different styles—simplicity, modesty, solemnity, vehemence, and so on—that was read and used by students well into the Renaissance.

Contemporary discussions of rhetoric often overlook the role played by ethical proofs, despite the fact that Americans are very much interested in the character and personal habits of public figures. Americans don't talk as much as they used to about persons having a good character, but apparently they still care about such things. The "character issue" is regularly raised in presidential elections, although in this case "character" ordinarily refers to a candidate's moral choices on matters having to do with sex: Has she been faithful to her spouse? What is her position on abortion or gay marriage? Ancient rhetoricians, in contrast, were interested in the virtues that counted in public affairs: courage, honesty, trustworthiness, modesty, intelligence, fair-mindedness.

The ancient interest in character is still useful because it highlights the role played by this important kind of proof in contemporary rhetorical exchanges. In this chapter, we review the ancient rhetorical advice about *ethos* that is still useful or interesting to modern rhetors, and we freely adapt some of it for contemporary use. Ethical rhetorical effects are varied and subtle, and we have not attempted to exhaust the enormous lode of ancient teachings about them. We have tried to give a sufficiently full treatment to alert our readers to the persuasive potential contained in this sort of rhetorical proof.

INVENTED *ETHOS*

Contemporary discourse is often composed for very large audiences, and so it is often the case that the rhetor does not know the people to whom she will speak or write. Thus she cannot use as a means of ethical proof whatever situated *ethos* she enjoys among those who know her. So she must rely upon invented *ethos*.

A rhetor who uses invented *ethos*, you will recall, constructs a character for herself within her discourse. In an essay in *Emerge* Magazine entitled "Finding My Place in Black America," Gloria Nauden invented an ethos for herself by recalling remarks made to her by others:

> "Excuse me, what are you?" As a person of mixed heritage, Black and Korean, I get asked this question several times a day. Sometimes rudely, most of the time innocently. But I'm always open to educating others about what it means to be Black and Asian.
>
> Among Blacks, I get this kind of reaction: "You look so exotic and different" (pickup line); "It's not too often you see an Asian person at a Black function" (ignorantly curious); "You know, I just got back from China" (So what?); and "My exgirlfriend was Black and Philipino" (So you have an Asian fetish?). Then there are the rude taunts. They go like this: "She thinks she's Black"; "I can't stand when Chinese people try to act Black."
>
> The worse incidents are when I'm called a "war baby," a reference to the children who were fathered by American soldiers and left behind in the streets and orphanages of Vietnam. In fact, my mother, who is Korean-born, met my father, an Army man, in her homeland, and came to the United States with me when I was a year old. They have been married for 30 years.
>
> Among the worst of all scenes is when I am called a "chink." Recently, I was at a new hot spot among young Black professionals, the BET SoundStage restaurant in Largo, Md., which is owned by BET Holdings Inc. I am the entertainment director and helped develop the restaurant. But one guest felt comfortable in trying to make me feel unwelcome.
>
> I was in "his" house, he said, taking great pride in this Black-owned venture. Chinese people have slanted eyes "because you're always squinting, being in everyone's business," the brother said. He complained that he was sick of "chinks" like me coming to the United States and trying to take over and that his people are responsible for building this country. Shocked and angry and hurt, as usual, I wanted to deck him. I wanted to let him know that I was the "sista" who had given the restaurant all its "flava." But even as I told him, "My father is Black, I am Black," he jeered and walked away while making an obscene jesture.
>
> I want people like him to know that I am a very confident, proud and passionate person. I want people to know that my generic code is Black and Korean, but I consider myself an African-American. This mostly has to do with how I was reared. Unlike Tiger Woods, who grew up in a predominantly White neighborhood, I grew up in a public housing complex in the Hill District of Pittsburgh. It was a Black neighborhood and my mother and I stuck out like sore thumbs. (1997, 67)

Nauden establishes that her identity is quite different and much more complex than the ethnic identities that others attempt to construct for her. In life, the situated *ethos* constructed for her by the community often contradicts her sense of who she is. In this text, however, her use of first person and her frank admissions about her anger invent an *ethos* that positions her as an honest and trustworthy narrator.

Aristotle taught that the character conveyed by a rhetor was most important in cases where the facts or arguments were in doubt, "for we believe fair-minded people to a great extent and more quickly [than we do others] on all subjects in general and completely so in cases where there is not exact knowledge but room for doubt" (I ii 1356a). In other words, people tend to believe rhetors who either have a reputation for fair-mindedness or who create an *ethos* that makes them seem fair-minded. This is especially true in cases where, as Aristotle said, there is room for doubt.

Aristotle saw three possible ways in which rhetors could make ethical mistakes. First, "through lack of practical sense they do not form opinions rightly." That is, rhetors could be so inexperienced or so uninformed that they simply don't draw the right conclusions. Second, "through forming opinions rightly they do not say what they think because of a bad character." That is, even though rhetors know the right answer or the right course, they may hide it from people because of some character flaw, such as greed or dishonesty. Third, "they are prudent and fair-minded but lack good will, so that it is possible for people not to give the best advice although they know what it is." That is, rhetors may not care about what happens to the people they represent, and so they do not give good advice even when they could. These, Aristotle wrote, are the only possibilities for a failed invented *ethos*.

The first ethical lapse still afflicts rhetors who, for some reason, offer impractical or unworkable solutions to community problems. But this lapse can usually be rectified by engaging in invention. Violations of the second and third requirements are far more damaging to an *ethos* because these mistakes describe behavior that is unethical in a moral sense. Dishonesty, greed, and selfishness were (and still are) considered immoral when practiced by anyone, rhetor or not. Unfortunately, it is possible for these vices to be reflected in a discursive *ethos*. A rhetorician named Ken Macrorie fabricated the following example of a failed invented *ethos*:

> Unquestionably the textbook has played a very important role in the development of American schools—and I believe it will continue to play an important role. The need for textbooks has been established through many experiments. It is not necessary to consider these experiments but, in general, they have shown that when instruction without textbooks has been tried by schools, the virtually unanimous result has been to go back to the use of textbooks. I believe, too, that there is considerable evidence to indicate that the textbook has been, and is, a major factor in guiding teachers' instruction and in determining the curriculum. (1984, 177)

The *ethos* in this piece fails all three of Aristotle's tests: the rhetor doesn't show evidence of having done the necessary homework, ("many experiments") and as a result, his honesty can be questioned, as can his good will toward his audience.

To put Aristotle's ethical requirements in positive terms, rhetors must seem to be intelligent, to be of good moral character, and to possess good will toward their audiences. Rhetors can construct a character that seems intelligent by demonstrating that they are well informed about issues they discuss. They project an appearance of good moral character by describing themselves or others as moral persons and by refraining from the use of misleading or fallacious arguments. Rhetors project good will toward an audience by presenting the information and arguments that audiences require in order to understand the rhetorical situation.

Demonstrating Intelligence by Doing the Homework

Rhetors can create a character that seems intelligent by demonstrating that they are informed about the issues they discuss, and by refraining from using arguments that are irrelevant or trivial. General audiences can be assumed to be relatively uninformed about difficult or technical issues, so in this case rhetors must take special care to convince an audience that they are well informed without overwhelming their listeners with details.

In the excerpt that follows, Andrew Sullivan details his impressions of Barack Obama, who was a candidate for the presidency in 2007:

> I went to see Obama last night. He had a fundraiser at H20, a yuppie disco/restaurant in Southwest DC. I was curious about how he is in person. I'm still absorbing the many impressions I got. But one thing stays in my head. This guy is a liberal. Make no mistake about that. He may, in fact, be the most effective liberal advocate I've heard in my lifetime. As a conservative, I think he could be absolutely lethal to what's left of the tradition of individualism, self-reliance, and small government that I find myself quixotically attached to. And as a simple observer, I really don't see what's stopping him from becoming the next president. The overwhelming first impression that you get—from the exhausted but vibrant stump speech, the diverse nature of the crowd, the swell of the various applause lines—is that this is the candidate for real change. He has what Reagan had in 1980 and Clinton had in 1992: the wind at his back. Sometimes, elections really do come down to a simple choice: change or more of the same?
>
> Look at the polls and forget ideology for a moment. What do Americans really want right now? *Change.* Who best offers them a chance to turn the page cleanly on an era most want to forget? It isn't Clinton, God help us. Edwards is so 2004. McCain is a throwback. Romney makes plastic look real. Rudy does offer something new for Republicans—the abortion-friendly, cross-dressing Jack Bauer. But no one captures the sheer, pent-up desire for a new start more effectively than Obama. ("Reagan," 2007)

Sullivan points out that he attended this event in person, which establishes his credentials both as a proximate witness and as someone who is interested in politics. As he tries to place Obama's candidacy in perspective, we learn that Sullivan is well versed in the major tenets of both conservative and liberal political ideologies. He shows as well that he is familiar with other candidates, their positions, and the current poll numbers, all of which attest, once again, to his being well-informed about the presidential race.

To seem well-informed is especially important when the audience is relatively well-informed themselves about the issue at hand. In this case, the rhetor must quickly assure them that he knows what he is talking about. He may do so by using language that suggests he is an insider, by sharing an anecdote that indicates he has experience or knowledge in a particular area, or by describing his qualifications. Here, in a book about training dogs, Mark Derr establishes that he has a good deal of personal experience in this area:

> In close to fifty years, I have never been without a dog, although I pledge occasionally to swear off them, because of the time required to care for them properly, I know I will not. . . . Like most people today, I do not work professionally with dogs, but I do train ours somewhat and exercise them for nearly two hours a day. I expect our dogs to come when called, to sit and stay, not to beg for food or jump on guests, and not to fight with other dogs or people unless physically threatened, and then I expect them to perform according to their nature, which they do. (2004, 4–5)

Derr's book presents dog training in the context of a heavily researched account of dog/human relationships, and so it is important that he establish his own firsthand experience with dogs, lest his philosophy seem out of touch to readers who just want their dogs to behave a little better.

In academic writing, it is common for authors to establish their professional *ethos* by listing their publications, thus establishing that editors and other scholars in the field have found the authors' previous work worthy of circulation. If our publisher follows ordinary practice, our academic credentials are probably listed somewhere in this book. The point of mentioning our advanced degrees in rhetoric, our lists of other publications on the history of rhetoric, and our teaching experience is to assure readers who buy this book that we have sufficient knowledge and teaching experience to give trustworthy information and advice.

A rhetor may also use specialized language to demonstrate her adeptness in a particular field, hence reassuring informed readers that what she has to say is worth their time. Richard Seager, a specialist in paleoclimatology, posted an article about droughts in North America on the Web site maintained by Columbia University. Here is part of that article:

> The causes of persistent droughts and pluvials over North America are still, ultimately, in question. But in the last few years scientists at, first, NASA's Goddard Space Flight Center and, second, the Lamont Doherty Earth Observatory of Columbia University have demonstrated that they are caused by subtle changes in sea surface temperatures (SSTs) of the tropical oceans, especially the tropical Pacific Ocean.
>
> Exactly why tropical SSTs should have this impact on precipitation in remote regions of the planet is easily understood. The warmest SSTs in the world occur in the tropics and have warm and moist air above. If air is warm and moist it tends to rise, the water vapor within it condenses and heats the air by latent heat release. The heating is balanced by expansion of air as it moves up to lower atmospheric pressure. The warmest regions of the planet are

potent heat sources for the global atmospheric circulation that, in combination with regions where the atmosphere is cooled (for example, by radiation to space over winter continental interiors), drive wind circulations that have global reach. The strongest heat sources are over the tropical west Pacific Ocean, central Africa, the Amazon, the summer monsoons and a globe-encircling near-equatorial strip called the Intertropical Convergence Zone (ITCZ) that lies above the warmest SSTs.

Tropical SSTs vary all the time. On the timescale of years to years, the eastern and central equatorial Pacific Ocean warms and cools as part of the El Nino–Southern Oscillation (ENSO), fundamentally a consequence of wind-driven ocean motions that redistribute the heat within the ocean. This causes eastward and westward shifts of the west Pacific warm pool and northward and southward shifts of the ITCZ. During the warm phase of ENSO, El Nino, the tropical troposphere also warms, as heat is released from the ocean, and it cools during the cold phase, La Nina. La Nina events are typically associated with dry winters in the southwest and also dry springs in the Plains. If they persist into summer they can also cause dry summers in the same regions. On the year to year timescale there are two basic reasons why cold tropical Pacific SSTs cause reduced precipitation over North America (and warm tropical Pacific SSTs cause increased precipitation). (2007)

Seager's first sentence betrays the caution that marks good scientific writing. He says, in effect, that "we're not entirely sure what causes droughts but we can make a good case for changes in sea temperature. Here it is." Because this article is posted on a Web site, where it will presumably reach a popular audience, it avoids highly technical language and/or tables and graphs. Nonetheless Seager's almost casual use of technical terms and acronyms (pluvials, SSTs, ITCZ) demonstrates his familiarity with the vocabulary scientists use to discuss droughts, thus enhancing his *ethos* as someone who knows a good deal about ocean temperatures. He also enjoys the situated *ethos* brought him by his connection to the Earth Observatory. As a result, readers are likely to trust his opinion.

We remarked earlier that rhetors who wish to appear intelligent and well-informed must demonstrate that they have done whatever research and contemplation is necessary to understand an issue, and they must avoid making irrelevant or trivial arguments as well. A rhetorical disaster may ensue when rhetors fail to establish themselves as well-informed about the issues they discuss. Here is an example of failed *ethos* we created to illustrate a lack of necessary research:

> Many students go to college to find a husband or wife. While there are some who attend for the purpose of getting themselves an education, these are few and far between. The majority of companion seekers are men because by the time they reach college most of them are ready to settle down after the bebop life of high school. In most cases, men are tied to home, security, and have problems in adjusting to being completely on their own. In the opinion of this author, men are looking to fulfill their need of security by finding a wife in college.

There is no hint here that the author did any research on this subject, even to the extent of asking one or two college men whether or not his conclusions were true. Audiences whose experiences and aims do not match the generalizations made here will feel excluded by the rhetor's assertive tone, while others may be offended by it. This tone is mitigated somewhat in the last sentence, where the rhetor tells us that these generalizations are his "opinion." Here is a revision of the passage:

> Although I have some friends who are here to get themselves an education, I know many students who come to college to look for a husband or a wife. For instance, my roommate is having problems adjusting to being completely on his own, and I think he's still tied to home and security. In fact, he has admitted to me that he is looking to find a wife in college who will give him the security he misses. This need for security seems to be the case with many of my male friends.

While talking with the author, his classmates discovered that the generalization about wife-seeking men was based on only one example—his roommate. They encouraged him to limit his generalization to what he knew from experience. As a result, the second version manifests a character who does not make claims about which he is uninformed.

A rhetor who wants to seem well-informed should always consider how much her audience knows about the issue she is discussing. Audiences who are not themselves well-informed about an issue may allow errors to go unremarked. But rhetors risk losing all credibility with better-informed audiences when they fail to do their homework. For instance, Melissa Kay Thompson has noticed that the authors who write children's novels often purvey stereotypes when they depict Native Americans: "children's book authors and critics typically stereotype indigenous peoples. Whether intentionally or not . . . they reinforce the legacy that traveled via Columbus to the Western hemisphere" (2001, 353). In order to substantiate this point, Thompson quotes a passage from a children's novel entitled *Danger Along the Ohio* (1997):

> An Indian stood on the cabin roof, clad only in breechcloth and leggings and carrying a hatchet. His lean body glistened in the glaring light. [The children] had seen Indians in Pittsburgh, shiftless, slouching men who loitered in doorways and begged money for whiskey. Their father had told them whiskey lured the Indians away from their own people. It made them useless and dependent on the white men. The man looming over Amos was different. He had a power and fierceness those begging Indians lacked, a fierceness that scared Amos to the ends of his toes. (17) [in Thompson 353]

Thompson comments on this passage as follows:

> In one paragraph at the beginning of her book . . . Patricia Willis manages to delineate the two major historical stereotypes: the "Indian" as savage beast and as drunken dependent. In Willis's book, indigenous peoples appear as two wooden personifications: the image of animals who attack peaceful white settlements for no other reason than pure savagery, and the more recent stereotype leveled at "city Indians"—that of homeless, alcoholic beggars.

The supposed moral and physical superiority of the White children is unmistakable throughout Willis's story, although Willis attempts to introduce some crosscultural camaraderie. The White children rescue an "Indian boy" from the river. They dub him "Red Moccasin," and Willis's narrator describes him as having the "eyes of the enemy" and the look of a "wounded wildcat" (89, 95). The boy, like the Indian depicted in the attack, is more animal than human. Willis portrays his physical and psychological subjugation by the White children in a scene where he relinquishes his knife: "Despite the look of outward calm, the boy appeared to shrink back within himself. He was beaten. He had shown weakness. In some strange way Amos understood. The boy had willingly given up his weapon to the enemy and it shamed him" (97). From start to finish in Willis's novel, the White children are portrayed as superior beings: they act magnanimously toward their alleged attacker, assign him a name rather than learning how to pronounce the boy's real name (thereby diminishing his "Indian" identity and voice), and remove his means of self-defense (leaving him "beaten" and "shamed"). (354–355)

Thompson argues, in other words, that Willis has not done her homework. In the venue of children's literature, this is a very serious failing because stereotypes of Native Americans depicted in her novel accord with powerful racist commonplaces, themselves derived from novels and films that unfortunately continue to circulate in American discourse. Audiences who are aware of this will not be impressed by Willis's ethical lapses.

Failed *ethos* in one situation can carry over into subsequent situations, shaping a rhetorical character that can hinder the reception of future messages, especially if the rhetor is under intense and constant public scrutiny. During a debate among Republican candidates for president in the spring of 2007, for instance, Libertarian Ron Paul claimed that the 9/11 plot was undertaken as retaliation against American foreign policy in the Middle East, policy which included a ten-year bombing campaign of Iraq. Rudy Giuliani, who was mayor of New York City when 9/11 occurred, took umbrage with Paul's analysis, saying that he had never heard such an argument before, and that it was ridiculous to suggest that America had "invited" attack. This response was greeted with wild applause by the audience in the auditorium. But in ensuing days, bloggers began to claim that Giuliani's remarks harmed his *ethos*. Some argued that he must know about the "blowback" thesis; here, for example, is Doug Mataconis, posting on a Libertarian blog:

> Giuliani's comment that he'd never heard the blowback argument before is either an indication that he knows little about foreign policy, or that he just doesn't pay attention to it. . . . The fact remains that the presence of American troops in the Middle East, and specifically in the Kingdom of Saudi Arabia was cited by Osama bin Laden as one of the grievances against the United States. And it's also true that America's history of intervention in the Middle East— whether in Iran, Lebanon, Iraq, or the Israeli–Palestinian conflict—has, more often than not, been fraught with missteps that have led to the loss of American lives. (2007)

Were it to circulate in larger venues the charge made by Mataconis—that Giuliani is ignorant or misinformed about foreign policy—could damage his *ethos* as someone who is well-informed enough to become president. Conservative blogger Andrew Sullivan suggested that Giuliani was so intent on refuting Paul's claim that he lied about it: "Giuliani, interestingly, openly lied about Ron Paul's position on 9/11. Paul specifically did not make a statement, as Giuliani immediately claimed, that the U.S. invited 9/11. I rewound to double-check" ("Palmetto," 2007). But the most critical estimates of the damage to Giuiliani's *ethos* came, as we might expect, from left and liberal bloggers. Here is Jeff Norman:

> Rudy Giuliani is a bully, and the best way to defang bullies is to fearlessly rebuke them. But after Giuliani arrogantly counseled Ron Paul to "withdraw" his supposedly unique contention that military intrusions breed resentment in the Middle East just as they do or would anywhere else, America's Mayor has been subjected to nothing sterner than the suggestion he ought to expand his reading list. Instead of cutely proposing that he edify himself, Giuliani's opponents should tell him he is not only ill-equipped to be president, but unqualified to participate in presidential debates. But unfortunately, there is nary a candidate with the nerve to say such a thing to the megalomaniac from New York.
>
> My criticism of Giuliani is not hyperbolic. Imagine a pro-choice advocate stating at an abortion debate that he or she had never before heard the standard pro-life position, and suggesting that the opposing argument be silenced. For that matter, imagine a pro-life exponent claiming to be unfamiliar with, and refusing to discuss, the widely known pro-choice position. Either way, such ignorance and unwillingness to address a contrary opinion, would render the advocate unfit to engage in a public disputation about abortion. Likewise, Giuliani doesn't belong in a debate about foreign policy, because whether or not Paul's analysis is correct, what the congressman said is nothing new (2007)

As of this writing it remains to be seen if Giuliani's remarks will permanently damage his *ethos*, and hence his campaign. The applause that greeted his remarks suggests that an audience does exist for his reading of the cause of 9/11—that America was attacked because members of Al-Qaeda resent our prosperity and freedom.

Establishing Good Character

There are probably as many ways to demonstrate good moral character as there are virtues—and vices. Cicero encouraged rhetors to extol their "merits or worth or virtue of some kind, particularly generosity, sense of duty, justice and good faith" (*On the Parts* viii 28). He also suggested that rhetors weaken charges or suspicions that had been cast upon their character and that they elaborate on misfortunes or difficulties that had befallen them in order to strengthen their audience's estimate of their ability to bear suffering (*On Invention* I xvi 22). When Cicero defended a man named Lucius Murena, he was accused of having a double standard—of holding other men to higher standards of conduct than he held for Murena. He responded by commenting on his own character:

> I have always gladly shown the restraint and forgiveness which nature herself has taught me; I have not been eager to wear the mask of dead seriousness and hardness, but I wore it willingly when the crisis of state and the solemn requirements of my office demanded. If, then, when the republic wanted force and uncompromising severity, I overcame my nature to become as ruthless as I was forced into being, not as I wished, may I not now respond to the sympathetic and humane qualities which all the motives in the case prompt in me and accord them my characteristic degree of energy and enthusiasm? (*Pro Murena* 3)

Here Cicero pictured himself as a sympathetic and softhearted man, forced by his duties into seeming hard-hearted. Contemporary rhetors are more subtle about displaying moral character than Roman rhetors were, but they still use moral standards as means of proof. Opponents of abortion characterize pro-choice advocates as "baby killers" and "murderers"; public officials are often charged with immoral behavior such as infidelity or harassment.

In order to establish their good moral standing, rhetors may cite approval of their character from respected authorities. Ordinary people establish their character in this way when they ask teachers or employers for letters of reference and when they list such persons' names on their resumes. References are often asked about the same qualities of character in prospective employees that concerned ancient rhetoricians: intelligence, honesty, and trustworthiness. Rhetors can also shore up an audience's sense of their character simply by refraining from the use of unfair discursive tactics: faulty reasoning or nonrepresentative evidence, threats, name-calling, or lies.

A slightly different interpretation of good character seems to be very persuasive in modern discourse. This is the *ethos* that conveys a person as an authority, either by virtue of respectable credentials or long experience in some activity. The covers or inside pages of books often list "other works by the same author" in order to establish the writer's history as a published author (and to sell more copies of her books). Advertisements for films often list previous performances by actors who perform in them. This is an attempt both to establish an actor's credentials as someone who is good at her work, and to associate her with other successful films as well. The tactic is ordinarily used when the producers think that actors' name recognition isn't tied closely enough to their face recognition—two kinds of *ethos* that are very important in the movie industry.

When *Time* magazine asked former Speaker of the House Newt Gingrich to write about Nancy Pelosi, he commented that "Speaker Pelosi, 67, is and will always be a historic figure. She is the first woman ever to become Speaker of the House—and she earned it. She spent years back home in California as a Democratic Party activist and fund raiser. When she won a congressional seat, she rose through the ranks of her colleagues by being a hardworking, smart and disciplined professional. No one should underestimate how much time, effort and courage went into her career." (2007). Given that it was written by a member of the opposing party, this brief history of Speaker Pelosi's accomplishments may convince readers that she values hard work and discipline—traits that are essential to a competent Speaker of the House.

Movie reviewers usually construct an *ethos* by showing us that they are experienced at viewing and reviewing films, and that they are familiar with the conventions used in film composition. Here, for example, is a selection from Michael Wilmington's review of *Pirates of the Carribean: At World's End:*

> *Pirates of the Caribbean* has had quite a ride, and I wouldn't bet that it's over, despite the seeming finality of *Pirates of the Caribbean: At World's End*, the most visually spectacular, action-packed and surreal of the adventures of Capt. Jack Sparrow (Johnny Depp).
>
> The movie begins with a terrifying image: a line of pirates and their accused confederates, shuffling on chained feet to the gallows, with a narrator citing an all-too-modern-sounding list of suspended rights. But this is no message movie. Soon we're on another wild ride from the tropics to the frozen wastes, as we pick up what happened since we last saw Jack in *Pirates of the Caribbean: Dead Man's Chest* (pulled into the deep in the clutches of a kraken) and follow the last battles between the free-roaming pirates and their allies against their nemeses from the East India Co., along with the final resolution of the contentious romance between Elizabeth Swann (Keira Knightley) and Will Turner (Orlando Bloom).
>
> The capper to 2003's *Pirates of the Caribbean: The Curse of the Black Pearl* and 2006's *Dead Man's Chest* was actually shot concurrently with the second (not incidentally, the third-highest international grosser of all time), and when they say "World's End," they're not kidding. The movie plunges us down to Davy Jones' locker, then hurls us into a series of violent voyages and confrontations in arctic wastes, South Sea isles and galleon-shredding gales, with Sparrow, the beauteous Swann, her sword-swain Turner and Sparrow's glibly treacherous rival captain Barbossa (Geoffrey Rush) clashing with their deadly 18th Century pursuers, led by the smugly murderous Cutler Beckett (Tom Hollander). . . .
>
> The movie is almost too much. Director Gore Verbinski and producer Jerry Bruckheimer have packed "World's End" with so much explosive action, opulent decor and surreal scenes of mayhem and madness—including a mass crab-and-ship exodus, an apocalyptic-looking waterfall and life-size and miniature hallucinatory clones of Capt. Jack, some capering around Depp's mane and shoulder—that sometimes it's overwhelming. This sequel is frenziedly imaginative, where the first "Pirates" was sunny, fey and friendly (like Sparrow) and the second a rollicking romp. . . .
>
> What we love about pirate movies and myths, of course, is their mix of adventure, freedom and naughtiness, and Verbinski and Depp again capture all three. In the end, *Pirates of the Caribbean: At World's End*, with its added doses of fantasy and even some piercing social comment (about Beckett and the government's rights-trampling tyranny), does its job. The movie, extravagant, amusing and exciting, may be only a ride, but it's a ride that dazzles. (2007)

Wilmington establishes that he has seen all three *Pirates* films, and his review of the third installment is filled with details suggesting that he paid close attention during its screening. He establishes his moral stance quite subtly, but it is evident nonetheless: he liked the last *Pirates* movie, but he wishes it had done more with the political theme introduced in the opening scenes. In other words he prefers complexity to spectacle, and this reinforces his *ethos* as a serious critic of film.

Securing Goodwill

Cicero wrote that goodwill could be won "if we refer to our own acts and services without arrogance; if we weaken the effect of charges that have been preferred, or of some suspicion of less honorable dealing which has been cast upon us; if we dilate on the misfortunes which have befallen us or the difficulties which still beset us; if we use prayers and entreaties with a humble and submissive spirit" (*On Invention* I xvi 22). While ethical tactics like these were persuasive to Roman audiences, they may be a bit too flamboyant for modern tastes. Modern rhetors can demonstrate their goodwill toward an audience by carefully considering what readers need to know about the issue at hand in order to follow the argument. They should supply any necessary information that audiences might not already have, but should be careful not to repeat information that the audience already knows.

Movie reviewers usually operate on the ethical principle of goodwill: they must assume that people will listen to or read their reviews in order to decide whether to see a given film. Since people put their trust (and their money) on the line when they take reviewers' advice, movie reviewers are obligated to have goodwill toward their audiences. They demonstrate this goodwill by telling audiences just enough about the plot or characters or direction to allow them to decide whether to see a film, but they don't give away the ending. They also demonstrate goodwill by providing audiences with their frank opinion about a film, as Wilmington does in the review cited earlier. Here is another review of *Pirates of the Carribean: At World's End*, written by Peter Travers, who is working from a very different *ethos*:

> The good news first: Keith Richards totally rocks it playing pirate daddy to Johnny Depp's Capt. Jack Sparrow. The deep rumble of his voice and those hooded eyes that narrowly open like the creaky gates of hell make him what the rest of this three-peat is not: authentically scary. It's fun to see Richards swagger, even sitting down. Watch him stage a macabre reunion for Jack and his dear old mum. Don't worry, I won't reveal her secret.
>
> So what's the bad news? Richards is onscreen for barely two minutes. The rest of *At World's End* left me at wit's end wading through nearly three hours of punishing exposition, endless blather (pirates take meetings—who knew?), an overload of digital effects and shameless setups for *Pirates 4*. I ask you people: Even if you like Depp (and who doesn't?), do you understand one bloody thing that's going on in this *Pirates* trilogy? The problem, I think, is that director Gore Verbinski and screenwriters Ted Elliot and Terry Rossio focus on Will Turner,

played by the aggressively bland Orlando Bloom, and his quest to find a personality. Kidding. Will wants to rescue his father (Stellan Skarsgard) from the tentacles of Davy Jones, a talking CGI fish with the luck to be voiced by the great Bill Nighy. Will still can't find the balls to make a move on Elizabeth Swann (Keira Knightley, working her skinny butt off trying to get a rise out of this putz), who spends her time trying to get Chow Yun-Fat, as the pirate lord of Singapore, to help save Jack. Confused? You should be, since Jack (why doesn't someone just tell him he's gay?) was swallowed whole by the Kraken in *Pirates 2*, but he steps lively here. He's trapped in Davy Jones' Locker, which resembles a hallucination out of *Being John Malkovich*, with multiple Jacks jabbering at each other.

I applaud the Oscar nomination Depp received for the first *Pirates*, but the third chapter proves that there can indeed be too much of a good thing. *Pirates 3* raises everything from the dead, except inspiration. A huge set piece in which a pirate ship pulls a Poseidon and turns upside down must have cost millions and still looks tacky. And until a wow of a climactic sea battle, the story plods along like a PBS special on the founding pirate fathers. Happily, Geoffrey Rush (absent from *Pirates 2*) encores his "arrghs" as Barbossa and shows how nostril-flaring acting should be done. This dude can steal scenes from a monkey, and does. At least Rush and Depp capture the pirate ethos that a lost boy can get older but stay immature forever. I haven't mentioned the heart cut out of Davy's chest. No reason. I just don't care. Being buried in an avalanche of cliches and incoherence will do that to a guy. Producer Jerry Bruckheimer does deserve a shoutout: It takes a kind of genius to sucker audiences into repeatedly buying the same party tricks. Know what? There really is no legit way to review *Pirates 3*. It's not a movie at all, it's a business proposition. (2007)

Travers immediately establishes his qualifications as an aficionado of popular culture with his remarks about Keith Richards—he is writing for *Rolling Stone*, after all. He also shows that he has done his homework with his references to the other films in the series. But he does not seem to care about establishing goodwill toward all of his readers, because some will warm to his *ethos* here only if they agree with his negative assessment of *At World's End*. Anyone who liked the movie will no doubt be put off by his snarky characterizations of the script and some of the performances. Travers establishes moral character at the very end of his review, when he implies that the film is less a work of art than a scheme to make money—scads of it.

The ethical criterion of goodwill poses interesting problems for public figures, particularly for those who have been in the public eye long enough to have made political blunders. After Hurricane Katrina devastated New Orleans and the Gulf Coast region, President George W. Bush and the federal Department of Homeland Security were widely criticized for their perceived failure to prepare for a disaster of this magnitude. When President Bush gave a speech from New Orleans a few days after the storm, he attempted to secure the goodwill of his audience:

> Good evening. I am speaking to you from the city of New Orleans—nearly empty, still partly under water, and waiting for life and hope to return. Eastward from Lake Pontchartrain, across the Mississippi coast, to Alabama and into Florida, millions of lives were changed in a day by a cruel and wasteful storm.

In the aftermath, we have seen fellow citizens left stunned and uprooted . . . searching for loved ones, and grieving for the dead . . . and looking for meaning in a tragedy that seems so blind and random. We have also witnessed the kind of desperation no citizen of this great and generous Nation should ever have to know—fellow Americans calling out for food and water . . . vulnerable people left at the mercy of criminals who had no mercy . . . and the bodies of the dead lying uncovered and untended in the street.

These days of sorrow and outrage have also been marked by acts of courage and kindness that make all Americans proud. Coast Guard and other personnel rescued tens of thousands of people from flooded neighborhoods. Religious congregations and families have welcomed strangers as brothers and sisters and neighbors. In the community of Chalmette, when two men tried to break into a home, the owner invited them to stay—and took in 15 other people who had no place to go. At Tulane Hospital for Children, doctors and nurses didn't eat for days so patients could have food, and eventually carried the patients on their backs up eight flights of stairs to helicopters. Many first responders were victims themselves—wounded healers, with a sense of duty greater than their own suffering. . . . (Sept. 15 2005)

President Bush's speechwriters subtly establish his courage by including details demonstrating that he toured the afflicted site in person. They show his sympathy with survivors and first responders, and his admiration for the heroes of this event. In other words, they underlined his human qualities, hoping by this means to establish his goodwill toward the victims of the disaster.

As another means of securing goodwill, rhetors can say why they think their presentation of an argument is important, and what benefits will accrue to those who read or listen to it. We made an ethical appeal of this sort at the beginning of this book when we suggested that the study of ancient rhetorics would, in essence, turn people into better citizens. Of course, this ploy works only if audiences do not suspect ulterior motives on a rhetor's part. A notorious television advertisement for life insurance began with scenarios depicting loved ones whose lives have been disrupted by the death of a provider who left no insurance. While the company that sponsored this ad seemed to have goodwill toward the audience insofar as they wished to protect people from harm, viewers knew that these companies also wanted to sell insurance. In this case, they did it by frightening people—a tactic that is marginally ethical.

Establishing goodwill is especially difficult to manage when students write for teachers, since in this case the audience is usually better informed than the rhetor. The best way to demonstrate goodwill in this case is to follow teachers' instructions.

VOICE AND RHETORICAL DISTANCE

We have been arguing that rhetors can create a character within a discourse and that such self-characterizations are persuasive. Ancient rhetoricians realized that very subtle ethical effects were available through the manipulation of stylistic features. Here is Hermogenes of Tarsus, for example, on how to convey an appearance of anger by means of word choice:

> Rough and vehement diction and coined words are indicative of anger, especially in sudden attacks on your opponent, where unusual words that seem to be coined on the spur of the moment are quite suitable, words such as "iambeater"or "pen-pusher." All such words are suitable since they seem to have been dictated by emotion. (*On Types of Style* 359)

Rhetors can still create self-characterizations by means of certain stylistic choices: modern rhetoricians give the name *voice* to this self-dramatization in style.[1] Of course, *voice* is a metaphor in that it suggests that all rhetorical situations, even those that use written or electronic media, mimic the relation of one person speaking to another. Written or electronic discourse that creates a lively and accessible voice makes reading more interesting. Like the characters of style, the repertoire of possible voices is immense: there are cheerful voices, gloomy ones, stuffy ones, homey ones, sincere ones, angry ones—the list is endless.

Voices affect the rhetorical distance that can seem to exist between rhetors and their audiences. Once again, the term *distance* is a metaphor representing the degree of physical and social distance that exists between people speaking to one another. But even in written or electronic discourse, rhetors can narrow or widen the rhetorical distance between themselves and their audiences by means of stylistic choice. When creating a voice, rhetors should consider the situation for which they are composing: how much distance is appropriate given their relationship to an audience; how much distance is appropriate given their relationship to the issue. As a general rule, persuasion occurs more easily when audiences can identify with rhetors. Identification increases as distance decreases.

> Intimate Distance = Closer Identification, More Persuasive Potential
>
> Formal Distance = Less Identification, Less Persuasive Potential

In the following brief excerpt from his regular column in the *New York Times*, Thomas Friedman writes about global warming—a serious subject in a respected news venue. And yet he uses a fairly informal voice:

> Surely the most glaring contrast in American political life today is the amount of words, speeches and magazine covers devoted to the necessity of "going green," "combating climate change" and gaining "energy security," and the actual solutions being offered by our leaders to do any of these things. You could very comfortably drive a Hummer through the gap between our words and our deeds.
>
> We are playing pretend—which, when you think about it, is really troubling (2007, 15).

The use of a familiar term ("Hummer") and the direct address ("you") closes the distance between rhetor and author, rendering this piece quite informal. Given that the issue of global warming is relevant to everyone, this familiar approach may be both appropriate and persuasive.

Rhetors who know an audience well, or whose audience is quite small, can use an intimate distance (unless some factor in the rhetorical situation prevents this). The distance created in personal letters, for example, is ordinarily quite intimate, while that used in business correspondence is more formal since rhetors either do not know their correspondents personally or because convention dictates that such relationships be kept at arm's length, so to speak. Compare the distance created by Michael Wilmington and Peter Travers in their respective reviews, appearing earlier in this chapter. Although both pieces are written in first person, Wilmington's tone is more distant and formal than Travers's. Wilmington achieves this by giving information about the film, while Travers delivers his opinion of it.

However, rhetorical situations can create exceptions to the distance-intimacy equation. Formal language is ordinarily appropriate in a courtroom, for example, even though an attorney, a defendant, and a judge constitute a very small group. In addition, the attorney may know both the judge and the defendant well. Nonetheless, she probably ought to use formal language in her conversations with both, given the official and serious nature of courtroom transactions. And sometimes very large groups are addressed in quite intimate language: performers at concerts and television evangelists, whose audiences number in the thousands or even millions, nonetheless occasionally address their audiences quite personally and intimately.

A rhetor's attitude toward the issue also influences distance. On one hand, where rhetors remain as neutral as possible, expressing neither a supportive nor rejecting attitude, distance tends to be greater. On the other hand, rhetors' strong expression of an attitude—approval or disapproval, for example—closes distance.

More Attitude = Intimate Distance

Less Attitude = More Formal Distance

In order to demonstrate the contrasting effects of distance created by more or less attitude, we examine three accounts of a current event. As we write, I. Lewis "Scooter" Libby, an aide to Vice President Richard Cheney, has been convicted of obstruction of justice in a federal court. This conviction was handed down after a controversial trial, and it has been much disputed. When a judge sentenced Libby to thirty months in prison, the argument about the justice of Libby's conviction and sentencing broke out anew. In order to demonstrate how attitude increases or decreases distance, we compare discussions of this issue that were published by news media against positions taken up by editorialists. To begin, here is National Public Radio's report of the sentencing:

> I. Lewis "Scooter" Libby, the former chief of staff to Vice President Dick Cheney, was sentenced Tuesday to 30 months in prison for obstruction of justice and perjury in the investigation into the leak of a CIA operation officer's identity. . . .
>
> Prosecutors have argued that leaking a CIA officer's name could endanger the life of the operative. They urged the judge to sentence Libby to prison, saying the nature of the investigation Libby obstructed was so serious that he should serve time.

> However, Libby's attorneys said probation was in order because no one was ever charged with the leak.
>
> In the end, [Judge] Walton sided with prosecutors, saying the serious nature of the investigation warranted a stiff sentence. "It's one thing if you obstruct a petty larceny. It's another thing if you obstruct a murder investigation," Walton said. . . .
>
> Walton also fined Libby $250,000 and ordered him to serve two years of probation following his release from prison.
>
> The events of the case date back to 2003 and the furor over the invasion of Iraq. CIA officer Valerie Plame's husband, former ambassador Joseph Wilson, was a leading critic of the White House's justification for the war. (2007)

Traditionally, straight news reporting confines itself to the facts of the matter. And so NPR's article displays no attitude about Libby's sentencing. No judgments are made, and most of the piece consists of facts and testimony that can be verified. This approach creates a relatively formal tone and increases the rhetorical distance between rhetor and readers.

In contrast, commentators are under no mandate to stick to the facts. Indeed, commentators are under some obligation to express opinions about events. Inevitably, then, their accounts close up rhetorical distance because they convey attitude. Here, for example, is Bill Kristol's response to Libby's sentencing:

> I feel terrible for Scooter Libby's family. Millions of Americans feel terrible for Scooter Libby's family. But we can't do anything about the injustice that has been done. Nor can we do anything to avert a further injustice looming on the horizon—Judge Reggie Walton seems inclined not to let Libby remain free pending appeal.
>
> Unlike the rest of us, however, George W. Bush is president. Article II, Section Two of the Constitution gives him the pardon power. George W. Bush can do something to begin to make up for the injustice a prosecutor appointed by his own administration brought down on Scooter Libby. And he can do something to avert the further injustice of a prison term.
>
> Will Bush pardon Libby? Apparently not—even if it means a man who worked closely with him and sought tirelessly to do what was right for the country goes to prison. Bush spokeswoman Dana Perino, noting that the appeals process was underway, said, "Given that and in keeping with what we have said in the past, the president has not intervened so far in any other criminal matter and he is going to decline to do so now."
>
> So much for loyalty, or decency, or courage. For President Bush, loyalty is apparently a one-way street; decency is something he's for as long as he doesn't have to take any risks in its behalf; and courage—well, that's nowhere to be seen. Many of us used to respect President Bush. Can one respect him still? (2007)

Kristol is the editor of *The American Spectator*, a conservative political journal. He begins this piece by noting his emotional response to Libby's sentencing, thus conveying his attitude toward it immediately. The mention of Libby's family, and the supposed millions of Americans who feel their suffering, also works to close the rhetorical distance between Kristol and his audience.

In his excoriation of President Bush's inaction, Kristol invokes a number of traditional values—loyalty, decency, and courage—implying that none of these are in play in this matter. There is lots of attitude here.

Compare Kristol's commentary to an opinion piece written by liberal blogger Jane Hamsher:

> It is customary for those found guilty to express contrition during the sentencing phase, a factor that judges take very seriously when determining jail time. Libby expressed none. Zero, zip, bupkis. It was my impression during the trial watching Libby that he thought himself a great man to whom a terrible wrong has been done. Today Scooter's career as a man on trial ended and his life as professional right wing victim began.
>
> Looking at the incredible collection of letters written in his defense is enough to give anyone bone chilling creeps, but it does offer some insight into the sickness governs beltway culture these days. . . .
>
> Because they, like Libby, don't believe he's done anything wrong. The modern Republican party is built on the construct that all government is bad, and once in power they set about bringing into fruition this self-fulfilling prophecy with ruthless efficiency. They destroy everything they touch, but they are very good at what they are good at: PR, partisan politics and preserving their own power. From where they stand, from where Scooter stands, there is no culpability in anything done in the service of this, and Scooter was just doing his job. Read through the letters. The presumption of extreme moral rectitude even in the absence of any kind of moral compass whatsoever is gobsmacking. . . .
>
> Today (Judge) Reggie Walton recognized what Scooter Libby and his cronies did not—Scooter is not a great man, he's a common crook and in the eyes of the law he ought to go to jail. This country will be just a little bit better tonight, a little bit healthier and closer to a place where faith in government and our system of justice can be restored because Libby and all his Very Important Friends were not able to hornswoggle Reggie Walton like they have been so many journalists who have fallen down on the job and failed to ask the kind of appropriate questions that should have kept us from getting to this place to begin with. (2007)

Hamsher also has very strong opinions about this matter, but her account is a bit more formal than Kristol's because she is interested in the larger questions the sentencing raises. She injects attitude into the piece primarily through her use of colloquialisms such as "gobsmacked" and "hornswoggle," which tend to close the rhetorical distance between her voice and her readers.

Grammatical Person

The prominent features of style that affect voice and distance are grammatical person, verb tense and voice, word size, qualifers, and—in written discourse—punctuation. There are three grammatical persons available in English: first person, in which the person or persons speaking or writing refer to themselves as "I" or "we"; second person, in which the audience is addressed by means of *you;* and third person, in which the rhetor mentions agents or issues but does not allude directly to herself or her audience.

> FIRST-PERSON REFERENCE: "I want you to do the dishes today."
> SECOND-PERSON ADDRESS: "Do these dishes today or else."
> THIRD-PERSON REFERENCE: "Someone must do these dishes today."

Composition textbooks (and teachers) often tell their students never to use first-person (*I* or *we*) or second-person *(you)* pronouns in the papers they write in school. No doubt teachers adhere to this rule because school writing is supposedly formal in tone, or because they want their students to sound objective—that is, they do not want their students' voices to take center stage in papers written for school. However, we think that this rule is far too simple and inflexible to respond to the great variety of rhetorical situations that people encounter.

Generally, first- and second-person discourse creates less distance between a rhetor and an audience than does third-person discourse, because the participants in the action are referred to directly. In third-person discourse, the issue or subject is instead foregrounded, and references to the rhetor or his audience tend to disappear. Thus third-person discourse creates the greatest possible rhetorical distance. First- and second-person discourse are used in situations where rhetors are physically proximate to audiences—in conversation and in more formal speech situations as well. In settings where spoken discourse is used, *I* and *you* actually refer to participants in the situation, even when the audience is very, very large, as it is at football games and open-air concerts. Third person is generally used by speakers only within quite formal contexts, or if convention dictates that it be used—at a conference of scientists, or engineers for instance.

First- and Second-Person Discourse

First- and second-person discourse are ordinarily used in speech when small groups of people are conversing. Clarity of pronoun reference is ordinarily not a problem in conversation because the persons to whom the pronouns apply are visible and audible to all participants. To see how important it is to maintain the relatively intimate distance necessary to conversation, try speaking about someone who is present in the third person (use her name; use the pronouns *she* and *her* to refer to her). Third-person pronouns create such a distance that the person so referred to may feel that she has suddenly become invisible.

First and second grammatical persons have interesting and complex ethical effects in writing and in electronic discourse, since the persons participating in these rhetorical acts are not physically proximate to each other.

Here is a fictional example of first-person discourse, from Benjamin Kunkel's novel *Indecision*:

> A week before Quito I was sitting up in bed in New York, the edges of my awareness lapped at by traffic. I was sitting there with one hand holding open the book I was reading, and the other hand placed above the head of sleeping Vaneetha. There I was, pinned in space and time like a specimen in a box.

Here is a version of the passage revised into third-person discourse:

> A week before he was to leave for Quito, Dwight was sitting up in bed in New York, the edges of his awareness lapped at by traffic. He was sitting there with one hand holding open the book he was reading, and the other hand placed above the head of sleeping Vaneetha. There he was, pinned in space and time like a specimen in a box.

By comparing the two versions, we see that the third-person passage increases the distance between reader and writer, as well as between readers and the subject of the novel, the post-9/11 "midlife crisis" of twenty-eight-year-old Dwight B. Wilmerding.

Since it is modeled on conversation, first-person discourse always implies the presence of a hearer or a reader, a "you" who is listening or reading, whether that "you" is explicitly mentioned or not. Prose that relies on an "I-you" relation indicates to members of an audience that a rhetor feels close enough to them to include them in a relatively intimate conversation:

> Dear folks: I know you may be worried about me, so I'm writing to say that I arrived safely. Please send money. Love, your son.

The author of this note gives no details at all about his arrival—when, where, how. He obviously feels so close to his audience that he assumes they need no more information than he supplies.

In relationships that are not intimate, the "I-you" voice has complex ethical effects. Novelist Fyodor Dostoyevsky's "Underground Man" provides a good instance of the ego-centeredness that may result from the use of first-person discourse, even when the rhetor is a fictional person, as he is in this case:

> I am a sick man . . . I am a spiteful man. I am an unpleasant man. I think my liver is diseased. However, I don't know beans about my disease, and I am not sure what is bothering me. I don't treat it and never have, though I respect medicine and doctors. Besides, I am extremely superstitious, let's say sufficiently so to respect medicine. (I am educated enough not to be superstitious, but I am). No, I refuse to treat it out of spite. You probably will not understand that. Well, but I understand it. Of course, I can't explain to you just whom I am annoying in this case by my spite. (1960, 1)

Here is a complaining neighbor, wrapped so deeply in his own troubles that he seems at first to be engaging in an ego-centered, aimless, and self-contradictory monologue. But suddenly he acknowledges the presence of an audience ("You probably will not understand"), a move that establishes a sort of back-fence intimacy. And the final sentence in the passage suggests that the relationship will become "us" against "them" before very long. The intimate "I-you" relationship includes Dostoyevsky's audience, whether they want to be this man's companion or not.

The ethical possibilities opened by grammatical person are endless. In *Desert Solitaire*, Edward Abbey used a combination of third and first persons to separate "us" from "them."

> There may be some among the readers of this book . . . who believe without question that any and all forms of construction and development are intrinsic goods, in the national parks as well as anywhere else, who virtually identify quantity with quality and therefore assume that the greater the quantity of traffic, the higher the value received. There are some who frankly and boldly advocate the eradication of the last remnants of wilderness and the complete subjugation of nature to the requirement of—not man—but industry. This is a courageous view, admirable in its simplicity and power, and with the weight of all modern history behind it. It is also quite insane. I cannot attempt to deal with it here.
>
> There will be other readers, I hope, who share my basic assumption that wilderness is a necessary part of civilization and that it is the primary responsibility of the national park system to preserve intact and undiminished what little still remains. (1968, 47)

Abbey referred to those who don't share his opinions in the third person, perhaps because he was pretty sure they wouldn't be among his readers. This tactic created a "we-they" relationship that gave Abbey's readers a sense of being allied with him against those who do not share his position.

"We," the plural first-person pronoun, shares in the complex rhetorical effects created by the use of "I." "We" may establish a level of intimacy that presumes much in common between rhetor and audience, even when, in fact, a great power differential exists between them. Here for example, is an excerpt from a speech by President Bush about foreign aid:

> We are a compassionate nation. When Americans see suffering and know that our country can help stop it, they expect our government to respond. I believe in the timeless truth, and so do a lot of other Americans, to whom much is given, much is required. We're blessed to live in this country. We're blessed to live in the world's most prosperous nation. And I believe we have a special responsibility to help those who are not as blessed. It is the call to share our prosperity with others, and to reach out to brothers and sisters in need.
>
> We help the least fortunate across the world because our conscience demands it. We also recognize that helping struggling nations succeed is in our interest. When America helps lift societies out of poverty we create new markets for goods and services, and new jobs for American workers. Prosperity abroad can be translated to jobs here at home. It's in our interest that we help improve the economies of nations around the world.
>
> When America helps reduce chaos and suffering, we make this country safer, because prosperous nations are less likely to feed resentment and breed

violence and export terror. Helping poor nations find the path to success benefits this economy and our security, and it makes us a better country. It helps lift our soul and renews our spirit. (2007)

Bush's arguments here are controversial among conservative members of his party who are isolationists, and so he uses an inclusive "we" to imply that all Americans share the values and beliefs he reviews here. This "we" cajoles the audience to accept his argument that aid to other countries strengthens the American economy at the same time as it makes the country safer.

We use the first-person pronoun throughout this book, even though to do so is unconventional in textbooks. We do so for three reasons. First of all, this voice seems to be more honest, since much of what we have to say here has developed from our own thinking about the usefulness of ancient rhetoric. As a result, writing in first person was easier for us since we didn't have to go searching for circumlocutions like "in the opinion of the authors" to express what we think. Second, when we take a position on a matter that is debated by scholars of ancient rhetoric, the first-person voice allows us to take responsibility for that position; third person makes flat statements about disputed matters seem far too authoritative and decisive in situations where opinions differ. Third, we hope that readers will identify more readily with a first-person voice. The material in this book is foreign and difficult and, by itself, puts quite a little distance between us and our readers. The use of a third-person voice would only widen that distance. Our choice of first person does create one problem, one that some readers may have noticed by now. Its use can create an ego-centered voice that excludes an audience. Whether this happens or not depends on the care taken by the rhetor to establish a respectable *ethos* and on his attitude toward his subject. We worried a good deal that our use of the plural first person *we* would take on authority we don't mean it to have. That is, we feared it would become the so-called "royal we," so-called because kings and queens use it when making official announcements.

There is yet another rhetorical problem inherent in the use of a first-person voice. First person often led us to want to write in second person as well, as in phrases like "Notice how . . ." and "You should do . . .". Since we wanted to avoid the instructional tone conveyed by the second person, we were often forced to substitute third-person circumlocutions for *you*—"the rhetor," "the writer," "the speaker," and so on.

Second-Person Discourse

Second-person discourse is the province of advertising. "Think different"; "Just do it"; "You're in good hands." Advertisers want their audiences to feel close to the companies they represent and the products they sell. The cozy second-person voices they establish cover over the fact that every ad gives instructions to its audience: use this, buy that. In other words, a potential rhetorical problem is inherent in second-person discourse, because rhetors who adopt it are giving directions. Obviously, this is true of recipes and directions for using or assembling something: "Add just a pinch of marjoram to the boiling sauce"; "Join tab A to slot B." The person who gives directions assumes a position of superiority to audiences. If readers are ready to be dictated to, as users of recipes usually are, this voice works.

When readers or hearers are not receptive to instruction, use of the second-person pronoun can increase distance rather than closing it. For example, when the chairwoman of the Congressional Black Caucus, Carolyn Cheeks Kirkpatrick, asked television talk-show host Don Imus if he understood that his language was offensive to black women, he responded in the affirmative. Then he said: "I can't get any place with you people." This would be funny if what it reveals weren't so horrible: Imus's use of the second person in the phrase "you people" is a palpable reminder of America's long history of segregation of black people, and its use created an alienating distance between himself and his audience—in this case a powerful black woman.

Third-Person Discourse

Third-person voice establishes the greatest possible distance between writer and reader. Use of this grammatical person announces that its author, for whatever reasons, cannot afford too much intimacy with an audience. Third person is appropriate when a rhetor wishes to establish herself as an authority or when she wishes to efface her voice so that the issue may seem to be presented as objectively as possible. In third-person discourse the relationship of both rhetor and audience to the issue being discussed is more important than the relation between them.

Here is a passage from Fredrich A. Hayek's *The Constitution of Liberty* that is written in third person:

> The great aim of the struggle for liberty has been equality before the law. This equality under the rules which the state enforces may be supplemented by a similar equality of the rules that men voluntarily obey in their relations with one another. This extension of the principles of equality to the rules of moral and social conduct is the chief expression of what is commonly called the democratic spirit—and probably that aspect of it that does most to make inoffensive the inequalities that liberty necessarily produces. (1960, 85)

Hayek did not qualify the generalizations put forward in this paragraph with an "I think" or even with an "Experience shows that .... " He may have had several reasons for choosing to write in this distancing fashion: to seem objective, to seem authoritative and therefore forceful, or to keep his subject—equality—in front of readers, rather than his personality. Since Hayek is a very-well-known political theorist, his status as an authority (his situated *ethos*) may be such that he doesn't have to qualify his generalizations.

Here's another example of third-person discourse from the first page of *How Institutions Think*, written by a well-known anthropologist, Mary Douglas:

> Writing about cooperation and solidarity means writing at the same time about rejection and mistrust. Solidarity involves individuals being ready to suffer on

behalf of the larger group and their expecting other individual members to do as much for them. It is difficult to talk about these questions coolly. They touch on intimate feelings of loyalty and sacredness. Anyone who has accepted trust and demanded sacrifice or willingly given either knows the power of the social bond. Whether there is a commitment to authority or a hatred of tyranny or something between the extremes, the social bond itself is taken to be something above question. Attempts to bring it out into the light of day and to investigate it are resisted. Yet it needs to be examined. Everyone is affected directly by the quality of trust around him or her. (1986, 1)

This third-person voice is a bit less distancing than Hayek's, because it does refer to people, rather than to abstractions. However, Douglas takes great pains not to name anyone, even though she is writing about intimate issues ("feelings of loyalty and sacredness"). Use of the third person forces Douglas to put rather vague words in the grammatical subject positions of her sentences: *writing, solidarity, it, they, anyone.* We have revised the passage into first person, making the author (*I*) the grammatical subject of most of the sentences:

If I write about cooperation and solidarity, I must write at the same time about rejection and mistrust. I define *solidarity* as the readiness of individuals to suffer on behalf of the larger group and their expecting other individual members to do as much for them. I have difficulty talking about these questions coolly, because they touch on intimate feelings of loyalty and sacredness. Since I have accepted trust and demanded sacrifice, and have willingly given them as well, I know the power of the social bond. I take the social bond to be above question; my commitment to authority or my hatred of tyranny are irrelevant to this question. Every time I attempt to bring it out into the light of day and to investigate it, people resist my efforts. Yet we need to examine it, because all of us are affected by the quality of trust around us.

We think the revision makes the passage clearer and more lively as well. Use of the first person also forces the author to take responsibility for the large generalizations she makes about the touchiness of this question. However, use of first-person discourse does lessen the authority carried by the original passage, because the generalizations made in the revision are less sweeping in scope. That is, they apply to "I" rather than to people in general.

Scientists, social scientists, and other scholars use third-person discourse in order to reinforce the impression that the facts speak for themselves, that human beings have had as little influence in these matters as possible. The warning label on cigarette packages, for example, used to read as follows: "Warning: The Surgeon General Has Determined That Cigarette Smoking Is Dangerous To Your Health." Even though the surgeon general probably did not conduct the research that discovered the connection between smoking and lung cancer, the message relied on the authority of that office to underscore the seriousness of the message. A later version of this warning reads: "Quitting Smoking Now Greatly

Reduces Serious Risks to Your Health." While the newer version is a bit more specific, it is also firmer, because it omits reference to an author and addresses the audience directly. It is probably safe to predict that this warning will never be couched in a first-person voice: "I think that smoking cigarettes is bad for you, and you ought to stop it. Mary Jones, M.D." The intimacy of first person undermines the authority that this serious message requires.

Our use of alternating male and female pronouns in this book has irritated some of our readers. Some who have complained about this practice would prefer that we stick to a single gender, thus reducing the number of occasions in which gender switches call attention to the rhetoric of our argument and hence distract readers from what we are saying. Other readers assert that consistent use of male pronouns would be less distracting. Calls for consistency in gender reference suggest that readers imagine a rhetorical actor or actors with whom they identify while reading. When that actor's gender is altered, the reader must stop in order to adjust her picture of the imagined actor (as in this sentence). Calls for sole reliance on the male gender, however, seem to us to stem from a commonplace: that rhetorical actors are, or ought to be, male. That is to say, the first objection to our practice is rhetorical; the second is ideological. We adopted the practice of switching the gender of pronouns referring to rhetorical actors in order to call our readers' attention to both the workings of rhetorical actors and the power of the commonplace. Some of our critics have said our second aim goes beyond our responsibilities as rhetoric teachers. What do you think?

Students often use third person when they write for teachers, on the correct assumptions that the formal distance lends authority to their work and that it is appropriate for the rhetorical situation that obtains in most classrooms. A curious thing sometimes happens within third-person prose, however: people write phrases like "the writer of this paper feels" or "in the opinion of this author." If these constructions emerge during the writing process, it may be that the issue demands that the rhetor express some opinions and take responsibility for them. In this case, first person may be a better choice. Third-person statements tend to have an authoritative flavor. When rhetors find themselves trying to add qualifiers about their opinions or attitudes, it may be the case that the third-person voice is inappropriate or even dishonest. Of course, dishonesty is disastrous if a reader detects it.

Verb Tense and Voice

The choice of grammatical person is the most influential element in establishing voice and distance. However, other stylistic choices, such as verb tense and voice, affect an *ethos* as well. Present tense has more immediacy than past tense; use of the present tense gives an audience a sense of participation in events that are occurring at the moment, while past tense makes them feel like onlookers in events that have already occurred. Compare your response to the following phrasings:

Present Tense: Quintilian teaches his students to . . .

Past Tense: Quintilian taught his students to . . .

The second example distances readers from Quintilian because it explicitly places his teaching in the past.

In English, verbs may assume one of two "voices"—active and passive. Passive verb constructions betray themselves through an explicit or implicit "by _____" phrase, as in "The door was left open (by _____)." Phrasing such a construction in active voice requires the rhetor to supply somebody (or some thing) who can act as an agent upon the door: John, the dog, the wind, as in "John left the door open." Active verb constructions tend to lessen distance, since the rhetor using them is forced to name either herself or somebody or something else as an actor in the sentence; usually this rhetorical subject (the actor) is also the grammatical subject of a sentence with an active verb construction. Passive constructions, in contrast, tend to create distance between rhetor and issue, since the grammatical subject of the sentence is usually not its rhetorical subject.

Active Voice: Mary did the dishes.

Passive Voice: The dishes were done (by Mary).

Active Voice: I take responsibility for these actions.

Passive Voice: Responsibility must be taken for these actions (by me).

Active constructions force rhetors to betray their presence as creator of the discourse; active voice also forces them to take overt responsibility for their assertions. Passive constructions permit rhetors to avoid taking responsibility for their statements. "The police were misled" is a passive construction that avoids mentioning the person who did the misleading.

Sometimes this strategy is useful, depending upon the rhetorical situation. If a rhetor does not know what he needs to know, he may want to disguise his ignorance by using passive constructions. Rhetors who do so, however, run the risk of damaging their audience's estimate of their intelligence, honesty, and goodwill. Take this passive sentence, for example:

Sometimes ridiculed for directing their presentation to the nonintellectual, television news coverage is obligated to give a concise, easily understandable, factual news report.

In this case, the use of third person creates distance between author and audience, since the passive construction allows the rhetor to disappear. She is nowhere in sight. Since nobody is around to take responsibility, readers might wonder just how authoritative this statement is. A reader might wonder: "Well, who obligates television news coverage to be concise, factual, and so on? Who says so? In my experience, Brit Hume and Candy Crowley and the rest don't always stick to the facts. . . ." If this happens, the rhetor might as well have never written at all, because important aspects of her *ethos*—that she seem well-informed and honest and that she have her audience's interest in mind—have been compromised. Active voice might have been a better choice, although it requires her to name some names and take some responsibility for her assertions:

> Critics sometimes ridicule television news coverage for directing their presentation to the nonintellectual. News writers couch the news in simple terms, however, because their duty as journalists obligates them to give a concise, easily understandable, factual news report.

Word Size

Other stylistic resources help to establish voice, as well. Word size seems to affect voice and distance. American audiences tend to assume that polysyllabic words (big words with lots of syllables, like polysyllabic) indicate that their user is well educated. Hence they are likely to award authority to a rhetor who uses them. Compare the effect of "It will be my endeavor in this analysis . . ." to that of "Here I will try to analyze. . . ."

When used carefully, polysyllabic words are generally more precise than smaller words: *polysyllabic* is more specific than *large* or *big; deconstructing* is both more impressive and precise than "taking apart"; *chlorofluorocarbons* is more precise, but less intimate, than "the stuff that causes holes in the ozone layer." Because of their greater accuracy, larger words tend to appear in formal discourse, in which rhetors are more concerned with accuracy than with establishing an intimate relation with readers. However, big words can have the disadvantage of making their user sound pompous; too many polysyllabic words can also discourage people from making the effort to plow through them, especially if their meanings are obscure to the intended audience. Here is a brief passage written by philosopher Jacques Derrida:

> On what conditions is a grammatology possible? Its fundamental condition is certainly the undoing of logocentrism. But this condition of possibility turns into a condition of impossibility. In fact it risks upsetting the concept of science as well. Graphematics or grammatography ought no longer to be presented as sciences; their goal should be exorbitant when compared to a grammatological knowledge. (1976, 74)

While Derrida writes simple sentences, he nonetheless litters his pages with polysyllabic terms whose meanings are unfamiliar to many readers (chiefly because Derrida coined many of them himself). One has to be very committed to read Derrida's work because it takes a long time to learn the meanings of the terms he employs.

Familiar words are effective in informal discursive situations where the audience is on fairly close terms with the rhetor; everyone shares common understanding that lessens the rhetor's obligation to be precise. "Cool!" is an example wherein precision of meaning is absolutely sacrificed to the establishment of intimacy. (As you can see, this phrase, which is ordinarily used in conversation, loses much of its effect in print). And while the meaning of "cool" has been readily understood by the readers of this book since its first edition, we might do better now to substitute another phrase for it such as "sweet!" or "awesome," which do similar kinds of work. Laudatory expressions such as these go in and out of fashion very quickly, because their utterance is the very mark of cool.

Qualifiers

Qualifiers like *some, most, virtually*, and *all* affect voice and distance. A qualifier is any term (usually an adverb or an adjective) or phrase that alters the degree of force or extent contained in a statement. Compare the relative distance achieved by the use of qualifiers in the following statements:

> All humans are created equal.
>
> It may be that most humans are created equal.
>
> I believe that very few humans are created equal.
>
> Virtually no humans are created equal.

The first statement is quite distant, because it makes a sweeping, authoritative judgment. No authors are present to identify with readers. The other statements are more intimate because they betray the presence of an author, modifying the extent or intensity of his judgment in each case.

As a general rule, the more qualifiers and the more intensity they convey, the more intimate the distance between rhetor and audience. Qualifiers have this effect because they indicate, however subtly, that someone is present making judgments about degrees of intensity. Compare this unqualified statement to the heavily qualified one that follows it:

> *Unqualified:* Three months after announcing it had settled a lawsuit filed against it by Bread and Butter Corporation, the City Council of Ourtown made the agreement public today.
>
> *Heavily Qualified:* Three long months after announcing it had tentatively settled one of the most expensive civil lawsuits in the city's history, today the City Council of Ourtown, with some trepidation, made public a proposed agreement between it and the gigantic Bread and Butter Corporation.

The first version creates more distance between author and readers because the writer expresses few judgments about the event under discussion. The author of the second version, is willing to qualify events by using adjectives and adverbs that express degree ("tentatively," "expensive," "gigantic").

Composition textbooks sometimes caution writers against the use of qualifiers, calling them "weasel words." However, cautious rhetors often find it necessary to use a few qualifiers in order to represent a position as accurately as possible. (The underlined words in the preceding sentence are qualifiers). Moreover, qualifiers can be effective in reducing distance between a rhetor and an audience in situations where an intimate distance is more persuasive than a more formal one. As a result, qualifiers can also make your work more interesting, and this effect is enhanced if the qualifiers add interesting detail to an account.

Here is a *New York Times* report of a study of the drug Avandia. We have underlined the qualifiers:

> Avandia was approved for sale in 1999 based on studies showing that it <u>could</u> lower blood glucose levels in patients suffering from Type 2 diabetes, also known as adult-onset diabetes. The assumption was that the drug <u>could</u> alleviate <u>some</u> of the <u>most damaging</u> effects of the disease, such as heart attacks and other cardiovascular ailments. But a paper <u>just</u> published in *The New England Journal of Medicine* suggests that Avandia <u>may</u> instead increase the risk of a heart attack <u>by 43 percent</u> and <u>perhaps</u> the <u>risk</u> of cardiovascular deaths as well.
>
> The study—an analysis of the combined results of 42 previous studies that compared people who took the drug with people who did not—is <u>not definitive,</u> and the <u>absolute</u> risk to any given patient is small. But the study points to a risk that <u>could potentially</u> harm thousands of patients a year. Its lead author was Steven Nissen, a cardiologist at the Cleveland Clinic, who blew the whistle on the cardiovascular risks of Vioxx, which adds to the sense of déjà vu. (2007)

The underlined terms show how careful scientific reports have to be. After all, an unqualified claim in a study such as this can result in a lawsuit; worse, a disproportionate assessment of the drug's effects can worsen an illness or even cause death.

Punctuation

Punctuation is an extremely subtle means of establishing voice and distance in written discourse. The more exotic marks of punctuation work to close distance between writers and readers; they do the work that gestures, facial expressions, tone, and pitch do for speakers. Dashes convey breathlessness or hurry—or a midthought—or an afterthought. Parentheses (like these) decrease distance, because they have the flavor of an interruption, a remark whispered behind the hand. Exclamation points indicate strong emotions at work! Textbooks say that quotation marks are to be used only to represent material that has been quoted from another source, but increasingly quotation marks are being used for emphasis. This example shows them doing both jobs: "We don't 'cash' checks." <u>Underlining</u> or **bold** or CAPITAL LETTERS convey emphasis or importance, and all of these graphic signals close the distance between rhetor and audience. In electronic discourse, text written in caps is taken as evidence that the user is SHOUTING, and the tactic is considered impolite unless used sparingly and for effect.

If you doubt that such small things do influence distance, note whether you are offended the next time you see them in a message e-mailed to you by someone you do not know. Contemporary decorum seems to dictate, in

short, that fancy or innovative punctuation should be used in intimate situations while discourse composed for more formal rhetorical situations
should feature only the standard punctuation used to mark sentences and
indicate possession (see Chapter 13, on delivery).

SITUATED *ETHOS*

Because rhetoric is embedded in social relations, the relative social standing of participants in a rhetorical situation can effect a rhetor's persuasiveness. A differential power relation inheres within any rhetorical situation
simply because rhetors have the floor, so to speak. As long as they are being
read or listened to they have control of the situation. But audiences have
power, too, particularly in the case of written rhetoric, in which readers are
relatively free to quit whenever they please. Few rhetors enjoy absolute
power over either hearers or readers. We all know how easy it is to mute
television commercials or to skip to the end of a murder mystery to see how
it turns out. Reader control is maximized on the Internet, where switching
from page to page is a simple matter of clicking a mouse.

But differential power relations exist outside of rhetorical situations,
and these affect the degree to which an invented *ethos* can be effective. In
other words, exceptions to Aristotle's generalizations about *ethos* occur in
rhetorical situations where a rhetor's *ethos* is either bolstered or compromised by his reputation or his position in the community. Such exceptions
apply most strongly to well-known people and especially to those who are
well known because they hold some authoritative or prestigious position in
the community. Ministers generally enjoy more cultural authority than bar-
tenders, at least in rhetorical situations where they are considered to have
expertise. A prior reputation as an *A* student or as a goof-off may affect a
teacher's reception of students' work no matter how carefully students
craft an invented *ethos*.

Rhetors and audiences may exist in unequal social relations to one
another for a variety of reasons. Within classrooms, for example, teachers
have more power than students, and usually teachers can silence students
whenever they think it's necessary or proper to do so. Within the culture at
large, in general, older people have more authority than younger ones, and
wealthy people have more power than poorer ones do, in part because they
have better access to the channels of communication. According to the
rhetorician Wayne Brockriede, there are three major dimensions in any
rhetorical situation: interpersonal, attitudinal, and situational. Each of
these dimensions can be used as a heuristic to help you determine the situated *ethos* at work in any given rhetorical situation.

The interpersonal dimension—the relations among persons who participate in a rhetorical act—has three characteristics: **liking, power,** and
distance. Liking has to do with how well the people who are engaging in a
rhetorical situation like each other. According to news reports, President
George W. Bush and British Prime Minister Tony Blair were great personal

friends during the time when both governed their respective countries. If this was so, according to Professor Brockriede, their personal relationship should have smoothed discussions of the difficult issues they had to face. Under the head of "liking," then, rhetors should ask:

1. Are the feelings of liking or disliking mutual among participants in this rhetorical situation or in arguments about this issue?

2. How intense are these feelings? Are these feelings susceptible to rhetorical change?

Brockriede defines *power* as "the capacity to exert interpersonal influence." Power may be the focus of a rhetorical act (as in "a power struggle"), or it may be a by-product of the act. A person may have power in a rhetorical situation for several reasons: because she has "charisma"; because of her position within the social system; because she has control over the channels of communication or other aspects of the rhetorical situation; because she can influence sources of information and/or the participants' ideology; or because she has access to other powerful people. President Ronald Reagan, who was frequently referred to as "the great communicator," was thought by his supporters to have great personal charm, or charisma (which was to be expected, perhaps, given his experience as an actor). John F. Kennedy was also thought to be a charismatic person, and many television evangelists owe their success to their personal charisma.

But not everyone has this somewhat mysterious quality called charisma. And so it is also important for rhetors to think about the power structure inherent in any rhetorical situation. Power is usually relatively shared between rhetors and their audiences. Few rhetors enjoy absolute power over their hearers or readers, even those, like the president of the United States, who can exert enormous power in other situations.

Rhetors who control the channels of communication have great situated power, because in extreme situations they can force people to become their audiences. When the president schedules a speech or a news conference on an important issue, for example, television networks are obligated to carry it even though it costs them money in lost advertising revenues to do so. People are obligated to listen and watch, unless they take rhetorical power into their own hands and turn the television off. Rhetorical power is obviously tied to access. Access (or lack of it) can either facilitate communication or disable certain possibilities for fruitful exchange.

Here are some questions to ask about the power structure of a rhetorical situation:

1. How disparate are the power positions of the various participants of a rhetorical act, and does the act increase, maintain, or decrease the disparity?

2. How rigid or flexible is the power structure, and does the rhetorical act function to increase, maintain, or decrease the stability?

As we have been saying, the rhetorical principle of distance examines how far apart, socially or situationally, participants are from one another in a rhetorical situation. When choosing a voice for a discourse, a rhetor should ask, Is this the optimal distance for persuasion, or should it be closed or opened up? Answers to these questions will depend in part on the quality of power relations between rhetor and audience.

The attitudinal dimension of rhetorical situations determines what predispositions exist among the participants in a rhetorical act that will influence their response to the situation. We can predict, roughly, that people will respond to a rhetorical proposition in one of three ways: acceptance, indifference, or rejection. Rhetors who are preparing to argue a case should ask:

1. What would or did it take to move someone who is/was indifferent toward acceptance or rejection of my position?

2. Can I move someone from a position of acceptance toward rejection, or vice versa?

3. People who do research on rhetorical situations have found that the more ego-involved a participant is, the less likely he is to be persuaded. Is or was this true in the situation you are analyzing?

People do not respond to a proposition out of context; their responses are determined by their ideology. Rhetors enjoy situated power if they are in a position to influence the ideology of participants in a rhetorical situation, as parents and clergy usually are. Rhetors also have situated power if they can suppress or divulge information that is crucial to understanding or deciding an issue. Press secretaries, spokespeople, and spin doctors enjoy this sort of power. What sorts of beliefs or ideological responses will your audience bring to your rhetorical situation?

RHETORICAL ACTIVITIES

1. Find a half dozen short pieces of professional writing. These can be selections from books, newspapers or magazines, fiction or non fiction. Read each passage carefully. How do the authors establish *ethos*? Specifically, how do they convince you that they are intelligent and well-informed? What tactics do the authors use to establish their good character? Their goodwill toward readers? Make lists of these tactics for future reference. Do any of the pieces display an *ethos* that is not successful?

2. Now analyze the pieces in terms of the rhetorical distance created by their authors' voices. Do the authors assume they know readers well, or do they establish a formal distance? How do they achieve this distance? Look at their uses of grammatical person, verb voice and tense, word size, qualifiers, and punctuation.

CHAPTER 6 / ETHICAL PROOF **231**

3. Write an e-mail or a letter to someone exhibiting bad *ethos*, violating some of the strategies discussed in this chapter.

4. For practice, try to alter the voice and rhetorical distance of two or three of the pieces. Change the grammatical person, the word size, the voice and tense; use more or fewer qualifiers; use more or less and different kinds of punctuation. What happens? Is the author's *ethos* altered? How? Does the distance change? How? Is your revision more or less effective than the original? Why?

5. To practice creating an effective *ethos*, write a letter to someone who is very close to you—a spouse, parent, or friend. Now write a letter that says the same thing to someone who is less close to you—a teacher, for example. Now write the letter to a company or corporation. What happens to your voice in each case? What features of your writing are altered?

6. Write a letter in the voice of someone else: someone you know or, better yet, a famous person such as a politician, a TV anchorperson, a movie star. Before you can do this successfully, you may have to watch and listen awhile to the person whose *ethos* you plan on imitating.

7. Try imitating the voice used by some writer you admire. (For more exercises of this kind, see the chapter on imitation.) How does the writer achieve ethical effects?

8. Look at several articles in a popular newspaper or news magazine such as *USA Today* or *Newsweek*. Who seems to be speaking? How do the authors of these articles establish *ethos*? Do they attempt to seem intelligent and well-informed? How do they get access to the information they pass along?

PROGYMNASMATA VI: COMPARISON AND CHARACTER

Comparison

Comparison is an exercise in which the composer implies that someone or something is greater than another. She does this by juxtaposing descriptions of both people or things. Comparison is similar to the exercise that precedes it, since a comparison is a double *encomium* or an *encomium* paired with an invective. Theon believed that two people or things compared should be relatively similar to start with: "comparison should be of likes and where we are in doubt which should be preferred because of no evident superiority of one to the other" (Kennedy 2003, 53). The point of the exercise, for Theon, is to aid in deliberation. Nicolaus the Sophist appears to have taken Theon a bit further by calling comparison an exercise in "double encomium" (Kennedy 2003, 163). Other ancients believed this exercise is useful, even if the difference between the people or things compared is vast. As Aphthonius counseled, "when comparing we should either set fine things beside good things or poor things beside poor things or good beside bad or small beside larger" (113–114, 2003). Hermogenes noted that comparison occurs in a number of other exercises, such as commonplace and *encomium*, as a means of amplification. He counted it as a separate exercise, however, because "some good authorities" had made comparison "an exercise by itself" (Kennedy 2003, 83).

With comparison we arrive at the portion of the rhetorical exercises that were practiced by mature rhetors. Plutarch's *Parallel Lives*, for instance, includes a number of exercises in comparison. Indeed, Plutarch probably learned the techniques used in the *Lives* when he practiced the school exercise called comparison.

Like Plutarch's *Lives*, ancient examples of comparison chiefly concern comparisons of persons. Aphthonius's example compared the Greek warrior Achilles to Hector, the Trojan warrior-prince. Hermogenes recommended comparison between the heroes Odysseus and Hercules. However, he warned that such an exercise required great skill, since the trickster Odysseus was a less-heroic figure than the mighty Hercules. The composer's goal in this case would be to praise Odysseus by showing that his virtues were even greater than those of the man who held the world on his shoulders. Hermogenes also suggested that comparisons could fruitfully be made between abstractions, such as justice and wealth.

The composing strategies used in comparison are the same as those used in *encomium* and invective. However, Aphthonius pointed out that the comparison should not treat all the details involved in one item and then move to the next; rather, it should compare the two items point by point. Here is Aphthonius's point-by-point comparison of Achilles and Hector:

A COMPARISON OF ACHILLES AND HECTOR

Seeking to compare virtue with virtue, I am going to measure the son of Peleus by the standard of Hector, for the virtues are to be honored in themselves. Compared, they become even more worthy of imitation.

Accordingly, both were born of not one land, but each alike sprang from one that is famous. One was of Phthia, whence came the name of Greece itself. The other was of Troy, whose builders were the first of the gods. To the degree that having been born in similar lands is not an inferiority in regard to commendation, by that degree Hector is not excelled by Achilles. And being born, the one as well as the other, of a praiseworthy land, both belonged to families of equal stature. For each was descended from Zeus. Achilles was the son of Peleus, Peleus of Aeacus, and Aeacus of Zeus; Hector, likewise, came from Priam and Laomedon, Laomedon from Dardanus, and Dardanus was a son of Zeus. And having been born with Zeus as a progenitor, they had forefathers nearly alike. For the ancestors of Achilles were Aeacus and Peleus, of whom the former freed the Greeks from want and the latter was allotted marriage with a goddess as a prize for his prowess in overcoming the Lapithes. On Hector's side, Dardanus was a forefather who formerly lived with the gods, and his father, Priam, was in command of a city whose walls were built by gods. To the degree that there was similarity in living with the gods and association with superior beings, by that degree is Hector about equal to Achilles.

And descended from such ancestors, both were brought up for courage. The one was reared by Chiron, while Priam was the tutor of the other by contributing lessons in virtue through his natural relationship. Just as an education in virtue is equal in both instances, so to them both does it bring equal fame.

When both arrived at manhood, they gained similar stature out of a single struggle, for in the first place, Hector led the Trojans and he was the protector of Troy as long as he survived. He remained in alliance with gods during that time, and when he fell, he left Troy lying vulnerable. Achilles, on the other hand, was the leader of Greece in arms; by terrifying all, he was prevailing against the Trojans, and he had the help of Athena in the contest, but when he fell, he deprived the Achaeans of gaining the upper hand. Overcome through Athena, the former [Hector] was destroyed; the latter [Achilles] fell, struck down at the hands of Apollo. And both, having sprung from gods, were taken off by gods; whence they drew their beginning, they also derived the end of their lives. To the degree that there was similarity in life and in death, by that degree is Hector on a par with Achilles.

It would be possible to say many other things on the virtue of both, except that both have nearly equal renown for their deeds.

Persons who are familiar with Homer's *Iliad* are likely to assume that Achilles was Hector's superior, since the Greek hero killed the Trojan prince in battle. However, Aphthonius's exercise demonstrates the persuasive potential of comparison, since his point-by-point consideration of the two heroes shows that Hector is as worthy of imitation as Achilles. Here is Plutarch's comparison of the two most famous orators in ancient times—Demosthenes and Cicero:

THE COMPARISON OF DEMOSTHENES AND CICERO

These are the most memorable circumstances recorded in history of Demosthenes and Cicero which have come to our knowledge. But omitting an exact comparison of their respective faculties in speaking, yet thus much seems fit to be said; that Demosthenes, to make himself a master in rhetoric, applied all the faculties he had, natural or acquired, wholly that way that he far surpassed in force and strength of eloquence all his contemporaries in political and judicial speaking, in grandeur and majesty all the panegyrical orators, and in accuracy and science all the logicians and rhetoricians of his day; that Cicero was highly educated, and by his diligent study became a most accomplished general scholar in all these branches, having left behind him numerous philosophical treatises of his own on Academic principles; as, indeed, even in his written speeches, both political and judicial, we see him continually trying to show his learning by the way. And one may discover the different temper of each of them in their speeches. For Demosthenes's oratory was without all embellishment and jesting, wholly composed for real effect and seriousness; not smelling of the lamp, as Pytheas scoffingly said, but of the temperance, thoughtfulness, austerity, and grave earnestness of his temper. Whereas

Cicero's love of mockery often ran him into scurrility; and in his love of laughing away serious arguments in judicial cases by jests and facetious remarks,
with a view to the advantage of his clients, he paid too little regard to what was
decent: saying, for example, in his defence of Caelius, that he had done no
absurd thing in such plenty and affluence to indulge himself in pleasures, it
being a kind of madness not to enjoy the things we possess, especially since the
most eminent philosophers have asserted pleasures to be the chiefest good. So
also we are told that when Cicero, being consul, undertook the defence of
Murena against Cato's prosecution, by way of bantering Cato, he made a long
series of jokes upon the absurd paradoxes, as they are called, of the Stoic set;
so that a loud laughter passing from the crowd to the judges, Cato, with a
quiet smile, said to those that sat next him, "My friends, what an amusing
consul we have."

And, indeed, Cicero was by natural temper very much disposed to mirth
and pleasantry, and always appeared with a smiling and serene countenance.
But Demosthenes had constant care and thoughtfulness in his look, and a serious anxiety, which he seldom, if ever, laid aside; and therefore, was accounted
by his enemies, as he himself confessed, morose and ill-mannered.

Also, it is very evident, out of their several writings, that Demosthenes
never touched upon his own praises but decently and without offence when
there was need of it, and for some weightier end; but upon other occasions
modestly and sparingly. But Cicero's immeasurable boasting of himself in his
orations argues him guilty of an uncontrollable appetite for distinction, his cry
being evermore that arms should give place to the gown, and the soldier's laurel to the tongue. And at last we find him extolling not only his deeds and
actions, but his orations also, as well those that were only spoken, as those that
were published; as if he were engaged in a boyish trial of skill, who should
speak best, with the rhetoricians, Isocrates and Anaximenes, not as one who
could claim the task to guide and instruct the Roman nation, the "Soldier full-
armed, terrific to the foe."

It is necessary, indeed, for a political leader to be an able speaker; but it is
an ignoble thing for any man to admire and relish the glory of his own eloquence. And, in this matter, Demosthenes had a more than ordinary gravity
and magnificence of mind, accounting his talent in speaking nothing more than
a mere accomplishment and matter of practice, the success of which must
depend greatly on the good-will and candour of his hearers, and regarding
those who pride themselves on such accounts to be men of a low and petty disposition.

The power of persuading and governing the people did, indeed, equally
belong to both, so that those who had armies and camps at command
stood in need of their assistance; as Charas, Diopithes, and Leosthenes of
Demosthenes's, Pompey and young Caesar of Cicero's, as the latter himself
admits in his Memoirs addressed to Agrippa and Maecenas. But what are
thought and commonly said most to demonstrate and try the tempers of /men,
namely, authority and place, by moving every passion, and discover every
frailty, these are things which Demosthenes never received; nor was he ever in
a position to give such proof of himself, having never obtained any eminent
office, nor led any of those armies into the field against Philip which he raised

by his eloquence. Cicero, on the other hand, was sent quaestor into Sicily, and proconsul into Cilicia and Cappadocia, at a time when avarice was at the height, and the commanders and governors who were employed abroad, as though they thought it a mean thing to steal, set themselves to seize by open force; so that it seemed no heinous matter to take bribes, but he that did it most moderately was in good esteem. And yet he, at this time, gave the most abundant proofs alike of contempt of riches and of his humanity and good-nature. And at Rome, when he was created consul in name, but indeed received sovereign and dictatorial authority against Catiline and his conspirators, he attested the truth of Plato's prediction, that then the miseries of states would be at an end when, by a happy fortune, supreme power, wisdom, and justice should united in one.

It is said, to the reproach of Demosthenes, that his eloquence was mercenary; that he privately made orations for Phornmion and Apollodorus, though adversaries in the same cause: that he was charged with moneys received from the King of Persia, and condemned for bribes from Harpalus. And should we grant that all those (and they are not few) who have made these statements against him have spoken what is untrue, yet that Demosthenes was not the character to look without desire on the presents offered him out of respect and gratitude by royal persons, and that one who lent money on maritime usury was likely to be thus indifferent, is what we cannot assert. But that Cicero refused, from the Sicilians when he was quaestor, from the King of Cappadocia when he was proconsul, and from his friends at Rome when he was in exile, many presents, though urged to receive them, has been said already.

Moreover, Demosthenes's banishment was infamous, upon conviction for bribery; Cicero's very honourable, for ridding his country of a set of villains. Therefore, when Demosthenes fled his country, no man regarded it; for Cicero's sake the senate changed their habit, and put on mourning, and would not be persuaded to make any act before Cicero's return was decreed. Cicero, however, passed his exile idly in Macedonia. But the very exile of Demosthenes made up a great part of the services he did for his country. for he went through the cities of Greece, and everywhere, as we have said, joined in the conflict on behalf of the Grecians, driving out the Macedonian ambassadors, and approving himself a much better citizen than Themistocles and Alcibiades did in the like fortune. And, after his return, he again devoted himself to the same public service, and continued firm to his opposition to Antipater and the Macedonians. Whereas Laelius reproached Cicero in the senate for sitting silent when Caesar, a beardless youth, asked leave to come forward, contrary to the law, as a candidate for the consulship; and Brutus, in his epistles, charges him with nursing and rearing a greater and more heavy tyranny than that they had removed.

Finally, Cicero's death excites our pity; for an old man to be miserably carried up and down by his servants, flying and hiding himself from that death which was, in the course of nature, so near at hand; and yet at last to be murdered. Demosthenes, though he seemed at first a little to supplicate, yet, by his preparing and keeping the poison by him, demands our admiration; and still more admirable was his using it. When the temple of the god no longer afforded him a sanctuary, he took refuge, as it were, at a mightier altar, freeing himself from arms and soldiers, and laughing to scorn the cruelty of Antipater. (1070–72).

While Plutarch's comparison supplied a good deal of information about both orators, it is not simply expository. Plutarch used his point-by-point comparison to evaluate the relative personal and professional merits of the two famous orators. In other words, comparison is a way of making judgments, of writing criticism. Shakespeare's Sonnet 18, which famously begins "Shall I compare thee to a summer's day?/Thou art more lovely and more temperate," is an interesting exercise because it compares a person to a day in summertime. Here again, an author used comparison to evaluate relative merits.

Comparisons frequently occur in the year leading up to an election. In the early weeks of 2007, the *Washington Post* published in its op-ed pages this comparison, written by E. J. Dionne, of two of the Democratic candidates:

HOW OBAMA VS. CLINTON SHAPES UP

Three differences and three similarities will define the contest between Hillary Rodham Clinton and Barack Obama.

The most important difference lies in where their respective political journeys began. After her early work as an advocate for children, Clinton came to political maturity in the South as part of her husband's efforts to rescue the Democratic Party from its low point in the 1980s. She was shaped by her party's need to win back moderate and conservative voters who had strayed to Ronald Reagan's banner.

The resulting Clinton project was a brilliant top-down effort to shape new Democratic ideas that would appeal to Southern whites and the Northern working class. This explains why both Clintons were drawn to the centrist Democratic Leadership Council, far more an elite policy shop than a grass-roots organization.

In a 2002 speech, Clinton signaled her respect for this approach by praising Al From, the DLC's founder and chief executive, for understanding "from the very beginning . . . that the right ideas were more important even than improving technology, organization or fundraising." Both Clintons have employed Mark Penn, the premier New Democratic pollster who is incessant in his efforts to locate the political center.

Obama, by contrast, began his political life as a community organizer in inner-city Chicago. His earliest experiences were of a bottom-up politics mobilizing the poor and the marginalized. This had the paradoxical effect of giving some of his ideas a decidedly progressive and activist tilt and others a more conservative tinge.

Consider two statements he made in 1997, shortly after his election to the Illinois Senate. On the one hand, Obama noted that welfare recipients "generally are not represented down here in Springfield," the capital, and that his job was to stand up for them.

But the organizer's emphasis on local and community responsibility sounded quite traditional when he declared the same year that "though we may be lobbying for more school funding, it's also important for us to bring education into the homes and ensure parents are checking children's homework, turning off the television, teaching common courtesy."

In keeping with his grass-roots background, Obama's campaign for the 2008 Democratic presidential nomination kicked off with a sense that it was a national movement, while Clinton, from the moment she announced her intentions on Saturday, commanded a well-established, well-staffed and well-financed national organization.

This second contrast can be exaggerated, since Obama will have ample financing. But the feel of the two campaigns is palpably different, with Obama enjoying an advantage on passion and Clinton on organization and discipline.

There are warnings for both candidates from the 1984 Democratic primaries, when Walter Mondale, the clear favorite, was nearly upended by the bright young upstart, Gary Hart. The danger for Clinton is that her front-running campaign will develop the habits of a cautious, inflexible behemoth. The bad news for Obama is that the solid Mondale had staying power and ultimately prevailed, though he lost in November.

There are, however, limits to the 1984 comparison, as a Clinton supporter noted over the weekend. Obama has been built up into a party savior a full year before the primaries—he will not enjoy Hart's element of surprise—even as expectations for Clinton have been defined downward by the incessant speculation about whether she can win.

Thus the third difference: Clinton, more than any other Democrat, has been both scarred and toughened by the partisan warfare of the past 15 years, while Obama is unscathed and untested.

This contrast was reflected in their announcement speeches. Obama attacked a politics that "has become so bitter and partisan" and pledged himself to "our common interests and concerns as Americans." Clinton spoke proudly of her ability to take on partisan foes. "I have never been afraid to stand up for what I believe in or to face down the Republican machine," she said. "I know how Washington Republicans think, how they operate and how to beat them."

Yet if Clinton and Obama present different profiles, they are, in certain respects, very much alike.

Both have displayed an unusually sophisticated and apparently genuine understanding of the role of religious faith in American politics. Both pride themselves on their ability, proven in their home states, to win over political moderates and voters not tethered to ideology.

And the woman who would become the nation's first female president and the man who would become its first African American president know how important the men and women of the white middle class will be to the outcome of the next election. Such voters will probably determine if either of them gets to become a national trailblazer—and also if any other Democrat can find a way to get in the middle of their fight.

This column helps illustrate the importance the exercise of comparison can play in rhetorical deliberation, a critical component of a democracy, as the ancients knew well. Contemporary students are familiar with this exercise in its guise as the "essay of comparison." In fact, comparison may be one of the few ancient exercises that survives in school rhetoric (description may be another). However, modern rhetoric frequently asks students to compose comparisons as noncontextualized exercises in exposition. Thus it misses an important point about the ancient exercise: comparisons are always persuasive, insofar as they praise someone or something by comparing it to a less praiseworthy person or thing.

PROGYMNASMATA: COMPARISON

1. Comparison in everyday life. We often make comparisons in everyday discourse. Think of the last time a friend asked you to weigh in on a choice between two activities or things: whether to wear a dress or pants, whether to attend a party with this person or that, or whether to major in one subject or another. Recount your advice in the form of a comparison.

2. Choose a favorite hobby or something you know a lot about and either a) compare two things within that hobby or b) compare the hobby to another. For example, if you choose cycling, you could compare two different makes of bikes or even road biking to mountain biking. Or you could compare basketball to tennis. Don't forget Aphthonius's recommended pattern to make comparisons point by point.

3. If there is an election going on—either nationally, locally in your city, or on your campus—research two candidates and compose a comparison. Which is the better of the two candidates? Which the lesser?

Character

Aphthonius defined this difficult exercise as "an imitation of the character of a proposed person." In other words, students using this exercise were to construct a characterization of some person, real or fictional, living or dead. In modern schools, this exercise, along with description and narration, is often taught by creative writers—persons who make their living writing poetry and fiction. But the ancients made no sharp distinctions among the composing skills required by rhetors, poets, historians, or novelists. Historians need to know how to depict character just as novelists and poets do. Furthermore, the establishment of a rhetor's character amounts to an important kind of proof in rhetoric.

Aphthonius divided characters into three kinds: *ethopoeia* (character-making), *prosopopoeia* (person-making) and *eidolopoeia* (image- or spirit-making). In the first kind, students depict the character of some person by imagining the words that a known person might say to another. The exercise becomes *prosopopeia* when students imagine a thing speaking or, according to Nicolaus the Sophist, when students create a fictionalized person and have him speak. In both instances a "person" gets made. Hermogenes' example from rhetorical history is when Aristides gives a speech in which "The Sea" addresses the Athenians. In the last kind of character, words are put into the mouth of an apparition or a person who has died. Shakespeare displayed his skill at *eidolopoeia* when he composed the speeches made by the ghost of Hamlet's father.

Both Aphthonius and Hermogenes taught that the compositions called "characters" could be either definite or indefinite. A definite character depicts specific persons, such as Andromache and Hector. Hermogenes would have classed these as indefinite characters, where the composer attempts to capture typical characteristics of a class of persons. We have already met with an example of indefinite *ethopoeia* where we quoted Theophrastus's characterization of a tactless person. Another example of an indefinite *ethopoeia* is given by Nicolaus the Sophist, who offers the exercise "what words a coward would say when going out to battle" (164). Hermogenes further classified characters as single or double. A single character depicts someone talking to himself, for example, "what a general might say on returning from a victory"; a double character represents another person or persons as well, as "what a general might say to his army after a victory."

Hermogenes also recommended that characterizations be appropriate to the persons and occasions being depicted: "for the speech of youth is not that of age, nor the speech of joy that of grief" (35). He pointed out that some characters depict a habit of mind, while others depict a passing mood or emotion. In the former kind, the composer should provide details that indicate a person's general habits of mind and action; what, for example, would a farmer say when seeing a ship or the sea for the first time? In the latter sort of character, the composer should portray the effects of powerful emotions on someone: for example, in portraying Achilles' response to the death of Patroclus, the composer should try to depict the hero's rage, pain, and grief.

The chronology of a characterization may be important in some rhetorical situations. Hermogenes suggested that composers "begin with the present because it is hard" (35) (Epic poems conventionally begin in the present, or *in medias res*—in the middle of things.) Then, Hermogenes said, the composer should "revert to the past because it has had much happiness; then make your transition to the future because what is to happen is much more impressive" (35). Characters need not involve consideration of past, present, or future, of course; they may depict a single moment in time.

One way to indicate character is to create conversation that gives clues about a person's responses to situations. Ancient teachers asked their students to indicate character by imagining what famous people in history or fiction might say on a given occasion: What would Queen Hecuba have said about the fall of her city? What would Medea say as she was about to slaughter her children? Here is a *prosopopoeia* written by Plutarch, in which he imagined Cleopatra standing over Marc Antony's grave:

> There was a young man of distinction among Caesar's companions named Cornelius Dolabella. He was not without a certain tenderness for Cleopatra, and sent her word privately, as she had besought him to do, that Caesar was

about to return through Syria, and that she and her children were to be sent on within three days. When she understood this, she made her request to Caesar that he would be pleased to permit her to make oblations to the departed Antony; which being granted, she ordered herself to be carried to the place where he was buried, and there, accompanied by her women, she embraced his tomb with tears in her eyes, and spoke in this manner: "O, dearest Antony," said she, "it is not long since that with these hands I buried you; then they were free, now I am a captive, and pay these last duties to you with a guard upon me, for fear that my just griefs and sorrows should impair my servile body, and make it less fit to appear in their triumph over you. No further offerings or libations expect from me; these are the last honours that Cleopatra can pay your memory, for she is to be hurried away far from you. Nothing could part us whilst we lived, but death seems to threaten to divide us. You, a Roman born, have found a grave in Egypt; I, an Egyptian, am to seek that favour, and none but that, in your country. But if the gods below, with whom you now are, either can or will do anything (since those above have betrayed us), suffer not your living wife to be abandoned; let me not be led in triumph to your shame, but hide me and bury me here with you, since, amongst all my bitter misfortunes, nothing has afflicted me like this brief time that I have lived away from you." (1151)

Plutarch uses a monologue to convey Cleopatra's character. In this short speech, we learn about the nature of her relationship to Antony.

In anticipation of the 2007 Cannes Film Festival, fiction writer Teddy Wayne wrote a piece that mixes *prosopopoeia* and *eidolopoeia*—putting words into the mouth of a living person (Joan Rivers) and a dead one (Julius Caesar) as he posits them interacting in Rome in 44 BC.

RED CARPETS THROUGHOUT HISTORY

JOAN RIVERUS Hail, Caesar! Over here! How are you?

JULIUS CAESAR Fantastic. Et tu, Joanie?

RIVERUS Super. You look positively divine, Julius.

CAESAR Thanks – this is really a simple, elegant white toga and strappy sandals designed by my talented dear friend for his label, Emporio Bruti.

RIVERUS I love what you've done with your hair.

CAESAR It's a new style – I'm calling it 'the Clooney.'

RIVERUS What are you up for tonight?

CAESAR Best Rhetorician. But, truly, it's an honor just to be given laurels alongside classic orators like Cicero and Mark Antony.

RIVERUS Any upcoming projects?

CAESAR I'm working with my collaborators—I've heard them call themselves 'conspirators,' for some reason—on a new oration for an Ides of March release. The tagline is: 'Beware. Be very wary.' (2007)

Rhetorical scholar John Poulakos composed several *eidolopoeia* for a symposium on ancient rhetoric. They are part of a play Poulakos is composing.

The play brings together Gorgias, Plato, Isocrates, and Aristotle, and its purpose is to "enact the four rhetorical perspectives" (2006, 176). Here are some outtakes:

> [Gorgias]: . . . as I have said repeatedly, there is no relation between words and things. Things do not have names; we are the ones who baptize them. Now Aristotle does have a point when he says that there are more things in the world than words, that each single thing does not have its very own name, and that some things have more than one name. For him this is a big problem but it does not trouble me at all. But rather than go on, let me tell you a story...
>
> [Plato]: Look, I, too, can do what my great rivals can do; indeed I can do it better than they. No Protagoras has invented myths as beautiful as mine; no dramatist such a vivid and captivating whole as my *Symposium*; no orator has written orations like those in my *Phaedrus*—and now I repudiate all this entirely and condemn all imitative art.
>
> [Aristotle]: I have no problem with people writing speeches, dialogues, comedies, or tragedies. I myself wrote some dialogues in my younger days and it's not my fault that they were lost. But any one particular speech, dialogue, or play does not tell us much. What we need is the bigger picture. And the bigger picture requires theory. (176–178)

Using *eidolopoeia* to imagine what these long-dead theorists of rhetoric might say to each other, Poulakos is able to explore with depth the theories put forth by these thinkers, while at the same time entertaining himself and others.

The playwright Tony Kushner makes use of *ethopoeia* in his plays. His very successful play *Angels in America* includes characters based on Roy Cohn, the McCarthy-era attorney made most famous for the trial that ended in the conviction and death sentence of Ethel Rosenberg for espionage. In the play, Rosenberg confronts Cohn in the form of a ghost, an example of *eidolopoeia*. Then in 2003 Kushner published *Only We Who Guard the Mystery Shall Be Unhappy*, a one-act play with a character named Laura Bush. The following year, Kushner composed an additional act in which Laura Bush confronts Kushner himself about the play. Here's an excerpt of that fictional exchange, published in salon.com:

> **LB:** What I think is you people are afraid of my husband, is what I think . . .
> **TK:** Oh, no argument about that, I mean . . .
> **LB:** [Overlapping, continuous from above.] You're afraid of George because, because well, first off you hate him because he *does things*. I mean actually likely to act, to act on his convictions. It's not his convictions—it's that he does stuff about it.
> **TK:** Well, no, it's that he does stuff about it and also his convictions really suck, his ideological . . .
> **LB:** You all can't stand his, well, let's call it *vividness* . . . Oh, sure, he's not a reader, I mean *tell me about it!* Sure, he can't get through the ingredients on the side panel of the cereal box in the morning without moving his lips, and sure, for people who read, for some people who read, this is like,

well, the mark of the devil because such people as yourself are snobs and you wear your reading like an expensive suit and you don't want to talk to people who just could give a flyin' flip about such things and who think "You wear your suit, and I wear my suit which I bought at Wal-Mart and so what, so what?"

TK: But you people are like *beyond rich*. You don't shop at Wal-Mart, you may eat pork rinds but you own the ranch!! You own the whole—And you're hardly uninterested in what other people are wearing, I mean you snoop and you pry and you try to get librarians to sign loyalty oaths and this whole laissez-faire—

LB: [Overlapping on "you snoop, etc."] But for people like you it's a precious badge of distinction notifying all other suit wearers, "Look at me, I have read enough to be muddleheaded enough not to do a frigging thing!" I mean, look at that gloomy old banana face you just nominated, and sorry to be name-calling but really, take a good look! Does *anyone* think he's likely to do anything other than marvel at the complexity of everything and hire people who are similarly awestruck and flabbergasted at the, at the whole magical mystery tour incomprehensibility of it all, and so you'll, you'll all get together in Washington like last time and you'll, you'll what, you'll *ban snowmobiles in Yellowstone Park* and then everyone in the Sierra Club'll take everyone in PETA out for a Sunday night pizza! (2004)

Some people will find Kushner's portrayal of Laura Bush distasteful; others will find it funny. And yet others will believe that the criticisms Kushner has the first lady utter are astonishingly accurate. The point here is that Kushner experimentally inhabits the character of a person. Doing so requires more than simply writing funny dialogue—it requires imaginative reflection on how a person speaks, what a person says, and how both of these things contribute to character. As rhetorical scholar Christy Desmet observes, for the ancients, "the success of *ethopoeia* in general depends on the fledgling orator's ability to identify with others—that is, to put himself in the 'place' of persons, real or imagined, who are remote from him in space and time" (2005, 201). Quintilian reminds us, too, that it is important to adapt one's style to the character being impersonated.

PROGYMNASMATA: CHARACTERIZATION

1. Try your hand at creating character (*ethopoeia*). Now imagine that one of the ancients discussed in this book is composing an introductory text for a social networking site such as MySpace or Facebook, called EthoRhetor. Write a brief first-person blurb in the voice of the ancient rhetoricians we discuss—e.g., Gorgias, Aristotle, Aspasia, or Cicero. What links might that figure include on the page? What "friends" might the figure list?

2. Choose a well-known public figure (a politician, a celebrity) and create a scenario to which this person responds.

3. Indefinite characterization, you'll recall, is character created in response to a specific situation or type. Imagine what a graduate of your institution might say to those who are in school right now if given the chance. Now try your hand at *prosopopoeia*. You might, for example, compose a brief plea from the earth for humans to ease up on mining its resources. Or write as a bird who has lost loved ones to cell phone towers.

4. In *eidolopoeia*, a rhetor composes a speech on behalf of a person no longer living. Think of a well-known person who has passed on and write a brief reflection about something happening today that this person would have cared about. Be sure to compose in the person's character.

NOTE

1. We are indebted to Walker Gibson's *Persona: A Style Study for Readers and Writers* and *Tough, Sweet, and Stuffy: An Essay on Modern American Prose Styles*.

WORKS CITED

Abbey, Edward. *Desert Solitaire*. Tucson: Arizona University Press, 1968.

Brockriede, Wayne. "The Dimensions of Rhetoric." *Quarterly Journal of Speech* 54 (1968): 1–12.

Bush, George W. "President Discusses Hurricane Relief in Address to the Nation." text available at http://www.Whitehouse.gov September 15, 2005.

Bush, George W. "President Bush Discusses United States International Development Agenda." The White House, May 31, 2007. http://www.whitehouse.gov/news/releases/2007/05/20070531-9.html (accessed May 31, 2007).

Cloud, John. "The Lavender Heart of Texas." *Time* 169, no. 22 (May 29, 2007): 55–58.

Derr, Mark. *Dog's Best Friend: Annals of the Dog-Human Relationship*. Chicago: University of Chicago Press, 2004.

Derrida, Jacques. *Of Grammatology*. Translated by Gayatri Chakravorty Spivak. Baltimore: Johns Hopkins University Press, 1976.

Desmet, Christy. "Progymnasmata." In *Classical Rhetoric and Rhetoricians: Critical Studies and Sources*, 296-304. Edited by Michelle Ballif and Michael G. Moran. Westport, Conn: Praegar, 2005.

Dionne, E. J. "How Obama vs. Clinton Shapes Up. "*Washington Post*, January 22, 2007, national edition, sec. A.

Dostoyevsky, Fyodor. *Notes From Underground*. New York: E. P. Dutton, 1960.

Douglas, Mary. *How Institutions Think*. Syracuse, N.Y.: Syracuse University Press, 1986.

Friedman, Thomas. "Our Green Bubble." *New York Times*, June 3, 2007, national edition, op-ed.

Gibson, Walker. *Persona: A Style Study for Readers and Writers*. New York: Random House, 1969.

———. *Tough, Sweet, and Stuffy: An Essay on Modern American Prose Styles*. Bloomington: Indiana University Press, 1966.

Gingrich, Newt. "Time 100: Nancy Pelosi." *Time*, April 27, 2007. http://www.time.com/time/specials/2007/time100/article/0,28804, 1595326_1615513_1615493,00.html (accessed May 31, 2007).

Hamsher, Jane. "Notes from the Libby Sentencing." *Firedoglake*, June 5, 2007. http://www.firedoglake.com/2007/06/05/notes-from-the-libby-sentencing (accessed June 9, 2007).

Hayek, Friedrich. *The Constitution of Liberty*. Chicago: Chicago University Press: 1960.

Kennedy, George, *progymnasmata: Greek Textbooks of Prose Composition and Rhetoric*. Leiden: Brill, 2003.

Kristol, William. "Who, Me? Bush Evades His Responsibility with Regard to Libby." *Weekly Standard*, June 5, 2007. http://www.weeklystandard.com/Content/Public/Articles/000/000/013/734azcei.asp (accessed June 9, 2007).

Kunkel, Benjamin. *Indecision: A Novel*. New York: Random House, 2006.

Kushner, Tony. *Angels in America*. New York: Theatre Communications Group, 2003.

———. "Only We Who Guard the Mystery Shall Be Unhappy." *Nation*, March 24, 2003. http://www.thenation.com/doc/20030324/kushner.

———. "First Lady Fights Back!" *Salon*, August 4, 2004. http://dir.salon.com/story/ent/feature/2004/08/04/kushner_scene/index. html.

Macrorie, Ken. *Writing to be Read*. 3rd rev. ed. Portsmouth, N.H.: Boynton Cook, 1984.

Mataconis, Doug. "Rudy Giuliani Distorts Ron Paul's Comments On Iraq." *Liberty Papers*, May 16, 2007. http://www.thelibertypapers.org/2007/05/16/rudy-giuliani-distorts-ron-pauls-comments-on-iraq/trackback/ (accessed June 6, 2007).

Nauden, Gloria. "Finding My Place in Black America." *Emerge: Black America's Magazine*, July/August 1997, 67.

New York Times. "Ignoring the Warnings, Again?" *New York Times*, May 25, 2007. http://www.nytimes.com/2007/05/25/opinion/25fri1.html?n=Top%2fOpinio n%2fEditorials%20and%20Op%2dEd%2fEditorials (accessed May 31, 2007).

Norman, Jeff. "Rudy the Bully." *Huffington Post*, May 31, 2007. http://www. huffingtonpost.com/jeff-norman/rudy-the-bully_b_50238. html? (accessed June 9, 2007).

Poulakos, John. "Testing and Contesting Classical Rhetorics." *Rhetoric Society Quarterly* 36, no. 2 (Spring 2006): 171–179.

Seager, Richard. "Persistent Drought in North America: a Climate Modeling and Paleoclimate Perspective." Lamont-Doherty Earth Observatory of Columbia University. http://www.ldeo.columbia.edu/res/div/ocp/drought/(accessed June 7, 2007).

Sullivan, Andrew. "Palmetto Punditry." *Atlantic*, May 15, 2007. http://andrewsullivan. theatlantic.com/the_daily_dish/2007/05/palmetto_pundit.html (accessed June 6, 2007).

Sullivan, Andrew. "The Reagan of the Left?" *Atlantic*, May 24, 2007. http://andrewsullivan.theatlantic.com/the_daily_dish/2007/05/the_reagan_of_t.html#more (accessed May 24, 2007).

Tedford, Deborah and Ari Shapiro. "Libby Sentenced to 2 1/2 Years in CIA Leak Case." National Public Radio. http://www.npr.org/templates/story/story.php?storyId=10741249 (accessed June 9, 2007).

Thompson, Melissa Kay. "A Sea of Good Intentions: Native Americans in Books for Children." *Lion and the Unicorn* 25, no. 3 (2001): 353–374.

Travers, Peter. Review of *Pirates of the Caribbean: At World's End. Rolling Stone,* May 27, 2007. http://www.rollingstone.com/reviews/movie/9474908/review/ 14756791/pirates_of_the_caribbean_at_worlds_end (accessed June 6, 2007).

Wayne, Teddy. "Red Carpets Throughout History." *New York Times,* May 27, 2007, national edition, sec. 4.

Wilmington, Michael. *Pirates of the Caribbean: At World's End. Chicago Tribune.* http://metromix.chicagotribune.com/movies/mmx-070525-movies-review-pirates,0,3970586,print.story?coll=mmx-movies_top_heds (accessed May 24, 2007).

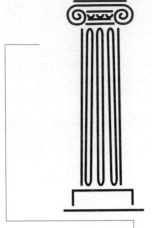

PATHETIC PROOF: PASSIONATE APPEALS

Speech is a powerful guide, which by means of the finest and most invisible body effects the divinest works: it can stop fear and banish grief and create joy and nurture pity . . . Fearful shuddering and tearful pity and grievous longing come upon its hearers, and at the actions and physical sufferings of others in good fortunes and in evil fortunes, through the agency of words, the soul is wont to experience a suffering of its own.

—Gorgias,
"Encomium of
Helen" 8

RHETORS CAN FIND arguments in the issue itself (*logos*), and a rhetor's character (*ethos*) can be persuasive, as well. According to Aristotle, a third kind of intrinsic proof is also available: rhetors can appeal to human emotion (*pathos*). In early Greek thought, the term *pathos* referred to a passive state we might call "experience"; later, in Greek plays called "tragedies," this state came to be associated with suffering. In the fifth century BCE Plato and Aristotle began to use the term *pathos* to discuss the emotions in general. *Pathos* is still used in English to refer to any quality in an experience that arouses emotions, and many English words are borrowed from the Greek term, including *sympathy* and *empathy*. Speakers of modern English generally use an adjective form, *pathetic*, to refer to anything that is pitiful or unsuccessful, as in the phrase "That's a pathetic excuse." But *pathetic* also refers to the arousal or expression of emotions, and that's the sense in which we use it here.

Aristotle and Cicero discussed the following sets of emotions: anger/calm, love/hate, fear/confidence, shame/shamelessness, compassion, pity/indignation, envy/emulation, joy, and hope (*Rhetoric* II 2–12; *De Oratore* II i 203). Emotions should be distinguished from appetites, such as pleasure and pain. They must also be distinguished from values, such as justice and goodness. However, people do hold values with more or less intensity, and this intensity is where the rhetorical force of emotional appeals resides. People respond emotionally when they or those close to them are praised or threatened; rhetorically, they also respond emotionally when their values are reinforced or threatened.

Of all the ancient kinds of rhetorical proofs, the appeal to the emotions seems strangest to contemporary rhetors, and perhaps a little bit shoddy as well. That's because of the modern reverence for reason and our habit of making a sharp distinction between reason and the emotions. In our culture, if you're emotional, you're irrational. Reason is associated with mind, and connotes a calm, studied approach to issues. Emotions are associated with the body and are thought to be superficial and dangerous. People tend to think of emotions as belonging to individuals, like opinions.

These prejudices are inaccurate and unfair. New research in neuroscience suggests that we can't think without emotions and that our emotional responses are intricately tied up with our beliefs, as well (Damasio 1994). Other research suggests that emotions can be shared among individuals, as is illustrated by the excitement shared by large crowds at concerts or sports events or the shared joy felt at a religious gathering (Brennan 2004). And anyone who has suffered the loss of a loved one knows that grief becomes more intense when shared with others who are suffering.

The ancients understood all of this, and hence they taught us that rhetorical appeals to the emotions were very effective. Contemporary advertisers and political spin artists also understand the important role played by emotion in our responses to their messages. The most obvious modern use of emotional appeals appears in advertisements that appeal to consumers' desire for success ("be all you can be;" "just do it!") or their fear of losing status in their communities ("don't let this happen to you!"). But emotional appeals appear in other sorts of discourse as well. Clearly, the nation's emotional response to the events of September 11 played a large role in Americans' support for the subsequent wars in Iraq and Afghanistan, support that was very strong immediately following the event but that has dwindled as time passed and the nation's grief and shock grew more muted. The diminishing support for these wars, interpreted as retaliation for September 11, suggests to us that as emotional intensity wanes, so does the persuasiveness of arguments based on emotional appeals.

For those of us who actually witnessed 9/11, though, accounts or images can still evoke the emotions we felt then. In his introduction to an anthology of essays about September 11, Phil Scraton recounts his own emotional responses on that terrible day, thus artfully drawing his readers into the scene:

> Trying to make sense—emotional, physical, political—of September 11, I return to my initial reactions and responses. Like so many others across the world, via satellite I witnessed truly horrifying scenes of scarcely believable atrocity. Filmed from every conceivable angle the second passenger aircraft imploded the twin tower. Its nose-cone, having passed through the building, was instantly

engulfed in flames. At that 'live by satellite' moment, the collapse of the entire World Trade Center inevitable, the realisation dawned that the dual crashes were no coincidence. Both aircraft had been piloted, purposefully and accurately, into their targets. As news broke, telling of two other planes crashing, one into the Pentagon, the second out of control in Pennsylvania, the immensity and significance of these disasters became apparent. They had to be the dreadful end-product of effective and efficient collaboration involving groups working together, carefully planning and acquiring skills. These were not random targets. The World Trade Center, bomb damaged just eight years earlier, and the Pentagon represented hugely symbolic as well as material targets.

In a Verona hotel room we watched the dramatic live transmissions from downtown Manhattan. Firefighters and rescuers raced into the disaster zone passing dust-covered, ghost-like workers coming from the opposite direction—running or staggering for their lives. Cameras homed in on others trapped in offices high above the flames, some throwing themselves from windows to avoid choking or burning to death. As the towers collapsed, clouds of grey toxic smoke covered all and everything in their path. Then came the first reports of agonised telephone calls made from one of the planes and by those facing death trapped in their offices. These were final goodbyes to loved ones. They reminded me of rescue workers recounting disaster scenes where the only sounds they could hear, as they listened for potential survivors, were those of mobile phones ringing from the debris as desperate relatives tried to make contact. (2002, 1)

ANCIENT TEACHERS ON THE EMOTIONS

Greek orators could find examples of the persuasive use of emotion in the texts of the poet Homer, whose two great epic poems, the *Iliad* and the *Odyssey*, were well known among the Greek people. In the last book of the *Iliad*, Homer depicted the Trojan king, Priam, appealing to Achilles, the Achean hero, to return the body of his son, Hector.

Perhaps you have seen the recent film, *Troy*, in which this scene is dramatized by Peter O'Toole, playing the aged king to Brad Pitt's Achilles:

> Remember your own father,
> Achilles, in your godlike youth: his years
> like mine are many, and he stands upon
> the fearful doorstep of old age. He, too,
> is hard pressed, it may be, by those around him,
> there being no one able to defend him
> from bane of war and ruin. Ah, but he
> may nonetheless hear news of you alive,
> and so with glad heart hope through all his days
> for sight of his dear son, come back from Troy,
> while I have deathly fortune. Noble sons
> I fathered here, but scarce one man is left me.
> Fifty I had when the Acheans came,
> nineteen out of a single belly, others
> born of attendant women. Most are gone.

FIGURE 7.1
PRIAM PLEADING FOR THE THE RETURN OF THE BODY OF HECTOR.
Source: The Art Archive/National Museum Beirut/Dagli Orti

> Raging Ares cut their knees from under them.
> And he who stood alone among them all,
> their champion, and Troy's, ten days ago
> you killed him, fighting for his land, my prince,
> Hector. It is for him that I have come
> among these ships, to beg him back from you,
> and I bring ransom without stint. Achilles,
> be reverent toward the great gods! And take
> pity on me, remember your own father.
> Think me more pitiful by far, since I
> have brought myself to do what no man else
> has done before—to lift to my lips the hand
> of one who killed my son. (XXIV 485–506)

Priam first arouses Achilles' sense of filial love by reminding him of his own
father and tries to arouse his pity for the plight of lonely old men whose

sons are missing or dead. Then he tells how his many children have been slain, hoping to rouse Achilles' pity for his misfortunes, and he mentions ransom, hoping to stimulate Achilles' greed. He reminds Achilles of the gods; this is a subtle attempt to make Achilles fearful, since he committed a serious religious transgression by refusing to bury Hector's body. Finally, he asks Achilles to pity him for the shameful position in which he, a king, has been placed by being forced to beg a soldier to return his son's body.

As this passage makes clear, emotional appeals are based on the assumption that human beings share similar kinds of emotional responses to events: fathers everywhere weep for lost sons; an old man who has lost his family is pitied by everyone, even his enemies. While this may not be true across wide cultural differences, it certainly is the case that people who live in the same community have similar emotional responses. If this were not true, governments would not be able to incite great numbers of people to volunteer for military service during wartime (which is an irrational thing to do, after all). In his history of the Peloponnesian War, Thucydides reported a speech made by Pericles, who had incited the Athenians to war against the Spartans. When this war did not go well, the people became angry. Pericles "called an assembly, wanting to encourage them and to convert their angry feelings into a gentler and more hopeful mood" (II 59). Pericles was only partially successful in quelling the anger of the people because the war had brought them great suffering. As this passage indicates, Pericles was quite aware that rhetoric could arouse or dispel emotional responses and that communities could share emotional responses to public events.

Ancient rhetoricians also treated the emotions as ways of knowing, thus associating them with intellectual processes. Gorgias argued in the "Helen" that the persuasive effect of verbal seduction is no different from physical force; Helen was blameless no matter whether she was abducted or her seducer simply persuaded her to flee her husband and country. Indeed, early rhetorical theorists like Gorgias and Plato characterized rhetoric as a *psychagogia*, a leader of souls, an enchanter. Gorgias argued that, given the right circumstances (*kairos*), a rhetor could alter an audience's emotional state of mind and thus change their assessment of reality, in essence helping them to see the world in new ways.

In other words, the ancients taught that emotions hold heuristic potential. The emotions even seem to be a means of reasoning: if someone becomes afraid, realizing that she is in a dangerous situation, she quickly assesses her options and takes herself out of danger as quickly as she can. Emotions can also move people to action: if someone feels compassion for someone else, he helps the suffering person.

Early sophistic treatises on rhetoric included topics for appealing to the emotions. For example, the *Rhetoric to Alexander* discussed appeals to friendliness, kindliness, and the like as a means urging an audience to act on behalf of the needy (1439b 15 ff). Since sophistic manuals were organized according to the parts or divisions of a discourse, they gave no systematic advice about arousing the emotions but rather included it in their discussions of introductions and conclusions.

Aristotle seems to have been the first rhetorician to provide a systematic discussion of emotional proofs. In Book II of the *Rhetoric*, he defined emotions as "those things through which, by undergoing change, people come to differ in their judgments" (II ii 1377b-1378a). This sounds very much like Gorgias's argument that emotional responses help people to change their minds. When a person experiences an emotion such as anger, pity, or fear, she enters a new state of mind in which she sees things differently. If she has become angry at someone, for example, she sees that person in a different light than she previously did. Perhaps she is angry with her supervisor because he mistakenly blamed her for something that was not her fault. Her angry reaction to this event will change her attitude toward her supervisor. She may even be moved by this new way of thinking to change her behavior toward him: she may, for example, vow to speak up for herself the next time she is unfairly accused; she may even decide to quit her job.

Aristotle realized that emotions are communal in the sense that they are usually excited by our relations with other people. We do not become angry in some general or vague way; ordinarily we are angry at someone else. We do not feel love toward nothing; we feel love for some persons or creatures. We can also communicate emotions to others—people who are afraid can make others fearful as well.

Most postclassical rhetorical treatises employed the sophistic habit of treating the emotions as suitable proofs only in the introduction and conclusion of a piece of discourse. Cicero's *De Oratore* and Quintilian's *Institutes* are exceptions to this general rule. While both rhetoricians adopted Aristotle's tripartite division of rhetorical proofs, neither added much of theoretical value to his discussion of *pathos*. However, their treatises do supply numerous examples of successful emotional appeals and give helpful suggestions on how to compose these. For these reasons, we rely on Aristotle for the theoretical part of our discussion of the emotions and turn to Cicero and Quintilian for advice on how to compose emotional appeals.

EMOTIONS AS RHETORICAL PROOFS

According to Aristotle, three criteria must be met if rhetors wish to understand how emotions are aroused or quelled. First, they must understand the state of mind of people who are angry, joyful, or indignant; second, they must know who can excite these emotions in people; third, they must understand the reasons for which people become emotional (II ii 1377b-1378a). People do not enter the state of mind called "anger" without a reason, and they become angry at someone, even if they don't know who the person is. If a person leaves his workplace feeling perfectly calm, this state of mind changes when he discovers in the parking lot that someone has put a dent in his car. The reason he becomes angry is that this situation leaves him with choices that are unpleasant: don't repair the dent, in which case it may rust and become worse, thus lowering the car's value; do repair the dent and pay for it out of his own pocket, since the repair will probably cost less than the deductible on his insurance. Note that his anger is not irrational in this case; it is a perfectly reasonable response to events.

Aristotle's first criterion is that rhetors must know the emotional states of mind of their hearers or readers. An audience may bring a certain emotional state of mind to a rhetorical situation, and if so, the rhetor needs to decide whether this state of mind is conducive to their acceptance of her proposition. If it is not, she needs to change their states of mind. Aristotle thought that emotional change came about through changes in the level of intensity with which emotions are felt (II ii 1377b–1378a). Emotional intensity alters in accordance with the spatial and temporal proximity of the people or situations that arouse them.[1] When the person with whom someone becomes angry is close, either physically or relationally, anger will be felt more intensely. If the person who dented the car is still in the lot when its owner arrives there, the owner focuses his anger more intensely on the culprit than if he can be only diffusely angry in general with people who dent parked cars and run. (In this case he may even refocus his anger on another car or on the traffic as he drives home.) If the culprit happens to be someone known to the owner of the dented car, the owner's emotional response will be intensified, as well, and the quality of their relationship may evoke other emotions in addition to anger. If the two are coworkers who don't like each other very much, the owner of the dented car may be more intensely angry than if the culprit is a friend. Their relationship may deteriorate even more. If the culprit is a supervisor, however, the owner of the dented vehicle may try to temper his anger with mildness. If the two are spouses or partners, however, things become enormously complex emotionally.

As this example demonstrates, the relation of spatial proximity to emotional intensity depends upon social hierarchy as well. As Aristotle noted, "People think they are entitled to be treated with respect by those inferior in birth, in power, in virtue, and generally in whatever they themselves have much of" (1378b). According to Aristotle's reasoning, people are less prone to be angry with those above or equal to them on a scale of social authority, while they are more prone to be angry with those below them on that scale. According to this analysis, then, if the supervisor who dented the car is a shop foreman, the car's owner may be more angry than he would be if the culprit were the president of the company.

Some emotions are also more intensely felt if people nearby are experiencing them, as well. This feature of emotional intensity is what makes horror fiction and films work, because the audience fears for the characters. The feeling of fear is intensified in a theater because others are sharing it. Joy and anxiety appear to be shareable emotions, and mob violence can be stimulated by shared hatred and/or rage. Communities can feel hope, as when it seems likely that a war is about to end, and they can also feel despair, as Americans did during the Great Depression, or they can share a sense of horror, as they did during and after the events of 9/11.

The intensity with which emotions are felt depends on the nearness of their objects in time, as well. Love tends to grow with time, but so can hatred. The intensity with which people feel joy depends very much on the temporal proximity of a joyful event, while sadness seems to linger through time. The intensity of grief fades, but it rarely disappears entirely. Anger tends to fade with time, unless the object of that anger is nearby in either time or space. The car owner's anger toward the person who dented his car will lessen over time, unless for some reason he fails to get the dent fixed. In that case, every time he sees it he may get angry all over again.

Proximity also influences the intensity with which fear is felt. Because people fear far-off dangers less than those that are closer in time and space, global warming may not intensely frighten people now because its visible effects on human culture will not occur for many years. And because proximity is related to emotional intensity, during wartime or when relations between nations are tense, governments try to stimulate fear of the enemy by bringing their images close to the people, altering them into objects of fear and thus disguising the fact of their spatial and temporal distance. In 1987, when relations between Iran and the United States were very tense, American media portrayed the Iranian leader, the Ayatollah Khomeini, as a crazed religious fanatic. Pictures of his stern, angry countenance were prominently featured on television and in news magazines. At the same time, students from Iran told us, the Iranian media portrayed the president of the United States, Ronald Reagan, as an idiotic warmonger, using close-up photographs of his smiling face. In other words, both parties to the conflict tried to personalize it for their citizens, because it is easier to make people afraid and angry toward a person than it is to make them afraid and angry toward an abstraction.

THE CHARACTERS OF AUDIENCES

In the *Phaedrus*, Plato instructed rhetors who wished to be persuasive to study the people in their audiences:

> Since the function of oratory is in fact to influence mens' souls, the intending orator must know what types of soul there are. Now these are of a determinate number, and their variety results in a variety of individuals. To the types of soul thus discriminated there corresponds a determinate number of types of discourse. Hence a certain type of hearer will be easy to persuade by a certain type of speech to take such and such action for such and such reason, while another type will be hard to persuade. (271d)

He might have meant, in part, that rhetors should study the emotions of their potential hearers or readers. In any case, some authorities think that Aristotle followed Plato's advice in Book II, chapters 12–17, of the *Rhetoric*, where he developed some general guidelines for evaluating the emotional states of audiences. He listed many Greek commonplaces about the differing attitudes held by young, middle-aged, and old people. For example, young persons are more passionate than older people, Aristotle wrote, but their emotions pass quickly. Older people, in contrast, tend to be suspicious because their hopes have often been dashed. He also provided commonplaces about the differing attitudes of rich and poor, powerful and powerless, and those who have good or bad luck.

In Cicero's *De Oratore*, one of the participants argues that it is desirable for an audience to "carry within them . . . some mental emotion that is in harmony with what the advocate's interest will suggest. For, as the saying goes, it is easier to spur the willing horse than to start the lazy one" (XLIV 185–186). He continued:

> This indeed is the reason why, when setting about a hazardous and important case, in order to explore the feelings of the tribunal, I engage wholeheartedly in a consideration so careful, that I scent out with all possible keenness their thoughts, judgements, anticipations and wishes, and the direction in which they seem likely to be led away most easily by eloquence. . . . If . . . an arbitrator is neutral and free from predisposition, my task is harder, since everything has to be called forth by my speech, with no help from the listener's character. (187)

In this passage Cicero anticipated the findings of some modern research about audiences. Roughly speaking, members of an audience may hold one of three attitudes toward an issue or a rhetor's *ethos*: they may be hostile, indifferent, or accepting. Communication researchers have found that it is easier to move people who care about an issue than it is to influence those who are indifferent. That is, it is easier to bring about a change of mind in those who are accepting or hostile than in those who are indifferent.

During the Vietnam war, people who opposed the war were called "doves" and those who approved it were called "hawks." Extreme doves wanted the war stopped and American soldiers brought home immediately. Extreme hawks wanted not only to escalate the war but to win it by whatever means were necessary. Many Americans subscribed to neither of these extremes but held more moderate positions. For instance, some doves wanted to scale down America's war effort, limiting it to guerilla skirmishes that would protect vital supply or communication lines. Other doves argued that a limited war should continue while peace was negotiated. Some hawks approved of bombing vital targets but stopped short of recommending large-scale bombing or the use of nuclear weapons. Early on in the war, many Americans were simply indifferent; that is, they held no position regarding it. These people presented both doves and hawks with their most difficult audiences, since those who were indifferent had to be convinced that the war was important to them before they could take up some other position on the issue. Indeed, it might be said that the war was finally ended, not because doves won the national argument about it but because a sufficient number of Americans finally abandoned their indifference toward the war when they saw the toll it took on American lives and resources.

Researchers have also discovered that a person's willingness to change her mind depends on two things: the emotional intensity with which she clings to an opinion and the degree to which her identity—her sense of herself as an integrated person—is wrapped up with that opinion. People who are intensely invested in a position are less likely to change their minds than those who are not. Someone who was hawkish on Vietnam, for example, might have been so for intellectual reasons: perhaps he saw the strategic importance of the Vietnamese peninsula to American rubber production and thus to capitalism. This is a value rather than an emotion, and so it is only partially relevant to his emotional state. Its relevance depends upon the emotional intensity with which he values capitalism, as well as the degree to which his identity and/or personal fortunes depend on its maintenance. Theoretically, this person would be easier to move away from hawkishness than someone who was emotionally invested in the position, who feared, for example, that an American pullout in Vietnam would exacerbate the spread of dangerous communist values across Asia. And if a hawkish person's identity were wrapped up with this position, theoretically at least it would be very difficult to move him away from it. This was apparently the case for some high-level military and State Department personnel whose careers depended upon successful maintenance of the war.

In sum, rhetors need to assess the emotional states of their audiences as well as the intensity with which they cling to those states. Rhetors need to decide as well whether those emotional states render their audiences receptive to themselves and/or their proposition. Next, they should decide whether an audience can be persuaded to change their minds and, if so, whether they will be moved by appeals to their current emotional states or to a different one induced by a rhetor.

Here is an excerpt from the text of a speech given by the former vice president Al Gore at the National Sierra Club Convention in San Francisco on September 9, 2005. Gore addressed the challenges and moral imperatives posed by Hurricane Katrina and global warming:

> Last year we had a lot of hurricanes. Last year, Japan set an all-time record for typhoons: ten, the previous record was seven. Last year the science textbooks had to be re-written. They said, "It's impossible to have a hurricane in the south Atlantic." We had the first one last year, in Brazil. We had an all-time record last year for tornadoes in the United States, 1,717—largely because hurricanes spawned tornadoes. Last year we had record temperatures in many cities. This year 200 cities in the Western United States broke all-time records. Reno, 39 days consecutively above 100 degrees.
>
> The scientists are telling us that what the science tells them is that this— unless we act quickly and dramatically—that Tucson tied its all-time record for consecutive days above 100 degrees. This, in Churchill's phrase, is only the first sip of a bitter cup which will be proffered to us year by year until there is a supreme recovery of moral health. We have to rise with this occasion. We have to connect the dots. When the Superfund sites aren't cleaned up, we get a toxic gumbo in a flood. When there is not adequate public transportation for the poor, it is difficult to evacuate a city. When there is no ability to give medical care to poor people, it's difficult to get a hospital to take refugees in the middle of a crisis. When the wetlands are turned over to the developers then the storm surges from the ocean threaten the coastal cities more. When there is no effort to restrain the global warming pollution gasses then global warming gets worse, with all of the consequences that the scientific community has warned us about.

My friends, the truth is that our circumstances are not only new; they are completely different than they have ever been in all of human history. The relationship between humankind and the earth has been utterly transformed in the last hundred years. We have quadrupled the population of our planet. The population in many ways is a success story. The demographic transition has been occurring more quickly than was hoped for, but the reality of our new relationship with the planet brings with it a moral responsibility to accept our new circumstances and to deal with the consequences of the relationship we have with this planet. And it's not just population. By any means, the power of the technologies now at our disposal vastly magnifies the average impact that individuals can have on the natural world. Multiply that by six and a half billion people, and then stir into that toxic mixture a mindset and an attitude that says it's okay to ignore scientific evidence—that we don't have to take responsibility for the future consequences of present actions—and you get a collision between our civilization and the earth. The refugees that we have seen—I don't like that word when applied to American citizens in our own country, but the refugees that we have seen could well be the first sip of that bitter cup because sea-level rise in countries around the world will mobilize millions of environmental refugees. The other problems are known to you, but here is what I want to close with:

This is a moral moment. This is not ultimately about any scientific debate or political dialogue. Ultimately it is about who we are as human beings. It is about our capacity to transcend our own limitations. To rise to this new occasion. To see with our hearts, as well as our heads, the unprecedented response that is now called for. To disenthrall ourselves, to shed the illusions that have been our accomplices in ignoring the warnings that were clearly given, and hearing the ones that are clearly given now.

Where there is no vision, the people perish. And Lincoln said at another moment of supreme challenge that the question facing the people of the United States of America ultimately was whether or not this government, conceived in liberty, dedicated to freedom, of the people, by the people, and for the people—or any government so conceived—would perish from this earth.

Gore knew that he had a sympathetic audience of environmentalists at the Sierra Club, and he knew as well that most members of this group were intensely interested in the issue of global warming. So he does not bother to define the term for them, assuming that they are well-informed and attentive at the outset. Rather, he recounts details that they might not know—the daily average temperatures in Reno and Tucson, for instance. He does raise a controversial interpretation at the end of his remarks, when he claims that human beings have a moral obligation to address the issues raised by global warming. Once he introduces this claim, his oratory becomes a bit more elevated: he uses a series of parallel infinitive phrases almost as an incantation to evoke a sense of moral, if not religious, commitment from his listeners. He then cites Abraham Lincoln, which is no doubt intended to evoke feelings of patriotism and to connect those emotions with the immediate need to stop global warming. The last two paragraphs of this excerpt, then, consist almost entirely of emotional appeals.

COMPOSING PASSIONATE PROOFS

We noted earlier that ancient rhetoricians named many emotions to which rhetors can appeal: anger, love, hate, fear, shame, compassion, pity, indignation, envy, joy, and hope. We cannot predict which of these emotions will be operative in the rhetorical situations with which our readers are working, and so we cannot forecast ways in which you can arouse these emotions, or calm them if they are already present in members of your audience. We can give some general advice about when and how to use emotional proofs, however.

Suppose that a rhetor who opposes the war in Iraq wishes to compose some suitable emotional appeals to use in her argument. She first needs to consider whether or not her audience will have an emotional response to this issue. Intense emotional responses are most likely if members of her audience are personally involved in the war—if they or family members are among the military personnel serving in Iraq, for instance. A strong emotional response is also likely if any members of the audience identify closely with the values the war is said to represent—America's safety from terrorism, for instance. If members of the audience feel strongly about the Iraq war, whether they agree with the rhetor's position or not, they will be interested in her argument.

People who are intensely supportive of a war, as well as those who intensely oppose it, probably take those positions because for some reason their identities and belief systems are closely wrapped up with their hawkish or dovish positions. If this is the case, emotions will run high when the issue is discussed. Such people are likely to read any departure from their preferred position as a challenge to their identities and beliefs, and this is why argument so often devolves away from rhetoric and into angry confrontation. Intense emotional attachment to claims can present serious barriers to rhetors who disagree with such claims. But ancient rhetoricians thought there were ways around and through such situations, and they provided us with a few bits of advice on how to navigate the emotional waters that surround the making of claims and arguments.

Enargeia

If an audience does not care about an issue in which a rhetor is interested, she will need to use emotional appeals to get their attention. In the case of an argument about the war in Iraq, she can do this by opening their eyes to the serious consequences of war—loss of innocent life, devastation of the countryside, ruin of the economy, the hatred and anger it creates and sustains. Ancient rhetoricians recommended that the most effective emotional appeals actually make an issue come alive for audiences, make them see vividly what is at stake in the issue. That is, emotional appeals can supply audiences with a reason for identifying with an issue, thus moving them away from indifference toward either acceptance or rejection of a position on it.

In *De Oratore*, Cicero's characters argued that emotional appeals are equal in importance to arguments from character *(ethos)* and from the issue itself *(logos)* (II xliv 185 ff). One of the characters, Antonius, argued further that it is important for a rhetor to feel the emotions he wants to arouse in his audience. He exemplified this point by recalling his defence of Manius Aquilius, who was accused of extortion:

> Here was a man whom I remembered as having been consul, commander-in-chief, honored by the Senate, and mounting in procession to the Capitol; on seeing him cast down, crippled, sorrowing and brought to the risk of all he held dear, I was myself overcome by compassion before I tried to excite it in others. (xlvii 195)

Cicero's rendering of this scene is so powerful that it still evokes compassion in people reading it two thousand years later. Cicero insisted that rhetors must somehow bring themselves to feel the emotions they wish to arouse in their audience. Quintilian echoed this advice in his discussion of emotional appeals, and he gave a useful hint about it. If a rhetor does not actually feel the requisite emotions while he is composing, he can draw on humans' shared emotions, their natural empathy with other human beings. Using these, he can imagine how events must have affected those who suffered them:

> I am complaining that a man has been murdered. Shall I not bring before my eyes all the circumstances which it is reasonable to imagine must have occurred in such a connection? Shall I not see the assassin burst suddenly from his hiding-place, the victim tremble, cry for help, beg for mercy or turn to run? Shall I not see the fatal blow delivered and the stricken body fall? Will not the blood, the deathly pallor, the groan of agony, the death-rattle, be indelibly impressed upon my mind? (*Institutes* VI ii 31)

Rhetors who can imagine the emotions evoked by a scene may stimulate similar emotions in their audiences by deploying the power of **enargeia**, a figure in which rhetors picture events so vividly that they seem actually to be taking place before the audience. Vivid depictions of events, Quintilian argued, stir the emotions of an audience exactly as if they had been present when it occurred. Perhaps Shakespeare had this advice in mind when he imagined Marc Antony's funeral oration for Julius Caesar, which, historians say, whipped the Roman people into a fury of anger at Caesar's murderers—Brutus, Casca, and Cassius. Shakespeare imagined his fictional Antony as standing before the crowd, holding up Caesar's bloodstained cloak for all to see. He put these words into Antony's mouth:

> You all do know this mantle. I remember
> The first time ever Caesar put it on.
> 'Twas on a summer's evening, in his tent,
> That day he overcame the Nervii.
> Look, in this place ran Cassius' dagger through.
> See what a rent the envious Casca made.
> Through this the well-beloved Brutus stabbed,
> And as he plucked his cursed steel away,

Mark how the blood of Caesar followed it,
As rushing out of doors, to be resolved
If Brutus so unkindly knocked, or no.
For Brutus, as you know, was Caesar's angel.
Judge, O you gods, how dearly Caesar loved him!
This was the most unkindest cut of all,
For when the noble Caesar saw him stab,
Ingratitude, more strong than traitors' arms,
Quite vanquished him. Then burst his mighty heart,
And, in his mantle muffling up his face,
Even at the base of Pompey's statue,
Which all the while ran blood, great Caesar fell. (*Julius Caesar* III ii)

Actors love this scene (our image shows Marlon Brando in the role of Antony). But even without all the trappings of the theatre, it is easy for readers to imagine this scene—Antony holding up the torn, bloodstained cloak, putting his hands through the holes made by the daggers that killed Caesar. Note also that he dwells on the emotional relationship between Brutus and Caesar—Antony implies that it was Brutus's ingratitude that actually killed Caesar, rather than the assassins' knives. By playing upon the crowd's shock and outrage at the bloody murder, he roused them to anger against the murderers.

FIGURE 7.2
Marlon Brando as Antony
Source: Photofest

Contemporary journalists often use *enargeia* to begin articles or books. Sportswriters are especially fond of this tactic. Here, for example, is Lynn Zinser, opening a piece on the Ottawa Senators professional hockey team:

> At a pep rally May 24 to celebrate the Senators' advance to the Stanley Cup finals, several thousand people filled the plaza at City Hall and the mayor declared Ottawa "Swaggerville," trying to wash away its image of the sleepy national capital full of easily bruised hockey fans.
>
> The Senators were far from the hoopla, practicing in their arena, Scotiabank Place, 20 miles south west of Ottawa in the suburb of Kanata. No fans were waiting in the parking lot for autographs and, aside from the banner for the Stanley Cup playoffs hanging on the side of the arena that faces the highway, there was little indication that the team being honored downtown was skating inside. (2007, 10)

Zinser manages to convey the emotional attitude of both the team and its fans with a few scenic details.

Blogger and journalist Marcy Wheeler begins her book about the trial of I. Lewis "Scooter" Libby with this *enargeia*:

> On January 28, 2003 when the sergeant at arms of the U.S. House of Representatives declared, "Mr. Speaker, the President of the United States," George W. Bush started slowly making his way through the chamber, shaking hands with those crowding the aisle, while Vice President Dick Cheney stood on the dais, quietly monitoring the proceedings. When Bush reached the dais, he turned to the two men—Cheney and Speaker of the House Dennis Hastert—standing above and behind him, and handed each a copy of the State of the Union speech he was about to deliver. Hastert put his copy to the side, almost carelessly. Cheney placed his directly in front of his seat, his fingers tapping it with satisfaction.
>
> On this occasion, President Bush handed a speech to Cheney that the vice president had created. The most important part of the speech, after all, would make the case to the American people for a preemptive invasion of Iraq. (2007, 11)

Wheeler's book is not about this State of the Union address, or at least it is not directly concerned with it. Nonetheless she begins with this dramatic *enargeia* of the first paragraph in order to establish the importance of her actual subject, which is an account of Scooter Libby's subsequent trial and conviction on charges of obstruction of justice. Libby was a top aide to Vice President Cheney during the run-up to the war in Iraq. Wheeler deftly uses this vignette to establish her version of Cheney's relationship to the president.

Honorific and Pejorative Language

Another way to evoke emotions is to use words that are honorific or pejorative. Honorific language treats people and things respectfully, while pejorative language disparages and downplays them.

That is, honorific and pejorative language conveys value judgments. In the passage that follows, written by James Wolcott, we have bolded the words that confer value terms:

> Rush Limbaugh, he's got the life. His days flick through the slot like postcards from paradise. Where most **gab-show** hosts report for duty at radio studios where candy bars get stuck in the vending machine and the carpeting is a **certain industrial shade of indifference**, Limbaugh—a man, a mission, **a mighty wind**—has carved out his own **principality** in Florida's Palm Beach, a **lion preserve** where he can roam undisturbed. Drinking in the rays, puffing on the **big-shot cigars, riding the range** in a golf cart—he's got the **complete Jackie Gleason how-*sweet*-it-is package deal**. But just as the Great One suffered from melancholia aggravated by alcohol, Limbaugh's **indulgence** in his own **creature comforts** hasn't been able to insulate him from the **demons within**. An addiction to painkillers reduced this **human boom box** of self sufficiency and strict enforcement—"If people are violating the law by doing drugs," he once lectured on his syndicated TV show, "they ought to be accused and they ought to be convicted **and they ought to be sent up" (up the river, that is)**—to the furtive, needy ploys of any other **junkie** who finds the medicine cabinet running dry. After he entered rehab, his third wife, Marta, reportedly vacated **the luxury estate** (they would later divorce), leaving Rush a **Tarzan without his Jane** in what the *Palm Beach Post* in 2004 called his "$24.2 million, 36,500 square-foot **secluded monster** at 1495 N. Ocean." (2007, 100)

Wolcott paints a subtly nasty portrait of Limbaugh with a series of tiny linguistic jabs, comparing him to the king of beasts, to Jackie Gleason, and to Tarzan. According to Wolcott, Limbaugh's cigars are too big and showy, he is self-indulgent, and he is addicted to drugs. We have rewritten the passage without the honorific and pejorative language so that you can see what is lost without it:

> Rush Limbaugh lives well, spending every day in Florida. Where most talk-show hosts report for duty at radio studios where equipment doesn't always work and where the carpets are not always clean, Limbaugh has made a space for himself in Florida's Palm Beach. He reminds one of Jackie Gleason, smoking cigars, driving a golf cart over the course. But just as Gleason suffered from depression and alcohol abuse, Limbaugh has his own problems with these issues. An addiction to painkillers rendered his remarks about drugs—"If people are violating the law by doing drugs," he once said on his syndicated TV show, "they ought to be accused and they ought to be convicted and they ought to be sent up"—similar to those made by others who are unable to stop using their drug of choice. After he entered rehabilitation, his wife, Marta, left the home they shared (they would later divorce), leaving Rush alone in the large house.

Without the pejorative language, much of the emotional appeal of the original passage disappears. The author's *ethos* changes as well, becoming more distant and formal.

Here is another passage, this time written by Ben Feller, a writer for the Associated Press. We have bolded the pejorative terms that appear in it:

WHITE HOUSE HITS BACK AT CARTER REMARKS

In a **biting rebuke,** the White House on Sunday **dismissed** former President Jimmy Carter as **"increasingly irrelevant"** after his **harsh criticism** of President Bush.

Carter was quoted Saturday as saying "I think as far as **the adverse impact** on the nation around the world, this administration has been the **worst in history.**"

The Georgia Democrat said Bush had overseen an "overt **reversal of America's basic values**" as expressed by previous administrations, including that of his own father, former President George H.W. Bush.

"I think it's **sad** that President Carter's **reckless personal criticism** is out there," White House spokesman Tony Fratto responding Sunday from Crawford, where Bush spent the weekend.

"I think it's **unfortunate,**" Fratto said, "And I think he is proving to be **increasingly irrelevant** with these kinds of comments."

Carter made the comments to the *Arkansas Democrat-Gazette* in a story that appeared in the newspaper's Saturday editions.

Carter spokeswoman Deanna Congileo confirmed his comments to *The Associated Press* on Saturday and declined to elaborate. (2007)

This report on a battle of words is a fine example of political mud-slinging. We revise the passage to eliminate the pejorative terms and indicate our amendments with bold text.

Carter was quoted Saturday as saying "I think as far as its **effects** on the nation and around the world, this administration has **not been the best we've seen** in the last few years of American history."

The Georgia Democrat said Bush had **departed from the practices and values** of previous administrations including that of his own father, former President George H.W. Bush.

"I think **it's to be expected** that President Carter **should have an opinion,**" White House spokesman Tony Fratto responded Sunday from Crawford, where Bush spent the weekend.

"I think it's **not unreasonable,**" Fratto said. "And I think he is proving **that he continues to be interested in the fate of the nation** with these kinds of comments."

Notice how the tone of the piece changes from harsh to neutral when the pejorative terms are made less negative or removed altogether. The revision is also far less interesting than the original, which suggests that pejorative terms are colorful and hence persuasive. In some cases, in order to remove the invective and soften the tone of this piece, we had to fudge the facts a bit—in other words, our revision is a fine example of spin, rather that rhetoric.

We encourage our readers to insert pathetic appeals into their own speaking and writing. We think that if you compose these carefully, with an eye toward the rhetorical situations you face, you will find that listeners and readers may respond to your propositions and arguments more warmly than they might have without your use of these appeals.

RHETORICAL ACTIVITIES

1. Try creating an emotional appeal to use in an argument you are work-ing on. If you are not working in a specific rhetorical situation at the moment, invent one. That is, describe an audience and an issue. Now decide what the emotional state of your designated audience is likely to be. Decide what emotions would rouse them to action, or at least move them to change their minds. Create an *enargeia*, a vivid scene, that is calculated to rouse the requisite emotions.

2. Select a proposition from your own repertoire of beliefs—that is, from your ideology. For example, perhaps you believe that the United States ought to intervene in the affairs of other countries for humanitarian reasons. Perhaps you support the legal status of abortion, or perhaps you oppose the death penalty. Now imagine an audience of one or more persons who are either hostile or indifferent to your proposition. Write a description of a rhetorical situation in which you attempt to persuade this audience to accept your proposition. Try to figure out why your audience is hostile or indifferent to you or to your proposi-tion. Compose a list of their possible emotional responses either to the issue or to your situated *ethos*. List some pathetic proofs you might use to persuade audience members to accept your premise or at least to examine it.

3. Think of a rhetorical situation in which an appeal to anger is appropri-ate. Compose the appeal. Now try composing appeals to other emo-tions discussed in this chapter. In what context would an appeal to shame be effective? Compassion? Hopelessness?

4. Advertisers often rely on fear—particularly the fear of losing status in the community—to get people to buy things. Find some examples of ads that do this. Do advertisers exploit other emotional appeals such as appeals to anger, dread, love, or hope?

5. Are Aristotle and Cicero's lists of emotions complete? That is, can you think of other emotions that are used in contemporary emotional appeals? For example, desire is often appealed to in contemporary rhetoric. Politicians say that "the American people want" this or that, and advertisers create extremely subtle appeals to desire, especially erotic desire. Perfume is a good example here—perfumes are often advertised with nothing but a photograph of a handsome actor's face and a bottle of perfume. Can you think of other examples? Is desire an emotion?

6. Keep a list of the honorific and pejorative terms that you come across in your reading. Once it has become long enough (fifty examples each of honorific and pejorative terms should do), study the list to deter-mine whether it tells you something about community values.

PROGYMNASMATA VII: DESCRIPTION

According to Aphthonius, a description (Greek *ekphrasis*) "is an expository speech, distinctly presenting to view the thing being set forth." Hermogenes wrote that descriptions bring "before one's eyes what is to be shown." Descriptions can be written of people, actions (a battle), times (peace or war), places (harbors, seashores, cities), seasons (spring, summer, a holiday), and many other things. Both teachers chose their examples of descriptions from Homer: "He was round in the shoulders, bronzed, with thick curling hair"; "crooked was he and halt of one foot." The ancient authorities recommended that composers follow some order when writing descriptions: a description of a person, for example, should move from head to foot; descriptions of places should distinguish between the places themselves and their surroundings. A description of the Vietnam Veterans Memorial in Washington DC, for example, might begin by describing the memorial itself; then it might move to the immediate surroundings—the people walking slowly past, the gifts left on the sidewalk in front of the memorial; then it might move outward toward less-immediate surroundings—the park, vendors selling war memorabilia, the Lincoln and Washington monuments. Vivid description comes in handy when making arguments about visual culture.

Like a description of a place, a description of an artifact or an object might distinguish it from its surroundings and from other objects around it. Visual scholar W. J. T. Mitchell offers this well-known poem—"Anecdote of a Jar"—by Wallace Stevens as a "pure example" of the ancient concept of *ekphrasis*:

> I placed a jar in Tennessee,
> And round it was, upon a hill.
> It made the slovenly wilderness
> Surround that hill.
> The wilderness rose up to it,
> And sprawled around, no longer wild.
> The jar was round upon the ground
> And tall and of a port in air.
> It took dominion everywhere.
> The jar was gray and bare.
> It did not give of bird or bush,
> Like nothing else in Tennessee. (1994)

Why is the description a "pure" example? Because it adheres to most of the ancients' descriptions of good *ekphrases*, which call for distinguishing objects from things around them—"The jar was gray and bare. . . . . Like nothing else in Tennessee." Clearly, Stevens's poem exemplifies Hermogenes' instructions for creating effective *ekphrases*: "the expression should almost create seeing through hearing" (86). That is to say, Stevens uses language to create a picture.

Much as the jar newly sets off what surrounds it, a description of a cataclysmic event can be made most startling by describing how it differs from the moments before and even after it. In a review of Don DeLillo's *Falling Man*, a novel about 9/11, Frank Rich offers his own description of the scene in New York on 9/11:

> No matter where you stood in the city, the air was thick after the towers fell: literally thick with the soot and stench of incinerated flesh that turned terror into a condition as inescapable as the weather. All bets were off. New Yorkers who always know where they're going didn't know where to go. Cab drivers named Muhammad were now feared as the enemy within; strangers on the street were improbably embraced like family under a canopy of fliers for the missing. Such, for a while anyway, was the 'new normal,' though the old normal began to reassert itself almost as soon as that facile catchphrase was coined. (2007, 1)

Here Rich captures scenes he perhaps recalls from that awful day, bringing it to life once again; for those of us who were not on the streets of Manhattan, who only watched on television, this report from a proximate witness is terribly compelling.

Ekphrasis is also important in other kinds of writing, including history, journalism, and ethnography. Here's an example of *ekphrasis* from an ethnography of capitalist activity in Bratislava, the capital of Slovakia, written by rhetoric scholar Catherine Prendergast:

> In 2001, the malls came to Slovakia: First, "Polus City Center," just west of downtown, then the sprawling "Aupark Bratislava Shopping Center," incongruously placed in front of miles of nearly identical concrete apartment buildings that had been erected by the communists to attract tens of thousands of workers to the country's most intelligentsia-rich city. Before I returned to Slovakia in 2003 after a nine year absence, Maria gave me this advance notice on the malls: "Really, if you are inside one of these malls, you will not be able to tell where you are, in Slovakia, or in America." With this comment Maria enunciated a common observation about the working of globalization: that certain features of the West's commercial landscape replicate themselves in many countries, seemingly with little regard for the locale. Certainly part of the confusion of place Maria alluded to resulted from the generous use of English in both malls. In Polus, for example, corridors were labeled in English: "5th Avenue" and "Regent Street." Such uses of English enabled local businesses to appear at least fictively as players in the global economy. That Polus had a corridor dubbed "Wall Street," for example, allowed the Slovak bank VUB to advertise on billboards that they could be found in Polus "na [on] Wall Street." (2008)

Such vivid description can lay the groundwork for—or actually make—an argument. Prendergast's book, for example, argues that citizens of Slovakia are deeply ambivalent about the new demand to learn English, and the description of the mall shows how a particularly Western version of capitalism has indeed arrived in Slovakia. Descriptions can also be persuasive, and so rhetors should know how to compose them (see also our comments about *enargeia* in the chapter on pathos).

PROGYMNASMATA: DESCRIPTION

1. It might be helpful to try a mode of what painters call "still life": compose a description of an object in the library, classroom, or in your apartment or dorm room. Compose a description of the most beautiful building in your city or on your campus. If the local architecture leaves a lot to be desired, then focus on landscaping or a favorite tree. Remember Hermogenes' observation that this exercise brings "what is being shown before the eyes." Try composing several of these "sketches." What visual details and textures might be drawn out in your description? Is there a particular style of describing that nicely suits the object?

2. Now find an instance of vivid description that you believe functions persuasively. Imitate this description, and connect your imitation to a broader issue that you are concerned about. (We give lots of advice about imitation in the sections of this book devoted to that exercise.)

NOTE

1. We are indebted in part to Craig R. Smith and Michael J. Hyde for our analysis of emotional appeals.

WORKS CITED

Brennan, Teresa. *The Transmission of Affect*. Ithaca, N.Y.: Cornell University Press, 2004.

Damasio, Anthony. *Descartes' Error: Emotion, Reason, and the Human Brain*. New York: Harper Collins, 1994.

Feller, Ben. "White House Hits Back at Carter Remarks." *Yahoo! Inc.*, May 20, 2007. http://news.yahoo.com/s/ap/20070520/ap_on_go_pr_wh/bush_carter (accessed May 23, 2007).

Gore, Al. "On Katrina, Global Warming." Common Dreams, September 12, 2005. http://www. commondreams.org/views05/0912-32. htm (accessed May 23, 2007).

Mitchell, W. J. T. *Picture Theory*. Chicago: University of Chicago Press, 1994.

Prendergast, Catherine. *Buying into English*. Pittsburgh: University of Pittsburgh Press, 2008.

Rich, Frank. "The Clear Blue Sky." Review of *Falling Man* by Don DeLillo. *New York Times*, May 27, 2007, national edition, sec. 7.

Scraton, Phil. "Introduction: Witnessing 'Terror,' Anticipating 'War.'" In *Beyond September 11: An Anthology of Dissent*. Edited by Phil Scraton, 1–10. London: Pluto Press, 2002.

Smith, Craig and Michael Hyde. "Rethinking 'the Public': The Role of Emotion in Being-with-others." *Quarterly Journal of Speech* 77 (November 1991): 446–66.

Wheeler, Marcy. *Anatomy of Deceit: How the Bush Administration Used the Media to Sell the Iraq War and Out a Spy*. Berkeley: Vaster Books, 2007.

Wolcott, James. "Rush to Judgment." *Vanity Fair* 561 (May 2007): 100–106.

Zinser, Lynn. "Rallying Support for an Ottawa Rally." *New York Times*, June 3, 2007, national edition, Sports.

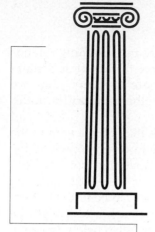

CHAPTER 8

EXTRINSIC PROOFS: ARGUMENTS WAITING TO BE USED

The material at the rhetor's disposal is twofold, one kind made up of the things which are not thought out by himself, but depend upon the circumstances and are dealt with by rule, for example documents, oral evidence, informal agreements, examinations, statutes, decrees of the Senate, judicial precedents, magisterial orders, opinions of counsel, and whatever else is not produced by the rhetor, but is supplied to him by the case itself or by the parties: the other kind is founded entirely on the rhetor's reasoned argument.

—Cicero, *De Oratore*
II xxvii 116–17

IN THE *RHETORIC*, Aristotle divided proofs into two kinds: intrinsic and extrinsic (I ii 1356a). Intrinsic proofs must be invented by a rhetor, and so we devoted the first few chapters of this book to them. Extrinsic proofs, on the other hand, do not need to be invented by a rhetor because they are found in the rhetorical situation. Extrinsic proofs include empirical evidence such as facts, **data**, artifacts, and the **testimony** of authorities and witnesses. While such proofs cannot be invented, rhetors may have to employ invention in order to decide how to use them in an argument.

Modern rhetoricians place a much heavier emphasis on extrinsic proofs than the ancients did. Today rhetors often assume that whatever is written down and published is accurate and trustworthy, since, in a sense, it represents someone's testimony about something. The version of rhetoric that is taught in school assumes that accounts based on empirical investigation are absolutely reliable. As a result, students are often taught that there are only two kinds of acceptable rhetorical proofs, testimony and data. Testimony provides audiences with accounts composed by people who for some reason have special access to relevant facts or arguments.

267

The English word *testimony* derives from a Latin phrase meaning "standing as a third," that is, serving as a witness. Hence testimony is a statement given by a witness about some event or state of affairs. Here we include citations from the work of scholars and other authorities under the category of testimony.

Data, in contrast, include any facts or statistics that are relevant to the rhetorical situation. This chapter is the only place in this book where the term *fact* is used in its current sense to mean something that has been empirically demonstrated. In this modern sense of the word, facts are grounded in experience. That is, the validity of a fact can be tested by personal observation, or at least we can imagine how such a test might be done. If someone remarks that the temperature has fallen below freezing, we can test this statement of fact by stepping outdoors; if we desire more accuracy, we can look at a thermometer.

Ancient teachers would have categorized both testimony and data as extrinsic to the art of rhetoric, because they are not invented according to its principles. Rhetors need only to find, select, and assemble the relevant extrinsic proofs. But, as we noted at the beginning of this chapter, sometimes the selection and assembly of such proofs does require invention, although it may not be the extensive sort of invention that we engage in when we first try to find suitable arguments to use in a rhetorical situation.

EXTRINSIC PROOFS IN ANCIENT RHETORICS

Scholars doubt that Aristotle invented the distinction between intrinsic and extrinsic proofs, even though most ancient authorities credit it to him. However, it also appears in the roughly contemporaneous *Rhetorica ad Alexandrum* (vii 1428a), which suggests that Aristotle may have found it in one or several of the treatises he gathered and studied in order to compose the *Rhetoric*.

Quintilian, noting that "the division laid down by Aristotle has met with almost universal approval," translated the Greek terms as "artistic" and "nonartistic" (V i 1). Translators have abandoned these terms, however, since *art* carries connotations of "high" or "creative" art to contemporary ears. In the chapter on *ethos* we called these two kinds of proof "invented" and "situated," since, as Aristotle wrote, intrinsic proofs have to be invented with the aid of rhetoric, while extrinsic proofs are situated within the circumstances of a case or issue, and have only to be used (I 2 1355b). We will use that terminology here, referring to extrinsic proofs as "situated."

Cicero stated that all extrinsic proofs rely chiefly upon the authority granted by the community to those who make them (*Topics* IV 24). In other words, Cicero defined all extrinsic proof as testimony. In keeping with Cicero's remark, we might argue that facts are a kind of testimony, since their accuracy depends upon the care taken by the person who establishes them as facts and upon his reputation in relevant communities, as well.

In any case, ancient authorities listed the following items as extrinsic proofs: laws or precedents, rumors, maxims or proverbs, documents, oaths, and the testimony of witnesses or authorities. Some of these were tied to ancient legal procedures or religious beliefs. If someone had refused to take an oath about a disputed issue, this refusal could be introduced in Athenian courts as evidence, for example, and the sayings of oracles were also cited as extrinsic support for arguments. Ancient teachers considered written documents to be extrinsic proofs because they were composed by someone other than the rhetor—usually a court official.

Ancient teachers knew that extrinsic proofs are not always reliable. For instance, they were quite aware that written documents usually required careful interpretation, and they were skeptical of their accuracy and authority as well. In Plato's *Phaedrus*, Socrates warned Phaedrus that written documents cannot always be trusted:

> Written words . . . seem to talk to you as though they were intelligent, but if you ask them anything about what they say, from a desire to be instructed, they go on telling you just the same thing forever. And once a thing is put in writing, the composition, whatever it may be, drifts all over the place, getting into the hands not only of those who understand it, but equally of those who have no business with it; it doesn't know how to address the right people, and not address the wrong. And when it is ill-treated and unfairly abused it always needs its parent to come to its help, being unable to defend or help itself. (275d)

The problem with written words, according to Plato, is that we don't always know their author: who his family was, what sort of work he did, what his reputation or ideological affiliation were. Because we don't know these things about authors, we cannot simply take their work at face value. Rather, we need to interpret it.

Furthermore, written documents that are central to a culture's definition of itself accrue a sediment of interpretation as time passes. Plato's *Dialogues* are themselves central to Western culture. When contemporary readers use very old documents like these, they must interpret them through thousands of years of readings and translations. There is no way to retrieve their original or authoritative meaning, as if, indeed, they ever had one.

A related kind of extrinsic proof—laws—provides good examples of the need to interpret written documents. In American jurisprudence, laws are written in general terms; that is, they describe the actions a community should take in case an instance occurs that fits within the general situation they describe. The legal debate over regulation of hateful speech hinges on whether uses of offensive speech should be interpreted as speech that is protected by the First Amendment or should be read as "fighting words" or as speech that provokes "imminent lawless action." When it is protected, of course, it cannot be regulated at all. If, however, an expression is interpreted as "fighting words" that "tend to incite an immediate breach of the peace," the courts may decide to allow its regulation. It all depends on how the law is read and how any instance of the use of hateful speech is interpreted.

In a famous case from Minnesota, for example, the Supreme Court struck down a municipal law against hateful speech, in the process pardoning young men who had burned a cross on the lawn of an African-American family. Here is Kermit Hall's account of that decision:

> In the early morning hours of 21 June 1990, Robert A. Viktora [sic] (R.A.V.), age seventeen, and Arthur Miller, age eighteen, along with several other teenagers allegedly burned a cross inside the fenced yard of a black family that lived across the street from the house where they were staying. Viktora's counsel in the trial court successfully moved to have the case dismissed on the ground that the St. Paul ordinance was substantially overbroad and impermissibly content-based and hence an unconstitutional limit on freedom of speech guaranteed under the First Amendment. The Minnesota Supreme Court, however, reversed the trial court judge and held that the measure was an appropriate means of accomplishing a compelling governmental interest in protecting the community of St. Paul from bias-motivated threats to public safety and order.
>
> Few high court cases have produced such dissent amid unanimity. Justice Antonin Scalia's opinion for the Court resoundingly condemned the St. Paul ordinance, although some of his colleagues, in various sharply worded concurring opinions, sought to limit the impact of Scalia's pronouncements. Scalia found the measure wholly incompatible with the First Amendment since it aimed to silence speech on the basis of its content. Scalia noted that the St. Paul ordinance singled out for limitation only speech that communicated a message of racial, gender, or religious intolerance. While such speech might be offensive, the actions of the city in punishing it effectively and inappropriately handicapped a particular form of expression. Thus, it was possible for persons to express hostility toward others based on political affiliation, union membership, or homosexuality and not be covered by the ordinance.
>
> Chief Justice William H. Rehnquist and Associate Justices Anthony M. Kennedy, David Souter, and Clarence Thomas agreed with the judgment, but did so on different grounds. For these four justices the ordinance failed because it was "overbroad," meaning that it could be used to limit speech or expression that would otherwise deserve constitutional protection.
>
> The remainder of the Court agreed with Scalia's decision, but they rejected entirely the rationale that he used in reaching it. Led by Justice Byron White, the three other members of the Court wanted to find a way to sustain the constitutionality of hate crime measures. As Justice Harry Blackmun, a resident of Minnesota, observed, "I see no Amendment values that are compromised by a law that prohibits hoodlums from driving minorities out of their homes by burning crosses on their lawns, but I see great harm in preventing the people of St. Paul from specifically punishing the race-based 'fighting words' that so prejudice their community" (p. 416). Blackmun's appeal to the concept of "fighting words" invoked *Chaplinsky* v. *New Hampshire* (1942), where the justices had held that certain words, along with obscenity and defamation,

were essentially outside the protection of the First Amendment. Justice Scalia recognized the importance of the fighting words exception but concluded that in this case they did not apply, a matter sharply disputed by White and his supporters. While they could not agree on the reasons, they did unite in the belief that the St. Paul ordinance was constitutionally unacceptable.

The decision cast doubt on the constitutionality of other state and local hate laws along with speech codes at public universities. The most specific outcome was an increasing practice by legislative bodies to write new ordinances in content-neutral ways. The impact of *R.A.V.*, then, was to slow but not altogether end the use of legislatively imposed limitations on hate speech.

Judges disagreed across levels about this law: the Minnesota state court found in favor of the African-American family, and while the justices of the Supreme Court agreed that St. Paul's law was unconstitutional, they disagreed among themselves about why this was so. This case demonstrates that laws must be interpreted and reinterpreted—that is why we have judges. This consideration suggests that Aristotle's distinction between intrinsic and extrinsic proofs is not absolute. Because of this, extrinsic proofs cannot always be inserted into an argument without art or skill. Rhetors must interpret and evaluate the worth of such proofs, especially when they contradict one another. Rhetors must also determine whether or not such proofs will be persuasive. By and large, the ancients recommended that rhetors follow this procedure in composing an extrinsic proof: state it; comment on its relevance to the issue; comment on its effectiveness; and make any arguments that are necessary to support it. This is good advice. A citation from an authority, inserted into a discourse without context, is usually useless to an audience.

TESTIMONY

Ancient rhetoricians generally distrusted the testimony of ordinary persons, especially those who testified in legal cases. The author of *ad Alexandrum* pointed out that "what is stated in evidence must necessarily be either probable or improbable or of doubtful credit, and similarly the witness must be either trustworthy or untrustworthy or questionable" (14). Rhetors could insert testimony into their discourse without comment, he wrote, only when a trustworthy witness stated a probability. Any combination of an untrustworthy or questionable witness with improbable or doubtful testimony required rhetors to supplement the testimony with an account of its worth. Aristotle developed a rule of disinterestedness for determining which witnesses were reliable: persons who had nothing to gain by testifying were more credible than those who stood to profit by doing so (I xv 16). Quintilian argued that rhetors need to know whether a witness favors or opposes a point of view and whether the witness has held this position for a long time or has only recently adopted it (V vii 13). In short, ancient rhetoricians never took anyone's testimony at face value.

Instead, they examined the motives of witnesses in order to determine whether their testimony was reliable.

Since testimony is a report made by someone about some state of affairs, it is valuable to the extent that audiences accept the authority and credibility of the witnesses who provide it. Today, audiences award authority to two sorts of witnesses: persons who are respected in the relevant community and persons who were in a position to observe some disputed state of affairs. We call the first kind **community authorities** and the second **proximate authorities.**

Community Authorities

Community authorities are persons whose words or actions have earned them respect within a given community. Rhetors use the words or examples of such persons to lend credibility to their *ethos* and authenticity to their positions. Aristotle wrote that "witnesses are of two kinds, ancient and recent" (I xv 1375b). In Aristotle's time, ancient witnesses were "the poets and men of repute whose judgments are known to all"—Homer, for example. Recent witnesses were "well-known persons who have given a decision on any point"—for example, Solon, who was a famous lawmaker in Athens (1376a).

Modern rhetors still rely upon the testimony of ancient witnesses, just as we have quoted or cited texts by Aristotle, Quintilian, and other ancient rhetoricians throughout this book to validate our interpretation of their theories and practices. It was important that we do so, because some of our interpretations are controversial among scholars and historians of ancient rhetorics. If we can support a doubtful or controversial position with a quotation from Cicero, we demonstrate that at least one ancient rhetorician took a position similar to ours (although it is always possible that we have misread a citation—scholars argue frequently with one another about how texts should be read). To quote from sources also suggests that we have read ancient rhetorical authorities carefully, which reinforces our *ethos.* Thus, citation of relevant authorities is an extrinsic or situated means of proof that may require artfulness in order to become useful one.

American rhetors often quote historical figures like Thomas Jefferson or Abraham Lincoln in support of a point of view, since both of these men are important figures in American political mythology. When Gerald Ford assumed the presidency in 1974 under difficult circumstances, he quoted both Jefferson and Lincoln in his inaugural address:

> Those who nominated and confirmed me as Vice President were my friends and are my friends. They were of both parties, elected by all the people, and acting under the Constitution in their name. It is only fitting then that I should pledge to them, and to you, that I will be the President of all the people. Thomas Jefferson said, "The people are the only sure reliance with the preservation of our liberty." And down the years Abraham Lincoln renewed this American article of faith asking, "Is there any better way for equal hope in the world?" (1974).

Ford's predecessor, Richard Nixon, had resigned under threat of impeachment. Thus it was important for Ford to reassure Americans that their democratic tradition of popular government was still intact. He did this in part by assuring his audience that his nomination and confirmation were fully constitutional and in part by quoting Jefferson, the architect of American democracy, and Lincoln, whose most famous utterances argue for the importance of government for and by the people.

Study of a community's choice of authorities often discloses the values held by its members. During a Democratic National Convention, for example, audiences are likely to hear speakers cite or quote Democrats and liberals noted for their courage or political skill, such as John F. Kennedy, Robert F. Kennedy, Martin Luther King Jr., Eleanor Roosevelt, Franklin Delano Roosevelt, Fannie Lou Hamer, or Rosa Parks. Hamer was a civil rights activist and a member of an African-American delegation to the 1964 Democratic convention that challenged discriminatory rules for delegate seating. Parks refused to give up her seat on a bus, and her example inspired the Montgomery bus boycott of 1955–1956. Martin Luther King Jr. was an activist in the civil rights movement, an advocate of nonviolent resistance who was assassinated in 1968. John F. Kennedy and Franklin D. Roosevelt were Democratic presidents, while Eleanor Roosevelt was an activist and philanthropist. Robert Kennedy, brother of John, was assassinated while running for president on the Democratic ticket in 1968. Democrats revere these people for their dedication to party ideals, particularly the furthering of civil rights. Interestingly, both Republicans and Democrats quote or cite Abraham Lincoln; indeed the Republican party styles itself "the party of Lincoln." Lincoln was a Republican, of course, and since he signed the Emancipation Proclamation, which purportedly "freed the slaves," he can be invoked by Republicans to signify their commitment to civil rights.

As Lincoln's case demonstrates, it is important that cultural authorities be invoked in support of a position only if they enjoy good reputations in the relevant community. Republicans are likely to cite Lincoln and Ronald Reagan, but they rarely mention Nixon, whose presidency ended in his resignation to avoid impeachment. The citation of authorities who are very well-known, such as American presidents, can be tricky because reputations represent a community's evaluation of someone's behavior; as a result, they do not always accurately represent that person's actual behavior. Some recent Democratic presidents, such as Lyndon Baines Johnson, Jimmy Carter, and Bill Clinton, are not often cited by contemporary Democrats as authorities, even though all were active in furthering civil rights legislation during their terms in office. Carter's stock as an authority has risen because he was awarded the Nobel Peace Prize in 2002, but recently it has fallen again because he has been an outspoken critic of the war in Iraq. And while many Democrats admire Johnson for his legislative skills, his reputation as a politician is tainted by his role in bringing on the Vietnam war. Clinton, of course, was thought to have engaged in scandalous behavior in the White

House, and it is doubtful that his reputation will recover in the near future despite his considerable talents as a statesman and politician.

A slightly different use of community authority appears in scholarly writing, including student writing, which relies heavily on the authoritative testimony of professionals or experts. In this case, the relevant community is a profession or discipline, such as physics or medicine or psychology or philosophy. Within communities of this kind, witnesses are ordinarily expected to hold the scholarly and/or research credentials authorized by the community: an M.D. for medical doctors, a D.V.M. for veterinarians, a Ph.D. for some scientists and for all scholars in the social sciences and humanities. Scholarly witnesses also accrue authority from the quality and extent of their research and/or publication, while their receipt of awards and prizes, such as a Nobel or a Pulitzer, increases their authority.

Rhetors who compose discourse to be used in professional or disciplinary communities are expected to cite persons who are defined as authorities within those communities. Such citations can easily be inserted into any discourse:

> Jane Doe, author of several books and many articles and winner of the coveted Status Prize for Weighty Authorities, agrees with my position.

Since we write chiefly for scholarly communities (students and colleagues), we try to cite an authority whenever we make a point that might be misunderstood or contested by an audience. We also try to comment immediately on every quotation we use. Commentary can include an interpretation of the quotation, or can show how the quotation is relevant to the argument in progress. We recommend this practice to our students, and we recommend it to you as well.

The scholarly habit of invoking authorities often frustrates beginning students who have not yet studied a discipline thoroughly enough to recognize the names of its authorities or to know their work. Another scholarly habit of citing authorities sometimes irritates those who are not initiates: using a person's name as shorthand for an ideology or a body of intellectual work. Within a given scholarly community, some thinkers are awarded such high status that they are no longer quoted but only named. Aristotle and Isocrates enjoy this status among historians of rhetoric, and the same is true of Émile Durkheim and Karl Marx in sociology or Claude Lévi-Strauss and Margaret Mead in anthropology or Sigmund Freud and Jacques Lacan in psychoanalysis. Reference to an authority by a last name only ("Marx," "Mead," or "Freud," as in "Mead says . . .") is a sure sign that he or she enjoys such status.

Evaluating Community Authorities

Since most scholarly and intellectual work relies heavily on the testimony of authorities, rhetors ought to know whether the authorities they cite or quote possess whatever credentials are required for entry to a discipline.

A scholar's credentials often appear on book jackets or at the end of books, and scholarly articles ordinarily list authors' credentials and accomplishments as well. If there is any doubt about the extent of a scholar's research, an author search in library holdings will show how often and where she has published. References to someone's work by other scholars in the same field also suggest that she is considered an authority.

Rhetors must also be concerned about an authority's accuracy. Authorities may produce inaccurate work for at least two reasons: either they were ignorant of some relevant information, or their ideological bias compromised their accuracy. The accuracy of a scholarly or intellectual authority is sometimes difficult to ascertain, especially for students who are new to a field of study. One way to check the accuracy of a source is to read reviews about it. Reviewers usually indicate whether an authority is trustworthy, and they may indicate as well whether his work is controversial. Another way to insure that authorities represent a reasonably accurate state of affairs in their work is to compare it with that of other scholars who discuss the same issues. Another is to use more recent accounts that correct errors in older works.

Students are sometimes surprised to learn that scholars disagree with one another. But they do. For example, historians of rhetoric argue over whether it is appropriate or accurate to group historical figures like Protagoras, Gorgias, and Isocrates together into a coherent rhetorical school called "the Sophists." Sometimes these arguments become quite heated. Arguments like these are important because their outcomes are ideological. In the case of the Sophists, if scholars can prove that their work was consecutive and widely recognized as such during the fifth century BCE, they have grounds for modifying Plato's negative comments about rhetoric, comments that have lent a negative coloring to rhetoric throughout the history of Western philosophy.

Some scholars believe that accuracy is insured if authorities are objective. Supposedly, authorities are objective if they have detached themselves emotionally or ideologically from issues and when they write or speak without bias or prejudice. We are skeptical about the ideal of objectivity, however. People ordinarily choose a field of study because they are interested in the issues raised within it. If people are interested in something, they have already foreclosed the possibility of their being objective about it. And since scholars also subscribe to ideologies, just like everybody else, their ability to approach any issue without bias is open to question. Given the role played by ideology in all thought, even in scholarly and intellectual rhetoric, *objectivity* is sometimes another name for orthodoxy ("straight thinking")—support of the intellectual status quo. That is, the so-called objective scholarly authority is thought to be so because she does not depart radically from the tenets held by her scholarly or intellectual community.

Like ancient rhetoricians who examined the motives of witnesses, then, modern rhetors ought also to inspect the motives and ideologies of even the most respected authorities if they plan to use them as extrinsic proofs.

Some authors acknowledge their motives and prejudices in a foreword or a preface.

Here is Senator Barack Obama, explaining in 2002 his reasons for opposing the war in Iraq:

> After September 11th, after witnessing the carnage and destruction, the dust and the tears, I supported this administration's pledge to hunt down and root out those who would slaughter innocents in the name of intolerance, and I would willingly take up arms myself to prevent such tragedy from happening again. I don't oppose all wars. And I know that in this crowd today, there is no shortage of patriots, or of patriotism.
>
> What I am opposed to is a dumb war. What I am opposed to is a rash war. What I am opposed to is the cynical attempt by Richard Perle and Paul Wolfowitz and other armchair, weekend warriors in this administration to shove their own ideological agendas down our throats, irrespective of the costs in lives lost and in hardships borne.
>
> What I am opposed to is the attempt by political hacks like Karl Rove to distract us from a rise in the uninsured, a rise in the poverty rate, a drop in the median income—to distract us from corporate scandals and a stock market that has just gone through the worst month since the Great Depression. That's what I'm opposed to. A dumb war. A rash war. A war based not on reason but on passion, not on principle but on politics.
>
> Now let me be clear—I suffer no illusions about Saddam Hussein. He is a brutal man. A ruthless man. A man who butchers his own people to secure his own power. He has repeatedly defied UN resolutions, thwarted UN inspection teams, developed chemical and biological weapons, and coveted nuclear capacity. He's a bad guy. The world, and the Iraqi people, would be better off without him.
>
> But I also know that Saddam poses no imminent and direct threat to the United States, or to his neighbors, that the Iraqi economy is in shambles, that the Iraqi military [is] a fraction of its former strength, and that in concert with the international community he can be contained until, in the way of all petty dictators, he falls away into the dustbin of history.
>
> I know that even a successful war against Iraq will require a US occupation of undetermined length, at undetermined cost, with undetermined consequences. I know that an invasion of Iraq without a clear rationale and without strong international support will only fan the flames of the Middle East, and encourage the worst, rather than best, impulses of the Arab world, and strengthen the recruitment arm of Al Qaeda. I am not opposed to all wars. I'm opposed to dumb wars.

Senator Obama could hardly be clearer about his motives for opposing the war in Iraq. He is also clear that he does not oppose war in general—that is, he is not a pacifist. Students should look for statements such as these in order to evaluate the bias of an authority before relying upon them.

Students should also get into the habit of reading the acknowledgments pages at the beginning of books, where writers cite the people to whose work they are indebted. A list of acknowledgments often tells a discerning reader who the author studied with, who her colleagues are, and whose scholarship she uses, admires, or disagrees with. Students can also determine a writer's ideological standpoint by looking for lists of the foundations or institutions that funded his work. These are usually listed in the acknowledgments or on the title page. Liberal or socialist foundations include Common Cause, the Brookings Institution, the Institute for Policy Studies, and the Center for the Study of Democratic Institutions; conservative or neoconservative foundations include the American Enterprise Institute, the Heritage Foundation, the Olin Foundation, the Scaife Foundation, and the Center for Strategic and International Studies. Publishing houses and magazines also have ideological biases. Sometimes they make these explicit, sometimes not. Among English-language publishing houses, Pantheon, South End Press, Beacon Books, International Publishers, Routledge, and Methuen are liberal or socialist, while Freedom House, Reader's Digest Books, Paragon House, and Arlington House are conservative or neoconservative. A book published by any of these houses is likely to reflect its ideological orientation.

People whose politics lean to the right of ours have objected to our assessments of the ideological leanings of these media. Our perspective is no doubt colored by our politics, because we also reject the current commonplace about "the liberal media." From where we stand, in America at present most mass-circulation media are centrist or just right of center; this is true of *Newsweek* and the major television networks, for example. Some cable channels, such as *Fox*, are extremely conservative. As we write, major Democratic candidates for the presidency are refusing to join a debate on that network because of its conservative leanings. The *Washington Post* and the *New York Times* are centrist but left leaning, while *Time* is further to the right, as are *US News and World Report*, the *Wall Street Journal*, and *Reader's Digest*. Some magazines are explicit about their ideological affiliation: *The Nation, Mother Jones,* and the *Village Voice* are solidly leftist, while *Commentary,* the *National Review,* and the *New American* are solidly ensconced on the right. Students can sometimes determine the ideology of an authority by looking for her use of the commonplaces associated with certain ideologies. See the chapter on commonplaces to learn about the typical beliefs of Americans whose ideologies can be called "rightist" or "leftist."

Proximate Authorities

Contemporary rhetoric includes a kind of testimony that was absent from ancient considerations: statements by persons who were physically present at an event. The authority of proximate witnesses derives not from their wisdom or their professional expertise but from the modern presumption that evidence provided by the senses is reliable and credible. And so someone who was physically present at an event is often thought to be a reliable source of testimony about that event.

Evaluating the worth of this sort of testimony is difficult. Rhetors can ask whether a proximate witness was in a position to observe the incident carefully: perhaps it was snowing or raining, preventing him from seeing or hearing clearly; perhaps he was hurrying to class, distracted with worry about an exam.

Rhetors who want to use the testimony of a proximate witness should also investigate that witness's freedom to report: perhaps some powerful group has urged her to come forward, when she would rather not become involved. Her testimony should be compared to that offered by other witnesses, and her motives should be examined to determine whether she has some kind of stake in the issue or event.

The worth of testimony offered by a proximate witness must pass several tests. First, a witness must be in a position to observe the events in question. Second, conditions must be such that a witness can adequately perceive an event. Third, the witness's state of mind at the time must be conducive to her accurate observation and reporting. If this is not the case, her testimony must be modified accordingly. Fourth, in keeping with modern faith in empirical evidence, testimony offered by a proximate witness is more valuable than evidence offered by someone who was not present. If the proximate witness gave his testimony to someone else (a policeman or reporter, for example), tests one through three must be applied to any testimony offered by the second person, as well.

People who claim to have been abducted by extraterrestrial beings often give compelling accounts of their experiences. Here is an account of the abduction of Travis Walton:

> Briefly the facts are these: In November 1975 Walton and a team of six other loggers were returning home to the town of Snowflake Arizona, when their pick-up truck was confronted by a glowing yellow object that hovered above the road in front of them. Gripped by a strange compulsion Walton leapt from the vehicle and ran straight towards the object. Ignoring his friends' pleas to turn back Walton was struck by an intense beam of light that knocked him off his feet. Terrified, his comrades left him for dead and made off in their truck. Several miles further on however a growing sense of guilt made them return to the place of the incident, though by this time there was no UFO, and no Walton to be found. . . .
>
> In the days that followed, a massive police search failed to turn up any clue as to Walton's whereabouts. The police suspected foul play and his friends came under intense suspicion. Then six days after the incident Walton's sister received a surprise phone call from her confused brother from a nearby town. Badly shaken, he was unable to explain what happened. Later under hypnosis however he was able to give a clearer account. In this testimony he claims to have been transported aboard the alien space ship and examined by three figures. In his own words: "It was weird. They weren't humans. They looked like foetuses to me, about 5 feet tall, and they wore tight-fitting brown robes. Their skin was white like a mushroom but they had no clear features."

Walton's experience is unusual given that his buddies in the truck were able to give testimony about his strange disappearance. But he was the only witness to supposed events aboard the alien vessel. Given that people who claim to have had these experiences are the only conceivable proximate authorities available, is there any way to verify these accounts?

DATA

Sometimes statements of fact are reliable and sometimes they are not. Rhetors who use them should be sure that facts come from a reputable and qualified source. They should also be sure that the facts were arrived at by means of some standard empirical procedure, such as random sampling. They should insure as well that any facts they use are current. They should provide all of this information—sources, method, date—to their audiences, especially if the issue they are arguing is controversial. Polling agencies qualify the results of their polls by telling audiences how the results were obtained ("We made 400 telephone calls to registered voters living in the New York City area between January 16 and 17, 2007"; "The poll is accurate to within plus or minus 3 percentage points").

In recent years it has become fashionable to determine the quality of a film by the level of its box office receipts. Here is a list from the Internet Movie Database (IMDB.com/chart) of the ten top-grossing American movies, along with the amounts of money (rounded up) they made in the United States as of May 2007:

1. *Titanic* (1997) $1,835,300,000
2. *The Lord of the Rings: The Return of the King* (2003) $1,129,219,252
3. *Pirates of the Caribbean: Dead Man's Chest* (2006) $1,060,332,628
4. *Harry Potter and the Sorcerer's Stone* (2001) $968,657,891
5. *Star Wars: Episode I - The Phantom Menace* (1999) $922,379,000
6. *The Lord of the Rings: The Two Towers* (2002) $921,600,000
7. *Jurassic Park* (1993) $919,700,000
8. *Harry Potter and the Goblet of Fire* (2005) $892,194,397
9. *Shrek 2* (2004) $880,871,036
10. *Harry Potter and the Chamber of Secrets* (2002) $866,300,000

(http://www.imdb.com/boxoffice/alltimegross?region=world-wide)

The amounts of money made by the movies named here are statements of fact. But such facts are often used to support an inference that is not always warranted: movies that make lots of money must be very good. By this reckoning, *Titanic* is somewhat better than the last installment of *The Lord of the Rings* and a great deal better than *Harry Potter and the Chamber of Secrets*.

Other interpretations of these facts are possible, however. First of all, it seems that movies aimed at families do very well at the box office: most of the films on this list had ratings that admitted all but very young children, and many of them, arguably, were aimed precisely at children. Second, all are adventure movies with lots of special effects. That is, they rely for their impact on what Aristotle called "spectacle" rather than more traditional indicators of film quality such as plot structure, character development, acting, direction, or cinematography. Last, with the exception of *Jurassic Park* and *Titanic*, all of these films are fairly recent—which may suggest that more people now go to movies than formerly or that movie tickets are more expensive than they used to be. (Both of these assertions are statements of fact.) In other words, the box-office success of a film may have to do with things other than its quality.

This impression is borne out by lists of the best movies of all times. Here is a list of the ten best movies ever made, in the opinion of users of IMDB.com and current as of May 2007:

1. *The Godfather* (1972)

2. *The Shawshank Redemption* (1994)

3. *The Godfather: Part II* (1974)

4. *Buono, il brutto, il cattivo, Il* (1966)

5. *Pulp Fiction* (1994)

6. *Casablanca* (1942)

7. *Schindler's List* (1993)

8. *Star Wars: Episode V - The Empire Strikes Back* (1980)

9. *The Lord of the Rings: The Return of the King* (2003)

10. *Shichinin no samurai* (1954)

(http://www.imdb.com/chart/top)

The users of IMDB.com are no doubt fans of film because they frequent this Web site. Most of the films they list as the best movies ever depend for their impact on plot and character development as well as skilled direction, acting, and cinematography. There are exceptions, such as *Star Wars* and *The Lord of the Rings*, which also feature dazzling special effects and lots of spectacle. A few are older, smaller movies filmed in black-and-white, and two are foreign-language films. Interestingly, only one top-grossing film appears on this list: *The Lord of the Rings: The Return of the King*.

Professional experts agree only in part with users of IMDB. Here is the list of ten best-ever films compiled by the American Film Institute, which claims that the list was put together by "a blue-ribbon panel of leaders from across the film community" (www.afi.com):

1. *Citizen Kane* (1941)

2. *The Godfather* (1972)

3. *Casablanca* (1942)

4. *Raging Bull* (1980)

5. *Singin' in the Rain* (1952)
6. *Gone With the Wind* (1939)
7. *Lawrence of Arabia* (1962)
8. *Schindler's List* (1993)
9. *Vertigo* (1958)
10. *The Wizard of Oz* (1939)

(http://connect.afi.com/site/PageServer?Pagenam=micro_100landing)

Clearly, the "leaders" in film who put this list together were unimpressed by box-office earnings. None of the films they list was a top-grossing film, and only two of the films they chose appear in a list of 250 top-grossing films in the United States (*Gone With the Wind* and *The Godfather*). These experts agree with the users of IMDB in only three cases, and their list of best films extends further back in time than does the users' list. Apparently professional filmmakers employ standards of excellence that are quite different from those of amateur film buffs and quite different still from those of ordinary film-goers. In short, while box-office receipts certainly reflect a film's popularity, they may or may not reflect its quality. Like all statements of fact, then, box-office receipts make sense only when they are contextualized within some network of interpretation.

Evaluating Data

Rhetors should never accept facts at face value. All data—and this includes statistics—have been discovered and assembled by someone. Rhetors who use data as proof should always ascertain who discovered the data and who vouches for their accuracy. Most important, rhetors should examine the networks of interpretation through which data are filtered. Networks of interpretation give meaning to facts; without such networks, facts are pretty much unintelligible and uninteresting as well.

This caution applies to printed materials as well as to information that circulates on the Internet. The speed with which information can be disseminated electronically makes it doubly important that owners of Web sites take great care to cite the sources of their information. The Web sites maintained by well-known newspapers such as the *New York Times* or the *Los Angeles Times* always cite their sources (usually the Associated Press [AP] or some other reputable news organization). But Web sites owned by private citizens do not always cite the sources of information contained there. Because of this a cautious rhetor will follow any links to other sites that are provided in order to determine the source of the information and its trustworthiness. If a Web site posts information that is neither cited nor linked, rhetors who want to use it should inform their listeners and readers of their uncertainty about its validity. It is also important to remember that many owners of Web sites have ideological axes to grind. Often such Web sites will clearly state their owner's beliefs or political leanings, but many others do not. The cautious rhetor will always try to establish the validity of any data cited from the Internet. The fact that data are in print does not make them reliable.

Educational technology specialist Andy Carvin tells an exemplary story about an unhappy state of affairs:

> With more than one million entries, Wikipedia is the largest encyclopedia on the Internet. But is it reliable? To begin exploring that question, we'll first have to talk about the JFK assassination and an English duke.
>
> John Seigenthaler Sr. certainly doesn't think it's reliable. In the summer of 2005, the award-winning journalist and publisher discovered that Wikipedia had an entry about him. It detailed his career, but included a particular paragraph that rattled him:
>
> John Seigenthaler Sr. was the assistant to Attorney General Robert Kennedy in the early 1960's. For a brief time, he was thought to have been directly involved in the Kennedy assassinations of both John, and his brother, Bobby. Nothing was ever proven.
>
> This paragraph was totally false—Seigenthaler had never been linked to the JFK assassination. To make matters worse, the offending paragraph had been on the Wikipedia site for several months, and was also picked up by several other websites that use Wikipedia as a source. Someone had decided to post the information to Wikipedia as a hoax, and it had propagated across the Internet.
>
> In November of 2005, Seigenthaler authored an opinion piece for *USA Today*. He pulled no punches:
>
> I had heard for weeks from teachers, journalists and historians about "the wonderful world of Wikipedia," where millions of people worldwide visit daily for quick reference "facts," composed and posted by people with no special expertise or knowledge—and sometimes by people with malice. . . .
>
> And so we live in a universe of new media with phenomenal opportunities for worldwide communications and research—but populated by volunteer vandals with poison-pen intellects. Congress has enabled them and protects them.
>
> When I was a child, my mother lectured me on the evils of "gossip." She held a feather pillow and said, "If I tear this open, the feathers will fly to the four winds, and I could never get them back in the pillow. That's how it is when you spread mean things about people."
>
> For me, that pillow is a metaphor for Wikipedia. (2006)

RHETORICAL ACTIVITIES

1. Listen to the propositions you hear advanced by friends and family or commentators in the media. How often are these propositions supported by testimony or data? From this investigation, can you determine whether testimony and data are considered necessary in popular rhetoric? If they are not, should they be? Reread something you have recently written. Did you use testimony and data? Were any available? Would their use have strengthened your argument?

2. In modern rhetoric, evidence of the senses—taste, touch, hearing, sight, smell—is sometimes regarded as indisputable. Can you think of instances in which such evidence might be unreliable? List some of these. Do you think the evidence of the senses—**empirical** evidence— is convincing, or do you accept the ancients' skepticism about such evidence? Find some arguments in which data or testimony is used and test its reliability using the criteria discussed in this chapter.

3. In modern rhetoric, the argument from experience also carries a good deal of rhetorical weight. People can stop arguments by saying something like this: "Well, I'm a Catholic and so I ought to know the Catholic position on abortion." The argument from experience assumes that persons who have lived through a series of experiences are authorities on any issues that are relevant to those experiences. What weight do you attach to such arguments? How can they be refuted?

4. Read the arguments you are working on. If any use testimony or data, determine how reliable this evidence is. Use the tests we recommend in this chapter to determine the reliability of these situated proofs.

PROGYMNASMATA VIII: THESIS AND INTRODUCTION OF LAW

Thesis

The last, and most difficult, of the *progymnasmata* were thesis and introduction of law. Hermogenes defined thesis as "a consideration of some subject viewed apart from any specific circumstances" (87). Quintilian wrote that "praise or denunciation of laws requires greater powers; indeed, they should almost be equal to the most serious tasks of rhetoric" (II iv 33).

We have met thesis before, in the chapter on stasis, and the school exercise is probably modeled on mature rhetors' use of the *staseis* in courtrooms and in legislative forums. In the context of the *progymnasmata*, however, a thesis is a composition that argues some general point. Ancient authorities distinguished thesis from hypothesis. Hypothesis presents an argument about a real person caught in real circumstances. The question whether Tom, Dick, or Mary ought to marry is a hypothesis (such specific arguments are, of course, the province of forensic argument—see the chapter on special topics). Thesis, by contrast, argues questions on a more general level. The favorite ancient example of a thesis was "should a person marry?" This question is a thesis because writers who use it must consider the benefits and disadvantages of marriage in general.

Aphthonius divided thesis into political and theoretical questions. Political questions "admit of an action that holds a city together; for example, whether one should marry, whether one should sail, whether one should build fortifications." Hermogenes added this example: "whether one should study rhetoric." In other words, political theses are questions that concern human activities.

Aphthonius distinguished this sort of thesis from theoretical theses, which "are considered by the mind alone; for example, whether heaven is spherical, whether there are many worlds." Cicero's Stoic Paradoxes are theoretical theses that explain and defend Stoic ethical beliefs such as "Only what is morally noble is good," and "Only the wise person is rich." Theoretical theses concern issues raised by philosophers, pure scientists, and theorists of all kinds.

Hermogenes and Quintilian both noted that an exercise in thesis may have a doubling or relative quality if in defending one side of an issue the writer must attack another. Quintilian mentioned the famous exercise in which a writer debates whether city life is to be preferred to country life as an example of the double or relative thesis (II iv 24). Other well-worn examples include the ancient debate about whether the active life was to be preferred to the contemplative life and whether soldiers are more worthy of merit than lawyers. Cicero composed an extended meditation on this thesis in his defense of Murena (9 ff). Cicero sometimes slipped into hypothesis in these passages, when he referred specifically to the lawyer Servius and the soldier Murena.

Since thesis is so much like actual argument, Aphthonius advised that theses display the standard arrangement and use of parts recommended for persuasive discourse in general (see the chapter on arrangement). Hermogenes disagreed about this, however. He pointed out that "theses are determined by the so-called final headings: justice, expediency, possibility, propriety." Hermogenes' final headings were drawn from the topics of invention. To use them in the thesis about marriage, a composer would show that marriage is just because married persons "make to life the contribution of life itself"; marriage is expedient because it brings "many consolations"; it is proper because married people must display calm dispositions; and so on.

Here is Aphthonius's example of a fully amplified thesis:

A THESIS: SHOULD ONE MARRY?

Let the one seeking to measure the entire question in a few words hold marriage in high esteem. For it came from heaven or, rather, it filled heaven with the gods and father was set up for them, whence originates the title of father. And having sired gods, marriage produced the natural powers to preserve them. Then, coming down to earth, it endowed all the other things with reproductive power. And bringing under its control those things that did not know how to be lasting, marriage cleverly devised the maintaining of them through their successors. First of all, it stirs men to bravery; it is through these [brave men], since marriage knows how to produce children and wives over whom war is fought, that marriage adds bravery to its gifts. Further, it provides righteous men along with the brave; it is through these [righteous men], since men who are anxious about the things in which posterity takes pride do those things justly, that marriage produces righteous men at the same time as brave men. Nay more, it makes men wise whom it inspires to provide for the dearest ones. And by way of paradox, marriage knows how to supply self-control, and moderation is mingled with the pursuit of pleasures; it is through these [temperate men], since it adds convention to the pleasures, that marriage supplies the pleasures of moderation in support of the convention; and that which by itself is brought as an accusation against itself is admired [when joined] with marriage. If, therefore, marriage produces gods and, after them, each of their descendants in succession, if it provides brave and just men at the same time, and if it furnishes wise and temperate men, how ought one not to esteem marriage as much as possible?

Antithesis. "Yes," he says, "but marriage is a cause of misfortunes."

Solution. You seem to me to be making a charge against fortune, not against marriage. For fortune, not marriage, produces things that men who fare badly encounter, whereas the things that marriage contributes to humankind are not at all those contributed by a desire of gain from fortune. Therefore, it is better to marvel at marriage for the fine things it encompasses, rather than to criticize it for the evil things fortune brings forth. But if we do, indeed, assign the worst of man's misfortunes to marriage, why should one rather refrain from marriage? There are those difficulties that you ascribe to business; these things would not by any means exert an influence toward an escape from business, would they? And let me examine one by one the activities to [each of] which is attributed what you are perhaps charging. Thunderbolts afflict those farming, and hailstorms harass them. Yet a thunderbolt does not spoil the soil for husbandmen, nor do they flee the soil, but they continue tilling it, even if something coming down from the heavens causes damage. On the other hand, seafarers are unfortunate, and attacking storms buffet their ships. Yet they do not thereafter abandon sailing on account of those things that they have suffered in turn, but they attribute the misfortune to chance and they wait for the passage provided by the sea. Furthermore, struggles and battles destroy the lives of the combatants; still, they do not avoid battles because by fighting they will fall; instead, because those fighting are admired, they have become reconciled to death and they join in concealing the attendant drawback because of the associated benefit. For one should not flee from whatever good things there are because of bad attributes, but because of the good things one should endure the worst. Surely then, it is unreasonable that on one side farmers, sailors, and as many as are serving in the army besides, should endure the difficulties arrayed against them for the sake of the praises associated with these activities, but that on the other side we should look down upon marriage because it brings with it a degree of vexation.

Antithesis. "Yes," he says, "but it introduced widowhood for wives and orphanhood for children."

Solution. These are the evils of death, and nature is cognizant of the misfortune; you seem to me to be critical of marriage on the ground that it does not make men gods and to censure marriage because it has not included mortal things for gods. Tell me, then, why do you criticize marriage for the things that death brings about? Why do you ascribe to weddings things such as those which nature [alone] understands? Grant that he who was born to die will die. Further, if men die because they have lived life's span and in dying bereave one dwelling in the same house and make an orphan of him, why will you say that marriage has finished off those things brought about by nature alone? I, on the contrary, hold that marriage corrects orphanhood and widowhood. To one a father is dead and thus a child is an orphan; but marriage brings in another father for the orphans, and this misfortune does not stem from marriage but is veiled completely by marriage, and marriage becomes the occasion of the disappearance of orphanhood, not the beginning of it. And so nature brought widowhood with death, but marriage effected a change with wedding songs. For marriage, as though standing guard over her gift, presents to a man in wedlock the one for whom death has accomplished a bereavement. For those things that it introduced from the first, it restores again when taken away; thus, marriage knows how to take away widowhood, not how to inflict it. Nay more, a father is deprived of children through death, but through the marriage he has a share of others. And he becomes a father for the second time who does not assent to being one but once. Why, therefore, do you pervert the fine things of marriage into a fault of marriage? Further, you seem to me not to be seeking to dishonor the wedding song but to be commending it. For by the very things you force us to enumerate as pleasures of the wedding songs, you have become an admirer, not an accuser of marriage, and you force us to be amazed at betrayers of marriage, and you make the accusations against marriage a list of good features.

Antithesis. "Yes," he says, "but marriage is wearisome."

Solution. And what is set up to halt drudgery like marriage? Whatever is some, through wedding songs it is taken away. Further, there is pleasure generally in coming together with a wife in intercourse. How pleasant it is for a man to go with a wife to the marriage bed! With how great pleasure is a child anticipated! And expected, does he appear! And having appeared, will he call a father! He is then started along his training with care and [soon] he is working with a father and addressing the people in the Assembly and taking care of a father; he becomes everything that it is necessary to be.

Epilogue. It is impossible to cover in a speech the favors that marriage knows how to bestow. A mighty thing is marriage, both for producing gods and for granting to mortals for whom it devises a means of continuing life, that they seem to he gods. And it guides those needing strict rules, it urges a consideration of self-control, and it seeks after pleasures, as many as are obviously not worthy of blame. Wherefore, it is established among all that marriage should be reckoned of the greatest worth. (Matsen, Rollinson, and Sousa 1990 284–286)

This thesis begins with an *encomium* to marriage. Then its author considers three topics: fortune, death, and boredom. Finally, the thesis concludes with another *encomium* listing other topics that might be considered.

Students have composed theses ever since this exercise was invented sometime during the fifth or fourth century BCE. Exercises in thesis were called "themes" during the European Middle Ages and throughout the Renaissance, when the standard question debated in ancient theses was sometimes turned into poetry: the first seventeen of Shakespeare's sonnets, for example, can be read as meditations on the advisability of marriage.

Papers written for university coursework are still sometimes called "themes," and thesis is a bit like the standard essay that students are asked to write in most American college composition courses. Indeed, one of the standard features of the modern college essay is the "thesis statement," a term that may owe its use to the ancient exercise. However, the ancient exercise differed substantially from the modern college essay because it was an exercise in the composition of persuasive discourse. The ancient exercise that is most like the modern college essay is probably the commonplace, since it is an exercise in exposition rather than persuasion. As Hermogenes pointed out, thesis differs from commonplace because commonplace deals with matters already settled while thesis "is an inquiry into a matter still in doubt." (The preceding paragraph, by the way, is a small exercise in comparison, complete with ancient testimony.)

PROGYMNASMATA: THESIS

---

1. Compose a brief thesis on the general question of whether one ought to exercise.

2. Compose a brief thesis on the general question of whether a community ought to help people with little or no money.

3. Compose a brief thesis on the general question of whether one ought to study rhetoric.

Introduction of Law

Students using this exercise defended or attacked existing laws. Aphthonius's example concerned an ancient law that required adulterers to be put to death on the spot. He argued that while the law rightly operated "against the crimes of adulterers," it was inexpedient because its provision for immediate punishment threatened the entire system of law. In other words, it allowed people to take the law into their own hands, as a character in a modern western might say.

Typically, according to Quintilian, this exercise centered on one of three issues: whether a law was clearly written and consistent with itself, whether it was just and expedient, and whether it could be enforced. The second of these two approaches is, clearly, the more interesting one, given that rhetors can use the topics of justice and expediency to elaborate their positions. Aphthonius's example demonstrated that a law can be just (if it is just to punish adulterers) at the same time as it can be inexpedient, if it threatens an entire system of justice.

This difficult exercise is still practiced in modern schools of law. However, its practice should not be limited to persons who have a professional interest in making and enforcing laws. All people who live in a community are subject to its laws, and hence they should be interested in arguments for and against them. This is as true for laws that affect individuals, like those recently passed in many states mandating stiffer penalties for conviction of drunken driving, as it is for laws that preserve the central tenets of American ideology, such as the First Amendment to the United States Constitution: "Congress shall make no law . . . abridging the freedom of speech." Rhetors' lives are affected every day by the laws of their community and the people who interpret them. That is why the ancient exercise called introduction of law is still interesting and useful.

For the exercise proper, Aphthonius recommended that an introduction of law include considerations of these four topics: constitutionality, justice, expediency, and practicability. The composition should also include an introduction and should then state a counterargument as well. We composed an example of an introduction to law according to Aphthonius's instructions, and we imitated his introduction and conclusion where possible:

AN OPPOSITION TO A LAW THAT PERMITS ASSAULT WEAPONS

(INTRODUCTION): The Second Amendment is a straightforward claim, elegant in its spareness: "A well-regulated militia being necessary to the security of a free State, the right of the people to keep and bear arms shall not be infringed." I do not wish to oppose Americans' right to bear arms. I support Americans' right to bear arms, but I wish to place emphasis on the collective hinted at by the plural—Americans. For too long, this law has been interpreted as a personal right, one tied to a spirit of self-protection.

(CONSTITUTIONALITY AND CONSISTENCY): We might, however, recall that the law itself invokes one kind of security: that "of a free State." A state that allows the sale of assault weapons—semiautomatic firearms designed expressly for individual use—risks pitting citizen against citizen and violates the very spirit of the Second Amendment's call for a "well-regulated militia."

(JUSTICE): Ironically, when the personal-rights interpretation of the Second Amendment leads to the manufacture and sale of assault weapons on the market, the very security the law seeks to sustain through the regulation of weapons use becomes compromised, and the value of another important constitutional law—the right to life—is threatened. That is, the right to bear arms, when extended to arms designed expressly for killing a human being, becomes unjust.

(EXPEDIENCY): It is not expedient to leave security and protection in the hands of individual citizens by allowing such deadly weapons as semiautomatic rifles, pistols, and shotguns to be attained so easily. Citizens are not law enforcement officers, nor are they soldiers.

(PRACTICABILITY): Assault weapons sold on the free market will end up in the hands of criminals, which then leads to widespread feelings of vulnerability among citizens, which leads to an interpretation of the Second Amendment as applying to each individual citizen. Handguns are expensive and require training for safe use, and it is therefore impractical for every citizen to own an assault weapon. The result is that the distribution of such weapons becomes highly irregular; and this irregular distribution runs counter to the "well-regulated militia" guaranteed by the law.

(CONCLUSION): In the spirit of safety and security, the free-market sale of assault weapons should be prohibited. Those who manufacture and sell assault weapons for purposes other than police work ought to be held accountable when those weapons are used to commit murder.

Introduction of law should not be considered overly specialized—it is not just for justices and attorneys. Practice at introduction of law helps reveal the complexity of laws. And attending to what the law actually says can lead to more careful and thoughtful arguments regarding the meaning and application of particular laws, activities for which citizens of democracies have been responsible ever since the fifth century BCE. We have, for example, left hunting out of our proposal—a conspicuous omission—because the authors of the Second Amendment failed to say anything about quail or deer (and because hunters do not need or use assault weapons). Again, we would underscore the importance of thinking about how laws apply to our everyday lives. In the wake of the 2007 shootings at Virginia Tech, countless people invoked the Second Amendment: journalists reporting on the tragedy, and parents who wanted their children to be able to carry guns to campus. The incident, like the shootings at Columbine High School in Colorado eight years earlier, caused people to think anew about kinds of firearms and the meaning of the Second Amendment.

Introduction of law invites you to attack, defend, or refine all manner of laws, large or small. Since the Bill of Rights was added to the United States Constitution in 1791, all of its amendments have been interpreted and reinterpreted as a result of court cases. Attorneys and judges have argued that in certain cases, observance of the amendments is neither just nor expedient. We reprint the full texts of four amendments to the American Constitution in order to illustrate the heuristic potential of the Introduction of Law.

> Article I: Congress shall make no law respecting an establishment of religion, or prohibiting the free exercise thereof; or abridging the freedom of speech or of the press; or the right of the people peaceably to assemble, and to petition the Government for a redress of grievances.

Many questions have been raised by cases appealing to this amendment: Is it just to interpret the use of prayer in public school as an abridgement of religious freedom? Is it expedient to ban prayer from public schools? Is it just to protect hateful speech on the grounds that it is free speech? Does freedom of the press extend to the publication of information about the private habits of public figures? Is it expedient to restrict the press from publishing the names of rape victims?

> Article II: A well-regulated militia being necessary to the security of a free State, the right of the people to keep and bear arms shall not be infringed.

People who oppose gun control appeal to the Second Amendment as their constitutional ground for doing so. Should the protection offered by this amendment include the possession of assault weapons? Can Congress or the states ban the possession of guns or impose limits on their distribution without violating this amendment?

> Article IV: The right of the people to be secure in their persons, houses, papers, and effects, against unreasonable searches and seizures, shall not be violated,

and no warrants shall issue but upon probable cause, supported by oath or affirmation, and particularly describing the place to be searched, and the persons or things to be seized.

The Fourth Amendment implies that people cannot be searched without proper procedures. Does this so-called right to privacy include persons who carry dangerous weapons in public places, such as airplanes? What about people who break laws in their homes, such as those who keep and deal drugs? Is it just that they be protected from searches by authorities? Is it expedient? Recently, someone videotaped a couple who were making love in their home. They were not aware that they were being watched or taped. Did the person who made the tape violate the couple's Fourth Amendment rights? If so, was he justified in doing so? Was his act expedient?

> Article VIII: Excessive bail shall not be required, nor excessive fines imposed, nor cruel and unusual punishments inflicted.

People who oppose capital punishment do so on the basis of the Eighth Amendment, because they define the death penalty as cruel and unusual punishment. Is their position just? Is it expedient? Is it practical?

Try your hand at composing introductions to law that expound, defend, or attack some question raised by these amendments.

PROGYMNASMATA: INTRODUCTION OF LAW

1. Select one of the amendments or visit the Web site of The National Archives at http://www.archives.gov/ to find another amendment or federal law that is of interest to you. Compose an introduction to law that expounds, defends, or opposes some question raised by these amendments.

2. We have used many controversial issues—and related court cases—as examples in this book. Do some research on one of the exemplary issues that has generated many court cases: abortion, hateful speech, gun control, capital punishment. Find the relevant laws in your region that govern the issue, and write an Introduction of Law that explains a law to someone who is wholly unfamiliar with it.

3. Now revise your Introduction of Law for an audience that is hostile to your interpretation of the law.

WORKS CITED

Carvin, Andy. "The Wild World of Wikipedia: A Study in Contrasts." *Public Broadcasting Service*, June 30, 2006. http://www.pbs.org/teachers/learning. now/2006/06/the_wild_world_of_wikipediaa_s.html (accessed May 22, 2007)

Ford, Gerald. "Gerald Ford's Remarks on Taking the Oath of Office as President." August 9, 1974. http://www.ford.utexas.edu/LIBRARY/speeches/740001.htm.

Hall, Kermit. "R.A.V. vs. City of St. Paul." Answers Corporation. http://www.answers.com/topic/r-a-v-v-city-of-st-paul-1 (accessed May 30, 2007).

Matsen, Patricia P., Rollinson, Philip, and Sousa, Marion, eds. *Readings from Classical Rhetoric*. Carbondale: Southern Illinois University Press, 1990.

Obama, Barack. "Remarks of Illinois State Sen. Barack Obama against Going to War with Iraq." *Obama for America*, October 22, 2002. http://www.barackobama.com/issues/iraq/ (accessed May 27, 2007).

Pseudo Quintilian. "The Poor Man's Bees." Major Declamations to trans. Lewis A. Sussman. Frankfurt: Lang, 1987.

"The Travis Walton Affair." *Atlantis Publishing* http://www.space-2001.net/html/abduction.html (accessed May 29, 2007).

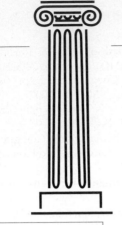

ARRANGEMENT: GETTING IT TOGETHER

For many arguments occur to us . . . but some of these are so unimportant as not to deserve notice, and some, even if they offer some amount of assistance . . . contain some flaw . . . while if nevertheless . . . there are numerous advantages and strong arguments, in my judgment those among them that are the least weighty or that closely resemble others that are weightier ought to be discarded and left out of the discourse: in my own case when I am collecting arguments for my cases I make it my practice not so much to count them as to weigh them.

—Cicero, *De Oratore*
II lxxvi 309

ANCIENT AUTHORITIES AGREED that arrangement was the second part of rhetoric and second in importance only to invention. In ancient rhetoric, arrangement primarily concerned two processes: selecting the arguments to be used and arranging these in an order that was clear and persuasive.

Ancient attitudes toward arrangement were very different from modern ones. In modern thought, the proper arrangement of a piece of discourse is often dictated by genre: there are formulas for arranging business letters, papers written in school, scientific reports, and even romance novels. The formulas are intended to insure that anyone who is used to reading these kinds of discourse can follow the argument without difficulty, since she knows what comes next if she knows the conventions.

While ancient discussions of arrangement were formal and prescriptive to some extent, ancient rhetors paid much more attention to rhetorical situations than to formal rules. For example, the composition of an introduction was determined by a rhetor's guess about the attitude of the targeted audience toward his *ethos* and his subject. Were they hostile to him or to his position? In this case he needed to diffuse this hostility somehow. If they were receptive, he could begin more directly. If audiences were familiar with the case, the rhetor did not need to tell them about its history. If they were uninformed and there was no skilled opponent, there was no need to anticipate and answer opposing arguments; thus a refutation was unnecessary in such a case. In other words, the composition and arrangement of the parts of a discourse were determined by a rhetor's informed guess about how listeners or readers would react to it and its author.

Arrangement, then, depends in large part on the rhetorical situation. Thus far, we've addressed *kairos* as a temporal concept, but for the ancients, it had a spatial dimension as well. In ancient literature, the term was used to indicate a vital part of the body. In fact, *kairos* indicated the critical spot or parts where wounds are fatal. In book 8 of the *Iliad*, for example, Nestor shoots Alexander "with an arrow upon the crown of the head where the foremost hairs of horses grow upon the skull, and where is the deadliest spot" (84, 326). In fact, the spatial dimension of *kairos* can be traced to the sport of archery, where it meant "a penetrable opening or an aperture" (White 1987, 13). It is easy to see how these earlier spatial meanings came to be used in the art of rhetoric as well; in Aeschylus's play *The Suppliant Maidens*, the King compared the act of speaking to archery, proclaiming that when a "tongue has shot arrows beside the mark," another speech may be necessary to make up for the words that weren't exactly on target (446).

Another way the spatial dimension of *kairos* informs the art of rhetoric is its usefulness for the canon of arrangement. The Greek term for arrangement, *taxis*, was originally used in military contexts to denote the arrangement of troops for battle. When considered this way, the connections between *kairos* and arrangement become clear: attention to *kairos* in arrangement means knowing when and where to marshal particular proofs. *Kairos* suggests the possibility of achieving an advantage with optimal placement of arguments, propitious timing, or a combination of the two. We believe that it is crucial to consider the spatial dimension of *kairos* along with Cicero's advice to weigh proofs and place them strategically. He wrote in *Orator* that "the results of [the orator's] invention he will set in order with great care" (xv, 50). Rhetors thus need to give careful attention to questions like these: Which of the arguments produced by invention should I use? Which should come first and which last? How should I order the others? Do I need to rehearse any information about the subject? Where should I do this? Do I need to address the audience? Where? What do I say to them? As always, the parameters of a rhetorical situation are determined by the time, the place, and the relevant actors: the rhetor and the audience.

ANCIENT TEACHINGS ABOUT ARRANGEMENT

Ancient discussions of arrangement were often lengthy and quite subtle, given the enormous range of possible rhetorical situations. As early as the fifth century BCE, sophistic rhetoricians may have realized that any discourse required several sections and that the need for certain sections of a discourse to perform certain tasks remained fairly constant in almost any situation. If so, they probably taught their students that a discourse required four parts: *prooemium* **(introduction), narration** (statement of the issue), proof, and conclusion.

In keeping with his general orientation toward simplicity of expression, Aristotle told his readers that a discourse really needed only two parts: a statement of the case and proof (*Rhetoric* III 13 1414a). The other parts were sometimes appropriate in certain kinds of discourse, but not in all. He grumpily dismissed the work of sophists like Theodorus and Licymnius, who, according to Aristotle, distinguished all sorts of "empty and silly" divisions of discourse, such as "narrative, additional narrative, preliminary narrative, refutation and additional refutation" (1414b). Aristotle agreed in this regard with his teacher Plato, who complained about the fancy elaborations of arrangement that had been invented by sophists, such as

> the exposition accompanied by direct evidence . . . indirect evidence . . . probabilities; besides which there are the proof and supplementary proof . . . and we are to have a refutation and supplementary refutation both for the prosecution and defense. . . . and covert allusion and indirect compliment and . . . indirect censure in mnemonic verse. (*Phaedrus* 266d–267a)

Perhaps intentionally, in this passage Plato confused sophistic topics, used in invention, with the sophists' teaching on arrangement. This was possible because sophistic treatises did not separate invention and arrangement, as Aristotle did; rather, they organized their treatises according to the parts of discourse and discussed the appropriate topics to be used within each part.

Aristotle's departure from this sophistic habit may have caused some confusion in later texts on rhetoric. Quintilian hovered between the two approaches. In books IV and V of the *Institutes*, he followed sophistic practice, discussing the topics that are appropriate to each part of a discourse. Then, in book VII, he started all over again, this time announcing that he would discuss arrangement as something separate from invention. But book VII turned out to be a discussion of *stasis* theory rather than of arrangement.

When Cicero was a young rhetoric student, rhetoric teachers apparently agreed that six parts were more or less standard in courtroom discourse. However, this division was often suggested for other sorts of discourse, as well. The six parts were an **exordium**, or introduction; a *narratio*, or statement of the issue; a *partitio*, or division of the issue into its constituent parts; *confirmatio*, where the rhetor's strongest arguments are made; *refutatio*, where arguments that can damage a rhetor's case are anticipated and refuted; and a *peroratio*, or conclusion.

Cicero's earliest work on rhetoric, *De Inventione*, included a clear and orderly exposition of this six-part division, and it adopted the sophistic habit of discussing appropriate topics within each part. Quintilian's approach was similar to Cicero's, although his treatment of arrangement is much fuller, since he gave rhetors subtle advice about artful arrangements that pointed up their rhetorical effects. As they did with invention, ancient commentators provided much more advice about arrangement than can ever be used in a given situation. In the rest of this chapter, we explore some of this rich advice, concentrating on a few topics and simply listing others that we suspect might kick-start the invention process for some readers on some occasions. As always, readers are urged to consult the relevant ancient texts if they find themselves wanting more advice about arrangement than we can provide here.

THE EXORDIUM

The term *exordium* comes from Latin words meaning "to urge forward." The English verb *exhort*, meaning "to urge earnestly," is descended from this term. Ancient rhetoricians gave copious advice for *exordia*, since this first part of a discourse often performs the important function of establishing an *ethos* (see Chapter 6). Indeed, Quintilian wrote that "the sole purpose of the exordium is to prepare our audience in such a way that they will be disposed to lend a ready ear to the rest of our speech" (IV i 5). However, in book III of the *Rhetoric*, Aristotle contended that the main purpose of the introduction was "to make clear what is the end *(telos)* of the discourse" (1415a). Other functions of introductions, according to Aristotle, include making the audience well disposed toward the rhetor and the issue and grabbing their attention. In any case, it is clear that ancient rhetoricians found many more uses for introductions than simply presenting the issue.

Apparently, ancient students sometimes tried to compose introductions before they had written a discourse to introduce, but Cicero warned his readers about the futility of composing the introduction first: "It does not follow that everything which is to be said first must be studied first; for the reason that, if you wish the first part of the discourse to have a close agreement and connection with the main statement of the case, you must derive it from the matters which are to be discussed afterward" (I xiv 19). In other words, you can't introduce arguments that haven't yet been composed. We suggest that you compose at least the narrative and the **confirmation** before you consider whether to include an exordium. Not all compositions require an introduction, and as we shall see, selection of the kind of introduction to be used depends upon the rhetorical situation.

Cicero suggested that, in general, *exordia* ought to be dignified and serious. They should not be vague or disconnected from the issues or the situation. Quintilian warned that students sometimes assume that audiences are acquainted with the facts of the case when they are not. If there is any doubt about how much an audience knows about a situation, the wisest course is to review the situation in the exordium in order to secure good-will of the audience.

The quality of the rhetor's case determines the kind of exordium required. Cicero discriminated five kinds of cases: **honorable, difficult, mean, ambiguous,** and **obscure**. An honorable case needs no introduction, since audiences will support it at once. All other sorts of cases need exordiums, since for some reason audiences will not receive them favorably. According to Cicero, a difficult case "has alienated the sympathy" of audiences, while audiences regard the mean case as "unworthy of serious attention" (*On Invention* I 20). In an ambiguous case, "the point for decision is doubtful, or the case is partly honorable and partly discreditable so that it engenders both goodwill and ill will." Last, a case is obscure either because the audience is too slow to understand it or because the case itself "involves matters which are rather difficult to grasp."

The Kinds of Cases

1. *Honorable:* has immediate support from audience.
2. *Difficult:* audience is unsympathetic to rhetor or to issues raised.
3. *Mean:* audience regards the rhetor or the issue as unimportant or uninteresting (in this context "mean" signifies "insignificant" or "trivial").
4. *Ambiguous:* audience is unsure about what is at issue; or issue is partly honorable and partly difficult.
5. *Obscure:* issue is too difficult for audience to understand, because they are uninformed or because it is complex.

Some cases are so difficult or controversial that they fall into several of these categories. In the present political climate, for instance, arguments about climate change can sometimes be controversial. Arguments made by the former vice president Al Gore, who advocates that the United States should adopt policies to halt global warming, are often made to indifferent or even hostile audiences. His case for climate change is difficult for two reasons: people who doubt the fact of climate change may also be dismissive of Gore himself because he was negatively portrayed by his opponents when he ran for president in 2000. The case may also be interpreted as a mean one because critics say there is no solid evidence of global warming. The case for global warming is also both ambiguous and obscure: it is ambiguous because audiences are not quite sure what will be expected of them if Gore's argument turns out to be correct; it is obscure in part because people cannot see immediate effects of global warming and in part because the case supporting global warming is very complex. For all these reasons, arguments concerning climate change require careful introduction at the present time.

Cicero recommended two sorts of exordia to handle this variety of cases: the introduction and the **insinuation.** An introduction "directly and in plain language makes the audience well-disposed, receptive and attentive." Introductions, on one hand, may be used in mean, ambiguous, and obscure cases, since here an audience is not hostile but only confused or

uninformed. Insinuation, on the other hand, should be used only in difficult cases, where an audience is hostile to a rhetor or to her position. Cicero
wrote that insinuation "unobtrusively steals into the mind" of audiences.
Using Cicero's definitions of the available kinds of cases, a rhetor should be
able to figure out whether she needs to compose an introduction or an
insinuation.

Introductions

As Cicero pointed out, honorable cases need no introduction of any kind,
because in such cases the rhetor is respected, the issue is not controversial,
and the audience is interested and attentive. Most other kinds of cases
require introduction. Difficult cases, however, may require insinuation
rather than introduction.

In a mean case, a rhetor must use the introduction to convince his audience that his position on the issue is important to them and, hence, make
them attentive. People who go door-to-door in order to sell a product or to
convert people to a new belief often find that the person who opens the
door considers their case to be a mean one. Experienced door-to-door pros-
elytizers usually begin their presentations with a dramatic question
intended to demonstrate that the audience is deeply implicated in whatever is being advocated—"are you tired of cleaning up your yard by yourself?" or "has someone in your family recently become ill or died?"
Another way to demonstrate the importance of a mean case is to heighten
its drama and impact on an audience. In his presentations about climate
change, for instance, Al Gore shows a series of dramatic and beautiful photographs that illustrate the effects of global warming—icecaps melting,
beaches eroding, polar bears struggling to find firm footing. The photographs are meant to demonstrate to audiences that climate change has
real effects that will in time affect their daily lives.

On occasion, mean cases are so trivial that writers must compose an
insinuation to introduce them. Here is George Meyer introducing a column
about his love of attending conferences:

> I have been called a voluptuary, a sybarite, a hedonist, a creep. I am all of these
> things. I cannot live without pleasure. It is my oxygen—though I must also
> have regular oxygen.
>
> Our existence is but an eyeblink. Why, then, should a man not chase down
> his passions, wrestle them to the dirt, and ride them like ostriches? He should,
> and I have.
>
> Speedboats have been a lifelong diversion. Scotch, a serious problem. Yet no
> vice bedevils me like my one desperate fixation, my shameful ravening itch: I
> simply must attend conferences.

Meyer keeps his readers attentive both by the sheer attractiveness of his
ethos and the cleverness of his writing. We read through three paragraphs
before we are introduced to the topic of the essay. And it's a good thing

too, because as a focus for an article, going to conferences isn't all that scintillating.

An ambiguous case is one where there is some doubt about the issue—that is, the audience for some reason does not understand the issue, has confused it with another issue, or has doubt about the morality of the issue (that is, the audience must be shown that the issue can be defended on moral grounds). In such a case, a rhetor should begin by clarifying the moral ambiguity.

Claims about the events of September 11, 2001 present rhetors with an ambiguous case because at least two accounts of these events are in circulation. The official account says that nineteen members of a militant group called Al-Qaeda, led by Osama bin Laden, hijacked four planes and crashed three of them into the World Trade Center and the Pentagon while the fourth crashed into a field in Pennsylvania. An alternative account of these events claims that they could not have taken place unless someone in the American government either let them happen or participated in their planning. This case is logically ambiguous because the available evidence and inferences that can be made from it, read one way, seem to support the official version while, read another, they may support the alternative version. For instance, the available facts show that none of the hijacked planes (with the possible exception of Flight 93, which crashed in Pennsylvania) were intercepted by American military aircraft. Is this defensive failure to be explained by incompetence (the official version) or something more nefarious (the revisionist version)? The case is also morally ambiguous because the several disasters that occurred on September 11 caused great harm, killing nearly three thousand people and damaging property that was both symbolically and financially important; clearly these acts were immoral. However, the moral consequences of incompetence are quite different than those accruing to complicity, and it is this difference that gives rise to moral ambiguity in this case.

One of the logical ambiguities raised in this argument is attached to the term *conspiracy*. People who doubt the official account of the events of September 11 are often denigrated as *conspiracy theorists*. In response, they point out that the official account is also a conspiracy theory, if *conspiracy* is defined as it is in *Webster's College Dictionary* as "planning and acting together secretly especially for a harmful or unlawful purpose, such as murder or treason." This objection does not always satisfy those who support the official account and who typically use *conspiracy theorist* as a synonym for *crazy*, however. And so those who support a revisionist account try to clarify the moral ambiguity inherent in the case by pointing out that debunkers of the official account may have a high moral purpose insofar as they are interested in finding out the truth of the matter. Indeed, these revisionists call themselves "The 9/11 Truth Movement."

David Ray Griffin, a prominent member of the 9/11 Truth Movement, clearly realizes the ambiguous nature of the group's argument. He begins one of his books on the issue by telling about his own reluctance to consider the evidence in favor of an alternate explanation:

Until the spring of 2003, I had not seriously looked at any of the evidence. I was vaguely aware that there were people, at least on the Internet, who were suggesting a revisionist account of 9/11, according to which US officials were complicit. But I did not take the time to find their websites. I was busy writing a history of American imperialism, which I had begun the day after 9/11. Having accepted the official account of the 9/11 attacks, I had also accepted the liberal interpretation thereof, according to which they were "blowback" for US foreign policy, especially in the Arab and Muslim worlds. This interpretation convinced me that the large book on global problems on which I had been working for several years would be incomplete without a separate chapter on American imperialism.

Studying this history probably helped me later change my interpretation of 9/11, because I learned that several of our nation's wars, such as those against Mexico, the Philippines, and Vietnam, had been justified by incidents that, although they were actually created by our own armed forces, were used to claim that we had been attacked. But this awareness did not lead me immediately to conclude that 9/11 had also been orchestrated as a pretext. Although that possibility did cross my mind, I did not take it seriously.

I maintained this mindset even after being introduced, late in 2002, to a professor from another country who said he was quite certain that 9/11 had been an inside job. I remember replying that I did not think the Bush administration—even the Bush administration—would do such a heinous thing. However, I added, I would be wiling to look at whatever he considered the best evidence. He directed me to some 9/11 websites, but I did not find them convincing. I do not know if they were bad sites or whether I looked at their evidence with less than a 30-percent open mind. In any case, I went back to working on American imperialism, assuming 9/11 not to be an instance thereof.

My response was quite different, however, a few months later when another colleague sent a different website, which had an abbreviated version of Paul Thompson's massive 9/11 timeline. Although this timeline was drawn entirely from mainstream sources, it contained hundreds of stories that contradicted one or another aspect of the official account of 9/11. Additional reading then led me to Nafeez Ahmed's *The War on Freedom: How and Why America Was Attacked September 11, 2001*. On the basis of the combined evidence summarized by Thompson and Ahmed, it took me only a short time to realize that there was strong prima facie evidence that the Bush administration had, at the very least, intentionally allowed the attacks to occur. Through additional study, I became aware that some of the strongest evidence indicated that forces within the government must have actually orchestrated the attacks. (2007, 1–2)

Griffin attempts to erase the ambiguity of the case posed by 9/11 by tracing the path of his own slow rejection of one explanation for the other. In the process, he manages to enhance his *ethos* as a reasonable person who has done his homework, reminding us that he did a lot of reading and tried to make careful judgments about that reading before he reached a decision.

In an obscure case, the audience for some reason cannot follow the arguments used in support of an issue. In this case, an audience may be made receptive if a rhetor states her case in plain language and briefly explains the points to be discussed. This should make her audience receptive, even though her arguments may be difficult for them to follow. Here is Michael Wolff's introduction to an article about private equity—which is surely an obscure issue for most people:

> I've started thinking about private equity, not as a financing concept or a professional undertaking, but as a way of life, an organizing social principle, a behavioral standard. Private equity—owning stuff with other people's money is a fairly good working definition—has become something that, as a reasonably educated, more or less adroit and socially well-adjusted person, you ought to naturally want, even fairly deserve, to be part of. Not taking part, not having such an ownership interest, starts to suggest you're odd, guileless, without pride. (2007, 108)

Early on Wolff provides a quick and simple definition of private equity. But the rhetorical effect of this introduction depends heavily on his construction of his *ethos*, as a regular guy who just wants to be part of a trend. If readers are made curious by his interesting definition, or if they find his *ethos* persuasive, they will continue to read despite their unfamiliarity with the issue of private equity.

Topics for Making Audiences Attentive and Receptive

It is necessary to explain to an audience why they should pay attention to a discourse if the issue taken up in the discourse is ambiguous, mean, or obscure. Cicero composed a list of topics for making an audience attentive in such cases. He recommended that rhetors show that "the matters we are about to discuss are important, novel, or incredible, or that they concern all humanity or those in the audience or some illustrious people or the immortal gods or the general interest of the state" (23). In other words, rhetors should tie their claims to something that the audience will think important or interesting.

Cicero also provided a list of topics for securing goodwill from the audience so that they will be receptive to the rhetor. He wrote that goodwill "is to be had from four quarters: from our own person, from the person of the opponents, from the persons of the jury, and from the case itself" (22). A rhetor's *ethos* may be a source of goodwill if she refers to her actions and services to the community; if she weakens any negative charges that have been made against her; if she elaborates on her misfortunes or difficulties; or if she humbly asks an audience for their attention. For example, a rhetor discussing climate change can say why she is interested in this issue. She can mention any experience that qualifies her as a knowledgeable person on the issue. If she is a member of a group that is interested in establishing policies for dealing with climate change, she can mention that, too. Or she can simply ask her audience to pay attention to the issue because it is important to their community.

Here are the opening paragraphs of a short piece on global warming written by biologist E. O. Wilson:

> Homo sapiens is not a physically imposing species—and in terms of biomass does not take up much room. If the bodies of all 6.5 billion human beings alive on earth today were log-stacked, they would fill less that a cubic mile. They could be lowered out of sight in some small corner or other of the Grand Canyon. Our musculature is even less imposing. Thin and wobbly-headed, we appear to have arisen by natural selection to run marathons across African savannas in pursuit of antelope and other strongly built but short-winded animal prey. (2007, 164)

Wilson immediately establishes his *ethos* as a person who is well-informed about the history of the human species by providing vivid details about our evolution. This *ethos* puts him in position to claim that human beings, despite their puniness, have "created a real mess" and are now in a position to wreck "our planetary world." His argument (and his *ethos*) are supplemented by a number of colorful maps developed by scientists at the universities of Michigan and Sheffield (UK) showing the depletion of plant life and the range of worldwide recycling efforts, among other things.

A rhetor can weaken the *ethos* of persons who oppose her point of view if she can "bring them into hatred, unpopularity, or contempt" (1.16.22), according to Cicero's *De Inventione*. She can do this by presenting their actions in a negative light; by showing that they have misused any extrinsic advantages they enjoy, such as "power, political influence, wealth, family connections" (1.16.22); or by revealing their unpreparedness on the issue. A rhetor who urges our attention to climate change can characterize those who deny its reality as obstructionist or ignorant, features that are especially serious if her opponents enjoy prestige or power. Or she can say that people who scoff at the reality of climate change are in denial and out of touch with the latest scientific assessments of the situation.

A rhetor can derive goodwill from the audience by showing his respect for them, or by stating "how eagerly their judgment and opinion are awaited" (1.6.22). Using this topic, a rhetor who supports policies that reduce global warming might urge his audience to examine his arguments, accept them, and join him in working against the resistance of those who deny the importance of his position. Last, goodwill may come from the circumstances themselves "if we praise and exalt our own case, and depreciate our opponent's with contemptuous allusions."

Topics for Making Audiences Attentive

1. Show importance of issue.
2. Show how issue affects audience.
3. Show how issue affects everyone.
4. Show how issue affects general good of the community.

Topics for Making Audiences Receptive

1. Strengthen your *ethos*.
2. Weaken *ethos* of those who oppose rhetor.
3. Show respect for audience.
4. Praise issue or position while denigrating position of opponents.

Notice how Adam Robinson follows Cicero's advice as he opens his book on Osama bin Laden:

> Imagine for a moment that you awoke one morning to discover that your relative—brother, cousin, uncle—was a mass murderer. Imagine that it was September 12, 2001, and the pendulum of guilt for the destruction of the twin towers of the World Trade Center in New York was swinging in the direction of a member of your family. Imagine, if you can, the revulsion and helplessness that you might feel—almost as strongly as those who lost friends and loved ones in the tragedy. Imagine your exemplary past crushed beneath the weight of those tragic towers.
>
> This numbing reality is what the Binladin family of Saudi Arabia faced. On that morning, on the other side of the world, the responsibility for this callous act of terrorism was being laid squarely at the door of one of their own clan, Osama bin Laden. (2001, 11)

Certainly bin Laden's importance is not in question, since he is widely thought to be the leader of a terrorist organization that plotted the horrible events of September 11, 2001. It is not difficult, then, to make audiences attentive to a book about this notorious man. The rhetor does have to make his audience receptive, though, because many readers will think of a book about bin Laden as a dishonorable case. Anyone who wants a receptive audience for a book about him has somehow to humanize its subject. Robinson does this by asking readers to sympathize with—perhaps even identify with—shocked and grieving members of bin Laden's family.

Insinuations

In a difficult case, if, on one hand, audiences are not completely hostile to a rhetor's point of view, he may risk composing an introduction that acquaints the reader with the issue and his position on it; on the other hand, if they are adamantly opposed, either to his *ethos* or his position on the issue, he should compose an insinuation. Cicero wrote that audiences are hostile if "there is something scandalous in the case," or if they are already convinced that a rhetor's point of view is wrong, or if they are weary. If there is something scandalous in the case, a rhetor should simply admit that he, too, is scandalized by it but should add that neither he nor his audience is tainted by the scandal. For example, if a rhetor thinks that the legal right to free speech is more important than the moral obligation to avoid hurting others, he might begin an argument as follows:

INSINUATION FOR A SCANDALOUS CASE

Like any other decent person, I am offended by hateful speech. Its use is ugly and hurtful. Nonetheless, as a good American I support Don Imus's First Amendment freedom to say whatever he likes, and thus I cannot support his being fired for making racist and sexist comments.

If an audience is hostile for ideological reasons, again, the rhetor should simply admit the difference of opinion, and be ready to attack the strongest argument against him or his position.

INSINUATION IN A CASE WHERE THERE IS A DIFFERENCE OF OPINION

I realize that you and I do not agree about the unfettered use of hateful speech on our nation's airways. However, I ask you to consider my arguments carefully before you dismiss them out of hand.

If an audience is weary, in contrast, a rhetor should promise to be brief.

INSINUATION IN A CASE WHERE AUDIENCE IS WEARY

Since I know that you are tired of hearing about this issue, I will keep my arguments short and to the point.

In sum, there are many available topics for composing an insinuation:

Topics for Insinuations
1. If audience is hostile, admit difference of opinion.
2. If issue is unsavory, admit this.
3. If audience is tired, promise to be brief.

THE NARRATIVE (STATEMENT OF THE CASE)

In the narrative, a rhetor states the issue as clearly and simply as she can. If the rhetor's argument centers on a conjectural issue, the narrative may be a simple statement of the conjecture:

SAMPLE NARRATIVES FOR CONJECTURAL CASE

Global warming is occurring.
   If global warming is occurring, its effects are not as massive as they have been made out to be.
   Global warming is a myth.

Any statement of the issue should depict a state of affairs in ways that favor the rhetor's position. Quintilian pointed out that statements of the case should be in keeping with the facts we desire to be believed: "We shall for instance represent a person accused of theft as covetous, accused of adultery as lustful, accused of homicide as rash, or attribute the opposite qualities to these persons if we are defending them; further we must do the same with place, time and the like" (IV ii 52). A rhetor who accepts that global warming is occurring, then, might compose a statement of the issue such as this one:

> To deny the evidence in support of global warming is to be pigheaded and obstinate.

A rhetor who doubts that global warming is occurring, on the other hand, might compose the statement of the case in this way:

> All of the evidence that has been marshaled in support of global warming is either mistaken or misapplied.

Here are some sample narratives for other kinds of cases:

1. *A definitive narrative:* Global warming may be defined as the increase in the average temperature of the earth's near-surface air and oceans in recent decades. Defined in this way, it is clear that the phenomenon is not new; the surfaces of the earth and its oceans have been hotter than they are now during many other periods in the planet's history. If this is the case, human beings may not be responsible for the current rise in the earth's temperature.
2. *A narrative about values:* Those who deny global warming place more importance on the greed of corporation than upon the lives of generations to come.
3. *A procedural narrative:* We must take immediate steps to reduce the level of greenhouse gas emissions in order to slow the process of global warming.

According to Cicero, the narrative may be omitted if the audience is familiar with the issue or if some other rhetor has already mentioned it. He recommended that it not be mentioned at all at the beginning of the discourse if the case were unpopular or if the audience were hostile to the rhetor's point of view. Quintilian disagreed vociferously on this point, however. To omit the statement of the case, he huffed, was tantamount to saying that it was worthless or dishonorable: "Nothing can be more easy, except perhaps to throw up the case altogether" (IV ii 66). If Quintilian is correct, audiences should be suspicious of discourse whose authors make no statement of their position on the issue at hand.

Ancient authorities agreed that the narrative should be clear, concise, and brief, as it is not meant to be persuasive and a clear statement of the issue lends credibility to a rhetor. Quintilian admired Cicero's use of seeming simplicity in his defense of Milo. Cicero stated the case as follows: "Milo, on the other hand, having been in the senate all day till the house rose, went home, changed his shoes and clothes, and waited for a short time, while his wife was getting ready" (57). This simple narrative not only indicated Milo's casual behavior on the day he supposedly murdered Claudio; Cicero's use of ordinary, everyday speech lulled the jury into thinking of Milo as an ordinary person, like themselves, going through an ordinary day.

For any number of reasons, a rhetor may not be satisfied with a simple statement of the case. Sometimes it is useful to give an audience some background or history about the issue so that they can understand why it is important to them. Cicero suggested that a narrative could contain an account of the reasons why an issue is being disputed; a digression to attack the opposition, amuse the audience, or amplify their understanding of the case by comparisons; and/or a true-seeming fiction that is analogous to the case, drawn either from history or literature or created by the rhetor. Sometimes it is very important to establish precisely why there is dispute about an issue.

The astronomer who wants a city to implement a dark-sky ordinance might compose a narrative like this:

> The police have expressed concern that a dark-sky ordinance will interfere with levels of light necessary to protect citizens at night; however, streetlights do not interfere with our astronomical observations. Our proposal, then, will not require nighttime lighting to be below safety levels, although it may impact other sorts of lighting such as illuminated advertisements.

This narrative explains exactly why the astronomer's proposal is controversial. Here is another example of a narrative that shows why a position is disputed by one or more opponents:

> There are still a few people who doubt that global warming is occurring, and among those who do accept it as fact, there are still some who doubt that the process is caused by human beings. I will show that prominent members of both of these groups are being paid by corporations whose profits will be reduced if greenhouse gas emission controls are widely adopted.

As the previous example illustrates, a rhetor may also use the narrative to attack the position of those who oppose him. Graydon Carter, the editor of *Vanity Fair*, began his introduction to the magazine's annual green issue with such a narrative: "It is an ongoing mystery to me why Republican administrations are such wretched protectors of our land, inasmuch as Republicans own so much of it" (2007, 46). This narrative takes two whacks at those who oppose environmental protections, suggesting that they are inept and greedy to boot.

A rhetor may also add a vivid historical or fictional example to the narrative. Such an example should be chosen for its relevance to the issue— that is, it should be analogous to the actual facts of the case. A rhetor who supports the adoption of polices that will curb global warming can paint a grim picture of how the world will look in 2050 if nothing is done to change the current levels of emissions. Or she can resort to a fabulous or historical example wherein environmental change caused disastrous results. From what we know of the earth's history, there are many of these examples, such as the disaster that wiped out the dinosaurs and the desertification of the African savannah. Many fictions depict the effects of environmental disaster; novels include David Brin's *Earth,* Ursula Le Guin's *Always Coming Home,* and Kurt Vonnegut's *Cat's Cradle;* films about environmental disasters include *The Day After Tomorrow* and *Waterworld.*

THE PARTITION

A partition can perform two functions: it can name the issues in dispute, and it can list the arguments to be used in the order they will appear. Not every argument requires a partition; if only one point is to be made, a narrative will suffice. In a complex argument, partition is very helpful to an audience. First of all, it clarifies for them which issues need to be addressed by any party to the argument. Second, it announces the order in which proofs appear, thus making the discourse easier to follow. These uses of a partition, then, have the ethical effect of making rhetors seem intelligent and well-disposed toward an audience. Partitions may list any number of arguments from one to many, depending on the length and complexity of the composition. On most speaking occasions, rhetors should not try to develop more than two or three lines of argument, and the same is true of short papers. Authors of books have more latitude, of course, and they often present outlines of chapters in their preface or introductory chapter; such an outline can serve as the partition for a lengthy argument.

Rhetors who have used stasis theory during invention should be quite clear about which issues need to be discussed and which do not. The rhetor who wishes to implement environmental policies that will slow or halt global warming, for example, should know whether anyone disputes that global warming is in fact taking place. If there is debate on this point (and there still is as of this writing), she is obligated to discuss the dispute and the grounds upon which people disagree about global warming, and she may say in a partition that she plans to do so. If all parties in the rhetor's target audience agree that global warming is occurring, she may move on to a disputed definition; if all agree about a definition of global warming, she may move to the issues of value that are involved in the discussion; and if all agree on those, she may then discuss procedures that ought to be used (or not) to regulate it.

PARTITIONS FOR A CONJECTURAL ARGUMENT

Global warming is occurring, and its effects will be disastrous for the population of the earth: in many parts of the world, the air will be unbreathable and the water undrinkable.

Global warming is occurring, and I will review the evidence that shows that this warming is caused at least in part by greenhouse gas emissions and the clear-cutting of forests.

A PARTITION FOR AN ARGUMENT OF DEFINITION

I define global warming as the increase in the average temperature of the earth's near-surface air and oceans in recent decades. The effects of this phenomenon include changes in the weather, the erosion of beaches, and the rising level of tides worldwide.

A PARTITION FOR AN ARGUMENT ABOUT QUALITY

Global warming will have disastrous effects on all the earth's species. Today I am concerned with its effects on marine life, particularly edible fish and shellfish.

A PARTITION FOR A POLICY ARGUMENT

The countries of the world must begin now to enact policies that will stem or curb global warming. In particular, all parties must sign the Kyoto protocol and begin implementing its provisions.

As we noted above, a partition may also announce the order in which supporting arguments appear in the discourse to follow. This is a courtesy to listeners and readers. Quintilian argued that this sort of partition

> not only makes our arguments clearer by isolating the points from the crowd in which they would otherwise be lost and placing them before the eyes of the judge, but relieves his attention by assigning a definite limit to certain parts of our speech, just as our fatigue upon a journey is relieved by reading the distances on the milestones which we pass. (IV v 22–23)

Ancient authorities agreed that a partition, like a narrative, ought to be clear and brief.

Here are the opening paragraphs of an essay about the death of Abraham Lincoln, written by Adam Gopnik. The partition appears at the very end of our excerpt:

> This all began on a very long plane ride, East Coast to West, when I was reading Doris Kearns Goodwin's *Team of Rivals*, her book about Abraham Lincoln and his political competitors, and how, in the course of the Civil War, he turned them into a collegial Cabinet. It is a well-told, many-sided story, which attempts to give context to Lincoln without diminishing him, to place him among his peers and place him above them, too.
>
> Coming to the end of the book, to the night of April 14, 1865, and Lincoln's assassination, I reached the words that were once engraved in every American mind. At 7:22 A.M., as Lincoln drew his last breath, all the worthies who had crowded into a little back bedroom in a boarding house across the street from Ford's Theatre turned to Edwin Stanton, Lincoln's formidable Secretary of War, for a final word. Stanton is the one with the long comic beard and the spinster's spectacles, who in the photographs looks a bit like Mr. Pickwick but was actually the iron man in the Cabinet, and who, after a difficult beginning, had come to revere Lincoln as a man and a writer and a politician—had even played something like watchful Horatio to his tragic Hamlet. Stanton stood still, sobbing, and then said, simply, "Now he belongs to the ages."

It's probably the most famous epitaph in American biography, and still perhaps the best; reading the words again, I felt a shiver. They seem perfectly chosen, in their bare and stoical evocation of a Lincoln who belongs to history alone, their invocation not of an assumption to an afterlife but of a long reign in the corridors of time, a man now part of eternity.

Overcome again by Lincoln's example—by the idea of a President who was at once an interesting mind, a tough customer, and a good writer—I decided to start reading the new Lincoln literature. It seemed to be multiplying by fission, as amoebas do, on the airport bookstore shelves. For the flight home, I picked up James L. Swanson's *Manhunt*, a vivid account of the assassination and the twelve-day search for John Wilkes Booth that followed. Once again, I came to the deathbed scene, the vigil, the gathering. The Reverend Dr. Gurley, the Lincoln family minister, said, "'Let us pray.' He summoned up . . . a stirring prayer. . . . Gurley finished and everyone murmured 'Amen.' Then, no one dared to speak. Again Stanton broke the silence. 'Now he belongs to the angels.' "

Now he belongs to the angels? Where had *that* come from? There was a Monty Python element here ("What was that? I think it was 'Blessed are the cheesemakers,'" the annoyed listeners too far from the Mount say to each other in *Life of Brian*), but was there something more going on? I flipped to the back of the book. In the endnotes, Swanson explained that his rendering was deliberately at variance with the scholarly consensus: "In my view, shared by Jay Winik, the most persuasive interpretation supports 'angels' and is also more consistent with Stanton's character and faith."

Well, that seemed circumspect enough. Even without having read Jay Winik, though, one could glimpse, just visible beneath the diaphanous middle of that endnote, the tracings of an ideological difference. Unlike Goodwin, a famous liberal, Swanson is a conservative legal scholar at the Heritage Foundation. And Stanton's words as they are normally quoted are (like the Lincoln Memorial) a form of American neoclassicism, at odds with the figure of Christian nobility prized by the right: Lincoln's afterlife lies not in Heaven but in his vindication by history. Does he belong to the angels or the ages? This small implicit dispute echoed, in turn, a genuine historical debate: between those historians who insist on a tough Lincoln, the Lincoln whom Edmund Wilson, in *Patriotic Gore*, saw as an essentially Bismarckian figure—a cold-blooded nationalist who guaranteed the unity of the North American nation, a stoic emperor in a stovepipe hat whose essential drive was for power, his own and his country's—and those who, like Goodwin, see a tender, soulful Lincoln, a figure of almost saintly probity and patience who ended slavery, deepened in faith as the war went on, and fought hard without once succumbing to hatred. A Lincoln for the ages and a Lincoln for the angels already existed. Now the two seemed to be at war for his epitaph. (2007, 30–31)

This introduction ends with a dual partition setting up the question that intrigued Gopnik: whether Stanton relegated Lincoln to the ages or to the angels. Gopnik is careful to establish the importance of this question for historians: how seriously religious was Lincoln? And did his friend Stanton want to convey Lincoln's religiosity? Or was he alluding to what he surely knew even then would be Lincoln's legacy as one of the greatest American presidents? He also uses the partition to classify the work of historians and to illuminate their different "takes" on Lincoln. Gopnik uses this dual partition to structure his essay, and it proves surprisingly useful to him as he reviews recent historical literature on Lincoln.

THE ARGUMENTS: CONFIRMATION AND REFUTATION

Once the statement of the case is clear, the rhetor presents the arguments she has derived by means of invention. Ancient rhetoricians called this portion of the discourse the "confirmation," since it confirms or validates the material given in the narrative and partition. As a reminder of the possibilities opened by invention, we list strategies discussed in earlier chapters of this book.

1. Consideration of the rhetorical situation: arguments from *kairos*, and from consideration of the relative power of rhetor and audience.
2. The *staseis*: issues of conjecture, definition, quality, and policy.
3. The common topics: arguments from conjecture, degree, and possibility.
4. The commonplaces: arguments in general circulation and arguments from ideologic.
5. *Logos:* arguments available in the issue itself—enthymemes, inductive arguments, examples, maxims, or signs.
6. *Ethos:* arguments from the rhetor's intelligence, good moral character, and goodwill toward the audience and arguments that establish the appropriate voice and distance for the rhetorical situation at hand.
7. *Pathos:* arguments that appeal to the emotions by painting vivid pictures and using honorific or pejorative language.
8. Extrinsic proofs: data and testimony from reliable authorities.
9. The sophistic topics: arguments found by means of definition, division, similarities, and contrasts.

A rhetor who has worked through some or all of these strategies for invention should have discovered most of the confirming arguments that are available for use in the rhetorical situation for which she is preparing to speak or write.

Not every argument that is available can or should be used, of course; rhetors should select only those arguments that will be most persuasive to a given audience, and they must keep time or length requirements in mind. Quintilian gave some advice for selecting and ordering arguments. He recommended that the strongest arguments be treated singly and at more length, while the weakest arguments (if they must be used) should all be grouped together. In this way, he wrote, "they may not have the overwhelming force of a thunderbolt, but they will have all the destructive force of hail" (V xii 5). Or a rhetor can alternate strong and weak arguments. In any case, Quintilian recommended that the weakest arguments not appear last.

Sometimes it is necessary for a rhetor to anticipate arguments that might damage her *ethos* or her case if her audience accepts them. The ancients called this process **"refutation."** Thorough attention to invention should disclose arguments that need to be anticipated and refuted. For instance, if a rhetor who supports the official account of the events of September 11, 2001 is speaking or writing to a group of people who are skeptical of that account, she must refute their likely assumption that she has some reason, beyond the factual or logical evidence, for denying government complicity in those events. That is, she must defend herself against the charge, spoken or unspoken, that she is ideologically or financially committed to the government's policies or practices. On the other hand, someone who accepts the revisionist account of 9/11 must refute the charge often made by supporters of the official account—that she is a conspiracy theorist (which is code for *nuts*)—before she can expect a respectful hearing of her position on the issue.

THE PERORATION (CONCLUSION)

According to Cicero, a rhetor may do three things in a peroration: sum up her arguments, cast anyone who disagrees with her in a negative light, and arouse sympathy for herself, her clients, or her case.

Composing a Summary

A summary, if included in the discourse, should review all the issues named in the partition and briefly recall how each was supported. Cicero and Quintilian both recommended that a summary be clear and brief. If a rhetor chooses to make emotional appeals or to enhance her *ethos* in the conclusion of her remarks, however, both rhetoricians recommended that she use all her art and skill on these parts of the discourse, since they constitute the last impression she leaves with an audience. As Quintilian wrote, rhetors who have spoken or written well are "in a position, now that we have emerged from the reefs and shoals, to spread all our canvas" (VI 1 52).

Composing Appeals to the Emotions

Cicero listed fifteen topics that could be used to appeal to the emotions in a peroration. The first of these was authority, in which a rhetor calls on whatever authorities are most revered in a community to establish the importance or urgency of her position. For Cicero's audiences, authorities were the gods as well as "ancestors, kings, states, nations, people of supreme wisdom, the senate, the people and authors of laws" (*On Invention* I 101). In American rhetoric, concluding appeals are often made to the authority of religious texts such as the Christian Bible or to historically important documents such as the Constitution. Rhetors appeal as well to the authority accorded to respected public figures (usually dead) such as Ben Franklin, Thomas Jefferson, or Martin Luther King Jr.

When Congressman Dennis Kucinich announced that he would run in the 2008 presidential election, he closed his speech by appealing to three different kinds of authority in as many paragraphs:

> Einstein once said "the significant problems we have cannot be solved at the same level of thinking with which we created them." Yet that is what we are in Washington with respect to Iraq. Even though we know that our presence in Iraq is totally wrong, we seem unable to do anything about it, except keep spending more money for the war. We must end this march of folly. Together we are going to change this and rescue our nation. This is a moment that we need to call our Democratic leaders to courage. This is about leadership, clear vision and integrity. The people were behind us in November. They are behind us now. We must stand by our word and bring the troops home now.
>
> I am the only member of the House and the Senate running for President who has consistently voted against funding for the war, based on a principled opposition.
>
> I was against the war then. I am against it now. A leader must have not just hindsight, but foresight. The prophet Isaiah said "Without vision, a people perish." I am stepping forth at this moment because I believe, as did Lincoln that "this nation, under God, shall have a new birth of freedom and that government of the people, by the people and for the people shall not perish from this earth." Thank you. (2006)

Perhaps Kucinich's choice to appeal to a mathematician, a prophet, and a well-regarded president is related to his relatively slim chances for being chosen as the Democratic candidate.

The second topic names people who are affected by the state of affairs promoted or deplored by the rhetor and vividly describes its effects on them. Under this topic the rhetor may comment on the size of the group affected; if it is very large, this is more serious than if it is very small. The effects of global warming are, of course, universal—all the peoples of the world, as well as all plant and animal species, will be affected by it if it is not slowed or stopped. The argument about what really happened on September 11 is most crucial to Americans, of course, but it too has global importance, particularly for people defined as "terrorists" in America's "War on Terror."

The third topic inquires what would happen if the state of affairs remains unchanged or if it is changed in the way recommended by the rhetor. For example, Brian Urstadt's investigation of the peak oil movement finds activists using this topic quite frequently. According to Urstadt, at a meeting in 2006, Richard Heinberg, "unofficial leader" of the peak oil movement, presents a grim picture of what will happen if we do not prepare for the depletion of fossil fuels:

> The economy will begin an endless contraction, a prelude to the "grid crash." Cars will revert to being a luxury item, isolating the suburban millions from food and goods. Industrial agriculture will wither, addicted as it is to natural gas for fertilizer and to crude oil for flying, shipping, and trucking its produce. International trade will halt, leaving the Wal-Marts empty. In the United States, Northern homes will be too expensive to heat and Southern homes will roast. Dirty alternatives such as coal and tar sands will act as a bellows to the furnace of global warming. In response to all of this, extreme political movements will form, and the world will devolve into a fight to control the last of the resources. Whom the wars do not kill starvation will. Man, if he survives, will do so in agrarian villages. (2006, 32)

Later in the piece, Urstadt offers a glimpse of alternatives presented at another group meeting. With planning, the argument goes, life might not be so bad: "One woman…suggested tearing up all the asphalt and turning the avenues into gardens. Bicycles would glide along paths in the shadows of the buildings. It was a beautiful image and it was roundly applauded" (34). With this topic, a rhetor presents undesirable scenarios resulting from inaction next to desirable scenarios resulting from following the rhetor's argument.

The fourth topic for peroration shows that the issue affects many people in other similar locations who will apply the outcome of this discussion to their own cases. When attorneys argue cases before the Supreme Court, for example, they often point out that any decision made by the justices will affect not only those Americans who are presently alive but will impact future generations as well.

The fifth topic warns "that in other cases a false decision has been changed when the truth was learned, and the wrong has been righted; but in this case, once the decision has been made it cannot be changed" (I lii 102). This possibility can be illustrated by the Supreme Court decision that stopped recounting of Florida ballots in the presidential election of 2000; once that decision was made, a winner was declared and the opponent felt he had no choice except to capitulate. Or, in another example of this topic, a rhetor who opposes regulation of hateful speech on the nation's airwaves might argue that imposition of such a policy would restrain talk show hosts from speaking their minds on important issues for fear their words would be construed as hateful speech.

The sixth topic addresses whether or not the state of affairs under discussion results from someone's intentions or whether it is unintentional or accidental; Cicero wrote that "misdeeds should not be pardoned, but sometimes inadvertent acts may be forgiven" (I lii 102). Certainly, innocent utterances can be mistakenly construed as hateful speech, and these should be treated differently than utterances meant to hurt or anger someone. The rhetor opposed to regulation could argue that a regulatory policy won't distinguish between these.

The seventh topic aims directly at increasing indignation toward those who oppose a rhetor's position: Cicero recommended showing the audience that "a foul, cruel, nefarious and tyrannical deed has been done by force and violence or by the influence of riches, and that such an act is utterly at variance with law and equity" (I lii 102–103).

Using the eighth topic, a rhetor may demonstrate the utter outrageousness of the state of affairs she opposes; this is especially effective if she can establish that the state of affairs violates some custom, value, or practice that is important to the community. As Cicero wrote, using this topic, the rhetor shows that the state of affairs is unjust toward "elders, guests, neighbors, friends, against those with whom you have lived, those in whose home you have been reared or by whom you have been educated, against the dead, the wretched or pitiable, against famous people of renown and position, against those who can neither harm another nor defend themselves" (I lii 103). Contemporary rhetors often mention the welfare of children in their closing remarks, in an attempt to arouse sympathy for those innocents who will be negatively affected if the rhetors' positions are not adopted.

The ninth topic compares or contrasts the state of affairs preferred by the rhetor with others, while the tenth creates a vivid picture of the suffering caused by the state of affairs or of the joy that might result if it can be altered according to the rhetor's proposal. The eleventh topic shows that those who oppose the rhetor ought to know better; the twelfth topic expresses indignation that the events have happened to the rhetor and no one else. The thirteenth shows "that insult has been added to injury," thus rousing resentment against haughtiness or arrogance. The fourteenth topic asks the audience "to consider our injuries as their own; if it affects children let them think of their own children…if the aged, let them think of their parents" (I liv 105). Under the fifteenth topic, the rhetor says "that even foes and enemies are regarded as unworthy of the treatment that we have received." In other words: "I wouldn't treat a dog in the way I have been treated."

Enhancing Ethos

Cicero mentioned a third option for the peroration: arguments that arouse the pity of the audience so they will identify with a rhetor or with his case. He listed sixteen topics for accomplishing this, all of which are intended to demonstrate to audiences that the state of affairs opposed by the rhetor affects them in some way. We mention only a few of these topics, since most of them reflect Roman customs or laws that perished long ago.

Using the first and second topics, a rhetor can show in her peroration that the state of affairs she opposes is much worse than it used to be, that currently things are very bad, or that they will continue to be deplorable in the future. In the third and fifth topics, a rhetor mentions examples or enumerates a list of things that demonstrate to the audience the specific ways in which they are harmed by the state of affairs she opposes, and she paints vivid pictures of their misery. In the thirteenth topic, the rhetor complains that the state of affairs she opposes causes bad treatment of others by those to whom it is least becoming. In short, there are myriad ways to end a speech or paper. As a handy review, we outline the currently applicable topics for perorations mentioned by Cicero in *De Inventione*:

Topics for Perorations

1. Summarize
   a. review issues
   b. briefly recall how each issue was supported
2. Make emotional appeals
   a. invoke authority
   b. point out the effects of success or failure
   c. show what happens if state of affairs unchanged
   d. point out effects elsewhere
   e. show that a decision can't be reversed
   f. show whether state of affairs is intentional or accidental
   g. arouse anger at opponents
   h. demonstrate that state of affairs violates community values
   i. compare/contrast state of affairs with similar one
   j. paint a vivid picture of effects
   k. imply ignorance on the part of opponents
   l. show how state of affairs is insulting as well as injurious
   m. ask the audience to identify with those injured or insulted
   n. show that injury or insult would not be applied to enemies
3. Enhance *ethos*
   a. show how state of affairs has deteriorated
   b. show that state of affairs will continue
   c. show audience how they are harmed by state of affairs
   d. paint a vivid picture of current misery
   e. show how state of affairs causes people to behave badly

We hope that our (admittedly sometimes sketchy) review of the available topics for arrangement will prove helpful to our readers. Ancient teachers developed a wealth of advice for beginning and ending a discourse, in particular, and we hope that some of it will prove useful to our readers on some occasions. As always, the rhetorical situation dictates which of these topics, if any, are appropriate for a given rhetor to use with a given audience.

AN EXAMPLE

We conclude our chapter on arrangement with an extended example of a piece of rhetoric that uses all six suggested parts of a discourse. In a *New York Times* editorial, Judith R. Shapiro, the president of Barnard College, voiced her concerns about parents' roles in higher education. We reprint the entire letter, dividing it into Cicero's principles of arrangement:

KEEPING PARENTS OFF CAMPUS

Exordium/Introduction: Every September I join our deans and faculty to welcome first-year students and their families to Barnard campus. It is a bittersweet moment; while parents are filled with pride, they also know they must now begin to let go of their children. Parents must learn to back off.

Narrative: Confidently, with generosity and grace, most parents let their children grow up. They realize that the purpose of college is to help young people stand on their own and take the crucial steps toward adulthood while developing their talents and intellect with skill and purpose.

But this truth is often swept aside by the notion that college is just one more commodity to be purchased, like a car or a vacation home. This unfortunate view gives some parents the wrong idea. Their sense of entitlement as consumers, along with an inability to let go, leads some parents to want to manage all aspects of their children's college lives—from the quest for admission to their choice of major. Such parents, while the exception, are nonetheless an increasing fact of life for faculty, deans and presidents.

Confirmation: Three examples, all recently experienced by my staff, illustrate my point. One mother accompanied her daughter to a meeting with her dean to discuss a supposedly independent research project. Another demanded that her daughter's academic transcript be sent to her directly, since she was the one paying the tuition bills. And one father called his daughter's career counselor so he could contact her prospective employers to extol her qualifications.

I have had my own awkward encounters on this front. I have met with parents accompanying their daughters on campus visits who speak in the "third person invisible." The prospective student sits there—either silently or attempting to get a word in edgewise—while the parents speak about her as if she were elsewhere. I always make a point of addressing the student directly; although this initially feels as if I were talking to a ventriloquist's dummy, I find that, if I keep at it, I can shift the conversation to one between the young woman and me.

Stories abound of parents horrified by a child's choice of major and ready to do battle with faculty or deans. These parents fail to understand that passion and curiosity about a subject, coupled with the ability to learn, are the best career preparation.

Refutation: We are living in times when educational pressures on families begin when children are toddlers and continue relentlessly through the teenage years. Four-year-olds today face a battery of tests to get into a desirable preschool. As they face the college admissions process, parents attuned to the barrage of media coverage believe that the best colleges accept only superhumans—a belief encouraged, admittedly, by some universities—and strive to prepare their sons and daughters accordingly. (One father even took a year off from his job to supervise the preparation of his daughter's admissions portfolio.)

By the time their children enter college, parents have become so invested emotionally in their success that they may not understand why it is crucial that they remain outside the college gates. The division of responsibility between parents and colleges during the undergraduate years is a complex matter, as is the question of how much responsibility young people should be expected to take for themselves. We have been hearing much of late about a return to the in loco parentis approach that fell out of favor in the late 1960's. The same baby boomers who fought to end these restrictions want to bring them back, perhaps out of dismay that their own children may have to make some of the same mistakes they did.

Colleges should do as much as they can to provide a safe and secure environment. More important, they must help students learn to take care of themselves and to seek guidance on life's tough decisions. Neither colleges nor parents can make the world entirely safe for our young people and, hard as it may be to accept, there are limits to our ability to control what life has in store for our children.

Peroration: Parents do best when they encourage their college-bound children to reach out enthusiastically for opportunities in the classroom and beyond. And if they can let go, they will see the results that they want and deserve: young people, so full of intelligence, spirit and promise, transformed into wonderful women and men. (2002)

Before analyzing Shapiro's arrangement strategies, we need to consider Shapiro's audience. The letter appeared in the *New York Times,* a newspaper with an audience so broad that her seeming intended audience (parents of Barnard College students) would be engulfed by the hordes of potential readers. A closer look, however, suggests that her letter is directed less to parents of Barnard College students exclusively, or even to parents of college students in general, than to parents with children of any age. We might even go so far as to say that Shapiro's letter, with its broad criticisms of attitudes toward education in general, could be of interest to all citizens. Shapiro's audience of *New York Times* readers, then, encompasses all sorts of groups, from Manhattan workers commuting on the subway, to parents readying their children to go off to college for the first time, to the college students themselves, to preschool teachers, to professors.

Shapiro's situated *ethos* is enhanced by her byline: she is the president of Barnard College, a prestigious women's college with a reputation for scholarly excellence. The timing of the letter's appearance is also notable. It was published in late August, just as new college students were likely packing their bags to head to campus. In anticipation of this moment, Shapiro opens the letter with a sentence about what happens this time every year. In keeping with Cicero's suggestions, the sentence is dignified. This sentence, however, does more work than just set the scene in a serious manner; it makes the audience receptive by building Shapiro's *ethos* in two important ways. First, it establishes Shapiro as someone who is experienced with this scene—"every September" she is on campus, meeting parents and students, preparing for a new school year. Secondly, the sentence presents Shapiro as someone with goodwill toward her own faculty, as well as Barnard students and parents: she "joins" with her deans and faculty to "welcome" new students and their families. The second sentence, by marking the moment as "bittersweet," builds this *ethos* even more by demonstrating an understanding of the emotional moment, thus making readers receptive. The third sentence of the piece strikes a much different tone: the short, terse sentence "Parents must learn to back off" works to make even the casual reader more attentive. This is a writer with a point to make. Even people without a direct stake in higher education might take notice and continue to read the editorial at this point.

In the narrative, Shapiro continues to argue why (and how) parents should "back off" by stating her wish more positively—that is, she wishes that parents would recognize the importance of letting children develop on their own and that they would do so with "generosity and grace." Next, in the third paragraph, the narrative states the problem clearly (as narratives should, according to Cicero): education is fast becoming a product to be bought and sold, like a sofa, rather than the vital process of transformation and development Shapiro thinks it should be.

The section Cicero would call "confirmation" begins by discussing three examples of overinvolved parents from Shapiro's own school. She moves from example to example without much discussion. The examples are sufficiently compelling that they don't require elaboration or discussion. Further, the quick movement from one to another to another has the effect of a barrage. While the examples she lists come from her faculty's experiences (but have no doubt been brought up to her as president), the next part of the confirmation presents a picture of how parents typically behave when Shapiro herself is around. Here, her *ethos* gets a boost, since her description shows how, unlike the parents, Shapiro seeks to engage the prospective student by speaking directly to—rather than about—her. The confirmation draws to a close with the general example about parents' attempts to choose their children's majors, followed by a diagnosis, which leads nicely into the refutation section.

In the refutation, Shapiro anticipates the arguments people will likely make in response to her case so far, arguments such as "sometimes young adults do not realize how crucial one's major can be, and they need parental guidance." Or "if we don't look after our children, who will?" Or, "this is a much different world now than when you went to college, Dr. Shapiro." Or even more likely, "I don't want my son/daughter making the same mistakes I did." Here, she moves to a general, cultural account of transformations that have occurred in attitudes toward education in past years, discussing the rise in competitive measures and acknowledging along the way that for parents, the stakes of their children's college education are high. She even ends the refutation by subtly acknowledging that members of the baby boom generation who went to college in the late 1960s (which most likely describes many of Shapiro's most invested readers) are becoming more conservative in their stance on education and would like their children to take a more businesslike approach to college than they perhaps did. She ends the refutation by devoting space to issues of safety and security, making sure to distinguish such issues from control and authority.

Finally, in her peroration Shapiro revisits the issue at hand by vividly describing the state of affairs she would like to see come about. She does this with one summative sentence followed by a description of the ideal result: "young people, so full of intelligence, spirit and promise, transformed into wonderful women and men." This focus on the students, in turn, boosts Shapiro's *ethos*, a strategy Cicero advised for the peroration. The concluding sentence, then, suggests that Shapiro has a vision, albeit an idealistic one, and her vision does not feature dollar signs, but people.

Judith Shapiro's letter provides an instance of discourse containing the Ciceronian elements and their appropriate topics. Shapiro's piece also exemplifies the important relationship between invention and arrangement. The generation of many effective proofs could be futile if they are ordered in such a way that they lose their persuasive force. Likewise, the most effective arrangement strategies will probably not help a rhetor who has not yet come up with good arguments. Again, a rhetor need not include all the parts of a speech outlined by Cicero and Quintilian; rather, the different parts, their functions, and the variety of topics presented for each part offers a wide range of choices to help a rhetor "assemble her troops" effectively.

RHETORICAL ACTIVITIES

1. Compose an exordium, narrative, partition, and peroration for some argument you are working on. Carefully consider the rhetorical situation before you begin: Is your audience receptive? Hostile? Indifferent? Does their attitude stem from their relation to the issue or to your *ethos*? Once you have answered these questions, you can decide whether you need an introduction or an insinuation and whether you need to make elaborate appeals in the peroration. Practice composing some brief arguments for a peroration, using Cicero's topics for establishing *ethos* and arousing emotion.

2. Examine a few speeches and essays produced by professional rhetors. (Collections of speeches by famous persons are available in most university libraries.) Can you find examples of insinuations, narratives, partitions, perorations? Examine enough pieces of discourse to determine whether modern rhetors feel it necessary to use any or all of these parts of a discourse.

3. Consider Judith Shapiro's rhetorical situation when she wrote the editorial on parental involvement in higher education. Do her choices in arranging her various arguments make sense? What different topics or proofs might Shapiro use if she were writing for another publication with a smaller, more clearly invested readership like Barnard's alumni newsletter? Would she write a different introduction? An insinuation? Write a new exordium for Shapiro's piece and rearrange its arguments (or generate new ones) so that the piece is suitable for a more specialized audience of Barnard graduates.

IMITATION I: ON THE USEFULNESS OF COPYING

Contemporary rhetors sometimes assume that great writers are born with an inherent creative ability that is denied to the rest of us. This myth about writing is so powerful in our culture that it sometimes discourages people from even trying to learn how to write better. But the myth isn't true. Ancient teachers thought that the ability to compose fluently and efficiently resulted from a lifetime of study and practice. Moreover, as Isocrates observed, study and practice are in some ways superior to talent:

> In the art of rhetoric, credit is won not by gifts of fortune, but by efforts of study. For those who have been gifted with eloquence by nature and by fortune, are governed in what they say by chance, and not by any standard of what is best, whereas those who have gained this power by study and by the exercise of language never speak without weighing their words, and so are less often in error as to a course of action. (*Antidosis*, 292)

In other words, the writer who is only gifted may produce good work on occasion. Study and practice, in contrast, guarantee the production of good work on every occasion.

Ancient orators and teachers of rhetoric everywhere extolled the virtues of study and practice. Demosthenes, the greatest ancient Greek rhetor, shaved half his head so that he would be too ashamed to go out of the house and leave his studies. Cicero, the greatest Roman rhetor, wrote that skill in rhetoric derived from "painstaking," which included "carefulness, mental concentration, reflection, watchfulness, persistence and hard work" (*De Oratore* II 35).

Students can learn an art by imitating the example of people who are good at it. Watching LeBron James or Diana Taurasi play basketball is an exhilarating experience, and we can learn some beautiful basketball moves by watching them play. But the examples set by outstanding models can be made clearer if we study with a coach or teacher. A coach can explain the rules of basketball, show us how each member of a team relates to the other, and develop game plans and strategies that may make up for lack of individual ability.

Another way to learn any art is to study its principles. A cookbook enhances and reinforces what we learn by watching Rachael Ray put together some exotic dessert, because the cookbook provides us with basic principles that Ray doesn't have time to mention: weights and measures, the effect of temperature on various foods, and so forth. In fact, study of principles has an advantage over learning from either models or teachers: principles can be studied anytime, anywhere. In the other modes of learning, students need a highly skilled or trained person to work with. If a model or a teacher is not available, students who have access to principles can continue their studies on their own.

If you have worked your way through this book, you have likely gathered that the ancients valued both principles and practice. The

ancients believed that regular practice put people in the habit of composing, so that they could begin easily and work without stopping.
Quintilian borrowed a Greek term, *hexis,* or habit, to describe the
"assured facility" with which capable writers use the strategies and
knowledge they possess (X i 1). A latin term for this supply of arguments
was *copia,* abundance. In his autobiography, Cicero remarked that he did
rhetorical exercises every day while he was studying philosophy (*Brutus*
310). He continued to compose rhetorical exercises throughout his lifetime, even after he had become an acclaimed public speaker. Ancient
teachers also thought that daily practice in speaking or composing was
crucial for the attainment and maintenance of *hexis* and *copia*; as
Quintilian remarked, "facility is mainly the result of habit and exercise"
(X vii 8). He compared the orator who had completed his course of study
to an athlete "who has learned all the technique of his art from his
trainer" and who then "is to be prepared by actual practice for the contests in which he will have to engage" (i 4).

ANCIENT RHETORICAL EXERCISES

Ancient students practiced a number of oral and written exercises intended
to enhance their skills and their stocks of rhetorical resources. These
included the *progymnasmata* as well as a variety of exercises in imitation,
translation, and paraphrase.

All of these exercises required students to copy the work of some
admired author or to elaborate on a set theme. Ancient dependence upon
material composed by others may seem strange to modern students, who
have been taught that their work should be original. As rhetoric and composition scholars Rebecca Moore Howard and John Logie have reminded
us, this notion of originality and ownership of ideas sprang up when technology reached a point where publication could become profitable (Howard
1995; Logie 2003). And so ancient teachers and students would have found
the notion of originality quite strange; they assumed that real skill lay in
being able to imitate or to improve on something written by others.
Language, after all, was available to all humans, and learning to use it well
was bound up with becoming an adult and a productive citizen.

Isocrates described ancient attitudes about original composition in a
passage from *Panegyricus*:

> Since language is of such a nature that it is possible to discourse on the same
> subject matter in many different ways—to represent the great as lowly or
> invest the little with grandeur, to recount the things of old in a new manner or
> set forth events of recent date in an old fashion—it follows that one must not
> shun the subjects upon which others have composed before, but must try to
> compose better than they. For the deeds of the past are, indeed, an inheritance
> common to us all; but the ability to make proper use of them at the appropri-
> ate time, to conceive the right sentiments about them in each instance, and to
> set them forth in finished phrase, is the peculiar gift of the wise. . . . We should

honor . . . not those who seek to discourse on subjects on which no one has discoursed before, but those who know how to use discourse as no one else could. (8–10)

Ancient teachers were not in the business of developing individual personalities or teaching self-expression. They knew that cultures were held together by important themes and that these themes are reproduced in speeches and writing on many different occasions. Thus they encouraged students of rhetoric to rework important themes and to imitate revered pieces of discourse as preparation for their roles as citizens. The rhetorical exercises that imitated or elaborated on the work of well-known authors had the double effect of acquainting students with the best products of their culture at the same time as they increased their stock of available arguments.

The rhetorical exercises are meant to be written, even though the discourses that result from them may eventually be delivered orally. Cicero and Quintilian were both great fans of writing practice as a means of attaining *copia*. In *De Oratore* Cicero's spokesman, Crassus, recommended that aspiring rhetors "write as much as possible. The pen is the best and most eminent author and teacher of eloquence" (I xxxii 150). Quintilian quoted this passage and added his own praise for writing practice: "We must therefore write as much as possible and with the utmost care. For as deep plowing makes the soil more fertile for the production and support of crops, so, if we improve our minds by something more than mere superficial study, we shall produce a richer growth of knowledge and shall retain it with greater accuracy" (X iii 2).

At first, these exercises may seem strange and uncomfortable to modern students, since, as we have said elsewhere, it is modern custom to aim at clarity and economy rather than at copiousness. The exercises become less strange and uncomfortable with practice, however. And the practice pays off: if you do a bit of composing every day, you should soon see a dramatic improvement in your powers of invention and arrangement and in your stylistic fluency as well.

IMITATION EXERCISES IN ANCIENT RHETORICS

Historians do not know exactly when ancient rhetoric teachers began to include formal exercises in their instruction. The use of imitation as a means of learning, at least, must be very old. Aristotle believed the inclination to imitate is the distinguishing characteristic of humans, and this is one of the reasons, he argues, that poetry itself exists:

> Poetry in general can be seen to owe its existence to two causes, and these are rooted in nature. First, there is man's natural propensity, from childhood onwards, to engage in mimetic activity (and this distinguishes man from other creatures, that he is thoroughly mimetic and through mimesis takes his first steps in understanding). (*Poetics* chapter 4, 1–5)

Similarly, Quintilian believed the desire to imitate is universal among humans, if not entirely natural:

> It is a universal rule of life that we should wish to copy what we approve in others. It is for this reason that children copy the shapes of letters that they may learn to write, and that musicians take the voices of their teachers, painters the works of their predecessors, and farmers the principles of agriculture which have been proved in practice, as models for their imitation. In fact, we may note that the elementary study of every branch of learning is directed by reference to some definite standard that is placed before the learner. (*Institutes* X ii 1)

Before the advent of writing, rhapsodes and actors must have learned their arts, in part, by studying and imitating their teachers as well as other rhapsodes and actors.

Most likely, imitation was introduced into the formal curriculum of rhetorical instruction by the Older Sophists, who taught by example rather than precept. That is, they composed and delivered specimen speeches, and their students attempted to imitate both the master's compositions and his delivery. According to Cicero, Gorgias and Protagoras composed lists of commonplaces; if so, students might have imitated these as well (*Brutus* 46–47). And surely the *"Dissoi Logoi"* and Antiphon's *Tetralogies*, both of which date from the fifth century BCE, are rhetorical exercises meant for imitation by students, since neither refers to any specific circumstances (as would be the case with speeches composed for actual use).

The sophistic practice of imitation remained popular throughout ancient times. Greek and Roman teachers of rhetoric developed a variety of exercises in which students copied or imitated the work of admired authors; these included reading aloud, **copying,** imitation, translation, and **paraphrase.** We treat the first two here and include the rest with other chapters in the book.

Reading Aloud and Copying

As we mentioned in the last chapter, silent reading is a modern practice. Throughout most of Western history, people read aloud, even when they were alone. Reading aloud develops an ear for sentence rhythm, and it strengthens reading skills as well. Reading aloud from the work of others may also enable you to absorb some habits of style that are not currently in your repertoire. Quintilian thought that it improved delivery too (*Institutes* II v 7). Try reading aloud from the work of writers you admire. Read aloud to yourself or to others. You can practice with any of the passages quoted in this chapter, or you may begin by reading your own work aloud. In fact, you should get in the habit of reading your own writing aloud; this will help you to spot places where punctuation is needed (or not) and to determine whether the rhythm of the sentence is pleasing to the ear.

Since ancient times, people have copied out passages from their reading that they wished to remember or to consult later. Malcolm X, who became one of the twentieth century's most compelling orators, used the ancient technique of copying as a means of learning:

I saw that the best thing I could do was get hold of a dictionary—to study, to learn some words. I was lucky enough to reason also that I should try to improve my penmanship. It was sad. I couldn't even write in a straight line. It was both ideas together that moved me to request a dictionary along with some tablets and pencils from the Norfolk Prison Colony school.

I spent two days just riffling uncertainly through the dictionary's pages. I'd never realized so many words existed! I didn't know which words I needed to learn. Finally, just to start some kind of action, I began copying.

In my slow, painstaking, ragged handwriting, I copied into my tablet everything printed on that first page, down to the punctuation marks.

I believe it took me a day. Then, aloud, I read back, to myself, everything I'd written on the tablet. Over and over, aloud, to myself, I read my own hand-writing.

I woke up the next morning, thinking about those words—immensely proud to realize that not only had I written so much at one time, but I'd written words that I never knew were in the world. Moreover, with a little effort, I also could remember what many of these words meant. I reviewed the words whose meanings I didn't remember. Funny thing, from the dictionary first page right now, that "aardvark" springs to my mind. The dictionary had a picture of it, a long-tailed, long-eared, burrowing African mammal, which lives off termites caught by sticking out its tongue as an anteater does for ants.

I was so fascinated that I went on—I copied the dictionary's next page. And the same experience came when I studied that. With every succeeding page, I also learned of people and places and events from history. Actually the dictionary is like a miniature encyclopedia. Finally the dictionary's A section had filled a whole tablet—and I went on to the B's. That was the way I started copying what eventually became the entire dictionary. It went a lot faster after so much practice helped me to pick up handwriting speed. Between what I wrote in my tablet, and writing letters, during the rest of my time in prison I would guess I wrote a million words. (1987, 172)

As Malcolm X points out, copying also enhances *copia* (or abundance) and is an aid to memory as well.

Even though we live in the age of electronic composing, the timeworn practice of copying by hand is still useful. Copying by hand is an aid to memory, for one thing. And if you want to use copying to enhance *copia*, you should get in the habit of doing a little copying every day. Handwriting works better than typing on a keyboard, because writing by hand slows you down and helps you to focus on the passage being copied. Handwriting can also work for its ease and portability. It's also the case that contemporary students are so accustomed to writing on computers that imitation would work by way of entering words and seeing them on the screen (we would discourage cutting and pasting, however). Copy passages you admire into a notebook, word for word. Since the aim of this exercise is the achievement of *copia*, try to copy short passages from many different authors. As Quintilian wrote, no single author displays the best wisdom or eloquence in every passage, and so "we shall do well to keep a number of different excellences before our eyes, so that different qualities from different authors may impress themselves on our minds, to be adopted for use in the place that becomes them best" (X ii 26). Ancient teachers helped their students with this exercise by analyzing selected passages before the students began to copy, but you can do this work for yourself. Read the whole passage carefully before you begin to copy, noting words that you may not know or structures that seem especially elegant or pleasing. Read each sentence before you begin to copy it. Above all, take your time and enjoy yourself. This is a different manner of reading than the kind of reading you tend to do for other classes: reading with the goal of gleaning information from a history text is different from reading with careful attention to the ways words and phrases fit together. (It's possible to accomplish both at once, of course, and since many historians write impressively, their work provides good models for emulation.)

A collection of copied passages is also useful, by the way, as a source of quotations and commonplaces that can be used in compositions. In premodern times, most rhetors kept written collections of copied passages; these were called *florilegia* (flowers of reading) in medieval times, and **commonplace books** during the Renaissance and into the eighteenth century. People often organized their commonplace books in the same way that ancient rhetors organized their trained memories. Erasmus, writing in the sixteenth century, recommended that students who wished to become educated begin by making a "full list of subjects" that they might read or write about (*De Copia* 636). He suggested, for example, that the list "consist partly of the main types and subdivisions of vice and virtue, partly of the things of most prominence in human affairs which frequently occur when we have a case to put forward, and they should be arranged according to similars and opposites." The first division might be "reverence" and "irreverence." Under the section of the commonplace book devoted to reverence, Erasmus suggested, writers could copy any items they ran across that had to do with patriotism, love for children, or respect for parents and teachers.

Apparently this advice about organizing commonplace books was, well, common. The poet John Milton kept multiple commonplace books, one each devoted to Theology and Law. He organized another under the headings of Ethics, Economy, and Politics. He divided each of these main headings into smaller subsections; under Ethics he copied passages dealing with Virtue, Chastity, and Courage, along with entries on Lust, Drunkenness, and Gluttony. A modern writer who wished to adopt this scheme might not be so interested in virtue and vice as people were in the sixteenth and seventeenth centuries. No matter. Whatever subjects or issues are of interest to a writer—business or politics or engineering or anything at all—can be listed and divided into their respective parts or into important issues. Whenever a writer hears or reads something that she wishes to remember or use later on in her own work, she can copy it down under the appropriate heading in the commonplace book.

But a commonplace book need not feature such elaborate arrangements. Writers' commonplace books can be organized in any way that suits their working habits. If you want to look at examples of commonplace books to see how others organize them, you can find copies of the commonplace books kept by well-known people, such as Ben Jonson or Thomas Jefferson, in many libraries.

Professional writers still carry notebooks that resemble common-place books. In keeping with this practice, we suggest that aspiring rhetors carry a notebook with them so that they can write down ideas that occur to them while they are engaged in doing other things. And when you are reading, or talking, or listening to others, you can use the notebook as a commonplace book, writing down comments or passages that you want to remember, copy, or imitate. As is evident from the list of historical figures who kept commonplace books, this practice is useful for rhetors at all levels of experience. One of us, for example, keeps a small notebook with her at all times. Whenever she hears a turn of phrase or word that is intriguing, she jots it down in her notebook. When she finds herself in a waiting room or in line with nothing to read, she takes out the book and reviews some of the things she heard, reminding herself to use the phrases when she gets a chance. As a result, the little notebook serves as a mini–memory pad for stylistic invention (see the chapters on style and memory). The other of us has for many years kept notebooks that include copied passages from her reading as well as her comments on the reading; she finds these notebooks invaluable when she is composing, trying to remember who first mentioned an idea with which she is working or in what source she found an invaluable lead to other useful research.

IMITATION EXERCISE: READING ALOUD AND COPYING

Select a passage from your favorite author. Copy it. Study it to learn why you admire it. Is the sentiment aptly expressed? Does its author make inno-vative use of some figure or trope? Is the argument original or exciting?

Bring the copied passage to class to read aloud to your classmates (either in small groups or to the entire class). You might practice reading it aloud before trying it in class.

WORKS CITED

Carter, Graydon. "On Borrowed Land." *Vanity Fair* 561 (May 2007): 46.

Gopnik, Adam. "Angels and Ages: Lincoln's Language and Its Legacy." *New Yorker*, May 28, 2007, 30–31.

Griffin, David Ray. *Debunking 9/11 Debunking: An Answer to Popular Mechanics and Other Defenders of the Official Conspiracy Theory.* Northampton, Mass: Olive Branch Press, 2007.

Howard, Rebecca Moore. "Plagiarisms, Authorships, and the Academic Death Penalty." *College English* 57, no. 7 (November 1995): 788–806.

Kucinich, Dennis. "Presidential Candidacy Announcement." Delivered December 12, 2006. Full text available at: http://kucinich.us/files/KucinichAnnouncement.pdf.

Logie, John. "'I Have No Predecessor to Guide My Steps': Quintilian and Roman Authorship." *Rhetoric Review* 22, 4 (2003): 353–373.

Malcolm X. *The Autobiography of Malcolm X*. New York: Ballantine, 1987.

Meyer, George, "My Undoing." The New Yorker, May 28, 2007: 45.

Robinson, Adam. *Bin Laden: Behind the Mask of the Terrorist*. New York: Arcade Publishing, 2001.

Shapiro, Judith. "Keeping Parents Off Campus." *New York Times*, August 22, 2002, national edition, op-ed.

Urstadt, Brian. "Scenes from the Apocalypse." *Harper's*, August 2006, 31–40.

White, Eric Charles. *Kaironomia*. Ithaca, N.Y. Cornell University Press, 1987.

Wilson, E. O. "Problems Without Borders." *Vanity Fair* 561 (May 2007): 164–166.

Wolff, Michael. "Serious Money." *Vanity Fair* 561 (May 2007): 108–117.

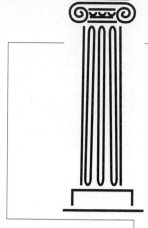

STYLE: COMPOSITION AND ORNAMENT

Cicero holds that, while invention and arrangement are within the reach of anyone of good sense, eloquence belongs to the rhetor alone. . . . The verb eloqui means the production and communication to the audience of all that the rhetor has conceived . . . and without this power all the preliminary accomplishments of rhetoric are as useless as a sword that is kept permanently concealed within its sheath.

—Quintilian, *Institutes* VIII Pr. 14–15

ANCIENT RHETORICIANS DEVOTED an entire canon of their art to the study of unusual uses or arrangements of words. They called this canon "style" (*lexis*, or "words," in Greek; *elocutio*, or "speaking out," in Latin). Defined as persuasive or extraordinary uses of language, style can be distinguished from grammar, which is the study of ordinary uses of language.

No one knows for sure when style emerged as the third canon of rhetoric. From earliest times, of course, poets and singers used unusual words and patterns in their work. Here, for example, are some lines from the *Iliad*, which is usually dated from the eighth century BCE—that is, two hundred years prior to Gorgias's trip to Athens during the sixth century BCE:

> Ah, Hektor,
> this harshness is no more than just. Remember, though,
> your spirit's like an ax-edge whetted sharp
> that goes through timber, when a good shipwright
> hews out a beam: the tool triples his power.
> That is the way your heart is in your breast.
> (III 58–62)

When he compared Hector's heart to an ax used by a strong shipbuilder, the poet employed a figure later called a simile, wherein two unlike things are placed together so that the attributes of one are transferred to the other. Notice how the simile adds meaning to the picture of Hector that the poet is painting; we learn from it that, like the strokes of an ax wielded by a strong man, Hector's courage is tireless, regular, and strong. As Quintilian remarked, such uses of language make things even more intelligible than does clarity alone (VIII ii 11).

Historians of rhetoric usually credit Gorgias with the discovery that extra-ordinary uses of language were persuasive in prose as well as poetry. Here, for example, is the opening passage of Gorgias's "Encomium to Helen":

> Fairest ornament to a city is a goodly army and to a body beauty and to a soul wisdom and to an action virtue and to speech truth, but their opposites are unbefitting. Man and woman and speech and deed and city and object should be honored with praise if praiseworthy but on the unworthy blame should be laid; for it is equal error and ignorance to blame the praiseworthy and to praise the blameworthy.

The first sentence shows careful attention to **sentence composition** in its use of balanced phrases ("to a body beauty" and so on). Both sentences contain examples of **antithesis,** wherein contrary or contradictory ideas are expressed in phrases that are grammatically alike ("to blame the praisewor-thy and to praise the blameworthy," for example). Even though Aristotle was skeptical about verbal pyrotechnics like these, he was aware of the per-suasive power of language. In fact, he was among the first teachers of rhetoric to recognize that extraordinary uses of language like Gorgias's could be systematically studied. In both the *Rhetoric* and the *Poetics,* he drew up rules for language use that exploited its tendencies to excite the emotions as well as its capacity to represent thought clearly. Some historians credit Aristotle's nephew, Theophrastus, with the realization that style could be studied separately from other closely related features of rhetoric, such as *ethos* or delivery, but other historians place the emergence of style as a separate area of study much later, during the Hellenistic period.

Stylistic ornament is still widely used. In an article on computer mod-eling of athletic anticipation written for *Wired,* Jennifer Kahn employed this **simile**: "Opponents struggling to anticipate Gretzky's next move often became disoriented, like hunters who think they're tracking a leopard, only to hear a twig crack directly behind them" (2007, 125). This example of **metaphor** appeared in a *New York Times* article about Katz's Delicatessen in Manhattan: "It's a strand of the city's DNA, a bridge between past and pre-sent that's no less a landmark than some bona fide architectural treasure" (Bruni 2007, 9). Here, the comparison between the historic lunch spot and genetic material—the basis of life and identity—borders on **personification**. Personification also crops up in the context of personal gadgets. It is almost commonplace these days, for example, to speak of iPods as having brains or hearts, such as when iPod user Revere Greist insists that his iPod "knows somehow when I am reaching the end of my reserves, when my motivation is flagging . . . It hits me up with 'In Da Club,' and then all of a sudden I am in da club" (Dodes 2004, G1). Apple ad writers encourage such attribution of human sensibility to Apple's digital music player by including this assertion in its features description: "After all, iPod loves music as much as you do" (Apple 2007, www.apple.com/ ca/ipod/features.html).

Ancient teachers of rhetoric combined Aristotle's philosophical view of language with Gorgias's sophistic view to argue that rhetorical language ought to be clear and that it ought to touch the emotions as well. Teachers helped their students to achieve stylistic excellence by teaching them about as many unusual uses of language as they could isolate and classify, by asking them to imitate famous authors and to practice composing their own examples of various **schemes** or **figures** (Greek *schemata;* Latin *figura,* "shape"). Ancient rhetoricians isolated four qualities of style that permitted them to distinguish a persuasive style from a less effective one. While there was some disagreement about which qualities ought to be included in a list of stylistic excellences, in the main, ancient authors agreed that a good style ought to manifest correctness, clearness, appropriateness, and ornament.

CORRECTNESS

The Greek and Latin words for correctness were *hellenismos* and *latinitas,* respectively. Sometimes translated as "purity," correctness meant that rhetors should use words that were current and should adhere to the grammatical rules of whatever language they wrote. In Greek and Latin, meaning depended to a great degree on word endings; nouns had different endings depending on their case, number, and gender, while verb endings indicated such things as tense and mood. Thus, the achievement of correctness in one of those languages was a more complex and interesting task than it is in English, which depends primarily on word order for its meanings.

Ancient rhetoricians ordinarily left instruction in correctness (and sometimes clarity as well) to the elementary school teachers, who were grammarians and students of literature. Cicero wrote in *De Oratore* that "the rules of correct Latin style . . . are imparted by education in childhood and fostered by a more intensive and systematic study of literature, or else by the habit of daily conversation in the family circle, and confirmed by books and by reading the old orators and poets" (III xii 48). Interestingly, Cicero agreed in this with the contemporary linguists, who argue that native speakers of any language internalize a good many of its grammatical rules while they are learning it. Since native speakers of a language have an intuitive grasp of its grammar, the **correctness rules** that trouble people today usually involve conventional niceties of written language such as spelling, punctuation, and some outdated rules of grammar and usage. Since these features of correctness govern choices that can be made while editing, we discuss a few of them in the chapter on delivery.

CLARITY

Clarity is the English word most often used for the Greek *sapheneia*, although it is sometimes translated "lucidity" (from Latin *lucere*, "to shine"), or "perspicuity" (from Latin *perspicere*, "to see through"). The Latin terms demonstrate that clarity once connoted language that lets meanings "shine through" it, like light through a window. As we noted earlier, however, rhetoricians like Gorgias were suspicious about the capacity of language to transfer meaning clearly from rhetors to audiences. For most ancient teachers, clarity simply meant that rhetors should use words in their ordinary or usual everyday senses unless they had some compelling reason to do otherwise.

According to Quintilian, rhetors could avoid the obligation to be clear only if they were compelled to refer to obscenities, unseemly behavior, or trivial matters. In any of these cases, they could resort to **circumlocution** (Greek ***periphrasis***, "speaking around"), a more roundabout means of reference. Terms like *restroom* or *powder room* are circumlocutions for *toilet*; it is a circumlocution to say that "Henry and the company decided to part ways" when Henry was fired. Clarity can also be obscured by the use of obsolete, technical, new, or colloquial words. Obsolete words are those that are no longer in popular use (*motored* for *drove*). Technical language (that is, jargon) is used by specialists in a profession or discipline (for example, *valorize* and *abjection* from current talk among academics). Quintilian also advised against the practice of coining of new words (neologism) since new words are not familiar to those who hear or read them. He told a funny story about a speaker who, in his anxiety to give a formal tone to his talk, used the phrase "Iberian grass" to refer to the plant known as "Spanish broom" (VIII I 2–3). The problem with "Iberian grass" was that the phrase puzzled everyone who heard it, which is, we must admit, an offense against clarity. Colloquial words are used in a very specific locale or culture. For example, *with it*, originally from the Beat culture of the 1950s, is colloquial and now obsolete as well. So are the "in" terms from the 1970s—*groovy* and *far out*. However, other colloquial terms, such as *hip* and *cool*, are amazingly tenacious: *hip* was "cool" in the sixties, while *cool* was "hip" in the fifties and the seventies; *cool* is still in popular use today, although *hot* seemed to be gaining on it for awhile; perhaps both will be replaced by *sweet*.

Modern composition textbooks tell writers to avoid colloquial or technical language altogether. This is nonsense. As Quintilian said, the best course is to call things by the names people ordinarily use, unless for some reason the name would puzzle an audience or give offense. In other words, rhetors should always use language that is familiar to their audiences, even if this language is colloquial or jargon ridden. A rhetor who addresses an audience that uses a dialect should use it if she is comfortable doing so. Former president Jimmy Carter, who was raised in Georgia, uses a Southern dialect of English. When he campaigned in the South, he told his audiences that they should elect him in order to have someone in the presidency who had no accent! Likewise, a rhetor who addresses literary critics should use whatever jargon is currently in vogue within that group, because jargon is ordinarily invented as a means of attaining precision—that is, clarity. A rhetor who is addressing teachers or bosses should try to use language that is familiar to those audiences. If this means learning a technical vocabulary, so be it.

APPROPRIATENESS: *KAIROS* AND STYLE

Once we move past correctness and clarity, we are working in more truly rhetorical realms of style—appropriateness and ornament.[1] Oddly enough, these realms are not often treated in modern composition textbooks, whose authors are more anxious that writers be correct and clear than that they be persuasive.

Appropriateness probably derives from the Greek rhetorical notion *to prepon*, meaning to say or do whatever is fitting in a given situation. Perhaps it is also descended from Gorgias's notion of *kairos*, seizing the right moment to speak, the moment when listeners are ready to hear. Cicero upheld appropriateness or propriety as the most important rule of thumb for effective rhetoric when he wrote that "the universal rule, in oratory as in life, is to consider propriety" (*Orator* xxi 71). But for Cicero, propriety was not something that can be made into a list of hard and fast rules. Cicero defined propriety as "what is fitting and agreeable to an occasion or person; it is important often in actions as well as in words, in the expression of the face, in gesture and in gait" (xxii, 74). So Cicero favored a situational propriety, one that comes closer to the Greek notion of *kairos*.

As we discussed in Chapter 2, on *kairos*, the mythical figure Kairos was often depicted balancing on some object—be it a razor blade or a ball or a wheel. Achieving a balanced style is one of the challenges rhetors often face. Cicero was well aware of this challenge as a central concern for rhetoric. He wrote: "When a case presents itself in which the full force of eloquence can be expended, then the orator will display his powers more fully; then we will rule and sway men's minds, and move them as he will, that is as the nature of the case and the exigency of the occasion demand" (xxxv, 125).

Cicero was not the only ancient who expressed a concern for propriety in rhetoric. Even Plato, who was skeptical about the value of rhetoric, emphasized the importance of using an appropriate style. In Plato's *Phaedrus*, the character Socrates tells Phaedrus that when a rhetor supplements an awareness of the audience with "a knowledge of the times for speaking and for keeping silence, and has also distinguished the favorable occasions *(kairous)* for brief speech or pitiful speech or intensity and all the classes of speech which he has learned, then, and not till then, will his art be fully and completely finished" (272–73). For Plato, then, attention to *kairos*—the nature of the subject matter, the general attitudes and backgrounds of the audience—helped the rhetor make decisions about an appropriate style. A young aspiring rhetor like Phaedrus, for example, might steer clear of using **hyperbole** (exaggeration of a case) in front of Socrates, the teacher of reason, for it would be in Phaedrus's best interest to establish himself as a reasonable rhetor. As you can see, concerns about style are linked to the ethical proofs, discussed in the chapter on *ethos*.

Like ethical proof, attention to *kairos* in style requires sensitivity to community standards of behavior, since appropriateness is dictated by the standards of the community in which we live. In our culture, for example, people do not generally pick their noses in public, because the community defines this as inappropriate behavior.

The community dictates the standards of rhetorical appropriateness as well. When ancient teachers of rhetoric counseled their students to use an appropriate style, they generally meant that a style should be suited to subject, occasion, and audience. This meant that rhetors had to understand the standards of behavior required by the occasion for which they composed a piece of discourse. Since every occasion for writing or speaking differs from the next, it is very difficult to generate rules to govern appropriateness. Cicero underscored this difficulty in *De Oratore*:

> Different styles are required by deliberative speeches, panegyrics, lawsuits and lectures, and for consolation, protest, discussion and historical narrative, respectively. The audience is also important—whether it is the lords or the commons or the bench; a large audience or a small one or a single person, and their personal character; and consideration must be given to the age, station and office of the speakers themselves, and to the occasion, in peace time or during a war, urgent or allowing plenty of time. (III iv 211–12)

In other words, the achievement of an appropriate style requires rhetors to pay attention to the conventional rules for verbal behavior in a given context, rules that have been laid down by their culture. If a rhetor has been asked to give a eulogy (a funeral speech), for example, his language should be dignified and subdued, because our culture dictates dignified and subdued behavior on such occasions. If he writes lyrics for country music, dignified and subdued won't cut it, since the style of country music is down-home and informal.

Ancient teachers distinguished three very general levels of style that were appropriate to various rhetorical settings: grand, middle, and plain.[2] According to the author of *ad Herennium*, discourse was composed in the grand style "if to each idea are applied the most ornate words that can be found for it, whether literal or figurative; if impressive thoughts are chosen, . . . and if we employ figures of thought and figures of diction which have grandeur" (IV viii 11). He supplied us with a fine example of the grand style, which we quote in part:

> Who of you, pray, jury members, could devise a punishment drastic enough for him who has plotted to betray the fatherland to our enemies? What offence can compare with this crime, what punishment can be found commensurate with this offence? Upon those who had done violence to a freeborn youth, outraged the mother of a family, wounded, or—basest crime of all—slain a man, our

> ancestors exhausted the catalogue of extreme punishments; while for this most savage and impious villainy they bequeath no specific penalty. In other wrongs, indeed, injury arising from another's crime extends to one individual, or only to a few; but the participants in this crime are plotting, with one stroke, the most horrible catastrophes for the whole body of citizens. O such men of savage hearts! O such cruel designs! O such human beings bereft of human feeling! (IV viii 12)

In keeping with our author's definition of the grand style, this passage concerns a lofty issue—treachery—and uses a great deal of ornament. It opens with two **rhetorical questions,** a figure in which a rhetor asks a question to which she doesn't really expect an answer. In fact, asking the question actually provides an opportunity to say more damning things about the traitors. The second rhetorical question also contains an **antistrophe** ("turning about"), the repetition of the same or similar words in successive clauses. Rather than referring to Rome by name, the speaker employs an **epithet**— *fatherland*—which is also a pun that reminds listeners about their dependent relationship on the state (*father* and *patriotism* have the same root, *patria,* in Latin). There are several examples of **isocolon** (balanced clauses), and the final passionate outbursts are examples of **apostrophe** ("turning away") to address absent persons or some abstraction—"O such cruel designs."

The middle style does not use ordinary prose, but it is more relaxed than the grand style. Cicero said that "all the ornaments are appropriate" to this style, especially metaphor and its relatives (*Orator* xxvi 91–96). A rhetor using the middle style develops arguments in leisurely fashion and as fully as possible and uses as many commonplaces as can be worked into the argument without drawing attention to their presence. The author of *ad Herennium* also provided an example of the middle style:

> men of the jury, you see against whom we are waging war—against allies who have been wont to fight in our defence, and together with us to preserve our empire by their valor and zeal. Not only must they have known themselves, their resources, and their manpower, but their nearness to us and their alliance with us in all affairs enabled them no less to learn and appraise the power of the Roman people in every sphere. When they had resolved to fight against us, on what, I ask you, did they rely in presuming to undertake the war, since they understood that much the greater part of our allies remained faithful to duty, and since they saw that they had at hand no great supply of soldiers, no competent commanders, and no public money—in short, none of the things needful for carrying on the war? (IV ix 13)

Here the rhetor used ordinary everyday language and loose sentence construction. While there are fewer ornaments than in the grand style, a few do appear: there is a fairly complex isocolon in the second sentence ("their resources, and their manpower, but their nearness to and their alliance with us"). "On what, I ask you" is another example of a rhetorical question.

According to the author of *ad Herennium,* the plain or simple style uses the "most ordinary speech of every day," almost as though it were conversation (IV x 14). Cicero elaborated on this bare description of the plain style, noting that it is "stripped of ornament" and "to the point, explaining everything and making every point clear rather than impressive" (*Orator* v 20). Usually the plain style employs straightforward narrative ("This happened and then this") or simple exposition of the facts, and it uses **loose** rather than **periodic sentences.**

Once again, rhetors should choose the level of style that is appropriate to their *ethos*, their subject matter, their audience, and the occasion. The grand style is certainly appropriate for ceremonial functions like weddings, funerals, and inaugurations. The plain style is appropriate when clarity is the main goal dictated by the occasion, while the middle style is appropriate for almost any discourse that will be published.

ORNAMENT

The last, and most important, of the excellences of style is ornament. Under this heading, ancient rhetoricians discussed uses of language that were unusual or extraordinary. They divided their study of ornament into three broad categories: **figures of speech** (Latin *figurae verborum*), **figures of thought** (*figurae sententiarum*), and **tropes** (Greek *tropi*, "turn"). Ancient grammarians and rhetoricians argued endlessly over the definitions and distinctions among these three sorts of ornament, and modern scholars haven't done much better at making sense out of the categories. As ancient rhetoric matured, the confusion grew. In some scholarly traditions, ornaments like **climax** and antithesis were classed under more than one heading (sometimes as figures, sometimes as tropes), while others, like **metaphor** and epithet, were often discussed both as single words (diction) and in terms of their effects in groups of words (composition).

Contemporary rhetors don't need to keep the categories straight, since discussions of figures and tropes no longer have to be memorized, as they did in Aristotle's time. However, rhetoricians should be able to distinguish among figures of language, figures of thought, and tropes. So, with Quintilian's help, we try to distinguish among these ancient categories.

Generally, a figure is any form of expression in which "we give our language a conformation other than the obvious and ordinary" (IX i 4). Sometimes Quintilian seems to mean the term *figure* literally; a figure is any piece of language that has a remarkable or artful shape. He likened the changes in language or meaning brought about by the use of figures to the changes in the shape of the body that came about "by sitting, lying down on something or looking back" (IX i 11). That is, use of a figure changes the shape of language, just as a change in posture or position changes the shape of the body. There are two kinds of figures. Figures of thought involve artful changes in ideas, feelings, or conceptions; these figures depart from ordinary patterns of moving an argument along (17). Figures of language, in contrast, involve unusual patternings of language, such as repetition or juxtaposition of similar words or constructions.

A trope is any substitution of one word or phrase for another. Grammatically speaking, a trope can transfer words or phrases from their proper place to another. This kind of grammatical trope is rare. Winston Churchill used it when he said "this is a kind of impertinence up with which I will not put." Here Churchill substituted an unusual word order for the ordinary pattern in order to make fun of the traditional grammatical rule that says prepositions may not appear at the end of sentences. Rhetorically speaking, a trope transfers the usual signification of a word or phrase to another, as in "My love is like a red, red rose." Here the poet (Robert Burns) transferred the meanings associated with roses (fragile, thorny, blooming briefly) to his love.

We review the ornaments of style in keeping with the ancient spirit of *copia*. Cicero wrote to his friend Trebatius, "As I have a guest with such a ravenous appetite for this feast of learning, I shall provide such an abundance that there may be something left from the banquet, rather than let you go unsatisfied" (*Topics* IV 25). Rhetors can study and practice using figures and tropes in order to enlarge their linguistic repertoire and, thus, to have them at hand whenever their use is appropriate to occasion, subject, audience, and *ethos*. But there are yet other reasons for their use. Quintilian argued that ornament, carefully deployed, contributes not a little to the furtherance of our case as well. For when our audience finds it a pleasure to listen, their attention and their readiness to believe what they hear are both alike increased, while they are generally filled with delight and sometimes even transported by admiration (VIII iii 5). A carefully chosen metaphor can make an argument clearer and more striking; a nicely balanced antithesis can lend emphasis to a point. Thus ornament enhances persuasion; indeed, it can also aid clarity.

Sentence Composition

We begin with ancient advice about sentence structure, since an understanding of ancient terms for parts of sentences is necessary to an understanding of figurative language. The ancient term for a sentence was **period** (Greek *periodos*, "a way around"). Modern scholars think that the ancient conception of a period as a whole made up of parts or **members** may derive from an analogy to the human body, which also has a main part—its trunk—from which the limbs or members branch off. In any case, ancient rhetoricians called any stretch of words that could stand on its own a "period," giving a sense of completeness (this is the source of our use of the term *period* to name a piece of punctuation that marks the end of a sentence). An ancient period is equivalent to a modern punctuated sentence: in other words, a period is any unit of prose that begins with a capital letter and ends with some mark of terminal punctuation (period, question mark, or exclamation point).

In order to grasp ancient thought about periods, it is helpful to think of any period as having a main part on which all the other parts depend—just like a tree or a human body. The main part of a period is meaningful all by itself, but this is usually not true of its members or branches.

John loves Mary.   (Main Part)

John loves Mary | even though he barely knows her.
   (Main Part)   (Member)

The stretches of language on either side of the | are logically different, because the left-hand one makes sense all by itself, while the one on the right needs more information to make complete sense.

Some periods consist only of one main part, with no additional members: "John loves Mary." It is also possible to string several main parts into a single period: "John loves Mary; Mary loves Fred; Fred despises everyone." Each section of this period is meaningful by itself. (Traditional grammarians call this a **compound sentence.** The ancients did not use this terminology, however.) It is also possible to add several kinds of dependent structures to the main part of any sentence. As the name implies, dependent structures are not meaningful by themselves. (Traditional grammarians call any sentence that has a main part and one or more dependent parts a **complex sentence.**) Ancient rhetoricians recognized two kinds of dependent structures: **colons** and **commas.**

Quintilian defined a colon (Latin *membrum,* "part" or "limb") as any expression that was rhythmically complete but meaningless if detached from the rest of the sentence. The author of *ad Herennium* gave these examples of colons:

On the one hand you were helping your enemy
and on the other you were hurting your friend. (IV xix 26)

Colons are not always equivalent to English clauses. Nevertheless, the structure known in English as a dependent or subordinate clause is a colon. Hence our use of the terms *semicolon* and *colon* to refer to punctuation marks that set off internal parts of sentences.

The term *comma* (Latin *articulus,* "part jointed on") referred to any set of words set apart by pauses (whence our term for the mark of punctuation, *comma,* which serves that very function in English sentences). Demetrius of Phaleron called a comma a "chip" since it was a piece cut or hacked off from a longer member (*On Style* I i 9). Quintilian defined it as an expression lacking rhythmical completeness or a portion of a colon (IX iv 122). A comma can consist of a single word, as in these examples from the *ad Herennium:*

By your vigour, voice, looks you have tarried your adversaries.
You have destroyed your enemies by jealousy, injuries, influence, perfidy.
(4.26)

In the first example, *voice* is a comma; in the second, *injuries* and *influence* are commas. In modern prose, commas are usually set off by punctuation. Since commas are very short, the English word *phrase* is usually a satisfactory translation.

Isocrates was widely regarded throughout antiquity as a master of art-ful composition. We use a sentence from his "Helen" to illustrate the ancient terms of composition:

> And although the Trojans might have rid themselves of the misfortunes which encompassed them by surrendering Helen, and the Greeks might have lived in peace for all time by being indifferent to her fate, neither so wished; on the contrary, the Trojans allowed their cities to be laid waste and their land to be ravaged, so as to avoid yielding Helen to the Greeks, and the Greeks chose rather, remaining in a foreign land to grow old there and never to see their own again, than, leaving her behind, to return to their fatherland. (50–51)

This is a very long sentence (ninety-four words) even by ancient standards. And yet it is still readable, because Isocrates (and his translator) paid care-ful attention to rhythm, internal punctuation, and the placement and bal-ance of its parts. We graph the sentence in order to indicate its parts and their relations:

> And although
> the Trojans might have rid themselves of the misfortunes which encom-passed them by surrendering Helen (COLON)
> and
> the Greeks might have lived in peace for all time by being indifferent to her fate (COLON)
> neither [the Trojans nor Greeks] so wished (FIRST MAIN PART)
> on the contrary (COMMA)
> the Trojans allowed their cities to be laid waste and their land to be ravaged (FIRST HALF SECOND MAIN PART)
> so as to avoid yielding Helen to the Greeks (COLON)
> and
> the Greeks chose (SECOND HALF SECOND MAIN PART)
> remaining in a foreign land to grow old there and never to see their own again
> rather than
> leaving her behind to return to their fatherland (COLON).

Traditional grammarians would call this a **compound-complex sentence,** since it has two main parts and each of these has dependent clauses attached. An ancient rhetorician, however, would have noticed the artful placement of the carefully balanced colons, as well as the rhythms built into the entire period. In order to appreciate these, you may have to read the sentence aloud. You can best appreciate the rhetorical effects of the other examples we provide for ancient figures of language if you read them aloud, as well, since they are intended to please the ear as well as the eye. Indeed, we recommend that you get into the habit of reading your own prose aloud in order to determine whether it has rhythm and shape. Reading aloud sometimes indicates the places where internal punctuation is needed, as well.

Paratactic and Periodic Styles

Ancient rhetoricians distinguished two types of sentences, which they called loose and periodic. Greek terms for a loose sentence can be translated "running" or "strung-on" or "continuous." Aristotle defined a style made up of loose sentences as having "no natural stopping-places." This style "comes to a stop only because there is no more to say of that subject" (III ix 9). He seems to have meant that the parts of a loose sentence are simply tacked onto one another. If we accept Aristotle's definition, a style made up of loose sentences might most accurately be called **paratactic** (Greek *parataxis*, "placed alongside"). A paratactic style gives the impression that the rhetor placed utterances somewhat carelessly side by side, just as they occurred to him. (The preceding sentence is an example.)

Later rhetoricians recommended this style for use in conversation and informal letters because of its simplicity and naturalness. They refined their discussions of the paratactic style to suggest that loosely constructed sentences also observe the ordinary or usual word order of the language in which they are written (as this very sentence does, or did, until we added this parenthesis). Paratactic style is frequently used in electronic mail, for this medium is fast, casual, and conducive to "chat" rather than to formal decrees. Since the paratactic style observes the natural word order of a language, its use does not constitute a figure unless a rhetor uses it to achieve some artistic effect, such as an impression of carelessness or breathlessness.

Aristotle thought that the paratactic style was unpleasant to read "because it goes on indefinitely—one always likes to sight a stopping-place in front of one. That explains why runners, just when they have reached the goal, lose their breath and strength, whereas before, when the end is in sight, they show no signs of fatigue" (*Rhetoric* III xi 1409a). For this reason, Aristotle preferred a style in which units of speech were more carefully demarcated and set off from one another. Like the rhetoricians who would later apply his terminology to all sentences, he called a unit of this kind a "period," and he defined it as "a portion of speech that has in itself a beginning and end, being at the same time not too big to be taken in at a glance" (35). Aristotle wrote that periods satisfied readers because they reached definite conclusions and they were easier to remember too. A periodic sentence, then, has an obvious structure; ordinarily its main part does not come at the beginning, as in a loose sentence. Its meaning may be distributed among several of its parts, as it is in the example from Isocrates, where the two main parts of the sentence are sandwiched between two groups of paired colons. Later rhetoricians dictated that rhetors should postpone the sense of the period until readers reached its final member, but this restriction was not usually a part of classical lore about style. In this example from Gorgias's "Helen," the main part of the period is placed last: "Who it was and why and how he sailed away, taking Helen as his love, I shall not say" (5). Hellenistic rhetoricians also dictated that periods could contain as few as one member or as many as four. Of course it is possible to write sentences that contain an infinite number of members, but ancient rhetoricians generally cautioned against such excess.

A style becomes periodic when readers have the sense that sentences are carefully constructed and satisfactorily "rounded off." Since the periodic style was appropriate to the most dignified and important occasions, most teachers also cautioned their students to use periodic sentences sparingly.

Figurative Language

In general, a paratactic style does not employ many figures of language, because it is structurally simple by definition. This is not true of the periodic style, however. Ancient rhetoricians compiled endless lists of variations on the use and arrangements of the basic parts of the period: these variations are the figures of language. Quintilian wrote that this group of figures has "one special merit, that they relieve the tedium of everyday stereotyped speech and save us from commonplace language" (IX iii 3–4). When they are used sparingly, they serve as a seasoning to any style.

We have divided the figures of language into two broad categories: those that interrupt normal word order and those that repeat words or structures for effect.

Figures That Interrupt Normal Word Order

Here is a periodic sentence from Gorgias's "Defense of Palamedes": "If then the accuser, Odysseus, made his accusation through good will toward Greece, either clearly knowing that I was betraying Greece to the barbarians or imagining somehow that this was the case, he would be best of men" (Sprague, 2001, 55).

> If then the accuser made his accusation through good will toward Greece
>   either
>   knowing clearly that I was betraying Greece to the barbarians
>   or
>   imagining somehow that this was the case
> he [Odysseus] would be the best of men.

Notice that Gorgias delayed the sense of the sentence until the very end (Odysseus is the best of men—if his motives are honest). The periodic structure keeps readers in suspense, heightening their curiosity about the author's opinion of Odysseus. Later on, Gorgias used a sentence constructed on similar lines to state another possibility: "But if he has put together this allegation out of envy or conspiracy or knavery, just as in the former case he would be the finest of men, so in this he would be the worst of men."

> But if he has put together this allegation out of envy or conspiracy or knavery
>   just as
> in the former case he would be the finest of men
>   so
> in   this   he would be the worst of men.

Again, the author's judgment of Odysseus's motives is postponed to the very end of the sentence. Taken together, the two sentences create an antithesis that works across several sentences.

Here is a periodic sentence from the nineteenth century written by Ralph Waldo Emerson in his essay "Nature": "Crossing a bare common, in snow puddles, at twilight, under a clouded sky, without having in my thoughts any occurrence of special good fortune, I have enjoyed a perfect exhilaration" (1983, 10).

> Crossing a bare common
>> in snow puddles
>> at twilight
>> under a clouded sky
>> without . . . good fortune
> I have enjoyed a perfect exhilaration.

Emerson postponed the point of the sentence (his achievement of perfect exhilaration) until its end, thus keeping readers in suspense and yet giving them the satisfaction of a firm closure when it finally arrives. He also used grammatically balanced commas (each is a prepositional phrase) inside a longish colon ("crossing . . . fortune") to build up suspense.

Here is a third example, a beautiful periodic sentence written by Alice Walker: "Wrapped in his feathered cape, his winged boots, he sent his soul flying to Zede while holding his body, his thought, his attentions on Carlotta, whom he did not cease to love" (1990, 24).

> Wrapped in his feathered cape
>> his winged boots
> he sent his soul flying   to Zede
>> while holding
>>> his body
>>> his thought
>>> his attentions on Carlotta, whom he did not cease to love.

Walker used parallel commas to emphasize her character's divided loyalties, which she reveals to readers only at the conclusion of the period.

News writers occasionally use periodic sentences, as well. This one appeared in a reflective essay on the history of racism in America, written by Jeffrey Gettleman: "Yet even at the height of segregation, when working-class whites clubbed black demonstrators in the streets of Birmingham and Atlanta, some white leaders were willing to question the old ways" (2002). The juxtaposition of the two contrasting but balanced comments about whites, with the second, more unexpected, clause coming last, demonstrates the force that a good period sentence can convey.

Rhetors can also interrupt normal word order by inserting a word or phrase inside a colon or period, as in this example, again composed by *New York Times* writer Jeffrey Gettleman, in an article about Somalia: "But confidence in the government—never very high—is rapidly bleeding away" (2007). Quintilian called this figure *interpositio,* but it is still known in English by its Greek name, *parenthesis* ("a statement alongside another"). As the interpolation in the previous sentence demonstrates, a parenthetical statement decreases distance, since it suddenly discloses the author's presence—as though she were speaking behind her hand. Parenthetical statements may appear between commas, like this, but they are more often punctuated by dashes—as we have done here—or with parentheses (as illustrated here). The novelist Robert Graves made interesting use of an almost wholly parenthetical style in the opening passage of his novel, *I Claudius:*

> I, Tiberius Claudius Drusus Nero Germanicus This-that-and-the-other (for I shall not trouble you yet with all my titles) who was once, and not so long ago either, known to my friends and relatives and associates as "Claudius the Idiot," or "That Claudius," or "Claudius the Stammerer," or "Clau-Clau-Claudius" or at best as "poor Uncle Claudius," am now about to write this strange history of my life. (1961, 3)

The parenthetical asides nearly swamp the main part of this sentence, inserted as they are between "I" and "am now about to write." Graves used them to suggest an important feature of Claudius's character: even though he wasn't very well organized, he was a stickler for detail.

Rhetors can interrupt normal word order in a number of other ways. The ancients gave such interruptions the generic name of *hyperbaton* ("a sudden turn"). A rhetor can attach a descriptive comma, as follows: "Mary, though reputed to be in love with John, is actually quite fond of Fred." The interpolated comma is an *appositio* ("putting off from," **apposition** in English), a phrase that interrupts the main part of the period to modify it or to add commentary about it. Or he can use an apostrophe to call on his audience or someone else: "I am, heaven help me, lost." In a very long sentence, it is sometimes helpful to sum up with an interrupter: "Invention, arrangement, style, memory, and delivery—these, the five canons of rhetoric—are all that occupy me now." The ancients called this figure *metabasis,* a summarizing transition.

Ancient rhetoricians also identified a pair of figures having to do with the use of connecting words between colons: **asyndeton** (no connectors) and **polysyndeton** (many connectors). Using the first figure, a rhetor eliminates connectors that ordinarily appear between colons or commas, as in this example from Cicero: "I ordered those against whom information was laid, to be summoned, guarded, brought before the senate: they were led into the senate" (quoted by Quintilian, IX iii 50). Cicero eliminated the *and*s that would ordinarily connect coordinate commas in order to give an impression of haste and vigor. Compare his version to a version that inserts connecting *and*s: "I ordered those against whom information was laid to be summoned and guarded and brought before the senate, and they were led into the senate." Gorgias used the opposing figure in the passage of his "Helen":

> What is becoming to a city is manpower, to a body beauty, to a soul wisdom, to an action virtue, to a speech truth, and the opposites of these are unbecoming. Man and woman and speech and deed and city and object should be honored with praise if praiseworthy and incur blame if unworthy, for it is an equal error

and a mistake to blame the praisable and to praise the blamable. (Sprague, 2001, 82.II, p. 50)

Here, both sentences contain examples of polysyndeton, in which the rhetor employs more conjunctions (*and* in this case) than are required by either grammar or sense. This figure enabled Gorgias to stretch out a series of words or phrases, thus calling attention to each item in the series and giving the whole a leisurely pace. To grasp the rhetorical effect of polysyndeton as compared to that of asyndeton, compare Gorgias's versions to a revision that substitutes punctuation for *and:*

> Fairest ornament to a city is a goodly army; to a body beauty; to a soul wisdom; to an action virtue; to a speech truth. Man, woman, speech, deed, city, object, should be praised.

Figures of Repetition

Modern composition textbooks often tell their readers to avoid repetition. Most likely, their authors worry that students rely on repetition because they do not have a sufficiently large vocabulary. But the advice to avoid repetition, however well meant, is not necessarily good advice. Since repetition is a means of calling attention to words and ideas that are important, rhetors should not be afraid to repeat words that are central to their arguments.

Artful repetition was available to speakers of Greek and Latin in single words. Rhetors could simply repeat a word in order to call attention to it, as Demosthenes is said to have done when asked what was the most important part of rhetoric. He replied: "Delivery, delivery, delivery." Gertrude Stein used repetition to make fun of poetic metaphors about roses: "A rose is a rose is a rose." In Chapter 2, on *kairos,* we encountered an instance of repetition in the speech by Governor George Ryan with which he commuted the sentences of death row inmates: "Our capital system is haunted by the demon of error, error in determining guilt and error in determining who among the guilty deserves to die" (2003). You can see how the ringing repetition of the word *error* marks the flawed system as that which drove Governor Ryan's landmark decision.

Another means of repeating words is **synomyny** ("the same name"), that is, using words that are similar in meaning as a means of repeating an important point: "call it treason, betrayal, sedition, or villainy—it is one." The author of *ad Herennium* gave these examples: "You have impiously beaten your father; you have criminally laid hands upon your parent" and "You have overturned the republic from its roots; you have demolished the state from its foundations" (IIV xxviii 38). A thesaurus can help when a rhetor wants to pile up similar words to create the figure of synonymy. A thesaurus should never be used to avoid repeating words, though; to do this is to commit the rhetorical sin of circumlocution. As the ancient rhetoricians repeatedly pointed out, repetition is not necessarily a bad thing. Artfully used, it constitutes a figure. A thesaurus supplies lists of words that are similar to one another (synonyms). But synonyms are not pure equivalents, despite their Greek name. No two words mean exactly the same thing, because meaning depends upon context and use. Students who use a thesaurus to avoid repetition or to find words that "sound fancier" than the ones they ordinarily use, then, are misusing the thesaurus, and they run the risk as well of saying something they don't mean.

There is another class of figures of language that use artful synonymy and exploit other similarities between words, as well. These are now known generically as **puns**. Puns allow rhetors to repeat something in an artful and often funny way: "He told the sexton and the sexton tolled the bell." The punch lines of shaggy dog stories were funny because they punned on some sober maxim: "Don't hatchet your counts before they chicken"; "People who live in grass houses shouldn't stow thrones." A practice currently in vogue is to give businesses punning names, such as "Shear Madness," a beauty shop in State College, Pennsylvania, and "The Great Impasta," an Italian restaurant in Champaign, Illinois. Ancient puns often do not survive translation, because the pun depends upon some similarity in word shape or sound. Quintilian quoted this one from the Roman poet Ovid: *"Cur ego non dicam, Furia, te furiam?"* ("Furia, why should I not call you a fury?"); and this one, which does survive translation, from *ad Herennium*: *"Nam amari iucundum sit, si curetur ne quid insit amuri"* ("To be dear to you would bring me joy—if only I take care it shall not in anguish cost me dear") (IV xiv 21; *Institutes* IX iii 69–70).

According to Quintilian, puns belong to the class of figures that "attracts the ear of the audience and excites their attention by some resemblance, equality or contrast of words" (IX iii 66). The ancient term for pun was *paronomasia,* which the author of *ad Herennium* defined as "the figure in which, by means of a modification of sound, or change of letters, a close resemblance to a given verb or noun is produced, so that similar words express dissimilar things" (IV xxi 29). Generally, puns exploit accidental resemblances among words.

The Fountains of Wayne Song "Hung Up on You" ("Ever since you hung up on me/I'm hung up on you") plays on both senses of the phrase "hung up"—the act performed with telephones and the "hang-up" or slight obsession. There are many varieties of this figure, but all have to do with using words that are similar to others, either in sound, shape, meaning, or function. In short, puns can exploit almost any accidental resemblance among the shapes, functions, sounds, spellings, or meanings of words.

When editors of the *Atlantic* asked readers to help them coin a word "to describe the moment of undignified vulnerability that people in airport security lines experience when they have to take off their shoes," they were flooded with puns about socks and shoes, including "insockurity," "sole-baring," "shoemiliation," "disshoeveled," "pedanoia" "footwary," "unshoddenfreude." The winner, as it turns out, was "toeing the line" (Wallraff 2007). Quintilian thought that this form of the figure was a "poor trick even when employed in jest" (Institutes of Oratory Ixiii. 73ff). Along with Quintilian, we often roll our eyes at puns.

Using *antanaclasis* ("bending back"), the rhetor repeats a word in two different senses: "I would leave this place, should the Senate give me leave" (*ad Herennium* IV xiv 21). "If we don't hang together, we'll hang separately" (Benjamin Franklin). Using *homoioteleuton* ("same ending"), the rhetor repeats words having similar endings: "You dare to act dishonorably, you strive to talk despicably; you live hatefully, you sin zealously, you speak offensively" (*ad Herennium* IV xx 28). This figure had more uses in Greek and Latin than it does in English, where only a few parts of speech, such as the adverbs illustrated here, have similar endings. Still, "The Confession Procession" titles a short piece by Nancy Gibbs on the absolution trend in politics (2007, 15).

Using **zeugma** and its relatives, the rhetor ties a number of commas or colons to the same verb. Quintilian quoted this example from Cicero: "Lust conquered shame, boldness fear, madness reason" (*"Pro Cluentio"* vi 15; *Institutes* IX iii 62). Modern rhetoricians like to cite Alexander Pope's use of zeugma in "The Rape of the Lock," whose heroine's confused values are such that she would just as soon "stain her honor, or her new brocade." Here is another zeugma from Pope:

> Here thou, great Anna! whom three realms obey
> Dost sometimes counsel take—and sometimes tea.

Pope's juxtaposition of the heavily political and the slightly domestic is funny (and it was possibly even funnier when *obey* actually rhymed with *tea*). Because zeugma turns the same verb in different directions, it is useful for dealing with complex issues. This feature, combined with its inherent economy, makes zeugma a favorite for writers of headlines like these: "Mercury, and Certainty, Rising" (Monastersky 2007, A16) and "Florida Girl Learns to Lift Weights, and Gold Medals" (Goodnough 2007).

There is another set of figures that depends upon repetition of words, but this group requires the composition of periods having two or more members. Rhetors using these figures repeat words that appear in similar positions in each of several members of a period. For example, words can be repeated at the beginning of successive colons expressing either similar or different ideas (**anaphora** or *epanaphora,* literally "carrying back"): "To you must go the credit for this, to you are thanks due, to you will this act of yours bring glory" (*ad Herennium* IV xiii 19). Sportswriter Steve Wulf uses anaphora in this opener to his article on apologies:

> Curt Schilling is sorry he said those things. Pacman Jones is sorry he did those things. Calvin Borel is sorry he thought he and Street Sense had the Preakness won. Dale Earnhardt Jr.'s crew chief is sorry he left the wrong brackets on the No. 8 car. Jason Giambi is sorry for "doing that stuff." Heck, we're sorry we made fun of Gil Meche when the Royals signed him. (2007, 28)

Or rhetors can repeat the last word in successive phrases *(epiphora):* "It was by the justice of the Roman people that the Carthaginians were conquered, by its force of arms that they were conquered, by its generosity that they were conquered." Or they can combine *epanaphora* and *epiphora* to get *symploke* ("tied together"): "One whom the Senate has condemned, one whom the Roman people has condemned, one whom universal public opinion has condemned, would you by your votes acquit such a one?" (xiv 20). Note also that this example postpones the rhetorical question, which carries the sense of the sentence, until the very end.

Yet another figure of language links colons or commas together by repeating words in each member (**anadiplosis,** "repeating two pieces"). Here is an example from *ad Herennium:* "You now even dare to come into the sight of these citizens, traitor to the fatherland? Traitor, I say, to the fatherland, you dare come into the sight of these citizens?" (IV xxviii 38). In a more complex use of anadiplosis, the rhetor repeats the last word of one member as the first word of the next. Here is a wonderful example from the journalist Tom Wolfe's *The Kandy-Kolored Tangerine-Flake Streamline Baby:*

> And there they have it, the color called Landlord's Brown, immune to time, flood, tropic heat, arctic chill, punk rumbles, slops, blood, leprotic bugs, cock-roaches the size of mice, mice the size of rats, rats the size of Airedales and lumpenprole tenants. (1999, 286)

Just when this very long sentence threatens to lose itself in a chaotic list, Wolfe brings some order to it by employing anadiplosis—he ends one item in the series with the word that begins the next.

When a period has a series of members that become increasingly important, it displays a figure called climax (Greek "ladder"). The author of the *ad Herennium* defined climax as "the figure in which the speaker passes to the following word only after advancing by steps to the preceding one" (IV xxiv 34). He gave this example: "Now what remnant of the hope of liberty survives, if those men may do what they please, if they can do what they may, if they dare do what they can, if they do what they dare, and if you approve what they do?" Here is another example, from Demosthenes' *On the Crown* (179), quoted by the author of the *ad Herennium* and by Quintilian as well: "I did not say this and then fail to make the motion; I did not make the motion and then fail to act as an ambassador; I did not act as an ambassador and then fail to persuade the Thebans" (IV xxv 34; IX iii 55–56).

Strictly speaking, climax uses anadiplosis, as all of these examples do. A less strict application of the figure refers to any placement of phrases or clauses in order of their increasing importance. An eighteenth-century rhetorician named George Campbell quoted this example of climax from the "Song of Solomon":

> My beloved spake and said to me, Arise, my love, my fair, and come away; for lo, the winter is past, the rain is over and gone, the flowers appear on the earth, the time of the singing of birds is come, and the voice of the turtle is heard in our land; the fig-tree putteth forth her green figs, and the vines, with the tender grape, perfume the air. Arise, my love, my fair, and come away. (II v 10–13)

Campbell noted that the poet begins with negative phrases indicating that winter has passed and moves toward positive indications of the coming of spring, arranged in order of their increasing importance (*Philosophy of Rhetoric* III i 1). Modern rhetoricians sometimes recommend that whole discourses feature the movement of climax, saving their most important or most persuasive point for last.

Commas or colons themselves can have ornamental effects when two or more that are similarly structured are repeated within a single period. This figure is called *isocolon* in Greek and "parallelism" in English. Here is a famous example from Abraham Lincoln's Gettysburg Address: "The world will little note nor long remember what we say here, but it can never forget what they did here." We graph this sentence in order to illustrate the balanced colons a little more clearly:

The world will	little note	what we say here,
	nor long remember	
but it	can never forget	what they did here.

In parallelism, verbs should be balanced against verbs, prepositional phrases against prepositional phrases, and so on. Some ancient authors claimed that the members of an *isocolon* should have a similar number of syllables so that the parallelism between them was nearly perfect. Here is an example from *ad Herennium:*

The father was meeting death	in battle;
the son was planning marriage	at his home. (IV xx 27)

Here is a modern example of parallelism, written by the nineteenth-century feminist Elizabeth Cady Stanton:

> I should feel exceedingly diffident to appear before you at this time, having never before spoken in public, were I not nerved by a sense of right and duty, did I not feel the time had fully come for the question of woman's wrongs to be laid before the public, did I not believe that woman herself must do this work; for woman alone can understand the height, the depth, the length, and the breadth of her own degradation. (1848)

Stanton repeated the phrase "did I not" in successive colons in order to emphasize her urgent reasons for violating the taboo against women speaking in public. She also used asyndeton to yoke the parallel commas in the last colon, thus vigorously and forcefully expressing the seriousness of women's situation.

In a slightly less serious context, this humorous instance of parallel construction appears on McSweeney's feature "Internet Tendency: Reviews of New Food," in a contribution by D. Paul:

> Now, as a college graduate who is enduring the humiliation of working for $8 an hour icing cakes and whose car is in a constant state of disrepair, whose boyfriend flirts with prettier, skinnier girls, whose parents are ashamed, whose apartment is a filthy hole of beer cans and liquor bottles, whose checking account hovers near the red, whose student-loan payments are past due, whose only comfort is the 30 minutes during the day when she can drive to the local park to cry, I find the mere prospect of $1,000 to be enough to inspire hope and a sense of overall well-being.

This lengthy sentence uses no fewer than eight dependent cola (each beginning with "who" or "whose") to provide details about a life while at the same time holding us in suspense until we come to its periodic ending. Ross Simonini used parallel construction to compose this tagline for an interview with singer/songwriter David Gates: "Distinguishing bluegrass from old-time, creativity from innovation, and criticism from fiction writing" (2007).

When the parallel members express logically contrary thoughts, as they do here, the figure is called an antithesis ("counterstatement"). In classical rhetorical theory, an antithesis occurred when either words or their meanings were opposed to one another. The author of the *ad Alexandrum* differentiated these two kinds of antithesis as follows: "Let the rich and prosperous give to the poor and needy" (opposition in terms only); "I nursed him when he was ill, but he has caused me a very great deal of harm" (opposition in meaning) (26 1435b). But the author of *ad Herennium* included any use of opposites or contraries under this figure. He illustrated its use with this jingling example:

> When all is calm, you are confused; when all is in confusion, you are calm. In a situation requiring all your coolness, you are on fire; in one requiring all your ardor, you are cool. When there is need for you to be silent, you are uproarious; when you should speak, you grow mute. Present, you wish to be absent; absent, you are eager to return. In peace, you demand war; in war, you yearn for peace. In the Assembly, you talk of valor; in battle, you cannot for cowardice endure the trumpet's sound. (IV xv 21)

All ancient authorities credit Gorgias with the invention of this figure, and its preference for stating balanced contraries is consonant with sophistic thought. In this example, from his "Helen," Gorgias combined antithesis with the figure of thought known as division: "For either by will of Fate and decision of the gods and vote of Necessity did she do what she did, or by force reduced or by words seduced or by love possessed" (6). Modern rhetors often use antithesis in order to express a contrast more effectively. The food writer John Mariani wrote this antithesis about culinary contrasts: "In Paris, you start the day with a great croissant and bad coffee; in Rome, with great coffee and a bad croissant" (2007, 54). John F. Kennedy's is perhaps the most famous: "Ask not what your country can do for you; ask what you can do for your country." This kind of antithesis—where the actual words are reversed—is called **chiasmus** ("arranged crosswise"; in the shape of the greek letter *chi,* which looks like an *X*). Sometimes a chiasmus uses more than two words, like this impressive example from novelist Richard Powers: "Data survive all hope of learning, but hope must learn how to survive the data" (2000, 88). Note the crisscross pattern in the language here:

data : hope : learning   ::   hope : learn : data

An even more complex use of antithesis appears in the figure called **antimetabole** ("thrown over against"). Here the rhetor expresses contrasting ideas in juxtaposed structures. Here are two examples from *ad Herennium:* "A poem ought to be a painting that speaks; a painting ought to be a silent poem"; "If you are a fool, for that reason you should be silent; and yet, although you should be silent, you are not for that reason a fool" (IV xxxviii 39). The best-known modern example was made popular by John Dean of Watergate fame: "When the going gets tough, the tough get going."

Figures of Thought

In *De Oratore* and *Orator* Cicero classed virtually all ornament under the head of figures of thought. This seems appropriate, since these figures (*sententia* in Latin) are the most rhetorical of the ornaments of style. By this we mean two things: first of all, the *sententia* are arguments in themselves; that is, they can function as proofs. Second, they can enhance a rhetor's *ethos* or appeal to an audience's emotions (*pathos*). As Quintilian noted, the figures of thought "lend credibility to our arguments and steal their way secretly into the minds of the judges" (IX i 19–20). Perhaps because they are so highly rhetorical, so obviously calling attention to themselves as artifice and to rhetoric as performance, the figures of thought are not often discussed by modern rhetoricians. This was not true of ancient authorities, however. Quintilian treated only those figures of thought that "depart from the direct method of statement," and he still managed to discriminate well over a dozen (IX ii 1). We have divided our discussion of the *sententia* among figures that call attention to the rhetor, figures that stimulate the emotions of an audience, and figures drawn from the argument itself.

Figures of Thought That Enhance Ethos

This group of figures allows rhetors to call attention to the fact that they are manipulating the flow of the discourse. As such, they strengthen the rhetor's *ethos;* in most cases, their use decreases distance between the rhetor and an audience, as well. (See the chapters on *ethos* and *pathos* for more information about these rhetorical appeals). Rhetors may use these figures to emphasize a point or to draw attention away from something, to hesitate, apologize, interrupt, attack opponents, make promises.

Rhetors often use questions (Latin *interrogatio*) to draw attention to important points. Quintilian gave the following example: "How long, Cataline, will you abuse our patience?" (IX 11 7–8). Notice that the effect of this differs from a flat statement: "You have abused our patience a long time, Cataline." Rhetors can also ask a question to which it is impossible or difficult to reply: "how can this be?" Or we may ask questions in order to belittle or besmirch the character of the person to whom it is addressed ("What would you have me do, you who have cut off my options?"), to excite pity ("Where will I go, what can I do?"), or to embarrass an opponent ("Can't you hear the cries of your victims?") (IX ii 9–10).

Today, the best-known figure of this group is the rhetorical question: "Do you really expect me to respond to such an outrageous accusation"? or "Who can tell the depths to which this treachery has sunk?" Here, of course, the rhetor does not expect a reply; indeed, she expects the audience to fill in the response for themselves, in the first case with "no" and in the second with the name of the person she hopes will be blamed for the treachery. Variations on rhetorical questioning include *hypophora* or *subjectio,* in which the rhetor asks what can be said in favor of those who oppose her ("Who, indeed, can support those who discriminate against the helpless poor?") or inquires what can possibly be said against her case ("On what grounds, my friends, can you object to so honorable a cause as mine?"). Use of this figure gives rhetors an opportunity to question the opinions or practices of those who oppose them or to anticipate and answer objections that might be made to their positions. Insofar as it allows rhetors to anticipate and answer objections that might be made to their positions, this figure is useful in refutation (see Chapter 9, on arrangement).

Asking a question to get information is not a figure; in order for a question to constitute a figure, it must be used to emphasize a point. Rhetors should also guard against using questions to which they don't know the answers. Audiences can usually discern when a rhetor is asking questions in order to avoid committing himself. The only effective rhetorical question, after all, is one to which the answer is so obvious that everyone, including the audience, can supply its answer. This figure depends for its effect on an audience's feeling that it is participating in the construction of the argument.

The author of *ad Herennium* mentions another *sententia* that depends on questioning. He calls it **reasoning by question and answer** (*ratiocinatio,* "reasoning"), wherein the rhetor inserts a question between successive affirmative statements. We quote a portion of his rather long illustration of this device. (The passage also displays several prejudicial commonplaces about women's characters, prejudices that have not entirely disappeared):

> When our ancestors condemned a woman for one crime, they considered that by this single judgement she was convicted of many transgressions. How so? Judged unchaste, she was also deemed guilty of poisoning. Why? Because, having sold her body to the basest passion, she had to live in fear of many persons. Who are these? Her husband, her parents, and the others involved, as she sees, in the infamy of her dishonor. And what then? Those whom she fears so much she would inevitably wish to destroy. Why inevitably? Because no honorable motive can restrain a woman who is terrified by the enormity of her crime, emboldened by her lawlessness, and made heedless by the nature of her sex. (IV xvi 23)

The use of *ratiocinatio* allowed the rhetor to repeat his charges. The repetitions hammer home the accusations, thus making them seem tenable whether they are or not. The device also calls attention to the ways in which the successive statements connect to each other, thus heightening the impression that the rhetor is proceeding rationally.

The author of *ad Herennium* pointed out that not all uses of interrogation are impressive or elegant. It is so when the points against the adversaries' cause have been summed up and it reinforces the argument that has just been delivered, as follows: "So when you were doing and saying and managing all this, were you, or were you not, alienating and estranging from the republic the sentiments of our allies? And was it, or was it not, needful to employ some one to thwart these designs of yours and prevent their fulfilment?" (IV xv 22). Fans of courtroom drama will easily recognize this device, which contemporary attorneys often use in their summations. The "were you or were you not" construction allows the person using it to repeat statements that may or may not be true without having to commit to them.

Anticipation (Greek *prolepsis,* "to take before") is a generic name given to any figure of thought wherein a rhetor foresees and replies to possible objections to her arguments. For example, a rhetor may anticipate that some point or points in her argument will seem weak or dishonorable to her audience. In his *Time* magazine article proposing that the *Bible* should be taught in public schools, David Van Biema offers this example of anticipation:

> To some, this idea seems retrograde. Citing a series of Supreme Court decisions culminating in 1963's *Abington Township School District v. Schempp,* which removed prayer and devotion from the classroom, the skeptics ask whether it is safe to bring back the source of all that sectarianism. But a new, post-*Schempp* coalition insists it is essential to do so. It argues that teaching the Bible in schools—as an object of study, not God's received word—is eminently constitutional. (2007, 42)

Van Biema's argument is no doubt controversial, and not all readers will be receptive, so the figure of anticipation is crucial for him to retain his audience's interest. Notably, this figure occurs fairly early on in the article. Cicero would approve. (See Chapter 9 on arrangement.)

Rhetors may also state that they will not speak or write about something all the while they are actually doing so (**paralepsis,** "to take alongside of"). Here is an example: "I will not here list all the negative effects of hateful speech: its divisiveness, its disruptiveness, its cruelty, its ugliness." A closely related figure is **hesitation** or indecision (Latin *dubitatio,* "doubt"). Using this figure, a rhetor pretends to be unable to decide "where to begin or end, or to decide what especially requires to be said or not to be said at all" (*Institutes* IX ii 19). A rhetor may express indecision over a word choice, for example: "Conservatives label pro-choice positions as 'anti-family,' but I am not sure that this is the most informative way to characterize those who favor abortion rights." Using *dubitatio,* a rhetor may point out that an issue is so vast that it can't be covered satisfactorily in the time or space allotted. Or he may express hesitation or doubt about introducing unpleasant or distasteful matters: "Most people are so sensitive about racism that I hesitate even to discuss it." Quintilian remarked that this figure lends "an impression of truth to our statements." Rhetors who use it can depict themselves as people who are sensitive to nuance and to the feelings of audiences as well.

Another similar figure of thought is **correction,** where a rhetor replaces a word or phrase he had used earlier with a more precise one. The author of *ad Herrenium* gave this example of *correctio:* "After the men in question had conquered—or rather had been conquered, for how shall I call that a conquest which has brought more disaster than benefit to the conquerors?" (IV xxvi 36). The rhetor's reconsideration makes him seem thoughtful and intelligent. In this example, the use of correction also emphasizes the point that the action being discussed can be read in more than one way. Here is another example: "I refer to hateful speech. However, things would be clearer if this practice were known by its rightful name—racism."

Figures of Thought That Involve Audience

Quintilian mentioned a set of figures of thought that involve the audience in the argument. He discussed these under the general heading of "communication." In these figures, the rhetor addresses the audience, taking them into her confidence: "No reasonable person can doubt the severe consequences of this practice." One form of this figure is concession, by which the rhetor concedes a disputed point or leaves a disputed point up to the audience to decide: "Of course I am aware that hateful speech hurts those it is aimed against. Nevertheless, the hurt felt by some does not justify the regulation of all." In suspension, the rhetor raises expectations that something bad or sensational will be mentioned and then mentions something much worse. Quintilian gave this example from Cicero: "What think you? Perhaps you expect to hear of some theft or plunder?" (IX ii 22). Cicero then went on to discuss serious crimes against the state.

The opposite of suspension is **paradox** ("contrary opinion"), in which the rhetor raises expectations and then mentions something trivial. The headlines on supermarket tabloids are paradoxes in this sense. In modern rhetoric, paradox has a different but related meaning. A paradox is any statement that seems self-contradictory but in some sense may be true: "There are none so credulous as unbelievers."

A related figure of thought is **oxymoron,** which yokes contradictory terms together, usually as adjective and noun: "cold heat," "eloquent silence." A favorite example of oxymoron comes from a professor of philosophy: "This passage in Heidegger is clearly opaque."

The author of *ad Herennium* discussed a figure of thought called *parrhesia* ("frankness of speech"). This figure occurs "when, talking before those to whom we owe reverence or fear, we yet exercise our right to speak out, because we seem justified in reprehending them, or persons dear to them, for some fault" (IV xxxvi 48). For example: "The university administration has tolerated hateful speech on this campus, and so to some extent they are to blame for its widespread use." An opposing figure is **litotes (understatement),** where a rhetor diminishes some feature of the situation that is obvious to all. The author of *ad Herennium* gave this example from the defense of a very wealthy person: "His father left him a patrimony that was—I do not wish to exaggerate—not the smallest" (IV xxxviii 50). Using litotes, the rhetor avoids stating the exact extent of the rich man's holdings, and the audience is led to admire his tact as well. Modern rhetoricians define litotes as any statement that denies its contrary statement: "She was not unmindful of my wishes." But the figure occurs in any deliberate understatement of a state of affairs wherein more is understood than is said: "Nuclear weapons are dangerous." Sometimes litotes is not deliberate, as when an American president brushed off "the vision thing" as inappropriate to his administration.

Figures of Thought That Arouse Emotion

According to Quintilian, "the figures best adapted for intensifying emotion consist chiefly in simulation" (IX ii 26). This group of figures requires more inventiveness from a rhetor than any other, since their persuasive quality depends upon skill in creating convincing fictions. As Quintilian remarked,

> Such devices make a great demand on our powers of eloquence. For with things which are false and incredible by nature there are but two alternatives: either they will move our hearers with exceptional force because they are beyond the truth, or they will be regarded as empty nothings because they are not the truth. (IX ii 33)

This group of *sententia* includes personification, *enargeia*, **irony,** and *ethopoeia.* Personification or impersonation "consists in representing an absent person as present, or in making a mute thing or one lacking form articulate" (*ad Herennium* IV liii 66). We may represent someone who has died as though she were present: "If my mother were alive, she would say . . ." We can represent animals or nature as having human qualities, as the poet John Milton did in this passage from *Paradise Lost:*

> Earth felt the wound, and Nature from her seat
> Sighing through all her Works gave signs of woe. (IX 529–30)

The advantage of this figure, according to Quintilian, is that we can display the inner thoughts of others as though they were present. He cautioned, however, that people and things must be represented credibly.

In *enargeia* (usually translated "ocular demonstration" or "vivid demonstration"), a rhetor paints a picture of a scene so vividly that it seems to be happening right in front of the audience. This is usually done by appealing to the sense of sight. Writer Barry Yeoman composed this *enargeia* of the pickup route to an organic farm:

> Several times a week a blue truck with a stainless steel collection tank drives up a newly blacktopped road in Guilford, Vermont, heading toward Mary Ellen and David Franklin's organic dairy farm. It rolls past a weathered white farmhouse roofed with Guilford and New York slate, past a sign advertising fresh eggs and grass-fed beef, until it arrives at the 19th-century barn where the Franklins do their milking. On both sides of the road, cows graze on pastureland that stretches beyond the Massachusetts line. The air is moist and earthy. (2007, 35)

Yeoman fills the description with images of old-fashioned, small-town farming in order to set up the article's intriguing incongruity: this organic farm's biggest customer is Wal-Mart.

Simply defined, irony occurs when an audience understands the opposite of what is expressed: someone says "Nice day, huh?" when it is windy and snowing; another asks "'Hot enough for you?" when everyone is obviously suffering from the heat. But irony can be extremely complex. As Quintilian put it, in this figure,

> the meaning, and sometimes the whole aspect of our case, conflicts with the language and the tone of voice adopted; nay, a man's whole life may be colored with irony, as was the case with Socrates, who was called an ironist because he assumed the role of an ignorant man lost in wonder at the wisdom of others. (IX ii 46)

Irony abounds in contemporary political rhetoric: "My opponent is an honorable woman, I am sure"; "The party of moral values is the party that brought us Watergate, the savings-and-loan scandals, and the Iran-Contra affair." Sometimes irony rebounds on its users. When a politician labels his opponent a draft dodger, the situation becomes ironic if the politician himself somehow escaped mandated military service. If this is discovered, his figure can backfire on him.

The philosopher Claire Colebrook has dubbed irony "the new critical idiom," and like us, she launches her discussion of irony by quoting Quintilian. Still, in the twenty-first century, the era of Jon Stewart and Stephen Colbert, irony has certainly made a return. Advertisers often use irony in their promotional campaigns, which can be a risky move with a vast audience. Irony finds a home on T-shirts, like the one featured in an episode of *Six Feet Under* when the character Billy wears a T-shirt that says "Ski Iraq," a deceptively simple tidbit of irony that entails a complex critique of the forces behind the invasion of Iraq. The T-shirts reading "T*** censorship" are also ironic because, well, they display a kind of censorship. Then there are the ironic T-shirts that read "[Insert Ironic Phrase Here]." Irony of ironies. Irony is very difficult to pull off in the more distant forms of writing such as memos and letters. And as David Shipley and Will Schwalbe write in their book *Send*, irony in e-mail—even when the two e-mail authors know each other quite well—can be very tricky indeed (2007, 175–179).

Ethopoeia, or character portrayal, consists in "representing and depicting in words clearly enough for recognition the bodily form of some person" (*ad Herennium* IV xlix 63). The author gave this example: "the ruddy, short, bent man, with white and rather curly hair, blue-grey eyes, and a huge scar on his chin." But character portrayal may deal with a person's qualities as well as her physical characteristics. The author of *ad Herennium* portrayed a rich man by depicting his habits:

> That person there . . . thinks it admirable that he is called rich. . . . Once he has propped his chin on his left hand he thinks that he dazzles the eyes of all with the gleam of his jewelry and the glitter of his gold. . . . When he turns to his slave boy here, his only one . . . he calls him now by one name, now by another, and now by a third . . . so that unknowing hearers may think he is selecting one slave from among many. (IV xlix 63)

It is not difficult to update this sketch: simply put a Rolex on the man's arm and substitute a personal secretary or a bodyguard for the slave. We have met this kind of *ethopoeia* before, in the character sketches of Theophrastus and also in the *progymnasmata* by the same name (see Chapter 6, on *ethos*). Quintilian treated this figure as a kind of imitation in which the rhetor copies or emulates someone's words or deeds. He recommended the use of *ethopoeia* because of its charm and variety. He also pointed out that depictions of character, since they seem natural and spontaneous, can make an audience more receptive to a rhetor's *ethos* or to the *ethos* of the person being described (IX ii 59). It is quite common for celebrity interviews to begin with a detailed description of the celebrity, like this opener from an interview with Olympic swimmer Michael Phelps:

> Because of the weather, a freak blizzard in late April that dumped a foot of snow on the streets of Colorado Springs, Colorado, Michael Phelps has ditched his usual flip-flops and boardshorts for a pair of scuffed Pumas and a rumpled tracksuit. With his backpack, iPod, and greasy Tigers cap, he could be any kid slouching around a college quad, another shaggy white boy banging hip-hop. But this isn't a college quad; it's the U.S. Olympic Training Center, and the kid in those baggy sweats is a coil of forward motion that might just be the greatest athlete alive. (Solotaroff 2007, 81)

With this *ethopoeia*, Solotaroff offers a vivid picture of Phelps's self-presentation. That picture will hang in the background of the question-and-answer session that follows.

Figures of Thought Borrowed from Invention and Arrangement

Quintilian disapproved of the practice of borrowing figures from invention or arrangement, and so he refused to treat them. In book IX of the *Institutes*, he huffed: "I will pass by those authors who set no limit to their craze for inventing technical terms and even include among figures what really comes under the head of arguments" (iii 99). Most ancient rhetoricians were not as fastidious as Quintilian, however. For example, the author of the *ad Herennium* treated reasoning by contraries (enthymeme or *conclusio*) as a figure of thought. As you can see from the Greek term for this figure, it is borrowed from invention. In the *ad Herennium,* reasoning by contraries is a figure when the rhetor uses one of two opposite statements to prove the other, as in the following: "A faithless friend cannot be an honorable enemy"; "George has never spoken the truth in private, and so he cannot be expected to refrain from lying in public." This figure resembles an enthymeme because it draws a conclusion (George will lie in public) from a statement that is not open to question (George lies to his friends). The author of *ad Herennium* liked it because of its "brief and complete rounding-off," and so he recommended that it be completed in one unbroken period (IV xviii 26).

Other figures of thought repeat on the sentence level the parts of arrangement suggested for whole discourses. Cicero was particularly fond of these as a means of helping the audience keep track of the progress of the argument. Along with other ancient rhetoricians, he recommended that complex topics be divided into parts and a reason for accepting the parts be attached to each (*divisio*). Here is an example from *ad Herennium:* "If·you are an upright man, you have not deserved reproach; if a wicked man, you will be unmoved" (IV xl 52). In this case, the rhetor divides alternatives into only two (the man is either upright or wicked); this allows the rhetor to select from among many characteristics that might be chosen and thus to control the audience's response to the man. This figure is closely related to **distribution** (*diairesis, distributio*), whereby the rhetor divides up possibilities and distributes them among different areas. Here is an example from *ad Herennium:* "The Senate's function is to assist the state with counsel; the magistracy's is to execute, by diligent activity, the Senate's will; the people's to choose and support by its votes the best measures and the most suitable men" (IV xxxv 47). The distribution makes this political arrangement seem fair and equitable. An Infiniti ad in the June 2007 issue of *Esquire* uses distribution to assert its car's desirability on multiple fronts: "Horsepower is what sends you against the back of your seat. Design is what makes the short journey more memorable."

Accumulation (*frequentatio*) is another figure of thought based on arrangement. Here the rhetor gathers together points that are scattered about and lists them all together. This has the effect of making a shaky conclusion seem more evident or reasonable. Interestingly, accumulation is forbidden in courtroom argument. In many cases, prosecutors are not allowed to introduce an accused person's past offenses into their argument on the grounds that a person should be tried only for the crime with which she is currently charged. This practice testifies to the rhetorical power of accumulation: while juries or judges might not be impressed by the evidence assembled to substantiate one instance of a crime, they are more likely to be impressed by evidence that testifies to the commission of a series of like or related crimes. Television uses a combination of images and speech to create the effect of accumulation, as when, for example, a sportscaster calls an NBA game a "dunkfest" while the rolling clips show twelve different slam dunks from the game. The accumulated images reinforce the credibility of the term.

Sometimes an argument about a relatively new trend will begin by accumulating instances of that trend, as with the movie *Super Size Me* (2004), which seeks to link America's rising obesity rate with the fast food industry's production of desire. The beginning of the documentary shows images of obese Americans, young and old, on the street, on the beach, some eating ice cream and some eating french fries. Written arguments about new trends can use accumulation to similar effect, as with this article in *Advertising Age* about the licensing of popular soft-drink names: "Dr. Pepper barbeque sauce. 7Up Bundt cakes. Mountain Dew lip balm. While primarily small soft-drink players such as Jones Soda Co. have for a long time licensed their brand name for products such as candy, the soda giants are increasingly breaking out of the beverage aisle in search of new revenue streams as soft drinks shrink" (MacArthur 2007, 10). Accumulation can also be used to create *enargeia*, as in this example written by David Sedaris: "The hut was a lot cozier than I'd imagined it. In the kitchen were the same sorts of things you'd find in the homes of any of our neighbors: a postal calendar picturing a kitten, a hanging copper saucepan turned into a clock, souvenir salt-and-pepper shakers in the shapes of castles and peasants and wooden shoes" (2007, 54).

Cicero and the author of *ad Herennium* also treated **transitions** as figures of thought (*Orator* xl 137; IV xxvi 35). A transition is any word or phrase that connects pieces of discourse. Cicero recommended that rhetors use transition to announce what is about to be discussed when introducing a topic *(propositio)* and sum up when concluding a topic *(enumeratio);* if both are used together, they constitute a smooth transition between topics. Using transition, a rhetor can briefly recall what has just been said and briefly announce what will follow.

Now that we have concluded our discussion of figures, we move to an analysis of tropes.

Tropes

Neither ancient nor modern rhetoricians have ever been able to agree about what distinguishes this class of ornament from figures. It is probably safe to say that tropes are characterized by the substitution of one word or phrase for another, but even this distinction does not clearly demarcate tropes from some figures of language, such as synonymy or puns. However, even though ancient rhetoricians could not agree about the definition of a trope, they knew one when they saw one. With the notable exception of Aristotle, who was ambivalent about every ornament except metaphor, major rhetoricians used a list of ten tropes that remained more or less standard throughout antiquity. The ten are: **onomatopoeia, antonomasia,** metonymy, periphrasis, hyperbaton, hyperbole, **synecdoche, catachresis,** metaphor, and **allegory.**

Onomatopoeia

According to the author of the *ad Herennium,* the rhetor who uses onomatopoeia ("making a new name") assigns a new word to "a thing which either lacks a name or has an inappropriate name" (IV xxx 42). This trope could be used either for imitative purposes, as illustrated by words like *roar, bellow, murmur, hiss* (*sibulus* in Latin), or for expressiveness. To exemplify this second use of onomatopoeia, the author coined a Latin word, *fragor,* which his modern translator renders as "hullabaloo": "After this creature attacked the republic, there was a hullabaloo among the first men of the state." (The 1960s gave us another onomatopoeia for a hullabaloo—*hootenanny.*) Readers who have been paying attention will notice that onomatopoeia bears a close resemblance to neologism—the coining of new words—a practice that was condemned by Quintilian as "scarcely permissible to a Roman." That quintessential Roman, Julius Caesar, warned us to "avoid, as you would a rock, an unheard-of and unfamiliar word" (notice the nice analogy here). Nonetheless, ancient rhetoricians agreed that onomatopoeia was the means by which language was invented, as their ancestors found names for things by emulating the noises those things characteristically made (*Institutes* VIII vi 31). Michael Lanza uses *onomatopoeia* in the classic sense to describe the sound of April snow hitting the top of his tent: "Pfft . . . pff" (2007, 90). Contemporary rhetoricians define *onomatopoeia* simply as words or language whose sound emulates or echoes their sense: "The brook babbled and murmured"; "Over the cobbles he clattered and clashed" (Alfred Noyes).

Antonomasia

In the trope called "antonomasia" ("another name"; Latin *pronominatio*), a rhetor substitutes a descriptive phrase for someone's proper name (or vice versa). When Quintilian referred to Cicero as "the prince of Roman orators," he used antonomasia (VIII vi 30). The author of *ad Herennium* suggested that, rather than naming the Gracchi, whose reputations were contested, a rhetor could more effectively refer to them as "the grandsons of Africanus," since Africanus's reputation was impeccable (IV xxxi 42). Antonomasia appears frequently in contemporary rhetoric. Elvis is "the King"; athletes acquire nicknames like "The Big Aristotle," "King James," and "Mr. Excitement." One of us even earned herself the epithet "Dr. Collision" on the ultimate frisbee field. The contemporary popularity of this trope is not limited to entertainment or sports. In 2006, President George W. Bush called himself "The Decider" in the context of the future of Donald Rumsfeld (who then was secretary of state), and the superhero-like name stuck. In an article about rock-and-roll star Little Richard, music writer Bob Mehr begins with a whole collection of *antonomasia:* "Before he was the Originator, the Innovator, the Emancipator, before he could claim his throne as the King, Queen or Quasar of Rock'n'Roll, Little Richard stood before a microphone in a cramped New Orleans studio and delivered his masterwork" (2007, 90). The rhetorical effects of this trope are obvious. It not only suggests that someone is so well-known that his name need not be used, thus cementing group loyalty; it also provides a rhetor with an opportunity to characterize the person he speaks or writes about in either positive or negative terms (see the discussion of honorific and pejorative language in Chapter 6, on *ethos*).

Metonymy

Metonymy ("altered name") names something with a word or phrase closely associated with it: "the White House" for the president of the United States or "the Kremlin" for the leadership of the former Union of Soviet Socialist Republics. The maxim "The pen is mightier than the sword" is a metonymy in which *pen* stands for persuasive language and *sword* for war. We refer to the works of an author by her name: "Morrison" or "McEwan" stand in for novels written by Toni Morrison or Ian McEwan. We use metonymy when we say "I like the Dixie Chicks," meaning that we like their music.

Periphrasis

We have already met the figure called "periphrasis" ("circling speech") under its Latinate name *circumlocution.* Quintilian defined uses of this fig- ure as "whatever might have been expressed with greater brevity, but is expanded for purposes of ornament" (VIII vi 61). He gave this poetic exam- ple from Virgil's *Aeneid:* "Now was the time / When the first sleep to weary mortals comes / Stealing its way, the sweetest boon of heaven" (ii 268). Virgil did not simply say "Night arrived." Rather, he embroidered on this simple observation to achieve the effect of calmness that sleep brings.

Quintilian worried that rhetors would use this figure simply to fill up space or to impress:

> Some rhetors introduce a whole host of useless words; for, in their eagerness to avoid ordinary methods of expression, and allured by false ideals of beauty they wrap up everything in a multitude of words simply and solely because they are unwilling to make a direct and simple statement of the facts. (VIII ii 17)

A contemporary rhetorician named Richard Lanham argues persua- sively that much contemporary American prose is written in what he calls the "Official Style." He gives this example:

> The history of Western psychological thought has long been dominated by philosophical considerations as to the nature of man. These notions have dic- tated corresponding considerations of the nature of the child within society, the practices by which children were to be raised, and the purposes of studying the child. (1992, 10)

In essence, this passage says that psychologists are interested in human nature and that this interest has led them to investigate childhood and child-rearing practices. In other words, users of the official style do exactly what Quintilian warned against—they pile up more words and phrases than are necessary in order to achieve an impressive effect. There is a big difference between using words to enhance an effect or to call attention to a point and simply failing to notice them.

Hyperbaton

Hyperbaton is the transposition of a word to somewhere other than its usual place: "Backward run sentences, until reels the mind" (a parody of the style of *Time* magazine). Strictly speaking, *hyperbaton* is a figure of language, since its effect depends upon a change in normal word order. But as Quintilian noted, it can be called a trope when "the meaning is not complete until the two words have been put together" (VIII vi 66). We parody our own writing by imposing a *hyperbaton* on the first sentence of this paragraph: "*Hyperbaton* is the transposition, to somewhere other than its usual place, of a word."

Hyperbole

Quintilian defined hyperbole ("thrown above"; "excess") as "an elegant straining of the truth" (VIII vi 67) and gives this wonderful example from

Cicero: "Vetto gives the name of farm to an estate which might easily be hurled from a sling, though it might well fall through the hole in the hollow sling, so small is it" (73). Aristotle gave these examples: speaking of a man with a black eye, "You would have thought him a basket of mulberries"; and of a skinny man, "He has legs like parsley" (*Rhetoric* III xi 1413a). In other words, hyperbole is exaggeration used for effect. People often use hyperbole to describe extreme weather conditions. During a Midwestern July heat wave, one of us heard this hyperbole: "hotter than the hinges on the gates of hell." Sportscasters, especially "color commentators," often use hyperbole to create excitement. When someone makes a long-range three pointer, for instance, the sportscaster might yell "From the parking lot!" or engaging in even more exaggerated hyperbole, he might say the shot came "From Downtown!" Hyperbole has made it into e-mail, instant messages, and text messages. While LOL is often not hyperbole, ROTFL usually is: a person can't typically type or text while rolling on the floor.

Synecdoche

In synecdoche ("to receive together") rhetors substitute the part for the whole (or vice versa) or cause for effect (or vice versa). Quintilian wrote that this figure occurred most commonly with numbers, as in "The Roman won the day," in which "the Roman" refers to an entire army. The author of *ad Herennium* gave this example of synecdoche: "Were not those nuptial flutes reminding you of his marriage?" (the flutes stand for the whole ceremony). Like hyperbole, this trope is common in everyday speech. We say "give me a hand," where *hand* refers to help or assistance, and we use the phrase "four hundred head" to refer to four hundred animals. When we say "check out my wheels," we usually mean the whole car, not just the tires.

Catachresis

Catachresis ("to use against") is "the inexact use of a like and kindred word in place of the precise and proper one" (*ad Herennium* IV xxxiii 45). The author gave these examples: "the power of man is short," "small height," "long wisdom," "mighty speech." In these examples adjectives are misapplied to nouns: we ordinarily speak of human power as limited rather than short, of wisdom as enduring rather than long, and so on. Quintilian defined this trope more narrowly as "the practice of adapting the nearest available term to describe something for which no actual term exists" (VIII vi 34). The Latin name for catachresis means "abuse," and novice rhetors might be wise to avoid it.

Metaphor

A metaphor transfers or substitutes one word for another. The Greeks have always taken metaphor seriously. If you visit modern Greece, you might notice a transfer truck bearing the label *metaphoros*. Some metaphors are so common in our daily speech that we no longer think about their metaphoric quality: we say that a disappointed lover "struck out" or "never got to first base," borrowing metaphors from baseball. When someone has exhausted all her alternatives, we say that she is "at the end of her rope," borrowing a grisly metaphor from executions. We say that the abortion question presents us with a thicket of difficult issues, borrowing a metaphor from nature. Truly striking metaphors appear in poetry. Here are two examples from a poem by Emily Dickinson:

> There is no frigate like a book
> To take us lands away,
> Nor any coursers like a page
> Of prancing poetry.

Dickinson compared a book to a ship and its pages to a pair of horses. In prose these comparisons don't make much sense, but they work beautifully in Dickinson's poem to evoke images and emotions.

Metaphor is often the only trope mentioned in traditional composition textbooks, giving the impression that modern writers should limit their use of ornament to a single trope. Aristotle, like other ancient rhetoricians, was more interested in metaphor than he was in other tropes or figures, and metaphor has received more attention from modern rhetoricians and literary critics than has any other trope or figure. In the *Poetics*, Aristotle defined metaphor as the movement of a name from its own genus or species to another genus or species (XXI vii 1457b). In the *Rhetoric*, he noted that metaphors borrowed from something greater in the same genus or species were complimentary, while those borrowed from something worse could be used to denigrate the person or thing to whom it was applied. Thus, pirates can be called "entrepreneurs" or "businesspeople," and someone who has made a mistake can be accused of criminal behavior (III ii 1405a). Humans often get compared to other species because of some shared characteristic that the rhetor wants to highlight. Women's National Basketball Association guard Theresa Weatherspoon, when asked about her stellar defensive game against the league's leading scorer, said: "She told me I was like a gnat, a pest who wouldn't go away." Here the comparison to a pesky insect conveys the frustration an offensive-minded player feels when guarded closely.

At another point in the *Rhetoric*, Aristotle classed metaphors among those tropes and figures he called witty or urbane sayings, and he developed a theory about why metaphors give us pleasure. They do so, he wrote, "because metaphors help us to learn new things, and learning is naturally pleasurable to humans" (x 1410b). In other words, since metaphors express ideas in new or unusual ways, they help us to see things in new ways.

Aristotle suggested that metaphors be taken from two sources: those that are beautiful, either in sound or effect, and those that appeal to the senses (ii 1405b). It would not do, he wrote, to substitute *red-fingered* or even *purple-fingered* in Homer's "rosy-fingered dawn." He told a funny story about Simonides, who at first declined to write a poem for a man who had won a mule race, on the ground that he did not want to celebrate half-asses.

When the man paid enough, however, Simonides accepted the commission and wrote "Hail, daughters of storm-footed mares!" Aristotle gave many examples of successful metaphors: citizens are like a ship's captain who is strong but deaf; ungrateful neighbors are like children who accept candy but keep on crying; orators are like babysitters who eat the baby's food and then moisten the baby's lips with their saliva (iv 1406b, 1407a).

Sometimes a good metaphor can launch and sustain an argument, like Jonathan Lethem's description of a novel: "Among the encompassing definitions we could give 'the novel' . . . is this: a novel is a vast heap of sentences, like stones, arranged on a beach of time" (2007, 1). Metaphors can be expanded and explored, and Lethem's allows him to account for the novel's readers as well: "The reader may parse the stones of a novel singly or crunch them in bunches underfoot in his eagerness to cross" (12). Lethem then deploys the stones-on-the beach metaphor in a terrific discussion of Ian McEwan's novel, which, as it happens, is set on a beach. As the Lethem example shows, the quest for an apt metaphor just might yield surprising insight. In other words, metaphors can be useful tools for invention. All tropes can be, for that matter.

Quintilian distinguished several kinds of metaphor. In one of these, a rhetor substitutes one living thing for another: "He is a lion"; "Scipio was continually barked at by Cato" (VIII vi 9). In another kind, inanimate things may be substituted for animate and vice versa. Quintilian thought this was most impressive when an inanimate object is spoken of as though it were alive, as in Cicero's "What was that sword of yours doing, Tubero?" or "The dam decided to collapse at that moment." Aristotle would have classed both of these kinds of metaphor under the head of species-to-species, in which a rhetor substitutes the name of one particular for another. Aristotle and Quintilian both named metaphors that substitute a part for a whole, or vice versa, as a separate class, but modern rhetoricians label such metaphors as synecdoches (for example, "Jane Doe" to represent all women).

In the *Poetics*, Aristotle writes, "In some cases of analogy no current term exists" (XXXI 1458a). The example he gives is this: "To release seed is to 'sow,' while the sun's release of fire lacks a name" (XXI 1458a). The resulting analogy, then, might be "the sun sowed fire on the morning." The contemporary novelist Richard Powers, writing just after September 11, 2001, offers a moving account of the tragedy while considering the very phenomenon Aristotle discusses—when "no current term exists"—to characterize something. The result, in such cases, is use of metaphor or simile (the most explicit kind of metaphor):

THE SIMILE

I was preparing to meet my undergraduate writing class at the University of Illinois when I heard the news. The day's topic was to have been figurative speech: metaphor and simile in fiction. On my way out the door, I saw the first headlines. Then the images and the repeating, unreal film. And every possible class lesson disappeared in that plume.

With the rest of the world, I found myself losing ground against the real. The anchors, the reporters, the eyewitnesses, the experts: all fighting against the onset of shock, all helpless to say what had happened, all working to survive the inconceivable. And when the first, stunted descriptions came, they came in a flood of simile. The shock of the attack was like Pearl Harbor. The gutted financial district was like Nagasaki. Lower Manhattan was like a city after an earthquake. The gray people streaming northward up the island covered in an inch of ash were like the buried at Pompeii.

And in this outpouring of anemic simile, again and again with startlingly little variation, people resorted to the most chilling refrain: like a movie. Like "Independence Day." Like "The Towering Inferno." Like "The Siege." Like bad science fiction. Like a Tom Clancy novel. (Clancy, talking to CNN, seemed to find the plot more unbelievable than any plot of his own.) The magnitude of this day could not be made real except through comparison to fiction. Nothing but the outsize scale of the imaginary was big enough to measure by.

Failed similes proliferated throughout the afternoon. Blocks like the apocalypse. Wall Street executives wandering like the homeless. Streets like Kinshasa. Rubble like Beirut or the West Bank.

No simile will ever serve. In its size and devastation and suddenness, the destruction of Sept. 11 is, in fact, like nothing, unless it is like the terrors experienced in those parts of the world that seemed so distant on Sept. 10.

I met my class, although I could pretend to no teaching. It was not like a wake; it was one. We shared the shortfall of our thoughts. "It's like a dream," my students said. And more frightening still, "Like waking from a dream." The America they woke to on Tuesday morning was, like the skyline of New York, changed forever. The always-thereness of here was gone.

The final lesson of my writing class came too soon. There are no words. But there are only words. To say what the inconceivable resembles is all that we have by way of learning how it might be outlived. No comparison can say what happened to us. But we can start with the ruins of our similes, and let "like" move us toward something larger, some understanding of what "is." (2001, 21–22)

Powers's piece gets to the heart of the ancient meaning of metaphor— "transference" or "transport"—the movement toward something through something else. And what is more portable or mobile, the word *metaphor* seems to ask, than language?

Aristotle also treated analogy as a kind of metaphor. In analogy, rhetors compare a relationship rather than items. Aristotle cited Pericles' saying that the young men killed in a recent war had vanished from Athens as though someone had taken spring from the year (III x 1411a). Analogies frequently come in handy when a physician questions a patient about his pain—"does the pain feel more like needles or a knife?"

Allegory

A metaphor becomes an **allegory** (literally "speaking otherwise"), when it is sustained throughout a long passage. One of the most well-known allegories is Plato's allegory of the cave in book VII of *The Republic*, where the darkness of the cave is made analogous to those who don't know philosophy.

In her book *Writing Permitted in Designated Areas Only*, English professor and rhetoric scholar Linda Brodkey uses allegory to compare the marking off of public smoking spaces to the marking off of writing spaces in American universities. We offer two excerpts from her book to illustrate the use of allegory:

> The international sign that bans smoking in public places can also be read as a sign of cultural hegemony, a frequent and forcible reminder that in democratic societies civic regulations commonly inscribe the will of the dominant culture. That there are two versions of the sign suggests that the dominant culture is of at least two minds when it comes to smoking in public places. One version of the sign prohibits smoking altogether, and the other regulates smoking by appending a note that may be more familiar to smokers than to nonsmokers: "Smoking Permitted in Designated Areas Only." This second sign, signaling the temporary segregation of smokers from nonsmokers, is part of the same expansionist public policy as the first, which seems likely to succeed eventually given the rapidly diminishing number and size of public spaces where smokers are still allowed to smoke. In the meantime, however—so long as they remove themselves to those designated areas—smokers constitute a literal and figurative body of evidence that a desire to smoke remains strong enough in some people to withstand the ever increasing pressure of social hostility and medical injunctions. That smokers commonly honor the signs, either by not smoking or by smoking only in designated areas, provides smokers and nonsmokers alike with continual public enactments of civil power, namely, the power of the professional-managerial middle class to enforce the public suppression of a desire it has recently identified and articulated via science as endangering its well being—as a class. (1996, 130)

Here Brodkey sets up one end of the allegory, the smoking signs and regulations with which her readers are already familiar. Boldly questioning the assumptions behind such regulation and its subscription to scientific ideology, Brodkey rearticulates the regulations as "cultural hegemony," the imposition of one group's will onto another group or groups. After developing her critique of smoking regulation a bit further, Brodkey moves to the other side of the allegory, the set of practices she wants to cast in a different light by way of the extended metaphor itself and a series of direct arguments: American writing instruction. Brodkey writes:

> Composition classrooms are the designated areas of American colleges and universities. Composition courses are middle-class holding pens populated by students from all classes who for one reason or another do not produce fluent, thesis-driven essays of around five hundred words in response to either prompts designed for standardized tests or assignments developed by classroom teachers. . . .
>
> It has always seemed to me gratuitous to regulate writing and writers via the contents of prompts and assignments, since a policy of coherence is already being "objectively" executed by assessing student writing on the basis of form and format: the grammar, spelling, diction, and punctuation

along with the thesis sentence, body paragraphs, and conclusion. Perhaps both are necessary, however, because while form identifies class interlopers (working-class ethnic and black students), content singles out class malcontents. While it seems to take longer in some cases than in others, composition instruction appears to have succeeded best at establishing in most people a lifelong aversion to writing. They have learned to associate a desire to write with a set of punishing exercises called writing in school: printing, penmanship, spelling, punctuation, and vocabulary in nearly all cases; grammar lessons, thesis sentences, paragraphs, themes, book reports, and library research papers in college preparatory and advanced placement courses. (135–136)

Through subtle language cues, Brodkey sustains the smoking metaphor throughout the passage—and the rest of the chapter (indeed, the metaphor permeates the entire book, thanks to the title). Words like "designated areas" and "regulate" carry over the arguments Brodkey made about regulating smoking to regulating student writing. The allegory enables Brodkey to clarify what bugs her most about prevailing practices in composition classes: writing is reserved for one place, she argues, and that very place is tainted by our culture, marked as the "lower" training ground for other university classes. In this schema, untrained writers—like smokers—are seen as potentially dangerous, threatening, or at least irritating to middle- and upper-class standards, hence necessitating strict regulation. The allegory certainly does powerful work for Brodkey and makes her argument all the more compelling, or at least we think so.

RHETORICAL ACTIVITIES

1. Go on a trope hunt. Between now and your next class meeting, locate a whole host of different kinds of tropes. You may wish to consult broadly: popular magazines, newspapers, Web sites, billboards, and advertisements are all fair game. Once you record the trope, use the information in this chapter to name it. Be on the lookout for particularly rare or artful tropes. Be prepared to tell the class why you've categorized the trope as you have.

2. Try your hand at composing figures and tropes. Find a passage of your writing and examine it to see whether you unconsciously used any of the figures or tropes discussed in this chapter. Rewrite any of the sentences in the passage, inserting figures or tropes where they are appropriate. Approach this task systematically over a few days or weeks; your eventual goal is to use each kind of figure or trope discussed in this chapter.

3. Revise a passage you've written in the plain style so that it is appropriate for a more formal rhetorical situation. Use complex sentence constructions, longer words, and lots of figures and tropes. For models of

highly ornate prose styles, you can turn to the work of composers from earlier periods of history. John Donne's sermons are good examples, as are those composed by American preachers such as Jonathan Edwards or Martin Luther King Jr.

4. We also recommend that rhetors as a practice be on the lookout for professional speakers and writers' uses of the various figures discussed in this chapter. When you find figures or tropes that you admire, write them down in a commonplace book. Practice imitating them. A modern handbook of the figures is a very useful aid to composers. We highly recommend Richard Lanham's *A Handlist of Rhetorical Terms*.

IMITATION II: INHABITING THROUGH PRACTICE

In addition to reading aloud and copying, ancient rhetoricians encouraged their students to imitate the work of authors they admired. Imitation differs from simple copying; the imitator may borrow the structures used in the imitated sentence, supplying her own material, or she may try to render the gist of the original passage in other words. The latter exercise is more aptly referred to as **paraphrase**, and we will practice paraphrasing at the end of the next chapter.

Most authorities agree that the proper procedure for imitation involved copying the model, studying it carefully, and imitating its structures. Here are some sample sentences, all taken from the work of professional writers. Our imitations of the samples are fairly close in that they borrow the grammatical structures of the originals. The samples are arranged in order of increasing grammatical complexity.

Simple Sentence

John loves Mary.

A simple sentence has only one colon. Simple sentences can be expanded in all sorts of ways: for example, by the insertion of *commata* set off by punctuation (as is done by James and Marquez in the samples that follow) or by the addition of prepositional phrases (as in the sample from Tuchman).

Sample 1

London was hideous, vicious, cruel, and above all overwhelming.

—Henry James

Imitation

Ourtown was ugly, empty, cold, and above all forbidding.

Analysis

James inserted two one-word *commata* into this simple sentence. The *commata*, separated by punctuation marks, slow readers down and help them to feel London's overwhelming atmosphere.

Sample 2

He remembered much of his stay in the womb. While there, he began to be aware of sounds and tastes. . . . Yet he was not afraid. The changes were right. It was time for them. His body was ready.

—Octavia Butler, *Adulthood Rites*

Imitation

She planned most of her day in the morning. At home, she recognized familiar sounds and smells. Yet she was not at home. The feeling was all wrong. The time was not ripe. She was not ready.

Analysis

Butler composed a string of plain simple sentences to convey the impressions felt by a sensitive young child. Strings of simple sentences can also convey other ethical effects, such as intense concentration.

Some Simple Sentences to Imitate

A phenomenon noticeable throughout history regardless of place or period is the pursuit by governments of policies contrary to their own interests.

—Barbara Tuchman, *The March of Folly*

The Antillean refugee Jeremiah de Saint-Amour, disabled war veteran, photographer of children, and his most sympathetic opponent in chess, had escaped the torments of memory with the aromatic fumes of gold cyanide.

—Gabriel Garcia Marquez, *Love in the Time of Cholera*

Early in the sixteenth century, Francis Bacon proposed that science consisted in the elevation of the authority of experiment and observation over that of reason, intuition, and convention.

—Marvin Harris, *Cultural Materialism*

Out of the back of the truck the city of San Francisco is bouncing down the hill, all those endless staggers of bay windows, slums with a view, bouncing and streaming down the hill.

—Tom Wolfe, "Black Shiny FBI Shoes"

Complex Sentence

John loves Mary even though she reads Milton.

In a complex sentence, one or more dependent colons are attached to one or more independent colons. A colon is dependent if it doesn't make sense by itself; it depends on another colon to make it complete.

Sample 1

Writing, reading, thinking, imagining, speculating. These are luxury activities, so I am reminded, permitted to a privileged few, whose idle hours of the day can be viewed otherwise than as a bowl of rice or a loaf of bread less to share with the family.

—Trinh T. Minh-ha, "Commitment from the Mirror-Writing Box"

Imitation

Aspen, sycamore, ponderosa, oak, laurel. These are the hardy trees, so I understand, classed among the privileged few, whose growth patterns in every season cannot be viewed otherwise than as a mere creeping along, a finely tuned adjustment to their surroundings.

Analysis

In this passage Minh-ha punctuated the first string of words as a sentence, even though a grammatical purist would deny them that status. In the second sentence, she interrupted the independent colon with another, brief independent colon ("so I am reminded") and attached a dependent colon at the end.

Sample 2

Cranes keep landing as night falls. Ribbons of them roll down, slack against the sky. They float in from all compass points, in kettles of a dozen, dropping with the dusk. Scores of *Grus canadensis* settle on the thawing river. They gather on the island flats, grazing, beating their wings, trumpeting: the advance wave of a mass evacuation. More birds land by the minute, the air red with calls.

—Richard Powers, *The Echo Maker: A Novel*

Imitation

Words keep crowding as sleep calls. Reams of them cram in, wound among the folds. Squeezed from the day's moments, in phrases and clauses, repeating with the broken fan. Hosts of figures dance in geometric shapes. They cluster on my end-table, calling, clacking their consonants, rounding: the condensed noise of a staged sit-in. More words tamp into seconds, the night thick with sense.

Analysis

The first three sentences build in complexity, beginning with two brief independent clauses joined by the word *as*. The next sentence has an independent clause to which a participial phrase is attached, and the next sentence adds yet another participial phrase ("dropping with the dusk"). The passage then returns to a simple sentence. The fourth sentence is the most elaborate of the bunch, beginning with an independent clause ("They gather on the island flats"), then three participial phrases in quick succession, and then, surprisingly, an independent clause. The final sentence returns to the opening pattern: a simple sentence appended by a descriptive, dependent clause.

Some Complex Sentences to Imitate

His name was Domenico Scandella, but he was called Menocchio. He was born in 1532 (at his first trial he claimed he was fifty-two years old) in Montereale, a small hill town of the Friuli twenty-five kilometers north of Pordenone at the foot of the mountains. Here he had always lived, except for two years when he was banished following a brawl.

—Carlo Ginzburg, *The Cheese and the Worms*

The effect was exactly what one expects that many simultaneous crashes to produce: the unmistakable tympany of automobiles colliding and cheap-gauge sheet metal buckling, front ends folding together at the same cockeyed angles police photographs of night-time wreck scenes capture so well on grainy paper; smoke pouring from under the hoods and hanging over the infield like a howitzer cloud; a few of the surviving cars lurching eccentrically on bent axles.

—Tom Wolfe, "Clean Fun at Riverhead"

Compound Sentences

John loves Mary but Mary despises John.

A compound sentence has two or more *cola* that are independent of one another. That is, each could stand alone as a simple sentence. Usually, the *cola* in a compound sentence are linked together by *and, but,* or *or.* In order to produce a different effect, however, writers can omit the words that ordinarily connect cola in a compound sentence and substitute punctuation instead (thus producing the figure asyndeton).

Sample 1

She was traveling alone and was too short to wield her roll easily. She tried once, and she tried twice, and finally I got up and helped her. The plane was packed: I'd never seen a plane quite so crowded before.

—Audre Lorde, "Notes from a Trip to Russia"

Imitation

Mary was working hard and was too tired to deal with John well. She put it off, and put it off again, and finally she gave in and called him. The conversation was trying: she'd never known how to do this sort of thing.

Analysis

In the first sentence in this passage, Lord connected the two *cola* in the standard way, with *and*. In the second, however, she used both punctuation and a connecting word, thus creating the figure polysyndeton. In the third sentence in the passage, she used a punctuation mark to connect the compound *cola*. Compound sentences can be used to pile up images or assertions; this piling up yields a variety of effects.

Sample 2

My father was dead, my mother was dead, I would need for a while to watch for mines, but I would still get up in the morning and send out the laundry.

—Joan Didion, *The Year of Magical Thinking*

Imitation

The impatiens were blooming, the clematis was climbing, I would need to have someone look for weeds, but I would still rent a car tomorrow and leave for vacation.

Analysis

Didion's sentence begins with asyndeton (linking the first three clauses with commas only). The effect is a kind of litany, a heaping up of painful circumstances. The word *but* breaks up the pattern before the final two clauses, and those are separated by the word *and*.

Some Compound Sentences to Imitate

The late eighteenth century abounded in schemes of social goodness thrown off by its burgeoning sense of revolution. But here, the process was to be reversed: not Utopia, but Dystopia; not Rousseau's natural man moving in moral grace amid free social contracts, but man coerced, exiled, deracinated, in chains.

—Richard Hughes, *The Fatal Shore*

Orlando's fathers had ridden in fields of asphodel, and stony fields, and fields watered by strange rivers, and they had struck many heads of many colours off many shoulders, and brought them back to hang from the rafters.

—Virginia Woolf, *Orlando*

We called the waiter, paid, and started to walk through the town. I started off walking with Brett, but Robert Cohn came up and joined her on the other side. . . . There were many people walking to go and see the bulls, and carriages drove down the hill and across the bridge, the drivers, the horses, and the whips rising above the walking people in the street.

—Ernest Hemingway, *The Sun Also Rises*

Compound-Complex Sentence

John loves Mary and remains faithful to her even though she reads Milton.

A compound-complex sentence contains at least two independent colons and at least one dependent colon.

Sample 1

This work came together in a slow way. Always something would get in the way—relationships ending, exile, loneliness, some recently discovered pain—and I had to hurt again, hurt myself all the way away from writing, re-writing, putting the book together.

—bell hooks, *Talking Back*

Imitation

Always events would block our progress—equipment failing, travel, illness, some newly discovered glitch—and we had to think again, rethink our work all the way back to the beginning, tinkering, improvising, putting our plans aside.

Analysis

The first sentence in this passage is, of course, a simple sentence. In the compound-complex sentence that follows, hooks inserts a comma between the two independent *cola*, punctuating it with dashes. She then repeats the verb of the second independent colon *(hurt)* to create a dependent colon that concludes with three participial phrases *(writing, re-writing, putting)*, thus creating the small parallelism that brings the sentence to a close.

Sample 2

In the nineteenth century, Parkinsonism was almost never seen before the age of fifty, and was usually considered to be a reflection of a degenerative process or defect of nutrition in certain "weak" or vulnerable cells; since this degeneration could not actually be demonstrated at the time, and since its cause was unknown, Parkinson's disease was termed an idiosyncrasy or "ideopathy."

—Oliver Sacks, *Awakenings*

Analysis

The first half of this sentence (before the semicolon) is a compound sentence. The second half begins with paired dependent *cola*, both beginning with *since*; these *cola* are attached to the independent colon that concludes the sentence.

Some Compound-Complex Sentences to Imitate

We all begin well, for in our youth there is nothing we are more intolerant of than our own sins writ large in others and we fight them fiercely in ourselves;

but we grow old and we see that these our sins are of all sins the really harmless ones to own, nay that they give a charm to any character, and so our struggle with them dies away.

—Gertrude Stein, *The Making of Americans*

There was a man and a dog too this time. Two beasts, counting Old Ben, the bear, and two men, counting Boon Hogganbeck, in whom some of the same blood ran which ran in Sam Fathers, even though Boon's was a plebeian strain of it and only Sam and Old Ben and the mongrel Lion were taintless and incorruptible.

—William Faulkner, "The Bear"

Of course, imitation need not be limited only to sentences. Actually imitation works best with short passages, because you can study the techniques writers use to move from sentence to sentence. Here, for example, is an interesting passage from Toni Morrison's *Song of Solomon:*

[1.] At that time of day, during the middle of the week, word-of-mouth news just lumbered along. [2.] Children were in school; men were at work; and most of the women were fastening their corsets and getting ready to go see what tails or entrails the butcher might be giving away. [3.] Only the unemployed, the self-employed, and the very young were available—deliberately available because they'd heard about it, or accidentally available because they happened to be walking at that exact moment in the shore end of Not Doctor Street, a name the post office did not recognize. (3)

Imitation

At that time of year, during the middle of winter, four-wheel drives just crept along. Cars with chains were sometimes seen; cars without were left at home; and most residents were putting on their warmest clothes and getting set to go out and see the drifts that rifted across their doorways. Only the old, the bold, and the quick-tongued were excepted—deliberately excepted because of infirmity, or grudgingly excepted because they were good at finding reasons why they should not shovel the snow piling ever higher outside, a place that at the moment they did not recognize as relevant to their lives.

Analysis

When we copied this passage, we noticed several interesting things. The first sentence is periodic. The second sentence begins with two balanced cola. These are connected to a third, much longer colon that itself contains two balanced pairs (the verbs *fastening* and *getting;* and the rhyming "tails or entrails"). The faint rhyming echo of *tails* and *entrails* is picked up again in the third sentence with *unemployed* and *self-employed* and the repetition-with-variation of *available.* The third sentence ends with a final colon that seems like an irrelevance or a digression (in fact, the rest of the passage elaborates on it). This carrying of reference across sentences is unusual (it may be one distinguishing mark of Morrison's style); most writers would begin a new sentence to discuss the post office's failure to recognize Not Doctor Street.

As you can see, imitation does not necessarily produce great writing. It does, however, enable rhetors to recognize and use patterns that they might not otherwise notice. If you use these patterns regularly in your own writing, they rapidly become second nature.

IMITATION EXERCISES

1. Return to the imitations and compose sentences following the authors we have offered for imitation.

2. Select a lengthy (half-page to a full-page) passage from your favorite author and imitate the style and structure. The point of imitation is to follow the syntactic structures employed by the original author, but the choice of subject, the voice, attitude, and the rest is up to you. You might alter the focus of the scene, or the kinds of characters.

NOTES

1. Like ancient rhetoricians, we think that correctness and clarity are not truly rhetorical considerations, and so we don't pay much attention to them in this book. We also think that Americans' obsession with correctness and clarity has kept them from studying and enjoying the more complex uses of language that are addressed here. There are plenty of books available that discuss correctness and clarity. Any good handbook for writers will demonstrate the correctness rules of traditional grammar. We recommend *The St. Martin's Handbook* by Andrea Lunsford (sixth edition, 2007). Dictionaries of usage are also available; Fowler's *Modern English Usage* is the standard reference work. Writers who are interested in achieving a clearer style can consult Joseph Williams's *Style: Lessons in Clarity and Grace* (ninth edition, 2006).

2. Writers who are interested in practicing this kind of stylistic appropriateness can consult the ancient treatises written by Hermogenes of Tarsus, usually called *The Ideas of Style* or *The Types of Style*, as well as that by Demetrius of Phaleron, called *On Style*. These treatises give copious advice about how to achieve such effects as solemnity, vehemence, simplicity, force, and the like.

WORKS CITED

Brodkey, Linda. *Writing Permitted in Designated Areas Only*. Minneapolis: University of Minnesota Press, 1996.

Bruni, Frank. "Go, Eat, You Never Know." *New York Times*, May 30, 2007, national edition.

Campbell, George. *Philosophy of Rhetoric*. Boston: Adamant Media Corporation, 2005.

Colebrook, Claire. *Irony: The New Critical Idiom*. New York: Routledge, 2004.

Dodes, Rachel. "Tunes, a Hard Drive, and Just Maybe, a Brain." *New York Times,* August 26, 2004, national edition, sec. G.

Emerson, Ralph Waldo. *Essays and Lecture.* New York: Library of America, 1983.

Gettleman, Jeffrey. "Southern Liberals Had Lott Moments, Too." *New York Times,* December 22, 2002, national edition, sec. 4.

—. "The New Somalia: A Grimly Familiar Rerun." *New York Times,* February 21, 2007, national edition, sec. A.

Gibbs, Nancy. "The Confession Procession." *Time,* March 26, 2007, 15.

Goodnough, Abby. "Florida Girl Learns to Lift Weights, and Gold Medals." *New York Times,* March 17, 2007, national edition, sec. A.

Graves, Robert. *I, Claudius.* New York: Vintage Books, 1961.

Kahn, Jennifer. "Mind Games." *Wired,* June 2007, 122–131.

Lanham, Richard. *Revising Prose.* New York: Macmillan Publishing Company, 1992.

Lanza, Michael. "Hells Canyon Wilderness." *Backpacker,* June 2007, 64–70.

Lethem, Jonathan. "Edward's End." Review of On Chesil Beach By Ian McEwan. *New York Times,* June 03, 2007, national edition, Book Review section.

MacArthur, Kate. "Soda Giants Expand Beyond the Fizz Biz." *Advertising Age,* June 4, 2007, 10.

Mariani, John. "The New Food Capital." *Esquire,* May 2007, 54.

Mehr, Bob. "In the Beginning Was the Word." *Mojo,* June 2007, 90 95.

Monastersky, Richard. "Mercury, and Certainty, Rising." *The Chronicle of Higher Education,* February 14, 2007, A16.

Morrison, Toni. *Song of Solomon.* New York: Vintage International, 2004.

Paul, D. "Taco Bell Cheesy Gordita Crunch." Timothy McSweeney, July–October 2003. http://www.mcsweeneys.net/links/newfood/(accessed June 1, 2007).

Powers, Richard. *Plowing the Dark.* New York: Farrar, Straus and Giroux, 2000.

—. "The Simile." *New York Times Magazine,* September 23, 2001, 21–22.

Ryan, George. "Excerpts From Governor's Speech on Commutations." *New York Times,* January 12, 2003, national edition, sec A.

Sedaris, David. "The Man in the Hut." *New Yorker,* June 4, 2007, 54.

Shipley, David, and Will Schwable. *Send. The Essential Guide to Email for Office and Home.* New York: Alfred Knopf, 2007.

Simonini, Ross. "David Gates." *Believer* 5, no. 5 (June/July 2007). Available at http://www.believermag.com/issues/200706/?read=interview_gates.

Solotaroff, Paul. "How do You Improve on Greatest Ever?" *Men's Journal,* July 2007, 80–84, 148.

Sprague, Rosamond Kent. *The Older Sophists.* Indianapolis: Hackett Publishing, 2001.

Stanton, Elizabeth Cady. "Speech at the Seneca Falls Convention" text available at http://ecssba.rutgers.edu/docs/ecswoman1.html

Van Biema, David. "The Case for Teaching the Bible." *Time,* April 2, 2007, 40–46.

Walker, Alice. *The Temple of My Familiar.* New York: Harcourt Brace Jovanovich, 1990.

Wallraff, Barbara. "Word Fugitives." *Atlantic,* July/August 2007, 160.

Wayne, Teddy. "Red Carpets Through History." *New York Times,* May 27, 2007, national edition.

Wolfe, Tom. *The Kandy-Kolored Tangerine-Flake Streamline Baby.* New York: Bantam, 1999.

Wulf, Steve. "Page 2." *ESPN The Magazine,* June 4, 2007, 28.

Yeoman, Barry. "The Wal-Mart Effect." *Audobon,* May–June 2007, 35–41.

MEMORY: THE TREASURE-HOUSE OF INVENTION

Now let me turn to the treasure-house of the ideas supplied by Invention, to the guardian of all the parts of rhetoric, the Memory.

—*ad Herennium*
III xvi 28

A RICH MAN NAMED Scopas once invited Simonides of Ceos, a magician and poet, to write a poem in celebration of a banquet he was hosting. When Simonides read his poem at the banquet, he praised the twin gods Castor and Pollux. Scopas was so angry that the poem praised someone other than himself that he paid Simonides only half the fee he had promised. After the banquet began, Simonides was given a message that two young men wished to see him outside the hall. While he searched for them outside, the hall collapsed and everyone inside was killed. When relatives came to collect the remains, they were dismayed to find that most of the banqueters had been crushed beyond recognition. However, Simonides was able to remember the exact place at the table where everyone had been sitting, thus making sure that the right relatives claimed the correct bodies. Of course, the two young men who had sent the message were Castor and Pollux. They repaid Simonides' praise by saving him from certain death.

From a rhetorician's perspective Simonides' prodigious feat of memory is the important part of this story. Ancient authors were so impressed with the powers of memory that they awarded it a place among the rhetorical canons. Both Cicero (*De Oratore* II 351–53) and Quintilian (*Institutes of Oratory* XI 2) retell the story of Simonides to begin their discussions of memory. Cicero goes on to list the ways memory mattered for the ancients, including not only retaining information or recalling the arrangement of a speech but also giving close attention to opponents' arguments so that all might be addressed, as well as recalling other arguments that have arisen in the past about the same topic, who made them, and where (355).

While memory is not as important in the age of print and electronic literacy as it was to the ancients, some ancient tactics for improving the memory can still work for us. In this chapter we also show how a variety of print and electronic technologies now constitute contemporary versions of the ancients' artificial memory systems.

MEMORY AND *KAIROS*

The legend of Simonides suggests memory's connection to the ancient concept of *kairos*. In fact, the entire story turns on propitious timing: Simonides got called away from the dining hall just in time, and returned just when he was needed by relatives of the victims. But Simonides' attunement to the dining hall surroundings is also suggestive of *kairos*. Quintilian focuses on preparing a "tappable" memory; that is, he suggests employing a system of signs or symbols so that a name, argument, or image will not get lost but will rather be readily available. Such signs and symbols, Quintilian averred, can help "jog" the memory (XI ii 19) when the time is right. He therefore promoted a "memory-ready" condition, not unlike the ready stance described in Chapter 2, on *kairos*. It seems paradoxical, but *kairos* and memory were partnered in several ways. First, both require a kind of "attunement" in that the rhetor who is gathering items for reserve in the memory must be thinking simultaneously about what's available now that might be useful later. Secondly, memory requires an attunement during the moment of speaking or composing, a recognition of the right time for recalling an illustrative example, an argument, and so on. Obviously, people who speak in public need reliable memories, especially if they are asked to speak without preparation, as politicians often are. Actors and comedians need large storehouses, as well. A recent documentary on Jerry Seinfeld, for instance, depicts the veteran of comedy pacing in his hotel room memorizing the order of the jokes he will tell.

Although the role of memory is not so apparent in written composition, writers do have to be able to remember information or to recall where it is located and, more broadly, to remember what arguments they have heard on a particular issue before. It is also of crucial importance to be aware of what events or knowledge might dominate the memories of a particular audience. We will treat this phenomenon a bit later under the head "cultural memory." All of these aspects of memory, we believe, connect to *kairos*, the ancient notion of timing and attunement.

MEMORY IN ANCIENT RHETORICS

It may be hard for us to grasp the importance of memory to premodern thinkers. Until the modern period, memory held a central place within rhetorical theory (and in most other intellectual endeavors, as well). Ancient rhetoricians distinguished between natural memory and **artificial memory.** An artificial memory is a memory that has been carefully trained to remember things. While every human being relies on natural memory to some extent, it is possible to enhance memory through training and practice. A person who possesses an artificial or trained memory has organized it into a set of orderly memory places into which she can locate relevant information so that she can retrieve it easily. (*Artificial* in this context simply means created by humans, something not given by nature; for ancient peoples something that was "artificed" was something made or created by human beings. The term did not carry its modern connotations of "fake" or "phony".) In ancient times even people who could write easily and well relied on their memories not merely as storage facilities but as structured heuristic systems.

In other words, memory was not only a system of recollection for ancient and medieval peoples; it was a means of invention. In ancient and medieval times, people memorized huge volumes of information, along with keys to its organization, and carried all this in their heads. Whenever the need arose to speak or write, they simply retrieved any relevant topics or commentary from their ordered places within memory, reorganized and expanded upon these, and added their own interpretations of the traditional material. People who had trained their memories could do this sort of composing without using writing at all. If they wanted to share their memorial compositions with others, they dictated them to scribes.

Some scholars think that ancient peoples invented memorial composition because writing materials were scarce and expensive. Certainly, literacy was not widespread until the modern period. But this explanation for the ancient interest in memory overlooks the fact that people relied on memory systems long past the time when printed books and libraries became accessible to most educated people. In fact, rhetors continued to use memorial composing strategies right up to the modern period. After all, unlike pen and paper or even a portable computer, a trained memory is always readily available as a source of invention. And Cicero, following Plato, compares a good memory to "inscribing letters on wax" (II lxxviii 360).

We shall probably never know whether artificial memory systems were in use prior to the fifth century BCE. It seems likely that they were, since the ability of the itinerant poets, called rhapsodes, to recall long poems cannot easily be explained in any other way. Perhaps rhapsodes used vivid mental images taken from the Homeric poems as memory aids; a trained memory could easily enough connect a vividly constructed mental image of the "wine-dark sea" either to events associated in the poems with seagoing or to the words and lines that narrated these events.

The sophists must have played an important role in establishing artificial memory as an important part of rhetorical training. The sophist Hippias was famous for his memory. According to the ancient historian Philostratus, "After hearing fifty names only once, [Hippias] could repeat them from memory in the order in which he had heard them"; he could do this "even in his old age" (*Lives of the Sophists* I 495). After writing came into general use, Hippias and the other sophists could store lists of topics in a manuscript as well as in memory. In fact, the handbooks mentioned in Aristotle's *Rhetoric* may have been memory aids as well as sources of invention. The handbooks arranged lists of topics in contradictory pairs, since the sophists taught their students how to argue both sides of any question. But students may have used mental images of the placement of these pairs on a roll of papyrus as a way of remembering what came next.

As we have seen, the sophistic *"Dissoi Logoi"* also contains several lists of commonplaces for use in public argument. The lists give possible variations on such topics as "What is true for one person is true for another." Rhetors could memorize this topic by connecting it to some vivid image and locating its variants in some orderly way. They would then be ready to invent arguments drawn from this topic for use on any occasion simply by combining and expanding upon the appropriate variations. A trained memory could house many such topics, along with their associated variations, if these were placed in some orderly manner. Composition, whether written or oral, would then amount to selection, combination, and amplification of appropriate topics and their variations to suit a particular occasion.

Scholars do not know when memory was added to the list of the rhetorical canons. Hellenistic teachers probably included formal instruction in artificial memory in their instruction; we possess a full treatment in the *Rhetorica ad Herennium*, which dates from the second century BCE, and as mentioned above, Cicero includes a brief discussion of memory in *De Oratore* (II 350 ff). Cicero's famous contemporary, Julius Caesar, must have practiced an art of memory; Caesar was famous in ancient times for prodigious feats of remembering. The historian Pliny wrote, "We are told that he used to write or read and dictate or listen simultaneously, and to dictate to his secretaries four letters at once on his important affairs—or, if otherwise unoccupied, seven letters at once" (*Natural History* VII xxv 92). Such feats would be impossible without the aid of a trained memory (and the Romans did not have Microsoft Word's handy cut-and-paste feature). Later Roman rhetors must have used memory arts as well; Quintilian gives a very full treatment of artificial memory in the *Institutes* (XI 2), and many rhetors of the Second Sophistic were famous for their memories.

ANCIENT MEMORY SYSTEMS

Ancient authorities agree that Simonides should be credited with the invention of artificial memory as an art that can be systematically studied and practiced. According to Cicero, Simonides taught

that persons desiring to train this faculty must select localities and form mental images of the facts they wish to remember and store those images in the
localities, with the result that the arrangement of the localities will preserve the
order of the facts, and the images of the facts will designate the facts themselves. (*De Oratore* II lxxxvi 354)

In other words, Simonides concluded that a mental construction, consisting
of a series of images connected in an orderly fashion to a series of mental
places, would allow people to remember lists of names or items if they simply associated each name or item with a mental place and/or its associated
image. A person had only to review each of the places, in order, to remember the images' names associated with it; a review of the images called up
the information being searched for. (The expression "in the first place" may
originate from this memory practice.)

This memory system took the notion of "place" literally. Its teachers
recommended that students visualize a street or a house with which they
were familiar. They were then to associate points along the street (say,
houses or buildings) or rooms inside the house with the items they wished
to remember. People who wish to use this memory system should choose
some arrangement or ordering of items that is quite familiar and thus easy
to walk through in memory. For example, if a rhetor wants to remember
three arguments, he can associate the first of these with the entryway to his
home. He then associates the second argument with the next room that he
enters in his house or apartment—say it is the living room—and the third
argument with the room that comes next—say, the kitchen. It is easy for a
rhetor to remember the order in which he enters each room of his house,
since he follows this order each time he goes in and out of the house.

Rhetors can use any geographical layout with which they are very
familiar as an ordering principle for memory. The main street of a town or
city was a favorite organizing device among ancient and medieval practitioners of artificial memory, for instance. It is important, however, that the
geographical layout contain memorable features; the hallways of modern
buildings are not very useful as an ordering principle, for instance, because
they contain a series of doors that all look alike.

The second task in this memory system was to place some striking or
memorable item within each of the ordered places. Teachers recommended
that the images be vivid and strange enough to be remembered easily and
that, if possible, the images be in some way associated with the items to be
remembered. For example, a rhetor might place a pair of red rubber boots
in the imaginary entryway of his house in order to remember his first argument about global warming: that if it is not stopped or slowed, the oceans
will continue to rise.

The *"Dissoi Logoi,"* the oldest rhetorical treatise we possess, gave
instructions for creating a second kind of artificial memory system:

The greatest and fairest discovery has been found to be memory; it is useful for
everything, for wisdom as well as for the conduct of life. This is the first step:
if you focus your attention, your mind, making progress by this means, will

perceive more. The second step is to practice whatever you hear. If you hear the same things many times and repeat them, what you have learned presents itself to your memory as a connected whole. The third step is: whenever you hear something, connect it with what you know already. For instance, suppose you need to remember the name "Chrysippos," you must connect it with *chrusos* (gold) and *hippos* (horse). Or another example: if you need to remember the name "*Pyrilampes*" you must connect it with *pyr* (fire) and *lampein* (to shine). These are examples for words. In the case of things, do this: if you want to remember courage, think of Ares and Achilles, or metal working, of Hephaistos, or cowardice, of Epeios. (Sprague 1968, 166–67)

This treatise counseled students of memory, first, to focus on things they wish to remember. Second, things to be remembered should be repeated many times. The third step resembled Simonides' system in part; here students were to associate the material to be lodged in memory with a vivid image that is connected either to words or to things. If he wished to remember the name *Chrysippos*, the rhetoric student might imagine a golden horse. Or he might imagine a fiery lamp in order to remember Pyrilampes' name. Both images should be vivid enough to be easily remembered.

If a rhetor wishes to remember the name of a person he meets, using this system, he should listen very carefully to the person's name when she is introduced to him. Then repeat the name aloud. Last, the rhetor should mentally associate the name with vivid and familiar images of objects in his memory. Say, for example, that the person's name is Patricia Smith. The rhetor can associate *Patricia* with a vivid image of an aristocratic person (a patrician) and *Smith* with an image of someone crafting metal, as a black-smith or locksmith does.

Memory for things is achieved by associating whatever is to be remembered—especially if it is an abstraction like courage or cowardice—with some mythological figure who is associated with that quality. So, if our rhetor learns that Patricia Smith is an astronaut, he can remember that by associating her in his memory with Icarus, who courageously flew all the way to the sun. (This example works only if mythological images are familiar and meaningful to the rhetor.) Or he can combine memory for words and memory for things: since the English term *astronaut* is formed from two ancient Greek words, *astron* ("star") and *nautes* (sailor), he can form a vivid image of a "star sailor" in order to remember Smith's occupation.

In the *Topics*, Aristotle recommended yet a third memory system. He counseled his students to memorize a "good stock of definitions," as well as a stock of premises to use in constructing enthymemes: "For just as in a person with a trained memory, a memory of things themselves is immediately caused by the mere mention of their places, so these habits too will make a man readier in reasoning, because he has his premises classified before his mind's eye, each under its number" (VIII 14 163b). In other words, Aristotle suggested that rhetors memorize the most often used commonplaces that serve as major premises for enthymemes. He also recommended that they group these into categories and give each category a number, so that premises can easily be recalled by mentally running through the numbered system. To use Aristotle's memory system, rhetors can group commonplaces on similar subjects under one mental category and invent a term to name the category. Then choose a key word from each commonplace, assign it a letter of the alphabet or a number, and organize the commonplaces in each category either alphabetically or numerically.

MODERN VERSIONS OF ANCIENT MEMORY SYSTEMS

Today, since many people are literate, they rely on writing and electronic storage systems to do the kind of work done by artificial memory among ancient peoples. People who use research in their writing, for example, take notes on their reading or make records of experiments while they are performing them; they refer to these notes and records when they begin writing up the results of their work. Thus the role played by memory in modern invention is not immediately obvious. Nevertheless, it is substantial.

When people begin to compose, they necessarily rely on their memories, no matter what composing strategies they use. Even if they take notes on experiments or reading, composers must rely on memory to reconstruct meanings for those notes. They must also remember commonplaces and other argumentative strategies. They must remember how they went about composing other pieces of discourse on other occasions, and they remember what they've been taught about usage and spelling. In other words, people do not begin composing as though nothing has ever happened to them or as though they remember nothing of their past lives.

Cultural Memory

The ancient notion of communal memory seems quite foreign to modern students because these days, people tend to think of their memories as narratives of their past lives, rather than as carefully organized depositories of common knowledge. Despite this belief, our memories are stocked with many things besides narratives of our experiences; we remember things we learn from teachers, parents, clergy, relatives and friends, the media and books, just as well as we remember experiences. Certainly we rely on our memories of all these kinds of teachings whenever we compose.

In a recent *New York Times* opinion piece entitled "A Lost Eloquence," Carol Muske-Dukes, an author and teacher, laments the decline of poetry memorization. "This long-ago discredited pedagogical tradition," she writes, "generated a commonplace eloquence among ordinary Americans who knew how to (as they put it) 'quote.' Poems are still memorized in some classrooms but not 'put to heart' in a way that would prompt this more quotidian public expression" (2002). Muske-Dukes writes further that she requires her students to memorize poetry. When discussing this requirement, Muske-Dukes's students usually protest that they are not capable of memorizing long poems, but she writes, "I ask them if they know the lyrics of 'Gilligan's Island' or 'The Brady Bunch,' and my point is made." Muske-Dukes's point, it seems to us, has to do with a kind of communal or cultural memory that exists either through explicit training (in the case of required memorization of poetry) or sheer repeated exposure (in the case of television theme songs). Cultural memory, to be sure, was partly why the ancients memorized Homeric epics and other poetry. Young Athenians and Romans were still memorizing lines from the *Iliad* and the *Odyssey* up to ten centuries after their appearance, well after they had been written down.

And this pedagogy of memorization was used in American schools as late as the twentieth century, as students were required to memorize parts of famous plays or poems. In fact one of us, while in college, was required to memorize the opening lines of Chaucer's *Canterbury Tales*—in Middle English.

Indeed, the ancient art of rhetoric is derived, at least in part, from earlier poetic traditions. Rhetorical scholar Jeffrey Walker argues that rhetoric's origins can be found within the poetic tradition. Poets such as Pindar and Sappho "sang" praises of people and deities, be they famous Olympic wrestlers, talented weavers, or Zeus, the god of thunder, and these songs of praise bear similarities to speeches of praise that Aristotle called epideictic rhetoric. Ancient poetry helped to create cultural memory, thus providing a ready pool of commonly known lines from which rhetors could draw in order to anchor their arguments.

World-changing events or situations help form cultural memories as well. The destruction of the World Trade Center on September 11, 2001 shook the United States to its core. Immediately thereafter, few rhetors could discuss anything without reference to the tragic events that happened on that date. To give a speech on October 4 without mentioning the event would have been thoughtless, if not impossible. Cultural memory was formed after 9/11 in myriad ways: the continuous replay on television of the disintegrating towers; photographs of victims pinned to every available nearby surface—storefronts, telephone poles, fences; widespread praise for heroic first responders; display of the American flag; expressed admiration for New Yorkers and how they were able to pull together in the face of such dreadful circumstances. In this way, monumental events and the memory of those events give rise to new commonplaces or resurrect old ones (such as the flag) in new ways. Even the Spiderman movie, released early the following year, played upon cultural memories of this event by showing the web-casting superhero swooping down beside a grand American flag, waving slowly.

Much like artificial memory, cultural memory thus oftentimes operates through visual images. Still, images require words in order to resonate in particular ways. While an image of the American flag generally provokes a feeling of love for country in most Americans, people whose politics lean left are more ambivalent about the flag than are people on the American right, because it sometimes seems to those leaning left to represent a desire to achieve empire and global economic domination. Either way, the visual symbol still functions powerfully as part of rhetorical memory and arguments.

Organizational Memory

Our memories also play a role in organizing things we remember. In an untrained memory, the organization of remembered material may seem chaotic and disjointed, just as it appears to us in dreams. But memories can be trained and organized, just as the ancients said. A little memory work can pay off handsomely if it teaches us how to find things in our memories more quickly.

Some very simple memory systems are available to everyone. The letters of the alphabet are quite useful in this regard. If, for example, you want to remember a list of items to buy at the grocery store, you can organize them in alphabetical order: apples, bananas, cheese, lettuce, pepper, vitamins, zucchini. It helps to repeat the list aloud a couple of times. When you arrive at the grocery store, simply skim through the alphabet letter by letter, searching your memory for any image you have attached to any letter. Another memory tactic, which resembles ancient geographical memory systems, is to organize your grocery list according to the floor plan of a grocery store in which you frequently shop. The first time you try this, you may need to walk through the store, noting the relation of its aisles to one another and making a mental place to coincide with each aisle. Then, when you make a grocery list, you can create the appropriate images and stash them on the appropriate aisles—carrots and potatoes on the vegetable aisle, milk at the back of the store, and so on. People who learn to do this don't need to make written grocery lists, and they never have to worry about leaving the grocery list at home. These simple memory systems also help writers and speakers to remember things that may be needed during composing. If you are like us, ideas often come to you when you are unable to write them down—while you are riding your bicycle, for example, or doing dishes or watching television or talking to someone. You can imprint such ideas on your memory by associating them with a letter of the alphabet and placing them in memory according to alphabetical order. Say that a rhetor has an idea about invention while she is having coffee with a friend. Rather than rudely interrupting the conversation to write this idea down, she can simply file the idea under "i" (for "invention") in her memory. This works even better if she mentally ties the idea to some vivid image. If, for example, she is having coffee with someone named "Ivan" she can conjure up his image, or an image of a coffee cup, or the odor of fresh coffee, to remember the idea filed under "i" when she needs it later. Better yet, she can create an image that is suitable to the idea. For example, she could associate her idea about invention with a vivid mental image of Thomas Edison, the inventor, getting a bulb to light up.

Since contemporary rhetors tend to associate memory with narratives of their lives, it might be useful for a composer to use his remembered chronology of his life as the organizing principle in a memory system. Young persons can use each year of their lives from age seven or so, while older persons might wish to divide the remembered chronology of their lives into five-year periods or decades. Assign each section of the chronology a letter of the alphabet or a number (such as *1990*). Try to characterize each section by associating it with something important that happened to you during that period of your life. Then, when you wish to remember something, mentally stash it in the section of your remembered chronology that is most relevant to it. This system is a variant of the one suggested by Aristotle, and it may work for people who have difficulty with memory systems that use places as organizing principles.

Literate Memory Systems

With the spread of literacy, the storage function of human memory was superseded. Public libraries and encyclopedias were developed during the modern period and, to some extent, took the place of artificial memory for things. Today people no longer need to remember information or arguments that they can easily look up in print or online. However, print storage cannot always tell you where to look for the information you need (something artificial memory can do). Electronic storage can usually tell you where to look, and for this reason it has now nearly superseded print storage systems. Print storage is still important, though, particularly for finding older material, and for this reason we provide some information here that may help you search it.

The organizational principles of literate storage systems have to be learned and memorized if they are to be of any help in locating materials. Libraries use systems such as the Library of Congress numbers to organize printed materials, and encyclopedias utilize the alphabet (along with other literate memory systems such as indexes). Books and periodicals use tables of contents, indexes, and bibliographies to help users determine whether the material they contain is relevant to the users' needs. Internet search engines usually attach a small blurb, or the first few words of a source, to an entry so that users can determine whether to pursue it. Students should get in the habit of reading cues, such as the organizational sections of printed materials, in order to save the time and energy that may be spent in reading irrelevant sources. It is also useful for students to get to know their way around the libraries they use most.

Books

The front and back matter of any book can help you to locate material within it more quickly. Books usually begin with a **title page** and a page that gives reference information—including its Library of Congress **call number**, its date of publication, and its publisher. Nonfiction books include a table of contents, which outlines the main headings of material discussed in the book. Read the table of contents to determine whether the book covers material that interests you. If you decide to use the book as a source, write down its author's name, its full title, its date of publication, and its library call number. You will need this information if you cite the book either in footnotes or a bibliography, and you need the call number in case you have to look something up later. If you plan to quote anything directly from the book, be sure to record the page numbers from which you took the quotation. If you get this information from an electronic source, you can print it out or save.

Books may optionally contain a **foreword**, sometimes written by someone other than the author, which introduces the book and places it in the context of other related work. Ordinarily, the author includes a **preface** (literally "a speaking before"). In a preface, an author may indicate her purposes in composing the book; she may outline her methods or indicate the scholarly or intellectual tradition to which she is indebted; and she may acknowledge those who helped her compose the work. Skimming a preface can tell you much about a book, and prefaces are often fun to read since authors sometimes feel they can be more informal in a preface than in the rest of the text.

At the back of most nonfiction books, you will find a **bibliography** and an **index**. In fact, if these are missing, you should doubt the scholarly quality of the book. The bibliography lists all of the works mentioned or used in the book, usually listed in alphabetical order by their authors' last names. Sometimes bibliographies will suggest related sources as well, and so you can use its entries to find more information. Indexes list persons' names and specific or technical terms used in the book, along with the page numbers on which these terms appear. Indexes are extremely valuable tools in literate storage systems. We often begin reading a book by looking at its index, to see if it lists any terms related to our current research or if it lists the names of persons who are important thinkers in the area we are researching. Sometimes notes appear at the back of a book; however, they sometimes appear at the bottom of pages (as footnotes) or at the ends of chapters. **Glossaries**, which explain the meanings of difficult or technical terms; **appendixes**; and other useful materials may also be included at the end of a book.

Periodicals

Librarians use the term **periodical** to refer to any literate materials that are published under the same name over a stretch of time. Periodicals include magazines, newspapers, and scholarly journals. Most periodicals include the organization information found in books: title pages, information pages, and tables of contents. Sometimes all of this information appears on a single page in a magazine or newspaper. Most periodicals have indexes, but these are issued periodically—once a year, or every three years, or the like. Before the advent of electronic storage, it was necessary to browse through one to three years' worth of journal issues to find out in which years they publish their indexes; now, however, journals usually post indexes to each volume on their Web sites. Periodical indexes are usually organized by author, title, and/or subject; they list all the materials published in the periodical over the time period covered by the index. The *New York Times*, for example, used to publish a yearly index of materials contained in that newspaper, and these volumes were usually housed in the reference rooms of large libraries. Now, however, most newspapers maintain an electronic index of the content of their issues.

Ordinarily, the publishers of periodicals assign a **volume number** to all the issues published in a given year. For example, Volume 42 of *Rhetors Monthly*, dated 2006, indicates that all issues of this journal published in 2006 will be bound together as volume 42; each issue will have a separate issue number. The volume number most likely indicates that *Rhetors Monthly* has been published for forty-two years. Its title indicates that this journal probably appears twelve times a year, so there will be twelve issues in each volume. The May 2006 issue, then, should be labeled "Vol. 42, No. 5." Sometimes page numbers are consecutive throughout a volume. The text of issue number one begins with page 1, but the text of the May issue begins with the number that comes after the number on the last page of the April issue.

Libraries

Libraries are to literate information storage what vivid images of city streets were to artificial memory. To be really useful, the literate storage systems used to organize libraries have to be memorized. Students who compose discourse in response to school assignments should study the indexing system used by the nearest library. Find out whether the library uses the Dewey decimal or the Library of Congress cataloging system. Get a copy of the library handout that explains the system and memorize as much of it as you can. Get a map of the library, and find the reference room.

Very few university libraries still catalog their holdings in large cases called **card catalogues**, although some libraries that have switched to electronic cataloging still retain card catalogues as resources for finding older holdings. Smaller public libraries and some private libraries may still rely solely on card catalogues, however. Both sorts of catalogues are ordinarily arranged according to three indexing systems: by author, by title, and by subject. E-catalogs can also be searched by many other means: by keyword, by date, by call number. If you are searching for materials on a given subject, you can use the alphabetical listing of standard subject headings used by the Library of Congress, which is usually available in the reference room. Other reference materials, such as the *Readers' Guide to Periodical Literature*, are also organized according to author, title, and subject.

If you need help in using these basic reference materials, take a library tour, or ask a reference librarian to explain the basic reference system to you. If the library you use is a large university library, walk through it in order to find where materials catalogued under each section of the system are stored.

Ask a reference librarian to tell you when the library's periodicals began to be stored on microforms. Memorize that date or write it down. This information can save you time otherwise spent walking between the rooms that house printed periodicals and those where microforms can be read. Today, many recent periodical articles can be found on-line, and libraries maintain lists of electronic databases that can help you find these articles. Older articles, alas, must still be found by hand (or foot, actually). If you do historical research, as we do, you may find yourself traipsing from one library storage facility to another, across campus or across town or across the country.

Most libraries divide their periodical holdings into two categories: bound and current. **Bound periodicals** are older issues of newspapers, magazines, and journals that have either been bound together into a book according to year of publication or volume number or that have been transferred to microforms for ease of storage. **Current periodicals** are piled on shelves just as they are; most libraries retain current issues of periodicals in their current periodical section for at least several months, depending on how often the periodical is issued. Daily newspapers, for example, are bound more often because they are so bulky. Bound and current periodicals are sometimes housed in different locations in a large library. The rooms and shelves that hold books are called **stacks**. Most public libraries allow everyone to browse the stacks, although some libraries close off some sections of the stacks to all but a few people. In that case, you have to get permission to use them. You can find books in the stacks by continually referring to the indexing system that is ordinarily posted or painted on walls, but library research goes much faster if you memorize at least the sections of the system to which you frequently refer. Once you have memorized the Library of Congress numbers that you use most often, you can use the system heuristically. That is, since you know where relevant materials are likely housed, you can find them by browsing the appropriate shelves in the library. If you know that most books and periodicals on rhetoric are housed under Library of Congress call numbers that begin with PN or PR, for example, you know immediately which floor of the library you need to get to, and if you use the same library frequently, a call number will tell you exactly which shelf you need to find (clearly relying on your artificial memory here). When a book or periodical is missing from its appointed place, even though the catalog shows it as "checked in" or "on shelf," search the space where it is supposed to be for a couple of feet in either direction. Look for a missing book or periodical on nearby carts and around copying stations as well. Knowing the call numbers is also helpful in electronic searching, since most libraries have systems that allow you to browse by call number.

ELECTRONIC MEMORY SYSTEMS

Electronic memory represents a vast improvement on both artificial memory and literate storage facilities. Computers can remember more information than any single human will ever need. The Web is a vast storehouse of information and images, available to anyone with access to a computer. Researchers no longer need to develop elaborate card systems to help them remember bibliographic information, since this information can be called up from the electronic **databases** of any good library at any time of the day or night and from any location where there are computer terminals. Software programs are available that help rhetors assemble their personal notes, footnotes, and bibliographies as well. Note taking can now be done wherever research takes place, at the keyboard of a portable computer. Copies of library materials may be made with a copier or scanner, and OCR (optical character recognition) programs can translate a scanned image of a document into text with very little need for editing. Oral composing can be done electronically with the aid of voice-activated word-processing programs that remember and store every sound uttered by a composer.

In other words, software is now available that serves the heuristic functions of ancient memory—something that literate storage could not do. Software programs can find where any file in an electronic system is located, even if their users can't remember the file's name, let alone where they stored it. Dictionaries, encyclopedias, thesauruses, collections of proverbs and quotations—reference materials of all kinds—are now available on disk. These electronic references have elaborate cross-referencing systems that are larger and far more subtle than human memory; they will search for related information in places where humans would never think to look. Electronic databases have all but eliminated the need to use literate cataloging systems; a researcher can simply type in a word or name or call number, and the database will display all related items held by that library or any others to which it is connected. Many libraries subscribe to more specialized databases that are organized by field or subject: business, humanities, sciences. Most such databases are user-friendly, providing users with step-by-step instructions for entering and using them. Libraries usually supply directions on paper as well, and librarians can always be called upon to help with a search of library holdings.

It is an open question whether electronic memory will replace human memory. It is probably more accurate to think of electronic memory as a supplement to, or expression of, human memory. The sci-fi image of the cyborg—part human, part machine—need no longer be limited to movie creations like *The Terminator*. Imagine Simonides seated before a speedy computer equipped with huge amounts of storage, plenty of memory and a fast graphics card, efficient word-processing software, a scanner, and quick access to the Web. We suspect that he would program his machine with one or several of the electronic memory systems that are now available, but he could program and install a version of the artificial memory system he created in the fifth century BCE, as well. Would he then quit using his mental memory system to remember things and their relations, relying instead only on his computer whenever he needed to remember something? We think not. We think he would continue to use both. In fact, interaction with his machine might stimulate Simonides to achieve even more dazzling feats of memory than those he displayed at Scopas's banquet.

IMITATION III: TRANSLATION AND PARAPHRASE

Anyone who can read in another language such as Spanish or Arabic knows that reading aloud is a lot easier than translating into English. This is because translation requires intimate knowledge of what is going on in the writing—from the word to the sentence and to the overall point of a passage. Less difficult, but still challenging, is paraphrasing, or stating something using different words. The ancients were fond of translation and paraphrase because they required careful attention to the passage that was being translated or paraphrased. These exercises, perhaps more than any others, asked students to delve into the writing—to inhabit it. The result is a better grasp of how language works for that author and in general.

Translation

Roman teachers regularly advised their students to translate passages from Greek into Latin and Latin into Greek. They argued that this exercise improved their students' understandings of both languages. Obviously, translation also improves one's grasp of the idioms used in a foreign language, something that is difficult to learn by studying its grammar. Translation, like imitation, also improves reading skills and enhances appreciation of good writing in any language.

Of course, translation is useful mostly for students who are bilingual or multilingual or for students who are trying to learn a second or third language. But translation can also move across levels of usage, and specialized pieces or writing for a particular audience can be translated for other audiences. A good example of this is contemporary science writing, in which writers take highly specialized reports from scientific journals and make their findings available and relevant to a broader readership. Here is an example of a recent study about smells and memory. We include the first part of the original study, written by Björn Rasch, Christian Büchel, Steffen Gais, and Jan Born and published in the journal *Science*, followed by the account of the study offered by science writer Benedict Carey in the *New York Times*. What are the main differences between the two versions?

ODOR CUES DURING SLOW-WAVE SLEEP PROMPT DECLARATIVE MEMORY CONSOLIDATION

Sleep facilitates memory consolidation. A widely held model assumes that this is because newly encoded memories undergo covert reactivation during sleep. We cued new memories in humans during sleep by presenting an odor that had been presented as context during prior learning, and so showed that reactivation indeed causes memory consolidation during sleep. Re-exposure to the odor during slow-wave sleep (SWS) improved the retention of hippocampus-dependent declarative memories but not of hippocampus-independent procedural memories. Odor re-exposure was ineffective during rapid eye movement sleep or wakefulness or when the odor had been omitted during prior learning. Concurring with these findings, functional magnetic resonance imaging revealed significant hippocampal activation in response to odor re-exposure during SWS.

Sleep facilitates the consolidation of newly acquired memories for long-term storage (1–3). The prevailing model assumes that this consolidation relies on a covert reactivation of the novel neuronal memory representations during sleep after learning (3–6). In rats, hippocampal neuronal assemblies implicated in the encoding of spatial information during maze learning are reactivated in the same temporal order during slow-wave sleep (SWS) as during previous learning (7, 8). The consolidation of hippocampus-dependent memories benefits particularly from SWS (9–11), and reactivation of the hippocampus in SWS after spatial learning has also been seen in humans observed with positron emission tomography (12). However, none of these studies experimentally manipulated memory reactivation during sleep. Therefore, its causal role in memory consolidation is still unproven.

References and Notes
1. P. Maquet, *Science* **294**, 1048 (2001).
2. R. Stickgold, *Nature* **437**, 1272 (2005).
3. J. Born, B. Rasch, S. Gais, *Neuroscientist* **12**, 410 (2006).
4. J. L. McClelland, B. L. McNaughton, R. C. O'Reilly, *Psychol. Rev.* **102**, 419 (1995).
5. G. Buzsáki, *J. Sleep Res.* **7**, 17 (1998).
6. G. R. Sutherland, B. McNaughton, *Curr. Opin. Neurobiol.* **10**, 180 (2000).
7. M. A. Wilson, B. L. McNaughton, *Science* **265**, 676 (1994).
8. D. Ji, M. A. Wilson, *Nat. Neurosci.* **10**, 100 (2007).
9. W. Plihal, J. Born, *J. Cogn. Neurosci.* **9**, 534 (1997).
10. M. Mölle, L. Marshall, S. Gais, J. Born, *Proc. Natl. Acad. Sci. U.S.A.* **101**, 13963 (2004).
11. L. Marshall, H. Helgadóttir, M. Mölle, J. Born, *Nature* **444**, 610 (2006).
12. P. Peigneux et al., *Neuron* **44**, 535 (2004).

STUDY UNCOVERS MEMORY AID: A SCENT DURING SLEEP

Scientists studying how sleep affects memory have found that the whiff of a familiar scent can help a slumbering brain better remember things that it learned the evening before. The smell of roses—delivered to people's nostrils as they studied and, later, as they slept—improved their performance on a memory test by about 13 percent.

The new study, appearing today in the journal *Science*, is the first rigorous test of the effect of odor on human memory during sleep. The results, whether or not they can help students cram for tests, clarify the picture of what the sleeping brain does with newly learned material and help illuminate what it takes for this process to succeed.

Researchers have long known that sleep is crucial to laying down new memories, and studies in the 1980s and '90s showed that exposing the sleeping brain to certain cues—the sound of clicking, for instance—could enhance the process. But it is only in recent years that scientists have begun to understand how this is possible. . . .

In the study, neuroscientists from two German institutions, the University of Lübeck and the University Medical Center Hamburg-Eppendorf, had groups of medical students play a version of concentration, memorizing the location of card pairs on a computer screen. Upon learning the location of each pair, the students received a burst of rose scent in their noses through masks they wore. The researchers delivered the fragrance in bursts because the brain quickly adjusts to strong smells in the air and begins to ignore them.

The students went to sleep about a half-hour later, with electrodes on their heads tracking the depth of their slumber. Neuroscientists divide sleep into stages, including deep (or slow wave) sleep and the shallow, dream-rich state called rapid eye movement (or REM) sleep.

The brain is thought to process newly acquired facts, figures and locations most efficiently in deep sleep. This restful state usually descends within the first 20 minutes or so after head meets pillow and may last an hour or longer, then recur once or more later in the night. The researchers delivered pulses of rose bouquet during this slow-wave state; the odor did not interrupt sleep, and the students said they had no memory of it. (2007)

Once again, the point of translation is to inhabit multiple rhetorical features at once—to simultaneously think about audience, about style, about arrangement, and nuance.

TRANSLATION EXERCISES

1. If you know another language, practice translating a passage from one language to another.

2. If you are lucky enough to use more than one variant of English, you may profit by translating your writing, as well as that of professional writers, into and out of both variants.

3. Find a highly specialized article—in science or another field—and translate it for a group of college students.

Paraphrase

In *De Oratore* Crassus described his favored rhetorical exercise: "This was to set myself some poetry, the most impressive to be found, or to read as much of some speech as I could keep in my memory, and then to declaim upon the actual subject-matter of my reading, choosing as far as possible different words" (I xxxiv 154). Here Crassus referred to the ancient exercise called paraphrase, which literally means "to express in other words."

Paraphrase is a very old exercise. A sophist named Theon, writing in the first century CE, provided us with some truly ancient examples of paraphrase:

> Paraphrasing Homer, when he says,
>
>> For such is the mind of men who dwell on earth
>> As the father of men and gods may bring for a day. [*Odyssey* 18.136–37]
>
> Archilochus says,
>
>> Glaucus, son of Leptines, such a spirit for mortal
>> Men is born as Zeus brings for a day.
>
> And again, Homer has spoken of a city's capture in this manner,
>
>> They kill the men, and fire levels the city,
>> But others lead away the children and deep-belted women. [*Iliad* 9.593–94]
>
> And Demosthenes, thus:
>
>> Now when we were on our way in Delphi, it was of necessity to see all these things, houses razed to the ground, walls taken away, a land in the prime of life, but a few women and little children and pitiable old men. [19.361]
>
> And Aeschines, thus:
>
>> But look away in your thoughts to their misfortunes and imagine that you see the city being taken, destruction of walls, burying of houses, temples being pillaged, women and children being led into slavery, old men, old women, too late unlearning their freedom. [3.157] (246)

These examples were all composed during or before the fourth century BCE. Throughout antiquity, rhetoric teachers believed that there were many, many ways in which to express any meaning. As Quintilian pointed out, the variety of expression available in language can never be used up:

> If there were only one way in which anything could be satisfactorily expressed, we should be justified in thinking that the path to success had been sealed to us by our predecessors. But, as a matter of fact, the methods of expression still left us are innumerable, and many roads lead us to the same goal. (X v 7–8)

This attitude toward the possibilities of paraphrase prevailed throughout the European Middle Ages and into the Renaissance. In his sixteenth-century textbook on *copia*, Erasmus demonstrated that there are over two hundred ways to write "Your letter pleased me mightily." He changed the word order: "Your letter mightily pleased me; to a wonderful degree did your letter please me; me exceedingly did your letter please" (the last version works better in Latin than it does in English). Then he added hyperbole (overstatement): "Your epistle exhilarated me intensely; I was intensely exhilarated by your epistle; your brief note refreshed my spirits in no small measure; I was in no small measure refreshed in spirit by your grace's hand; from your affectionate letter I received unbelievable pleasure; your affectionate letter brought me unbelievable pleasure" (349). If you wish to see how far Erasmus was able to extend these variations on a theme, find a copy of his *De Copia* and see for yourself.

Paraphrase was still in use in modern times as a means of improving writing skill. In a famous passage from the first chapter of his *Autobiography*, Benjamin Franklin described the paraphrasing exercises he did as a young man:

> About this time I met with an odd volume of the *Spectator*. It was the third. I had never before seen any of them. I bought it, read it over and over, and was much delighted with it. I thought the writing excellent, and wished, if possible, to imitate it. With this view I took some of the papers, and, making short hints of the sentiment in each sentence, laid them by a few days, and then, without looking at the book, try'd to compleat the papers again, by expressing each hinted sentiment at length, and as fully as it had been expressed before, in any suitable words that should come to hand. Then I compared my *Spectator* with the original, discovered some of my faults, and corrected them. But I found I wanted a stock of words, or a readiness in recollecting and using them, which I thought I should have acquired before that time if I had gone on making verses; since the continual occasion for words of the same import, but of different length, to suit the measure, or of different sound for the rhyme, would have laid me under a constant necessity of searching for variety, and also have tended to fix that variety in my mind, and make me master of it. Therefore I took some of the tales and turned them into verse; and, after a time, when I had pretty well forgotten the prose, turned them back again. I also sometimes jumbled my collections of hints into confusion, and after some weeks endeavored to reduce them into the best order, before I began to form the full sentences and compleat the paper. This was to teach me method in the arrangement of thoughts. By comparing my work afterwards with the original, I discovered many faults and amended them; but I sometimes had the pleasure of fancying that, in certain particulars of small import, I had been lucky enough to improve the method or the language, and this encouraged me to think I might possibly in time come to be a tolerable English writer, of which I was extremely ambitious. My time for these exercises and for reading was at night, after work or before it began in the morning, or on Sundays, when I contrived to be in the printing-house alone, evading as much as I could the common attendance on public worship which my father used to exact on me when I was under his care, and which indeed I still thought a duty, though I could not, as it seemed to me, afford time to practise it. (1895)

Franklin knew the importance of *copia*, a "stock of words," to anyone who wishes to become "a tolerable English writer." His method was similar to Crassus's, except that Franklin took notes on the material he read rather than retaining it in memory.

In order to demonstrate how paraphrase works, we performed one of the exercises recommended by Franklin. The *Spectator* was a popular newspaper published in London between 1711 and 1714. It contained essays about morals, current events, education, and good taste, among other things. Essay number 157, written by Richard Steele, was a meditation on the use of corporal punishment in British elementary schools. At the time Steele wrote this essay, such punishment was frequently used with students who failed to memorize or recite their lessons correctly. Here is the text of his essay:

I am very much at a Loss to express by any Word that occurs to me in our Language that which is understood by *Indoles* in Latin. The natural Disposition to any particular Art, Science, Profession, or Trade, is very much to be consulted in the Care of Youth, and studied by Men for their own Conduct when they form to themselves any Scheme of Life. It is wonderfully hard indeed for a Man to judge of his own Capacity impartially; that may look great to me which may appear little to another, and I may be carried by Fondness towards my self so far, as to attempt things too high for my Talents and Accomplishments: But it is not methinks so very difficult a Matter to make a judgment of the Abilities of others, especially of those who are in their Infancy. My common-place Book directs me on this Occasion to mention the Dawning of Greatness in Alexander, who being asked in his Youth to contend for a Prize in the Olympick Games, answered he would if he had Kings to run against him. Cassius, who was one of the Conspirators against Caesar, gave as great a Proof of his Temper, when in his Childhood he struck a Play-fellow, the Son of Sylla, for saying his Father was Master of the Roman People. Scipio is reported to have answered (when some Flatterers at Supper were asking him what the Romans should do for a General after his Death), Take Marius. Marius was then a very Boy, and had given no Instances of his Valour; but it was visible to Scipio from the Manners of the Youth, that he had a Soul formed for the Attempt and Execution of great Undertakings. I must confess I have very often with much Sorrow bewailed the Misfortune of the Children of Great Britain, when I consider the Ignorance and Undiscerning of the Generality of School-masters. The boasted Liberty we talk of is but a mean Reward for the long Servitude, the many Heart Aches and Terrours, to which our Childhood is exposed in going through a Grammer-School: Many of these stupid Tyrants exercise their Cruelty without any Manner of Distinction of the Capabilities of Children, or the Intention of Parents in their Behalf. There are many excellent Tempers which are worthy to be nourished and cultivated with all possible Diligence and Care, that were never designed to be acquainted with Aristotle, Tully, or Virgil; and there are as many who have Capacities for understanding every Word those great Persons have writ, and yet were not born to have any Relish of their Writings. For want of this common and obvious discerning in those who have the Care of Youth, we have so many Hundred unaccountable Creatures every Age whipped up into great Scholars, that are for ever near a right Understanding, and will never arrive at it. These are the Scandal of Letters, and these are generally the Men who are to teach others. The Sense of Shame and Honour is enough to keep the World it self in Order without Corporal Punishment, much more to train the Minds of uncorrupted and innocent Children. It happens, I doubt not, more than once in a Year, that a Lad is chastised for a Blockhead, when it is good Apprehension that makes him incapable of knowing what his Teacher means: A brisk Imagination very often may suggest an Errour, which a Lad could not have fallen into if he had been as heavy in conjecturing as his Master in explaining: But there is no Mercy even towards a wrong Interpretation of his Meaning; the Sufferings of the Scholar's Body are to rectify the Mistakes of his Mind.

I am confident that no Boy who will not be allured to Letters without Blows, will ever be brought to any thing with them. A great or good Mind must necessarily be the worse for such Indignities: and it is a sad Change to lose of its Virtue for the Improvement of its Knowledge. No one who has gone through what they call a great School, but must remember to have seen Children of excellent and ingenuous Natures, (as has afterwards appeared in their Manhood;) I say no Man has passed through this Way of Education, but must have seen an ingenuous Creature expiring with Shame, with pale Looks, beseeching Sorrow, and silent Tears, throw up its honest Eyes, and kneel on its tender Knees to an inexorable Blockhead, to be forgiven the false Quantity of a Word in making a Latin Verse: The Child is punished, and the next Day he commits a like Crime, and so a third with the same Consequence. I would fain ask any reasonable Man whether this Lad, in the Simplicity of his native Innocence, full of Shame, and capable of any Impression from that Grace of Soul, was not fitter for any Purpose in this Life, than after that Spark of Virtue is extinguished in him, tho' he is able to write twenty Verses in an Evening?

Seneca says, after his exalted Way of talking, As the immortal Gods never learnt any Virtue, tho' they are endued with all that is good; so there are some Men who have so natural a Propensity to what they should follow, that they learn it almost as soon as they hear it. Plants and Vegetables are cultivated into the Production of finer Fruit than they would yield without that Care; and yet we cannot entertain Hopes of producing a tender conscious Spirit into Acts of Virtue, without the same Methods as is used to cut Timber, or give new Shape to a Piece of Stone.

It is wholly to this dreadful Practice that we may attribute a certain Hardness and Ferocity which some Men, tho' liberally educated, carry about them in all their Behaviour. To be bred like a Gentleman, and punished like a Malefactor, must, as we see it does, produce that illiberal Sauciness which we see sometimes in Men of Letters.

The Spartan Boy who suffered the Fox (which he had stolen and hid under his Coat) to eat into his Bowels, I dare say had not half the Wit or Petulance which we learn at great Schools among us: But the glorious Sense of Honour, or rather Fear of Shame, which he demonstrated in that Action, was worth all the Learning in the World without it.

It is methinks a very melancholy Consideration, that a little Negligence can spoil us, but great Industry is necessary to improve us; the most excellent Natures are soon depreciated, but evil Tempers are long before they are exalted into good Habits. To help this by Punishments, is the same thing as killing a Man to cure him of a Distemper; when he comes to suffer Punishment in that one Circumstance, he is brought below the Existence of a rational Creature, and is in the State of a Brute that moves only by the Admonition of Stripes. But since this Custom of educating by the Lash is suffered by the Gentry of Great Britain, I would prevail only that honest heavy Lads may be dismissed from slavery sooner than they are at present, and not whipped on to their fourteenth or fifteenth Year, whether they expect any Progress from them or not. Let the Child's Capacity be forthwith examined, and he sent to some Mechanick Way of Life, without Respect to his Birth, if Nature design'd him for nothing higher; let him go before he has innocently suffered, and is debased into a Dereliction of Mind for being what it is no Guilt to be, a plain Man. I would not here be supposed to have said, that our learned Men of either Robe who have been whipped at School, are not still Men of noble and liberal Minds; but I am sure they had been much more so than they are, had they never suffered that Infamy. (1711)

We read Steele's essay carefully, and one of us copied it out by hand. Then we made notes about important points. The next day we read it again and wrote the following paraphrase:

No word in English is a satisfactory translation of the Latin term *indoles*. Perhaps *nature* or *natural disposition* come closest. A person's natural disposition, if there is such a thing, needs to be taken into account in her education and in her choice of a profession. It is difficult for anyone to know what her own natural aptitudes are, although others can sometimes determine these with ease. History abounds with examples of persons whose early activities hinted at their later greatness. George Washington's honesty about the cherry tree presaged his later courage in the face of difficulties. Abraham Lincoln demonstrated his persistence and ambition as a young man, when he worked long hours and walked many miles to study law.

But bright lights like these can easily be extinguished by ignorant and brutal teachers. It is difficult to believe that the freedom we prize so highly is often purchased at the expense of long years of terror and heartache in school. Ignorant teachers do not distinguish between the able and the less able, but punish all alike for failure to perform correctly. The truth is that many people are not suited for the study of letters. Despite this lack of natural inclination, such persons are beaten into diligence. Often it is these persons who become teachers themselves.

Students' combined senses of honor and shame should suffice to drive them to study. Punishment for failure to give the correct answers does not serve the aim intended for it. Because of their active imaginations, students sometimes give answers that are correct, but are not the answers that teachers were looking for. Students who do this are punished nonetheless. As a result, punishment often extinguishes the scholarly virtue of imagination, while it reinforces the belief that scholarship amounts to absorbing and parroting back trivial bits of information.

Quintilian remarked that "study depends on the good will of the student, a quality that cannot be secured by compulsion" (I iii 8). We do not recklessly prune fruits or vegetables while we are encouraging them to grow; rather we care for them, making sure they have enough water and sunlight. Teachers should shape young minds with the same care and attention that sculptors use to shape pieces of marble into works of art.

Punishment breeds a certain brutishness in even the best-educated persons. Using punishment to force people to learn is like killing someone to cure him of a cold. This method turns people into brutes who only work when they are forced to. Punishment extinguishes rational behavior, rather than encouraging it.

Given these considerations, it makes sense that children who are not cut out to be scholars should be allowed to quit school when they have learned all they can. Those whose natural dispositions incline them away from learning should be encouraged to follow other career paths. I am not saying that our current crop of intellectuals, who were educated in this way, are not fine and upright people. However, I am sure they would have been persons of even more liberal and noble character had they been better treated while they were in school.

This paraphrase is fairly accurate; it condenses Steele's essay and renders it in more modern English. Since we do not agree with much of what Steele wrote in this number of the *Spectator*, this exercise was difficult. However, writing it did stimulate us to think about the issues it raises—more so than simply reading the essay would have done—and so it may be that paraphrase can occasionally jump-start invention.

We recommend that writers paraphrase anyone whose work they admire. A paraphrase can be longer or shorter than the original; it can use a different voice or arrangement; it can have more figures or fewer; it can develop fuller characterizations and add more detail; or it can be as spare as possible—in which case it is more accurately called a summary or precis. All choices like these are up to the paraphraser.

Here is a method for paraphrasing: Read a passage carefully. Copy it into a commonplace book, wait awhile, and then without looking at the original again, try to compose another passage that captures the sense of the original. Or you can make notes on the original passage, and use these to compose a paraphrase.

These days students encounter paraphrase in the context of citation practices, making sure to paraphrase if not using quotation marks. While these exercises in paraphrase might assist with such information extraction, they nevertheless have different goals having to do with style, arrangement, delivery, and yes, even invention. The ancients had serious reasons for recommending paraphrase to their students. Paraphrase encourages us to look for words and structures that do not appear in the original, thus increasing our stocks of both. Because it requires us to rely on our own linguistic resources, paraphrase is more challenging than imitation. Indeed, Quintilian recommended it precisely because of its difficulty (8).

Paraphrasing Poetry

In the passage quoted earlier, Benjamin Franklin mentioned another exercise in paraphrase that was also recommended by Quintilian: turning poetry into prose. According to Quintilian, this exercise is useful because "the lofty inspiration of verse serves to elevate the rhetor's style" (X v 4). In other words, writers of prose may find unusual uses of language in poetry that they can borrow. But paraphrase of poetry into prose may also teach us something about arrangement as well. Certainly it helps us to read poetry more carefully.

Here is Aesop's fable of the stag and the horse, as told in prose by Aristotle:

> A horse had a meadow to himself. When a stag came and quite damaged the pasture, the horse, wanting to avenge himself on the stag, asked a man if he could help him get vengeance on the stag. The man said he could, if the horse were to take a bridle and he himself were to mount on him holding javelins. When the horse agreed and the man mounted, instead of getting vengeance the horse found himself a slave to the man. (*Rhetoric* II xx 1393b)

Now here is the same fable, told in poetry in 1688 by a poet named John Ogilby (we have modernized Ogilby's English):

Long was the war between the hart and horse
Fought with like courage, chance, and equal force;
Until a fatal day
Gave signal victory to the hart; the steed
Must now no more in pleasant valleys feed,
Nor verdant commons sway,
The hart who now o'er all did domineer,
This conquering stag,
Slights like a nag,
The vanquished horse, which did no more appear.
In want, exiled, driven from native shores,
The horse in cities human aid implores,
To get his realms again.
Let man now manage him and his affair,
Since he not knows what his own forces are.
Thus sues he for the rein;
For sweet revenge he will endure the bit,
Let him o'erthrow
His cruel foe,
And let his haughty rider heavy fit.
He takes the bridle o'er his yielding head.
With man and arms the horse is furnished,
And for the battle neighs.
But when the hart two hostile faces saw
And such a centaur to encounter draw,
He stood awhile at gaze.
At last known valor up he roused again,
More hopes by fight
There was, than flight;
What's won by arms, by force he must maintain.
Then to the battle did the hart advance;
The horse a man brings, with a mighty lance
Longer than the other's crest;
The manner of the fight is changed, he feels
No more the horse's hoof, and ill-aimed heels;
They charge now breast to breast.
Two to one odds 'gainst Hercules; the hart,
Though strong and stout,
Could not hold out,
But flies, and must from conquered realms depart.
Nor longer could the horse his joy contain,
But with loud neighs, and erected mane,
Triumphs after fight;
When to the soldier mounted on his back,
Feeling him heavy now, the beast thus spake;
Be pleased good sir to light.

Since you restored to me by father's seat,
And got the day,
Receive your pay,
And to your city joyfully retreat.
Then said the man; This saddle which you wear
Cost more than all the lands we conquered here,
Beside this burnished bit,
Your self, and all you have, too little are
To clear my engagements in this mighty war;
Till that's paid, here I'll sit:
And since against your foe I aided you,
Can you deny
Me like supply?
Come, and with me my enemy subdue.
Then sighed the horse, and to the man replied;
I feel thy cruel rowels gall my side,
And now I am thy slave;
But thank thy self for this, thou foolish beast,
That for revenge to foreign interest
Thy self and Kingdom gave.
Amongst rocky mountains I had better dwelled,
And fed on thorns,
Gored by the hart's horns,
Than wicked man's hard servitude have felt. (1688)

As you can see, Ogilby elaborated the basic story a good deal in his paraphrase, providing more plot detail and giving the horse and stag more character than Aristotle cared to (after all, Aristotle was interested in the moral of the story, while Ogilby wished to entertain his readers). But a prose paraphrase does not need to be as spare as Aristotle's version; a faithful prose paraphrase of Ogilby's poem would be at least twice as long as Aristotle's rendering of the fable. As Quintilian remarked, the duty of a paraphrase is not to replicate an original exactly but rather "to rival and vie with the original in the expression of the same thoughts" (X v 5).

Here are poetic renderings of two more of Aesop's fables, suitable for paraphrasing into prose:

THE NORTH WIND AND THE SUN

Between the North Wind and the Sun
A quarrel rose as to which one
Could strip the mantle from a man
Walking the road. The wind began,
And blew, for in his Thracian way
He thought that he would quickly lay
The wearer bare by force. But still
The man, shivering with the chill,

Held fast his cloak, nor let it go
The more the North Wind tried to blow,
But drew the edges close around,
Sat himself down upon the ground,
And leaned his back against a stone.
And then the Sun peeped out, and shone,
Pleasant at first, and set him free
From the cold blowing bitterly,
And next applied a little heat.
Then suddenly, from head to feet,
By burning fire the man was gripped,
Cast off his cloak himself, and stripped.

THE TWO PACKS

      Among the gods when time began
Prometheus lived. He made a man
All molded out of earth and plaster,
And thus produced for beasts a master.
He hung on him two packs to wear,
Filled with the woes that men must bear,
With strangers' woes the one before,
But that in back, which carried more,
Was filled with evils all his own.
Hence many men, I think, are prone
To see the ills some other bears
But still be ignorant of theirs.

              —Dennison B. Hull, 1960

Try paraphrasing these fables into prose. If you wish, you can compare your prose version to any of the hundreds of modern translations of Aesop's fables that can be found on the Internet. For further practice, you can turn your prose paraphrase back into poetry, or you can try to write a poetic version in imitation of Ogilby's seventeenth-century style. Once again, this exercise is useful because it demands that writers find new words and structures to express something already written by someone else.

If you find paraphrase to be fun and/or useful, we recommend that you practice paraphrasing your favorite poetry into prose. We are aware that this exercise may offend the sensibilities of persons who think that great poets have found the best and only way to express anything. This is a quite modern notion, having to do with Romantic attitudes toward originality and the uniqueness of creative ability. The ancients viewed creativity in a far different light: they thought that craft played a large role in the production of fine writing and that craft could be learned through practice. Nor did they believe that any poem or piece of prose was so good that it couldn't be improved upon. As Quintilian remarked, a paraphrase may "add the vigor of oratory to the thoughts expressed by the poet, make good his omissions, and prune his diffuseness" (X v 4–5).

Writers need not imitate or paraphrase only the work of others, however. Quintilian recommended that writers get in the habit of paraphrasing their own work: "For instance, we may specially select certain thoughts and recast them in the greatest variety of forms, just as a sculptor will fashion a number of different images from the same piece of wax" (X v 9–10). In fact, self-paraphrase can become a method of composition. It works like this: after you have written a draft of a composition, set it aside for awhile. Then read it over and quickly write a second draft. Compare the two drafts, take what you like from each, and compose a third. Continue with this process until you achieve a draft that satisfies you.

The reasons for using paraphrase are many: it promotes *copia* and it may stimulate invention. Paraphrase also turns people into more careful readers, and it may make reading more enjoyable too (X v 8). Plus there's always the chance that a paraphrase will turn out better than the original. In that case, paraphrase provides writers with rare chance to congratulate themselves.

Examples of Paraphrase

During the seventeenth and eighteenth centuries CE, accomplished poets practiced their art by imitating, translating, or paraphrasing poetry composed by ancient and medieval poets. We conclude this chapter with some examples of their art, suitable for imitation or paraphrase.

At the age of fifteen, John Milton paraphrased Psalm 114 in English, probably as a school exercise. Here is a modern English version of Psalm 114 that purports to be a literal translation of the Hebrew original:

> After Israel went out of Egypt,
> the house of Jacob from a barbaric people,
> Judah became his sanctuary,
> Israel his dominion.
> When the sea saw him, it fled,
> the Jordan turned back.
> The mountains leaped like rams,
> the hills like lambs of the flock.
> What ailed you, O sea, that you fled?
> O Jordan, that you turned back?
> O mountains, that you leaped like rams?
> O hills like lambs of the flock?
> In the presence of the Lord writhe, O land,
> in the presence of Jacob's God.
> Who turned rock into a pool of water,
> flint into a flowing spring.

Here is Milton's "A Paraphrase on Psalm 114":

> When the blest seed of Terah's faithful Son,
> After long toil their liberty had won,
> And past from Pharian Fields to Canaan Land,
> Led by the strength of the Almighties hand,

Jehovah's wonders were in Israel shown,
His praise and glory was in Israel known.
That saw the troubled Sea, and shivering fled,
And sought to hide his froth becurled head
Low in the earth, Jordan's clear streams recoil,
As a faint Host that hath receiv'd the foil.
The high, huge-bellied Mountains skip like Rams
Amongst their Ewes, the little Hills like Lambs.
Why fled the Ocean? And why skipt the Mountains?
Why turned Jordan toward his Chrystal Fountains?
Shake earth, and at the presence be agast
Of him that ever was, and ay shall last
That glassy floods from rugged rocks can crush,
And make soft rills from fiery flint-stones gush. (1623)

Try paraphrasing both poems in prose. Or tell the story of the Israelites' escape in more detail.

Here is a love poem by the ancient Greek Sappho; this modern translation is by Suzy Q. Groden:

As equal to the gods, he seems to me,
the man who, with his face toward yours,
sits close and listens to the whispers of
your sweet voice and enticing laugh.
To watch has made my heart pounding hammer in my breast.
For as I look at you, if only for an instant,
my voice no longer comes to me.
My silent tongue is broken,
and a quick and subtle flame
runs up beneath my skin.
I lose my sense of sight, hear only drumming in my ears.
I drip cold sweat,
and a trembling chases all through me.
I am greener than the pale grass
and it seems to me that I am close to death. (1967, 10)

The English playwright Ben Jonson imitated Sappho's poem and included his imitation in one of his plays, "The New Inn." Here is Jonson's imitation:

Thou dost not know my sufferings, what I feel,
My fires and fears are met; I burn and freeze,
My liver's one great coal, my heart shrunk up
With all the fibres, and the mass of blood
Within me is a standing lake of fire,
Curled with the cold wind of my gelid sighs,
That drive a drift of sleet through all my body,
And shoot a February through all my veins.
Until I see him I am drunk with thirst,
And surfeited with hunger of his presence.

> I know not where I am, or no, or speak,
> Or whether thou dost hear me. (V ii 45–56)

Try paraphrasing Jonson's poem in modern English. Or compose a paraphrase in prose.

The Roman poet Horace was a great favorite for imitation among English poets. Here is a prose version of the fifth ode of book I of Horace's *Odes*, translated into English during the nineteenth century by one C. Smart:

> To Pyrrha,
>
> What dainty youth, bedewed with liquid perfumes caresses you, Pyrrha, beneath the pleasant grot, amid a profusion of roses? For whom do you bind your golden hair, plain in your neatness? Alas! How often shall he deplore your perfidy, and the altered gods; and through inexperience be amazed at the seas, rough with blackening storms, who now credulous enjoys you all precious, and, ignorant of the faithless gale, hopes you will be always disengaged, always amiable! Wretched are those, to whom thou untried seemest fair! The sacred wall [of Neptune's temple] demonstrates, by a votive tablet, that I have consecrated my dropping garments to the powerful god of the sea.(1979, 12–13)

Now here is John Milton's translation/paraphrase of Horace's poem:

> What slender Youth bedew'd with liquid odors
> Courts thee on Roses in some pleasant Cave,
> Pyrrha for whom bindst thou
> In wreaths thy golden Hair,
> Plain in thy neatness; O how oft shall he
> On faith and changed Gods complain: and Seas
> Rough with black winds and storms
> Unwonted shall admire:
> Who now enjoys thee credulous, all Gold,
> Who always vacant always amiable
> Hopes thee; of flattering gales
> Unmindful. Hapless they
> To whom thou untried seem'st fair. Me in my vow'd
> Picture the sacred wall declares t' have hung
> My dank and dropping weeds
> To the stern God of Sea.

Whose version do you prefer? Again, you can paraphrase Milton's version in modern English, or you can paraphrase either version in prose.

We now quote the opening lines, in Latin, of Horace's Sixth Satire, Book II, in order to demonstrate the freedom with which poetry may be paraphrased.

> Hoc erat in votis; modus agri non ita magnus,
> Hortus ubi, et tecto vicinus jugis aquae fons,
> Et paulum sylvae super his foret: auctius atque
> Dii melius fecere: bene est: nil amplius oro,
> Maia nate, nisi ut propria haec mihi muner faxis. (1926, II.i)

Here is C. Smart's prose translation of these lines:

> This was ever among the number of my wishes: a portion of ground not over-large, in which was a garden, and a fountain with a continual stream close to my house, and a little woodland besides. The gods have done more abundantly, and better, for me than this. It is well: O son of Maia, I ask nothing more save that you would render these donations lasting to me. (1979, 158)

Now here are Jonathan Swift and Alexander Pope collaborating in 1737 on an imitation of the opening lines of Horace's satire entitled, appropriately enough, "The Sixth Satire of the Second Book of Horace Imitated." Their version is almost twice as long as Horace's original, because Pope adds an observation about his own situation under English law at the time:

> I've often wish'd that I had clear
> For life, six hundred pounds a year,
> A handsome House to lodge a Friend,
> A River at my garden's end,
> A Terras-walk, and half a Rood
> Of Land, set out to plant a Wood.
> Well, now I have all this and more,
> I ask not to increase my store;
> But here a Grievance seems to lie,
> All this is mine but till I die;
> I can't but think 'twould sound more clever,
> To me and to my Heirs for ever. (1835, 33)

Try composing a loose paraphrase of these lines that indicates your hopes for your retirement.

PARAPHRASE EXERCISES

1. Make a simple sentence like Erasmus's "Your letter pleases me very much" and see how many variations you can compose. We suggest going for twenty-five, but with a little more time students have been known to write fifty, and even one hundred. If you are at a loss for a sentence, choose one from a paper you have written recently, or make an observation about something on campus or about your friend. Here are some examples: "Our school has a lot of school spirit" or "Caiti is anxious about her exam."

2. Return to the Odes of Horace (quoted earlier), as well as to Pope's paraphrase. Now try composing a loose prose paraphrase of these lines that indicates your hopes for your retirement.

3. Read the following poem written by Edna St. Vincent Millay (1892–1950). Set aside the book and write a summary of the poem. Then, consulting the poem more carefully, compose a paraphrase of the

poem, converting it into prose. Did you encounter any difficulty? How did you manage?

I, BEING BORN A WOMAN AND DISTRESSED

I, being born a woman and distressed
By all the needs and notions of my kind,
Am urged by your propinquity to find
Your person fair, and feel a certain zest
To bear your body's weight upon my breast:
So subtly is the fume of life designed,
To clarify the pulse and cloud the mind,
And leave me once again undone, possessed.
Think not for this, however, the poor treason
Of my stout blood against my staggering brain,
I shall remember you with love, or season
My scorn with pity,—let me make it plain:
I find this frenzy insufficient reason
For conversation when we meet again. (1923)

WORKS CITED

Carey, Benedict. "Study Uncovers Memory Aid: A Scent During Sleep." *New York Times*, March 9, 2007, national edition, sec. A.

Franklin, Benjamin. "Autobiography. From Revolution to Reconstruction—An HTML Project." Available at: http://odur.let.rug.nl/~usa/B/bfranklin/frank1.htm (accessed on June 15, 2007).

Horace. *Satires, Epistles, Ars Poetica*. Cambridge: Loeb Classical Library, 1926.

Millay, Edna St. Vincent. "I, Being Born a Woman and Distressed." in *Anthology of Modern American Poetry*, ed. Cary Nelson, New York: Oxford University Press, 2000, p. 320.

Muske-Dukes, Carol. "A Lost Eloquence." *New York Times*, December 29, 2002, national edition, Op-ed.

Pope, Alexander. *The Poetical Works of Alexander Pope*. London: William Pickering, 1835.

Rasch, Björn, Christian Büchel, Steffen Gais, and Jan Born. "Odor Cues During Slow-Wave Sleep Prompt Declarative Memory Consolidation." *Science* 315, no. 5817 (March 2007): 1426–1439.

Sappho, *Poems*, trans. Suzy Q. Groden. Indianapolis: Bobbs-Merrill Co. 1967.

Smart, C. *Christopher Smarts Translations of Horace's Odes*. Victoria, B.C.: English Literary Studies, 1979.

Sprague, Rosamund Kent, trans. "*Dissoi Logoi*." *Mind* 78 (April 1968): 155–187.

Steele, Joseph. "Essay 157." *Spectator* 157 (August 30, 1711).

Walker, Jeffrey. *Rhetoric and Poetics in Antiquity*. New York: Oxford University Press, 2000.

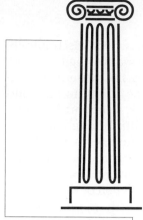

DELIVERY: ATTENDING TO EYES AND EARS

What a great difference there is in persuasiveness between discourses which are spoken and those which are to be read. . . . The former are delivered on subjects which are important and urgent, while the latter are composed for display and gain. . . . When a discourse is robbed of the prestige of the speaker, the tones of his voice, the variations which are made in the delivery, and, besides, of the advantages of timeliness and keen interest in the subject matter . . . when it has not a single accessory to support its contention and enforce its plea . . . in these circumstances it is natural, I think, that it should make an indifferent impression upon its hearers.

—Isocrates, "To Philip" 25–27

FOR ANCIENT RHETORS and rhetoricians, spoken discourse was infinitely more powerful and persuasive than was written composition. Most discourses were composed in order to be performed, and as ancient lore about memory makes clear, composition could be accomplished without the aid of writing.

The ability to write was not widespread in ancient cultures. While most members of classical Greek aristocracy could read, it was not fashionable to do one's own writing, and so those who did compose dictated their work to a scribe. Those who could write probably edited the scribe's work, especially if they planned to publish a written version of a composition. Nonetheless, they may have done this orally as well, by asking the scribe to read his copy aloud. These practices remained in vogue within Roman culture even among people who wrote easily, like Cicero.

But the relative importance of spoken discourse was not only related to the scarcity of writing ability. Rhetoric was invented for use within very small cultures, where citizens knew one another by sight, if not personally. The agora and the forum were not large by the modern standards set by such arenas as Madison Square Garden or the Astrodome. Of course, the ancients had few ways to amplify their voices, as is done electronically today, and so the sites of public gatherings were necessarily small.

Ancient rhetoricians would be very surprised by the modern association of intelligence and education with literacy—the ability to read and write. For them, writing was an accessory technology, a support for memory as a way of storing information (*Institutes* XI xi 10). Throughout antiquity, discourse was primarily composed to be spoken. As a result, the ancients were very concerned about how speeches ought to be delivered: the proper management of the voice, bodily movement, and gestures. Because of this concern, they made delivery the fifth canon of rhetoric. But this does not mean that delivery was ranked fifth in importance. Quintilian, in fact, boldly proclaimed: "I would not hesitate to assert that a mediocre speech supported by all the power of delivery will be more impressive than the best speech unaccompanied by such power" (XI iii 5). And when Demosthenes was asked to name the most important aspects of oratory, he apparently answered, "Delivery, Delivery, and Delivery" (Quintilian, *Institutes* XI iii 6). Modern rhetoric, for the most part, has neglected aspects of delivery, opting for a "set format" for compositions (a certain number and order of paragraphs; a certain style of writing; strict adherence to grammar rules). Under such conditions, delivery tends to collapse into arrangement and style.

In the twenty-first century, page literacy is slowly giving way to electronic literacy, particularly because of television and the Internet. These mediums have reduced distance between rhetor and audience, replicating to some degree the conditions of ancient culture. Television makes certain faces and certain styles of delivery as familiar as those of members of one's family. One important difference between us and the ancients, then, is that people are more likely to stay home to watch TV or surf the Web than to venture out to listen to speakers in the town square or a nearby auditorium. Nevertheless, delivery remains an important canon of rhetoric, despite the fact that most of the public voices we hear, along with the news and commentary we read, are electronically mediated.

ANCIENT COMMENTARY ON DELIVERY

The Greek word for delivery was *hypokrisis,* and yes, the English word *hypocrisy* is a direct descendant. The term comes from a verb (*hypokrinesthai*) used to describe the work of the actor who responded to the chorus in Greek tragedy. Later, the term *hypokrites* meant simply "actor." There are many stories about ancient orators learning the craft of delivery from famous actors. Plutarch recounted this one about Demosthenes:

> When the assembly had refused to hear him, and he was going home with his head muffled up, taking it very heavily, they relate that Satyrus, the actor, followed him, and being his familiar acquaintance, entered into conversation with him. To whom, when Demosthenes bemoaned himself, that having been

the most industrious of all the pleaders, and having almost spent the whole strength and vigor of his body in that employment, he could not yet find any acceptance with the people, that drunken sots, mariners, and illiterate fellows were heard, and had the hustings for their own, while he himself was despised, "You say true, Demosthenes," replied Satyrus, "but I will quickly remedy the cause of all this, if you will repeat to me some passage out of Euripides or Sophocles." Which when Demosthenes had pronounced, Satyrus presently taking it up after him, gave the same passage, in his rendering of it, such a new form, by accompanying it with the proper mien and gesture, that to Demosthenes it seemed quite another thing. By this, being convinced how much grace and ornament language acquires from action, he began to esteem it a small matter, and as good as nothing for a man to exercise himself in declaiming, if he neglected enunciation and delivery. Hereupon he built himself a place to study in under ground (which was still remaining in our time), and hither he would come constantly every day to form his action and to exercise his voice; and here he would continue, often times without intermission, two or three months together, shaving one half of his head, that so for shame he might not go abroad, though he desire it ever so much. (1025–1026)

However much rhetors could learn from actors, there was still a difference between their arts. As Cicero pointed out, orators act in real life, while actors mimic reality (*De Oratore* III lvi 214–15). Furthermore, Cicero suggested that delivery might have had its roots not just in acting but also in athletics. Here is the character Crassus in *De Oratore:*

> But all these emotions must be accompanied by gesture—not this stagy gesture reproducing the words but one conveying the general situation and idea not by demonstration but by hints, with this vigorous manly throwing out of the chest, borrowed not from the stage and the theatrical profession but from the parade ground or even from wrestling. (III liv 220)

Given that gladiators and wrestlers occupied a powerful place in Roman culture, it makes sense that Cicero would see overlap between rhetorical delivery and sporting activities. Rhetoric, after all, for the Romans, was highly competitive, culturally important; and most of all, like the arts of gladiators and wrestlers, rhetoric was performed by bodies.

Modern scholars are not sure when delivery began to be included among the rhetorical canons. The fourth-century *ad Alexandrum* included only invention, arrangement, and style. Aristotle briefly discussed delivery, however (*Rhetoric* III i 1402b–1404a). In a very interesting aside, he noted that no systematic treatment of delivery had yet been composed, and he speculated that this was the case because "originally, the poets themselves acted their tragedies." What this means is that by the time Aristotle composed the *Rhetoric* (ca. 330 BCE), professional actors had replaced poets as reciters of tragedies. These actors must have learned to recite tragedies in one of two ways: either by memorizing them while the poets recited or by memorizing written copies produced by scribes. In other words, by this time performance could be separated from composition; the person who composed the play did not need to be the same person who delivered it.

Now the actor was copying the words composed by the poet, but he did not have to copy the poet's performance into the bargain. Likely, actors imbued their performances with their own interpretations, and this mimicry is what set Aristotle's teeth on edge.

This state of affairs lends another level of meaning to the term *hypokrites:* an actor is someone who pretends to be somebody else. It also means that acting and delivery could now become arts, with principles that could be learned and transmitted to others. Once these arts were written down, they could be learned without the example of a teacher, although in the case of delivery (as suggested by the example of Demosthenes) a teacher's example is always helpful.

In his comments on delivery in the *Rhetoric*, Aristotle remarked in passing that performers who give careful attention to delivery "are generally the ones who win poetic contests; and just as actors are more important than poets now in the poetic contests, so it is in political contests because of the sad state of governments" (III i 1403b). This analogy—actors are to poets as orators are to statesmen—indicates a quite conservative attitude toward Athenian democracy on Aristotle's part. Just as poets are somehow the "real" owners and creators of their compositions, aristocrats are the "real" owners and creators of government. With the establishment of acting and rhetoric as arts that anyone could learn, poetic compositions, like political decision making, were available to anyone, and not just to those who fancied they had some natural talent or hereditary claim to them. This state of affairs apparently dismayed Aristotle.

Even though he thought delivery was a "vulgar matter," Aristotle nevertheless paid it some attention. He wrote that delivery "was a matter of how the voice should be used in expressing each emotion." The expression of emotion could be altered by variations in volume, pitch, and rhythm. He also distinguished between oral and written delivery, noting that "where there is most need of performance, the least exactness is present" (III xii 1414a). In other words, written discourse must be more precise than spoken discourse.

Aristotle's student, Theophrastus, was widely credited throughout antiquity with having written a treatise on delivery. But this treatise, if it ever existed, has been lost. While Hellenistic rhetoricians regularly remarked that delivery was the most important of the canons, they didn't have much to say about it. Indeed, the author of *ad Herennium* stated flatly that no consistent treatment of delivery had ever been composed, and he provided us with the oldest account that we possess.

While the author of *Rhetorica ad Herennium* does not agree with Demosthenes that delivery is the most important of the five canons of rhetoric, he nonetheless believes that it effectively strengthens the other four parts of ancient rhetoric: "For skillful invention, elegant style, the artistic arrangements of the parts comprising the case, and the careful memory of all these will be of no more value without delivery" (III xi 19). Cicero and Quintilian both argue that the proper delivery can excite the emotions. As Cicero put it in *De Oratore*, "Nature has assigned to every emotion a particular look and tone of voice and bearing of its own; and the whole of a person's frame and every look on his face and utterance of his voice are like the strings of a harp, and sound according as they are struck by each successive emotion" (III lvii 216). People who have watched great actors at work know that emotions can be powerfully conveyed by facial gestures and tone of voice.

According to Quintilian, "All delivery . . . is concerned with two different things, namely, voice and gesture, of which one appeals to the eye and the other to the ear, the two senses by which all emotion reaches the soul" (XI iii 14). It is fair to say, then, that delivery is that part of rhetoric that extends most explicitly to the audience, as it attends to their eyes and ears, the visual and the aural. In what follows, we will consider the different ways in which rhetors reach out to eyes and ears in oral discourse, written discourse, and finally, electronic discourse.

DELIVERY OF ORAL DISCOURSE

In the context of oral discourse, the ears of the audience tune into the voice of the rhetor, and the eyes focus on the rhetor's facial and bodily gestures (or lack thereof). The *ad Herennium* author offers an intriguing theory of voice and divides the concern of vocal delivery into three considerations: volume, stability (a calm, composed voice), and flexibility (varying intonations). For the ancients, these areas all reflect and produce *ethos*: a calm but not monotonous voice, for example, implies a calm yet somewhat lively speaker even as it soothes hearers while maintaining their interest. The *ad Herennium* author makes specific suggestions, such as using a calm tone in the introduction, calling a bellowing tone "disagreeable." He notes too that pauses can help "strengthen the voice" and that they serve to separate thoughts, in order to give each thought its due attention and to let the audience reflect.

In general, the ancients recommended that speakers use a modulated tone and speak slowly and clearly. The ancients gave a great deal of attention to the use of tone and pitch to convey emotions; but since contemporary audiences prefer that a speaker's tone and pitch reflect those that occur in conversational speech, today speakers needn't worry about such matters. Ancient rhetoricians also recommended that speakers vary the volume of their voices throughout the speech, using a louder voice to emphasize important words. The appropriate volume to use is determined to some extent by the size of the room and the audience. People who are asked to speak in a room that does not have electronic amplification should check it out ahead of time. As an acquaintance sits in the back row, deliver a few lines of your speech from the front in order to determine whether you can be heard throughout the room. If you are using a microphone, try to maintain the same distance from it throughout your talk, so that your voice does not fade in and out.

Wise rhetoric teachers insist that anyone who speaks in public should rehearse her remarks out loud. This is good advice, and we follow it whenever we are asked to speak in a formal setting. Rehearsal is important for several reasons. First of all, practice allows a speaker to time her remarks. Adhering to set time limits is professional and considerate when others are speaking after you, and it is a necessity for those who speak in public broadcasting. Second, rehearsal helps you decide where to pause and where you can look up at your audience in order to establish contact with them. Third, reading aloud helps you to hear the rhythms of the sentences you have written. We often read our work aloud while we are revising it. Sometimes this practice tells us where a sentence construction has gone wrong, but more often it helps us to determine which sentences are too long to read or hear easily. Sentences composed for oral delivery should never be so long that they cannot be uttered in a single breath, unless they are carefully punctuated. Long sentences are elegant if their internal punctuation, balance, and rhythm signal the relations of their parts to readers and listeners. Where this is not the case, long sentences can confuse and ultimately tire an audience. In order to consider the listener's "ear," composers and practitioners of oral discourse need to pay attention to all aspects of verbal delivery, especially volume, tone, pace, and length.

When thinking of the audience's eyes, however, a different set of concerns comes to the fore. The *ad Herennium* author advises speakers to consider physical gestures to go along with the tone of the speech. As with voice, the use of gestures should be appropriate to the rhetorical situation: bodily delivery should be subdued on formal occasions but animated in the courtroom or legislature, especially when vigorous debate is in progress. The importance of appropriate bodily delivery is underscored if we consider the standards of decorous delivery that obtained in Roman rhetoric. Apparently it was appropriate (and expected) that Roman orators would strike their brows, stamp their feet, tear their clothing, and slap their thighs. (This last gesture served to keep the crowd awake as well.) Such antics would excite only laughter or anxiety in modern audiences, who expect restrained delivery from their public performers. The convention of restrained delivery applies even to actors today; the only performers we exempt from this rule are stand-up comedians. Yet with the exception of newscasters, rhetors don't often simply just stand and speak with an expressionless face.

The ancients gave elaborate advice about facial and bodily gestures. Since a speaker's face and movement could not be electronically amplified in ancient settings, gestures were very important means of amplifying the speaker's mood and conveying it to distant members of an audience. However, since modern audiences do not care for elaborate facial and bodily gestures, a very limited repertoire of these will suffice in most settings. The most important consideration is use of the eyes. As Cicero wrote, "By action the body talks . . . nature has given us eyes, as she has given the horse and the lion their mane and tail and ears, to indicate the feelings of the mind" (*De Oratore* III lix 222–23). If you are speaking to a live audience, look at them as frequently as you can. If you are speaking before a camera, be sure to look directly into it whenever possible. Today, gestures should be as natural and spontaneous as possible. Live audiences respond surprisingly well to a few hand gestures, such as pointing the index finger to underscore an important remark or slicing the hand downward to indicate a conclusion.

If for some reason you are interested in improving your oral delivery, you can do no better than to take Quintilian's advice to memorize a few passages of written discourse and practice reciting them aloud whenever you can. Or carefully watch speakers you admire and try to imitate their facial gestures and vocal control. The anchors on national network news are very good speakers and are worthy of imitation. If you want to imitate more flamboyant deliveries, watch able politicians, attorneys, and clergy.

If composing a speech for oral delivery, then, it makes sense to think about the most appropriate tones and gestures to go along with the speech. What points might need a bit of bodily, facial, or tonal emphasis? As rhetors compose and subsequently practice their speeches, it's a good idea, following the ancients, to consider these aspects of oral delivery, and to even practice different tones or gestures in the mirror to see what may or may not work in the speaking situation. Attention to delivery is crucial for conveying points and establishing and maintaining *ethos*. At the close of his discussion of delivery, the *ad Herennium* author underscores this point: "One must remember: good delivery ensures that what the orator is saying seems to come from the heart" (III xv 28).

DELIVERY OF WRITTEN DISCOURSE

Are rhythm and physicality confined to the spoken word? Does written discourse extend to the eyes and ears of the audience? Certainly it is impossible to stomp one's feet in written prose, yet there are ways in which written discourse nevertheless attends to the ears and eyes of the audience. As we mentioned earlier, in ancient times, writing was always read aloud, whether in a public forum, as with the speech Gorgias delivered at the Olympic games, or in private. It wasn't until about the fourth century CE that silent reading practices emerged in the context of the monastic tradition (Parkes 1993, 9).

Also interesting is that, early on, Greek writing had no punctuation. Instead, the text was written in one long stream, breaking a line when necessary (as at the end of the papyrus or stone). This kind of writing—without breaks or other distinguishing marks—is called *scriptio continua*. As reading became more common, teachers and authors began to worry about how students and readers would interpret a text with no breaks, so they developed systems of punctuation. Teachers, then, were among the very first to use punctuation in order to assist young boys in their early attempts at reading aloud.

There was therefore a kind of correspondence between spoken and written discourse, and in order to preserve this correspondence, the ancients started tinkering with systems of punctuation. Rhetors, for example, marked places where speakers would pause to take a breath. The early origins of punctuation were therefore rhetorical, and while punctuation functions these days to mark more than pauses for breathing, it is nonetheless important to bear in mind the rhetorical value of punctuation. It seems to us that practitioners of modern rhetoric sometimes forget the rhetoric of punctuation in favor of rules about sentence structures.

In his dialogue *De Oratore*, Cicero makes the link between rhythmic speaking and writing by referencing Isocrates and his forebears:

> For they thought that in speeches the close of the period [sentence] ought to come not when we are tired out but where we may take breath . . . and it is said that Isocrates first introduced the practice of tightening up the irregular style of oratory which belonged to the early days, so his pupil Naucrates writes, by means of an element of rhythm, designed to give pleasure to the ear. (III 173)

In another dialogue, Cicero asserts the importance of rhythm more strenuously:

> Hence this must be used, call it composition, or finish or rhythm as you will— this must be used if you wish to speak elegantly, not only, as Aristotle and Theophrastus say, that the sentence may not drift along vaguely like a river . . . but for the reason that the periodic [or rhythmic] sentence is much more forceful than the loose. (*Orator* lviii 228)

Here, the notion of rhythmic prose harkens back to the notion of rhetorical style—remember, the five canons were interconnected. Still, in the context of delivery, we would draw attention to the rhetorical function of punctuation: the way in which dashes, commas, and periods mimic the pauses, stops, and connections of speech and, as such, attend to the reader's "ear." The first-century-BCE rhetorician Dionysius of Halicarnassus, in his treatment of written composition, even discusses the rhythmic, musical qualities of language, since, as he puts it, "rhythm plays no small part in a dignified and impressive composition" ("On Literary Composition" 17).

In written discourse, attending to the "ear" of the audience has to do with editing a discourse so that it is accessible and pleasant to read. **Editing** is the very last stage in the composing process. Writers should not attempt it until they are 95 percent sure that they have finished working through the other canons. Nothing stifles composing quite so quickly as trying to edit too soon. Three issues face modern rhetors during the editing process: correctness rules, **formatting**, and **presentation**.

Correctness Rules I: Spelling and Punctuation

Obviously, spelling and **punctuation** present no problems to speakers, but they can be troublesome for writers. People who are chronically bad spellers often think of themselves as bad writers. However, there is no connection between one's ability to spell and one's ability to write. Furthermore, if you are a bad speller, this does not (and should not) reflect negatively on your character.

People have trouble spelling English words because English spelling is irregular and erratic; it is irregular and erratic because it reflects accidents of linguistic history. For example, the "gh" in words like *light* and *bright* is there because it used to be pronounced. The written forms of these words are slowly conforming to their current pronunciation: *lite, brite.* Soon, everyone but traditional grammarians will have forgotten that they were ever spelled differently.

Happily, inability to spell is no longer a problem for people who can afford the technology, since portable spell-checkers and electronic dictionaries are now available, and most word-processing programs have spell-checkers and dictionaries built into their files. If you can't afford to get electronic help, read as much as you can. When you come across words that are difficult for you to spell, write them down. Once a week, organize the words in alphabetical order and memorize your list (see Chapter 11, on memory). Use the words as often as you can when you write. This method won't turn you into a champion speller overnight, but it works for most people.

Traditional grammar books contain lists and lists of rules for the use of punctuation. Some of these are necessary and some are not. Most are simply confusing. There are four kinds of punctuation in written discourse. The first indicates where pauses would occur if the discourse were spoken (for example, commas and periods). A second group of punctuation marks indicate the logical relations of parts of sentences (semicolons and colons, parentheses and dashes). The third indicates the graphic or logical relations of larger parts of discourse (paragraphs, headers). The fourth indicates insertions or omissions.

The best advice we can give about the first and second sorts of punctuation is this: read your writing aloud, like the ancients did, and mark the places where you pause. Then put punctuation in these places. Better yet, ask someone else to read your writing aloud while you follow along on another copy. Mark the places where your reader pauses, and put punctuation there when you revise. If your reader falters, mark the passage. Usually, readers falter when writers haven't punctuated clearly enough. Wait to put in larger marks of punctuation, like paragraphs and headers, until you've drafted the entire discourse at least once. Then outline it and use indentations and headers to mark the divisions of the discourse.

If the "play it by ear" method does not work for you, then you should resort to a grammar handbook that will help you understand how to punctuate and refer to it when you reach the editing stage of composing. Or you can refer to the quick and dirty advice we offer here. We should warn you: sticklers for correctness do not approve of some of the recommendations that follow.

Punctuation That Marks Internal Pauses

These marks can appear inside punctuated sentences. In English, a punctuated sentence is a stretch of words that begins with a capital letter (also called an "uppercase letter") and ends with some terminal mark of punctuation—a period (.), a question mark (?), or an exclamation point (!).

1. The comma (,) marks a relatively weak internal pause. Commas are used to set off short phrases that would interfere with readers' understanding of the sentence, like this, if not so marked.

2. The semicolon (;) marks a stronger internal pause; like this. Semicolons are generally used to set off clauses from one another. Clauses are sentences that appear inside bigger sentences; they can be recognized because they sound like complete sentences.

3. The colon (:) marks the strongest available internal pause: like this. Generally colons are used to announce that some sort of division or partition is coming next: in this case semicolons usually appear at the end of each part of the division; except for the last part, which is marked with a period. Take, for example, this famous line from Julius Caesar: I came; I saw; I conquered.

4. One dash (—) can be used to set off some loosely connected clause or phrase from the main part of a sentence—as though it were an afterthought. Paired dashes—used to set off any interruption of the main sentence, like this—are appearing more frequently in modern prose. Parentheses (like these) serve essentially the same function as paired dashes (that is, they interrupt or comment on the main point of the sentence).

Punctuation That Marks External Pauses

These pieces of punctuation are used to mark the beginnings and ends of sentences.

1. In modern written English, a capital letter (Latin *caput*, "head" or "chief") ordinarily marks the beginning of a sentence. But a capital letter can also mark the beginning of a fragment. Like this. (In Early Modern Written English, Things were Easier, because Capitals were Used to Mark most of the Important Words. Written German still Employs this Convention.)

2. A period (.) marks the end of any punctuated sentence that makes a statement. It is also used to mark fragments that are statements. Such as this.

3. A question mark (?) marks the end of any punctuated sentence that asks a question. It also marks fragments that are questions. Got it?

4. An exclamation point (!) marks the end of any punctuated sentence that expresses some strong emotion. It also marks fragments that express strong emotion. How about that! Exclamation points are seldom used in formal discourse because they express too much emotion, thus closing the distance between rhetor and audience in a manner that may be inappropriate to the rhetorical situation.

5. Indentation (the writing begins five or six spaces from the left margin). Indentation is used to mark the beginning of a new paragraph.

During the Middle Ages, when people wrote everything by hand, and when paper was scarce and expensive, scribes copied text onto every bit of space available on paper or vellum. Hence it became necessary to mark off sections of longer discourses in some way so that handwritten texts would be intelligible. Medieval scribes invented a mark for such sections, and they called it a paragraph (Greek "written separately"). Eventually the name for the mark got transferred to the section of discourse itself. Paragraphs are a necessity only in written texts, and they are a product of page literacy. During the nineteenth century, a logician named Alexander Bain invented all sorts of artificial rules for paragraphs. Bain thought that every paragraph should represent a single idea (whatever that is) and this notion morphed into the rule that every paragraph should have a topic sentence and a set number of sentences that specified the topic sentence, among other things. Studies of written discourse have since shown that few professional writers follow Bain's rules (Bain wasn't any Cicero—he hoped that everyone would learn to write like a logician so that rhetoric would disappear from the face of the earth). So if you were taught these rules, you should try to forget them and let paragraphs develop by intuition as you write. Some writers actually create paragraphs after they have finished a piece of writing, and they break long sections into paragraphs in order to make the page look nice and readable—which was the original function of the paragraph, after all.

Headers serve exactly the same function as paragraphs except that they mark larger pieces of text. We used them in this book to indicate the relations of one part of a chapter to another. But to some extent, we must confess, the choice of where to put headers is arbitrary, having as much to do with their relative length as with any internal logic of the discourse. We cheerfully confess that the larger divisions of a discourse never become very clear to us until we are almost finished composing.

Punctuation That Marks Omissions and Insertions

1. The mark of punctuation called an **apostrophe** (') should not be confused with the figure of the same name (see the chapter on style). Apostrophes appear only in written English, and they are there to prevent confusion. In modern English, apostrophes have three uses. First, they indicate that someone or something possesses something else, as in "Colleen's cat" or "the audience's response." If the apostrophe did not appear, readers might take the words to be plurals. In this use, apostrophes can cause their own brand of confusion if the word in which they appear ends with an *s* or an *x*. At the moment, there is considerable debate about how to mark this occurrence in written English. Should one write "Socrates' socks" or "Socrates's socks"? We prefer the former, but many authors like the latter.

    Second, apostrophes substitute for an omitted letter. This occurs most frequently in contractions, such as *isn't* for "is not" or *don't* for "do not." They are also used, mostly in poetry, to mark the figure called "ellipsis," where a letter has been omitted to make the meter come out right (*e'en* for *even*). Third, apostrophes are used to form the plural of numbers, symbols, letters, and abbreviations: *Ph.D.'s*; "There were three e's in the word"; "I counted eight occurrences of 8's."

2. Quotation marks (" ") are used chiefly to indicate material that has been borrowed from some other text; throughout this book we have used them this way when quoting Aristotle or Cicero, for example. A second use of quotation marks shows that the words they enclose are being referred to, as they are in this sentence and the next, where we put "scare quotes" in quotation marks. A third use of quotation marks is called "scare quotes": scare quotes are intended to show an ironic distance on the author's part, as in this sentence:

   The president claimed again today that we are "winning" the war in Iraq.

   As you can see, things can get complicated with quotation marks. Take this infamous sentence: "We don't 'cash' checks." In that example we put double marks around the entire sentence to signify that we were referring to it, and we put single quotation marks around the word *cash* to signify that it is in scare quotes. The rule on single quotation marks is this: When you quote or emphasize something that is already within quotation marks, use single quotation marks to indicate the quote within a quote.

3. Ellipses (. . .) are used to mark places in quoted material where stuff has been omitted.

   As we said earlier, if this list doesn't work for you, get hold of a handbook on style and read the chapters on punctuation. Memorize as much as you can. If necessary, refer to these chapters when you edit your writing (but not before—trying to edit while you are inventing is the surest way we know to bring both processes to a dead halt). Or hire or beg somebody to edit your work for you.

Correctness Rules II: Traditional Grammar and Usage

Every native speaker of a language has intuited the grammar rules of her language by the time she is five years old. Why is it, then, that grammar has to be taught in school? For many years, American teachers made their students adhere to the rules laid down in traditional grammar, which is an artificial grammar imposed on English during the eighteenth century and which observes grammatical rules borrowed from Latin. (Latin was then thought to be the language that intellectuals ought to use.) But unlike Latin, which now has no native speakers, English is a vibrant spoken language whose grammar rules change over time; certainly they have changed a great deal since the eighteenth century. The grammar of Latin was never a very good fit with written English in the first place, because the two languages have very different histories. But teachers and traditional grammarians tried to make them fit, nonetheless.

The rules of traditional grammar include this one: infinitive verbs should not be split (write "to speak carefully" rather than "to carefully speak"). In Latin, infinitive verbs could not be split, because they were a single word (*dicere*, "to speak"; *scribere*, "to write"). In English, of course, infinitives are composed of two words, which allows rhetors to insert words in between them if they wish. But this important difference doesn't stop traditional grammarians from imposing an archaic rule on writers. And so students can be penalized for writing "to eagerly go" rather than "to go eagerly."

Again, our advice concerning such traditional niceties is this: rely on your intuitive grammatical sense about your native language when you write, and upon your ear when you read your work aloud. This is good advice unless, of course, your teacher or boss is a traditional grammarian. In that case, get hold of a handbook that lists traditional rules about grammar, and use it when you edit your work, or hire someone to edit it for you, if you can afford to. If you are not a native speaker of English, continue to do what your second-language teachers told you to do: read and listen to the English used by native speakers whenever you can. Nonnative speakers of English, and people who use dialects of English, have an advantage over the many Americans who are monolingual or monodialectical because they can use the ancient exercise of **translation** to improve their grasp of both languages or dialects. Ancient rhetoricians recommended translation from one language to another as a useful means of understanding the grammar of a second language, as well as its rhythmic patterns.

Usage is another matter altogether. Usage can be defined neutrally as the customary ways in which things are done within written discourse. A more biased and yet more accurate definition is this: usage rules are the conventions of written English that allow Americans to discriminate against one another. Questions of usage are tied to social attitudes about who is intelligent and well educated and who is not. A person who says "I ain't got no idea" obviously learned to say this somewhere, probably in the community into which she was born. If she were to say this in other settings or to write it down she risks being marked as illiterate, uneducated, and possibly stupid into the bargain. This is manifestly unfair, since her usage is perfectly appropriate in her native community. Despite their manifest unfairness, however, usage rules exist; they are enforced by people with power; and so they must be observed in situations where they have been decreed to be important.

Because of its social aspect, usage differs from natural grammar, which describes the rules people use to form utterances in their native languages. Many of the rules of "correct" usage are drawn not from the language people use but from traditional grammar. Its rules represent an attempt to freeze the language in time, to create a standard for "good English" that allows people who care to do so to mark deviations from it. Nevertheless, utterances that are deemed bad usage in terms of traditional grammar may be perfectly grammatical (and appropriate) in the language or dialect from which they are drawn. One of us remembers growing up in the Midwest, where people typically said "Leave it be" when they wanted someone to stop messing with something, or "Leave us go" when they were ready to depart. According to traditional rules, both usages are incorrect; but to try to erase them from someone's verbal repertoire, in our opinion, is to deny her the use of linguistic resources that are both charming and appropriate in certain times and places.

The usages that raise the hackles of traditional grammarians involve perceived misuses of verb forms, pronouns, and adverbs. Some English verbs persist in being irregular, meaning that they don't form their past and participial tenses in the regular way that most verbs do. *Try* and *fail* are regular verbs; their past and past-participle forms are formed by adding -ed: *tried* and *failed*. *Shoot* and *buy* are irregular verbs; their past and past-participle forms are *shot* and *bought*. These two verbs, like most irregular verbs, still retain vestiges of the inflected forms that all verbs had when English first emerged as a distinct language. Most native speakers of English know all this stuff, having learned it as children; but if for some reason you struggle with verb forms, you might want to find a list of irregular English verbs and study it.

Verb forms can also pose problems to users of dialectical varieties of English when they write for teachers or bosses who are traditional grammarians. "She gone over to Mom's house" is perfectly acceptable in dialectical English, but advocates of traditional grammar prefer "She went to Mom's house." Verb agreement is a matter of grammar rather than usage, strictly speaking, but insuring that nouns and verbs agree in number can be tricky. The general rule is: if the noun is singular, the verb is singular; if the noun is plural, the verb is plural. This is not an issue for native speakers except in a few instances. The proper choice of verb can get sticky when a class noun (*none, everyone, faculty*) is the main noun in a sentence; does one write "The faculty is in revolt" or "The faculty are in revolt"? "None dares call it treason," or "None dare call it treason"? In both sets of examples, use of the singular verb (*is, dares*) changes the meaning of the sentence slightly. In the first example, the singular verb (*is*) suggests that the entire group of people called "the faculty" is (are?) involved in a revolution; the plural (*are*) suggests that perhaps a few faculty members are holding out.

The use of objective-case nouns in subjective positions is a usage error: "Her and him dropped by Mom's house"; "Me and him have tickets to the game." This archaic rule really irritates us, because case endings are not necessary to preserve meaning in English, as they were in Latin, and so they are not often observed in spoken English. People answering a phone don't often say "It is I" or "This is she"; they say "It's me" and "This is her" and are perfectly understood. But the usage police disapprove of case switching, and we are obliged to report this to you.

Another traditional rule of usage cautions writers to avoid double or triple negatives ("I *ain't* got *no* idea," "It *don't* make me *no never* mind"). Of course, absolute observance of this rule would make it impossible to use the ancient figure called litotes ("This is *not unexpected*"). Standard usage doesn't let you double up on comparative adverbs, either ("He dropped by Mom's house acting *more crazier* than ever"). It also dictates that writers avoid substituting adjectives for adverbs, especially with the pair *good* (adjective) and *well* (adverb). "He upset Mom real good" is not acceptable in standard usage, because *good* modifies *upset*, which is a verb, and as every good member of the usage police knows, only adverbs can modify verbs, and only adjectives (and pronouns) can modify nouns.

So there. Those are the usage rules that pretty much bother everyone who sets (set?) themselves up as arbiters of right and wrong uses of the written language. There are a few others that bother the real strict usage police (we committed a usage error in that sentence—can you spot it?). The first of these is sentence fragments. Some people don't like other people to write sentences that don't have subjects or verbs: "So there"; "Even though she reads Woolf." This nonsense derives from an eighteenth-century super-stition about sentences, that supposed that every sentence represents a complete thought. Whatever that is. Usually, reading your writing aloud will tell you when you have committed a fragment. You need to answer two questions about any fragment that appears in your writing: Did you commit it intentionally? Will your audience love and appreciate it as much as you do? If the answers to both questions are "no," attach the fragment to some nearby sentence by means of internal punctuation. An opposite breach of usage rules occurs when a sentence has two members, or an inter-nal comma, that have not been marked off by internal punctuation. This is often called a "run-on" or "fused" sentence. This can be cured by reading aloud and paying careful attention to the places where pauses occur. Mark them with internal punctuation. Or break the offending sentence into two sentences. If all this talk of participles and the objective case gives you the heebie-jeebies, or if you have difficulty understanding why these problems are problems, or how to correct them, get hold of a guide to style or a gram-mar handbook that devotes sections to traditional grammar and usage.[1] Read the explanations. Do the exercises. Consult them when you edit. If you don't commit any of these breaches of usage, throw a party and forget about them.

VISUAL RHETORIC

Our discussion of the delivery of written discourse has thus far been lim-ited to what we are calling, following Quintilian, issues of "the ear"—that is, how words sound when they're fit together on a page, connected and separated by punctuation, and so forth. But what about how written work looks? These days, many scholars are concerned with something called "visual rhetoric," a branch of rhetorical studies that considers all aspects of the visual—from the persuasive force of images to words and how they function as images. We believe this contemporary field fits most appropri-ately under the canon of delivery.

"Ocular Demonstration"

One aspect of visual rhetoric enters through how words help the audience "see" through use of descriptive language and the like. The author of *ad Herennium* calls this general aspect of language "ocular demonstration." He writes: "It is Ocular Demonstration when an event is so described in words that the business seems to be enacted and the subject to pass vividly before our eyes" (IV lv 68). The author continues: "This we can effect by including what has preceded, followed, and accompanied the event itself, or by keeping steadily to its consequences or the attendant circumstances." This example is a thick description of the orator Gracchus approaching the assembly: "In a sweat, with eyes blazing, hair bristling, toga awry, he begins to quicken his pace, several other men joining him." The description continues, but you get the picture. Ocular demonstration is another term for what the Greeks called *enargeia*, discussed in the chapter on *pathos*, and is also closely tied to *ekphrasis* (description), the *Progymnasmata* at the end of Chapter 7. Such vivid description of actual events can help to create *kairos* by recreating a scene anew. Of course language is inherently visual in this way, as Aristotle pointed out with metaphor when he wrote, "Metaphors therefore should be derived from what is beautiful either in sound, or in signification, or to sight, or to some other sense" (*Rhetoric* 1405b 13). So written delivery connects back to style insofar as writing style plays to the ears and eyes of the reader.

Textual Presentation

Yet another aspect of visual rhetoric is the way words look on a page. When it comes to physical presentation of the written text, contemporary rhetors are faced with a variety of choices; indeed, textual features and page layouts are an "available means of persuasion," to use Aristotle's definition of rhetoric. Choosing a font style and size is no longer the province of the person at a printing press, since standard word-processing programs offer several kinds of fonts and various styles (italic, bold, underline, shadow).

In design-speak, fonts are categorized as either serif or sans serif. Serif type features a fine line that finishes off the main strokes of a letter, as in the font used in this book. The term *sans serif* means "without serifs," and looks like this. Generally, though, serif type is thought to be more reader-friendly, for the enhanced edges of each letter help the eyes move more easily through the words. Serif type is also considered to be more traditional and formal, while sans serif looks more contemporary. Design experts also claim that serif and sans serif designs put forth a particular character; specialists Sam Dragga and Gwendolyn Gong, for instance, claim that "serif type seems artistic, designed with grace and flourish; sans serif type looks clean, objective, direct" (1989, 143).

In rhetorical terms, fonts present a particular *ethos*. Whether because of their historical associations or simply the rhetorical effect of their image, certain fonts can be symbolically charged. The German Fraktur font, for example, because it was a favorite of the Third Reich, is often associated with the Nazi party. Some fonts, like the ones designed to resemble the type used in comics, are not really appropriate in serious matters. We once saw a flyer advertising a lecture on the Holocaust designed entirely in the comic strip font, thus undermining the seriousness of the issue and the *ethos* of the designers. *Kairos,* or attention to the situation, becomes an important consideration here, as font designers (also known as fontographers) are well aware. The designer of a mid-1990s font called "Jackass," for example, cautions that Jackass is only useful in "select situations" (Heller and Fink 1997, 26).

Typefaces are available in different sizes and styles. The measuring unit for a typeface is points; there are 72 points in an inch, so a capital letter in 72-point type will be about an inch high. A readable type size is 10- to 12-point type; smaller than 8-point type may strain readers' eyes. Many writers, especially journalists, use large fonts as a way of drawing the reader's eyes to important material. The more urgent the news headline, the larger the type size of the headline, and readers' eyes are trained to recognize this correlation of size to importance.

Typestyles are another way to assist readers by adding emphasis. Some basic typestyle choices include plain, **bold**, *italic*, outline, and shadow. Plain, bold, and italic are the most commonly used typestyles. The bold style usually indicates emphasis or importance; for example, we use boldface type to draw attention to the key terms in this text. Italics also indicates emphasis, sometimes enforcing a particular forceful tone on the italicized word or words. Earlier in the book, we wrote, "In short, *kairos* is not about duration, but rather about a certain *kind* of time." Our use of italics in this instance emphasizes the difference between *kairos* and the other concept for time, *chronos*. As you can see from the previous sentence, italics are also used to indicate non-English words.

The main thing for rhetors to remember when experimenting with typeface and style is consistency; if bold is used for headings and italics for subheadings, then this should be a constant textual feature. Inconsistent or arbitrary changes in typestyle can be distracting for readers.

Another element of textual presentation is page layout. The most common page size is 8½" × 11", and once rhetors allow room for at least one-inch margins all around, the landscape of the page becomes 6½" × 9". The major layout issues deal with general organization of information and page format, but they also extend to the use of visual aids (photographs, charts, tables). We believe that good page layout works together with typeface to guide the reader's eye across and down the page, providing textual cues to indicate important information. Moreover, a well-laid-out page is one that achieves visual balance—that is, the text works together with the white space and other layout elements, such as visuals, to focus readers' attention.

White space can be an effective rhetorical tool; room left in the margins and spaces between the typed lines makes the page look more inviting to read, and lots of readers (especially teachers, supervisors, and editors) like to have space in which to write comments. While too little white space can make a text seem crowded and intimidating, too much white space can cause the text to get lost on a page or send certain signals to readers. If the bottom margin, for example, is larger than the top margin, then the reader may think he has reached the end of the discourse and might not turn the page. Headers and subheaders are useful in longer arguments to "chunk" texts and allow extra space for readers to pause and consider important shifts in arguments.

As much as anyone, college students have figured out what typestyles can do for their campus flyers, event announcements, and even for their class assignments. Since the advent of word processing, students have played with font sizes and styles (and margins and line spacing) in order to stretch a four-page paper onto that all-important fifth page or to shrink a long-winded response down to the requested limit. This kind of manipulation is not of interest here. Rather, it's the more stylized use of the digital that holds promise for rhetorical invention, style, and delivery. Richard Lanham, a modern rhetorician whose 1993 book, *The Electronic Word*, has become a classic in scholarship on writing technologies, treats digital formatting as a kind of inventional "tinkering":

> When inspiration lags, *I'll be* tempte*d* t@ s*ee* what a new type style m*i*ght do for m*e*. I can reformat a text to make it easier to read, or, using a dozen transformations, make it harder, or just different, to read. I can literally color my colors of rhetoric. I can heal the long hiatus of silent reading and make the text read itself aloud. At present this reading sounds a little funky, but it will become an expressive parameter as agile and wide as the others. I can embolden my own special key words and places. I can reformat prose into poetry. I can illuminate my manuscript in ways that would make a medieval scribe weep with envy. And when I have finished, I can print it out on my Linotron 300 electronic typesetter by pushing a keystroke or two. (7)

This paragraph was written over a decade ago, in the early 1990s, when desktop publishing was just entering rhetorical scholarship (and when scholars of technology used Linotron 300s). The passage, nonetheless, touts the visual aspects of processed words by emphasizing the way they function as changeable images. When Lanham suggests that he can "make the text read itself aloud" he points out ways in which textual presentation these days can combine the senses of sight and sound we have been discussing in this chapter: words, more than ever, act as images. Quintilian would have been intrigued.

Picture Theory

So words and how they're gathered on a page have a visual aspect of their own, but they may also interact with nondiscursive images such as drawings, paintings, photographs, or moving pictures. Most advertisements, for example, use some combination of text and visuals to promote a product or service. On this topic, Gorgias once observed that

Whenever pictures of many colors and figures create a perfect image of a single figure and form, they delight the sight. How much does the production of statues and the worksmanship of artifacts furnish pleasurable sight to the eyes! Thus it is natural for the sight sometimes to grieve, sometimes to delight. ("Encomium to Helen" 18)

The ancients were very aware of an image's capacity to move someone to action—the rhetorical force of the visual. While visual rhetoric is not entirely new, the subject of visual rhetoric is becoming increasingly important, especially since we are constantly inundated with images and also since images can serve as rhetorical proofs. "Picture theorist" W. J. T. Mitchell considers the relation between image and word because, as he points out, they often accompany each other (1994, 4–5). Like Mitchell, we are curious about visual images, specifically how they function rhetorically—that is, how they work in tandem with words or on their own to make or support arguments. Much of our language about rhetoric, after all, draws on visual metaphors. In spoken and written discourse, words like *see* and *show* abound—"Do you *see* what I mean?" "I'll *show* that the president's new tax policies are unfair to the working class."

When you incorporate visuals into written text, balance is an important consideration. Consider, for example, the opening page to each chapter in this book. In Western cultures, the reading eye moves from left to right and top to bottom. Note how the opening page to each chapter offers a graphic—the top of a classical column—at the upper left corner of the page. This column draws in the reader's eye and directs it to the epigraph, written in italics, underneath the column. Then next to the column, in a larger type size and bold style, is the chapter title. The title is followed by a significant amount of white space in order to let the readers pause momentarily before diving into the introductory portion of the chapter. Because the page layout seems fairly complicated—featuring a graphic, three different typestyles, and two columns of text—we provided ample white space to allow a "break" from the written text, thus guiding readers' eyes slowly down the page. We don't use a lot of other images in this book, because our original editor thought that a book about ancient rhetorics should look weighty and serious. We agreed.

The order and way in which people will "read"—that is, move their eyes across—the images should be taken into consideration. If you incorporate images into a text you're working on, it's a good idea to show the page with images to someone for a few seconds, remove it, and ask the viewer what she notices and remembers.

WEBRHETORS

Americans have moved into an era when words are "processed," stored, and retrieved electronically, an era when words more noticeably exist as and alongside images, and one when much political action and communication transpires on screens rather than, as in the ancient world (or even early America, for that matter), face-to-face at an assembly or a town meeting (Welch 1999, 192).

Now that we have moved squarely into the digital age, it seems important for us to consider ways ancient rhetoric can be brought to bear on technology, or what contemporary writers are calling "new media," a term often used to refer to recently created and rapidly changing forms of communication that combine computer and telecommunications technology. "New media" can refer to browser-based technologies, e-mail, and all the various forms of interactive media.

But what in the world could ancient rhetoric have to offer Webrhetors, rhetors for whom BCE refers to that archaic age "before computers existed"? We believe the canons of ancient rhetoric are quite useful for using new media to read, write, and generally engage the world. The Greeks themselves, after all, rehabilitated many of their rhetorical approaches and guidelines as they moved between oral and written discourse. While media change, as we have seen with the move from oral to literate cultures, different concerns come to the fore.

First, though, let's think about how new media are different from spoken or written rhetoric and how they incorporate features of both. Think of the way the television screen looks when it's set on CNN's channel—there might be live action shots in the upper-left corner, a newscaster in the center, the Dow report down the right side, and ribbons of headlines at the bottom. Similarly, the Web version of the *New York Times* displays the Dow report in one margin; an index of other sections of the paper in the other; the day's headlines with short blurbs in the center; photos with links and special reports covering any number of topics; hotlinks to the day's weather, charities, sponsoring organizations, all interspersed with advertisements for new movie releases—all this on the initial page. These media are digital, interactive, multimedia, nonlinear, hypertextual, and packed with information. They also include recognizable features of rhetoric treated so far in this book.

Contemporary rhetors Jay David Bolter and Richard Grusin use the term *hypermediacy* to describe a visual presentation style that, like CNN or the Web version of the *New York Times,* uses icons, hotlinks, layers of windows, and a browser format. One of the goals of such hypermediacy, according to Bolter and Grusin, is to "engage all the senses" (2000, 68). In an odd way, then, the hypermediacy of this millennium shares similar qualities with ancient rhetoric, for, as we've suggested in this chapter, the senses were often foremost on the minds of rhetors from Gorgias to Quintilian. This attention to multiple senses has all but disappeared from modern theories of rhetoric, which, as we have indicated previously, often rely solely on principles of reasoning and lockstep methods of composing. It could be, in fact, that an age of hypermediacy provides a comfortable "home" for ancient rhetorics. Bolter and Grusin have a term for this process of replacing or combining an old delivery system with a new one—for example, the placement of the day's news in both newspaper (old media) and Web (new media) formats. They call the process "remediation." What follows considers some ways in which ancient rhetoric itself is becoming remediated with new technology.

As we saw earlier with the Richard Lanham passage, with electronic writing technologies, delivery can become an inventional tool—that is, new media features, such as the availability of a variety of typefaces, pictures, moving images, and sounds, can sometimes prompt new directions in writing and argument. This does not mean, however, that concerns like *ethos* drop out of the picture. Far from it. We believe that a well-conceived, carefully created, navigable Web site helps produce strong *ethos*.

Kairos is obviously a major component of new media. With the new "just in time" economy, many businesses have moved online to meet the rising demand for immediate supply. News stories can be broadcast online just as quickly as they can be broadcast on television, and more quickly than they can appear in print media. In this way, new media seem more analogous to the speaking situation, with their immediate, "in your face" visual style.

Perhaps one of the most intriguing ways new media are "remediating" rhetoric is in the area of arrangement. The first screen or home page of a Web site, for example, shares common features with the exordium, Cicero's word for the first section of a speech (see Chapter 9, on arrangement). That is, the home page establishes the tone and *ethos* of the site through its use of fonts and images and, of course, its writing style. From there, though, the differences between new media and spoken or written discourse become apparent. Beyond the home page, more information is generally made available via hotlinks, which move to other pages. Some Web authors design links to move directly from one to another, by installing a "next" button at the bottom right of the page, thus preserving the linear style of oral and written discourse. Others, however, favor the "choose your own adventure" style of writing, presenting the links in a nonlinear form (perhaps in a circle or even moving). This capacity to defy linear arrangement presents the rhetor with interesting inventional possibilities.

We have also noticed the way language about the Internet resembles artificial memory systems, with their emphasis on the spatial. Recall from the memory chapter how the ancients trained their memories by making the parts of a speech into places in a building. The Web shares these qualities as well—we "visit" Web *sites* and can usually "return" to *home*. When we talk about Web logs (or blogs), we often say "over at luvspuppybreath," or, increasingly, "I was on Facebook the other day." Such discourse may mark the return of spatialized discourse.

We believe that the canon of delivery in new media presents an interesting amalgamation of issues discussed in the oral and written discourse sections, which appear earlier. Just as speakers think about facial and bodily animation, sound, and so forth, Webrhetors may incorporate digital features that simulate these very qualities. They may use an avatar—an animated icon—to "guide" users through a site, for example. They can install movies, sound clips, or images to convey a certain kind of *ethos* or present information in an attention-getting (or annoying!) way.

The design choices available for delivering information on the Internet are virtually limitless. In addition to the typographical choices available for the printed page, rhetors may choose background patterns and colors, and they have easy access to all kinds of dynamite graphics—blinking icons, moving pictures, fun sounds—that can enhance the design of texts online. Since there is already a flood of information available on Web design, at the end of this chapter we offer a guide to available resources for rhetors interested in spinning their rhetorical abilities onto the Web.

RHETORICAL ACTIVITIES

1. Choose a punctuation marker—the dash, the comma, the semicolon, or any marker discussed in this chapter—and do a little research on how it is used. Consult a variety of textual sources: magazines, a newspaper article, a textbook, ads in buses and trains, bumper stickers, instructions on the back of a shampoo bottle. Note the instances in which writers use that particular punctuation mark. From the usages you observe, compose a one-page analysis of the various functions of the marker. Did different writers use the same marker in contradictory ways? What rhetorical effects did the various usages have on you?

2. Tape-record a conversation with a group of friends and transcribe it, using only periods to punctuate. Then go back through the transcription while replaying the tape, and place the various punctuation markers where you hear distinctive pauses and the like. Write a brief analysis of the editorial choices you made: How did you decide to use a semicolon? Did you use any dashes? If so, why?

3. Look at a piece of writing you did before reading about delivery. Examine the layout, including your choice of font, use of headers, and indentation. Why did you make those choices? Now look at your use of punctuation. Would you change anything?

4. Explore the relationship between design choices and *ethos* by examining a few different magazines, focusing on the typography, page layout, and spacing. What effects do the design choices have on you as a reader? Is there a connection between the ideology of the publication and the font choices?

5. Log onto the Internet and examine the delivery of several different Web sites. Click on a few links that look interesting, then return to the home page. What kind of *ethos* does the Web page foster? That is, what pictures do you have of the Web site creator or organization that it represents? What is the apparent purpose of the Web site (education? self-promotion? resource hub?)? Now look at links and other features. What background colors and patterns are conducive to reader-text interaction? What font colors work well? How do pictures help facilitate

communication? Is spacing used efficiently? Which sites look cluttered and why? What are some rhetorical effects of cluttering? What kind of movement does it foster?

6. Choose a proof developed in another essay, and find a way to make the same argument visually. You may either find an image already in existence or create your own. What barriers did you encounter? Is the argument more or less powerful when rendered visually?

7. Choose an argument you have written for this course or for another venue and "remediate" it—that is, design a plan for moving it onto one of the new media. (If you are proficient with Web design, create a Web site for it.) Be sure to let hypertext/Web technology play into your inventional strategies. What kinds of arguments does a "linked" essay (linked both among its parts and to other pieces of writing) enable? How might the visual play into your essay?

NOTE

1. We highly recommend Martha Kolln's *Rhetorical Grammar* and Joseph Williams's *Ten Lessons in Clarity and Grace* in this regard.

WORKS CITED

Bolter, Jay David, and Richard Grusin. *Remediation: Understanding New Media.* Cambridge: MIT Press, 2000.

Dragga, Sam, and Gwendolyn Gong. *Editing: The Design of Rhetoric.* Amityville, N.Y.: Baywood Publishing Company, 1989.

Heller, Steven, and Anne Fink. *Faces on the Edge: Type in the Digital Age.* New York: Van Nostrand Reinhold, 1997.

Kolln, Martha. *Rhetorical Grammar: Grammatical Choices, Rhetorical Effects.* 5th ed. New York: Longman, 2006.

Lanham, Richard. *The Electronic Word: Democracy, Technology, and the Arts.* Chicago: Chicago University Press, 1993.

Mitchell, W. J. T. *Picture Theory: Essays on Verbal and Visual Representation.* Chicago: Chicago University Press, 1994.

Parkes, M. P. *Pause and Effect: An Introduction to the History of Punctuation in the West.* Berkeley: University of California Press, 1993.

Welch, Kathleen. *Electric Rhetoric: Classical Rhetoric, Oralism, and a New Literacy.* Cambridge: MIT Press, 1999.

Williams, Joseph. *Style: Lessons in Clarity and Grace.* 9th ed. New York: Longman, 2006.

GLOSSARY

accumulation a figure wherein a rhetor gathers scattered points and lists them together.

active voice a grammatical construction available in English, in which the grammatical subject is the actor in a sentence.

allegory (AL a gor ee) an extended metaphor.

ambiguous case (am BIG you us) case that is partly honorable, partly dishonorable in the eyes of an audience; or a case wherein the audience is not sure of the rhetor's position.

amplification the ancient art of saying a great deal about very little.

anadiplosis (a na di PLO sis) a figure wherein the last word of a phrase, clause, or sentence is used to begin the next phrase, clause, or sentence.

analogy (an AL o gee) a comparison, either of particulars or of relations; also, a proof developed by Aristotle wherein a rhetor compares one hypothetical example to another.

analysis a kind of definition; analytic definition divides the term to be defined into parts and lists all of these.

anaphora (a NAF o ra) a figure wherein the same word is repeated at the beginning of several successive phrases, clauses, or sentences.

antanaclasis (an tan ACK la sis) a figure wherein a word is used in at least two different senses.

anticipation a general name for figures wherein a rhetor foresees and replies to objections.

antihimera (an tee HI mer a) a figure wherein one part of speech is used as another.

antimetabole (an tee ma TAB oh lee) a figure that expresses contrasting ideas in juxtaposed structures; also called **chiasmus**.

antistrophe (an TIS troe fee) a figure wherein the same or similar words are repeated in successive phrases or clauses.

antithesis (an TITH a sis) a figure wherein contrary ideas are expressed in grammatically parallel structures.

antonomasia (an toe no MAS ya) a trope wherein a rhetor substitutes a descriptive phrase for someone's name.

apostrophe (a PAWS tro fee) a figure wherein a rhetor addresses some absent person; also, a mark of punctuation that signals possession or omission.

appendix additional material included at the back of a book.

apposition any phrase that interrupts a period to modify or comment on it.

argument in this book, a rhetorical situation in which the people who are involved disagree about something; also used here as an equivalent term for proof.

arrangement the second canon of rhetoric; concerns the selection and ordering of parts in a discourse.

art any set of productive principles or practices.

artificial memory the ancient term for a memory that has been carefully trained to increase its potential.

asyndeton (ah SYN da tun) a figure wherein normal connectors between words (usually "and") are eliminated.

atechnoi (AY tek noy) Greek term meaning without art or skill.

audience any persons designated by a rhetor as hearers or readers of a discourse.

authorities any persons or sources called upon by a rhetor to support his or her arguments.

BCE abbreviation for "before the Common Era." In the Western calendar, indicates years prior to the year 1. Years BCE are counted backwards, as in "323 BCE, 322 BCE."

bibliography (bib lee OG ra phee) a list of the works used to compose a discourse, usually appearing at the end of the discourse.

bound periodical older issues of journals or newspapers bound together into a book, usually according to year of issue.

call number the number used by libraries to identify books and other materials; printed on the cover and an inside page.

canon ancient term for a division or part of the art of rhetoric.

card catalogue drawers containing cards that list all the books and other materials kept in a library; usually found in the library's reference room.

case a rhetor's proposition and proofs developed for use in a specific rhetorical situation.

catachresis (kat a KREE sis) a trope wherein a rhetor intentionally substitutes a like or inexact word in place of the correct one.

cause to effect any argument that reasons from causes to effects or vice versa; an ancient sophistic topic.

CE abbreviation for Common Era. In the Western calendar, indicates years since the year 1.

character a rhetor's habitual way of life or reputation in the relevant community; *ethos*; also an elementary exercise, or *progymnasmata*.

chiasmus a figure that expresses contrasting ideas in juxtaposed structures; also called **antimetabole**.

chreia (KRAY ya) an elementary exercise, or *progymnasmata*, in which the rhetor elaborates on a famous event or saying.

circumlocution literally, speaking around; a figure wherein a rhetor avoids naming an unsavory issue or term.

class Latin *genus*; a group, kind, sort.

classification a sophistic topic wherein items are grouped under a single general head.

climax a figure in which terms or phrases are arranged in order from least to most important.

colon ancient term for meaningful phrase that was shorter than a sentence but longer than a comma.

comma ancient term for short phrase; in modern English, punctuation that marks an internal pause in a sentence.

commonplace any statement or bit of knowledge that is commonly shared among a given audience or a community; also, an elementary exercise, or *progymnasmata*.

commonplace book a notebook kept by a rhetor as a storehouse of materials to be remembered or quoted.

common topics means of invention developed by Aristotle that are useful for developing arguments on any issue or in any field of discourse; they are conjecture, degree, and possibility.

community authority any person who is judged as an expert or is qualified to offer testimony based on a good reputation in the relevant community.

comparison in the sophistic topic called comparison, rhetors place two similar items together and examine their similarities; also, an elementary exercise or *progymnasmata*.

complex sentence a sentence that contains at least one independent colon and one dependent colon.

compound sentence a sentence that contains at least two independent colons.

compound-complex sentence a sentence that contains at least two independent colons and at least one dependent colon.

concession a figure wherein a rhetor concedes a disputed point or leaves a disputed point to the audience to decide.

conclusion modern term for the peroration, or final part of a discourse.

confirmation the part of a discourse that elaborates arguments in support of a rhetor's position.

conjecture in stasis theory or in Aristotle's topical theory of invention, any issue or topic that considers a proposed state of affairs.

context the words and sentences that surround any part of a discourse and help to determine its meaning; also, the rhetorical situation and background of an issue that help to determine the meaning of any text.

contraries a sophistic topic wherein a rhetor compares unlike items, situations, or events.

contrast a sophistic topic wherein a rhetor compares opposites.

copia (KO pee ya) abundant and ready supply of language; arguments or figures available for use on any occasion.

copying an ancient exercise used to enhance *copia*.

correction a figure wherein a rhetor replaces a word or phrase with a more correct one.

correctness rules standards of grammar and usage drawn from traditional grammar.

cultural memory a type of collective memory stemming from shared cultural experiences, historical events, educational practices, or social customs.

current periodical any recent issue of a periodical.

data a type of proof based on the evidence of the senses, or empirical proof; also includes statistics.

database a computer program that accesses information.

declamation (deck la MAY shun) an art of debating practiced by Roman rhetors and students.

deduction an ancient means of invention; a method of reasoning wherein a conclusion is derived from comparison of general to particular premises.

definite issue Greek hypothesis (hy POTH a sis); an issue involving specific persons, places, events, or things.

definition in stasis theory, any issue that considers how something should be defined or classified; also, a sophistic topic that sets limits to a term.

degree a common topic that requires rhetors to approach an issue with comparative questions of size, magnitude, and value.

delivery the fifth canon of rhetoric; concerns use of voice and gesture in oral discourse or editing, formatting, and presentation in written discourse.

description one of the elementary exercises, or *progymnasmata*; discusses attributes or appearance of something or someone.

dialectic a heuristic that proceeds by question and answer.

differences   in the sophistic topic of definition, a list of ways in which the term to be defined differs from other members of its designated class; also, a sophistic topic that generates a list of ways in which similar items differ.

difficult case   a case that is not honorable or to which an audience is hostile.

distance   a metaphor for the discursive relation obtaining between rhetor and audience; see **rhetorical distance**.

distribution   a figure wherein a rhetor divides a whole into parts and assigns each part to a different field.

division   a sophistic topic that separates out and lists the parts of any whole; also, a figure that does the same.

editing   stage of composing wherein the rhetor corrects errors and makes sure discourse conforms to conventions of formatting and presentation.

eidolopoeia   (eye doe low PO ee ya) an exercise wherein the character of a spirit or an image is depicted.

empirical proof   proof derived from the senses.

enargeia   (en AR gay uh) figure in which rhetor creates a vivid scene.

encomium   a discourse that praises someone or something.

energia   (en ERG ya) a Greek term meaning to energize or actualize.

entechnoi   (EN tek noy) Greek term meaning within or embodied in an art.

enthymeme   (EN thee meem) a means of proof within which the rhetor places probable premises together in order to establish a probable conclusion.

enumeration   a means of definition that lists relevant attributes or parts of the term to be defined.

epanaphora   (ep an AF o rah) a figure wherein a rhetor repeats words at the beginning of successive colons; the repeated words are used in different senses.

epideictic   (eh pi DIKE tick) one of Aristotle's major divisions of rhetoric oratory that praises or blames.

epiphora   (eh PYF o rah) a figure wherein a rhetor repeats the last word in successive clauses.

epistemology   (eh pis tem OL o gee) any theory of how people know; any theory of knowledge.

epithet   a figure in which a rhetor calls someone a name.

ethical proof   proof that depends upon the good character or reputation of a rhetor.

ethics   any set of guides or standards for human conduct.

ethopoeia   (ee tho PO ee ya) character portrayal; Greek term for discourse that creates a character; also, an ancient exercise wherein rhetors invented a set of traits to describe a kind of person.

ethos   the character or reputation of a rhetor.

etymological definition   a definition that supplies a history of a term to be defined.

etymology   the history of a word.

example   a specific instance; a particular; one member of a class; also, a rhetorical proof developed by Aristotle.

exigence   the force or impetus in a rhetorical situation that gives rise to use or practice of rhetoric.

exordium   (ex OR di yum) Latin term for the first part of a discourse.

expediency   an ancient topic of value; considers whether a course of action is useful, efficient, or suited to the circumstances.

extended example   a fully developed rhetorical example.

extrinsic proof   proof that is available within the circumstances of the case; does not have to be invented.

fable   a fictional story meant to teach a moral lesson.

facts   bits of knowledge derived from sensory perception; also, bits of knowledge agreed to by all concerned parties.

fictional example   a rhetorical example drawn from a tale, fable, short story, or novel.

figure   generic term for artful uses of language.

figure of language   any artful patterning or arrangement of language.

figure of thought   Greek *sententia* (sen TEN shya); any artful presentation of ideas, feelings, concepts; figures of thought that depart from the ordinary patterns of argument (also called figure of speech).

foreword   a discourse that introduces another discourse.

format   conventional means of presentation; includes spacing, margins, and headers.

general issue   Greek *thesis*; in stasis theory, an indefinite issue.

general/specific relations   an ancient method of reasoning that treats whatever is under investigation as a class composed of specifics or particulars.

generalization   any statement about a group or class.

genus   (GEE nus) the Latin word for class; a group or kind.

genus/species   an ancient mode of definition.

gesture   a persuasive facial or bodily movement; part of delivery.

glossary   a list of terms used in a discourse; supplies definitions (and sometimes pronunciations) of technical or specialized terms.

goodness   an ancient common topic of degree.

grammatical person   a grammatical feature of English that indicates who is speaking or writing, and/or the relation of the user to hearers/readers and/or issues; there are three grammatical persons in English.

greater/lesser   a common topic developed by Aristotle; here called "degree."

hesitation   (also indecision or *dubatio*) a figure wherein a rhetor pretends to be unable to decide what to say or write.

heuristic   (hyur IS tick) any system of investigation.

homoioteleuton   (home ee o TEL you ton) a figure wherein a rhetor repeats words with similar endings.

homonym   (HOM i nim) words that sound the same but that have different meanings.

honor   an ancient common topic of degree.

honorable case   a case that is respected by the audience.

honorific language   language that respects or glorifies.

hyperbaton   (high PER ba tun) a figure in which language takes a sudden turn; usually an interruption; also, a trope that transposes a term to somewhere other than its usual place.

hyperbole   (high PER bo lee) exaggeration.

hypophora   (high POF o rah) a figure wherein a rhetor asks what can be said in favor of the opponents.

hypothesis   (high PAH tha sis) in stasis theory, a specific issue.

identification   an ideal rhetorical situation in which an audience feels close to a rhetor.

ideologic   chain of reasoning by commonplaces that makes up ideological arguments and positions.

ideology   any body of beliefs, doctrines, values held by a single individual or by a group or a culture.

imitation   an ancient rhetorical exercise wherein students copied and elaborated on the work of revered or admired authors.

indefinite issue   Greek *thesis*; in stasis theory, an issue or question that is general or abstract.

index   list of important names or topics in a discourse, with page numbers; appears at end of discourse.

induction   an ancient method of invention; a rhetor collects a number of instances and forms a generalization that is meant to apply to all instances.

insinuation   the introduction to a difficult case.

instance   an example or particular.

interest   the reason or reasons why someone takes a given position on an issue; these may be ideological or unconscious.

intrinsic *ethos*   proofs from character that are invented by a rhetor or are available by virtue of the rhetor's position on an issue.

intrinsic proof   argument generated through use of the art of rhetoric.

introduction   the first part of a discourse, called **exordium** in ancient rhetorics.

introduction of law   the last and most difficult of the elementary exercises, or *progymnasmata*.

invective   a discourse that casts blame on somebody or something.

invented *ethos*   proofs from character that are invented by a rhetor or are available by virtue of the rhetor's position on an issue.

invented proof   any proof discovered through use of the principles of rhetoric.

invention   the first of the five canons of rhetoric; the art of finding available **arguments** in any situation.

irony   (EYE ron ee) a trope in which an audience understands the opposite of what is being expressed.

isocolon   Greek term for grammatically balanced phrases or clauses.

issue   matter about which there is dispute; point about which all parties agree to disagree.

justice   an ancient common topic.

kairos   (KY ross) Greek term meaning the right time, opportunity, occasion, or reason.

lines of argument   related issues and proofs that open up when rhetorical situation is systematically investigated.

litotes   (LIE toe tees) a figure in which the rhetor understates the situation.

logical proof   an argument found in the issue or the case.

logos   (LO gose) in archaic Greek, speech, voice, breath, or even spirit; in Aristotle's rhetoric, any arguments found in the issue or the case.

loose sentence   a sentence whose word order follows the word order of whatever language it is expressed in; phrases and clauses are tacked on haphazardly.

major premise   the first statement in an enthymeme; a general statement about probable human action.

maxim   a familiar saying; a bit of community wisdom.

mean case   a case in which the audience regards the rhetor or the issue as unimportant or uninteresting.

member   a phrase or clause; in ancient rhetoric, any part of a sentence.

memory   the fourth canon of rhetoric.

memory places   invented mental categories used to store information and images of an artificial memory.

metabasis   (meh TAB a sis) a summarizing transition.

metaphor   (MET a for) a trope wherein one word is substituted for another.

metonymy (me TAH na mee) a trope wherein something is named by words frequently associated with it.

microforms written materials that have been photographed and reduced in size; libraries use microforms to reduce the space taken up by printed documents. There are two kinds of microforms: film, which is stored on a reel like video or movie film; and fiche, which is stored on a flat surface.

minor premise a statement in an **enthymeme** that names a particular instance.

narrative the second part of a discourse; it states the issue and may supply a history of the issue.

neologism (knee OL o jism) a new or coined word or phrase.

network of interpretation any interpretive framework used to make sense of an array of data or knowledge; **ideology**.

obscure case a case that is unclear to the audience.

onomatopoeia (on o ma to PO ee ya) a trope that uses words to suggest sounds.

oxymoron (oks ZIM o ron) a figure wherein unlike or opposite terms are used together.

paradox (PAIR a docks) a figure wherein a rhetor raises expectations then mentions trivia; also, any seemingly self-contradictory statement.

paralepsis (pair a LEP sis) a figure wherein a rhetor refuses to mention something, all the while doing so.

parallel case an argument that treats two or more instances as similar.

parallelism a figure wherein similar grammatical constructions house different words.

paraphrase imitation with elaboration; imitating sense of a discourse in words other than those used by original author; an ancient rhetorical exercise.

paratactic style (pair a TACK tick) a string of loose sentences.

parenthesis a figure in which the rhetor interrupts the train of thought; in modern English, punctuation that has the same function.

paronomasia (pare oh no MAZ ee ya) pun; words or phrases sound alike but have different meanings; often the juxtaposition is funny.

parrhesia (pah REEZ ya) frankness of speech.

particular a single item or a member of a class.

partition the third part of a discourse; divides the issue into relevant areas.

passive voice a grammatical structure available in English wherein the grammatical subject of the sentence is not the actor.

past/future fact a common topic developed by Aristotle; here called **conjecture**.

pathetic proof proof that appeals to the emotions or motives of an audience.

pathos (PAY those) Greek term for emotions or passions.

pejorative language language that disparages or downplays.

period Greek term for the sentence; in modern English, the punctuation that marks the termination of declarative sentences.

periodical magazines, journals, or books issued regularly and published under the same name over a period of time.

periodic sentence sentence with obvious structure; meaning is distributed among several members or saved until last.

periphrasis (pair i FRAA sis) trope wherein the rhetor substitutes other words for the term under discussion.

peroration   the final part of a discourse; may summarize, arouse emotions, or enhance rhetor's ethos.

persona   (per SO nah) Latin term used by Cicero for *ethos*.

personification   a figure that attributes the qualities of living things to things that are not alive, at least in the conventional sense.

phrase   a short string of words; equivalent to the Greek comma.

policy   the fourth stasis; investigates possible actions in a given situation.

polysyndeton   (pol ly SIN dee tun) a figure wherein the rhetor inserts all possible connectors between words, phrases, or sentences.

possibility   a common topic.

possible/impossible   common topic developed by Aristotle; here called possibility.

power relation   the social, economic, or ethical relationship that obtains between a rhetor and an audience.

practical issue   in stasis theory, an issue having to do with human action.

preface   a discourse that may introduce a book, an author's methods and rationale; appears at beginning.

premise   a statement laid down, supposed, or assumed before an argument begins.

presentation   how a manuscript looks; depends on width of margins, use of headers, and the like.

probability   a statement about what people are likely to do.

procedure   in stasis theory, any issue that considers how people ought to proceed.

progymnasmata   (pro ghim NAS ma ta) the elementary rhetorical exercises used in ancient schools of rhetoric.

prooemium   (pro EEM ee yum) Greek term for the exordium or first part of any discourse.

proof   any statement or statements used to persuade an audience to accept a proposition; also, the section of a discourse where arguments are assembled; in this book, used interchangeably with **argument**.

proposition   any arguable statement put forward for discussion by a rhetor.

prosopopoeia   (prose oh POE ee ya) an exercise wherein the character of a fictional person is depicted.

proverb   any well-known saying; a bit of community wisdom.

proximate authority   someone who is in a position to offer testimony because of having been close to the events in question.

pun   artful and sometimes funny **synonymy**.

punctuation   graphic marks used to represent features of spoken language in writing.

qualifier   word in English that mitigates the force of other words.

quality   in stasis theory, any issue that considers values.

reasoning   Aristotle's term for deduction; here, any method of comparing statements in order to draw conclusions.

reasoning by contraries   a figure wherein a rhetor uses one of two opposing statements to prove the other.

reasoning by question and answer   a figure wherein a rhetor inserts a question between successive affirmative statements.

refutation   the part of a discourse wherein a rhetor anticipates opposing arguments and answers them.

representative theory of language   theory of language that assumes language is transparent—that it allows meaning to shine through it clearly and without distortion.

rhetor   (RAY tor in Greek; REH ter in English) anyone who composes discourse that is intended to affect community thinking or events.

rhetoric   (REH ter ick) the art that helps people compose effective discourse.

rhetorical distance   metaphor for the degree of physical and social distance created between a rhetor and an audience by creation of an *ethos*.

rhetorical question   a figure wherein rhetors ask questions to which they and the audience already know the answers.

rhetorical situation   the context of a rhetorical act; minimally made up of a rhetor, an issue, and an audience.

rhetorician   (reh to RISH an) someone who studies or teaches the art of rhetoric.

scheme   generic term for artful use of language.

sensus communis   (SEN sus co MUNE is) Latin phrase for common knowledge shared among members of a community.

sentence composition   in ancient rhetorics, the artful construction of sentences.

sign   facts or events that usually or always accompany other facts or events.

similarity   a relation between items that emphasizes their likenesses or resemblances.

simile   (SIM i lee) a figure wherein two unlike items are compared.

simple sentence   a sentence that has one independent clause and no other clauses.

situated *ethos*   proof from character that depends on a rhetor's reputation in the relevant community.

sophist   (SOF ist) in ancient times, name given to any rhetor who taught by example; when capitalized, refers to any of a group of rhetoric teachers who worked in and around Athens in the fifth and fourth centuries BCE; in modern English, term for a **rhetor** who may use fallacious or tricky arguments.

sophistic topics   sources of arguments that depend on regular patterns or arrangements of material.

sophistry   (SOF ist ree) term applied to the rhetorical theory and practice of the Older Sophists; in modern times names tricky or fallacious rhetorical practices.

special topics   a means of invention developed by Aristotle; arguments drawn from specific arts such as politics or ethics.

species   Greek term for an example, an instance, or a particular.

species/genus   an ancient method of definition.

specific issue   in stasis theory, an issue that deals with a particular or individual.

stacks   shelves in a library where books are stored.

staseis   (STAS ay is) Greek term for issues.

stasis   (STASE is) a stand; place where opponents agree to disagree.

stasis theory   theory of invention developed by Hermagoras of Temnos.

style   the fourth canon of rhetoric; has to do with sentence composition and the use of ornament.

style sheet   list of editing conventions used by a specific professional group.

suspension   a figure wherein a rhetor raises expectations.

syllogism   (SILL o jiz im) name for a deductive argument in logic.

symploke   (SIM plo key) a figure that combines *epanaphora* and *epiphora*.

synecdoche   (sin ECK doe key) a trope wherein a part of the whole is referred to as though it were the whole.

synonymy   (sin ON o mee) a figure wherein a rhetor uses similar words as means of repetition.

table of contents   page or pages that list chapter headings or subtitles in a book or journal.

tale   a short narrative; an ancient elementary exercise or *progymnasmata*.

techne   (TEK nay) Greek term for an art; any set of productive principles or practices.

testimony   a person's account of an event or state of affairs.

theoretical issue in stasis theory   any wide-ranging philosophical issue not involved with specific human actions.

thesis   (THEE sis) in stasis theory, a general or indefinite issue; also, an elementary exercise or *progymnasmata*.

title page   the page of a book that gives its title and author's name.

topic   Greek term for a commonplace; literally, place where arguments are located.

traditional grammar   artificial grammar imposed on English in eighteenth century CE; observes grammatical rules borrowed from Latin; treated as grammatical standard by some.

transition   any word or phrase that connects pieces of discourse.

translation   ancient rhetorical exercise wherein rhetors translated discourse from one language or dialect to another.

trivial case   a case wherein an audience is not convinced that the issue is important or the rhetor worth paying attention to.

trope   any artful substitution of one term for another.

understatement   figure in which a rhetor deliberately makes a situation seem less important or serious than it is.

usage   customary ways of using language.

value   anything that is deemed desirable or worthy by a community.

verb tense   grammatical feature of English that identifies time of action, such as present, past, or future.

verb voice   grammatical feature of English that allows user to identify the grammatical subject with an actor in the sentence (active voice) or to substitute some other word in the grammatical subject position (passive voice).

visual rhetoric   a burgeoning branch of rhetorical studies that considers images as rhetorical in the way they function to persuade, whether alongside words or on their own as images.

voice   persuasive use of loudness and tone of voice.

volume number   number given to all issues of a periodical published during a given span of time, usually one year.

whole/part relation   an ancient method of reasoning that treats whatever is under investigation as a whole that can be divided into parts.

word size   feature of English that influences **rhetorical distance**.

zeugma   (ZOOG mah) figure wherein the same word is used in different senses in grammatically similar constructions.

APPENDIX

Archaic Rhetoric

ca. 1250 BCE: battle of Troy

ca. 1150–850 BCE: Homer composes the *Iliad* and the *Odyssey*; ancient rhetoricians thought that the speeches in these poems demonstrated the great antiquity of rhetoric.

Greek Rhetoric in the Classical Period (500–323 BCE)

494–434: Empedocles, a teacher, scientist, and magician, may have been a teacher of the sophist Gorgias. Some authorities say he invented rhetoric.

490–429: Pericles, a great statesman and orator, participates in the formation of direct democracy at Athens; everybody who is anybody is a member of his circle, including the famous woman rhetorician, Aspasia, and wealthy, ambitious young men like Alcibiades.

470–450: Corax/Tisias practice rhetoric in Sicilian capital of Syracuse; both apparently wrote *techne*, or arts of rhetoric, that are now lost. These may have been collections of sample arguments, introductions, and conclusions. Some authorities say that Gorgias studied with Tisias.

460–400: Thucydides writes his great history of the Peloponnesian War, which contains many speeches that demonstrate his knowledge of rhetoric.

The Older Sophists

483–375: Gorgias of Leontini, a teacher and theorist of rhetoric, arrives in Athens in 427 as an ambassador from Sicily and takes the Greek city by storm with his fiery displays of stylistic elegance. Like Protagoras, Gorgias was a philosophical skeptic, more interested in ethics, rhetoric, and politics than in metaphysics. We have two entire speeches ("Helen" and "Palamedes") and several fragments of his work. See also Plato's dialogue *Gorgias,* where the sophist is made to look like an unethical fool.

481–411: Protagoras authors the famous phrase "Man is the measure of all things," which some contemporary scholars take to mean that

Protagoras scorned the metaphysical speculations of the pre-Socratic philosophers and perhaps of Plato, as well. He apparently contributed the notion of *dissoi logoi* to sophistic rhetoric, the notion that competing or contradictory statements can be made about any issue. We have only a few fragments of his work, plus the unflattering portrait of him that appears in Plato's dialogue *Protagoras*.

470–399: Socrates is an itinerant teacher and the famous interlocuter in Plato's *Dialogues*. Although modern philosophers might be shocked to find Socrates in a list of Sophists, some contemporary scholars think that he should be included here as being responsible for an inventional scheme called eristic. Socrates was condemned to death in 399 for corrupting the youth of Athens.

436–338: Isocrates founds a very successful school of rhetoric in Athens that competed for students with Plato's Academy. He apparently wrote no systematic treatise on rhetorical theory, but many of his complete orations have been preserved, indicating that people have thought them worth reading ever since his own time. Since he had weak vocal cords, Isocrates did not practice rhetoric for very long, but he was a capable writer of speeches for others—that is, he was a *logographer,* or ghostwriter.

Other persons sometimes classed as Older Sophists are Antiphon, Hippias of Elis, Prodicus of Ceos, and Thrasymachus.

A Handbook

ca. 341: Anaximines (?) writes a textbook called the *Rhetoric to Alexander* (*Rhetorica ad Alexandrum*). The work was given this title because its author pretended to be Aristotle writing a textbook on rhetoric for his student, Alexander the Great. Its importance is that it probably represents the typical instruction given to students by fourth-century sophistic teachers.

Academic and Peripatetic Rhetorics

420–348: Plato develops an anti-Sophistic theory of rhetoric (chiefly in the dialogue *Phaedrus*), which posits that rhetoricians must know the truth before they speak, must be able to separate true knowledge from opinion, must know the souls of humans, must be able to define and divide topics for discussion, and must be able to develop orderly principles of arrangement. In other words, he turns rhetoric into philosophy.

384–322: Aristotle contributes a very full and systematic theory of invention to the history of rhetoric in his *On Rhetoric*. Aside from this text, Aristotle apparently wrote an early treatise on rhetoric, the *Gryllus* (which is now lost), and collected treatises by other teachers into the *Synagoge Technon,* also now lost but known to Cicero, who consulted it to write the history of rhetoric contained in his *Brutus*.

Famous Greek Rhetors of the Classical Era

384–322: Demosthenes, the exact contemporary of Aristotle, is acknowledged by all classical authorities to be the greatest of the Greek rhetors. He is best known now for his clash with Aeschines, which is preserved for us in the speeches *On the Crown*. During Roman times, scholars developed a canon of famous Greek orators (The Attic Orators) whose works had been preserved and who were thought worthy of imitation. They are: Antiphon, Andocides, Lysias, Isaeus, Isocrates, Demosthenes, Aeschines, Hyperides, Lycurgus, and Dinarchus. Most of these orators supported themselves by appearing in court on behalf of wealthy clients and by working as logographers.

Greek Rhetoric in the Hellenistic Period (323–37 BCE)

Rhetoric becomes the focus of higher education in Greece and elsewhere. During this period teachers of rhetoric elaborated and sometimes conflated Aristotelian and sophistic theories of rhetoric. We have no Greek manuscripts from Hellenistic teachers, although many later accounts of their teachings exist. Only one major theoretical contribution occurs during this period—stasis theory. However, teachers of rhetoric were interested in refining their study of style, and some developed theories about the levels, or kinds, of style.

ca. 370–285: Theophrastus, a student of Aristotle, advances the study of style and perhaps invents systematic study of delivery. He writes a series of character studies demonstrating the construction and use of *ethopoeia*, which is still extant.

345–283: Demetrius of Phaleron writes "On Style," in which he claims that there are four types of style: the plain, the grand, the stately, and the powerful.

Mid-second century BCE: Hermagoras of Temnos apparently invents stasis theory, which will compete for first place in rhetorical handbooks with Aristotlean and sophistic theories of invention throughout antiquity and into the European Renaissance.

Latin Rhetoric

Roman intellectuals come into contact with Greek rhetoric during the second century BCE, and they adopt Greek rhetorical theory almost intact, only later refining its precepts in order to accommodate the Latin language.

Early first century BCE: Cornificius (?) writes the *Rhetoric for Herennius* (*Rhetorica ad Herennium*), a very full discussion of Hellenistic rhetorical theory and pedagogy. This treatise contains a discussion of memory, the most complete and oldest available to us.

106–43 BCE: Cicero, who combines an interest in rhetorical theory with skill in speaking, sets stylistic and persuasive examples that will be emulated at least until the Renaissance. Cicero is well acquainted with Greek rhetoric and philosophy, and he writes several important works of rhetorical history and theory: *On Invention, Brutus, On the Parts of Oratory,* and his masterpiece, *Of Oratory.*

35–ca. 90 CE: Quintilian writes the *Institutes of Oratory,* the most complete treatise on rhetorical education available from antiquity.

First century CE: Longinus writes "On the Sublime," wherein he defines *hypsos,* "elevation" or "sublimity," as the quality of excellence found in Greek orators and poets. The sublime has five qualities that are reminiscent of the five canons of rhetoric.

First century CE: Hermogenes of Tarsus writes *On Ideas of Style,* wherein he catalogues the "ideas" or virtues of style: clarity, grandeur, beauty, vigor, ethos, verity, and gravity. Hermogenes' theory is important in rhetorical instruction throughout later antiquity and into the Renaissance.

Rhetorical Exercises

The *progymnasmata* were a series of school exercises used by teachers to hone students' skill in composition. Students imitated, amplified, and composed proverbs, fables, narratives, and arguments drawn from the works of classical authors.

Declamation was a school exercise as well as a popular form of entertainment among Roman adults. Declamation took at least two forms: *suasoriae,* where the speaker took the role of some historical or mythological person; and *controversiae,* where a real or imaginary law was cited alongside a real or imaginary case, and the speaker adopted the role of one of the persons in the case or became one of the person's advocate.

Greek Rhetoric in Later Antiquity

The Second Sophistic

During the first four centuries of the Common Era, Greek rhetors traveled throughout the Roman Empire, teaching and demonstrating their mastery of the art of rhetoric by declaiming, whenever asked, on any subject whatsoever. If they taught, they did so by means of example; their students watched them declaim and then did likewise. Most historians of rhetoric claim that the Sophists of this period were more interested in artistry and stylistic display than in public discussion of important issues—something that was very dangerous, after all, in the last days of the Roman Empire.

BIBLIOGRAPHY

CITATION SOURCES OF ANCIENT TEXTS

Aesop. *Aesop's Fables Told by Valerius Babrius.* Translated by Denison B. Hull. Chicago: University of Chicago Press, 1960.

Aesop. *The Fables of Aesop, Paraphrased in Verse.* John Ogilby. Los Angeles: Augustan Reprint Society (UCLA), 1965. (Originally printed 1668).

Antiphon. *Tetralogies.* Translated by J. S. Morrison. In *The Older Sophists*, 136–63. Edited by Rosamond Kent Sprague. Columbia, South Carolina: U of South Carolina P, 1972.

Aphthonius. *Progymnasmata.* Translated by Ray Nadeau. In *Speech Monographs* 19 (Nov. 1952): 264–85. Reprinted in *Readings from Classical Rhetoric*, 267–88. Edited by Patricia P. Matsen, Philip Rollinson, and Marion Sousa. Carbondale: Southern Illinois UP, 1990.

Aristotle. *Aristotle on Rhetoric: A Theory of Civic Discourse.* Translated by George A. Kennedy. New York: Oxford UP, 1991.

Aristotle. *On Interpretation.* Translated by E. M. Edghill. In *The Works of Aristotle.* Edited by W. D. Ross. Vol I. London: Oxford UP, 1966.

Aristotle. *Posterior Analytics.* Translated by G. R. G. Mure. In *The Works of Aristotle.* Edited by W. D. Ross. Vol. I. London: Oxford UP, 1966.

Aristotle. *Rhetoric.* Translated by John Henry Freese. Loeb Classical Library. Cambridge, Mass.: Harvard UP, 1926.

Aristotle. *The Rhetoric of Aristotle.* Translated by Lane Cooper. New York: Appleton-Century-Crofts, 1932.

Aristotle. *Topics.* Translated by W. A. Pickard-Cambridge. In *The Works of Aristotle.* Edited by W. D. Ross. London: Oxford UP, 1966.

Cicero. *Against Verres.* Translated by Palmer Bovie. New York: New American Library, 1967.

Cicero. *Brutus.* Translated by G. L. Hendrickson. Loeb Classical Library. Cambridge: Harvard UP, 1971.

Cicero. *In Defense of Murena.* Translated by Palmer Bovie. New York: New American Library, 1967.

Cicero. *On Invention.* Translated by H. M. Hubbell. Loeb Classical Library. Cambridge: Harvard UP, 1968.

Cicero. *On Oratory.* Translated by E. W. Sutton and H. Rackham. 2 vols. Loeb Classical Library. Cambridge: Harvard UP, 1976.

Cicero. *On the Parts of Oratory.* Translated by H. Rackham. Loeb Classical Library. Cambridge: Harvard UP, 1982.

Cicero. *Oratore.* Translated by H. M. Hubbell. Loeb Classical Library. Cambridge: Harvard UP, 1971.

Cicero. *Topics.* Translated by H. M. Hubbell. Cambridge: Harvard UP, 1968.

Demetrius. *On Style.* Translated by W. Rhys Roberts. Loeb Classical Library. Cambridge: Harvard UP, 1982.

Demosthenes. *On the Crown.* Translated by John J. Keany. In *Demosthenes'* On the Crown: *A Critical Case Study of a Masterpiece of Ancient Oratory.* Edited by James J. Murphy. New York: Random House, 1967.

Diogenes Laertius. *Lives of the Eminent Philosophers.* Translated by R. D. Hicks. 2 vols. Loeb Classical Library. Cambridge: Harvard UP, 1972.

"Dissoi Logoi." Translated by Rosamond Kent Sprague. *Mind* 78 (Apr. 1968): 155–67. Reprinted in *The Older Sophists,* 279–293. Edited by Rosamond Kent Sprague. Columbia: South Carolina UP, 1972.

Gorgias. *Gorgias.* Translated by George Kennedy. In *The Older Sophists.* Edited by Rosamond Kent Sprague. Columbia: South Carolina UP, 1972.

Homer. *Iliad.* Translated by Robert Fitzgerald. Garden City, N.Y.: Anchor Press, 1975.

Hermogenes. *On Types of Style.* Translated by Cecil W. Wooten. Chapel Hill: North Carolina UP, 1987.

Hermogenes. *Progymnasmata.* Translated by Charles Sears Baldwin. In *Medieval Rhetoric and Poetic,* 23–38. New York: Macmillan, 1928.

Isocrates. *Isocrates.* Translated by George Norlin. 3 vols. Loeb Classical Library. Cambridge: Harvard UP, 1980.

Lucian of Samasota. *Works.* Translated by H. W. Fowler and F. G. Fowler. 4 vols. Oxford: Clarendon Press, 1905.

Ovid. *The Metamorphoses.* Translated by Horace Gregory. New York: New American Library, 1960.

Philostratus. *The Lives of the Sophists.* Translated by Wilmer Cave Wright. Loeb Classical Library. Cambridge: Harvard UP, 1922.

Plato. *The Collected Dialogues.* Edited by Edith Hamilton and Huntington Cairns. Princeton: Princeton UP, 1971.

Plutarch. *The Lives of the Noble Grecians and Romans.* Translated by John Dryden. New York: Random House, 1932.

Priscian. *Fundamentals Adapted from Hermogenes.* Translated by Joseph M. Miller. In *Readings from Medieval Rhetoric,* 52–68. Edited by Joseph M. Miller, Michael H. Prosser, and Thomas W. Benson. Bloomington: Indiana UP, 1973.

Quintillian. *The Institutes of Oratory.* Translated by H. E. Butler. 4 vols. Loeb Classical Library. Cambridge: Harvard UP, 1980.

Rhetoric to Alexander. Translated by H. Rackham. Loeb Classical Library. Cambridge: Harvard UP, 1957.

Rhetoric to Herennius. Translated by Harry Caplan. Loeb Classical Library. Cambridge: Harvard UP, 1981.

Seneca the Elder. *Declamations.* Translated by M. Winterbottom. 2 vols. Loeb Classical Library. Cambridge: Harvard UP, 1974.

Theon. *Progymnasmata.* Translated by Patricia P. Matsen. In *Readings from Classical Rhetoric.* Edited by Patricia P. Matsen, Philip Rollinson, and Marion Sousa. Carbondale: Southern Illinois UP, 1990.

Theophrastus. *The Characters.* Translated by J. M. Edmonds. Loeb Classical Library. Cambridge: Harvard UP, 1961.

Thucydides. *The Peloponnesian War.* Translated by Benjamin Jowett. In *The Greek Historians.* Edited by Francis R. B. Godolphin. 2 vols. New York: Random House, 1942.

Virgil. *Georgics.* Translated by H. Rushton Fairclough. Loeb Classical Library. Cambridge: Harvard UP, 1942.

Xenophon. *Memorabilia.* Translated by E. C. Marchant. Loeb Classical Library. Cambridge: Harvard UP, 1979.

Suggestions for Further Reading

Armstrong, Edward. *A Ciceronian Sunburn: A Tudor Dialogue on Humanistic Rhetoric and Civic Poets*. Columbia: U of South Carolina P, 2006.

Atwill, Janet M. *Rhetoric Reclaimed: Aristotle & the Liberal Arts Tradition*. Ithaca: Cornell UP, 1998.

Ballif, Michelle, and Michael G. Moran. *Classical Rhetorics and Rhetoricians: Critical Studies and Sources*. Westport, CT: Praeger Publishers, 2005.

Benson, Thomas W., and Michael Prosser. *Readings in Classical Rhetoric*. Boston: Allyn and Bacon, 1969.

Brody, Miriam. *Manly Writing: Gender, Rhetoric, and the Rise of Composition*. Carbondale: Southern Illinois UP, 1993.

Cole, Thomas. *The Origins of Rhetoric in Ancient Greece*. Baltimore: Johns Hopkins UP, 1991.

Consigny, Scott. *Gorgias: Sophist and Artist*. Columbia: U of South Carolina P, 2001.

Enos, Richard Leo. *Greek Rhetoric Before Aristotle*. Prospect Heights, IL: Waveland Press, 1993.

———. *Roman Rhetoric: Revolution and the Greek Influence*. Prospect Heights, IL: Waveland Press, 1995.

Fredal, James. *Rhetorical Action in Ancient Athens: Persuasive Artistry from Solon to Demosthenes*. Carbondale: Southern Illinois UP, 2006.

Gleason, Maud. *Making Men: Sophists and Self-Presentation in Ancient Rome*. Princeton: Princeton UP, 1995.

Glenn, Cheryl. *Rhetoric Retold: Regendering the Tradition from Antiquity through the Renaissance*. Carbondale: Southern Illinois UP, 1997.

Gross, Alan G., and Arthur E. Walzer. *Rereading Aristotle's Rhetoric*. Carbondale: Southern Illinois UP, 2000.

Haskins, Ekaterina V. *Logos and Power in Isocrates and Aristotle*. Columbia: U of South Carolina P, 2004.

Hawhee, Debra. *Bodily Arts: Rhetoric and Athletics in Ancient Greece*. Austin: U of Texas P, 2004.

Jarratt, Susan C. *Re-Reading the Sophists: Classical Rhetoric Refigured*. Carbondale: Southern Illinois UP, 1991.

Kennedy, George A. *The Art of Persuasion in Greece*. Princeton: Princeton UP, 1963.

———. *The Art of Rhetoric in the Roman World*. Princeton: Princeton UP, 1972.

———. *A New History of Classical Rhetoric*. Princeton: Princeton UP, 1994.

Kerford, G. B. *The Sophistic Movement*. Cambridge: Cambridge UP, 1981.

Keuls, Eva C. *The Reign of the Phallus: Sexual Politics in Ancient Athens*. New York: Harper & Row, 1985.

Loraux Nicole: *The Invention of Athens: The Funeral Oration in the Classical City*. Cambridge: Harvard UP, 1976.

Lunsford, Andrea, ed. *Reclaiming Rhetorica: Women in the Rhetorical Tradition*. Pittsburgh: U of Pittsburgh Press, 1995.

Marback Richard. *Plato's Dream of Sophistry*. Columbia: U of South Carolina P, 1999.

Marrou, H. I. *A History of Education in Antiquity*. Madison: U of Wisconsin P, 1982.

Matsen, Patricia P., Philip Rollinson, and Marion Sousa. *Readings from Classical Rhetoric*. Carbondale: Southern Illinois UP, 1990.

Poulakos, John. *Sophistical Rhetoric in Classical Greece*. Columbia: University of South Carolina Press, 1995.

Poulakos, Takis. *Speaking for the Polis: Isocrates' Rhetorical Education*. Columbia: U of South Carolina P, 1997.

Poulakos, Takis, and David J. Depew, eds. *Isocrates and Civic Education*. Austin: U of Texas P, 2004.

Romilly, Jacqueline de. *The Great Sophists in Periclean Athens*. Trans. Janet Lloyd. New York: Oxford UP, 1992.

Rorty, Amelie. *Essays on Aristotle's Rhetoric*. Berkeley: U of California P, 1996.

Schiappa, Edward. *Protagoras and Logos: A Study in Greek Philosophy and Rhetoric*. Columbia: U of South Carolina P, 1991.

———. *The Beginnings of Rhetorical Theory in Classical Greece*. New Haven: Yale UP, 1999.

Too, Yun Lee. *Education in Greek and Roman Antiquity*. Leiden and Boston: Brill, 2001.

———. *Isocrates*. Austin: U of Texas P, 2000.

Walker, Jeffrey. *Rhetoric and Poetics in Antiquity*. Oxford: Oxford UP, 2000.

Welch, Kathleen. *Electric Rhetoric: Classical Rhetoric, Oralism, and a New Literacy*. Cambridge: MIT Press, 1999.

TEXT CREDITS

Photo Credits

INDEX